CONCISE HISTORY OF WESTERN MUSIC

Barbara Russano Hanning

THE CITY COLLEGE OF NEW YORK
CITY UNIVERSITY OF NEW YORK

BASED ON

Donald Jay Grout & Claude V. Palisca

A History of Western Music

FIFTH EDITION

W · W · NORTON & COMPANY · NEW YORK · LONDON

The text of this book is composed in Minion & Optima
with the display set in Elizabeth-Ann & Optima
Text composition by University Graphics, Inc.
Music composition by David Budmen
Manufacturing by Quebecor, Kingsport Press
Book design by Jack Meserole
Cover illustration: Instruments de musique, by Raoul Dufy. © 1997 Artists Rights Society
(ARS), NY/ADAGP, Paris

Library of Congress Cataloging-in-Publication Data

Hanning, Barbara Russano, 1940–
    Concise history of western music / Barbara Russano Hanning : based on Donald Jay
  Grout & Claude V. Palisca, A history of western music, fifth edition.
      p.   cm.
    Includes bibliographical references and index.
    ISBN 0-393-97168-6
    1. Music—History and criticism.   I. Grout, Donald Jay.   History of western
music. II. Title.
  ML 160.H2827 1997
  780′.09—dc21
                                                        97-19815
                                                       (MN)

W. W. Norton & Company, Inc., 500 Fifth Avenue, New York, N.Y. 10110
http://www.wwnorton.com

W. W. Norton & Company Ltd., 10 Coptic Street, London WC1A 1PU

3 4 5 6 7 8 9 0

CONTENTS

PREFACE   xi

MUSIC IN ANCIENT GREECE AND EARLY CHRISTIAN ROME   1   1
PRELUDE 1 • Music in Ancient Greek Life and Thought 4 •
The Early Christian Church: Musical Thought 8 • The Early
Christian Church: Musical Practice 12 • *Window:* Sounding
and Silent Harmony 14 • POSTLUDE 16

CHANT AND SECULAR SONG IN THE MIDDLE AGES,
400–1450   18   2
PRELUDE 18 • Roman Chant and Liturgy 19 • Classes, Forms,
and Types of Chant 24 • Medieval Music Theory and Practice
32 • Nonliturgical and Secular Monody 35 • *Window:*
Eleanor of Aquitaine and Her Courts of Love 40 • POSTLUDE 42

POLYPHONIC MUSIC FROM ITS BEGINNINGS THROUGH
THE THIRTEENTH CENTURY   43   3
PRELUDE 43 • Early Organum 45 • Notre Dame Organum
48 • Polyphonic Conductus 54 • The Motet 56 • *Window:*
The Motet as Gothic Cathedral 58 • POSTLUDE 61

4   FRENCH AND ITALIAN MUSIC IN THE FOURTEENTH
CENTURY   62

PRELUDE 62 • The *ars nova* in France 64 • Italian *trecento*
Music 70 • Theory and Practice in Fourteenth-Century Music
77 • *Window:* The Subtler Art 78 • Instruments 81 •
POSTLUDE 82

5   ENGLAND AND THE BURGUNDIAN LANDS IN THE FIFTEENTH
CENTURY: THE BEGINNINGS OF AN INTERNATIONAL STYLE   83

PRELUDE 83 • English Music and Its Influence 86 • Music in
the Burgundian Lands 91 • POSTLUDE 98

6   THE AGE OF THE RENAISSANCE: MUSIC OF THE LOW
COUNTRIES   99

PRELUDE 99 • The Musical Culture of the Renaissance 101 •
Northern Composers and Their Music 105 • *Window:* The
"Gutenberg Bible" of Music Printing 106 • Josquin and His
Contemporaries 111 • POSTLUDE 118

7   THE AGE OF THE RENAISSANCE: NEW CURRENTS IN THE
SIXTEENTH CENTURY   120

PRELUDE 120 • The Generation after Josquin (1520–1550) 121 •
The Rise of National Styles: Italy 124 • The Italian Madrigal
125 • *Window:* Caravaggio Paints a Performer 127 • The
Rise of National Styles: Secular Song outside Italy 135 • The
Rise of Instrumental Music 140 • Categories of Instrumental
Music 143 • POSTLUDE 149

8   CHURCH MUSIC OF THE LATE RENAISSANCE AND
REFORMATION   150

PRELUDE 150 • The Music of the Reformation in Germany
151 • Reformation Church Music outside Germany 153 •
Window: Music as a Symbol for Human Frailty 154 • The
Counter-Reformation 158 • POSTLUDE 168

MUSIC OF THE EARLY BAROQUE PERIOD   170 9

PRELUDE 170 • General Characteristics of Baroque Music
172 • Early Opera 176 • Vocal Chamber Music 186 •
Window: Barbara Strozzi, Renaissance Woman 190 • The
Venetian School 192 • Genres of Sacred Music: Catholic and
Lutheran 193 • *Window:* The Ecstasy of Saint Teresa 196 •
Instrumental Music 198 • POSTLUDE 207

OPERA AND VOCAL MUSIC IN THE LATE
SEVENTEENTH CENTURY   208 10

PRELUDE 208 • Opera 209 • Vocal Music for Chamber and
Church 218 • POSTLUDE 225

INSTRUMENTAL MUSIC IN THE LATE BAROQUE PERIOD   227 11

PRELUDE 227 • Music for Organ 228 • Music for
Harpsichord and Clavichord 233 • Ensemble Music 237 •
Window: Queen Christina of Sweden and Her Circle 244 •
POSTLUDE 247

MUSIC IN THE EARLY EIGHTEENTH CENTURY   249 12

PRELUDE 249 • Antonio Vivaldi 250 • Jean-Philippe Rameau
255 • Johann Sebastian Bach 260 • George Frideric Handel
276 • *Window:* Farinelli, the Adored Castrato 280 •
POSTLUDE 285

THE EARLY CLASSIC PERIOD: OPERA AND INSTRUMENTAL
MUSIC IN THE EIGHTEENTH CENTURY   287 13

PRELUDE 287 • General Characteristics of the New Style 291 •
Opera buffa 294 • Opera seria 298 • Opera Reform 302 •
Instrumental Music: Sonata, Symphony, and Concerto 305 •
POSTLUDE 313

THE LATE EIGHTEENTH CENTURY: HAYDN AND MOZART   315 14

PRELUDE 315 • Franz Joseph Haydn 316 • Haydn's
Instrumental Music 316 • Haydn's Vocal Works 331 •
Wolfgang Amadeus Mozart 334 • Mozart's Years in Salzburg
335 • Mozart's Vienna Years 338 • *Window:* Mozart and His
Father 346 • POSTLUDE 349

15 LUDWIG VAN BEETHOVEN   350

PRELUDE 350 • First Period 352 • Second Period 356 • Third Period 365 • *Window:* The Immortal Beloved 366 • POSTLUDE 372

16 ROMANTICISM AND NINETEENTH-CENTURY ORCHESTRAL MUSIC   373

PRELUDE 373 • Romanticism 374 • Orchestral Music 375 • *Window:* The Symphony Orchestra 380 • POSTLUDE 388

17 SOLO, CHAMBER, AND VOCAL MUSIC IN THE NINETEENTH CENTURY   391

PRELUDE 391 • Solo Music for Piano 392 • *Window:* A Ballad of Love 398 • Chamber Music 401 • Vocal Music: The Lied 406 • POSTLUDE 410

18 OPERA, MUSIC DRAMA, AND CHURCH MUSIC IN THE NINETEENTH CENTURY   412

PRELUDE 412 • French Grand (and Not-So-Grand) Opera 413 • Italian Opera 416 • Giuseppe Verdi 418 • German Romantic Opera 422 • Richard Wagner and the Music Drama 423 • Church Music 429 • POSTLUDE 432

19 EUROPEAN MUSIC FROM THE 1870s TO WORLD WAR I   433

PRELUDE 433 • The German Tradition 434 • Nationalism 444 • New Currents in France 451 • *Window:* Impressionism 456 • Italian Opera 459 • POSTLUDE 460

20 THE EUROPEAN MAINSTREAM IN THE TWENTIETH CENTURY   462

PRELUDE 462 • Ethnic Contexts 464 • The Soviet Orbit 469 • England 473 • Germany 475 • Neo-Classicism in France 479 • Stravinsky 481 • *Window:* Nijinsky's Lost Ballet 486 • POSTLUDE 491

ATONALITY, SERIALISM, AND RECENT DEVELOPMENTS IN
TWENTIETH-CENTURY EUROPE   492   **21**

PRELUDE 492 • Schoenberg and His Followers 493 •
Window: Expressionism 502 • After Webern 504 •
Recent Developments 506 • POSTLUDE 514

THE AMERICAN TWENTIETH CENTURY   515   **22**

PRELUDE 515 • Traditional Music 517 • Vernacular Styles
520 • Foundations for an American Art Music 526 • Since
1945 535 • POSTLUDE 551

GLOSSARY   553

INDEX   567

COLOR PLATES

I   GIOTTO (1266–1337) St. Francis receiving the stigmata / FACING   82

II   ANONYMOUS (14TH CENTURY) Portrait of Francesco Landini / FACING   83

III   VERONESE (1528–1588) *The Marriage Feast at Cana* / FACING   130

IV   ANONYMOUS (16TH CENTURY) A vocal quartet reading from partbooks / FACING   131

V   CARAVAGGIO (1571–1610) *The Lute Player* / FACING   178

VI   HANS MIELICH (1516–1573) Orlando di Lasso leading his chamber ensemble / FACING   179

VII   GIOVANNI LORENZO BERNINI (1598–1680) *The Ecstasy of Saint Teresa* / FACING   226

VIII   JEAN ANTOINE WATTEAU (1684–1721) *The Sheperds* / FACING   227

IX   FRANCESCO GUARDI (1712–1793) Concert at the Casino dei Filarmonici, Venice / FACING   274

X   JOHN HENRY FUSELI (1741–1825) *The Nightmare* / FACING   275

XI   J. M. W. TURNER (1775–1851) *Music Party, East Cowes Castle* / FACING   418

XII   CLAUDE MONET (1840–1926) *Impression: Sunrise* / FACING   419

XIII   MATTHIAS GRÜNEWALD (D. 1528) *Temptation of St. Anthony* from the Isenheim altarpiece / FACING   466

XIV   ERNST LUDWIG KIRCHNER (1880–1938) *Street Scene* / FACING   467

XV   THOMAS HART BENTON (1889–1938) *The Sun-Treader* (portrait of Carl Ruggles) / FACING   538

XVI   FRANK STELLA (B. 1936) *Six Mile Bottom* / FACING   539

Preface

In response to the needs of some music history courses around the country, I was asked to abbreviate and partially to restructure the Fifth Edition of *A History of Western Music.* The result is a book that is briefer and easier to use, and I hope no less authoritative than HWM. Although this volume still covers the entire sweep of Western music history, it concentrates on the main avenues of musical activity, omitting several of the byways while at the same time augmenting the picture with some new, ancillary material.

In abbreviating the narrative, I have eliminated more from the earlier chapters than the later ones, thereby redistributing the balance of attention in favor of the more recent periods of music history. In every chapter I have placed some content into boxed "études," which students can be asked to read or not, as the instructor sees fit. The basic text is complete without these passages, but some will want to use them to investigate details of form (such as sequence, ballade, virelai, rondeau, each described with a diagram as well as verbally), the workings of a particular piece or style (such as Mahler's Fourth Symphony or Palestrina's counterpoint), or the characteristics of a certain genre (such as Anglican Church music or the Lutheran Passion).

The partial restructuring consists in my having given each chapter a similar shape: an introductory "Prelude," which weaves into its narrative the subheadings (highlighted in color) of the topics covered in the chapter; the main body of the chaper, which presents the topics in the order laid out in the Prelude; and a closing "Postlude," which usually summarizes or otherwise reflects on the materials just covered, and sometimes serves as a transition to the next chapter. In addition to the vignettes that enliven the historical account with contemporaneous commentary, each chapter also includes a chronology, which helps to provide a context for the events narrated in the text. In an effort to achieve some continuity from one chapter to the next, certain events are retained and new ones added; in each subsequent chronology the new items—those actually mentioned or discussed within the chapter—are marked by asterisks.

Another new feature is the inclusion of "windows," brief essays on various topics that serve to broaden the student's perspective on music history. Some of these focus on art and iconography, others address biographical matters, still others relate to architecture and dance history—but all of them supplement some aspect of musical culture suggested in the main text and bear cross-references to the pertinent chapter discussions and illustrations.

The relationship of this book to the two-volume *Norton Anthology of Western Music* (Third Edition) is the same as that of the Fifth Edition of HWM: references to musical works presented in the *Anthology* are referred to by number whenever they are mentioned in the history text. However, while other pieces have not been altogether excluded, I have elaborated especially on the core set of works appearing in the *Concise Norton Recorded Anthology of Western Music* (a set of four CDs or cassettes) and my discussions of these pieces overlap with—but avoid repeating in their entirety—the detailed musical essays that accompany them in the *Anthology* volumes. A new *Study and Listening Guide,* also focusing on the sixty-nine works in the *Concise Recorded Anthology,* has been prepared by J. Peter Burkholder to aid in the use of this text.

My heartfelt thanks go to a number of people who have sustained me throughout this project: to Claude Palisca, for his unfailing support and generous advice; to Michael Ochs, music editor at Norton, and Kathy Talalay—both of whom edited the text with great care—as well as the music assistant, Martha Graedel, for their cheerful and expert guidance; to many of my colleagues and students in the Music Department of The City College of New York, for their genial encouragement and helpful suggestions; and finally to my family—especially my parents, Helen and George Russano—and friends, who listened patiently and lovingly, sometimes with exceeding forbearance, as I recounted in excruciating detail the labors of each stage in the book's production.

Barbara Russano Hanning
New York, New York

Pitch Designations

In this book, a note referred to without regard to its octave register is designated by a capital letter in italics (*A*). A note in a particular octave is designated in the following way:

by *C, D,* etc.   by *c′, d′,* etc.

by *c, d,* etc.   by *c″, d″,* etc.

CONCISE HISTORY OF WESTERN MUSIC

1

MUSIC IN ANCIENT GREECE
AND EARLY CHRISTIAN ROME

PRELUDE

Why study music history? Because in music as in all other realms of human endeavor, the past influences and informs the present. Never in music history has this been more true than in our own time, when scholars have retrieved and restored so much music from the past, performers have brought it to life, and recordings, radio, and television have disseminated it more widely than ever before. Our great-grandparents had access only to music that was performed live by their parents, teachers, friends, and local entertainers. If they could read music and afford lessons, they might also have become acquainted with a few works by Bach, Beethoven, Chopin, and other composers whose music was in print, including the tunesmiths of Tin Pan Alley. In contrast, the technological revolution has made an overwhelming number of works available to us: ten centuries of written music as well as the (often unwritten) musical styles of cultures from around the globe.

Composers and musicians have always been influenced by all the sounds around them, regardless of how limited or varied these sounds were. Today, the possibilities are almost infinite; they range from the folk music of various cultures and ethnic groups to popular music broadcast over the airwaves, even to the raw sounds of nature (such as whale songs) harnessed by modern technology. These influences are absorbed almost unconsciously, and are either unintentionally or purposely incorporated into new works. Furthermore, throughout history composers of one generation have engaged in a conscious and determined struggle to define themselves in opposition to, or in sympathy with, the sounds and styles of previous generations. Like children growing away from their parents, composers sometimes rebel and strike out on their own, only later to acknowledge and embrace or transform the ways of their predecessors. We find this tension—between rejecting the immediate past and accepting or reinterpreting it—in every era of music history. In fact, it mirrors a pattern we recognize in all fields of learning and the arts since the beginning of recorded history. In more recent times, however, the restoration of works from the more remote past has complicated the issue for creative artists by providing an awesome array of additional models and stylistic possibilities.

In itself, the influence of a rich past may not offer enough reason to study music history. After all, we can enjoy *Over the Rainbow*, *Yesterday*, or the latest Top-10 music videos without knowing who wrote them, when they were first performed, or what forces induced their creation. But if we want to understand *why* the music we hear was composed to sound the way it does, we look to music history for explanations. For example, as much as we may enjoy listening to Beethoven, we cannot really *understand* or *appreciate* his work without knowing the music of Haydn or Bach. Similarly, the music of Ellington or Stravinsky, to name two important composers of the twentieth century, owes much of its distinctiveness to a particular ancestry. Ellington's musical parentage included the ragtime and jazz idioms of African-American music as well as some European traditions. And Stravinsky reached not only into his own Russian past for inspiration, but as far back as the fourteenth century to the works of Guillaume de Machaut, which became available to modern listeners only during Stravinsky's lifetime.

To tell the story from its beginning, the history of Western European music—that is, the art music of Europe and the Americas, as opposed to the musics of many Eastern and other cultures—starts in ancient Greece and Rome. Like many aspects of European and American culture, such as philosophy, literature, visual arts, and government, Western music has tangible connections to these early civilizations, links that go back more than three thousand years. We acknowledge these connections when we design our Supreme Court and other civic buildings to look like ancient Greek temples, when we talk about *Platonic* love, and when we explain father-son conflicts in terms of the *Oedipus* complex.

Unlike the statues and architectural ruins of antiquity, however, the musical works themselves have vanished, except for a small number of songs and hymns (praise-songs) that were not identified until the sixteenth century or later. But the Greco-Roman musical heritage was transmitted to modern civilization through written descriptions and through images that survived in painting or sculpture, on vases, buildings, tombs, and other ar-

tifacts from the ancient world. We will see that Western music has much
in common with **Music in Ancient Greek Life and Thought**. Then, as now,
music was used in religious ceremonies, as popular entertainment, and as
accompaniment to drama. Greek music theory—especially its ideas concerning pitch—became the basis for Western music theory and was passed
on to the ancient Romans. During the first and second centuries, when the
Roman Empire was in its heyday, cultivated people were supposed to be
educated in music just as they were expected to know Greek and Latin.
Many of the emperors were patrons of music, and one—Nero—even
aspired to personal fame as a musician.

With the decline of the Roman Empire, the musical heritage of ancient
Greece and Rome was transmitted to the West, if incompletely and imperfectly, through **The Early Christian Church**, specifically in the writings of
the church fathers and other scholars who tried to understand and preserve
this enormous body of information about music and other subjects. As the
public rituals and musical practices of the early church spread from Jerusalem to Asia Minor and westward into Africa and Europe, they picked up
musical elements from different areas of the Mediterranean region. At first
there was little standardization; but as the prestige of the Roman emperor
declined, the importance of the Roman bishop (eventually, the pope) increased, and Christians began to acknowledge the authority of Rome in
matters of faith and discipline. This Roman dominance gradually led to the
regulation and standardization of the Christian liturgy, or worship service,
and to the organization of a repertory of melodies for singing sacred texts
now known as Gregorian chant.

C H R O N O L O G Y

		1 C.E.	
800 B.C.E.	Rise of Greek city-states (800–461 B.C.E.)		Crucifixion of Jesus (ca. 33 C.E.)
700	Homer, *Iliad* and *Odyssey* (700 B.C.E. or earlier)		Nero becomes emperor of Rome (54)
			Temple at Jerusalem destroyed (70)
500		300	
	Pythagoras dies (ca. 497 B.C.E.)		Constantinople established as new capi-
	Euripides, *Iphigenia in Tauris* (ca. 414 B.C.E.)		tal of Roman Empire (330)
			St. Ambrose introduces responsorial
400			psalmody in Milan (386)
	Plato, *Republic* (ca. 380 B.C.E.)		Separation of Eastern and Western Ro-
	Aristotle, *Politics* (ca. 330 B.C.E.)		man Empires (395)
	Aristoxenus, *Harmonic Elements* (ca. 320 B.C.E.)	400	
			St. Augustine (354–430)
100		500	Boethius, *De institutione musica* (ca. 500)
	Julius Caesar becomes dictator (46 B.C.E.)		Election of Pope Gregory I (the Great; ca. 540–604) (590)
	Vergil, *Aeneid* (26–19 B.C.E.)		

Music in Ancient Greek Life and Thought

In Greek mythology, music had a divine origin: its inventors and earliest practitioners were gods and demigods, such as Apollo, Amphion, and Orpheus, and their music had magical powers. People thought it could heal sickness, purify the body and mind, and work miracles. In the Hebrew Scriptures similar powers were attributed to music: we may recall the stories of David curing Saul's madness by playing the harp (1 Sam. 16:14–23), or of the trumpet blasts and shouting that toppled the walls of Jericho (Josh. 6:12–20).

Extant Greek music

The few surviving examples of ancient Greek music come from relatively late periods. Among the complete works or substantial fragments that survive we have the Epitaph of Seikilos, a drinking song from about the second century B.C.E. inscribed on a tombstone (see illustration, page 6, and its transcription, NAWM 1). From this and similar examples, and from what was written about Greek music, we may guess that it resembles music of the early Christian era. It was primarily monophonic—that is, melody without harmony or counterpoint—but instruments often embellished the melody while a soloist or an ensemble sang it, thus creating heterophony. Greek music, moreover, was almost entirely improvised. Its melody and rhythm were intimately linked to the sound and meter of Greek poetry. Despite the similarities between Greek and early Christian music, we have no evidence of any continuity in practice from the earlier culture to the later one.

Greek theory

By contrast, Greek theory profoundly affected the music of western

▼ Woman playing the double-aulos in a drinking scene. Usually a single-reed but sometimes a double-reed instrument, the aulos was typically played in pairs; here the player seems to finger identical notes on both pipes. Red-figured drinking cup ascribed to the Attic vase painter Oltos, 525–500 B.C.E. (*Archivo Fotografico, Museo Arqueologico Nacional*)

Ancient Greek Instruments: Kithara and Aulos

From earliest times music was an inseparable part of religious ceremonies. The lyre became the characteristic instrument for the cult of Apollo, and the aulos for followers of the god Dionysus. Both instruments probably came to Greece from Asia Minor; they were played solo and as accompaniment to the singing or recitation of epic poems. The lyre and its larger counterpart, the kithara, used five to seven strings (later as many as eleven). The aulos, a single- or double-reed instrument sometimes incorrectly identified as a flute, often appears with twin pipes. It was used to accompany the singing of poems in the worship of Dionysus as well as in theatrical performances of the great Greek tragedies by Aeschylus, Sophocles, Euripides, and others, in which choruses and other musical portions combined or alternated with the sounds of the aulos.

From the sixth century B.C.E. or even earlier, both the lyre and the aulos were independent solo instruments. Contests of kithara and aulos players, as well as festivals of instrumental and vocal music, became increasingly popular. As instrumental music grew more independent, the number or virtuosos multiplied and the music itself turned more complex. Alarmed by this trend, the philosopher Aristotle warned against too much professional training in general music education. A reaction against technical virtuosity and musical complexity set in, and by the beginning of the Christian era, Greek music as well as its theory was simplified.

➤ Kitharode singing to his own accompaniment on the kithara. His left hand, which supports the instrument with a sling (not visible), is damping some of the strings, while his right hand has apparently just swept over all the strings with the plectrum. A professional musician like this one wore a long, flowing robe (*chiton*) and a mantle (*himation*). Detail of an Attic red-figured amphora from the fourth century B.C.E., attributed to the Berlin Painter. (*Courtesy, The Metropolitan Museum of Art, Fletcher Fund, 1956. [56.171.38] All Rights Reserved*)

◄ Tomb stele from Aidin, near Tralles, Asia Minor. It bears an epitaph, a kind of *skolion*, or drinking song, with pitch and rhythmic notation, identified in the first lines as being by Seikilos, probably first century C.E. See the transcription in NAWM 1. (*Copenhagen, National Museum, Department of Classical and Near Eastern Antiquities, Inventory No. 14897*)

Europe in the Middle Ages. From the ancient philosophers and theorists we know much more about Greek musical thought than about the music itself. Philosophers such as Plato and Aristotle wrote about the nature of music, its place in the cosmos, its effects on people, and its proper uses in human society. Greek theorists, from Pythagoras (ca. 500 B.C.E.) to Aristides Quintilianus nine hundred years later, not only discovered numerical relationships between pitches but also developed systematic descriptions of the materials of music and the patterns of musical composition. In both the philosophy and the science of music, the Greeks achieved insights and established principles that have survived to this day. Here we will discuss only those that were most characteristic of, and important for, the later history of Western music. We will also discover that the word *music* had a much wider meaning to the Greeks than it has today.

Music and number

Pythagoras and his followers taught that music was inseparable from number, which was supposed to be the key to the entire spiritual and physical universe. According to legend, Pythagoras discovered the ratios of certain musical intervals when he heard hammers of different sizes pounding on an anvil in a blacksmith shop. More likely, he observed that when a vibrating string was stopped (held fixed) in the middle—and thereby divided into lengths expressed by the simple ratio 2:1—it produced a sound one octave above the open (unstopped) string. Similarly, the ratios 3:2 produced a fifth, and 4:3 a fourth. Musical sound, then, being controlled by number, reflected the harmony of the entire universe, including the motion of the planets and the character of the human soul (see window, pages 14–15).

Music and poetry

The close union between music and poetry is another measure of the Greeks' broad conception of music. For them, the two were practically synonymous: Plato, for example, held that song (*melos*) was made up of speech, rhythm, and harmony (which he defined as an agreeable succession of pitches in a melody). "Lyric" poetry meant poetry sung to the lyre; the original Greek word for "tragedy" incorporates the noun *ōdē*, "the art of singing." Many other words that designated different kinds of poetry, such as *hymn*, were musical terms. In the Epitaph of Seikilos referred to above (NAWM 1), the musical rhythms of each line of the poem follow the text rhythms very closely. And if we knew the correct pronunciation of the ancient Greek verses, we might well discover that the contours of the melody match the rising and falling inflections of the words.

Underlying the doctrine of *ethos* (the Greek word for character) is the belief that music possessed moral qualities and could affect a person's character and behavior. Because of the Pythagorean view that the same mathematical laws governing music operate throughout the cosmos, the human soul was also thought to be kept in harmony by numerical relationships. Music, then, could penetrate the soul and, indeed, the inanimate world. The legendary musicians of mythology, it was believed, owed their ability to perform miracles to this power of music.

> *The doctrine of ethos*

Closely related to the doctrine of ethos is Aristotle's theory of imitation, which explains how music affects behavior. Music, he writes, imitates (that is, represents) the passions or states of the soul, such as gentleness, anger, courage, temperance, and their opposites. Music that imitates a certain passion also arouses that passion in the listener, and so habitual listening to music that stirs up ignoble passions, for example, warps a person's character. In short, the wrong kind of music makes you the wrong kind of person, and the right kind tends to make you a better person. Aristotle argues, for example, that those being trained to govern should avoid melodies expressing softness and indolence, and should listen instead to melodies that imitate courage and other similar virtues.

> *Theory of imitation*

Both Plato and Aristotle believed that a public system of education that stressed gymnastics to discipline the body and music to discipline the mind could create the "right" kind of person. In his *Republic*, written about 380 B.C.E., Plato insists that these two educational components must be balanced: too much music makes a man effeminate or neurotic while too much athletics makes him uncivilized, violent, and ignorant. Plato recommends two *modes* (styles of melody)—Dorian and Phrygian—because they fostered the passions of temperance and courage. He excludes other modes from his ideal Republic and deplores current styles that rely on too many notes, scales that are too complex, and the mixing of incompatible genres, rhythms, and instruments. He disapproves of changing established musical conventions, saying that lawlessness in art and education inevitably leads to license in manners and anarchy in society. Aristotle, in the *Politics* (ca. 330 B.C.E.), is less restrictive than Plato about particular modes and rhythms. He holds that music can be used for amusement and intellectual enjoyment as well as for education. But he also believes that music is powerful enough, especially in combination with drama, to arouse certain emotions, like pity and fear, in people and thus to relieve them of those same emotions through a process similar to medical purgation or katharsis.

> *Music in education*

Music and
politics

In limiting the kinds of music they would allow in the ideal society, Plato and Aristotle showed what they disliked of Greek musical life, including orgiastic ritual rhythms, elaborate instrumental music, and professional virtuosos. These philosophers appreciated the great power music held over people's intellectual and emotional well-being. In later centuries, the church fathers also warned regularly against certain kinds of music. Nor is the issue dead: in the twentieth century, dictatorships, both leftist and rightist, attempted to control the musical tastes and activities of their people. Educators and many ordinary citizens today still express concern about the kinds of music (and pictures, lyrics, and performances) to which young people are exposed.

The harmonic
system

The Greek discipline of *harmonics*, or the study of matters concerning pitch, laid the foundation for our modern system of music theory and its vocabulary. Concepts such as notes, intervals, scales, and modes were defined and explored by Greek writers including Aristoxenus around 320 B.C.E. (*Harmonic Elements*) and Cleonides, who lived some five or six hundred years later. Intervals, such as tones, semitones, and ditones (thirds), were combined into scales. Certain intervals, such as the fourth, fifth, and octave, were rec-

Tetrachords

ognized as consonant. The scale's principal building block was the tetrachord, made up of four notes spanning the interval of a fourth. Theorists recognized three kinds, or genera, of tetrachord: diatonic, chromatic, and enharmonic, the last involving intervals smaller than a semitone. Such variety allowed for a broad range of expression and many different nuances within melodies.

Early Christian writers about music transmitted some of these Greek concepts to the Middle Ages unchanged. Other concepts were poorly understood and survived only after being adapted to the musical practice of Gregorian chant. Still others were forgotten altogether until their rediscovery by the great Renaissance humanist scholars of the fifteenth and sixteenth centuries (see Chapter 6).

The Early Christian Church: Musical Thought

Rome's decline

By the fifth century the Roman Empire, which had for a time imposed peace on most of western Europe and on large parts of Africa and Asia as well, declined in wealth and strength. Unable to defend itself against invaders from the north and east, it was too large and weak to continue. The common civilization it had fostered throughout Europe splintered into fragments that would take many centuries to regroup and, eventually, to emerge as modern nations (compare maps, pages 9 and 37).

As the Roman Empire declined, however, the Christian Church gained strength, becoming the main—and often the only—unifying force and channel of culture in Europe until the tenth century. When the last Roman emperor finally left the throne in 476 C.E. after a terrible century of wars and

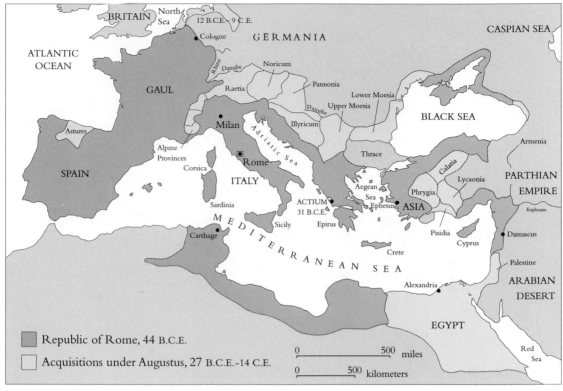

▲ The Roman Empire at the death of Augustus in 14 C.E.

invasions, the power of the papacy was already established. With the help of
the church fathers, highly influential Christian writers and scholars who interpreted the Bible and set down some guiding principles, the church took
over Rome's mission of civilizing and unifying the peoples under its sway.
Writing in Greek (Clement of Alexandria, Origen, St. Basil, and St. John
Chrysostom) or in Latin (St. Ambrose, St. Augustine, and St. Jerome), they
saw in music the power to inspire divine thoughts and also to influence, for
good or evil, the character of its listeners (a version of the Greek doctrine of
ethos).

Church fathers

Philosophers and church leaders of the early Middle Ages disdained the
idea that music might be enjoyed solely for its play of sounds, something we
now take for granted. Without denying that the sound of music could be
pleasurable, they held to the Platonic principle that beautiful things exist to
remind us of divine and perfect beauty, not to inspire self-centered enjoyment
or desire of possession. This view forms the basis for many of the pronouncements against music made by some church fathers (and, later, by some theologians of the Protestant Reformation; see Chapter 8). Others, however, not
only defended pagan art, literature, and music but found themselves so deeply
affected by them that they actually feared their own pleasure in listening to
music, even in church. St. Augustine (354–430) expresses this dilemma in a
well-known passage from his *Confessions* (see vignette, page 10).

Dangers of music

Saint Augustine on the Pleasures and Dangers of Music:

66 When I remember the tears I shed at the psalmody of Thy church, when I first recovered my faith, and how even now I am moved not by the singing but by what is sung, when it is sung with a clear voice and apt melody, I then acknowledge the great usefulness of this custom. Thus I hesitate between dangerous pleasure and approved wholesomeness, though I am inclined to approve of the use of singing in the church (yet I would not pronounce an irrevocable opinion upon the subject), so that the weaker minds may be stimulated to devout thoughts by the delights of the ear. Yet when I happen to be moved more by the singing than by what is sung, I confess to have sinned grievously, and then I wish I had not heard the singing. See the state I am in! Weep with me, and weep for me, you who can control your inward feelings to good effect. As for those of you who do not react this way, this is not a concern of yours. But Thou, O Lord my God, listen, behold and see, and have mercy upon me, and heal me—Thou, in whose sight I have become a problem to myself; and this is my weakness. 99

Saint Augustine, *Confessions* 10:33.

Transmission of Greek music theory

The music theory and philosophy of the ancient world—or whatever could still be found after the collapse of the Roman Empire and the invasions from the north—were gathered up, summarized, modified, and transmitted to the West during the early centuries of the Christian era. Most notable in this process were the writers Martianus Capella and Boethius.

Martianus Capella

Martianus produced an appealing textbook on the seven liberal arts in his encyclopedic treatise *The Marriage of Mercury and Philology* (early fifth century). It covered grammar, dialectic (or logic), and rhetoric; then geometry, arithmetic, astronomy, and harmonics (or music). The first three—the verbal arts—were called the *trivium* (three paths), while the last four were named the *quadrivium* (four paths) by Boethius and consisted of the disciplines based on number.

Boethius

Anicius Manlius Severinus Boethius (ca. 480–524) was the most revered and influential authority on music in the Middle Ages. His *De institutione musica* (The Fundamentals of Music), written in the first years of the sixth century, is a compendium of music within the scheme of the quadrivium. Together with similar texts on geometry, arithmetic, and astronomy, it prepared students for further studies in philosophy. The music treatise contains little original material: Boethius used Greek sources that he had at hand, mainly a long treatise by Nicomachus that has not survived, and the first book

Boethius's *Fundamentals*

*I*n the opening chapters of *De institutione musica*, the most original part of the treatise, Boethius divides music into three kinds. The first is the inaudible *musica mundana* (cosmic music), which is apparent in the orderly numerical relations seen in the movement of the planets, the changing of the seasons, and the combination of elements. The second is *musica humana*, which controls the union of body and soul and their parts. Because music could influence character and morals, Boethius assigned it an important place in the education of the young, as the Greek philosophers had before him. Last is *musica instrumentalis*, audible music produced by instruments and the human voice, which exemplifies the same principles of order as the other kinds of music, especially in the numerical ratios of its musical intervals.

In placing *musica instrumentalis*—the art of music as we commonly understand it now—in the third and presumably lowest category, Boethius indicated that like his predecessors he saw music first as a science. Music, he wrote, is the discipline of examining the diversity of high and low sounds by means of reason and the senses. Therefore, the true musician is not the singer, nor someone who makes up songs by instinct without understanding the nature of the medium, but rather the theorist, or critic, who can use reason to make discoveries and judgments about the essence and the art of music.

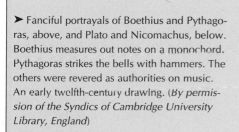

➤ Fanciful portrayals of Boethius and Pythagoras, above, and Plato and Nicomachus, below. Boethius measures out notes on a monochord. Pythagoras strikes the bells with hammers. The others were revered as authorities on music. An early twelfth-century drawing. (*By permission of the Syndics of Cambridge University Library, England*)

of Ptolemy's *Harmonics*. It also echoes ideas set forth by Pythagoras, Euclid, and Aristoxenus. Although medieval readers may not have realized how much Boethius depended on other authors, they understood that his statements rested on the authority of Greek mathematics and music theory. They came away with the message that music was a science of number, because numerical ratios determined the melodic intervals, the consonances, the composition of scales, and the tuning of instruments and voices.

The Early Christian Church: Musical Practice

During its first two or three centuries, the Christian Church absorbed features of Greek music and the music of other cultures bordering on the eastern Mediterranean Sea. But the church definitely rejected the idea of cultivating music purely for enjoyment. It also disapproved of the forms and types of music connected with great public spectacles such as festivals, competitions, and dramatic performances, as well as the music of more intimate social occasions. It was not that leaders of the church disliked music itself; but, they wanted to wean converts away from anything associated with their pagan past, even banning for a time all instrumental music.

The Judaic heritage

Christianity also had a Judaic heritage. Scholars have seen some parallels between the ritual sacrifice of the Temple service and the symbolic sacrifice of the Christian Mass. In the Temple service of the biblical era, a lamb was usually sacrificed in a ritual performed by priests and Levites—including musicians—and witnessed by lay Israelite citizens. Depending on the occasion, priests and even lay worshipers ate some of the "burned" animal. Part of the ceremony involved a choir of at least twelve Levites, who sang a specific *psalm* (a prayer-poem from the Old Testament Book of Psalms) for each day of the week, accompanied by string instruments. On important festivals, a wind instrument resembling an aulos joined in the string accompaniment.

Christian Mass

In the Christian sacrifice of the Mass, the priest and early worshipers partook of both the blood of Christ, in the form of a cup of wine, and the body of Christ, in the form of bread that was shared. Some scholars believe that the Mass also commemorates the Last Supper, in imitation of the festive Jewish Passover meal, which was accompanied by music in the form of psalm singing.

Psalms and hymns

As the early church spread from Jerusalem to Asia Minor, North Africa, and Europe, it continued to pick up other musical influences. For example, the monasteries and churches of Syria were important in the development of psalm singing and the use of hymns. Both psalms and hymns traveled from Syria by way of Byzantium (in Asia Minor) to Milan (Italy) and other Western centers. Hymn singing is the earliest recorded musical activity of the Christian Church (Matt. 26:30; Mark 14:26).

In 395 the political unity of the ancient world was formally divided into Eastern and Western Empires, with capitals at Byzantium and Rome. The city of Byzantium (later Constantinople, now Istanbul), at the crossroads between Europe and Asia Minor, remained the capital of the Eastern Empire for more than a thousand years, until its capture by the Turks in 1453 (see map, page 37). During much of this time, Byzantium, located on the northern rim of the Mediterranean Sea, flourished as a cultural center that blended elements of Western, African, and Eastern civilizations. But in the absence of a strong central authority, Christian churches in the various regions of the Eastern Empire developed different liturgies. Although no manuscripts prior to the ninth century exist to reveal the music used in these Eastern rites, we can still make inferences about early music in the Byzantine churches. Byzantine musical practices left their mark on Western chant, particularly in the classification of the repertory into eight modes, or melody types, and in a number of hymns borrowed by the West between the sixth and ninth centuries.

Eastern churches

In the West, as in the East, local churches were relatively independent at first. Although they shared a large area of common practice, including the use of Latin for the chanting of sacred texts, each Western region probably received the Eastern heritage in a somewhat different form. These original differences, combined with local variations, produced several distinct liturgies and bodies of liturgical music between the fifth and eighth centuries. During the seventh and early eighth centuries, western Europe was controlled by various peoples who inhabited what is now Italy, France, and Germany, and each of these political divisions developed its own repertory of melodies for singing sacred texts in Latin. We call these melodies *chants*, and the different regional styles may be called *dialects* by analogy to language. Gaul (approximately the same area as modern France) had the *Gallican* chant; southern Italy, the *Beneventan*; Rome, the *Old Roman* chant; Spain, the *Visigothic*, or *Mozarabic*; and the area around Milan, the *Ambrosian*. Later, England developed its own dialect of chant, called the *Sarum* (Salisbury) *Use*, which persisted from the late Middle Ages to the Reformation. Eventually most of the local versions either disappeared or were absorbed into the single uniform practice for which the central authority was Rome. From the ninth to the sixteenth centuries, in theory and in practice, the liturgy of the Western church was increasingly Romanized.

Western churches

Chant dialects

One exception to this process was Milan, a flourishing city with close cultural ties to Byzantium and the East. Its chant dialect was named after St. Ambrose, the Bishop of Milan from 374 to 397, who first introduced responsorial psalmody to the West. In this manner of singing the psalms, a soloist or reader sings the first half of a psalm verse and the congregation responds by singing the second half. Because of Milan's importance and St. Ambrose's energy and high profile, the Milanese liturgy and music exerted a strong influence not only in France and Spain but also in Rome, where responsorial psalmody was incorporated into the Roman Mass. Some of the Ambrosian liturgy and music survives in present-day Milan and many of the Ambrosian

Ambrosian chant

Responsorial psalmody

chants are similar to those of the Roman Church, indicating either an interchange or a derivation from a common source.

How did the thousands of chant melodies associated with Christian worship survive over so many centuries? Throughout Christian lands, monasteries preserved the order of worship and the sacred texts and melodies and passed them on from one generation to the next. Eventually these texts and melodies were written down and copied by hand into manuscripts that were housed in monastic libraries. During the ninth century, Frankish monks—from

Window

SOUNDING AND SILENT HARMONY:
MUSIC AND ASTRONOMY

For many thinkers of the ancient world, music had a close connection with astronomy because mathematics dominated the study of both subjects. In fact, Pythagoras (fifth century B.C.E.), who recognized the numerical relationships that govern musical intervals, is better known for his discovery of specific mathematical laws, such as the familiar Pythagorean theorem. Ptolemy (second century C.E.), the most systematic of the ancient Greek theorists of music, was also the leading astronomer of antiquity. Numerical proportions were thought to underlie the systems both of musical intervals and of the heavenly bodies, and certain modes and notes were believed to correspond with particular planets, their distances from each other, and their movement in the heavens. Plato gave this idea poetic form in his myth of "the music of the spheres" (*Republic* 10.617), the unheard music produced by the harmonious relationships among the planets as they revolved around the earth.

In the Middle Ages, music was defined as the discipline that deals with numbers in their relationship to sounds. Medieval Christian philosophers from St. Augustine (fourth to fifth centuries) to St. Thomas Aquinas (thirteenth century) believed that a knowledge of proportion and number was essential to understanding God's universe. Seen as one of the seven liberal arts, music was grouped with the mathematical and speculative sciences in the quadrivium, the path of learning that led to the contemplation of philosophy. In this curriculum, music had a place of honor next to astronomy because, through numerical analogies and ratios, it could help explain connections between things perceived by the senses (such as sound), things knowable only through reason and speculation (such as the movement of heavenly bodies), and things that could never be known because they belonged to the modern-day Switzerland, France, and western Germany—played a crucial role in this process. But Rome remained the dominant musical force, in part because the popes took special measures to organize, revise, and preserve this body of sacred melodies. A papal choir existed as early as the sixth century, and by the eighth century the city of Rome had a *Schola cantorum*, a designated group of teachers responsible for training boys and men as church singers. Supposedly, Pope Gregory I (the Great; reigned 590–604) began regulating and standardizing the liturgical chants, but the resulting repertory,

Rome's musical dominance

realm of the divine (such as the mysteries of the human soul). So, the numerical relationships that regulated both music and astronomy provided the foundation for knowledge about the order and system of the entire universe.

Pythagorean and Platonic ideas about cosmic harmony and music of the spheres continued until the end of the Renaissance and persist even into the modern era. Along the way these ideas strongly influenced astronomers, physicians, architects, and poets, including Dante, Shakespeare, and Milton. In addition, astronomy and music had close ties to astrology, which has maintained a considerable appeal since antiquity, despite arousing the suspicion of Christian philosophers and theologians through the ages and the derision of scientists and other rationalists today. Boethius's popular notions about *musica mundana* and *musica humana* (see page 11), which affirmed Greek theories about the relationship between the music of the spheres and music's influence on human character and morals, left the door wide open for astrology in the Middle Ages; then, as now, astrology professed to interpret the influence of the heavenly bodies on human affairs. In astrological symbolism, the planets Venus and Mercury hold particular sway over the musical attributes of humans and for this reason, depictions of Venus often include musical instruments in medieval and Renaissance art.

➤ Venus and Cupid making music. Detail from Jan Brueghel the Elder (d. 1625). *Hearing.* From the series of five senses. Museo del Prado, Madrid. (*Scala/Art Resource, NY*)

> ### The Restoration of Gregorian Chant
>
> *G*regorian chant has been restored for modern times by the scholarly efforts of a monastic community in France. Benedictine monks at the Abbey of Solesmes began in the 1880s to publish facsimile editions, with commentaries, of the manuscript sources of Gregorian chant. They also issued modern editions of chants which the Vatican proclaimed in the early 1900s to be official. But since the Second Vatican Council (1962–65) elected to modernize the liturgy by substituting local, vernacular languages for Latin in the Roman Catholic Mass, the chants in these books are seldom used in modern services and the books themselves are rarely reprinted. For an example of a chant from the modern edition of the all-purpose *Liber usualis*, a book containing the chants that were most commonly used until the Second Vatican Council, see page 24.

Gregorian chant ▸ called Gregorian chant, was more likely named for Pope Gregory II (reigned 715–31). Whether or not he or even a group of popes should be credited with this reorganization, the fact is that particular items of the liturgy and their music were assigned to the various services throughout the year in an order that remained essentially unchanged until the sixteenth century.

POSTLUDE

Although many details are uncertain, we know that in the ancient world: (1) music consisted essentially of a single melodic line; (2) melody was intimately linked with the rhythm and meter of words; (3) musical performances were improvised (not read from notation) in keeping with accepted conventions; (4) philosophers believed that music was an orderly system interlocked with the system of nature and a force in human thought and conduct; (5) a scientifically based acoustical theory was in the making; (6) scales were built up from tetrachords; and (7) musical terminology was well developed. The last three elements of this heritage (Nos. 5, 6, and 7) were specifically Greek; the others were common also among other cultures in the ancient world.

This heritage was transmitted to the West, if incompletely and imperfectly, through the Christian Church, the writings of the church fathers, and early medieval scholarly treatises that dealt with music and other subjects. The awesome powers attributed to music by the ancient Greeks were still convincing to St. Augustine, who confessed his fears about the pleasure he experienced while listening to music. Boethius wrote an influential treatise based on the Greek view of music as a science of numerical ratios and an important educational force. In practice, early Christian church music absorbed elements from many cultures, and local variants of the liturgy and its chant existed throughout the Byzantine and Western Roman Empires. Eventually, the practices of the Roman Church prevailed and the body of melodies later known as Gregorian chant became the established repertory in the West.

2

CHANT AND SECULAR SONG IN THE MIDDLE AGES, 400–1450

PRELUDE

Two distinct bodies of song, one sacred (religious) and the other secular (worldly), flourished side by side during the Middle Ages—the thousand-year period that began with the fall of the Roman Empire in the fifth century. The sacred repertory, known as plainchant (eventually, Gregorian chant; see page 16), was created for ceremonial use and served as a principal element in the communal liturgy, or worship service, of the Roman Church; it was essentially musical prayer, its devotional words heightened through melody and rhythm. Nonsacred song, known in this period as secular monody, was intended mainly for entertainment. These songs, like those of any age, gave voice to the celebration of heroes, the expression of protest, and, especially, the pain and pleasure of love. Both the sacred and secular repertories are primarily monophonic, although for secular song instrumental accompaniments were probably improvised from the beginning. Both repertories originated in oral cultures, and their texts and melodies were initially performed from memory according to formulas handed down by older singers or invented by new poet-composers. Chants and songs were transmitted this way for many centuries before they were eventually written down in a gradually evolving notation that developed in order to preserve the music, more or less accurately, for future generations.

As we read in Chapter 1, Rome increasingly dominated the practices of the early Christian Church. But **Roman Chant and Liturgy** itself changed and expanded over time, even after it was stabilized by the popes and written down in manuscripts. Therefore, we need to know the basic elements of the Roman liturgy, especially the Catholic Mass, if we are to understand the various **Classes, Forms, and Types of Chant** and how they were used in medieval ceremonial context. Another important factor in the transmission and preservation of these melodies was their classification into church modes. Learned theorists who interpreted (and sometimes misinterpreted) Boethius, as well as teachers responsible for training student monks (who did not necessarily have any musical aptitude) to sing plainchant, patiently created a system of **Medieval Music Theory and Practice** partly based on concepts inherited from the ancient Greek science of music. Other elements of this medieval system were newly invented—such as the syllables associated with sight singing, which are still used in the classroom today.

Like plainchant, the repertory of song outside the church, known as **Nonliturgical and Secular Monody**, also comprised many different types and forms that had distinct functions and differing conventions. One kind was intended for performances of medieval drama (which included both religious and secular subjects), while another was epic or lyric in style. Among the most artful and refined were the songs of the twelfth- and thirteenth-century poet-composers—called troubadours (male) or trobairitz (female, singular and plural) and trouvères—who also wrote their own lyrics in either of the two principal French dialects of the time. Some features of these medieval lyrics are echoed in nineteenth-century art song (see Chapter 17) and even in modern rap: they all often deal openly with sensual subject matter, use coded language, and address some sort of coterie—a group of aristocrats at court, a closed circle of friends, or a commercial audience of fans.

Roman Chant and Liturgy

The chants of the Roman Church rank among the great treasures of Western civilization. Like Romanesque architecture, they stand as a memorial to religious faith in the Middle Ages, embodying the sense of community and the aesthetic values of the time. Not only does this body of plainchant include some of the oldest and noblest melodies ever created, it also served as the source and inspiration for much Western art music until the sixteenth century.

Because plainchant is musical prayer, its shape cannot be separated from its verbal message or from its place in the worship service. Musically, it can be as simple as a recitation on a single pitch or as elaborate as a long, winding

C H R O N O L O G Y	
500 Boethius, *De institutione musica* (ca. 500)	*Chanson de Roland* (ca. 1075)
Election of Pope Gregory I (the Great; ca. 540–604) (590)	First Crusade (1095–99)
600	**1100**
Muslim conquests in Asia, North Africa, and southern Europe (completed by 719)	Second Crusade (1147–49)
	*Hildegard of Bingen (1098–1179)
	*Bernart de Ventadorn (ca. 1150–ca. 1180)
700	*Eleanor of Aquitaine (ca. 1122–1204)
800 Charlemagne (742–814) crowned Holy Roman Emperor (800)	Third Crusade (1189–92)
900	**1200**
	*Beatriz de Dia (d. ca. 1212)
*Monks at St. Gall compose tropes and sequences (Notker Balbulus, ca. 840–912; Tuotilo, d. 915)	**1300** The Plague devastates Europe (1348–49)
	1400
1000	Gutenberg (1398–1468) invents printing from movable metal type (1454)
*Guido of Arezzo (ca. 955–1050), writings on music	**1500**
*Goliards flourish	*Hans Sachs (1494–1576)

*Asterisks indicate persons or items of musical significance that are newly presented and discussed in each chapter.

melody that requires a highly trained soloist to perform. The degree of musical elaboration depends on the solemnity of the occasion, the function of the words in the ritual, and who is singing the chant—a soloist, a trained choir, or the untutored congregation. The position of the chant in the liturgy determines all this.

Liturgy

The body of texts and rites that make up a sacred service is known as the liturgy. It varies according to the saints, events, feast days, or seasons of the church year that are marked or remembered by the prescribed readings, prayers, and songs. In the Roman liturgy two main types of service exist: the Office and the Mass. The Divine Office, or Canonical Hours, comes from the Jewish practice of collective praying and singing of psalms. The Mass centers around a ritual commemorating the Last Supper of Jesus and his disciples as recounted in the New Testament.

The Office

The Office, or Canonical Hours, first codified in the *Rule of St. Benedict* (ca. 520), consists of a series of eight prayer services celebrated daily at specified times by the clergy and members of religious orders. By calling a monastic community to pray collectively every few hours, the Office provides the ritual around which life in a monastery is structured. It consists of prayers, recitation of scriptural passages, and songs.

The chief musical features of the Office are the chanting of psalms (from the Old Testament Book of Psalms) with their *antiphons* (chants that serve as frames for the simpler psalms), the singing of hymns and canticles (praise-songs), and the chanting of Scripture with additions called *responsories*. From a musical standpoint, the most important Canonical Hours are Matins (sung before daybreak), Lauds (at sunrise), and Vespers (at sunset), immediately followed by Compline. Matins includes some of the most ancient chants of the church. Vespers incorporates the canticle *Magnificat anima mea Dominum* (My soul doth magnify the Lord; Luke 1:46–55; see NAWM 4n, part of the Office of Second Vespers for Christmas Day, given complete in NAWM 4). In the history of sacred music Vespers is especially significant because it was the only part of the Office to use polyphonic song from early times. Compline always requires the singing of one of the four Marian antiphons (chants honoring the Blessed Virgin Mary), such as *Salve Regina* (Hail, O Queen, Example 2.1, page 25).

The Mass remains the most important service of the Catholic Church. The word "Mass" (Latin, *Missa*) comes from the end of the service, where the celebrant dismisses the congregation with the words *Ite, missa est* (Go, it is concluded). In other Christian churches the service is also known as the Eucharist, the Liturgy, Holy Communion, and the Lord's Supper, but all of them culminate in a symbolic reenactment of the Last Supper (Luke 22:19–20; 1 Cor. 11:23–26) in which the celebrant blesses the bread and wine and offers one or both to the faithful. An outline of the Catholic Mass, as it has been practiced since the late Middle Ages, appears below, with the most important musical items marked with asterisks.

The Mass

THE MASS OF THE ROMAN LITURGY		
	Proper	**Ordinary**
Introductory prayers	Introit*	
		Kyrie*
		Gloria*
	Collects	
Liturgy of the Word	Epistle	
	Gradual*	
	Alleluia/Tract*	
	Sequence* (now rare, common in the Middle Ages)	
	Gospel	
	[Sermon]	
		Credo*
Liturgy of the Eucharist	Offertory*	
	Preface	
		Sanctus*
		Agnus Dei*
	Communion*	
	Post-Communion	
		Ite, missa est*

◄ Gregory the Great (ca. 540–604) alternately listens to the dove (symbolizing the Holy Spirit) revealing the chants to him and dictates them to a scribe. The scribe, puzzled by the intermittent pauses in the pope's dictation, has lowered his slate and is peeking from behind the screen.

The liturgy of the Mass falls into three successive stages: introductory prayers; the Liturgy of the Word, during which the congregation listens to passages read or intoned from the Old Testament prophets and from the apostles and gospel writers of the New Testament; and the Liturgy of the Eucharist, during which the bread and wine are consecrated and distributed. Within these three stages, some prayers remain the same from one day to the next while others change according to the season or the particular occasion being celebrated. The variable prayers, called the *Proper of the Mass*, include the *Introit, Collects, Epistle, Gradual, Alleluia,* and others. The unchanging texts (each of which, however, may be sung to several different melodies throughout the year), called the *Ordinary of the Mass*, are the *Kyrie, Gloria, Credo, Sanctus, Agnus Dei,* and *Ite, missa est.*

The notation of chant

Systematic notation of the chant melodies coincided with a determined campaign by political leaders to promote a uniform liturgy and music in order to consolidate the entire population of worshipers throughout their lands. Numerous liturgical-musical "missionaries" traveled between Rome and the north in the late eighth and ninth centuries, and a potent weapon in their propaganda was the legend of St. Gregory, who, guided by divine inspiration in the form of a dove singing in his ear, wrote down the chant melodies. Notating the melodies helped assure that the chants would be sung the same way wherever the Roman liturgy was in use. Notation, then, was both the result of a striving for uniformity and a means of perpetuating that uniformity.

Modern Chant Books and Notation

The music for the Office is collected in a liturgical book called the *Antiphonale* (named for the antiphon, the type of chant that appears most frequently in the Canonical Hours), while the music for the Mass, both Proper and Ordinary, appears in the *Graduale* (after the Gradual, the most musically elaborate chant in the Mass). The *Liber usualis*, a modern publication that is now out of print, contains a selection of the most frequently used chants from both the *Graduale* and *Antiphonale*. An example of a chant in modern plainchant notation from the *Liber* appears on page 24; its transcription is given as Example 2.1, page 25.

As most chants have a range of less than an octave, the staff in early and modern plainsong notation has only four lines, one of which is designated by a clef as either *c'* (♭) or the *f* immediately below it (♯). These clefs do not indicate absolute pitches but rather the relative distance from one note to the next. Today it is usual to interpret all the notes (called *neumes*) as having essentially the same duration, regardless of shape. A dot after a neume doubles its value. A neume may carry only one syllable of text. Two or more neumes in succession on the same line or space, if on the same syllable, are sung as though tied. A horizontal dash above a neume means the note should be slightly lengthened. Scribes in medieval times, whose task was to compile or copy music and other manuscripts by hand, often used symbols and abbreviations in their work to save time and to limit the use of parchment (which was very expensive) or paper (nearly unobtainable). Certain neumes represented two or more notes sung to the same syllable, thereby uniting sounds that belonged together or were slurred. These *composite* neumes are read from left to right, except for the symbol (♯), in which the lower note is sung first. An oblique neume (♮) indicates two discrete notes. Flat signs, except in a signature at the beginning of a line, are valid only until the next vertical division mark or until the beginning of the next word. The partial note at the end of a line heralds the first note in the following line. An asterisk in the text shows where the chorus takes over from the soloist, and the signs *ij* and *iij* indicate that the preceding phrase is to be sung twice or three times.

➤ The Antiphon to the Blessed Virgin Mary, *Salve Regina mater misericordiae* (Hail, O Queen, Mother of mercy) as notated in a modern book of the most frequently used chant of the Mass and Offices, the *Liber usualis*.

Classes, Forms, and Types of Chant

Chants are classified in different, overlapping ways: (1) by their texts, which may be biblical or nonbiblical, prose or poetry; (2) by their manner of performance, which may be antiphonal (sung by alternating choirs), responsorial (with a choir responding to a soloist), or direct (simply by one choir); and (3) by their musical style, which may be syllabic (one note per syllable of text) or melismatic (many notes per syllable). This distinction is not always clear-cut, as chants that are mostly melismatic usually include some syllabic sections or phrases, and many syllabic chants have occasional short melismas of four or five notes on some syllables, passages that are sometimes called neumatic.

Text setting   In general, the melodic outline of a chant reflects the way the Latin words were pronounced, with prominent syllables set to higher notes or to a melisma. But in florid chants, the word accent often takes a backseat to the

EXAMPLE 2.1   Antiphon: *Salve Regina*

Hail, O Queen, Mother of mercy, our life, our sweetness and our hope! To thee we cry, banished children of Eve; to thee we send up our sighs, mourning and weeping in this vale of tears. Turn then, our Advocate, thine eyes of mercy toward us; and after this our exile, show unto us the blessed fruit of thy womb, Jesus. O clement, O loving, O sweet Virgin Mary.

This modern transcription reproduces certain signs that accompany the neumes in the manuscript. The asterisk indicates where the chant alternates between soloist and choir, or between the two halves of the choir. The straight lines under some pairs of notes are extensions of the sign for a slight lengthening of the notes. The small notes correspond to a sign probably indicating a light vocalization of the first ("voiced") consonant in such combinations as *ergo* and *ventris*. The wavy line represents a sign that probably called for a slight ornamenting of the note, perhaps something like a short trill or mordent.

melodic curve, resulting in long melismas on weak syllables, such as the final "a" of "alleluia" or "e" of "Kyrie." In such cases, the most important words or syllables of a phrase are emphasized with syllabic treatment that makes them stand out against the rich ornamentation of the unstressed syllables. Plainchant calls for word repetition only where it exists in the text of the prayer itself (such as the phrase "Kyrie eleison"; see page 29). The melody is always adapted to the rhythm of the text, to its general mood, and to the liturgical function of the chant. Rarely does the melody realize emotional or pictorial effects. Even so, chant is highly expressive in proclaiming the text, sometimes straightforwardly and other times ornately.

Melodic structure

Every chant melody is divided into phrases and periods corresponding to the phrases and periods of the text. In modern chant books these sections are marked off by vertical lines that resemble partial bar lines, shorter or longer according to the importance of the subdivision. The melody is most often shaped to follow the curve of an arch, beginning low, rising to a higher pitch, perhaps remaining there for a while, then descending at the end of a phrase. This simple and natural design occurs in a great variety of subtle combinations—extending over two or more phrases, for example, or including many smaller arches within its span. A less common melodic design, characteristic of phrases beginning with an especially important word, starts on a high note and descends gradually to the end.

Chant forms

We can distinguish three main forms in the chant repertory. One, exemplified in the psalm tone, consists of two balanced phrases that correspond to the two halves of a typical psalm verse (see Example 2.2, page 27). In the second form—such as strophic form in hymns—the same melody is sung to several stanzas of text (as in NAWM 4k). A third is free form, which may be entirely original or may combine traditional melodic formulas, possibly incorporated into an otherwise original composition.

We will now look at the important types of chants used in the Mass and Office, beginning with syllabic and proceeding to more melismatic styles.

Chants of the Office

Psalm tones

The formulas for chanting the Psalms, called psalm tones, are among the oldest chants of the liturgy. There is one tone (formula) for each of the eight church modes (see page 33) and an extra one called the *Tonus peregrinus*, or "wandering tone." In the Office a psalm may be sung to any one of the tones, chosen to match the mode of its prescribed antiphon (see, for example, NAWM 4b and c).

A psalm tone consists of five separate melodic elements. It begins with an *initium* (used only in the first verse of the psalm), rises to its *reciting tone*, or *tenor* (a single note that is repeated), bends at the midpoint of the verse for a semicadence, or *mediatio*, continues on the reciting tone for the second half-verse, and concludes at the end of the verse by descending to a cadence, or *terminatio* (see Example 2.2). This formula is repeated for each verse of the psalm. The final verse usually leads into the Lesser Doxology, an expression of praise to the Trinity tacked on to "christianize" the psalms, originally a body of Hebrew poetry inherited from the Jewish liturgy. The words of the Doxology are fitted to the same psalm tone as the psalm verses. Every psalm in the Office is framed by a different antiphon, attached to it solely for one particular day of the calendar year. So, although all 150 psalms are sung in the course of a week's cycle of Canonical Hours, each will have a new antiphon the following week and thereafter throughout the year. A model for the chanting of Antiphon and Psalm in the Office is outlined in Example 2.2. (The full text of the antiphon *Tecum principium* [Thine shall be the dominion] and Psalm 109 may be found in NAWM 4b and c.)

Doxology

EXAMPLE 2.2   Outline of the Psalmody of the Office

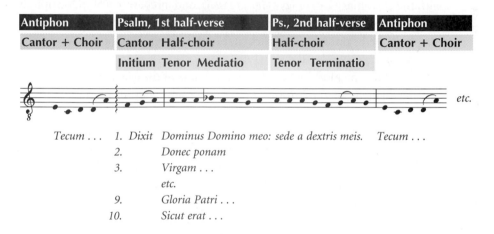

Antiphon	Psalm, 1st half-verse		Ps., 2nd half-verse	Antiphon
Cantor + Choir	Cantor	Half-choir	Half-choir	Cantor + Choir
	Initium	Tenor Mediatio	Tenor Terminatio	

Tecum . . .   1. *Dixit*   *Dominus Domino meo: sede a dextris meis.*   *Tecum . . .*
 2.   *Donec ponam*
 3.   *Virgam . . .*
    etc.
 9.   *Gloria Patri . . .*
 10.   *Sicut erat . . .*

This kind of psalmodic singing is called antiphonal (from the Greek for "sounding against") because the half-verses alternate between two choirs or between a half-choir and the full choir. The practice, believed to imitate ancient Syrian models, was adopted early in the history of the Christian Church.

Antiphonal psalmody

In earliest times, the antiphon, a verse or sentence with its own melody, was probably repeated after every verse of a psalm, like the phrase "for His mercy endureth forever" in Latin Psalm 135 (English 136). Eventually, only the intonation (opening phrase) of the antiphon was sung before the psalm, with the entire antiphon performed after the psalm.

Antiphons

Antiphons are more numerous than any other type of chant; about 1,250 appear in the modern *Antiphonale*. However, many antiphons employ the same melody, using only slight variations to accommodate the text. Since antiphons were originally intended to be sung by a group rather than a soloist, the older ones are usually syllabic or only slightly florid, with stepwise melodic movement, comparatively simple rhythm, and a limited melodic range. Some of the more elaborate antiphons developed into independent chants—for example, Introits, Offertories, and Communion chants, all belonging to the Proper of the Mass—retaining only a single psalm verse or none at all. Many antiphons were composed for additional feasts introduced into the church calendar between the ninth and thirteenth centuries. This same period produced a number of antiphons that were not attached to particular psalms, for use in processions and at special occasions. The four Marian antiphons—liturgically not antiphons at all but independent compositions—are of comparatively late date (see, for example, the *Salve Regina*, Example 2.1).

Chants of the Mass

Introit

As noted above, the Introit was originally a complete psalm with its antiphon. In the course of time, this opening part of the service was shortened so that today the Introit consists only of the original antiphon, a single psalm verse with the customary Doxology (*Gloria Patri*), and a repetition of the antiphon. The Communion, coming near the end of the Mass as a counterpart to the Introit at the beginning, is a short chant, often consisting of only one scriptural verse.

Musically, the most highly developed chants of the Mass are the Graduals, Alleluias, Tracts, and Offertories, probably because they occur at moments in the service that are more meditative than active. The Tract was originally a solo song, replacing the Alleluia during periods of penitence or mourning. The Gradual and Alleluia are responsorial, intended for soloist and choir in alternation. Each has only one psalm verse, framed by a separate melody and text known as a *respond*. Most likely, the Offertory began as an antiphonal chant, but no trace of the original psalm remains today and what must have been the original antiphon is performed as a responsorial chant by soloist and choir.

Gradual and Alleluia

Graduals came to the Frankish churches (in what is now France) from Rome in a form that was already highly evolved. Their melodies and those of the Alleluia are very florid and have a similar structure (see the outline of an Alleluia, below). The soloist (or group of soloists) sings the framing respond, which the choir then picks up. The soloist sings the psalm verse, with the choir joining in on the last phrase. Certain melismatic formulas recur in different Graduals at similar points in the chant, such as intonations, internal cadences, and terminations. Some melodies consist almost entirely of such formulas, pointing to an earlier, pre-notational time when singers had to rely on their memories; recurring patterns made performing that much easier. In the Alleluias, the respond text is always the single word "alleluia" with the final syllable "ia" receiving an effusive melisma called a *jubilus* (see NAWM 3e). The Alleluia proceeds as follows: the soloist (or solo group) sings the word "alleluia," up to the asterisk; the chorus repeats it and continues with the jubilus; the soloist then sings the psalm verse, with the chorus joining in at the last phrase; then the entire "alleluia" is repeated by the soloist with the chorus joining in again at the jubilus.

Responsorial performance

Soloist			Soloist		
	Chorus			Chorus	Chorus
Alleluia	** Allelu-ia* . . . (jubilus) . . .		*Ps. verse* . . .*	. . . *Allelu-ia*	(jubilus)

Many Alleluias have the character of music that was carefully planned and composed rather than improvised. For example, they often include what might be termed "musical rhyme," in which matching phrases occur at the ends of sections. Alleluias were written throughout the Middle Ages and spawned important new forms.

The chants for the Mass Ordinary probably started out as simple syllabic melodies sung by the congregation. After the ninth century, these were replaced by more ornate settings. The syllabic style was retained for the Gloria and Credo, which have the longest texts. The Kyrie, Sanctus, and Agnus Dei, because of the nature of their texts, have three-part sectional arrangements. The Kyrie, for example, suggests the following setting (see NAWM 3b):

Chants of the Ordinary

Kyrie

> A *Kyrie eleison*
> B *Christe eleison*
> A *Kyrie eleison*

Since each exclamation is uttered three times, there may be an *aba* or *aba′* form within each of the three principal sections. More sophisticated versions of the Kyrie may have the pattern A B C, with motivic interconnections. (For the complete music and text of the Mass on Christmas Day, see NAWM 3.)

Later Developments of the Chant

Between the fifth and ninth centuries, the peoples of western and northern Europe converted to Christianity and adopted the doctrines and rites of the Roman Church. The official "Gregorian" chant was established in the Frankish Empire before the middle of the ninth century, and from then until nearly the close of the Middle Ages, all important developments in European music took place not in Rome but north of the Alps. This shift in musical centers occurred partly because of political conditions. The Muslim conquests of Syria, North Africa, and especially Spain, completed by 719, left the southern Christian regions either in the hands of occupying forces or under constant threat of attack. Meanwhile, various cultural centers arose in western and central Europe. Between the sixth and eighth centuries, missionaries from Irish and Scottish monasteries established schools in their own lands and abroad, especially in what is now Germany and Switzerland. A resurgence of Latin culture in England early in the eighth century produced scholars whose reputation extended to continental Europe. An English monk, Alcuin of York, helped Emperor Charlemagne in his project to revive education throughout the Frankish Empire. One result of this eighth- and ninth-century renaissance was the development of important musical centers, including the famous monastery of St. Gall in Switzerland. Here, the northern, Frankish influence on plainchant is evident in melodic lines with greater use of leaps, especially thirds, and in the introduction of both new melodies and new forms of chant, such as *tropes* and *sequences*. The same period saw the rise of secular monodic song and the earliest experiments in polyphony, developments to be taken up shortly.

Tropes

Tropes originated as newly composed additions, usually in neumatic style and with poetic texts, to Introits and other antiphonal chants of the Proper (see NAWM 7 and page 28). Later, such additions were also made to chants of the Ordinary, especially the Kyrie and Gloria. We find three kinds of tropes: text added to existing melismas; music extending melismas or adding new ones; and new words and music added to a regular chant. Many fine tropes were written by Tuotilo (d. 915), a monk at the monastery of St. Gall, which became an important center of troping. Trope composition flourished especially in monastic churches in the tenth and eleventh centuries; in the twelfth it fell out of favor, although tropes continued in use until the Council of Trent (1545–63) banned them from the liturgy four hundred years later.

Sequences

Sequences probably began as text additions to the jubilus in Alleluias, but

Structure of the Sequence

A sequence typically begins with a text statement (versicle or strophe) set to its own phrase of music; this is followed by a pair of versicles or a double strophe (each having the same number of syllables and pattern of accents), set to a single new phrase of music that is heard twice. A varying number of paired statements follows, each sung to a new and repeating musical phrase that matches the number of syllables and accents in the text. The final phrase of music, like the opening one, is stated only once, to a single versicle or strophe. This pattern may be represented in the following diagram, where N and x represent the last, unpaired statement of text and music.

Versicle or strophe:	1	2	3	4	5	6	7	. . . N
Music:	a	b	b	c	c	d	d	. . . x

In some sequences, the composer has unified the different melodic segments with similar cadential phrases, as we may see in *Victimae paschali laudes* (Praises to the Paschal Victim, NAWM 5), the sequence for the Mass of Easter Day.

they quickly became independent compositions. Notker Balbulus (his name means "the stammerer"; ca. 840–912), another Frankish monk of St. Gall, describes how he learned to write words syllabically under long melismas to help him memorize them. The sequence was an important creative outlet from the tenth to the thirteenth centuries and later. Popular sequences were even imitated and adapted for secular genres, both vocal and instrumental, in the late Middle Ages. Nevertheless, most sequences were banned from the Catholic service by the liturgical reforms of the Council of Trent. The five that survived hold vital places in the liturgy, such as the celebrated *Dies irae* in the Requiem Mass (Mass for the Dead).

Liturgical drama also originated in troping. One of the earliest of these dramas, *Quem quaeritis in sepulchro* (Whom do you seek in the tomb?), was based on a tenth-century troped dialogue preceding the Introit for Easter Sunday Mass. In the dialogue, the three Marys come to the tomb of Jesus. The angel asks them, "Whom do you seek in the sepulchre?" They reply, "Jesus of Nazareth," to which the angel answers, "He is not here, He is risen as He said; go and proclaim that He has risen from the grave" (Mark 16:5–7). According to contemporary accounts, the dialogue was sung responsorially and the scene was acted out. The Easter trope and a similar one for Christmas, *Quem quaeritis in praesepe* (Whom do you seek in the manger? NAWM 7 and illustration below), were performed all over Europe. Other plays survive from the twelfth century and later. The early-thirteenth-century *Play of Daniel* from Beauvais and *The Play of Herod*, concerning the slaughter of the innocents, from Fleury, have now become staples in the repertories of early-music ensembles. The music for these plays consists of a number of

Liturgical drama

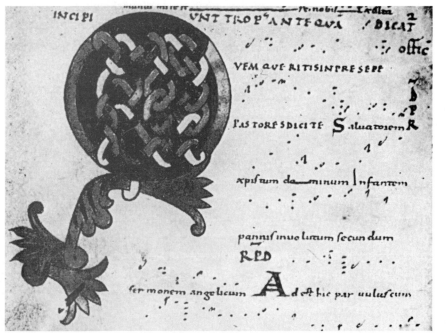

◄ The earliest surviving copy of the Christmas dramatic trope *Quem quaeritis in praesepe*, in a troper from St. Martial de Limoges. For a transcription, see NAWM 7. (*Paris, Bibliothèque Nationale, MS 1118, fol. 8v.*)

chants strung together, with processions and actions that approach theatrical representation. A few manuscripts give evidence that the works were staged, with scenery, costumes, and actors drawn from the clergy.

Hildegard of Bingen

Although most liturgical dramas from this period are anonymous, we have a unique, nonliturgical but sacred music drama by Hildegard of Bingen (1098–1179). In her morality play *Ordo virtutum* (The Virtues, ca. 1151), all the parts—such as the Prophets, the Virtues, the Happy Soul, the Unhappy Soul, and the Penitent Soul—except the Devil's are sung in plainchant. The final chorus of the Virtues (NAWM 6), in the composer's typically expansive melodic style, overflows the normal limits of its mode. Founder and abbess of the convent at Rupertsberg in Germany, Hildegard stands out among authors of tropes and sequences because she composed the melodies as well as the verse.

Medieval Music Theory and Practice

Treatises in the age of Charlemagne and in the later Middle Ages reflected actual practice to a greater extent than the more speculative earlier writings. They always spoke of Boethius with reverence and passed along the mathematical fundamentals of scale building, intervals, and consonances that he transmitted from the Greeks. But reading Boethius did not help solve the immediate problems of how to sing intervals, memorize chants, and, later, read notes at sight. Theorists addressed these goals in establishing the system of eight modes, or *toni* ("tones"), as medieval writers called them.

The church modes

The medieval modal system developed gradually, achieving its complete form by the eleventh century. It encompassed eight modes, each defined by the sequence of whole tones and semitones in a diatonic octave built on a *finalis*, or final. In practice, this note was usually the last note in the melody. The modes were identified by numbers and grouped in pairs; the odd-numbered modes were called *authentic*, and the even-numbered modes *plagal* (collateral). A plagal mode always had the same final as its corresponding authentic mode. The authentic modal scales may be thought of as analogous to white-key octave scales on a modern keyboard rising from the notes *D* (mode 1), *E* (mode 3), *F* (mode 5), and *G* (mode 7), with their corresponding plagals (modes 2, 4, 6, and 8) a fourth lower (see Example 2.3). These notes, of course, do not stand for specific "absolute" pitches—a concept foreign to plainchant and to the Middle Ages in general; they are simply a convenient way to distinguish between the interval patterns of different modes. The modes became a primary means for classifying chants and arranging them in books for liturgical use. However, because many of the chants existed before the theory of modes evolved, their melodic characteristics do not always conform to modal theory.

EXAMPLE 2.3   The Medieval Church Modes

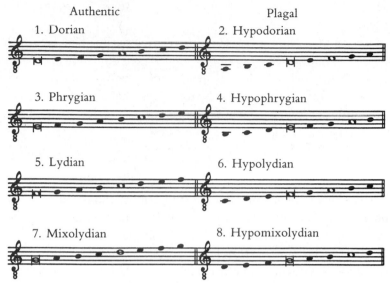

More about the Medieval Church Modes

The finals of each mode are shown in Example 2.3 as boxed whole notes. In addition to the final, each mode has a second characteristic note, called the *tenor* or *reciting tone* (shown in Example 2.3 as whole notes), as in the psalm tones. The finals of the corresponding plagal and authentic modes are the same, but their tenors differ. A handy way to identify the tenors using the scheme of Example 2.3 is to remember that in the authentic modes the tenor is a fifth above the final, except that whenever a tenor falls on the note *B*, it is moved up to *C* (to avoid outlining the tritone *B–F* in the melody); and in the plagal modes the tenor is a third below the tenor of the corresponding authentic mode, with the same exception.

The final, tenor, and range all contribute to characterizing a mode. Although a plagal mode (for example, mode 2) has the same final as its corresponding authentic mode (mode 1), the two have different tenors and ranges. In contrast, modes 1 and 8 have the same range, but different finals and tenors.

Under certain conditions, the *B* was flatted in modes 1 and 2, making their octave-scales analogous to the modern natural minor; modes 5 and 6 could similarly be made to resemble the modern major. Accidentals were necessary, of course, when a modal melody was transposed; if a chant in mode 1, for example, were written on *G*, a flat would be required in the signature.

In the tenth century a few authors, misreading Boethius, applied the names of the Greek *tonoi* to the church modes, even though the two systems were not at all parallel. Although neither medieval treatises nor modern liturgical books refer to the modes by the Greek names (preferring numerals), their original ethnic designations appear in modern textbooks on counterpoint and analysis, modes 1 and 2 being called Dorian and Hypodorian, modes 3 and 4 Phrygian and Hypophrygian, and so forth (see Example 2.3).

Solmization

For teaching sight singing, the eleventh-century monk Guido of Arezzo proposed a set of syllables, *ut, re, mi, fa, sol, la*, to help singers remember the pattern of whole tones and semitone in the six steps that begin on *G* or *C*. In this pattern (for example, *C–D–E–F–G–A*), a semitone falls between the third and fourth steps, and all other steps are whole tones. The syllables were derived from a two-hundred-year-old hymn text *Ut queant laxis*, that Guido himself may have set to music to illustrate the pattern. Each of the six phrases of the hymn begins with one of the notes of the pattern in regular ascending order—the first phrase on *C*, the second on *D*, and so on (Example 2.4). (Rodgers and Hammerstein used the same procedure in "Doe, a deer," a song from their 1959 musical *The Sound of Music*.) The initial syllables of these six phrases became the names of the scale steps. The so-called solmization (from *sol-mi*) syllables are still employed in teaching, except that in English we say *do* for *ut* and add a *ti* above *la*.

EXAMPLE 2.4   Hymn: *Ut queant laxis*

Ut que-ant la - xis *re*-so-na-re fi-bris *Mi* - ra ge-sto-rum *fa*-mu-li tu-o - rum,

Sol - ve pol-lu - ti *La* - bi - i re - a-tum, San - cte Jo-an-nes.

That thy servants may freely sing forth the wonders of thy deeds, remove all stain of guilt from their unclean lips, O Saint John.

The Guidonian hand

Followers of Guido developed a pedagogical aid called the "Guidonian hand." Pupils were taught to sing intervals as the teacher pointed with the index finger of the right hand to the different joints of the open left hand. Each joint stood for one of the twenty notes that made up the musical system of the time; any other note, such as *F♯* or *E♭*, was considered to be "outside the hand." No late-medieval or Renaissance music textbook was complete without a drawing of this hand.

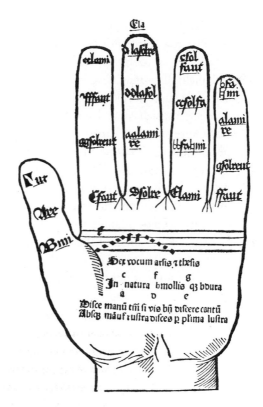

➤ The "Guidonian hand," a mnemonic device used for locating the pitches of the diatonic scale, particularly the semitones *mi-fa*, which occupy the four corners of the polygon containing the four fingers. Although credited to Guido, the hand was probably a later application of his solmization syllables.

The musical staff, already in use by Guido's time, not only enabled scribes to notate (relative) pitches precisely but also freed music from its dependence on oral transmission. The achievement was as crucial for the development of Western music as the invention of writing was for literature.

The staff

Nonliturgical and Secular Monody

Music outside the Church spawned as many different types and forms of song as plainchant; a few of them will be described here. The oldest written specimens of secular music are songs with Latin texts, among them the Goliard songs from the eleventh and twelfth centuries. The Goliards—named after a probably fictitious patron, Bishop Goliath—were students or footloose clerics who migrated from one school to another in the days before the great universities existed. Their vagabond way of life, scorned by respectable people, was celebrated in their songs, gathered into numerous manuscript collections. The texts are drawn largely from three topics of interest to young men of the time: wine, women, and satire. In most cases, the music does not survive in a notation precise enough to permit accurate modern transcriptions and performances.

Goliard songs

Conductus

Another kind of monophonic song from the same period—the eleventh, twelfth, and thirteenth centuries—is the *conductus* (plural also *conductus*). Conductus straddle the vague dividing line between sacred and secular music. Originally they may have been sung when a cleric in a liturgical drama or a celebrant in a liturgical service was formally "conducted" from one place to another; most have a distinct rhythmic pulse—almost like a march. Their texts were metrical verses in Latin, like those of sequences from the same period. But their connection with the liturgy was so loose that by the end of the twelfth century, the term *conductus* applied to any serious, nonliturgical Latin song with a metrical text on any sacred or secular subject. An important feature of the conductus was that, as a rule, its melody was newly composed, not borrowed or adapted from plainchant.

Chanson de geste

The secular spirit of the Middle Ages comes through clearly in the songs with vernacular texts. One of the earliest known types was the *chanson de geste*, or "song of deeds," an epic narrative poem recounting the exploits of national heroes, sung to simple melodic formulas. A single formula serves unchanged for each line throughout long sections of the poem. The poems, transmitted orally, were written down comparatively late; but virtually none of the music has been preserved. The most famous *chanson de geste* is the *Song of Roland*, the national epic of France, which dates from about the second half of the eleventh century, though its story is set three hundred years earlier, in the age of Charlemagne.

Jongleurs

The people who sang the *chansons de geste* and other secular songs in the Middle Ages were the *jongleurs* or *ménestrels* (minstrels), a class of professional musicians who first appear in about the tenth century. These men and women wandered singly or in small groups from village to village and castle to castle, earning a precarious living by singing, playing, performing tricks, and exhibiting trained animals. They were social outcasts, often denied the protection of the law and the sacraments of the church. With the economic recovery of Europe in the eleventh and twelfth centuries, society became more stably organized and towns sprang up. The minstrels' situation improved, though for a long time people continued to regard them with a mixture of fascination and revulsion. In the eleventh century, they organized themselves into brotherhoods, which later developed into guilds of musicians offering professional training, much as we find in a modern conservatory.

The minstrels were not poets or composers in the usual sense. They sang, played, and danced to songs composed by others or taken from the popular repertory, no doubt altering them or making up their own versions as they went along. Their professional traditions and skill played a role in an important development of secular music in western Europe—the body of song known today as the music of the troubadours and the trouvères.

Troubadours and trouvères

Troubadours (male) or *trobairitz* (female, singular and plural) were poet-composers who flourished in the south of France and spoke Provençal (also called the *langue d'oc* or *Occitan*). *Trouvères* were their equivalent in northern

France. (The verb *trobar* in the southern dialect and the corresponding northern word *trouver* mean "to find"; thus troubadours and trouvères were finders or inventors of songs.) Their art, taking its inspiration from the Arabic love poetry cultivated in Moorish Spain, spread quickly northward, especially to the provinces of Champagne and Artois. There the trouvères, active throughout the thirteenth century, spoke the *langue d'oïl*, the medieval French dialect that became modern French (*oïl = oui*, yes).

Neither troubadours nor trouvères constituted a well-defined group. They flourished in generally aristocratic circles; some were kings, others of lower birth but accepted into a higher social class because of their talent. Many of the poet-composers not only created their songs but sang them as well; those who did not entrusted the performance to a minstrel. The songs are preserved in collections called *chansonniers*, some of which appear in modern editions or facsimiles. About 2,600 troubadour poems and about one-tenth as many melodies are preserved. By contrast, we have some 2,130 trouvère poems, but at least two-thirds of their melodies are known.

Types of songs

The poetic and musical structures of the songs show great variety and ingenuity. Some ballads are simple, others dramatic, suggesting two or more characters. Some of the dramatic ballads were probably intended to be mimed; many obviously called for dancing. The dance songs may include a

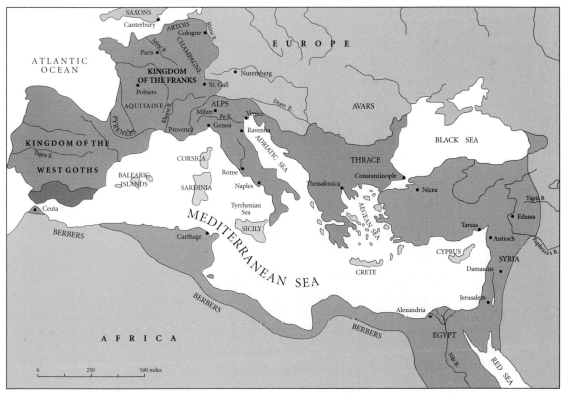

▲ Medieval Europe, ca. 600 C.E.

refrain sung by a chorus of dancers. An important structural feature of numerous trouvère songs, the refrain is a line or two of poetry that returns with its own music from one stanza to another. The troubadours, especially, wrote songs of love, the subject par excellence of their poetry. But they also wrote songs on political and moral topics, and songs whose texts debate or argue esoteric points of chivalric or courtly love. Each type of song includes many subtypes that followed certain conventions about subject matter, form, and treatment.

Pastourelle

A favorite genre, the *pastorela* or *pastourelle*, told a variation on the following story: a knight pursues a shepherdess who succumbs after due resistance, or the shepherdess screams for help, whereupon her brother or lover rushes in, thrashes the knight and drives him away. In the earliest pastourelles, a narrator told the story. It was a natural step, however, to turn the text into a dialogue between the knight and the shepherdess. Later, the dialogue was acted as well as sung. If one or two episodes were added, and if the rescuing shepherd appeared with a group of rustic companions and the performance was decked out with incidental songs and dances, the result was a little musical play. The most famous of such musical plays was *Jeu de Robin et de Marion* (ca. 1284) by Adam de la Halle, the last and greatest of the trouvères (NAWM 8).

Provençal lyrics

The pastourelles and other narrative songs adapted folk material. The Provençal love songs, by comparison, were aristocratic creations. Many were openly sensual; others hid sensuality under a veil of courtly love. The object of the passion they expressed was a real woman—usually another man's wife—but she was adored from a distance, with such discretion, respect, and

◄ Portrait of Adam de la Halle in a miniature from the Chansonnier d'Arras, which contains six of his chansons. The legend says, "Adans li bocus made these songs." His family, from Arras, was known by the name "le Bossu" (the hunchback). (*Arras, Bibliothèque Municipale*)

humility that the lover is made to seem more like a worshiper content to suffer in the service of his ideal Love. The lady herself is depicted as so remote, calm, lofty, and unattainable that she would be stepping out of character if she condescended to reward her faithful lover. It is typical of the indistinct line between sacred and secular music that we find trouvère songs praising the Virgin Mary in the same style, using the same vocabulary, and sometimes employing the very same melodies that were used to celebrate earthly love.

Among the best preserved songs is *Can vei la lauzeta mover* (When I see the lark beating, NAWM 9) by the troubadour Bernart de Ventadorn (ca. 1150–ca. 1180), one of the most popular poets of his time. Stories about his life assert that he rose from low birth as the son of a serf and baker in the castle of Ventadorn to become the great lover of three noble ladies, including Eleanor of Aquitaine (see window, pages 40–41). Of the eight stanzas of *Can vei la lauzeta mover*, the second displays especially well the complaints, the contradictions, and the emotional and erotic tensions that characterize this repertory.[1]

Bernart de Ventadorn

Ai, las! tan cuidava saber	Alas! I thought I knew so much
d'amor, e tan petit en sai,	of love, and I know so little;
car eu d'amar no·m posc tener	for I cannot help loving
celeis don ia pro non aura.	a lady from whom I shall never obtain any favor.
Tout m'a mo cor, e tout m'a me,	She has taken away my heart and my self
e se mezeis e tot lo mon;	and herself and the whole world;
e can se·m tolc, no·m laisset re	and when she left me, I had nothing left
mas dezirer e cor volon.	but desire and a yearning heart.

Like Bernart's song, or *canso*, the typical troubadour and trouvère text is strophic, with all the stanzas sung to the same through-composed melody. The settings are generally syllabic with an occasional short melismatic figure near the end of a line. Such a simple melody invites improvised ornaments and other variants as the singer passes from one stanza to the next. The range is narrow—a sixth, perhaps, or an octave. Because the songs were written chiefly in the first and seventh church modes and their plagals, the entire body of works displays a certain coherence. The notation yields no clue to the rhythm of the songs: they might have been sung in a free, unmeasured style, or in long and short notes corresponding to the accented and unaccented syllables of the words. Most scholars now prefer to transcribe them as they do plainchant—in neutral note values without bar lines.

Typical song structure

Each poetic line receives its own melodic setting. Through variation, contrast, and the repetition of short, distinctive musical phrases, a variety of

---

1. Text and translation are from Hendrik van der Werf, *The Chansons of the Troubadours and Trouvères* (Utrecht: A. Oosthoek, 1972), pp. 91–95, which presents versions of the melody from five different sources, showing surprising consistency of readings. The dot splitting two letters of a word, as in no·m, stands for contraction.

Window

ELEANOR OF AQUITAINE
AND HER COURTS OF LOVE

A most fascinating woman of her time, Eleanor (1122?–1204) was born into an aristocratic family that presided over an immense realm in the south of France. Her grandfather was William IX, seventh count of Poitiers and ninth duke of Aquitaine, the first troubadour whose songs we have. Descended from a first-rate poet-composer (who is sometimes regarded as the originator of the courtly love lyric), Eleanor became a great patron of troubadours and trouvères, some of whom addressed her in their lyrics as the lofty lady of their heart's desire. Legend has it that she took Bernart de Ventadorn as her lover for a time (see page 39).

Eleanor was also married to two kings, Louis VII of France, whom she accompanied on the Second Crusade and later divorced, and Henry II (Plantagenet) of England, by whom she bore three daughters and five sons, two of whom also became kings of England: Richard I and John. When Richard, also called Coeur de Lion (Lion-Heart, 1157–1199), was taken prisoner on his return from the Third Crusade, she energetically collected the ransom to pay for his freedom. (Richard was also a trouvère, and the story of his imprisonment for two years in an Austrian dungeon is commemorated in moving lines from his song *Ja nus hons pris*, including "Never will a prisoner speak his mind fittingly unless he speaks in grief.")

formal patterns emerges. Many of the troubadour and trouvère melodies repeat the opening phrase or section before proceeding in a free style—for example, a b a b c d e f. Phrases are modified on repetition, and elusive echoes of earlier phrases appear, but the main impression is one of freedom, spontaneity, and simplicity, although in fact both the music and poetry are very skillfully crafted.

Beatriz de Dia

Some of these features are illustrated in another canso, composed by the twelfth-century trobairitz Comtessa Beatriz de Dia (d. ca. 1212). A *vida*, or biographical tale, written about a century later describes Beatriz as a "beautiful and good woman, the wife of Guillaume de Poitiers. And she was in love with Rambaud d'Orange and made about him many good and beautiful songs." In *A chantar* (To sing, NAWM 10) the comtessa berates her unfaithful lover and reminds him of her own worthy qualities. The song uses four distinct melodic components, arranged in the form a b a b c d b.

Probably an educated musician herself, Eleanor was a smart and strong-minded woman. Because of Henry's infidelities, her relations with him grew strained, and in 1170 she left London and established a court of her own in Poitiers, a geographic center of her native region, Aquitaine. She assisted her sons in an unsuccessful revolt against Henry in 1173 and was herself imprisoned by him for fourteen years, but her efforts eventually helped Richard secure the throne.

In the course of her long and tempestuous career, Eleanor attracted many artists, trouvères, and writers, some of whom–like Bernart–dedicated works to her. All sorts of artistic monuments to Eleanor still exist, ranging from a regal twelfth-century likeness of her head (supposedly paired with that of King Henry; see illustration) carved onto one of the capitals of a church near Bordeaux in Aquitaine and now in the Romanesque chapel of The Cloisters in New York, to a 1968 movie called *The Lion in Winter*, for which Katharine Hepburn in the role of Queen Eleanor won an Oscar. There is also a wonderful biography by Amy Kelly, *Eleanor of Aquitaine and the Four Kings* (1950; new ed., 1957).

Minnesinger

The troubadours served as the model for a German school of knightly poet-musicians, the *Minnesinger*, who flourished between the twelfth and fourteenth centuries. The love (*Minne*) of which they sang in their *Minnelieder* (love songs) was even more abstract than troubadour love and sometimes had a distinctly religious tinge. The music is correspondingly more sober. Some of the melodies are written in the church modes, while others tend toward major tonality. Based on the rhythm of the texts, scholars think that the majority of the tunes were sung in triple meter. As in France, strophic songs predominated. Their tunes, however, were more tightly organized through melodic phrase repetition. A typical German poetic form called *Bar* (aab) inspired a common musical pattern: the melodic phrase *a* is sung twice for the stanza's first two units of text, while the remainder, *b*, which is longer and sung only once, contains new melodic material.

Both the French and the German texts include loving depictions of the glow and freshness of spring. There are also dawn songs, or watcher's songs, sung by the faithful friend who stands guard and warns the illicit lovers that dawn is approaching. And in both languages there are songs of religious devotion, many inspired by the Crusades (Christian military expeditions to recover the Holy Land from the Muslims).

Meistersinger

The Minnesinger were succeeded by the *Meistersinger* (singular and plural), staunch merchants and artisans of German cities. Just as the art of the trouvères in France had passed from the nobility to cultured middle-class citizens, a similar change took place in Germany during the course of the fourteenth, fifteenth, and sixteenth centuries. Hans Sachs is a typical figure—a sixteenth-century shoemaker in Nuremberg who composed thousands of poems and the tunes for singing them. Although Sachs's work includes some fine examples, the art of the Meistersinger was so bound by rigid rules that their music seems stiff in comparison to the Minnelieder. The Meistersinger's guild enjoyed an extraordinarily long life until it was finally dissolved in the nineteenth century.

POSTLUDE

The spread and stabilization of the Roman rite through western Europe during the Middle Ages resulted in the creation of a Gregorian chant repertory that survives to this day. This repertory includes many different types of song, each with a distinct function within the liturgical celebration of the Office and the Mass. It also contains many chronological layers, having evolved from pre-Christian times (witness the Psalms) until about the thirteenth century, when some types of chant (such as tropes and sequences) were still being written. Chants were classified into eight church modes and written down in a notation that gradually evolved as a means of teaching and standardizing its performance.

Secular songs also flourished, especially with the growth of cultural centers and courts in the later Middle Ages. These songs, in a variety of strophic forms often including refrains, had many different uses, sometimes involving dance. Some were narrative or dramatic, others lyrical. The body of love songs created by troubadours and trouvères as a monument to the sentiments and ideals of courtly love remains unequaled for its sheer beauty and artfulness.

3

POLYPHONIC MUSIC FROM ITS BEGINNINGS THROUGH THE THIRTEENTH CENTURY

The years 1000–1200 saw an increase in trading and commerce throughout western Europe, as its growing population began to build modern cities. The Normans (a warrior people originally from Scandinavia who had settled Normandy in northern France) crossed the English Channel to conquer England, while Spain was seeking to liberate itself from Muslim conquerors. The First Crusade united Christian ruling families from all over Europe in a successful campaign to drive the "infidel" Turks from Jerusalem. After centuries of political instability and limited literacy, Europe enjoyed a cultural revival, which included music and all the arts; we have seen some of its effects in the thriving love songs of the troubadours and trouvères. Scholars translated important works from Greek antiquity and the Arab world into Latin, encouraging the development of music theory. Places of teaching and learning that eventually became universities sprang up in Paris, Oxford, and Bologna. Large Romanesque churches, built on the architectural principle of the round arch of the Roman basilica, began to dominate the landscape, just as Gregorian chant and the Roman rite prevailed in the liturgy. Literature and philosophy in Latin and in the spoken languages, such as Italian, French, and Spanish, asserted their independence from pagan antiquity. The rivalry between the Western and Eastern churches reached a crisis in 1054, when the Roman pope excommunicated the patriarch of Constantinople after Norman invaders captured Byzantine-held territory in southern Italy. The patriarch of Constantinople returned the discourtesy, and Christendom has been divided ever since.

As we have noted, many of these events had a positive influence on the development of music. In this chapter, we will trace another outcome of the cultural revival: the growth of polyphony in the church. By polyphony in this period we mean music in which voices sing together not in unison or octaves but in diverging parts. When, in the eleventh century, singers improvising according to certain rules departed from simple parallel motion to give these parts some independence, they set the stage for the next nine hundred years of Western music history. As the parts were combined in more complex ways, refinements in notation permitted the music to be written down and performed repeatedly. Written composition could now replace improvisation as a way of creating musical works, and notation could replace memory as a means of preserving them. Music became more consciously structured and was made to follow certain precepts, such as the theory of the eight modes and the rules governing rhythm and consonance. Such precepts were eventually set down in learned treatises.

These changes came about gradually; there was no sudden, sharp break with the past. Monophony remained the principal medium of both performance and new composition. Indeed, some of the finest monophonic chants, including antiphons, hymns, and sequences, were produced as late as the thirteenth century. Then, too, musicians continued to improvise during the eleventh century and beyond, and many stylistic details of the newly composed, polyphonic music grew out of improvisational practice.

After tentative beginnings in the eleventh century, two types of polyphonic composition gained a secure place in France by 1250: organum and conductus. A third type, the motet, soon augmented the repertory of polyphonic genres. **Early Organum** (pronounced ór-ga-num; Latin pl., órgana) grew out of the practice of troping the chant (described in Chapter 2). But now, instead of attaching a melodic trope to the beginning or end of an existing chant—a horizontal extension—organum offered composers and performers the possibility of adding new layers of melody in a vertical dimension. This polyphonic elaboration of plainchant reached its most sophisticated level in Paris at the Notre Dame Cathedral, which was being built in the soaring, new, Gothic style of the twelfth century. By creating different rates of motion among the voice parts, composers of **Notre Dame Organum** forced a breakthrough in rhythmic notation, which until then had been vague at best. The most famous of these composers, Léonin and Pérotin, devised a notational system known as the rhythmic modes (not related to the eight church modes). They also began writing **Polyphonic Conductus** and, through the creative outlet offered by troping, developed **The Motet**, which eventually became the dominant genre of both sacred and secular polyphonic music.

Polyphony

Composition

Early Organum

We have good reasons to believe that European musicians used polyphony in nonliturgical sacred music, and perhaps in folk music as well, long before it was first unmistakably described in a ninth-century treatise called *Musica enchiriadis* (Music Handbook). The anonymous author examines and illustrates two distinct kinds of "singing together," both designated by the term *organum*. In one species of this early organum (Example 3.1), a plainchant melody in the "principal voice" (*vox principalis*) is duplicated, at a fifth or a fourth below, by an "organal voice" (*vox organalis*). Either voice or both may be further duplicated at the octave (Example 3.2). Of course, singing in parallel fourths sometimes results in a tritone (as might have occurred in "-les" of "Te humiles" in Example 3.3), so a rule was devised to prevent the organal voice from going below *G* in this situation (or below *C* when the principal voice was heading for an *F*). Remaining on one note avoided the tritone until it was safe to proceed in parallel fourths again. In this procedure, called organum with oblique motion, the organal part became melodically differentiated from the plainchant, and a variety of simultaneous intervals came into use, including dissonances.

EXAMPLE 3.1   Parallel Organum

You of the father are the everlasting son (from the *Te Deum*).

EXAMPLE 3.2   Modified Parallel Organum in Four Voices

EXAMPLE 3.3   Organum with Oblique Motion

[Your] humble servants, worshiping with pious melodies, beseech you, as you command to free them from diverse ills (from the sequence *Rex coeli*).

As contrary and oblique motion became regular features in eleventh-century music, we find increasing melodic independence and more equality between the two voices. The vox organalis usually sings above the vox principalis (though the parts often cross) and occasionally sings two notes against one of the vox principalis (Example 3.4). Consonant intervals—the unison, octave, fourth, and fifth—prevail, while others occur only incidentally. The rhythm is identical to plainchant, which forms the basis for all these pieces.

EXAMPLE 3.4   Eleventh-Century Organum

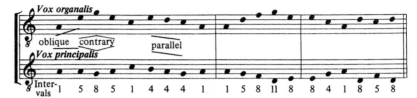

Winchester Troper

The Winchester Troper, the oldest large collection of organum-style pieces, consists of two eleventh-century English manuscripts used at Winchester Cathedral. The "troping" appears mainly as an additional organal voice. Unfortunately, the two voices are notated without staff lines, so the intervals can only be approximated, but the existence of a later manuscript with more precise notation has allowed us to reconstruct some melodies.

In the eleventh century, polyphony was applied chiefly to the troped plainchant sections of the Mass Ordinary (such as the Kyrie and Gloria), to certain parts of the Proper (especially Graduals, Alleluias, Tracts, and Sequences), and to responsories of the Office. Because polyphony demanded trained soloists who could follow rules of consonance while improvising or reading the approximate notation, only the soloists' portions of the original chant were embellished polyphonically. In performance, then, polyphonic sections alternated with monophonic chant, which the full choir sang in unison. The solo sections from the *Alleluia Justus ut palma* (NAWM 14) are preserved in a set of instructions headed *Ad organum faciendum* (To make organum) and dating from about 1100. The added voice proceeds mostly note-against-note above the chant, but toward the end of the opening "Alleluia," the performer sings a melismatic passage against a single note of the chant (Example 3.5)

EXAMPLE 3.5   Organum: *Alleluia Justus ut palma*

Florid organum

A new type of organum, more florid in style, appeared early in the twelfth century in Aquitaine, a region in southwestern France. In this type, the lower voice, usually an existing chant but sometimes composed anew, sustains long notes while the upper (solo) voice sings phrases of varying length. Pieces in this new style resulted in much longer organa, with a more prominent upper part that moved independently of the lower one. The chant, meanwhile, became elongated into a series of single-note "drones" that supported the melismatic elaborations above, therefore completely losing its character as a recognizable tune. The lower voice was called the *tenor*, from the Latin *tenere* ("to hold"), because it *held* the principal, that is, the first or original melody. For the next 250 years, the word *tenor* designated the lowest part of a polyphonic composition.

Writers in the early twelfth century began distinguishing between two kinds of organum. The style just described, in which the lower voice sustains long notes while the upper voice moves more ornately, they now termed *organum*, *organum duplum*, or *organum purum* ("double" or "pure organum"). The other kind, in which the movement is primarily note against note, they called *discantus* ("discant"). When the Notre Dame composer Léonin was praised by a contemporary writer as *optimus organista*, he was not being called an "excellent organist," but an "excellent composer of organa" (see vignette, page 53). The same writer described Pérotin as the best *discantor*, or maker of discants.

Organum purum

Discant

We can see a good example of florid, Aquitanian organum in the three-voice *Benedicamus Domino* trope, illustrated below and transcribed in Example 3.6 (see NAWM 15 for complete version). Typically, the upper part displays little bursts of melisma when the three parts meet on some consonant syllables. But this trope is also atypical because the middle part is not melismatic like the upper one; rather, it moves note-against-note with the lower part.

◀ A three-voice *Benedicamus Domino* trope, *Congaudeant catholici*, late twelfth century, attributed to Magister Albertus of Paris. An example of florid polyphony in the Aquitanian style. For a transcription, see page 48 and NAWM 15. (*Santiago de Compostela Cathedral, Codex Calixtinus, fol. 185*)

EXAMPLE 3.6   Albertus of Paris, *Benedicamus Domino* Trope: *Congaudeant catholici*

Con - gau - de — ant ca - tho - li - ci, le - ten - tur

ci — ves ce - li - ci di — e

Let us all rejoice together, let the heavenly hosts be glad [on this day].

Notation of organum

When organum purum was written down (which ordinarily it was not), one part sat above the other, fairly well aligned as in a modern score, with the phrases marked off by short vertical strokes on the staff. Two singers, or one soloist and a small group, could not easily go astray. But when the rhythmic relation between the parts was complex, singers had to know exactly how long to hold each note. As we have seen, the late medieval notations of plainchant and of troubadour and trouvère songs did not indicate duration. Indeed, no one felt a need to specify it, for the rhythm was either free or was tied to that of the words. Uncertainty about note duration was not a serious concern in solo or monophonic singing but could cause chaos when two or more melodies were sung simultaneously. Composers in northern France solved this problem by devising a system of rhythmic modes (see facing page).

Notre Dame Organum

Léonin

Two early composers of polyphony, both clerics associated with Notre Dame Cathedral in Paris, were Léonin (ca. 1135–1201), a poet-musician, and Pérotin (1180–ca. 1207), a singer. Léonin compiled the *Magnus liber organi* (Great Book of Organum), a cycle of two-part Graduals and Alleluias of the Mass, and Office responsories for the entire church year, some or all of which he himself composed. The organa of the *Magnus liber* are set to the solo portions of the responsorial chants for certain major feasts. The Easter chant *Alleluia Pascha nostrum* was elaborated not only by Léonin but also by later composers, making it ideal for tracing the layers of polyphonic embellishment bestowed on Alleluias. A sampling of these layers is presented and discussed in NAWM 16.

A Summary of the Rhythmic Modes

The so-called rhythmic modes, developed by eleventh- and twelfth-century composers to notate rhythm, proved adequate for all polyphonic music until well into the thirteenth century. The system differs fundamentally from modern notation, which shows relative durations by means of different note symbols. Instead, rhythmic modes use certain combinations of single notes and ligatures—groups of notes written as units—to indicate different rhythmic patterns. By about 1250, these patterns were codified into six rhythmic modes, identified simply by number:

I. ♩ ♪   IV. ♪♩ ♩.

II. ♪♩   V. ♩. ♩.

III. ♩. ♪♩   VI. ♪♪♪

The patterns correspond roughly to the arrangements of long and short syllables that characterize French and Latin verse. While Mode I (which moves in trochaic meter) and Mode V were used most often, Modes II (iambic) and III (dactylic) were also common. According to the system, a melody in rhythmic Mode I follows the pattern throughout, each phrase ending with a rest:

♩ ♪♩ ♪│♩ ♪♩ ⁊│♩ ♪♩ ♪│ etc.

In practice, however, the rhythm was more flexible and therefore less monotonous. Composers could divide notes into shorter units or combine them into one longer note, and take advantage of other means to vary the basic patterns. A melody in a given rhythmic mode might also be sung over a tenor whose long notes were not strictly measured or were organized in the pattern of a different mode, as in the following example (the melody is in Mode I and the tenor in Mode V):

I. ♩ ♪♩ ♪│♩ ♪♪♪♪│♩. ♩. │♩. ⁊ │ etc.

V. ♩. ♩. │♩. ⁊ │♩. ♩. │♩. ⁊ │ etc.

An actual melody read as in Mode I may be seen in the upper voice of Example 3.9 at "nostrum."

The system of rhythmic modes was based on a threefold unit of measure   *Perfection*

Ligatures

that theorists called a *perfectio* (perfection), which permitted any mode to be combined with any other. This ternary division of the "beat" produced what we would recognize as $\frac{6}{8}$ or $\frac{9}{8}$ meter. To let singers know which rhythmic mode was in force, notators used ligatures, plainchant neumes written in clusters that grouped two or more tones under a single syllable of text. In melismatic chant, especially, differently shaped ligatures often occurred, though in no particular order. In polyphony, however, in order to signify a rhythmic mode, ligatures appeared in definite patterns, as in Example 3.7a. Here, a three-note ligature followed by a series of two-note ligatures cues the singer to perform the melody as in Example 3.7b. In other words, the particular arrangement of ligatures in Example 3.7a tells the singer to use the first rhythmic mode. The other rhythmic modes were evoked in similar ways.

EXAMPLE 3.7   Use of Ligatures to Indicate a Rhythmic Mode

If we compare a setting of the Alleluia in the organum manuscripts (NAWM 16b; see illustration, page 51) with the original chant (NAWM 16a), we see that the *Magnus liber* provided music only for the sections of the chant sung by soloists, while the choir was expected to sing the rest of the chant in unison, either from memory or from another book.

Soloists		Chorus	Soloists		
Organum duplum		Plainchant	Organum duplum	Discant	Organum duplum
Alleluia _____		*Alleluia* __	*Pascha* _____	*no-strum* (melisma)	*immo-la-*

Soloists (cont.)		Chorus	Soloists	Chorus
Discant		Plainchant	__ Discant	Plainchant
[*la*](melisma)-*tus* (melisma) *est Christus.*			*Alle-lu- ia.* _____	

The responsorial Alleluia chant by itself displays contrasts in form and sound that are emphasized in Léonin's elaboration when we pass from plainchant to organum to discant (compare diagram in Chapter 2, page 29). The different styles of polyphonic composition, then, build further contrasts into the new sections. The opening intonation "Alleluia" (Example 3.8) resembles the older melismatic or florid organum: the plainsong melody is stretched out into unmeasured long notes to form the tenor, against which solo voices sing melismatic phrases, broken at irregular intervals by cadences and rests.

➤ Organum duplum by Léonin of the Alleluia verse *Pascha nostrum*. It includes an ambiguously notated—probably rhythmically free—organum purum on *Pascha* and a clausula on *nostrum*, in which both parts are in modal rhythm. For one possible transcription, see NAWM 16. (*Florence, Biblioteca Medicea-Laurenziana, MS Pluteus 29.1*)

The original notation (see illustration above) suggests a free, unmeasured rhythm. The fluid melody—nonperiodic and loosely organized—smacks of improvisatory practice.

EXAMPLE 3.8   Léonin, *Organum duplum*: First Section of *Alleluia Pascha nostrum*

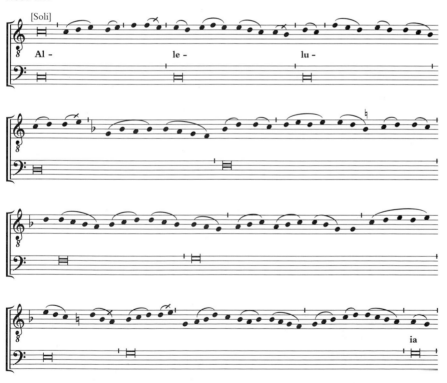

After the choir responds "Alleluia" in unison, the two-voice solo texture in organum purum resumes with the psalm verse on "Pascha." But beginning with the word "nostrum," a different style takes over (Example 3.9). The tenor now sings in strictly measured rhythm while the upper voice, which

EXAMPLE 3.9   Léonin, Beginning of Verse from *Alleluia Pascha nostrum*, with Anonymous Clausula on "nostrum"

Clausula

moves in still faster notes, likewise assumes the character of discant. This section constitutes a *clausula*, a closed form in discant style. In this case a chant melisma appears twice in the tenor (marked in Example 3.9 by Roman numerals I and II).

The term *clausula* (plural, *clausulae*) means a grammatical close but, like the English word "period," also stands for the section of prose or music falling between two punctuation marks (what we would call a clause, period, or phrase). Each clausula is distinct, terminating in a definite cadence. The Léonin *Alleluia Pascha nostrum* includes three clausulae in discant style: on "nostrum"; on "-latus" of the word "immolatus"; and on "-lu-" of the final "Alleluia." All three occur where there are melismas in the original chant. (If sections of discant were not used and the polyphonic setting were entirely in organum purum, the result would be a rhapsodic work of excessive length.) Between these clausulae are contrasting sections of organum purum. Since it was common to substitute new clausulae for old ones, these examples were probably not written by Léonin but by a later composer. After the final discant section, the chorus concludes the piece with the last few phrases of the original plainsong Alleluia.

Composers of Léonin's generation evidently liked juxtaposing old and new elements—passages of florid organum with the livelier discant clausulae. But in the course of the thirteenth century, singers gradually abandoned organum purum in favor of discant. The clausula sections became quasi-independent pieces that in time evolved into a new form, the motet.

Pérotin and his contemporaries continued the work Léonin had begun, abbreviating and updating the *Magnus liber*. The basic formal structure of the

Pérotin

Anonymous IV Compares the Achievements of Léonin and Pérotin:

❝ Note that Master Leonin, according to what was said, was the best composer of *organa*, who made the great book of *organum* from the gradual and antiphonary to elaborate the divine service. And it was in use up to the time of Perotin the Great, who edited it and made very many better *clausulae* or *puncta*, since he was the best composer of discant, and better than Leonin. But this is not to be said about the subtlety of the *organum*, etc.

But Master Perotin himself made excellent *quadrupla*, like 'Viderunt' and 'Sederunt,' [NAWM 17] with an abundance of colors of the harmonic art; and also several very noble *tripla*, like 'Alleluia posui adiutorium,' 'Nativitas,' etc. He also composed three-part conductus, like 'Salvatoris hodie,' and two-part conductus, like 'Dum sigillum summi patris,' and even monophonic conductus [*simplices conductus*] with several others, like 'Beata viscera,' etc. ❞

Jeremy Yudkin, *The Music Treatise of Anonymous IV: A New Translation*, MSD 41 (Neuhausen-Stuttgart: AIM/Hänssler-Verlag, 1985), p. 39. The author of the treatise, a pupil of Johannes de Garlandia, is the fourth anonymous writer represented in C.-E.-H. de Coussemaker's collection of medieval treatises (Paris, 1864–76).

C	H	R	O	N	O	L	O	G	Y

1000		1180	*Pérotin at Notre Dame of Paris (until ca. 1207)
	Norman conquest of England (Battle of Hastings, 1066)		Richard Coeur de Lion (1157–1199) becomes king of England (1189); Third Crusade (1189–92)
	First Crusade (1095–99)		
1100		1200	
	Second Crusade (1147–49)		
1150	Hildegard of Bingen (1098–1179) founds a convent at Rupertsberg		St. Francis of Assisi (1182–1226) founds Franciscan order (1209; see Plate I, facing page 82)
1160			
	Cornerstone of Notre Dame of Paris laid (1163)	1210	
	*Léonin (ca. 1135–1201) in Paris (1163–90)		Magna Carta signed (1215)
1170	Eleanor of Aquitaine (ca. 1122–1204) establishes her court in Poitiers	1280	*Franco of Cologne, *Ars cantus mensurabilis* (ca. 1280)

organum—alternating unison chant and polyphonic sections—remained unchanged, but musicians of Pérotin's time preferred to combine modal rhythm in the upper voices with the slower-moving tenor notes. The older florid organa often yielded their place to discant clausulae, and many of the older clausulae in turn were replaced by newer, so-called "substitute" clausulae in definite and stylized rhythmic patterns. In his organa Pérotin characteristically laid out the tenor in a series of repeated rhythmic motives (usually those of Modes III or V). And because his tenor melodies use shorter notes than Léonin's, they were often repeated, at least in part, to make a section long enough to suit the composer. We will meet these two kinds of repetition—of rhythmic motive and of melody—again in motets of the later thirteenth century.

> **Substitute clausulae**

> **Triple and quadruple organum**

Composers of Pérotin's day expanded organum's dimensions by increasing the number of voice parts, first to three and then to four. We find an astonishing example of Pérotin's four-voice organum—which stretches out the first word of the respond to extraordinary melismatic lengths—in the Gradual for St. Stephen's Day, *Sederunt* (NAWM 17). Since the second voice was called the duplum, by analogy the third was called the *triplum* and the fourth the *quadruplum*. These same terms also designated the composition as a whole: a three-voice organum came to be called an *organum triplum*, or simply *triplum*, and a four-voice organum a *quadruplum* (see vignette, page 53). The triplum, which became the standard in the Pérotin era, remained in favor for a half century.

Polyphonic Conductus

The conductus, among the most lively and independent compositions of the Middle Ages, grew out of quasi-liturgical genres such as the hymn and the sequence, but later admitted secular words. In a polyphonic conductus, two or more voices sing the same words in essentially the same rhythm, resulting in a texture that sounds more modern. Its texts, like those of the earlier monophonic conductus (see Chapter 2), consist of metrical Latin poems, rarely liturgical though often on sacred themes. Secular conductus texts deal with current or historical events or with moral and ecclesiastical issues.

The polyphonic conductus by Pérotin and other composers of the Notre Dame era were written for two, three, or four voices. As in organum, the vocal range is narrow and the voices cross and recross, forming mostly octaves, fourths, and fifths, and in some pieces, thirds. In addition to the simultaneous motion of its voices, two other features distinguished the polyphonic conductus of the early thirteenth century. First, by setting the words syllabically (each syllable to a different note, for the most part), composers allowed the strongly metrical lines of rhyming poetry to organize the music into phrases of equal length. An exception occurs in conductus that introduced *caudae* (literally, tails), which are fairly long, untexted passages placed at the beginning, at the end, or just before important cadences. Second, composers of Notre Dame conductus also supplied many of their own tenors instead of "borrowing" a plainchant or some other preexisting melody, thereby creating the first completely original polyphonic works. In the manuscripts, the conductus are notated like the organa in score arrangement, with voice parts aligned vertically and the text written only under the lowest (tenor) part.

The conductus *Ave virgo virginum* (Hail, virgin of virgins; see Example 3.10 and NAWM 18), which addresses the Virgin Mary, was probably used

EXAMPLE 3.10   Early-Thirteenth-Century Conductus: *Ave virgo virginum*

Hail, virgin of virgins, shrine of the word made flesh, who for men's salvation pours out milk and honey. You have borne the Lord; you were a rush-basket to Moses.

Florence, Biblioteca Medicea-Laurenziana, MS Pluteus 29.1, fols. 240–240v.

in special devotions and processions. The composer set the first two couplets identically in all the voices and used the same music for all three strophes.

The nearly homorhythmic writing displayed in this example has been called "conductus style." Two- or three-part settings of hymns, sequences, and secular songs in this style flourished throughout the twelfth and thirteenth centuries. Both organum and conductus gradually dropped out of favor after 1250, leaving the polyphonic field to the motet.

The Motet

A clausula section of organum, cut loose from its larger setting, could enjoy a second life as a separate piece when Latin or French words were added to the upper voice. This new type of work, originating like earlier genres in the familiar troping procedures, was called a *motet* (from the French *mot*, meaning "word"). The Latin form, *motetus*, also designates the second voice—the original duplum, now sporting its own text—in three and four-part motets, while the third and fourth voices carry the same names, triplum and quadruplum, they had in organum.

The motet originated, then, when composers troped the substitute clausulae of Pérotin and others. These clausulae had earlier belonged to the family of works known as organum, which in turn featured newly composed melodies layered above old chants. Indeed, a defining characteristic of the motet

Cantus firmus

was its use of borrowed chant material in the tenor. Such a tenor was known as the *cantus firmus* (Lat., plain chant; pl. *cantus firmi*). Because substitute clausulae could be used interchangeably in the liturgical service, different composers wrote new clausulae using the same favorite cantus firmi. Similarly, of the thousands of motets written throughout France and western Europe during the thirteenth century many derived from a common stock of motet melodies—both tenors and upper parts—that lay in the public domain. Without acknowledgment, composers and performers helped themselves to the music of their predecessors and altered it for their own purposes. In the process the plainchant tenor lost its connection with a specific place in the church service and became raw material for composition.

Since motets were intended for nonliturgical use, and the upper voices could have vernacular texts, there was no point in singing the original Latin text of the cantus firmus, so the tenor was often played on instruments. By 1250 it was customary to use different but topically related texts in the two upper voices. These motets are identified by a compound title made up of the *incipit* (the first word or words) of each voice part, beginning with the highest, as in Example 3.11.

Both the original and the substitute clausulae of the organum *Alleluia Pascha nostrum* (NAWM 16b) in the *Magnus liber* were reworked as motets

EXAMPLE 3.11   Motet: *Amours mi font souffrir—En mai, quant rose est florie—Flos filius*

Triplum: **Love wrongly makes me suffer pain,**
because my lady, who is killing me . . .
Duplum: **In May, when the rose blooms,**
and I hear the birds sing . . .
Tenor: **[The Virgin, Mother of God, is the branch,] the son its flower.**

by having Latin or French texts added. For example, the duplum voice of the clausula on *nostrum* (NAWM 16c) received a Latin text, *Gaudeat devotio fidelium,* that expands on the meaning of Christ's sacrifice and turns the clausula into a motet (16d). Similarly, the duplum of the clausula on *-la-* of *immolatus* (NAWM 16e) acquired a Latin text, *Ave Maria, Fons letitie,* which praises the mother of the sacrificed "lamb" celebrated in the Alleluia (16f).

In the earlier motets, all the upper parts were written in one melodic style. Later composers distinguished the upper voices from each other as well as from the tenor. In this new kind of motet, called "Franconian" (after Franco of Cologne, a composer and theorist who was active from about 1250 to 1280), the triplum bears a longer text than the motetus and features a fast-moving melody with many short notes in brief phrases of narrow range. Against this, the motetus sings a broader, long-breathed, lyrical melody. Toward the end of the thirteenth century even the tenor's rigid rhythmic scheme was relaxed in favor of a flexible style approaching that of the other two parts (see illustration and window, pages 58–59).

Franconian motet

A charming Franconian motet is *Amours mi font souffrir—En mai, quant rose est florie—Flos filius* (Example 3.11 and NAWM 19). All the voices are based on the first rhythmic mode, consisting of a long followed by a breve (short note). The tenor goes twice through the chant melody, which is broken into a short, repeating rhythmic pattern (two measures of the transcription). As we have seen in other motets, the music of the motetus was first composed as the duplum of a clausula for two voices, and the French text was fitted to it afterward, as a trope. This sequence of events accounts for the uneven lengths of poetic lines and the irregular rhyme scheme of the motetus text. The triplum's text and melody are more independent, and its textual-musical

THE MOTET AS GOTHIC CATHEDRAL

A distinctive feature of music is its movement through time. But in order to understand time, we must be able to measure it. Composers of polyphony in the twelfth and thirteenth centuries devised a way of ordering time so that it could be manipulated and controlled. The motet, wholly a creation of French composers, illustrates this accomplishment better than any other genre of the era. (See, for example, NAWM 19, *Amours mi font/En mai/ Flos filius* and the discussion on page 57.)

Each voice of a motet moves in its own rhythmic framework, yet is perfectly compatible with each of the others. In the case of a three-voice motet, for example, the tenor measures the passage of time in long note values, while the middle voice superimposes its own rhythmic design, consisting of shorter values, on the support created by the tenor. Meanwhile, the highest voice articulates its relationship with time differently from its two partners, usually in notes that move even more quickly than the middle voice and with phrases that coincide with (or sometimes overlap) the ends of the phrases below. The result is a three-tiered structure in which each layer is quite independent of, yet completely coordinated with, the other two layers.

If we look at the interior space of a typical Gothic cathedral (see illustration of Laon Cathedral), created by French architects during the very period in which the medieval motet flourished, we see a formal design remarkably similar to the structure just described. Along either side of the nave, or central aisle of the church, are huge columns, placed at regular intervals to define the length of the cathedral and support its soaring height. Along the next higher story are the arches of the triforium gallery, where space is measured by an arcade of shorter columns supporting bays of double arches. Superimposed atop this layer, just below the level at which walls give way to windows, is a third tier of still smaller, triple arches, more ornamental than functional, independent of and yet perfectly harmonized with the rest.

The similarities described here are not accidental; the architects of the Gothic style codified their principles of design from the same mathematical laws that the creators of modal rhythm and the composers of motets used in establishing their theories of proportion and measure. The results of their efforts are, on the one hand, a glorious edifice in which we can "hear" a kind of silent music, and on the other, a genre of polyphonic composition that allows us to "see" the harmonious plan of its underlying structure.

Neo-Gothic churches are still being built in our day. The Gothic style, which many regarded with outright disdain for over three centuries, came back into favor about a hundred years ago, influenced by the completion of Germany's Cologne Cathedral in 1882. The chapel at West Point, Princeton University chapel, St. Thomas's Episcopal Church and the huge Cathedral of St. John the Divine in New York City, the National Shrine in Washington, D.C., and more than a hundred other American churches testify to the inspiring grandeur of the Gothic style, which continues to strengthen the faith of believers and to fill even the most casual visitors with wonder. As Winston Churchill observed, "We fashion our buildings and then they fashion us."

◄ Nave of Laon Cathedral, looking west. This Gothic cathedral was built during the third quarter of the twelfth century. (*Giraudon/Art Resource, NY*)

Thirteenth-Century Notation

*A*s composers of the later thirteenth-century motets used more syllables, livelier rhythms, and shorter note values, they realized that the notation evolved for modal rhythm no longer worked. Around 1280, Franco of Cologne in his *Ars cantus mensurabilis* (The Art of Measurable Music) codified a complicated though more practical system in which the relative time values of individual notes, ligatures, and rests are clearly laid out and, as in our modern system, some notes take on different shapes depending on their duration. These notational refinements allowed for both greater rhythmic flexibility and greater precision. The Franconian system remained in use until the 1320s and many of its features survived for an additional two hundred years.

The new motet style created a further notational change. The earliest motets were written in score, like the clausulae from which they derived. But as the upper voices acquired longer texts and as each syllable had to have a separate note-symbol, composers and scribes soon found these voices taking much more room than the tenor, a part that had fewer notes and, being melismatic, could be expressed in the compressed modal notation of ligatures. In a score, there would be long vacant stretches on the tenor staff, a waste of space and costly parchment. And since the upper voices sang different texts anyway, it seemed natural to separate them. So, in a three-voice motet, the triplum and the motetus came to be written either on facing pages or in separate columns on the same page, with the tenor on a single staff extending across the bottom. This pattern, known as *choirbook* format, remained the usual way of notating polyphonic compositions from 1230 until the sixteenth century.

lines do not match those of the motetus but sometimes overlap. This feature, together with the breaking up of the rhythmic mode into shorter notes, assures constant animation and averts the stops and starts of many motets dating from this period.

At the beginning of the thirteenth century, nearly all polyphonic music was sacred. By the end of the century, composers were setting secular texts as well, in much the same style. Motets of the late thirteenth century mirrored both the rationalism and the cultural diversity of the time: we find a motley collection of love songs, dance tunes, popular refrains, and sacred hymns, held together by strict rhythmic patterns and plainchant tenors.

POSTLUDE

The history of polyphony in the Middle Ages parallels in many ways the development of monophonic song, including plainchant. Initially improvised, polyphony was eventually "composed" in notations devised to control its performance. The body of composition gradually expanded through the process of troping, whereby new melodies and/or texts were added to, or layered above, the original monophonic lines. By the late twelfth and early thirteenth centuries we find three main genres: organum, conductus, and motet. In organa and motets, composers elaborated on chant tenors; conductus were freely composed. Styles of organum evolved from parallel organum (where added voices merely duplicated the contour of the chant melody) to more florid pieces (where the added voices assumed greater melodic and rhythmic independence from the cantus firmus). Sections of discant-style organa, called clausulae, became separate works and, with added texts, gave rise to the motet, a new genre that dominated the polyphonic scene by the mid–thirteenth century.

These genres and conventions would soon be outmoded, however, because of the newer motet styles. The rhythmic modes gradually became obsolete, and the chant tenor was relegated to a purely formal function, elevating the triplum to the status of a solo voice against the accompanying lower parts. The road was open to a new musical style, a new way of composing (*ars nova*), in an age that would look back on the music of the latter half of the thirteenth century as the antique, outdated way (*ars antiqua*).

4

French and Italian Music
in the Fourteenth Century

Where the thirteenth century had been an era of relative stability and unity, the fourteenth was one of change and diversity, as we can see in the status of the papacy. In the thirteenth century people had looked to the church, long centered in Rome, as the supreme authority in matters of faith and morals and even in most intellectual and political affairs; in the fourteenth this authority, and especially the supremacy of the pope, was widely questioned. Early in the century, King Philip V ("the Fair") of France had engineered the election of a French pope, who never went to Rome because of the hostility there to foreigners. Instead, from 1305 until 1378 the popes resided in Avignon, a city in southeastern France. The papacy in Avignon was more like a princely court than a religious community, and the surviving music from this Avignon period is almost entirely secular. The political situation became even more complicated when Italian factions elected their own pope, and between 1378 and 1417, there were two, sometimes three rival claimants to the papal throne. This state of affairs, as well as the perceived and actual corruption in the lives of the clergy, drew increasingly sharp criticism, which we see expressed in polemical writings, in motet texts of the time, and in the rise of divisive and dissenting movements that foreshadowed the Protestant Reformation. When the papacy finally moved back to Rome, it brought French music with it.

Europeans in the thirteenth century could generally reconcile revelation and reason, the divine and the human, the claims of the kingdom of God and those of the political states of this world. By contrast, the separation in the fourteenth century between religion and science and between church and state emerged as doctrines that are still held today. Philosophers made a distinction between divine revelation and human reason, each prevailing only in its own sphere. In other words, the church cared for people's souls while the state looked out for their earthly concerns.

A healthy growth of literature in the spoken languages of Europe testifies to the new importance of secular pursuits. Dante's *Divine Comedy* (1307), Boccaccio's *Decameron* (1353), and Chaucer's *Canterbury Tales* (1387) remain with us today as great literary landmarks of the fourteenth century. The same period saw the beginnings of humanism and a renewed interest in classical Greek and Latin literature, a most important force in the culture of the Renaissance (see Chapter 6). In painting, Giotto (ca. 1266–1337) broke away from the formalized Byzantine style toward a more natural representation of objects (see Plate I, facing page 82). Literature, education, and the arts all moved from the relatively stable, unified, religiously centered viewpoint of the thirteenth century toward the human concerns of this world.

In music, too, composers consciously struck out in a new direction. The French musician, poet, and bishop of Meaux, Philippe de Vitry (1291–1361), wrote a treatise he called *Ars nova* (The New Art; early 1320s). The term *ars nova* fit so well that it came to denote the French musical style in the first half of the fourteenth century. But the change had its opponents. The Flemish theorist Jacques de Liège vigorously defended the *ars antiqua* (the old art) of the late thirteenth century against the innovations of the "moderns" in his encyclopedic *Speculum musicae* (The Mirror of Music, ca. 1325; see vignette, page 66).

Philippe de Vitry

The innovations of **The *ars nova* in France** centered on rhythm and its notation, areas which became the playground of the fourteenth-century French composer. The motet, where many of these experiments occurred, continued to be a favorite genre of composition, although now its function was less devotional and more political, and it was structurally more complex than it had been in the thirteenth century. Earlier advances in polyphony had generally been associated with sacred music; but as the arts became more secularized during this period, the production of sacred music seems to have declined. At the same time, composers wrote lots of secular music in both French and Latin, including polyphonic settings of love songs in the traditional refrain forms of the trouvères.

The 1300s in Italy were known as the *trecento* (short for *mille trecento*, or 1300). Composers of **Italian *trecento* Music** avoided the complicated textures and subtle structures of the motet and instead cultivated the short, sensuously lyrical forms typical of Italy's native poets and musicians. By contrast, French music of the late fourteenth century became ever more refined and complex, catering to the somewhat extravagant tastes of polished performers and educated, courtly audiences.

Important issues in the **Theory and Practice in Fourteenth-Century Music** involved the notation of duple divisions of the beat and the use of accidentals. Although composed and notated music until now tended to be vocal, we know from pictorial and literary sources that **Instruments** and instrumental ensembles played an important role in entertainment at court, both indoors and in festivities held out-of-doors.

The *ars nova* in France

Motet

Roman de Fauvel

Even before the end of the thirteenth century the motet, a genre originally associated with sacred music because of its dependence on plainchant, had become largely secularized. This trend continued in such works as the *Roman de Fauvel*, a satirical poem interpolated with 167 pieces of music (of which thirty-four are motets) and preserved in a beautifully decorated French manuscript dating from 1310–14. The collection provides a veritable anthology of thirteenth- and early-fourteenth-century music, much of which is still monophonic—strophic songs with refrains and a variety of plainchant melodies. Many of the motet texts denounce the clergy, while others refer to political events. Such allusions came to characterize the fourteenth-century motet, as they earlier had the conductus. Indeed, the motet in the 1300s often commemorated ecclesiastical or secular occasions, and it continued to do so through the first half of the fifteenth century.

The isorhythmic motet

Philippe de Vitry wrote five of the motets in the *Roman de Fauvel*, and their tenors provide the earliest examples of a musically unifying device called *isorhythm*. These tenors are laid out in sections of identical rhythm, which might recur as many as ten times in one piece, thus producing an *iso-rhythmic* ("same-rhythm") motet. We have already seen this principle at work in some late-thirteenth-century motets where a certain number of repetitions verifies the rhythmic formula. But now, all this takes place on a much larger scale. The tenor is longer, the rhythms are more complex, and the whole line moves so ponderously against the faster notes of the upper voices that it can no longer be recognized as a melody. Rather, the abstract isorhythmic design, superimposed on the borrowed tenor or cantus firmus, functions as a foundation for the entire polyphonic structure and lends coherence to a relatively long composition that had no other formal organization. (An isorhythmic motet by de Vitry from *Roman de Fauvel* may be seen in NAWM 20.)

Under de Vitry's influence, composers and theorists recognized two recurring elements in the motet tenors, one melodic and the other rhythmic.

➤ A charivari, or noisy serenade, awakens Fauvel and Vaine Gloire after their wedding in the
Roman de Fauvel (1310–14), a poem by Gervais
du Bus with many musical interpolations. Fauvel
is an allegorical horse or ass that incarnates the
sins represented by the letters of his name: flat-
terie, avarice, vilainie, variété (fickleness), envie,
and lâcheté (cowardice). (*Paris, Bibliothèque
Nationale, MS Fr. 146*)

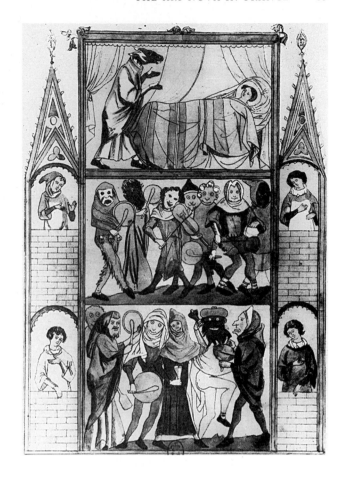

They called the repeating statement of the cantus firmus the *color*, and the
long recurring rhythmic unit the *talea* (a "slice" or segment). Color and talea
could coincide, beginning and ending together over the course of the piece.
Or the color could extend over two, three, or more taleae, with the two factors
still coinciding. But if the endings of color and talea did not concur, then the
two would overlap; for example, a repetition of the color might begin in the
middle of a talea. Upper voices could also be organized isorhythmically, and
the technique was occasionally applied to compositions in other genres, as
illustrated by the section of Machaut's Mass (NAWM 22) discussed below.

Guillaume de Machaut

The leading composer of the *ars nova* in France, Guillaume de Machaut (ca.
1300–1377), was fully involved in the political, intellectual, and ecclesiastical
worlds of his time. Born in the province of Champagne in northern France,
he was educated as a cleric and took Holy Orders. In his early twenties he
became secretary to King John of Bohemia, whom he accompanied on mil-

Jacques de Liège Rails against the *ars nova*:

66 In a certain company in which some able singers and judicious laymen were assembled, and where modern motets in the modern manner and some old ones were sung, I observed that even the laymen were better pleased with the ancient motets and the ancient manner than with the new. And even if the new manner pleased when it was a novelty, it does so no longer, but begins to displease many. So let the ancient music and the ancient manner of singing be brought back to their native land; let them come back into use; let the rational art once more flourish. It has been in exile, along with the corresponding method of singing, as if violently cast out from the fellowship of singers, but violence should not be perpetual. Wherein does this studied lasciviousness in singing so greatly please, by which, as some think, the words are lost, the harmony of consonances is diminished, the value of the notes is changed, perfection is brought low, imperfection is exalted, and measure is confounded? 99

From *Speculum musicae*, ca. 1325, Book 7, chapter 46, trans. by James McKinnon in Strunk, *Source Readings in Music History*, rev. ed. (1997).

itary campaigns over many parts of Europe during the early stages of the Hundred Years' War. After King John died in battle in 1346, Machaut entered the service of the French court and eventually ended his days as a canon (an official of the church) at Rheims. Machaut was famous not only as a musician but also as a poet; in fact, his reputation in France equaled that of Chaucer in England. His musical works, written in most of the genres then current, reveal a composer of both conservative and progressive tendencies.

Motets

Most of Machaut's twenty-three surviving motets followed the traditional texture in which an instrumental liturgical tenor supports two upper voices with different texts. Like other motets of the time, Machaut's were longer, more secular, and more rhythmically complex than earlier examples. They are pan-isorhythmic, that is, the isorhythmic structure involves all three voices, and Machaut frequently emphasized the talea's recurrences by the clever use of a rhythmic device called *hocket*, which also serves to animate the polyphonic texture. In hocket (French *hoquet*, "hiccup"), rests interrupt the flow of melody in one voice while another voice interjects the notes that are "missing" in the first, resulting in a rapid exchange of rests and notes. Although Machaut did not invent the technique, he used it to great effect.

Fourteenth-century composers typically produced much more secular music than sacred, and Machaut was no exception. The church itself dis-

C H R O N O L O G Y	
1300	**1350** Boccaccio (1313–1375), *Decameron* (ca. 1349–53)
Giotto (1266–1337), frescoes in the Arena chapel, Padua (1305)	Death of Petrarch (b. 1304), Italian poet laureate (1374)
Dante (1265–1321), *The Divine Comedy* (ca. 1307)	**1375**
Clement V moves papal headquarters to Avignon (1309)	*Death of Guillaume de Machaut (b. ca. 1300) (1377)
*Philippe de Vitry (1291–1361), *Ars nova* (ca. 1322–23)	Start of papal schism (1378)
1325	Chaucer (ca. 1340–1400), *The Canterbury Tales* (ca. 1387–1400)
Beginning of Hundred Years' War (1338)	*Death of Francesco Landini (b. ca. 1325) (1397) (see Plate II, facing page 83)
The Plague devastates Europe (1348–49)	
	1400

couraged elaborate musical settings in its services. From the twelfth century on, numerous ecclesiastical pronouncements railed against complicated music and displays of virtuosity by singers; such practices were thought to distract worshipers by turning the Mass into a form of entertainment, obscuring the words of the liturgy, and making the chant melodies unrecognizable. Nevertheless, Machaut left us a majestic monument to his faith and the splendor of his church in his *Messe de Notre Dame*, one of the earliest polyphonic settings of the Mass Ordinary. Given the spacious dimensions of his Mass, its control of consonance and dissonance in a four-part texture, and its carefully planned isorhythmic structures, Machaut must have composed it for an occasion of unusual solemnity and magnificence, perhaps for the coronation of the French king Charles V in 1364.

> *Mass*

Machaut's Mass is exceptional in that the composer set the six prayers of the Ordinary as one artistic work rather than as six separate pieces, which was the custom. Unlike some later Masses, Machaut's is not unified by a single cantus firmus—he chose a different chant for each of four movements. Instead, Machaut's unity of compositional techniques and style as well as some recurring motives and cadence tones hold the movements together. The Kyrie, Sanctus, Agnus Dei, and Ite, missa est are in motet style, each using a different cantus firmus that is organized isorhythmically. The Gloria and Credo, having longer texts, are written in conductus style—that is, with no cantus firmus and a syllabic, note-against-note setting—although both movements end with elaborate isorhythmic Amens. The Agnus Dei (NAWM 22) is typical of the isorhythmic movements. The tenor melody is the Agnus Dei from the plainchant Mass numbered XVII in modern chant books (*Liber usualis*, p. 61). The isorhythmic structure begins at the words "qui tollis," that is, after the intonation of each Agnus. Example 4.1 shows the placement of the color and its repetition. It also illustrates how each color is subdivided by the repetition of a different talea.

EXAMPLE **4.1**   Tenor of Machaut, Agnus Dei from *Messe de Notre Dame,* Showing Isorhythmic Structure

In addition to the tenor, the triplum and contratenor (in the same range as the tenor) are also wholly or partly isorhythmic. The two upper parts enliven the rhythm with almost constant syncopation, another innovation brought about by the preoccupation that *ars nova* composers had with rhythm. (See NAWM 22 for a fuller discussion.)

Love songs

Although clearly the leading practitioner of the New Art in France, Machaut was also the last great poet-composer of courtly love songs in the trouvère tradition. In his songs a new lyricism speaks through the finely fashioned, supple melodic line of the solo voice, imparting warmth even to the stylized language of chivalric verse. His monophonic chansons comprise nineteen *lais* (a twelfth-century form similar to the sequence), and about twenty-five *chansons balladées,* called *virelais.* Machaut also wrote seven polyphonic virelais in which the vocal line, performed solo, is accompanied by an instrumental tenor.[1] These works display an occasional melodic correspon-

1. Examples of Machaut's monophonic and polyphonic virelais may be found in HAM (*Historical Anthology of Music* [Cambridge, Mass.: Harvard University Press, 1950]) Nos. 46a and b; and in *Polyphonic Music of the Fourteenth Century* (Monaco: Éditions de l'Oiseau-Lyre, 1956–58; reprint 1975), Vols. 2–3, ed. Leo Schrade.

dence between the endings of the two halves of the piece; also seen in some types of plainchant, this subtle structural device has been called musical rhyme.

Ars nova tendencies appear most clearly in Machaut's polyphonic virelais, rondeaux, and ballades—the so-called *formes fixes* ("fixed forms"), in which text and music have particular patterns of repetition that are determined by the poetic structure. All three are strophic and involve the use of refrain, but each form differs in its details from the other two (see "Standard Forms of Fourteenth-Century Chansons," page 71). One hot issue debated by advocates of the new and old styles was whether a duple, or "imperfect," division of note values should be allowed along with the traditional triple, or "perfect," division. Machaut often exploited the possibilities of the new duple division of time. In the rondeau *Rose, liz* (NAWM 21), for example, he organized the rhythm into what we would call duple meter, with a triple subdivision of the beat. Although his chansons do not employ isorhythmic techniques—the poetic forms provide their formal organization in every case—they do indulge in other rhythmic complications characteristic of the motet style, such as chains of syncopation and, occasionally, hocket.

One of Machaut's most important achievements was his development of

> **Ars nova *traits***

▲ Guillaume de Machaut in his study is visited by Amour, who introduces his three children, Doux Penser (Sweet Thoughts), Plaisance (Pleasure), and Espérance (Hope). Miniature from the atelier of Jean Bondol in a manuscript of Machaut's works. (*Paris, Bibliothèque Nationale, MS Fr. 1584*)

The ballade and ballade style

the "ballade" or "cantilena" style, in which the top part, or cantus, carries the text alone and dominates the three-part texture, while the two lower voices are most often performed instrumentally. His polyphonic virelais and rondeaux, as well as the forty-one *ballades*, exhibit this hierarchy of parts. Machaut wrote ballades with two, three, and four parts and for various combinations of voices with instruments, but his typical settings were for high tenor solo or duet with two lower parts. Those for two voices, each with its own text, are called *double ballades.*[2]

Rondeau

The rondeau captivated poets and musicians of the late Middle Ages. Machaut's elegant *Rose, liz* (Rose, lily, NAWM 21) is characteristic of all these songs, with its long melismas that extend the sensual lyricism of the melody. Melismas occupy as many as four measures at the beginning or, sometimes, in the middle of lines. Although they may fall on unimportant words and even on unaccented syllables, the melismas have a formal, decorative function and generally convey the mood of the text.

Machaut's rondeaux are highly sophisticated musically. One in particular, *Ma fin est mon commencement et mon commencement ma fin* (My end is my beginning and my beginning my end), stands out for its ingenuity. The melody of the tenor is the same as the topmost voice sung backward, and the second half of the contratenor's melody is the reverse of its first half.

Italian *trecento* Music

Italian music in the *trecento* developed differently from French music because of Italy's social and political climate. Where France had a monarchy with increasing power and stability, Italy was a collection of city-states, each with its own political, cultural, and linguistic traditions and alliances. Composers who were associated with the church and trained in notation and counterpoint wrote secular polyphonic pieces as entertainment for the elite. But many other types of music remained in unwritten form. Even polyphony was still largely improvised in fourteenth-century Italian churches. At the courts, Italian *trovatori* of the thirteenth century followed in the footsteps of the troubadours, singing their songs from memory. The only music of the people to survive in manuscripts are the monophonic *laude*, or processional songs (see page 124).

The main centers of Italian *trecento* music were in the central and northern regions, notably Bologna, Padua, Modena, Milan, Perugia, and above all Florence, an especially important cultural center from the fourteenth through

---

2. An example of a three-part ballade by Machaut may be seen in HAM No. 45, as well as in the volumes of *Polyphonic Music* cited previously.

Standard Forms of Fourteenth-Century Chansons

*C*haracteristic of the virelai is the form AbbaA in which A stands for the refrain (a phrase or section that repeats both words and music), b the first part of the stanza (which is immediately repeated with new words), and a the last part of the stanza (which uses the same melody as the refrain but different words). If there are several stanzas, the refrain A may be repeated after each. A typical virelai strophe is represented below:

Virelai

	Refrain		Stanza				Refrain	
Lines of poetry:	1	2	3	4	5	6	1	2
Sections of music:	A		b	b	a		A	

The form of Machaut's ballades, inherited in part from the trouvères, consists of three or four stanzas, each sung to the same music and each ending with a refrain. Within each stanza the first two lines (or pairs of lines) have the same music (a a), although often with different endings (a^1 a^2); the remaining lines and the refrain have a different melody, whose close might echo that of the first section. One possible scheme for the ballade is represented below (where C stands for a refrain that reappears only in successive strophes):

Ballade

	Stanza						(Refrain)	
Lines of poetry:	1	2	3	4	5	6	7	8
Sections of music:	a		a		b			C

Like the virelai, the rondeau has only two musical sections with the refrain containing all of the music; unlike any of the other formes fixes, however, the rondeau refrain partially returns midway through the piece. The form is ABaAabAB (again, capital letters indicate that both the music and the text of the refrain are sung). The following diagram matches Machaut's four-part rondeau, *Rose, liz* (NAWM 21):

Rondeau

	Refrain					Half-Refrain					Refrain		
Lines of poetry:	1	2	3	4	5	6(1)	7(2)	8	9	10	11(1)	12(2)	13(3)
Sections of music:	A		B	a		A			a	b	A		B

Giovanni Boccaccio, from the *Decameron*:

66 The tables having been cleared away, the queen commanded that instruments be brought in, for all the ladies knew how to do the round dance, and the young men too, and some of them could play and sing very well. Upon her request, Dioneo took a lute and Fiammetta a viol and began sweetly to play a dance. Then the queen together with other ladies and two young men chose a carol and struck up a round dance with a slow pace—while the servants were sent out to eat. When this was finished, they began to sing charming and merry songs. They continued in this way for a long time, until the queen thought it was time to go to sleep. 99

Giovanni Boccaccio, *Decameron*, Day One, Introduction.

the sixteenth centuries. Florence is the birthplace of two celebrated works of literature, the *Decameron* by Giovanni Boccaccio (1313–1375) and the *Paradiso degli Alberti* by Giovanni Gherardi da Prato (ca. 1367–ca. 1444). From these writings and others of the time, we learn how music, both vocal and instrumental, accompanied nearly every aspect of Italian social life (see vignette above).

Squarcialupi Codex

Very few examples of Italian polyphony from before 1330 have survived, but after that date we find several fourteenth- and fifteenth-century manuscripts written either in Italy or southern France. The most copious source is the magnificent Squarcialupi Codex, named for an early owner, the Florentine organist Antonio Squarcialupi (1416–1480). This collection, copied about 1420, is written on vellum (animal hide) and is richly ornamented in bright colors. It contains 354 pieces, mostly for two and three voices, by twelve composers of the *trecento* and early *quattrocento* (1400s). A miniature portrait of each composer appears at the beginning of the section containing his works (see Plate II, facing page 83). Three types of secular Italian composition are represented in the Squarcialupi Codex and other manuscripts: *madrigale, caccia*, and *ballata*.

Madrigale

Madrigals were idyllic, pastoral, satirical, or love poems usually set for two voices. Jacopo da Bologna's *Fenice fù* (A phoenix was I, NAWM 23) is a hauntingly beautiful example of this *trecento* form (see diagram on page 75). Its two voices, which reveal occasional bits of imitation, convey the same nostalgic text in similar, undulating melodies, although the upper voice is slightly more florid.

Caccia

Written for two equal voices in canon at the unison, the *caccia* parallels the French *chace*, a popular-style melody set in strict canon to lively words describing or imitating some sort of bustling scene. Unlike its French and Spanish counterparts, the caccia usually has a free instrumental part in slower motion added below. A typical text describes a hunt or some other animated scene, such as a fishing party, a busy marketplace, a group of girls gathering flowers, or a battle. Vivid details—shouts, bird songs, horn calls, exclamations, dialogue—are all brought out with spirit and humor in the music, often with the aid of hocket and echo effects.[3]

The polyphonic *ballata*, which flourished later than the madrigale and caccia, shows some influence of the French ballade style. The word "ballata" originally signified a song to accompany dancing (from the Italian *ballare*, to dance). Thirteenth-century ballate (of which no musical examples are known today) were monophonic dance songs with choral refrains, and in Boccaccio's *Decameron* the ballata is still associated with dancing. Although a few early-fourteenth-century monophonic ballate have survived, most of the examples we find in the manuscripts are for two or three voices and date from after 1365. In form, these lyrical, stylized, polyphonic ballate resemble the French virelai. (See "Standard Forms of *trecento* Song," page 75, for a description of all three types of Italian lyric poetry discussed here.)

Ballata

Francesco Landini (ca. 1325–1397) was the leading composer of ballate and the foremost Italian musician of the *trecento*. Blind from boyhood as a result of smallpox, Landini nevertheless became an esteemed, well-educated poet (like de Vitry and Machaut) and a master of music theory. He was also a virtuoso performer on many instruments and was known especially for his

Francesco Landini

Giovanni da Prato, from *Paradiso degli Alberti*, ca. 1425:

❝ Now the sun rose higher and the heat of the day increased. The whole company remained in the pleasant shade, as a thousand birds sang among the verdant branches. Someone asked Francesco [Landini] to play the organ a little, to see whether the sound would make the birds increase or diminish their song. He did so at once, and a great wonder followed. When the sound began many of the birds fell silent and gathered around as if in amazement, listening for a long time. Then they resumed their song and redoubled it, showing inconceivable delight, and especially one nightingale, who came and perched above the organ on a branch over Francesco's head. ❞

Il Paradiso degli Alberti, ed. A. Wesselofsky (Bologna, 1867), pp. 111–13, trans. D. J. Grout.

3. A caccia by Ghirardello da Firenze, a contemporary of Landini, may be seen in HAM No. 52.

skill at the organetto, a small portative organ (see Plate II, facing page 83). Although he left no known sacred music, he may have improvised organ music in church or written sacred vocal music that is now lost. Landini is a principal character in Giovanni da Prato's *Paradiso degli Alberti*. This book, though written around 1425, supposedly records scenes and conversations from the year 1389 (see vignette, page 73).

Landini's ballata *Non avrà ma' pietà* (She will never have mercy, NAWM 24) typifies this genre's form and style (see "Standard Forms of *trecento* Song," page 75). Like the French formes fixes, the ballata is strophic and incorporates a refrain. Melismatic passages decorate the ends (and sometimes the beginnings) of lines, but never interrupt the middle of a verse, showing an early concern for text declamation—a characteristic feature of Italian music. The

Landini cadences

end of every line (and often a structurally important internal point as well) is marked by a cadence, usually of a type now known as the "Landini" cadence. Here the progression from the major sixth to the octave is ornamented by a lower neighbor leaping up a third in the top voice (see measures 3–4, 5–6, 10–11 of Example 4.2, which shows the first line of the refrain). A great appeal of Landini's music, in addition to its graceful vocal melody, lies in the sweetness of its harmonies. Sonorities containing both the intervals of the third and fifth or of the third and sixth are plentiful, though they never begin or end a section or piece.

EXAMPLE 4.2   Francesco Landini, Ballata: *Non avrà ma' pietà*

She will never have pity, this lady of mine . . . Perhaps by her [the flames] will be extinguished . . .

Polyphonic Music of the Fourteenth Century, IV, p. 144 (Monaco: Éditions de l'Oiseau-Lyre, 1958).

Standard Forms of *trecento* Song

Madrigale

*T*he madrigale consists of several three-line stanzas, followed by a closing pair of lines. All the stanzas were set to the same music; the additional pair of lines, called the *ritornello*, was set to different music with a contrasting meter. The following diagram corresponds to Jacopo da Bologna's *Fenice fù* (NAWM 23):

	Stanza			Stanza			Ritornello	
Lines of poetry:	1	2	3	4	5	6	7	8
Sections of music:	a			a			b	

Caccia

The poetic form of the caccia is irregular, although, like madrigali, many caccie have ritornellos that are not always in canonic style. The French word *chace* and the Italian *caccia* both mean "chase" or "hunt." In the case of the caccia, the name refers not only to the pursuit of one voice by the other but also to the subject matter of the text, which often evokes the excitement of hunting or the liveliness of other outdoor scenes.

Ballata

In the Italian ballata, a three-line refrain (*ripresa*) is sung both before and after a seven-line stanza. The first two pairs of lines in the stanza, the *piedi*, have their own musical phrase, while the last three lines, the *volta*, uses the same music as the refrain. The form, exemplified by Landini's *Non avrà* (NAWM 24), may be represented as follows:

	Ripresa			Stanza (2 piedi + volta)							Ripresa		
Lines of poetry:	1	2	3	4	5	6	7	8	9	10	1	2	3
Sections of music:	A			b		b		a			A		

French influence

Unlike their French counterparts, Italian composers of the early *trecento* did not use isorhythm or any other textural and rhythmic complications associated with the motet, such as different layers of text and chains of syncopations. In the late 1300s, however, the music of Italian composers began losing its specific national characteristics and started to absorb the contemporary French style. The trend was especially noticeable after the papal court moved from Avignon—where it had been for most of the century—back to Rome in 1377. Italians wrote songs to French texts and in French genres, and we often find their works written down in French notation. Toward the end of the century, northern composers began to settle in Italy, beginning a parade of Flemish, Netherlandish, French, English, and (later) Spanish musicians who flocked to that country in the course of the fifteenth century. Not only were they warmly welcomed, for many years foreigners filled nearly every important musical post in Italy. Unquestionably, the music of these composers was influenced by what they heard and learned in Italy.

Later fourteenth century

In a paradox typical of the later fourteenth century, the papal court at Avignon left its mark more on secular composition than on sacred. There and at other courts across southern France, trends begun earlier in the century were continued and became increasingly fashionable. Sometimes composers carried their fascination with rhythmic complexity and notational subtlety to extremes that made their works devilishly challenging for performers: beats subdivided in unusual ways, phrases broken by hocket or stretched out in chains of syncopations, voices moving simultaneously in contrasting meters and different groupings within the beat. A rondeau from this period by Baude Cordier illustrates some of these intellectually playful tendencies in a fanciful, yet relatively moderate way—both in the music and its notation (see illustration and window, pages 78–79). The musical complication in this rondeau, *Belle, bonne, sage* (Fair lady, good and wise, NAWM 25), results from the use of hemiola (a relationship between note values of 3 to 2), as we may see in Example 4.3. At measure 9 of the cantus part, each of the quarter notes of the $\frac{3}{4}$ measure is subdivided into three eighth notes, converting it to a $\frac{9}{8}$ measure. Meanwhile the contratenor in measures 8–11 has two measures of $\frac{3}{2}$ against four measures of $\frac{3}{4}$ in the upper part. These metrical shifts are notated by means of red notes in the manuscript (see facsimile, page 79). Adding

EXAMPLE 4.3 Baude Cordier, Rondeau: *Belle, bonne, sage*

further color and visual interest, the word "heart" in the text is replaced with a red heart, and, of course, the entire piece is notated in the shape of a heart, a pun on the composer's name (Latin *cor*, meaning heart).

Theory and Practice in Fourteenth-Century Music

The practice of raising or lowering certain notes by a half step, known as *musica ficta* (false or feigned music), gave a special flavor to fourteenth-century French and Italian music and continued in use through much of the sixteenth century. Such alterations, implied or indicated in manuscripts by accidentals, made cadential points more emphatic and melodic lines more supple. These accidentals were common at cadences where a minor sixth (demanded by the mode) was raised to a major sixth before a cadential octave (as at the cadence on *D* in Example 4.4a and b). Composers, singers, and theorists apparently also agreed that a third contracting to a unison should be made minor. Actually, cadences of the type shown in Example 4.4b would have *both* upper notes of the penultimate chord raised to avoid the tritone or augmented fourth, resulting in a *double leading-tone cadence* (Example 4.4c). Cadences on *G* and *C* were altered similarly. In cadences on *E*, however, the penultimate outer interval already formed a major sixth, so no alteration was required (see Example 4.4d). This succession of chords, in which the lower voice descends by semitone, is called a *Phrygian cadence*.

Pitches were also raised or lowered to avoid sounding the augmented fourth against the lowest note of a texture, to avoid the tritone interval *F–B* in a melody, or simply to make a smoother melodic line. Such alterations in fourteenth-century music would present no difficulty to modern performers if composers and scribes had written the sharps, flats, and naturals in the manuscript. Unfortunately for us, they often did not, or they did so inconsistently. In view of these uncertain factors, conscientious modern editors of this music include only those accidentals found in the original sources and indicate in some way (usually above or below the staff) those they believe should be additionally applied by the performers.

Musica ficta

Accidentals

EXAMPLE 4.4   Alteration at Cadences

a. Strict modal forms

b. Chromatically altered forms

c. Form with double leading tones

d. Modal (Phrygian) cadence on *E*

Window

THE SUBTLER ART

The sophisticated music we find in the southern French courts of the late fourteenth century was intended for professional performers and highly cultivated listeners. Because of its formidable rhythmic and notational complexities, sometimes carried to extremes by composers fascinated with their own technical skills, modern scholars have dubbed this highbrow music the *ars subtilior* (the subtler art). Its super-elegant style is matched by the elaborate appearance of the pieces themselves in the manuscript pages, often teeming with fanciful decorations, intermingled red and black notes, ingenious notation, and other unusual devices. Baude Cordier's rondeau notated in the shape of a heart, *Belle, bonne, sage* (NAWM 25), is a good example.

The upper half of the heart, with its delightful double curve, presents the texted cantus or song part (not so named in the manuscript); its many short note values and lengthy melismas—the first one appears where the note-shapes seem to crowd together at the dip in the middle of the line—take up two complete staves. Below these are the tenor and contratenor lines, so identified by their enlarged initial letters at the left. They are notated without text, on one long and two shorter staves respectively, each staff becoming more narrow than the one above it as the heart tapers to a point. The words **T**enor and **C**ontra mark their parts' separate starting points, followed by the text incipit, *Belle bonne*. The placement of the C-clef at the head of each staff depends on the melodic range: for the cantus, the clef wraps around the second line so that the higher notes of this part can fit on the staff; but for the tenor and contratenor (which share the same, lower range) the clef is placed on the fourth line. Each of the three parts begins after a different number of rests (indicated by the vertical lines after the clef), but each takes up the same melodic idea (visible in the matching patterns of notes after the rests) in an early instance of imitation. Patches of red notation in all three parts (seen here in purple) indicate the subtle shifts in rhythmic organization that are discussed in NAWM 25.

The remainder of the text (lines 5–6 and 9–12, not numbered in the manuscript but so identified in the NAWM transcription) neatly fills the bottom point of the heart. If we look closely, we can see the repeated words *Belle bonne* twice more—once at the end of the second line of text and again at the lowest point—indicating the position of the rondeau's refrains. The small red heart, which appears just left of center under the second line of the cantus, not only replaces the word "heart" in the text but also sums up the witty premise of the whole chanson.

Baude Cordier, whose name is boldly proclaimed above the rondeau, undoubtedly wrote the text himself, a common practice at the time. In this case, however, the words of the refrain make his authorship especially clear, not only by punning on the composer's own name (*cor*, meaning heart) but also by revealing his amorous and virtuosic intentions:

> Fair lady, good, wise, pleasant, and nice,
> on this day when the year is renewed
> I make a gift of a new song
> within my heart which presents itself to you.

▲ The rondeau *Belle, bonne, sage* by Baude Cordier (after 1400) in a supplement to the Chantilly manuscript. (*Musée Condé, MS 564*)

Fourteenth-Century Notation

*I*nnovations in notation in the fourteenth century allowed for both triple and duple subdivision of longer notes, the introduction of many new short note values, and the greater rhythmic flexibility that marked the music of the latter part of the century. This French system of mensuration (or measured music) expanded on Franconian principles of the late thirteenth century. The long (¶), the breve (■), and the semibreve (◆) could each be divided into either three or two notes of the next smaller value. The division of the long was called *mode* (*modus*), that of the breve *time* (*tempus*), and that of the semibreve *prolation* (*prolatio*). Division was *perfect* or *major* if it was triple, *imperfect* or *minor* if duple. Two new note forms were introduced to indicate values shorter than the semibreve: the *minim*, ♩, one-half or one-third of a semibreve; and the *semiminim*, ♪, one-half of a minim. The system may be plotted as follows:

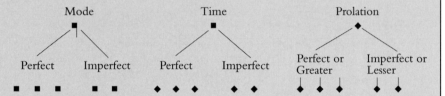

Eventually, signs for time and prolation were devised that approximated time signatures. A circle indicated perfect time and a half-circle imperfect time; the latter became our modern sign for $\frac{4}{4}$ time. A dot inside the circle or half-circle indicated major prolation and the absence of a dot, minor prolation. Thus, four "prolations" were recognized and represented as follows:

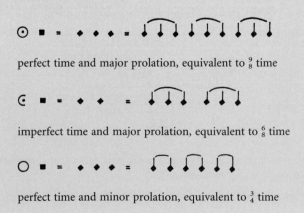

perfect time and major prolation, equivalent to $\frac{9}{8}$ time

imperfect time and major prolation, equivalent to $\frac{6}{8}$ time

perfect time and minor prolation, equivalent to $\frac{3}{4}$ time imperfect time and minor prolation, equivalent to $\frac{2}{4}$ time

In addition to the signs shown above, the French employed other notational devices. They used dots and "colored" notes; red notes, for example, served a multitude of purposes, among them to show perfection or imperfection where the normal reading would indicate the opposite interpretation. White—or outline–note forms replaced black notation about 1425, and black was then used to signal special meanings. However, the basic system of stems and flags introduced in the fourteenth century remains essentially unchanged today. Even the Latin names assigned to the different note values are still used in some countries; for example, in England a whole note is called a semibreve, and a half note is called a minim.

Instruments

A full and accurate account of instrumental music in the fourteenth and fifteenth centuries is impossible for the simple reason that the music manuscripts rarely even tell us whether a given part is instrumental or vocal, let alone specify the instruments. Composers were content to rely on musicians' habits and on tradition.

We know from painting and literature of the fourteenth and early fifteenth centuries that polyphonic music was usually performed by a small vocal or instrumental ensemble or a combination of the two, with only one voice or instrument to a part. We also have evidence that the solo voice part of pieces in cantilena style was doubled by an instrument that added embellishments. The Latin tenors in isorhythmic motets and the textless tenors in Landini's three-part ballate were almost surely instrumental rather than vocal. But beyond making a few suppositions like these, we can say only that performance probably varied according to circumstances, depending on the singers or players who happened to be available and on their tastes.

Out-of-doors music, dancing, and especially festive or solemn ceremonies called for relatively larger ensembles and louder instruments. The fourteenth-century distinction between "high" (*haut*) and "low" (*bas*) instruments referred to loudness, not pitch. The most common soft instruments were harps, vielles, lutes, psalteries, portative or portable organs, transverse flutes, and recorders. Among the loud instruments were shawms (double-reed woodwinds similar to the oboe), cornetts (early trumpets made of hollowed-out wood, with finger holes and a brass-type mouthpiece), slide trumpets, and sackbuts (early trombones). Percussion instruments, including kettledrums, small bells, and cymbals, often appeared in ensembles of all kinds. Motets

Loud and soft instruments

and other vocal pieces were sometimes performed by instruments alone. A large repertory of instrumental dance music also existed, but as these pieces were generally either improvised or played from memory, few written examples survive.

Keyboard instruments

Although the fourteenth century saw the invention of the earliest keyboard instruments of the clavichord and harpsichord type, they were not commonly used until the fifteenth. In addition to the portative organ, or organetto, chamber organs (also called positive organs) were frequently employed, and large organs installed in churches. Organs in Germany sprouted pedal keyboards in the late 1300s. A mechanism of stops enabling the player to select different ranks of pipes at will and the addition of a second manual keyboard were both innovations of the early fifteenth century.

POSTLUDE

The musical landscape of the fourteenth century revealed a variety of new forms and practices, some resulting from a pronounced shift of interest from sacred music to secular composition. *Ars nova* musicians developed a sophisticated system for rhythmic notation, which in turn allowed for greater freedom and flexibility of rhythmic play. At the same time, French composers created the structural device of isorhythm to control and organize their seemingly unlimited choices. The principal types of polyphonic composition in France were the isorhythmic motet, which had a rather abstract structure and a complicated, layered texture; and the secular love songs in the fixed poetic forms inherited from the trouvères, which had very obvious structures involving refrains and simpler, songlike or cantilena textures. These chanson types—chief among them the virelai, ballade, and rondeau—made use of a more melodic-harmonic idiom as composers aimed for a sensuously appealing sound. New genres of composition emerged. Some, like the Italian caccia and madrigale, probably derived from popular musical practice and remained simpler and more lyrical in style than their French counterparts. The ballata and other songs with refrains, inherited from the thirteenth century, can also be traced back—though more remotely—to popular models.

Two very different composers of equally great renown dominated the scene in their respective countries: Machaut in France and Landini in Italy. By the year 1400, however, the French and Italian musical styles, formerly distinct, had started to merge, moving toward an international style. As we will see in the next chapter, this new style became diversified in the fifteenth century by influences from other sources, chiefly England and the Low Countries.

I. Giotto (1266–1337) signed this canvas of St. Francis receiving the stigmata—that is, the marks impressed on his body in semblance of the wounds on the crucified Christ. Below are other episodes in the life of St. Francis, modeled on frescoes in the Bardi Chapel of Santa Croce in Florence and in the Church of St. Francis in Assisi. At left is the *Dream of Innocent III*, a vision of St. Francis propping up the Church of San Giovanni in Laterano (Rome); in the center he receives *The Confirmation of the Rule*, and at right he is preaching to the birds. Giotto distinguished himself from his predecessors in the naturalness of facial expressions and posture and in the depth achieved by placing figures and objects at different planes of the pictorial space. (*PARIS, MUSÉE DU LOUVRE / SCALA / ART RESOURCE, NY*)

II. Anonymous portrait of Francesco Landini playing a portative organ in the initial letter, *M*, of the madrigal *Musica son* (I am music). From the "Squarcialupi Codex," an early fifteenth-century manuscript named for its fifteenth-century owner Antonio Squarcialupi. (*FLORENCE, BIBLIOTECA MEDICEA-LAURENZIANA, MS PALATINO 87, FOL. 121V*)

5

ENGLAND AND THE BURGUNDIAN LANDS IN THE FIFTEENTH CENTURY: THE BEGINNINGS OF AN INTERNATIONAL STYLE

PRELUDE

Music in the fifteenth century continued its move toward an international European style, retaining some characteristics of French and Italian music of the fourteenth century and incorporating new ingredients as well. English composers contributed decisively to this new style early in the century, but by 1500, Continental composers from areas ruled by the wealthy and powerful dukes of Burgundy had become its chief practitioners. These composers continued to favor secular genres, whose songlike cantilena texture (see page 70) even influenced settings of the Mass and the motet (which had itself become a quasi-secular and ceremonial genre).

English victories during the Hundred Years' War, such as the Battle of Agincourt in 1415, left a strong English presence in France. The conquerers brought with them not only government and military personnel, but also composers and musicians to sing the Mass and entertain them during their occupation. Thus **English Music and Its Influence** spread throughout the Continent, and a large number of British works were copied into Continental manuscripts during the first half of the fifteenth century. Its qualities made quite an impression on the French, particularly the sound of its "lively [imperfect] consonances." A French poem of the early 1440s enthusiastically describes this new *contenance angloise* (English guise or manner), citing especially the "marvelous pleasingness" that made their music so "joyous and remarkable" (see vignette, page 90).

Toward the middle of the century, **Music in the Burgundian Lands**—the

◄ An outdoor entertainment at the court of Duke Philip the Good (1396–1467) of Burgundy. Musicians play for the duke (center) and his company. In the foreground couples dance, while in the background hunters are chasing game. Detail from a sixteenth-century copy of an anonymous fifteenth-century painting. (*Musée National du Château de Versailles*)

parts of France and the Low Countries ruled by the dukes of Burgundy— became the chief conduit for the new, international style that had blended Italian, French, and English elements. Although the Burgundian dukes were technically beholden to the kings of France, they virtually equaled them in power and influence. During the second half of the fourteenth century and the early 1400s, the ruling dukes acquired vast territories— adding to their original area of Burgundy, in east central France, most of the present-day Netherlands, Belgium, northeastern France, Luxembourg, and Lorraine—and presided over the whole until 1477 as though it were an independent kingdom. Nearly all the leading composers of the late fifteenth century came from these regions, and many of them had some connection or other with the Burgundian court and chapel.

Chapels were musical establishments with salaried composers, singers, and instrumentalists who furnished music for church services and court entertainments. When going on a journey, the ruler often took along his chapel, which might include as many as thirty professionals, and other members of the court. Chapels were springing up all over fifteenth-century Europe, as popes, emperors, kings, and princes competed for the services of eminent musicians. The court and chapel of Philip the Good, duke of Burgundy (ruled 1419–67), and his successor Charles the Bold (ruled

146/–77) were the most resplendent. Most of their musicians came from northern France, Flanders, and the Low Countries. In addition to his chapel, Philip the Good maintained a band of minstrels—trumpeters, drummers, viellists, lutenists, harpists, organists, and players of bagpipes and shawms—which included musicians from France, Italy, Germany, and Portugal. Charles the Bold, an amateur instrumentalist and composer, was particularly keen on music and issued detailed regulations for his chapel (see vignette, page 87).

Foreign musicians were constantly visiting the courts, enriching their cosmopolitan atmosphere. Also, members of the chapel themselves were continually moving from one court to another as better job opportunities arose. Inevitably, these circumstances fostered an international musical style. At the same time, the Burgundian court enjoyed such great prestige that its music influenced other European musical centers as well. A Flem-

➤ Among the painters who enjoyed the patronage of the dukes of Burgundy was Jan van Eyck (1390–1441), whose depiction of the angels' instruments in his Ghent altarpiece is so vivid that modern instrument makers have used them as models for reconstruction. Shown here are a positive or chamber organ, a harp, and a vielle or tenor fiddle, all belonging to the category of soft (*bas*) instruments discussed on pages 81–82. (*Ghent, Church of St. Bavon. Giraudon/Art Resource, NY*)

1400

Battle of Agincourt (1415)
End of papal schism (1417)
Philip II (the Good) begins his reign as duke
   of Burgundy (1419)

1425

Joan of Arc executed (1431)
*Dufay's motet *Nuper rosarum flores* written
   for the dedication of Filippo Brunelleschi's
   dome of Santa Maria del Fiore in Florence
   (1436)

1450

Lorenzo Ghiberti completes doors of
   Baptistry in Florence (1452)

End of Hundred Years' War; fall of Constan-
   tinople (1453)
*Death of John Dunstable (1453)
Johann Gutenberg (1398–1468) invents
   printing from movable metal type (1454)
Charles the Bold of Burgundy succeeds
   Philip II (the Good) (1467)
*Death of Guillaume Dufay (b. ca. 1400)
   (November 27, 1474)

1475

Battle of Nancy, death of Charles the Bold;
   end of duchy of Burgundy (1477)

ish theorist writing about 1475 tells how the honor and riches offered to prominent musicians stimulated the growth of talent so much that music in his day seemed like "a new art, the source of which was among the English, with Dunstable at their head, and, contemporary with him in France, Dufay and Binchois." These are the very composers who will be introduced in this chapter.

English Music and Its Influence

From earliest times, England's sacred and secular art music, like northern Europe's generally, kept close connections with folk styles. It leaned toward major tonality as opposed to the modal system, used homophonic discant (or note-against-note) style rather than independent lines with divergent texts, and favored thirds and sixths over the perfect fourths, fifths, and octaves and the dissonances of the French motet. With its special penchant for these imperfect consonances, English discant also had a fuller sound than music of the Continent, where French polyphony favored the more hollow-sounding perfect consonances. Then, too, English conductus and carols (songs in strophic forms) reveal a new stylistic feature: successions of simultaneous thirds and sixths in parallel motion. Such writing, which reflected the English taste for bright, harmonious textures, appeared as early as the thirteenth century and played an important role now, two hundred years later.

Fauxbourdon

Perhaps through hearing English discant, Continental composers from about 1420 to 1450 became fascinated with successions of thirds and sixths. This manner of writing, called *fauxbourdon* ("false bass") affected every genre of composition. Most important, it stimulated the emergence around 1450 of a new way of writing both sacred and secular music for three parts in which

The Organization of the Chapel of Charles the Bold in 1469:

❝ Ordinances of the House of My Lord Duke of Burgundy

... that henceforth his domestic chapel in his house be maintained and governed by 25 persons named below, that is, 13 chaplains, 6 clerks,[1] 5 *sommeliers*,[2] and 1 *fourrier*,[3] who shall be salaried and shall perform daily the divine service. ...

My Lord shall have: five battle trumpets ... six minstrel trumpets ... three players of soft instruments. ...

My Lord intends that among the twelve chaplains some may not be priests yet shall have all the wages of a chaplain ... and according to the merit of their voices and good services, clerks and *sommeliers* may rise from one rank to another, that is, from *sommelier* to clerk and from clerk to chaplain. ...

My Lord wishes and orders that all the said twelve chaplains, clerks, *sommeliers*, and *fourrier*, be obedient to the first chaplain. ...

Item: each day of the year at a suitable hour an ordinary high mass shall be celebrated by the said chapel by these chaplains, clerks, and other servants in chant and discant. ...

Item: for singing [polyphony] from the book there will be at least 6 trebles, 3 tenors, 3 bass contras and 2 middle contras without counting the 4 chaplains of the high masses or the *sommeliers*, who, if they are not occupied at the altar or otherwise will be expected within reason to serve with the others.

... [members of the chapel] should avoid all company of dissolute persons, or those suspected of vice, all card and dice games, and others prohibited by holy decrees ... going around at night making noise and tumult, or singing and shouting in the streets night or day. ...

Item: they shall expressly avoid all concubinage and not keep with or near them nor bring or have brought to them suspicious women. ... ❞

Trans. from David Fallows, "Specific Information on the Ensembles for Composed Polyphony, 1400–1474," in *Studies in the Performance of Late Mediaeval Music*, ed. Stanley Boorman (Cambridge: Cambridge University Press, 1983), pp. 146–51.

1. A clerk (*clerc*) was a singer of rank immediately below that of chaplain (*chapelain*).

2. *Sommeliers*, besides singing, read the Epistle at certain High Masses and assisted at the altar and at Offices of the hours, prepared the altar, guarded the jewels and wine, and performed other duties.

3. A *fourrier* arranged lodgings, guarded the door, provided seating, candles, etc.

A Closer Look at Fauxbourdon

*A*s written, a fauxbourdon originally consisted of a chant accompanied by a lower voice in parallel sixths, each phrase ending with an octave. Against these written parts, a middle voice improvised a fourth below the top part, creating intervals of a third with the lowest part. The actual sound of French fauxbourdon, then, resembled passages of English discant—chains of what today we would call sixth chords—although the principal melody was in the treble rather than in the middle (as in the English compositions, called *faburden*), or in the lowest voice (where the chant was traditionally placed in written discant). A kind of updated version of parallel organum, fauxbourdon technique was used chiefly for settings of the simpler Office chants—hymns and antiphons— and of psalms and psalmlike texts, such as the Magnificat.

EXAMPLE 5.1   Guillaume Dufay, Hymn: *Conditor alme siderum*

the voices move together melodically and rhythmically and participate almost equally in a harmonious texture.

Dunstable   John Dunstable (ca. 1390–1453), named in Martin Le Franc's poem (see vignette, page 90), was the leading English composer of his time. He spent part of his career in France serving the English duke of Bedford, who was regent of France from 1422 to 1435 and commander of the English armies that Joan of Arc tried to drive off French land. Among Dunstable's seventy or so known compositions, we find examples of all the principal types and styles of polyphony that existed in his lifetime: isorhythmic motets, Ordinary Mass sections, secular songs, and three-part settings of miscellaneous liturgical texts. His twelve isorhythmic motets show that this old form was still in fashion. Some of the Mass sections, which make up about one-third of Dunstable's surviving works, also use isorhythm. We know of only a few secular songs by Dunstable; some of these illustrate the expressive lyrical melodies and clear harmonic profile common to the English music of his time.

Historically, Dunstable's three-part sacred pieces—settings of antiphons, hymns, and other liturgical or biblical texts—remain his most important works. Some use a cantus firmus in the tenor or an ornamented chant melody in the treble (see Example 5.2). Others have florid treble lines and borrowed melodies in the middle voice, with the tenor moving mostly in thirds and sixths below. Still others are freely composed, without any borrowed thematic material. The antiphon *Quam pulchra es* (How fair you are, NAWM 26) exemplifies this last approach.

*Dunstable's
motets*

EXAMPLE 5.2   John Dunstable, Treble of Motet: *Regina caeli laetare*, with the Original Plainsong Melody

The three voices of *Quam pulchra es*, similar in character and nearly equal in importance, move almost homophonically. The musical texture resembles a conductus that incorporates passages of fauxbourdon (see measures 12–15, for example). The short melisma at the end of the word "alleluia" animates the conclusion. Dunstable chose not to restrict himself to a cantus firmus or an isorhythmic scheme; instead, he allowed the accents and phrasing of the highly sensuous text to determine the form of the music. Compared to the French-style motets of the time, this composition sounds astonishingly fresh, revealing even greater melodic and harmonic suavity than some of the secular songs of the day.

Quam pulchra es is usually classified as a motet, even though it has no borrowed tenor. As we have seen, a motet was originally a composition on a liturgical text and cantus firmus, for use in church. The isorhythmic motet was already becoming an anachronism in the fifteenth century—retaining

Martin Le Franc Describes the Music of His Time in *Le Champion des dames*, 1440–42:

Tapissier, Carmen, Cesaris	Tapissier, Carmen, Cesaris
Na pas longtemps si bien chanterrent	not long ago sang so well
Quilz esbahirent tout paris	that they astonished all Paris
Et tous ceulx qui les frequenterrent;	and all who came to hear them.
Mais oncques jour ne deschanterrent	But the day came when they did not discant
En melodie de tels chois	such finely wrought melody—
Ce mont dit qui les hanterrent	so those who heard them told me—
Que G. Du Fay et Binchois.	as G. Dufay or Binchois.
Car ilz ont nouvelle pratique	For they have a new practice
De faire frisque concordance	of making lively consonance
En haulte et en basse musique	both in loud and soft music,[4]
En fainte, en pause, et en muance	in feigning,[5] in rests, and in mutations.[6]
Et ont prins de la contenance	They took on the guise
Angloise et ensuy Dunstable	of the English and follow Dunstable
Pour quoy merveilleuse plaisance	and thereby a marvelous pleasingness
Rend leur chant joyeux et notable.	makes their music joyous and remarkable.

French text in C. Van den Borren, *Guillaume Dufay: son importance dans l'évolution de la musique au XVe siècle* (1926), pp. 53–54.

4. This distinction was explored in Chapter 4, p. 81.

5. The word refers to the application of musica ficta; see Chapter 4, p. 77.

6. A reference to shifting from one set of six scale steps (hexachord) to another in the solmization system devised by Guido; see Chapter 2, p. 34.

older characteristics such as tenors taken from chant melodies, multiple texts, and strongly contrapuntal or layered texture—and it disappeared entirely by 1450. Meanwhile, the term *motet* was being used to describe liturgical or even secular works in the newer musical style of the time, whether or not they used a cantus firmus. This broader meaning of the word is still current today: a motet is now almost any polyphonic composition on a Latin text other than the Ordinary of the Mass, including settings of antiphons, responsories, and other texts from the Proper and the Office. The somewhat explicit text of Dunstable's antiphon (given with translation in NAWM 26) was adapted by the Church from the Old Testament Song of Songs as an allegory of Christ's love for the individual soul.

Music in the Burgundian Lands

The foremost composers of music in the Burgundian style were Guillaume Dufay and Gilles Binchois, seen conversing in the miniature illustration, from Martin Le Franc's poem, reproduced on page 92. Although both composers wrote in all the main genres of their day, Dufay stands out for his contributions to sacred music and Binchois for his secular songs.

Guillaume Dufay (also du Fay, ca. 1400–1474) is commonly associated *Guillaume Dufay* with the Burgundian court, although he was probably not a regular member of the ducal chapel. Born about 1400 in or around Cambrai in northern France, Dufay became a choirboy at the cathedral there in 1409. As a young man he served at various Italian courts and chapels, including the papal chapel, and in Savoy (a region that at the time comprised parts of Italy, Switzerland, and France). From at least 1439 until 1450, Dufay's home base was Cambrai, where he was made a church dignitary at the cathedral by Pope Eugene IV. After another stint as choirmaster with the duke of Savoy, he returned to Cambrai, where he died in 1474. We can assume from Dufay's "résumé" that he played an important part in forming the new, international style. Not only was he well traveled, he was also exceptionally well educated, having attended a cathedral school, and received a degree in canon law from the University of Bologna. He gained appointments to influential offices in the church, not because of his music—although he was greatly admired as a composer—but because of his learning.

Gilles Binchois (ca. 1400–1460) stood at the center of musical life in the *Gilles Binchois* Burgundian court, serving in the chapel of Duke Philip the Good from the 1420s until 1453. He did not travel widely and remained in this one post for three decades, which probably accounts for the consistency of his style. Binchois composed more than fifty songs, among them some of the greatest "hits" of the fifteenth century, as measured by their frequent use as tenors for Masses by other composers (see page 95). His chansons express the tender melancholy, touched with sensuous longing, so typical of the courtly love song. Binchois continued the ballade or cantilena style of the fourteenth century, but his flowing and gently arching melodies avoided rhythmic complications.

Composers of the Burgundian period produced four principal types of *Genres and style* work: Masses, Magnificats, Latin motets, and French secular chansons; all but the Magnificat will be discussed in this chapter. Voice combinations were the same as in the French ballade and the Italian ballata: tenor and contratenor both moving within the same small range, and a treble or discantus spanning about a tenth. Larger works, such as Masses and some motets, often had a fourth, texted part. As in fourteenth-century music, each line has a different function and a distinct timbre, with the principal melody in the discantus.

◄ Guillaume Dufay, next to a portative organ, and Gilles Binchois, holding a harp, in a miniature from Martin Le Franc's poem *Le Champion des dames* (1440–42; see vignette, p. 90). (*Paris, Bibliothèque Nationale, MS Fr. 12476*)

The typical discantus line flows in warmly expressive lyrical phrases, ordinarily in a lilting triple meter, breaking into graceful melismas when it approaches important cadences. Even though fauxbourdon was frequently used and essentially homophonic, the texture nonetheless allowed for a certain amount of melodic freedom and contrapuntal independence, including occasional points of imitation.

Cadences

The preferred cadence formula was still a major sixth expanding to an octave (Example 4.4, page 77), often with the "Landini" embellishment figure (Example 4.2, page 74). In a newer version of this cadence, found in three-part writing, the lowest voice under the sixth-to-octave progression skips up an octave, so that the ear hears the effect of a bass rising a fourth (as in the modern dominant-tonic cadence; see Example 5.3a and b).

EXAMPLE 5.3　Cadential Formulas

a. Dufay, Motet　　　　　　　　　　**b.** Binchois, Rondeau

In the fifteenth century, the term *chanson* stood for any polyphonic setting of a French secular poem. Burgundian chansons were, in effect, accompanied solo songs with texts—nearly always love poems—that most often took the complicated form of the rondeau, with its traditional two-line refrain. Composers also continued to write ballades in the typical a a b C form. (For more on both forms, see page 71.) In keeping with the refined ballade tradition of the fourteenth century, the vocal part is much more florid than it is in the rondeau. For example, in Dufay's ballade *Resvellies vous et faites chiere lye* (Awake and be merry, NAWM 28), each line ends with a melisma that occupies eight or ten bars of the transcription.

Burgundian chansons

At first no distinctive sacred style emerged; motets and Masses were written in the manner of the chanson. A freely melodic treble dominates, supported by a tenor and contratenor in the usual three-voice texture. The treble might be newly composed, but often it was an embellished version of a chant. For example, Dufay's *Alma Redemptoris Mater* (Gracious mother of the Redeemer) has such an embellished chant melody in the treble.[7] Dufay's hymn settings, such as *Conditor alme siderum* (Bountiful creator of the stars, NAWM 29), also have the chant in the treble. In the hymns, as in the fauxbourdon tradition, the two outer voices were written down, and the middle voice improvised in parallel motion to fill out the harmony (see Example 5.1). Only the even-numbered stanzas were sung polyphonically; the others were performed as plainchant.

Burgundian motets

In addition to motets in the modern chanson style and fauxbourdons, Dufay and his contemporaries still wrote occasional isorhythmic motets for solemn public ceremonies, following the convention that an old-fashioned musical style was more fitting for ceremonial and state occasions. Dufay's magnificent *Nuper rosarum flores* (Roses recently [came]) was such a work; it was performed in 1436 at the dedication of Filippo Brunelleschi's amazingly large dome for the church of Santa Maria del Fiore (the "Duomo") in Florence. Pope Eugene IV officiated. A writer who attended the ceremony described the bright-robed company of trumpeters, viellists, and other instrumentalists, and the singing choirs that struck the listeners with awe, so that the sound of music, the aroma of incense, and the sight of the beautiful pageant filled the spectators with wonder.

Isorhythmic motets

For the Mass the Burgundian composers eventually developed a specifically sacred musical style. As we have noted, the number of polyphonic settings of the Mass increased in the late 1300s and early 1400s. Until about 1420, the various sections of the Ordinary were nearly always composed as separate pieces (Machaut's Mass and a few others excepted), though occasionally the compiler of a manuscript would group such separate items together. In the course of the fifteenth century, it became standard practice for composers to set the Ordinary as a musically unified whole. Writing a Mass

Masses

7. Ed. in HAM 65.

▲ The Cathedral of Santa Maria del Fiore, in Florence. Dufay wrote the isorhythmic motet *Nuper rosarum flores* for the consecration of the church in 1436.

became the supreme challenge to a composer's creative ingenuity, much as designing a chapel or painting an altarpiece was for an artist of the time.

Some musical unity resulted simply from composing all five parts of the Ordinary in the same general style, though at first each movement was based on a different chant (which usually appeared in ornamented form in the treble). Unity, then, derived from two factors: liturgical association—all movements were part of the cycle of prayers constituting the Mass Ordinary—and compositional procedure. But composers soon achieved a more perceptible and effective musical interconnection by using the same *thematic* material in all sections of the Mass. At first, this connection consisted only in beginning each movement with the same melodic motive, usually in the treble. Since the Ordinary sections do not follow one another in unbroken succession, a Mass that uses such a "head-motive," or "motto," signals to the listener that a particular section "belongs with" the other sections of the Ordinary.

Tenor Mass

The motto technique was soon superseded by, or combined with, another: constructing each movement around the same cantus firmus, which was placed in the tenor. The resulting cyclical form is known as a *cantus firmus Mass*, or *tenor Mass*. English composers wrote the earliest cantus firmus Masses, but the practice was soon adopted on the Continent and by the second half of the fifteenth century had become customary.

Placing the borrowed melody in the tenor followed the medieval motet tradition but created compositional problems. The sound-ideal of the fifteenth century needed the lowest voice to function as a foundation, particularly at cadences. Letting the lowest voice carry a chant melody that could not be altered would have limited the composer's ability to provide such a foundation. The solution was to add a part below the tenor, called at first *contratenor bassus* (low contratenor) and later simply *bassus*. A second contratenor called *contratenor altus* (high contratenor), later *altus*, sounded above the tenor. The highest part was the treble, called variously the *cantus* (melody), *discantus* (discant), or *superius* (highest part). These four voice parts became standard by the mid-1400s and remain so today.

The practice of writing the tenor cantus firmus in long notes and in an isorhythmic pattern was a holdover from the medieval motet. When the chosen melody was a plainchant, a rhythmic pattern was imposed on it and repeated if the melody was repeated. When the borrowed melody was a secular tune, the song's original rhythm was retained, but in successive appearances the pattern could be made faster or slower in relation to the other voices. As in the isorhythmic motet, the identity of the borrowed tune might therefore be thoroughly disguised, the more so now that it lay in an inner voice. Obscuring the cantus firmus in this way did not diminish its power to unify the five divisions of the Mass. Borrowed chant melodies came from the Proper or the Office, secular ones most often from the tenors of chansons. In neither case did they have any liturgical connection with the Ordinary, but the Mass usually owed its name to the borrowed melody, as in Dufay's *Missa Ave regina caelorum*, based on the Marian antiphon; such a connection would also have made this particular setting suitable for performance at any Mass in honor of the Blessed Virgin.

One of the most beautifully integrated tenor Masses is Dufay's *Missa Se la face ay pale*, based on the tenor of his own ballade, *Se la face ay pale* (If my face is pale [the reason is love], NAWM 30a). The practice of using one's own (presumably popular) love song as the basis for a liturgical composition may seem inappropriate to us today. But in the fifteenth century, when court and chapel composers were one and the same, it was motivated at least in part by pride of authorship—the desire of composers to mark works as their own, and in a way that would be unmistakable to their employer and other listeners. Similarly, using a cantus firmus borrowed from another's song was a way of paying tribute to a colleague or, perhaps, acknowledging the influence of a teacher.

In the Kyrie, Sanctus, and Agnus Dei of Dufay's Mass, the value of each note of the ballade melody is doubled. In the Gloria (NAWM 30b) and Credo, the cantus firmus is heard three times, first in notes that are triple their normal values, then in doubled note values, and finally at their original note values, so that the melody becomes easily recognizable only at the third hearing. In this way, Dufay applied the principles of the isorhythmic motet on a larger scale. In Example 5.4a, we see the first phrase of the song in very long notes

Missa Se la face ay pale

in the tenor at "Adoramus te," its first appearance in the Gloria. The next time this opening phrase occurs, at "Qui tollis peccata mundi" (4b), the note values are doubled. The third time, at "Cum sancto spiritu" (4c), the song is heard at its normal tempo. By speeding up the tenor's cantus firmus and imitating some of its motives in the other parts, Dufay heightened the excitement of the closing Amen.

Layered texture in Dufay's Masses

The diverse character of the voices in Dufay's Mass nearly overshadows the unity achieved by the threefold statement of the chanson melody in the

EXAMPLE 5.4   Guillaume Dufay, *Missa Se la face ay pale*: Gloria

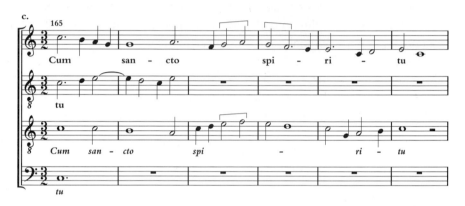

tenor. As in the old-fashioned French motet, each voice exists as an independent layer having its own melodic and rhythmic logic and function. The top two voices—the superius and the contratenor altus—maintain smooth melodic contours and occasionally exchange motives, while the contratenor bassus, more angular though still vocal, provides a harmonic foundation. This texture prevails in other Masses by Dufay as well.

Consonance and dissonance are also carefully controlled rather than used haphazardly. The stronger dissonances appear as suspensions and resolve downward by step, as at measure 33; this treatment of dissonance became standard, and was considered "proper" practice in the sixteenth century. Other dissonances, mainly between beats, pass quickly. Otherwise, Dufay favors thirds and sixths sounding with octaves, fifths, and fourths, producing many combinations of triads (as they were later called) on the beats.

Dufay's four-part cantus firmus (or tenor) Masses are late works, dating for the most part after 1450. Their structural procedures distinguish them from the earlier chansons and chansonlike motets and Masses. As opposed to the "easy-listening" qualities of the Burgundian chanson, some of their new features reflect an extremely artful or "learned" musical style, one that rose to prominence after the middle of the century.

Consonance and dissonance in Dufay's Masses

POSTLUDE

The Burgundian musical style cast such a spell that it lingered in Europe long after the duchy of Burgundy had ceased to exist as an independent political power. Burgundian composers played a large role in the formation and dissemination throughout Europe of an international musical language, which had been fused from French, Italian, and English elements. An overly simple description of the new style—but one that does not distort the truth entirely—might attribute its rhythmic suppleness to the French, its melodic suavity to the Italians, and its clear, crisp harmonies to the English. The full consonant sound of sixths and thirds, sometimes in parallel succession, was adopted on the Continent as fauxbourdon. This new sound strongly influenced all types of composition and prompted composers to write homophonic or homorhythmic textures that emphasized the similarity among the parts rather than their differences. After about 1430, then, certain characteristic features of the new style emerged in the Burgundian orbit: predominantly consonant sonorities including sixth-third successions, control of dissonances, equal importance of the voices, melodic and rhythmic identity of lines, four-part textures, and occasional use of imitation. These features represented a departure from the musical style of the late Middle Ages and looked forward to the new age of the Renaissance.

6

THE AGE OF THE RENAISSANCE: MUSIC OF THE LOW COUNTRIES

The word *Renaissance* (which appears in the title phrase of this chapter and the next) means "rebirth" in French. It was first used in 1855 by the historian Jules Michelet in his *Histoire de France*, then adopted by historians of culture, by art historians, and eventually by music historians, who applied it to the 150 years spanning 1450 to 1600. The concept of rebirth was appropriate to this period because of the renewed interest in ancient Greek and Roman culture that began in Italy and then spread throughout Europe; scholars and artists of the fifteenth and sixteenth centuries wanted to restore the learning and ideals of the classical, pre-Christian civilizations of Greece and Rome. So, the idea of rebirth also involved a rededication to human—as opposed to spiritual—values. Fulfillment in life became a desirable goal, and expressing the entire range of human emotions and enjoying the pleasures of the senses were no longer frowned on. Artists and writers now turned to secular as well as religious subject matter and sought to make their works understandable and appealing to men and women as well as acceptable to God.

These changes in outlook deeply affected **The Musical Culture of the Renaissance**—how people thought about music as well as the way music was composed, experienced, discussed, and disseminated. To be sure, they could see the architectural monuments, sculptures, plays, and poems that were being rediscovered but they could not actually hear ancient music. Yet they could read the writings of classical philosophers, poets, essayists,

99

and music theorists that were becoming available in translation. They learned about the power of ancient music to move the listener and wondered why modern music did not have the same effect. For example, the influential religious leader Bernardino Cirillo (see vignette, page 102) expressed disappointment with the learned music of his time. He urged musicians to follow the example of the sculptors, painters, and architects who had rediscovered ancient art, and the scholars who had restored Greek and Roman literature, and to reclaim the power of the classical musical styles and modes.

We should think of the musical Renaissance more as a general cultural movement and state of mind than as a specific set of musical techniques. Furthermore, music changed so rapidly during this century and a half—though at different rates in different countries—that we cannot define a single Renaissance style. Still, the beginnings of an international European style had emerged at the end of the fifteenth century, as we have seen, from the variety of compositional techniques practiced in England and on the Continent. Because of the influence of the Burgundian court, it spread chiefly from the Low Countries—regions of northeastern France, Belgium, and the Netherlands—to other areas of western Europe. For the first hundred years or so of the Renaissance, **Northern Composers and Their Music** dominated the courts and chapels of France, Italy, and the Holy Roman Empire (which included Spain, Germany, Bohemia, and Austria). In this chapter the northern composers are referred to variously as French, Franco-Flemish, or Netherlandish, depending on where they were born. Each new generation built on the musical accomplishments of the previous one, and composers of the same generation competed with one another in writing Masses, motets, and chansons.

The chapter will close with a discussion of **Josquin and His Contemporaries**. Of the large number of first-rank composers active around 1500, Josquin des Prez (ca. 1440–1521) was surely the greatest.[1] Few musicians have enjoyed higher renown while they lived, or exercised more profound and lasting influence. Among his contemporaries Martin Luther acknowledged Josquin's complete technical and expressive control of his art by calling him "master of the notes." Others hailed him as "the best of the composers of our time," the "father of musicians." Cosimo Bartoli wrote in 1567 that Josquin had been without peer in music, even as Michelangelo (d. 1564) was in architecture, painting, and sculpture: "Both opened the eyes of all those who now take pleasure in these arts and shall find delight in the future."

---

1. Josquin's name, like that of many other composers of earlier times, is spelled in various ways: des Prez, Desprez, Despres; similarly, Dufay's name is often seen as du Fay. Such flexibility resulted no doubt from the different pronunciations, alphabets, and customs in the many countries in which they worked, and from the absence of standardized spelling, which came about only after the gradual increase in printing and literacy made it an issue.

The Musical Culture of the Renaissance

Humanism—the retrieval and revival of the culture of antiquity—was the most characteristic intellectual movement of the Renaissance. It touched music later than the other arts, but this delay was not so great as some writers have claimed. As early as 1424 at the court of Mantua, students were reading the music treatise of Boethius (see Chapter 2) as a classical text rather than as a basis for professional training. This change in approach marked a rebirth of interest in music theory's Greek past. Over the next half century, Greeks emigrating from Byzantium and Italian manuscript hunters brought the principal Greek treatises on music to the West. Among these were the music treatises of Aristides Quintilianus, Claudius Ptolemy, Cleonides, and Euclid. Also newly available were passages by Plato and Aristotle on music. By the end of the fifteenth century, all of these treatises were translated into Latin, although some of them were commissioned for the private use of scholars and were not in general circulation.

> *Humanism*

Franchino Gaffurio (1451–1522) was one musician-scholar who owned

> *Gaffurio*

	C H R O N O L O G Y		
	End of Hundred Years' War; fall of Constantinople (1453) Johann Gutenberg (1398–1468) prints Bible from movable type (ca. 1454)		Henry VIII (1491–1547), king of England (1509–47) Desiderius Erasmus (1466–1536), *In Praise of Folly* (1511)
1460	*Josquin des Prez singer at Milan Cathedral (1459–72) Death of Dufay (November 27, 1474) Battle of Nancy, death of Charles the Bold; end of duchy of Burgundy (1477) *Johannes Tinctoris (ca. 1435–ca. 1511), *Liber de arte contrapuncti* (1477) Lorenzo de' Medici ("Il Magnifico") becomes ruler of Florence (1478)		Niccolò Machiavelli (1469–1527), *The Prince* (1514) Sir Thomas More (1478–1535), *Utopia* (1516) Martin Luther (1483–1546), ninety-five theses (1517) Charles V (1500–1558), Holy Roman Emperor (1519–56)
		1520	
1480	Tudor dynasty in England (1485–1603) First voyage of Columbus to America (1492) Leonardo da Vinci, *The Last Supper* (1495) *Franchino Gaffurio, *Practica musice* (1496) *Death of Ockeghem (February 6, 1497)		*Death of Josquin des Prez (b. ca. 1440) (August 27, 1521) Sack of Rome (1527) Baldassare Castiglione (1478–1529), *The Courtier* (1528) Nicolaus Copernicus (1473–1543), *De revolutionibus orbium coelestium* (publ. 1543) (ca. 1530)
1500	*Petrucci publishes *Odhecaton* (1501) Leonardo da Vinci (1452–1519), *Mona Lisa* (1503) Michelangelo Buonarotti (1475–1564), *David* (1504)	**1540**	Council of Trent (1545–63) *Gioseffo Zarlino (1517–1590), *Le istitutioni harmoniche* (1558)

A Critical View of Polyphonic Music Is Expressed by Bernardino Cirillo in a Letter of 1549:

❝ You know how much music was valued among those good ancients as the finest of the fine arts. With it they worked great effects that today we do not, either with rhetoric or oratory, in controlling the passions and affections of the soul. With the power of song it was easy for them to move any sage mind from the use of reason and drive it to fury and rage. . . . With the efficacy of song the lazy and lax would become aggressive and quick, the angry peaceful, the dissolute modest, the afflicted consoled, the joyful sad. . . . I see and hear the music of today, which is said to have arrived at an ultimate refinement and perfection such as never was or could be known before. Yet I do not hear or see any part of those ancient modes. . . . Kyrie eleison means 'Lord, have mercy upon us.' An ancient musician would have expressed this affection of asking God's pardon in the Mixolydian mode, which would have crushed as well as made contrite a heart and soul and moved every stony disposition if not to tears at least to a pious affection. Thus he would have adapted similar modes in keeping with the texts and made the Kyrie different from the Agnus Dei, and the Gloria from the Credo, or the Sanctus from the Pleni, and these from the psalms and motets. Today all such things are sung in a promiscuous and uncertain genus. . . . In short, when a Mass is sung in church, I should like the music to consist of certain harmonies and rhythms apt at moving our sentiments to religion and piety according to the meaning of the words. . . . Today every effort and diligence is bent on making a work in strict fugue so that when one says 'Sanctus,' another pronounces 'Sabaoth,' while a third sings 'Gloria tua,' with certain wails, bellows, and bleating that at times they sound like cats in January. . . . ❞

Letter of February 16, 1549 to Ugolino Gualteruzzi, from *Lettere volgari di diversi nobilissimi huomini*, ed. Aldo Manuzio, Vol. 3 (Venice, 1564), fols. 114r–115r. Cirillo was the head or archpriest of the famous shrine and destination for pilgrimages, the Santa Casa of Loreto.

some of these translations and incorporated many concepts of Greek learning and theory into his own treatises: *Theorica musice* (Theory of Music, 1492), *Practica musice* (The Practice of Music, 1496), and, most of all, *De harmonia musicorum instrumentorum opus* (A Work Concerning the Harmony of Musical Instruments, 1518). Gaffurio's writings were the most influential of his time. They stimulated new thinking on matters such as the modes, consonance and dissonance, the tonal system, tuning, word-music relations, and the harmony of music and its relationship to the body, the mind, and the cosmos. Some of these topics will be taken up briefly here, and new ones will be introduced.

Learning what the ancient philosophers had thought about the modes—especially their belief that the choice of mode could affect the listener's emotions—stirred up interest once again in the Greek modal system. Both Plato and Aristotle had insisted that various modes had different ethical effects (we may recall the discussion about *ethos* in Chapter 1). But Renaissance theorists and composers mistakenly assumed that the old Greek modes were identical to the similarly named church modes and that the legendary powers of the former could be attributed to the latter. The Swiss theorist Heinrich Glareanus (1488–1563), in his famous book *Dodekachordon* (The Twelve-String Lyre, 1547), added four new modes to the traditional eight: the Aeolian and Hypoaeolian with the final on *A*, and the Ionian and Hypoionian with the final on *C*. With these additions, he brought the theory of the modes in line with the practice of composers, who had frequently employed the modes on *A* and *C*. By analyzing a number of Josquin's motets Glareanus also demonstrated how the music of des Prez (see below) utilized the power of the modes. But his claim of having reestablished Aristoxenus's tonal system was unfounded.

Despite the increased use of thirds and sixths, these imperfect consonances sounded rough in the tuning system of the mid–fifteenth century. But by the beginning of the sixteenth century, instrumental tunings were adjusted to make thirds and sixths sound quite acceptable. Until that time only perfect consonances (fourths, fifths, and octaves) were allowed on the final beat of a cadence; in the sixteenth century, triads appeared there more frequently.

As thirds and sixths became theoretically as well as practically acceptable, a sharper distinction was drawn between consonance and dissonance, and masters of counterpoint devised new rules for controlling dissonance. The outstanding fifteenth-century instruction book on counterpoint—composing melody against melody—was the *Liber de arte contrapuncti* (A Book on the Art of Counterpoint, 1477) by Johannes Tinctoris (ca. 1435–ca. 1511), a Flemish composer who settled in Naples at the court of King Ferrante I in the early 1470s. He deplored the works of the "older composers in which there were more dissonances than consonances" and proclaimed in his preface that nothing written more than forty years earlier was worth hearing. Tinctoris devised very strict rules for introducing dissonances, restricting them to unstressed beats and to syncopated passages (or what we call suspensions) at cadences. These rules were further refined in later treatises by Italian authors and finally synthesized in the great work of Gioseffo Zarlino, *Le istitutioni harmoniche* (Harmonic Foundations) of 1558.

Because humanists believed that music and words could derive added force from each other, they succeeded in bringing music into closer alliance with the literary arts, especially poetry. The image of the ancient poet, singer, and accompanist united in a single person inspired both poets and composers of the Renaissance to seek a common expressive goal. Authors became more

Power of the ancient modes

Glareanus

Tuning

Consonance and dissonance

Tinctoris

Music and words

concerned with the sound of their verses, and composers with matching and projecting that sound. The grammatical structure of a text guided the composer in shaping its musical setting and in placing cadences (that had more or less finality) according to the text's punctuation. Inspired by the poet's message and images, composers tried new ways to dramatize the content of the text. They made it a rule to follow the rhythm of speech and not to violate the natural accentuation of syllables, whether in Latin or the vernacular. Where previously singers had been responsible for matching syllables with the notated pitches and rhythms, composers were now more careful to ensure that the words and music were correctly aligned in the written sources.

Music printing

During the fifteenth century, every city, court, or chapel compiled music manuscripts to suit the local repertory. Copies of these manuscripts, sumptuously decorated and illuminated, were also made and presented as gifts at weddings, anniversaries, and other occasions. This process, although slow and expensive, did not always transmit the composer's music correctly. But with the advent of printing, much wider and more accurate dissemination of written music became possible. In fact, the arrival of the printing process completely transformed the musical culture of the Renaissance—first by printing books and treatises, which helped spread the ideas of antiquity and, later, music.

Petrucci

The first collection of polyphonic music printed entirely from movable type was brought out in 1501 by Ottaviano Petrucci in Venice (see page 112). Under a monopoly granted by the Venetian authorities, Petrucci went on to publish fifty-nine volumes (including reprints) of vocal and instrumental music in the next twenty-two years. His publications are models of clarity and accuracy, especially the earliest ones, which show no trace of being at the experimental stage (see facsimile and window, pages 106–7).

Why Italy?

Why did the Renaissance begin in Italy? One reason surely was geography: Italy was close to, or even at the very source of, the learning and art objects that inspired the movement. Another reason was Italy's commercial dominance: its trade with Byzantium, its wealthy families (like the Medici, who were bankers), and its profusion of secular princes all spurred the growth of a worldly culture, as opposed to the ecclesiastical culture fostered by the great monasteries and cathedrals of northern Europe. The Italian peninsula in the fifteenth century was made up of a collection of city-states and small principalities that were often at war with each other. The rulers, many of whom had gained their positions by force, sought to glorify themselves and magnify their cities' reputations. They did so in a variety of ways: by erecting impressive palaces and country houses decorated with newly commissioned artworks and recently unearthed artifacts from ancient civilizations; by maintaining chapels of talented singers and ensembles of gifted instrumentalists; and by lavishly entertaining neighboring potentates. Meanwhile the citizenry, no longer in feudal service to a lord and free of military duties (wars were fought mostly by mercenaries), accumulated wealth through commerce, banking, and crafts. Although they prayed and attended church, these people gave priority to earthly matters. They wanted prosperity for their families, property and prestigious art for themselves and their heirs, and education for their children along classical rather than religious lincs. Personal fulfillment through learning, public service, and accomplishment motivated their individual lives as well as their social contacts and institutions.

Just as the dukes of Burgundy had made their court a magnet for talented artists and musicians, the wealthy and powerful Italian dukes and princes recruited and attracted the most accomplished composers and musicians from France, Flanders, and the Netherlands to their cities. Thus the Medici in Florence, the Este in Ferrara, the Sforza in Milan, and the Gonzaga in Mantua, to name only some of the Renaissance ruling families, became patrons to the learned singer-composers who had been trained in the magnificent cathedrals and chapels of the north.

Northern Composers and Their Music

Although the migration of musical talent across the Alps to Italy had already begun in the fifteenth century (and was to continue for another three hundred years), Johannes Ockeghem (ca. 1420–1497) was one northern composer who was known there only by reputation. More than a half century after his death, the Italian writer Cosimo Bartoli paid him a tribute comparable to the one he gave to Josquin des Prez (quoted above, page 100): "I know well that Ockeghem was, so to speak, the first who in these times rediscovered music, which had almost entirely died out—not in other wise than Donatello, who in his time rediscovered sculpture."

Ockeghem

◄ Title page of Silvestro Ganassi's instruction book in recorder playing, *Opera intitulata Fontegara*. A recorder consort and two singers perform from printed partbooks. In the foreground are two cornetti and on the wall three viols and a lute.

Window

THE "GUTENBERG BIBLE" OF MUSIC PRINTING

The expanding musical culture of the Renaissance created a demand for music from which to play and sing, and this in turn spurred the development of printed music. Petrucci's first printed collection of polyphonic music, the *Odhecaton* of 1501 (see page 112), consisted not of learned Masses or motets (although he published plenty of these later) but rather of chansons—small forms for a few parts that could easily be performed at home or in the company of friends (see Plate IV, facing page 131). Petrucci had cleverly sized up the market and collected what he judged to be the best secular music of his own and previous generations.

If his taste was impeccable, so too was his technology. The *Odhecaton* and Petrucci's subsequent volumes were printed entirely from specially cast movable type, which meant that notes could be assembled in any order, rearranged, and reused. (Although plainchant had for years been printed from movable type, the *Odhecaton* was the "Gutenberg Bible" of secular music printing.) Each page of music required a triple-impression process, that is, both sides of every sheet went through the press three times: once to print the staff lines, then to print the notes, and finally to print the words. The procedure was long, difficult, and expensive, and Petrucci soon reduced it to two impressions, one for the staff lines and words and one for the music. Printing from a single impression—using pieces of type that printed staff, notes, and text in one operation—was developed in the early 1520s and first applied on a large scale by the Parisian Pierre Attaingnant in 1528. But anything less than the triple-impression process often resulted in imperfectly joined staff lines that appear broken or wavy on the page. In Germany, movable-type music printing began in 1507 and later in the Netherlands. Venice, Rome, Nuremberg, Paris, Lyons, Louvain, and Antwerp were the principal centers in the sixteenth century.

Most ensemble music published in the sixteenth century was printed in the form of oblong partbooks—one small volume for each voice, so that a complete set was needed to perform any piece. Partbooks were intended for

Ockeghem sang in the choir of the cathedral at Antwerp in 1443. Several years later he turned up in France, serving Charles I, duke of Bourbon. In the 1450s he was appointed *premier chapelain* at the royal chapel of the king of France and probably held that position until he retired, having served three kings. A charming miniature in a French manuscript shows Ockeghem in his use at home or in social gatherings (see Plate IV, and illustration, page 105). Most church choirs continued to use the large handwritten choirbooks (see illustration, page 109). New ones were still being hand-copied in the sixteenth century, even as printed collections began appearing, because there was not enough demand for these large books to make printing them economical.

Like Gutenberg's innovation half a century earlier, movable-type music printing had far-reaching consequences. Instead of a few precious manuscripts laboriously copied by hand and liable to all kinds of errors and variants, a plentiful supply of new music in copies of uniform accuracy (or, for that matter, inaccuracy) was now available—not exactly at a low price, but still less costly than equivalent manuscripts. Moreover, the existence of printed copies meant that many more works would become known more widely and would be preserved for performance and study by later generations. Petrucci devoted three volumes to the publication of Josquin's Masses, but no more than one volume to any other composer. For this reason, we might say that Josquin des Prez became the first composer whose reputation was made in his own time by a kind of mass medium—the presses of a discriminating Venetian publisher, interested in commercial gain, but whose good judgment was ultimately confirmed by posterity.

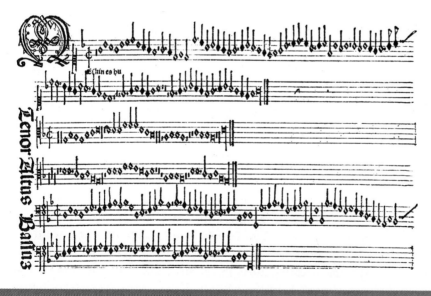

◄ The four-part song *Meskin es hu*, from *Harmonice musices odhecaton A*, a collection of 96 polyphonic settings of mostly French songs, published by Petrucci in 1501. In this music book, the first such to be printed from movable type, the incipit of the text appears only under the cantus part.

chapel surrounded by singers (see illustration, page 109). He was celebrated as a composer as well as a teacher of the next generation's leading musicians, including Josquin, who wrote a moving lament on his death.

Ockeghem's known output comprised only thirteen Masses, ten motets, and some twenty chansons. Most of his Masses resemble each other in their general sonority: four voices of essentially like character interact in a contra-puntal texture of independent melodic lines. He extended the bass, which before 1450 rarely moved below *c*, downward to *G*, *F*, and even *C* in special combinations of low voices. Ockeghem achieved a full, thick texture that gives his works a darker and more homogeneous sonority. Reinforcing this effect, Ockeghem spun out long-breathed melodic phrases in a very flexible rhyth-mic flow (much like that of melismatic plainchant), with few cadences or rests (see Example 6.1).

EXAMPLE 6.1   Johannes Ockeghem, Agnus Dei from *Missa Caput*

Masses

Some of Ockeghem's Masses, like Dufay's *Missa Se la face ay pale*, are based on a cantus firmus, using a given melody as the framework for every movement. For example, the Mass *De plus en plus* takes as its cantus firmus the tenor part of a chanson by Binchois. To vary the sonority, Ockeghem followed the example of earlier fifteenth-century composers and scored whole sections for trios or duets. Sometimes he set one pair of voices against another pair, a device that later composers adopted enthusiastically for both sacred and secular music. He used imitation only occasionally in his Masses, and when he did, he seldom involved all the voices.

In the fifteenth and sixteenth centuries, Masses without a cantus firmus sometimes took their titles from the mode in which they were written (for example, *Missa quinti toni*—"Mass in Mode 5"). Ockeghem's *Missa mi-mi*

➤ This miniature from a French manuscript of about 1530 shows Ockeghem and eight musicians of his chapel singing a Gloria in the usual fashion of the time, from a large manuscript choirbook on a lectern. (*Paris, Bibliothèque Nationale, MS F. 1587, fol. 58v.*)

derives its name from the first two notes of the bass voice, *e-A*, both of which in solmization were sung to the syllable *mi*. Some Masses, including Ockeghem's *Missa prolationum* and *Missa cuiusvis toni*, were named for a structural feature, in these cases a canon (see "Mensuration Canons in an Ockeghem Mass," page 111). A Mass having neither a cantus firmus nor any other identifying peculiarity, or one whose source the composer wanted to keep under wraps, was often called a *Missa sine nomine* (Mass without a name, the musical equivalent of "untitled" in modern art).

Although Ockeghem did not use imitation all that much, he made a conspicuous exception for canons. In the method prevailing at the time, the composer wrote out a single vocal part and left instructions explaining how the singers should derive the additional voices from that part. It was the written instruction itself that was called *canon*, which means "rule" or "law." For example, the "canon" might tell the second voice to join in with the same melody starting a certain number of beats after the original, at the same or at a different pitch; it might direct the second voice to invert the first—that is, move by the same intervals but in the opposite direction; or it might require that the second voice join in with the melody sung backward—a type called a *retrograde* or *cancrizans* (crab) canon.

Another possibility was to instruct the two voices to move at different

Canon

Mensuration canons

rates of speed. Canons of this sort are called *mensuration* canons, and they could be notated by prefixing two or more different mensuration signs to a single written melody, as in Example 6.2a.

EXAMPLE 6.2   Ockeghem, Kyrie II from the *Missa prolationum*

In prestige and craft, writing secular music did not lag far behind Mass composition. Composers expanded the miniature proportions typical of the early Burgundian chanson into larger musical forms. Chansons from 1460 to 1480 show more and more use of imitative counterpoint, at first between the superius and tenor voices, later among all three parts. Most of Ockeghem's chansons, as well as those of his equally famous contemporary Antoine Busnois (d. 1492), made use of the traditional formes fixes of courtly poetry. For example, Ockeghem's *D'ung aultre amer* (To love another, NAWM 31) follows the medieval rondeau form, ABaAabAB (see page 71), and is still

Ockeghem's chansons

Mensuration Canons in an Ockeghem Mass

Ockeghem's *Missa prolationum* is an amazing technical tour de force in which every movement is a double mensuration canon (that is, two different mensuration canons go on at once) involving different intervals and various combinations of time signatures in each section. For the second Kyrie, for example, the original notation includes two parts, each with two mensuration signatures—Ȼ and ○ in the superius, ☉ and Ȼ in the contra—and two C-clefs (Example 6.2a). Each singer must figure out and then observe the pertinent clef and mensuration sign at the beginning of one of the two written parts. The soprano reads the notes of the superius part using the sign Ȼ and the C-clef on the lowest line while the alto uses ○ and the C-clef on the second line. Similarly, the tenor and bass read the contra part. We can see in the transcription (Example 6.2b) how the four voices are derived and how they fit together. For Ockeghem's singers, performing the *Missa prolationum* was like working out an elaborate puzzle, with each section of the Mass presenting a new challenge, and without having the "solutions" written down.

basically an accompanied love song for one texted voice and two instruments. The chansons of Ockeghem, Busnois, and their successors were immensely popular: certain favorites appear again and again in manuscripts and prints from many different countries. Composers freely altered their own and others' chansons, rearranged them, and transcribed them for instruments. Above all, the chansons provided an inexhaustible supply of material for Masses, which might be based on either the superius or the tenor of the original.

Josquin and His Contemporaries

Many of the next generation of Franco-Flemish composers could call themselves direct or indirect pupils of Ockeghem. The three most eminent figures were Jacob Obrecht (ca. 1452–1505), Heinrich Isaac (ca. 1450–1517), and Josquin des Prez (ca. 1440–1521). All born around the middle of the century, they received their earliest musical training and experience in the Low Countries. Each one traveled widely, working in various courts and churches in different parts of Europe, including Italy. Consequently, their careers illustrate the lively interchange in musical matters between northern and southern

Ockeghem's pupils

Europe, that is, between the Franco-Flemish centers and those of Italy and later Spain. Obrecht, from the Dutch town of Bergen op Zoom, died in Italy of the plague (at age fifty-three) while a member of the ducal chapel in Ferrara, where Josquin was also employed for a time. Isaac, Flemish by birth, also ended his years in Italy serving the Medici rulers of Florence. It is no surprise, then, that their music mixes and even combines northern and southern elements: the serious tone, rigid structure, intricate polyphony, and subtly flowing rhythms of the north; the more spontaneous mood, simpler structure, homophonic texture, more distinct rhythms, and more clearly articulated phrases of the Italians.

Odhecaton

The *Odhecaton*, the first printed anthology of chansons, illustrates how deeply northern music penetrated into Italy. It contains works dating from about 1470 to 1500 by composers ranging from the late Burgundian era to the generation of Obrecht, Isaac, and Josquin. Petrucci published the volume in Venice in 1501 under the title *Harmonice musices odhecaton A* (One Hundred Songs [actually there are only ninety-six] of Harmonic Music [that is, part-music, or polyphony]; see facsimile and window, pages 106–7). The letter "A" indicates that this was planned as the first in a series. The publication of two more chanson volumes, *Canti B* in 1502 and *Canti C* in 1504, allowed Petrucci to corner the market on the most up-to-date and popular secular music. Over the next half century he and other Italian music printers issued a great number of such anthologies by French and Franco-Flemish composers.

Chansons

More than half of the chansons in the *Odhecaton* are for three voices, written primarily in the older styles. In the four-voice chansons, however, we see the genre developing toward a fuller texture, a more completely imitative counterpoint, clearer harmonic structure, and greater equality of voices. Duple meter replaced the more common triple meter of the Burgundian period. Many of these pieces, like the Masses of the time, were based either on a popular tune or on a single voice from some earlier chanson.

During the first two decades of the sixteenth century, Franco-Flemish composers at the French royal court in Paris cultivated various types of chanson. Some were entirely original compositions; others incorporated preexisting melodies. By contrast with Ockeghem, Josquin des Prez virtually abandoned the formes fixes, choosing instead strophic texts and simple four- or five-line poems. The polyphonic fabric of his chansons is not formed from independent layers, like Ockeghem's, but is unified and interwoven with imitation. Instead of the tenor-cantus pair serving as the skeleton of the music with the other voices filling in, all the parts are now equal.

Josquin's chansons

Every voice is essential in Josquin's *Mille regretz* (A thousand regrets, NAWM 32a), because it is not an accompanied song. A pair of voices sometimes answers another pair, as at the words "et paine douloureuse" (Example 6.3, measures 20–24), or two voices move in imitation, as the cantus and alto do on "brief mes jours definer" (measures 27–30). All the voices are meant to be sung. Among Josquin's last chansons, perhaps written for Charles V in

EXAMPLE 6.3   Josquin des Prez, *Mille regretz*

I feel so much sadness and painful distress that soon my days will seem to decline.

Reprinted by permission from *The Chanson and Madrigal*, ed. James Haar (Cambridge, Mass.: Harvard University Press). Copyright © 1964 by the President and Fellows of Harvard College.

1520, *Mille regretz* became one of the most popular after his death. It was reworked in a Mass by a Spanish composer, Cristóbal de Morales (ca. 1500–1553), and arranged for vihuela (a plucked and fretted string instrument) by another Spaniard, Luys de Narváez (fl. 1530–1550; see NAWM 32b).

Josquin des Prez

The greatest composer of his generation, Josquin was born about 1440, probably in France across the border from Hainaut, which belonged to the Holy Roman Empire. He sang at Milan Cathedral from 1459 to 1472 and then joined the ducal chapel of the Sforza family. After that he served at the papal chapel in Rome, then moved to France, perhaps to the court of Louis XII. He was appointed *maestro di cappella* at the court of Ferrara in 1503, at the highest salary in the history of that chapel, but again left Italy for France the following year, escaping the plague that was to take the life of one of his contemporaries, Jacob Obrecht. From 1504 until his death in 1521, Josquin

Career

resided at Condé-sur-l'Escaut, in his region of birth, where he was provost of Notre Dame. A large number of sixteenth-century printed and manuscript anthologies contain his compositions, which include some eighteen Masses, one hundred motets, and seventy secular vocal works.

Motets

The high proportion of motets in Josquin's output is noteworthy. In his day the Mass was still the traditional form for composers to demonstrate mastery of their craft. But the Mass's liturgical formality, unvarying text, and established musical conventions left little room for experimentation. Motets, on the other hand, could be written on a wide range of relatively unfamiliar texts that offered interesting new possibilities for word-music relationships. For a Renaissance composer of Josquin's stripe, the motet became the most challenging and inviting genre of sacred composition.

Text and music

In keeping with humanist ideals, Josquin and his contemporaries tried to make the music communicate the meaning of the texts. They carefully fit the musical stress to the accentuation of the words, whether Latin or vernacular, and wanted the words to be heard and understood. The highly florid lines of Ockeghem and other Franco-Flemish composers gave way to more direct syllabic settings in which a phrase of text was presented as an uninterrupted thought. Composers turned to the chanson and the Italian popular genres as models for their vocal writing.

Hearing the note-against-note harmony of Italian popular music (to be discussed in Chapter 7), with its root-position chords, must have made Josquin particularly aware of the potential that resided in this style. His motet *Tu solus, qui facis mirabilia* (You alone, who do wonders, NAWM 33), from his early years in Italy, reflects this attraction. Sections of four-part, homorhythmic music in declamatory style alternate with episodes in which pairs

Falsobordone

of voices imitate each other. The homophonic sections (Example 6.4) use a technique practiced in Italy and Spain known as *falsobordone*, in which the declamatory reciting formula in the top voice was harmonized by root-position triads; such sections appeared typically in psalms, Magnificats, and

EXAMPLE 6.4   Josquin des Prez, Motet: *Tu solus, qui facis mirabilia*

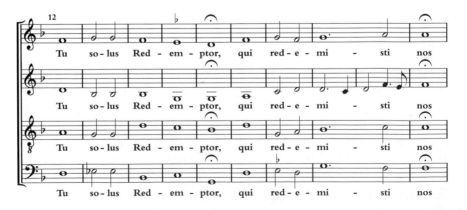

Lamentations. (By contrast, the cognate term *fauxbourdon,* as we saw in the last chapter, describes a northern technique, applied mainly to hymns, in which the chant was accompanied by sixths and thirds expanding to octaves and fifths at cadences.) This homophonic technique allowed listeners to hear and understand the text. During the course of his career, Josquin developed many other ways of setting texts expressively and clearly. In his late motets he explored every resource then available to a composer to enliven the meaning of the words.

A splendid example, believed to date from the last twenty years of Josquin's life, is his setting of Psalm 129, *De profundis clamavi ad te* (English 130: Out of the depths I cried to thee, NAWM 34). Deeply expressive of its text and wedded to it on several levels, the music is appropriately scored for low voices and shaped throughout according to the form, rhythm, accentuation, and meaning of the words. Josquin captured the spirit of the whole psalm in the opening line of the superius (Example 6.5). The music outlines a descending minor triad, leaping down a fifth for the word "profundis" (depths) and reaching up to the minor sixth above for "clamavi" (I cried out), creating a perfect image of a soul sinking into despair and calling for help, straining to be heard. The other voices imitate the first five pitches and durations exactly.

EXAMPLE 6.5   Josquin des Prez, Motet: *De profundis clamavi ad te*

◄ Woodcut purported to be a portrait of Josquin des Prez, from Petrus Opmeer, *Opus chronographicum*, 1611.

IOSQVINVS PRATENSIS.

We can also see Josquin's typical approach to motet writing in an earlier work, *Ave Maria . . . virgo serena*,[2] one of the composer's most widely copied pieces. Its main method of construction is fugal imitation: each phrase of text is assigned a musical subject that is then taken up by each voice, one after the other. The subject is usually imitated exactly at the unison, octave, fifth, or fourth. The first voices to enter either drop out after stating the subject, as in the opening of this motet (Example 6.6), or continue with free counterpoint until they reach a cadence. Before the last voice has finished its phrase, a different voice (or voices) begins the next phrase of text with a new subject. In this way Josquin avoids a cadence and so preserves the continuity of the words in the music. For example, the phrase "Ave Maria" progresses to "gratia plena" without a cadence, then "plena" is linked to "Dominus tecum" through a weak cadence at measure 16, where the two phrases overlap. At "virgo serena," the final phrase of the sentence, all the voices sing together for the first time, pushing forward to the cadence with increasing rhythmic activity.

Fugal imitation

Masses

Not all of Josquin's work is so forward-looking. As we might expect, he employs conservative styles most conspicuously in his Masses, which abound in technical ingenuity. Most use a secular tune as a cantus firmus. In the *Missa L'homme armé super voces musicales*, Josquin transposed a familiar fifteenth-century tune to successive degrees (or syllables—*voces musicales*) of the scale, beginning on *C* for the Kyrie, *D* for the Gloria, and so on. This Mass also includes a mensuration canon.

Josquin's Masses employ many of the techniques commonly used in the sixteenth century. The theme of the *Missa Hercules dux Ferrariae* offers an example of a *soggetto cavato dalle vocali*, a "subject [theme] drawn from the

2. *The Norton Scores: A Study Anthology*, Vol. 1, 7th edition, ed. Kristine Forney (New York: Norton, 1995), pp. 26–33.

EXAMPLE 6.6   Josquin des Prez, Motet: *Ave Maria . . . virgo serena*

Hail Mary, full of grace, the Lord be with you, serene maiden.

vowels" of a word or sentence, or in this case, a name, by letting each vowel indicate a corresponding syllable of the scale, thus:

Imitation Mass

The subject honored Hercules, or Ercole I, duke of Ferrara from 1471 to 1505, and Josquin's employer at one point in his career.

Another of Josquin's works, *Missa Malheur me bat*, illustrates a procedure that became more common later in the sixteenth century. Instead of basing the Mass on a single voice of a chanson, the composer subjected all its voices to free fantasy and expansion. In the process, such a Mass could take over many attributes of the preexisting work, including its characteristic motives, fugal statements and answers, and even its general structure. Although the resulting composition has also been called *parody Mass*, it is best termed *imitation Mass*, which does not imply the use of motivic imitation; instead it acknowledges that in Josquin's time, this Mass would have been called "Mass *in imitation of* the music of *Malheur me bat*."

The amount of borrowing in an imitation Mass varies, as does the composer's originality in treating the borrowed material. The full-fledged imitation Mass not only borrows musical material to a significant extent but also makes something new out of it, weaving its motives into an original contrapuntal texture with systematic imitation among all the voices. The imitation Mass replaced the cantus firmus Mass as the dominant type around 1520.

POSTLUDE

The Renaissance was an era of rediscovery and rapid change that affected the way educated people lived and thought about their own times and culture. It had far-reaching consequences in all the arts and brought about new attitudes toward the creation, consumption, and reception of music. The international style that had begun to emerge from the variety of compositional techniques practiced in England and on the Continent during the 1400s now spread to Italy and the lands of the Holy Roman Empire.

Although the Renaissance did not produce a single, specific musical style, it did influence many features of European art music. More and more, composers let the structure of the text determine the structure of the music. Polyphonic parts were written to be sung—even if they ended up being played—and became nearly equal in importance. The quest by composers for full harmonies, singable melodies, and motivic relationships between the voices influenced the texture of sacred as well as secular pieces. Borrowed melodies, whether sacred or secular, were still used to unify large compositions, but the borrowed material was distributed among the voices rather than confined to the tenor or superius. Although the tenor remained a key voice in the structure, the bass took over the foundation of the harmony. Cadences continued to close in perfect consonances, but between them composers strove for full triadic sonorities. Simplification and standardization of rhythm favored duple measure organized by the value of the breve (alla breve). The preferred sacred genres were the cyclical Mass and the motet. The chanson, breaking out of the formes fixes, was cast in new shapes and its texture was gradually pervaded by imitation. Hidden and esoteric structural devices, such as isorhythm and mensuration canon, gave way to transparent textures, principally that of overlapping fugal or imitative sections, relieved occasionally by homophonic ones. These trends gave composers greater flexibility than they had had before and, aided by the success of music printing, more opportunity to communicate with a wider audience. Many of the trends discussed in this chapter continued throughout the sixteenth century.

7

THE AGE OF THE RENAISSANCE: NEW CURRENTS IN THE SIXTEENTH CENTURY

PRELUDE

By the time of Josquin's death in 1521, the international language of the artful or learned composer was the Franco-Flemish style. During the next thirty years this dominant style changed, absorbing the latest trends and, in turn, creating novel types and forms of vocal music. One reason for the change was the continued migration of northern composers and musicians into southern Germany and across the Alps to places that offered plentiful employment. In **The Generation after Josquin** (1520–50), many composers such as Adrian Willaert from Flanders, continued to write contrapuntal Masses and motets. But they too were influenced by the musical idioms and theoretical ideas of their adopted homes. Willaert eventually settled in Venice and trained many eminent musicians, who spread his fame and influence all over Italy.

The sixteenth century also witnessed **The Rise of National Styles**, or native musical idioms. These local idioms, more popular than the sophisticated art of the foreign composers, gradually came into their own, eventually transforming the international style, especially in Italy. The merger of native and foreign styles created a new type of vocal piece, **The Italian Madrigal**, which became the main focus for musical experimentation in the sixteenth century. By the end of the century, Italy not only replaced France and the Low Countries as the center of European musical life but also maintained its dominant position for two hundred years. At the same time, other countries also developed national styles, which generated new types of **Secular Song outside Italy**.

Finally, although music with words continued to receive the most attention from composers and patrons, **The Rise of Instrumental Music** in the sixteenth century initiated a process that led, centuries later, to its complete domination. During this period, instrumental music increased in both importance (see, for example, Plate III, facing page 130) and quantity and was also affected by the migration of musicians as well as by the changing character of vocal music. **Categories of Instrumental Music** became more and more distinct.

The Generation after Josquin (1520–1550)

For a time church music remained relatively unchanged by the new currents. Northern composers continued to supply polyphonic Masses and motets for the courts and chapels of their southern employers. The smooth polyphonic textures established by Josquin and his contemporaries persisted, but their scoring expanded from four to five or six voices. Chant melodies still served as subjects for Masses and motets, but composers gradually abandoned the old technique of basing a Mass on a single cantus firmus usually assigned to

C H R O N O L O G Y		
1525	Martin Luther (1483–1546), ninety-five theses (1517) Charles V (1500–1558), Holy Roman Emperor (1519–56) Death of Josquin des Prez (b. ca. 1440) (August 27, 1521)	**1575**
1550	*Adrian Willaert becomes director of music, St. Mark's, Venice (1527) *Attaingnant publishes first collection of chansons in Paris (1528); Baldassare Castiglione (1478–1529), *The Courtier* *Jacques Arcadelt (ca. 1505–ca. 1568), first book of four-part madrigals (1539)	*Concerto delle donne* established in Ferrara (1580) *Nicholas Yonge (d. 1619) issues *Musica transalpina* (1588) Edmund Spenser (1552–1599), *The Fairie Queene*, Books 1–3 (1590) *Gesualdo (d. 1613) marries Leonora d'Este of Ferrara (1593) *Death of Orlando di Lasso (b. 1532) (1594) William Shakespeare (1564–1616), *Romeo and Juliet* (1594) Caravaggio (1571–1610), *The Lute Player* (see Plate V, facing page 178, and window, page 127) (ca. 1595)
	Gioseffo Zarlino (1517–1590), *Le istitutioni harmoniche*; Elizabeth I (d. 1603) becomes queen of England (1558) *Death of Adrian Willaert (b. ca. 1490) (December 17, 1562) Tasso's *Aminta* first performed in Ferrara, starting the pastoral fashion that sweeps Europe (1573)	**1600** *Morley issues *Triumphes of Oriana* (1601) *Claudio Monteverdi (1567–1643) publishes fifth book of madrigals (1605) *Monteverdi appointed director of music, St. Mark's, Venice (1613)

the tenor. Instead, they now favored newer methods, such as treating the chant melody more freely and allowing it to be shared, through imitation, by all the voices. And humanism (see page 101), particularly strong in Italy, continued to influence composers in many ways, but especially in their careful treatment of text.

Adrian Willaert

Adrian Willaert (ca. 1490–1562), among all the Franco-Flemish composers of the generation after Josquin, was most deeply affected by the humanist movement and by Italian musical practices. After studying composition in Paris and holding various musical positions in Rome, Ferrara, and Milan, Willaert became director of music at Venice's St. Mark's Church in 1527. He remained in this most prestigious musical post until his death thirty-five years later. A whole new generation of Italian composers learned from his teaching and followed his example as a composer of both sacred and secular music. Among his pupils, the Italian theorist Gioseffo Zarlino became the greatest counterpoint teacher of the century, and the Flemish composer Cipriano de Rore outclassed all his contemporaries in writing Italian madrigals.

Attention to text

In Willaert's sacred compositions, which outnumber his other works, the text determines every dimension of the musical form. Willaert insisted that his printer place the syllables under their proper notes instead of randomly under the staff. Similarly, Willaert paid scrupulous attention to the correct pronunciation of the words by matching long notes to accented syllables, and carefully planned his compositions to suit the structure and meaning of the

Cadences

text in every detail. For example, he never allowed a rest to interrupt a word or thought within a voice line and brought the voices to a cadence only at the end of a unit of text. Full cadences—in which the major sixth moves to the octave and the bass rises a fourth or descends a fifth—Willaert saved for significant textual breaks and used weaker cadences or evaded cadences at lesser points of rest.

In the evaded cadence, which plays an important part in Willaert's technique, the voices seem to be leading to a perfect or full close, but instead turn in a different direction. These cadences contribute to the clarity of the counterpoint while avoiding the frequent resting places characteristic of earlier imitative pieces. They also permit some voices to continue the imitative texture after others have come to a halt. Example 7.1a shows evaded cadences from the motet *O crux, splendidior cunctis astris* (O cross, shining more brightly than all the stars; 1539). The two-voice outline of the typical polyphonic cadence—the major sixth moving to the octave—underlies most of these evaded cadences, but other voices proceed in a way that disguises the finality of the cadential formula. Willaert often marked important cadences with a series of close imitations, multiple suspensions, and strategically placed dissonances, as we find at the end of the first part of this motet (Example 7.1b).

EXAMPLE 7.1   Adrian Willaert, *O crux, splendidior*

a. Evaded cadences

b. Close of *prima pars*

New texture

Although *O crux* is based throughout on the plainchant antiphon (see *Liber usualis*, page 1453), it illustrates some of the newer techniques of sacred composition mentioned above. No one voice monopolizes the borrowed melody (as in the older cantus firmus procedure); instead, motives from the chant serve as subject matter for an extremely free imitative development. In Example 7.2, the Tenor (at measure 1), Altus (measure 2), Quintus (measure 7), and Bassus (measure 7) all paraphrase the chant melody, but each does so in a different way.

EXAMPLE 7.2   Willaert, Opening of Motet *O crux, splendidior*

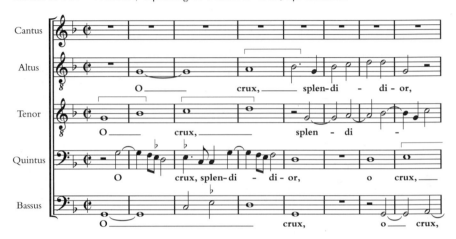

O cross, shining more brightly than all the stars, renowned throughout the world

Adherence to mode

Just as sensitive text treatment was important to Renaissance composers grounded in humanism, so too was the preservation of the church modes. They thought of the modes as a link between the Christian tradition and the legendary emotional effects of ancient music. Few composers succeeded in capturing the essence of a mode as Willaert did. In *O crux* he adopted the chant's mode 1 but transposed it up a fourth by applying one flat (see Example 7.2). In the opening melodies of all the voices he stressed certain intervals that are characteristic of mode 1: the rising fifth, *G–D*, and the fourth, *D–G*. He also made sure that each of the perfect cadences, which mark major points of punctuation, closed on *G*, the final of the transposed mode 1. With good reason did the eminent theorist Zarlino believe that Willaert had achieved perfection in his sacred music.

The Rise of National Styles: Italy

Frottola and lauda

In Italy two types of native song prevailed when the northerners arrived, and others developed during the sixteenth century. The two earlier types, the *frottola* and *lauda* (plural, *frottole* and *laude*) were both strophic, four-part homophonic songs, with the melody in the upper voice, simple diatonic harmonies, and words set syllabically to catchy rhythmic patterns that repeat from one line to the next. Frottole, composed and sung for entertainment in the sophisticated Italian courts of Ferrara and Mantua (see map, page 229), sounded earthy and satirical. Laude, performed at semi-public gatherings of the faithful, were religious and devotional. Neither bore any resemblance to the intricate style of Franco-Flemish polyphony. Petrucci, the great Venetian music printer, published thirteen collections of these highly popular tunes (eleven of frottole and two of laude) within a span of ten years in the early sixteenth century. (For an example of the frottola see NAWM 36.) Historically important as a forerunner of the Italian madrigal, the frottola may also have influenced the emerging Parisian chanson (see page 135).

Later in the century, composers in Italy also cultivated other types of light secular song. The *canzon villanesca* (peasant song), or *villanella* for three voices, was a lively little strophic piece in homophonic style. It flourished chiefly in the Neapolitan area and sometimes mimicked the more sophisticated madrigal. Two other important forms existed—the *canzonetta* (little song) and the *balletto*. The balletto, as the name suggests, was intended for dancing as well as singing or playing, and its typical "fa-la-la" refrains made their way into English songs of the period. In fact, German as well as English composers imitated both canzonette and balletti in the late sixteenth century.

Villanella

Canzonetta and balletto

Native Italian song was intimately bound up, naturally enough, with native Italian poetry. Early in the century, a renewed appreciation for the great fourteenth-century Italian poet Francesco Petrarch (1304–1374) sparked a movement during which the poet's sonnets and other poems were analyzed, discussed, edited, and imitated. Critics praised Petrarch for his remarkable ability to match the sound qualities of his verses to the sense of their meaning. For example, harsh sentiments were expressed with words containing gruff consonants, while tender thoughts were couched in phrases that used soothing vowels and liquid consonants. The Petrarchan movement soon attracted the attention of composers, who found inspiration in the sonic values conveyed by Petrarch's verse. Many of the early madrigalists, including Willaert and his pupil Cipriano de Rore, turned to Petrarch for their texts. In fact, even though the madrigal arose from the merger of native and foreign musical styles—the frottola and Franco-Flemish polyphony—it owes its elevated tone and serious subject matter to the Petrarchan movement.

Petrarchan movement

The Italian Madrigal

The popularity of the Italian madrigal, which dominated secular music in the sixteenth century, allowed Italy to assume a leading role in European music for the first time. Unlike the *trecento* madrigal—a strophic song with a refrain—the sixteenth-century madrigal was a through-composed setting of a short poem. The word "through-composed" says it all: for every line of poetry a different musical setting reflected the rhythm and sense of the words. In contrast with the poetry of the frottola, madrigal poetry sounded more artful and dignified, and borrowed its amorous situations and erotic allusions from the pastoral genre, which was all the rage in the sixteenth century. Many madrigal texts were written by major poets, including Petrarch (who had been crowned poet laureate in Rome in 1341), Jacopo Sannazaro (1457–1530), Ludovico Ariosto (1474–1533), Torquato Tasso (1544–1595), and Giovanni Battista Guarini (1538–1612). They indulged in both heroic and sentimental subjects, which became more and more sensual as the century progressed. Unlike the simple frottola—essentially a tune for singing strophic poetry with harmonic accompaniment—the madrigal setting displays greater invention and variety in its homophonic and contrapuntal textures. Most important, madrigalists tried to match the gravity or playfulness of the poetry with the elegance or wit of their music in order to communicate the poem's ideas and passions.

Social setting

All sorts of courtly social gatherings featured madrigals—especially meetings of academies (societies organized in the fifteenth and sixteenth centuries for the study and discussion of literary, scientific, or artistic matters). In these circles the performers were mainly amateurs, but around 1570 princes and other patrons began to employ professional groups of virtuoso singers. The formation of chamber concerti or ensembles of professional or semiprofessional singers encouraged composers to write more difficult music that demanded the execution of florid runs, trills, and turns and a variety of attacks, dynamics, and vocal color. In 1580, Duke Alfonso d'Este of Ferrara established the most famous of these ensembles, the *concerto delle donne* (women's ensemble)—a group of trained singers (Laura Peverara, Anna Guarini, and Livia d'Arco) appointed as ladies in waiting to his music-loving wife Margherita Gonzaga. Their performances at court, frequently together with professional men singers, attracted so much attention and praise that the Gonzagas of Mantua and the Medici of Florence formed ensembles to rival Ferrara's (see vignette, page 129). Madrigals also adorned plays and other theatrical productions. Because of the great demand for this music, some two thousand collections (counting reprints and new editions) were published between 1530 and 1600, and its popularity continued well into the seventeenth century.

Concerto delle donne

Voices

Most of the early madrigals, dating from about 1520 to 1550, employed four voices; after the middle of the century five voices became the rule, and settings for six or more parts were not unusual. The word "voices" should be taken literally: by definition the madrigal was a vocal chamber work intended for performance with one singer to a part. As always in the sixteenth century, however, instruments often doubled the voices or took their place. Toward the end of the century, madrigals were also performed in arrangements intended for more intimate settings in which a soloist sang one part and performed a reduced version of the others on an instrument such as the lute (see Plate V, facing page 178, and window on facing page).

CARAVAGGIO PAINTS A PERFORMER

The first thing to notice about *The Lute Player* (see Plate V, facing page 178), a painting by Michelangelo Merisi da Caravaggio (1571–1610), is that its conventional title is misleading, for this musician is both playing *and sing-ing*. The painting originated in the 1590s, precisely when the new fashion of solo singing was gaining attention and the practice of singing madrigals as solo songs with instrumental accompaniment was still in vogue. The painter Caravaggio lived in Rome in the home of his patron, Cardinal del Monte, who was a passionate music lover and collector of instruments and books. Del Monte undoubtedly commissioned the painting to show off his expensive and beautiful instruments as well as to document one kind of performance that took place in his apartments.

Can we know more about what the young musician is singing and playing? Indeed, scholars have identified the music as the bass part of a madrigal by Jacques Arcadelt, a composer popular during the cardinal's youth (see page 128). Once we realize that the madrigal was published fifty years earlier, in Arcadelt's First Book (1539), and we observe the yellowing condition of the book's pages, we may reasonably assume that the cardinal provided Caravag-gio with a set of partbooks from his own collection of first editions to use in the painting. That only the bass part is visible reflects the up-to-date perfor-mance practice of the time: the performer would have sung the highest part and its text from memory, while rendering on the lute a simple accompani-ment improvised from the bass line.

The highly specific character of *The Lute Player*, with its array of instru-ments and partbooks, suggests that the painting was conceived both as a plausible representation of a musical performance, and as a public record of such a performance, an evocative reminder for the friends and guests who once heard it. But the work is more than the portrait of a concert; it also belongs to a tradition of Renaissance paintings that allegorized the art of music. Some clues may be seen in the caged songbird—barely noticeable in the dark, upper left-hand corner of the canvas—perhaps a reference to the sense of hearing; in the androgynous features and suggestive tunic of the performer, who might consequently represent a generic personification of Music rather than a specific musician; and in his dreamy, somewhat erotic expression, which reminds us that music was recognized from Plato's time as having enormous sensual power.

Whether portrait, allegory, or a combination of both, Caravaggio's paint-ing helps us not only imagine one set of possible circumstances for music's performance in the late Renaissance but also begin to understand its powerful network of symbols and associations.

Arcadelt

The leading Italian madrigal composers, initially emigrants from the north such as Adrian Willaert, also worked as church musicians and transferred their skills in sacred polyphony to the writing of secular madrigals. The northerner Jacques Arcadelt (ca. 1505–ca. 1568) headed the pope's chapel for a time and later joined the royal chapel in Paris. Arcadelt's madrigal *Ahimè, dov'è 'l bel viso* (Alas, where is the beautiful face, NAWM 37), published about 1538, illustrates a transitional style between the homophonic frottola and the later, more imitative madrigal. It is full of subtle expressive touches. The emotion-laden words "mio caro thesoro" (my dear treasure; Example 7.3) stand out because the composer turned from a C-major to a sustained B♭-major chord, which lies outside the mode of the piece and causes a cross-relation with the previous harmony. The passage on the phrase "Oimè chi me'l ritiene" (Alas, who keeps it from me; measure 25) presents a plaintive series of parallel sixth-chords and introduces imitation at the same time. But the influence between madrigal and sacred genres was mutual. Bernardino Cirillo, who criticized the church music of this period for failing to move listeners with the message of the sacred texts (see vignette, page 102), saw in this madrigal a ray of hope, a sign that composers would soon turn away from complicated polyphony to music's primary goal of communicating feeling.

EXAMPLE 7.3   Jacques Arcadelt, Madrigal: *Ahimè, dov'è 'l bel viso*

My dear treasure, the greatest good. Alas, who keeps it from me, who hides it from me?

Vincenzo Giustiniani on the Women's Vocal Ensembles of Ferrara and Mantua:

❝ [The dukes of Ferrara and Mantua] took extreme delight in music, especially in having numerous women and the leading ladies [of the court] appear singing and playing excellently. They sometimes spent entire days in little sitting rooms elegantly decorated for this purpose with pictures and art works. There was much rivalry between the women of Mantua and of Ferrara, who competed not only in the timbre and natural quality of their voices but in aptly introducing exquisite runs [*passaggi*], yet not excessively (as the falsetto Giovanni Luca [Conforti?] of Rome, who also served in Ferrara, was guilty of doing). They moderated or increased the voice—forte or piano—making it thinner or ampler, and, as the occasion demanded, sustaining the voice, cutting it off with a gentle sigh, or drawing out long, smoothly flowing, clearly articulated passages of embellishment [*passaggi*], turns [*groppi*] and trills [*trilli*], both long and short. Sometimes they sang the passages sweetly and softly, at other times echoes were suddenly heard answering. They accompanied the music and the text with appropriate glances and gestures, and above all without unbecoming movements of the body, lips, or hands that did not contribute to the success of the performance. They articulated the words in such a way that you could hear the very last syllable of every word when it was not interrupted or smothered by passages of embellishment or other ornaments. They sang with many other special tricks and subtleties that would be detected by those more experienced than I. ❞

Vincenzo Giustiniani, *Discorso sopra la musica de' suoi tempi* (Discourse Concerning the Music of His Time), ed. in Angelo Solerti, *Le origini del melodramma* (Turin: Fratelli Bocca, 1903), pp. 107–8.

Cipriano de Rore (1516–1565), like his teacher Willaert, also admired the poetry of Petrarch, whose verses he matched with great subtlety of expression and technique. Flemish by birth, Rore worked in Italy, chiefly in Ferrara and Parma, and briefly succeeded Willaert as music director at St. Mark's in Venice. He became the leading madrigalist of his generation and set the trends that madrigal composers would follow later in the century.

Rore

In his madrigal *Datemi pace, o duri miei pensieri* (1557; Give me peace, O my jarring thoughts, NAWM 39), Rore imbued every detail of the music with the sense and feeling of Petrarch's sonnet. The setting shifts from homophony to imitation, from triple to duple, and from long to short note values depending on the words. Note how Rore contrasts the first and second halves of the opening line (Example 7.4)—between the coveted peace and the painful thoughts that disturb it. In the first half, "Datemi pace" (Give me peace), serene, root-position harmonies and cheerful triple rhythms dominate (as in popular songs or villanelle); in the second half, "o duri miei pensieri" (O my jarring thoughts), staggered rhythms, bleak $^6_3$ and $^6_4$ chords, and an archaic fauxbourdon-like cadence spell out the poet's distress. These kinds of contrasts, which followed the clashing sentiments in the verse, became typical of madrigal settings. Rore's contemporary, Zarlino, devoted an entire chapter of his book *Le istitutioni harmoniche* (Harmonic Foundations, 1558) to instructing composers how to set words to music effectively and faithfully (see vignette on facing page).

EXAMPLE 7.4   Cipriano de Rore, Madrigal: *Datemi pace*

Give me peace, O my jarring thoughts.

Other northerners

Among the many northern madrigal composers who wrote after the middle of the century, Orlando di Lasso, Philippe de Monte, and Giaches de Wert made important contributions to the genre. Orlando di Lasso (1532–1594) excelled as a church composer, but was equally at home with the madrigal, the chanson, and the German part-song, or lied. Like Lasso, Philippe de Monte (1521–1603) was enormously productive in both sacred and secular domains. He began writing madrigals while a young man in Italy and continued uninterrupted throughout his many years serving the Habsburg emperors in Vienna and Prague. He published thirty-two collections of secular madrigals and several books of *madrigali spirituali*. Giaches de Wert (1535–1596), though born near Antwerp, spent nearly his entire life in Italy; he continued to develop the style of madrigal composition begun by Rore. His late style, full of bold leaps, speechlike declamation, and extravagant contrasts, exercised a marked influence on Monteverdi.

Marenzio

Toward the end of the century the leading madrigalists were native Italians, not the northerners who first dominated the field of madrigal composition. Luca Marenzio (1553–1599), who spent most of his career in Rome in the service of several cardinals, depicted contrasting feelings and pictorial details in his music with artistry and virtuosity. Like other madrigal composers of the late sixteenth century, Marenzio favored pastoral poetry, but he was

III. Paulo Caliari, called Veronese (1528–1588), painted this vast canvas, *The Marriage Feast at Cana*, for the refectory of the Benedictine abbey of San Giorgio Maggiore in Venice in 1562–63. It illustrates the account in John 1:2 of the first public sign that Jesus gave of his divine powers. At a wedding banquet in Galilee to which Jesus, his mother, and his disciples were invited, the steward ran out of wine. Jesus instructed the servers to fill the wine jugs with water, which, once poured, had turned to wine. Musicians around the center table in the lower foreground play tenor viols, a contrabass viol, a cornetto, and a violin, while a fifth holds a sackbut. The viol player in white is said to be a self-portrait of the artist, who was noted for his grand conceptions, brilliant colors, and fastidious architectural details.   (*PARIS, MUSÉE DU LOUVRE / ERICH LESSING / ART RESOURCE, NY*)

IV. A vocal quartet reading from partbooks, with the man leading. The rich costumes suggest that these are aristocratic amateurs performing for their own pleasure in the privacy of an idyllic island. Detail from an anonymous sixteenth-century painting.   (*MUSÉE DE L'HÔTEL LALLEMANT À BOURGES*)

Zarlino on Suiting the Harmony to the Words, 1558:

❝ When a composer wishes to express harshness, bitterness, and similar things, he will do best to arrange the parts of the composition so that they proceed with movements that are without the semitone, such as those of the whole tone and ditone. He should allow the major sixth and major thirteenth, which by nature are somewhat harsh, to be heard above the lowest note of the concentus, and should use the suspension [*sincopa*] of the fourth or the eleventh above the lowest part, along with somewhat slow movements, among which the suspension of the seventh may also be used. But when a composer wishes to express effects of grief and sorrow, he should (observing the rules given) use movements which proceed through the semitone, the semiditone, and similar intervals, often using minor sixths or minor thirteenths above the lowest note of the composition, these being by nature sweet and soft, especially when combined in the right way and with discretion and judgment.

It should be noted, however, that the cause of the various effects is attributed not only to the consonances named, used in the ways described above, but also the movements which the parts make in singing. These are two sorts, namely, natural and accidental. Natural movements are those made between the natural notes of a composition, where no sign or accidental note intervenes. Accidental movements are those made by means of the accidental notes, which are indicated by the signs ♯ and ♭. The natural movements have more virility than the accidental movements, which are somewhat languid. . . . For this reason the former movements can serve to express effects of harshness and bitterness, and the latter movements can serve for effects of grief and sorrow. ❞

Gioseffo Zarlino, *Le istitutioni harmoniche*, Book III, chapter 31, trans. Vered Cohen in Zarlino, *On the Modes*, p. 95.

by far the most prolific, publishing eighteen collections of his own madrigals over a period of only two decades.

Ferrara, the city renowned as the home of the original *concerto delle donne*, also boasted several important madrigal composers, all Italians. Nicola Vicentino (1511–ca. 1576) explored chromatic passages in his madrigals, inspired by the chromatic and enharmonic types of Greek tetrachords. To promote his theories Vicentino not only published a treatise, *L'antica musica ridotta alla moderna prattica* (Ancient Music Adapted to Modern Practice, 1555), but he also designed a specially constructed harpsichord and organ (an *arcicembalo* and *arciorgano*) on which to perform his experimental music. Vicentino was succeeded by the madrigalist Luzzasco Luzzaschi (1545–1607), who became a master at improvising on Vicentino's chromatic-enharmonic keyboards. Luzzaschi in turn influenced the madrigal composer most asso-

Vicentino

Luzzaschi

ciated with chromaticism at the end of the century—Carlo Gesualdo, prince of Venosa (ca. 1561–1613).

Gesualdo was a picturesque character whose fame as a murderer preceded his reputation as a composer. In 1586 he married his cousin Maria d'Avalos, who soon took a lover, the duke of Andria. Discovered in their lovemaking by her husband, the couple was murdered on the spot. Gesualdo weathered the scandal and married Leonora d'Este, the niece of Duke Alfonso II of Ferrara, in 1593, thereby entering the Ferrarese court circle.

Gesualdo's prevalent chromaticism was no mere affectation of antiquity but a deeply felt response to the text, as we may observe in the madrigal *"Io parto" e non più dissi* ("I depart" and I said no more, NAWM 40). For the lover's exclamation "Dunque ai dolori resto" (Hence I remain in suffering; Example 7.5), Gesualdo combined melodic half-step motion with ambiguous successions of chords whose roots are a third apart. Although he fragmented the poetic line Gesualdo achieved continuity by avoiding conventional cadences. Despite departing from the diatonic system, he emphasized the main

EXAMPLE 7.5   Carlo Gesualdo, Madrigal: *"Io parto" e non più dissi*

Hence I remain in suffering. May I not cease [to languish in painful laments.]

steps of the mode on *E* at key points—rhythmic pauses and the beginnings and ends of lines—providing the madrigal with some of its coherence.

The madrigal had a special place in the career of Claudio Monteverdi (1567–1643), whose compositions made a crucial stylistic transition in this genre—from the polyphonic vocal ensemble to the instrumentally accompanied song for solo, duet, or larger forces. Born in Cremona in 1567, Monteverdi received his earliest training there from Marc' Antonio Ingegneri, who directed the music in the cathedral. In 1590, Monteverdi entered the service of Vincenzo Gonzaga, duke of Mantua, and eventually became head of the ducal chapel. From 1613 until his death thirty years later, he held the most prestigious musical position in Italy—choirmaster at St. Mark's in Venice—a post once occupied by Willaert.

Of Monteverdi's eight books of madrigals, the first five, published between 1587 and 1605, are monuments in the history of the polyphonic madrigal. Without going to such extremes as Gesualdo, Monteverdi demonstrated remarkable expressive power through his smooth combination of homophonic and contrapuntal part-writing, his faithful reflection of the text, and his free

Monteverdi

Monteverdi's Reply to Artusi, 1605:

❝ Don't be surprised that I am giving these madrigals to the press without first replying to the objections that Artusi made against some very minute portions of them. Being in the service of this Serene Highness of Mantua, I am not master of the time I would require. Nevertheless I wrote a reply to let it be known that I do not do things by chance, and as soon as it is rewritten it will see the light under the title, *Seconda pratica overo Perfettione della moderna musica* [Second Practice, or the Perfection of Modern Music]. Some will wonder at this, not believing that there is any other practice than that taught by Zerlino [*sic*]. But let them be assured concerning consonances and dissonances that there is a different way of considering them from that already determined, which defends the modern manner of composition with the assent of the reason and the senses. I wanted to say this both so that the expression *seconda pratica* would not be appropriated by others and so that men of intellect might meanwhile consider other second thoughts concerning harmony. And have faith that the modern composer builds on foundations of truth.

Live happily. ❞

From C. V. Palisca, "The Artusi-Monteverdi Controversy," in *The New Monteverdi Companion*, ed. Denis Arnold and Nigel Fortune (London, Boston: Faber & Faber, 1985), pp. 151–52.

use of chromaticism and dissonances. But certain features—only suggested in the music of his contemporaries—indicate that Monteverdi was moving swiftly and confidently toward the new style of the seventeenth century. For example, many of his musical motives are not melodic but declamatory, in the manner of the later recitative; the texture often departs from the medium of equal voices and becomes a duet over a harmonically supporting bass; and ornamental dissonances and embellishments that previously would have occurred only in improvisation are written into the score.

Cruda Amarilli (Cruel Amaryllis, NAWM 41) exemplifies the flexible and lively style of Monteverdi's polyphonic madrigals. The sound is rich in musical invention, humorous yet sensitive, and audacious yet perfectly logical in its harmonies. Although this madrigal was first published in Monteverdi's fifth book (1605), it must have been in circulation before 1600, the year that Giovanni Maria Artusi attacked, in print, Monteverdi's style. His commentary, *L'Artusi overo delle imperfettioni della moderna musica* (The Artusi, or Imperfections of Modern Music), harshly criticized Monteverdi for the grating dissonances and contrapuntal liberties in this piece (see Example 7.6,

EXAMPLE 7.6   Claudio Monteverdi, Madrigal: *Cruda Amarilli*

Cruel Amaryllis, who with your name, to love alas, [bitterly you teach . . .]

measures 2 and 6). Monteverdi defended himself in a brief response (see vignette, page 133), calling his approach a *seconda pratica* (second practice) that permitted composers to violate the strict rules of counterpoint (the first practice) in order to express a text.

The Rise of National Styles: Secular Song outside Italy

French composers of the early sixteenth century continued to write Masses and motets in a modified international style. But during the long reign of Francis I (1515–47), composers working in and around Paris developed a new type of chanson, often called the "Parisian chanson," that was more distinctively national in both poetry and music. The first French music printer, Pierre Attaingnant (ca. 1494–ca. 1551), brought out more than fifty collections of chansons—about fifteen hundred pieces altogether—and other publishers soon followed his lead. Hundreds of chanson transcriptions for lute and arrangements for voice and lute, published during the sixteenth century in both France and Italy, affirm the popularity of the genre.

French chanson

Attaingnant

The typical "Parisian chanson" of the earliest Attaingnant collections resembles the Italian frottola in that it is a light, fast, strongly rhythmic song for four voices. The texts, written in a variety of verse forms, frequently revolve around amatory situations that allow for double meanings, although serious subjects are not excluded. Composers treated the words syllabically, with many repeated notes, and placed the melody in the highest voice. They also favored duple meter, a homophonic texture with short points of imitation, and forms with distinct, compact sections that recurred in easily grasped patterns, such as a a b c or a b c a.

Parisian chanson

Tant que vivray by Claudin de Sermisy (ca. 1490–1562) illustrates some of these traits (Example 7.7; for the entire song, see NAWM 42). The harmony

Sermisy

EXAMPLE 7.7   Claudin de Sermisy, *Tant que vivray*

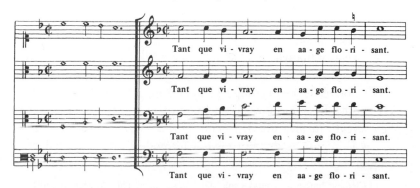

As long as I am able bodied, I shall serve the potent king of love through deeds, words, songs, and harmonies.

consists of thirds and fifths with only an occasional sixth. Instead of syncopation at the cadence, the note that becomes a dissonance—for example the *c″* in measure 3—coincides with the downbeat, giving an "appoggiatura" effect. The end of each line of text corresponds with a relatively long note or with repeated notes, thereby emphasizing the form of the poetry.

Janequin

The two principal chanson composers represented in the first Attaingnant collections were Sermisy and Clément Janequin (ca. 1485–ca. 1560). Janequin excelled at writing descriptive chansons, featuring imitations of bird calls, hunting calls, and street cries. His most celebrated piece, *La Guerre* (War), supposedly about the Battle of Marignan (1515), foreshadowed later "battle" pieces. The decidedly humorous *Le Chant des oiseaux* (Song of the Birds)[1] abounds in vocal warbling and chirping.

Franco-Flemish chanson

Besides Attaingnant and his colleagues in Paris, an important chanson publisher of the 1530s to 1550s was Tilman Susato in Antwerp. Susato focused on Franco-Flemish composers, whose works combined the French trend toward homophony with the older chanson tradition. Franco-Flemish chansons were more contrapuntal than those from Paris, with fuller texture, more melismatic lines, and a less obvious rhythmic beat.

English madrigal

The golden age of secular part-song occurred later in England than in the Continental countries. It began in 1588, when Nicholas Yonge published *Musica transalpina* (Music from across the Alps), a collection of Italian madrigals translated into English. According to Yonge's preface, these madrigals were already part of a singing repertory of gentlemen and merchants who met daily at his home. This anthology and others that appeared throughout the next decade sparked a period of English madrigal composition that flourished from the 1590s to the 1630s. Leading figures were Thomas Morley (1557–1602), Thomas Weelkes (ca. 1575–1623), and John Wilbye (1574–1638).

Morley

Morley, the earliest and most prolific of the three, wrote delightful madrigals as well as lively balletts and canzonets. Modeled on the Italian balletti, Morley's balletts are mainly homophonic with the tune in the topmost voice and, as the name suggests, dancelike in meter. Full cadences mark off distinct sections, which repeat in patterns such as a a b b and the like. A refrain, sung to the syllables *fa-la*, further characterizes the pieces so sharply that they were sometimes called *fa-las*.

Weelkes

The presence of the syllables "fa-la" in a madrigal sometimes disguises its serious message, as in *O Care, thou wilt despatch me* (NAWM 44) by Weelkes. Particularly notable is the opening (Example 7.8), with its learned imitations in direct and contrary motion, and a chain of suspensions (including a diminished seventh in measure 3) to convey the poet's complaint. Weelkes's harmony is as intense as some of his Italian models, but its overall effect is one of liquid vocality and majestic breadth. He achieved a smooth progression

---

1. Ed. in Clément Janequin, *Chansons polyphoniques*, ed. A. Tillman Merritt and François Lesure, 1 (Monaco: Éditions de l'Oiseau-Lyre, 1965): 5–22.

EXAMPLE 7.8   Thomas Weelkes, Madrigal: *O Care, thou wilt despatch me*

to the gleeful fa-las by introducing their music as early as the second line, producing the pattern a b b c d d.

In 1601, Thomas Morley published a collection of twenty-five English madrigals by different composers modeled after a similar Italian anthology called *Il trionfo di Dori* (1592). He called his *The Triumphes of Oriana* in honor of Queen Elizabeth I (reigned 1558–1603). Each madrigal in Morley's collection ends with the words "Long live fair Oriana," a name from the conventional vocabulary of pastoral poetry often applied to Elizabeth. These works combine expressive and pictorial traits with accurate, lively declamation of the English texts. Each voice independently accentuates the words so that the ensemble produces a sparkling counterpoint of continuous rhythmic vitality that simultaneously drives the musical line forward. The collection highlights one of the important ways in which English madrigals differed from their Italian prototypes: the overall musical structure received greater attention.

Madrigals, balletts, and canzonets were all written primarily for ensembles of unaccompanied solo voices, though many of the published collections of

The Triumphes of Oriana

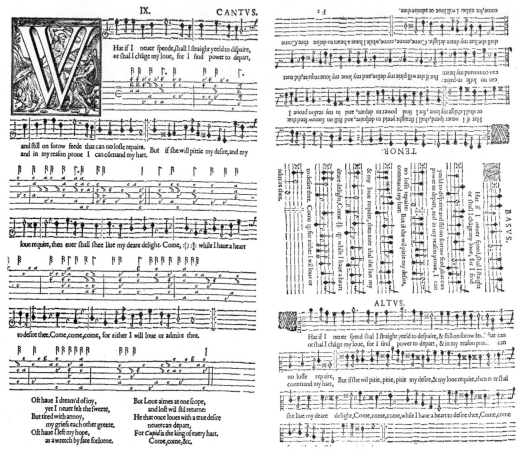

▲ John Dowland's song *What if I never speede*, as printed in his *Third and Last Book of Songs or Aires . . .* (London, 1603), may be performed either as a soprano solo with lute accompaniment or as a four-part arrangement, with or without lute accompaniment. The parts are so arranged that singers around a table can read from a single book. (*London, British Library. By permission of the British Library*)

partbooks indicate on the title page that the music is "apt for voices and viols," presumably in any available combination. This flexibility made them ideal for amateurs. Ability to read a part, either vocally or instrumentally in such pieces, was expected of educated persons in Elizabethan England and elsewhere (see Plate IV, facing page 131).

English lute songs   Solo songs with lute and viol accompaniment, which had flourished on the Continent for nearly a century, became popular in England with the decline of the madrigal during the early 1600s. The most notable composers of lute songs were John Dowland (1562–1626) and Thomas Campion (1567–1620). The melodies of Dowland, especially, are remarkable for their subtle and sensitive treatment of the text. The lute accompaniments, while always carefully subordinated to the voice, maintain a rhythmic and melodic independence. The voice and lute parts are usually printed on the same page in vertical alignment, allowing singers to accompany themselves. In some collections the songs appear both this way and in an alternative version, with three additional vocal parts so arranged on the page that performers sitting around a table could read from the same book (see illustration, page 138). The alternative four-part version, which sometimes resembled a madrigal, could be performed with either voices or instruments or both.

The remarkable *Flow, my tears* (NAWM 45), Dowland's air best known to Elizabethans, from his *Second Book of Ayres* (1600), spawned a whole generation of variations and arrangements (see, for example, *Pavana Lachrymae* [Tearful Pavane], NAWM 47). Its form is a compromise between strophic (typical of Dowland's airs) and through-composed. A performer sings the first two stanzas to the first strain, or section of music, the next two to the second, and the final stanza twice to the third strain, resulting in the musical pattern aabbCC. This duplicates the pattern of the *pavane*, a sixteenth-century Italian processional dance, and suggests that Dowland's air was conceived as a dance-song. Even though the repeats prevent any concrete expression of individual words and phrases, Dowland managed to capture the dark mood that pervades all five stanzas.

Dowland

Because of the entrenched monophonic art of the Meistersinger and their guilds, which flourished in Germany throughout the sixteenth century, secular polyphony developed later in that country than in the rest of Europe—only after 1530, when Franco-Flemish music finally arrived. Then, with the rise of a prosperous merchant class in the cities, came the *Lied* (pl. *Lieder*), a German song set in a polyphonic style derived from the Franco-Flemish tradition. Ludwig Senfl (ca. 1486–1542/3) transformed the simple German lied into an artful genre, similar to the exquisitely crafted motets of northern composers.[2] Senfl also wrote many shorter songs on folklike tenor tunes; though filled with pictorial or witty touches, they also exhibit a certain earthy, serious quality.

German lied

Music printers in Nuremberg, a leading center of German culture in the sixteenth century, issued many collections of German lieder. Among them were highly polished lieder by Nuremberg's own Hans Leo Hassler (1564–1612), who also composed pieces for instrumental ensemble and keyboard, canzonets and madrigals with Italian texts, Latin motets and Masses, and settings of Lutheran chorales. When German taste moved toward Italian madrigals and villanelle after 1550, the lied declined in importance or took on Italianate characteristics. Until then, however, it provided a musical model and a great deal of musical material for Lutheran church chorales (see Chapter 8).

In the later sixteenth century, Munich hosted the great Franco-Flemish Orlando di Lasso (see page 130) who, like Hassler, studied in Italy. Among the vast number of Lasso's compositions were seven collections of German lieder. Instead of surrounding a familiar tune in the tenor with a web of

2. See, for example, Nos. 32 and 48 in his *Sämtliche Werke*, Bd. 2, ed. A. Geering and A. Altwegg.

counterpoint (as in earlier German lieder), he set many in the manner of the Italian madrigal, with all parts participating equally in the interplay of motives.

The Rise of Instrumental Music

During the hundred years between 1450 and 1550, distinct styles, genres, and forms of instrumental music emerged. Independent instrumental music existed earlier, of course, in the form of dances, fanfares, and the like, but since performers played from memory or with improvised embellishments, the music has not survived or has survived only in an approximate state. Although there appears to be a greater emphasis on instrumental music after 1450, it is, perhaps, an illusion: it may mean only that more of it was written down. In addition, only a small portion of the instrumental music in manuscripts and prints from the Renaissance exists today.

Then, too, a great deal of vocal music was often performed instrumentally, and instruments had participated with voices in the performance of polyphonic music since the Middle Ages. Throughout the sixteenth century, much instrumental music remained closely associated, both in style and performance, with vocal music. Instruments doubled or replaced voices in secular and sacred polyphonic compositions. For example, the lowest parts of a madrigal or chanson were often reduced for lute or keyboard, becoming in effect an accompaniment to the melody performed by a solo voice. (See window, page 127, and Plate V, facing page 178.) Portions of a hymn or sections of the Mass (especially the Kyrie and Gloria) alternated with short organ pieces that substituted for the passages normally sung, incorporating some or all of the chant melody they replaced. Composers also wrote organ pieces on liturgical or other cantus firmi as independent works, comparable to vocal motets.

Two different tendencies, then, governed the rise of instrumental music in the Renaissance: (1) the exploitation of compositional styles and genres peculiar or idiomatic to the instruments themselves and functionally independent of vocal music; and (2) the reliance on preexistent vocal genres, including mere substitution of instruments for voices, instrumental transcriptions and arrangements of vocal compositions, and newly composed instrumental works either based on, or otherwise inspired by, vocal models. These two tendencies cut across the five categories of instrumental music discussed below; some categories show signs of incorporating both, as in William Byrd's *Pavana Lachrymae* for harpsichord (NAWM 47; see the discussion about variations on page 147). On the one hand, the piece itself bears no stylistic resemblance to vocal music and reveals a style idiomatic of the instrument. On the other hand, it betrays a reliance on vocal genres because the variations build on the melody of Dowland's very popular air, *Flow, my tears* (see page 139 and NAWM 45). Sometimes the two tendencies merged: because Dow-

Instruments Used during the Renaissance

From illustrations of the period we learn of an extraordinary number and variety of instruments, many of which were built in sets or families, so that one uniform timbre was available throughout the entire range, from soprano to bass. A complete set, called a "chest" or "consort"—of viols or recorders, for example—consisted of four to seven instruments.

Besides recorders, the principal wind instruments were shawms (double-reed forerunners of the oboe); the capped-reed instruments, such as the krummhorn, kortholt, and rauschpfeife; transverse flutes, and cornetts (made of wood or ivory, with cup-shaped mouthpieces); trumpets; and sackbuts (ancestors of the modern trombone). Most of the winds were softer in tone than their modern counterparts.

Wind instruments

◀ Holy Roman Emperor Maximilian I (reigned 1486–1519), surrounded by his musicians. Among the instruments are pipe organ, harp, spinet, drums, kettledrum, lute, sackbut, flute, krummhorn, recorders, viol, and marine trumpet. Woodcut by Hans Burkmair (1473–1531).

Among bowed stringed instruments, the viols differed in many details of construction from the present-day violin family: the neck was fretted, there were six strings tuned a fourth apart with a major third in the middle (as $A–d–g–b–e'–a'$), and the tone, played without vibrato, was more delicate, finer, and less taut.

By far the most popular household solo instrument of the Renaissance was the lute, originally from African and Arabian lands and known throughout Europe for more than five hundred years. Before the end of the sixteenth century they came in various sizes, often made of costly materials and with exquisite workmanship. Except for the *vihuela de mano*, a Spanish type of lute with a guitarlike body, the standard instrument was pear-shaped. It had one single and five double strings, tuned $G–c–f–a–d'–g'$ and plucked with the fingers. The neck was fretted and the pegbox turned back at a right angle (see Plate V, facing page 178). Chords, melodies, runs, and ornaments of all kinds, eventually even contrapuntal pieces, were performed on the lute, and a skilled player could produce a great variety of effects. Lutenists performed solos, accompanied singing, and played in ensembles. We can guess the extent to which the lute developed independently of vocal music from its special kind of notation known as *tablature*, which shows not the pitch of each sound (as in vocal music) but the fret at which the finger stopped the string to produce the required pitch (see illustration, page 138, and NAWM 45).

The organ created a full-bodied sound that covered a broad range with a uniform sonority. The tone of the organ changed over time with the addition of solo and other stops. By about 1500, the large church organ was similar in essentials to the instrument we know today, although the pedal keyboard was employed in Germany and the Low Countries long before it was adopted elsewhere. The medieval portative organ had gone out of fashion, but there were small positive organs (without pedals), including the regal, which had reed pipes of a quietly strident tone.

Two types of stringed keyboard instruments held sway, the clavichord and the harpsichord. In the clavichord, a metal tangent (wedge) struck the string and remained in contact with it; the tone was very soft, but within narrow limits the performer could control the volume and could even produce a vibrato. Instruments of the harpsichord type used a quill to pluck the string. They came in different shapes and sizes known under various names—virginal, spinet, clavecin (in French), and clavicembalo (in Italian), among others. The tone, more robust than the clavichord's, could not be shaded. Rather, different timbres and degrees of loudness were achieved by adding a second manual or a stop mechanism, which allowed coupling with another string, usually tuned an octave higher. The clavichord was essentially a solo instrument suitable for small rooms. The harpsichord served both solo and ensemble playing in spaces of moderate size.

land's air is itself in the form of a particular dance (a pavane), Byrd's keyboard elaboration of it may be associated with two of the five categories given below—variation and dance.

Categories of Instrumental Music

It is useful to separate the emerging instrumental genres of the Renaissance into five categories: 1) dance, 2) improvisatory pieces, 3) contrapuntal works, 4) canzona or sonata, and 5) variation. To some extent these categories are artificial because many pieces combined features from more than one, as illustrated by Byrd's *Pavana Lachrymae*, mentioned above. But as instrumental music continued to flourish and eventually came into its own during the seventeenth century, these same categories and the traditions they represent not only persisted but became even more distinct, as we will soon discover in Chapter 9.

1. Dance Music

Social dancing was widespread and highly regarded in the Renaissance, and people of breeding were expected to be accomplished dancers. Much sixteenth-century instrumental music consisted of dance pieces for lute, keyboard, or ensembles. As in the late Middle Ages, improvisation still prevailed, but many publishers—notably Petrucci and Attaingnant—issued instrumental pieces in tablatures or partbooks. As befits their purpose, these pieces contain distinct sections with clearly marked, regular rhythmic patterns.

Social dancing

Dance was probably the earliest type of instrumental music to gain independence from vocal music because it functioned so differently. Early-sixteenth-century composers, therefore, developed a characteristic instrumental style in writing dance pieces. Some dances were simple arrangements of tunes for popular use, but the majority served a more highbrow function as entertainment for social occasions at the homes of the bourgeoisie or at the courts of the aristocracy. The ballet, which had flourished earlier in the Burgundian and the Italian courts, now reached France. The earliest surviving French ballet music, composed and staged for the *Ballet comique de la reine* (The Queen's Dramatic Ballet), was performed in Paris in 1581.

Ballet

Dances were commonly grouped in pairs or threes, foreshadowing the later dance suite—pieces retaining the characteristic rhythms and general outlines of dance music but not actually intended for dancing. A favorite combination was a slow dance in duple meter followed by a fast one in triple meter on the same tune, the second dance being a variation of the first. One such pair, the *pavane* (*pavana, paduana*) and *galliard*, became a favorite in sixteenth-century France. Another popular pair in Italy was the *passamezzo* and *saltarello*. In both combinations, the first dance was a stately processional

Dance medleys

➤ At a party in the court of Duke Albrecht IV in Munich, three couples dance a stately pavane, accompanied by a flute and drum visible in the left balcony, while the right balcony holds a kettledrum player and two trumpeters, whose instruments are hung up. In the background the duke and a lady play cards. Engraving by Matthäus Zasinger, ca. 1500. (*Dresden, Staatliche Kunstsammlungen*)

in duple time, while the second dance displayed a more lively movement in triple time, usually based on the same melody. The English excelled in writing artful pavanes and galliards not intended for dancing. The *allemande* or *alman*, a dance in moderate duple meter, came into favor about the middle of the sixteenth century, along with the *courante*; these two endured in stylized form and later became regular components of the dance suite.

2. Improvisatory Pieces

Written dance music tells us much about improvisatory practice. It offers evidence of two ways in which sixteenth-century performers improvised: they ornamented a given melodic line, or they added one or more contrapuntal parts to a given melody. Improvisation was an important aspect of a musician's training. In fact, instrumentalists performed the favorite courtly dance of the late fifteenth and early sixteenth centuries, the *basse danse*, by improvising over a borrowed tenor. Later basses danses, however, such as those published by Attaingnant in the 1530s, keep the melody in the top line, as in NAWM 46. Attaingnant notated the basses danses in duple time, but the choreography often called for a mixture of duple and triple to form twelve-beat units. The *branle gay* was a type of basse danse in triple time (see NAWM 46b).

Basse danse

Other improvisatory genres

Compositions resembling improvisations but not meant for dancing rank among the earliest examples of instrumental music for solo players. They proliferated under various names: *prelude* or *preambulum*, *fantasia*, or *ricercare*. Not based on any preexisting melody, they unfold freely, often in a somewhat rambling fashion, with varying textures and without adhering to a definite meter or form. The fantasias of Luis Milán (ca. 1500–ca. 1561), preserved in his *Libro de musica de vihuela de mano intitulado El Maestro* (Book of Music for Vihuela Entitled The Teacher; Valencia, 1536), give us an idea of the improvisations that lutenists might have played before accompanying themselves or a singer in a lute song or another type of vocal piece. Each of the fantasias is in the same mode as the vocal piece that follows it and sounds much like a preparatory warm-up. Some incorporate brilliant rapid scale passages that add tension and suspense before the final chord.

The *toccata* was the chief form of improvisatory keyboard music during the second half of the century. This name, from the Italian verb *toccare* (to touch), carries the suggestion of a lutenist exercising on the fingerboard. The toccatas by the Venetian organist Claudio Merulo (1533–1604) exemplify the transfer of the genre to the keyboard (Example 7.9).[3]

Toccata

EXAMPLE 7.9   Claudio Merulo, Toccata from *Toccate, Libro secondo* (1604)

etc.

---

3. Ed. in HAM No. 153, it was published in Merulo's *Toccate, Libro secondo* (1604).

In the opening succession of broadly conceived harmonies centered on *F* (Example 7.9), Merulo took advantage of the organ's power to sustain tones, closing first on the final and then moving to a half cadence on the fifth degree. The numerous suspensions and other prolonged and repeated dissonances are idiomatic to the organ. Embellishments and scale passages in freely varied rhythms animate the polyphonic texture. Pieces of this sort did not necessarily contain fugal or imitative sections, nor were they uniformly labeled toccatas—they were also called *fantasia, intonazione,* and *prelude.*

3. Contrapuntal Genres

Ricercare

One type of prelude, the *ricercare* or *ricercar* (pl. *ricercari*), evolved into a motetlike succession of fugal sections. The term *ricercare*—an Italian verb meaning both "to seek out" and "to attempt"—probably comes from lutenists' jargon for picking out—*ricercare*—notes on the instrument and testing the tuning. The earliest ricercari, for lute, were brief and improvisatory; when transferred to the keyboard, the genre acquired occasional imitative sections. Later composers clarified the form with repeated phrases and paired imitation. By 1540, the ricercare consisted of successive themes without marked individuality or contrast, each developed in imitation and overlapping with the next at the cadence—in effect, a textless imitative motet. Compared with their vocal counterparts, these ricercari displayed freer voice leading and offered embellishments that were more typically instrumental. Most ricercari were intended for ensemble playing, but some were still written for keyboard instruments and for lute. English fantasias, or "fancies," exhibited similar contrapuntal leanings. Many other instrumental compositions that derived from polyphonic vocal models were nothing more than transcriptions of madrigals, chansons, or motets, decorated by turns, trills, runs, and other embellishments.

4. Canzona or Sonata

Canzona

The Italian *canzone da sonar* (songs to be played), also called *canzone alla francese* (chansons in the French manner), appeared for both ensembles and solo instruments. The canzona, whose very name suggests a work derived from vocal models, began as an instrumental composition in the style of a French chanson—it was light, fast-moving, strongly rhythmic, with a fairly simple contrapuntal texture. From the chanson as well, composers adapted the typical opening rhythmic figure that occurs in nearly all canzonas: —∪∪ or long, short, short. More lively and entertaining than the sober and somewhat abstruse ricercare, the canzona became the leading genre of contrapuntal instrumental music in the late sixteenth century. The earliest Italian examples (apart from mere transcriptions) were for organ. Ensemble canzonas made their appearance about 1580 and eventually developed into the seventeenth-century *sonata da chiesa* (church sonata). The essential step in this development was the division of the canzona into more or less contrasting sections, each based on a distinct theme.

Sonata

From the fifteenth century on, the term *sonata* described a variety of pieces for instrumental ensembles or solos. The Venetian sonata of the late 1500s—the sacred version of the canzona—consisted of distinct sections, each based on a different subject or on variants of a single subject. This sectional character links it to the later sonata da chiesa, which in the seventeenth century was made up of movements in different tempos, meters, and moods. Giovanni Gabrieli (ca 1557–1612), organist at St. Mark's in Venice, left seven sonatas in addition to some thirty-six canzonas.

Innovative Venetian composers adapted their polychoral medium to instruments. (For a discussion of Gabrieli's polychoral vocal music, see Chapter 8.) The famous *Sonata pian' e forte*[4] from Gabrieli's *Sacrae symphoniae* (1597) is essentially a double-chorus motet for instruments. This composition claims a prominent place in music history because it stands among the first instrumental ensemble pieces to designate specific instruments in the printed parts. The first choir names a cornett and three sackbuts, the second, a violin and three sackbuts. The sweet tone of the cornett blended well in an ensemble. Sackbuts, which came in five sizes from soprano to bass, also had a relatively mild tone. Another innovation in the printed music was the indication *pian[o]* or *forte*, appearing either when each choir was playing alone (soft) or when both were sounding together (loud)—one of the earliest instances of dynamic markings in music.

5. Variations

Improvising on a tune to accompany dancing has ancient roots. Actual written-out variations on pavane tunes appeared early in the sixteenth century in published lute tablatures. In a related practice, composers and performers wrote and improvised variations on *ostinato* patterns—short bass lines repeated over and over—such as the *passamezzo antico* and *moderno*, both deriving from the pavane. (These were prototypes of the later chaconne and passacaglia.) Composers also created sets of variations on standard melodic formulas for singing verses, such as the *Romanesca, Ruggiero*, and *Guardame las vacas* (see page 187). Spanish lute and keyboard composers carried the art of making variations on popular tunes to a level of great refinement.

English virginalists

In the late sixteenth century an extraordinary flowering of the variation form took place among a group of English keyboard composers called *virginalists*, after *virginals*, the name applied at the time to all plucked keyboard instruments. The leading composer of this group was William Byrd (1543–1623). Of the many English manuscript collections of keyboard music dating from this period, the most comprehensive remains the *Fitzwilliam Virginal Book* (modern edition, 1963). Its pages contain nearly three hundred com-

---

4. Ed. in HAM No. 173.

➤ Title page of *Parthenia*, a collection of music for virginals by William Byrd, John Bull, and Orlando Gibbons presented to Princess Elizabeth and Prince Frederick on their wedding in 1613. The title—*parthenia* were Greek maidens' choral dance-songs—alludes whimsically to the bride, the instrument's name, and to the fact that this is the first such collection ever published.

positions from the late sixteenth and early seventeenth centuries, among them transcriptions of madrigals, contrapuntal fantasias, dances, preludes, descriptive pieces, and many sets of variations. Most of the variations in the *Fitzwilliam Virginal Book* are on slow dance tunes or on familiar songs or folk tunes of the time.

Themes   Melodies that served as a basis for sets of variations were generally short, simple, songlike, and regular in their phrasing, with a clear binary (two-part) or ternary (three-part) pattern marked by distinct cadences. A set consisted of an uninterrupted sequence of variations, numbering from a half-dozen to more than twenty. Each variation preserves the phrase structure, harmonic plan, and cadences of the theme. The melody may be presented intact throughout an entire set of variations, passing occasionally from one voice to another; more often, it is broken up by decorative figuration, so that its original profile is only suggested. Sometimes variations are paired; often the degree of rhythmic animation increases as the sections succeed one another. Some of the passage work demands a high degree of virtuosity.

Variation technique may be studied in the pavane for keyboard (*Pavana Lachrymae*, NAWM 47) that Byrd wrote on Dowland's air *Flow, my tears* (NAWM 45). The air itself exhibits the typical form of a pavane, that is, three strains, each immediately repeated. Byrd added a variation after each strain; he retained the outline of the tune in the right hand while adding short accompanying motives or decorative turns, figurations, and scale patterns that are imitated between the hands.

POSTLUDE

Developments in the sixteenth century included the continued cultivation of sacred polyphony by northern composers who settled in Italy and the emergence of new secular genres—madrigal, chanson, and lied—as the sophisticated international style encountered native traditions in Italy, France, and Germany. Among the composers following Josquin's generation, Willaert and Arcadelt in Italy were driven by the spirit of humanism to seek a close rapport between music and text. In both his sacred and secular compositions, Willaert shaped the music to follow the syntax and rhythms of the Latin and Italian language; in his secular works he went beyond this to represent musically the essence of a text's message. Yet he remained faithful to the inherited ideal of modal, diatonic counterpoint, equality and independence of voices, full harmony, controlled dissonance, and clarity of form.

Willaert's pupils and their contemporaries—Vicentino, Rore, and Lasso, for example—sought an even closer bond between music and text, but they tilted the balance, at least in the madrigal, toward the expression of a poem's varied feelings and images, sacrificing a certain cohesion and homogeneity of style. At the same time, the madrigal became more dramatic and declamatory as composers attempted to convey the sentiments of the text to a wider audience. During the last decades of the century, composers found new ways to express intense passions and the clever conceits of modern poetry. Gesualdo explored chromaticism, while Monteverdi experimented with dissonance and new textures and rhythms. In Paris, chanson composers turned from serious motetlike polyphony to a light, tuneful, treble-dominated song. A number of English composers enthusiastically took up the new Italian trends, but the most characteristic genre to emerge from the widespread cultivation of vocal chamber music in the British Isles was the air and consort song.

During this same period, instrumental music emerged from the shadows cast by vocal music and improvisation. Dance music dominated the field as before, but by the end of the 1500s, many other independent genres of written instrumental music could be distinguished by their functions and procedures. First identified with a particular instrument, most of these genres spread to other instruments and to ensembles—for example, the toccata, ricercare, prelude, fantasia, canzona, sonata, and variations. Around 1600 English lute and keyboard composers took the lead in instrumental writing until, as we shall see, Italian composers turned their attention to instrumental music in the seventeenth century.

8

Church Music of the Late Renaissance and Reformation

PRELUDE

When Martin Luther nailed his ninety-five theses to the door of a church in Wittenberg in 1517, he had no idea that his action would result in a group of Protestant religious sects completely separating themselves from Rome, the center of Western Christianity. The liturgical changes that eventually ensued from the Reformation naturally brought about musical changes, which differed from country to country according to the degree of reform advocated by the various Protestant leaders: Luther in Germany; Calvin and his followers in France, the Low Countries, and Switzerland; and Henry VIII in England.

At first, **The Music of the Reformation in Germany**, written by Lutheran composers, remained very close to the traditional Catholic sources and styles of plainsong and polyphony. Some music retained the original Latin texts, other works used German translations, and still others had new German texts fitted to the old melodies (resulting in *contrafacta*). The Lutheran Church's most distinctive and important musical innovation became the strophic hymn, called *Choral* or *Kirchenlied* (church song) in German and *chorale* in English, intended for congregational singing in unison. Just as plainchant was the basis for musical expansion and elaboration for Catholic composers, so too the repertory of chorales became the starting point for a great deal of Lutheran church music from the sixteenth century until the time of Johann Sebastian Bach (1685–1750) and beyond.

Reformation Church Music outside Germany developed along similar

150

lines, except that Calvin and leaders of other Protestant sects opposed certain elements of Catholic ceremony much more strongly than Luther had. They distrusted the allure of art in worship services and prohibited singing of texts not found in the Bible. As a result, the only notable contributions to music from the Calvinist churches were their Psalters—rhymed metrical translations of the Book of Psalms set to newly composed melodies or, in many cases, to tunes of popular origin or from plainchant. Since the Calvinists discouraged musical elaboration, they seldom expanded the Psalter tunes into larger vocal or instrumental forms. In England, under Henry VIII, the Anglican Church's separation from Rome in 1534 happened more for political than for religious reasons; so English church music was less affected and remained closer to Catholic musical traditions (except that English replaced Latin in the liturgy).

The Catholic Church met the defection of its northern brethren by starting its own program of internal reform known as **The Counter-Reformation**. This movement not only gave birth to many liturgical reforms, it also reaffirmed the power of music to affect the hearts and minds of the faithful through an appropriately sacred style of polyphony. Indeed, one of its goals was to win back those who had left the Catholic Church, appealing to their senses through the sheer beauty of its liturgy and ceremonial music. Among all the Catholic composers of sacred music to succeed in this strategy, the Roman Giovanni Pierluigi da Palestrina (1525 or 1526–1594) was the most important. Not only did he capture the essence of the musical Counter-Reformation, but his style also became a model for church music composition—one that serves teachers and students of counterpoint to this day.

The Music of the Reformation in Germany

The central position of music in the Lutheran Church reflects Luther's own convictions. He was a singer, a composer of some skill, and a great admirer of Franco-Flemish polyphony, especially the works of Josquin des Prez. He believed strongly in the educational and ethical power of music and wanted the entire congregation to participate in the music of the services. Although he altered the words of the liturgy to conform to his own views on certain theological points, Luther also wished to keep Latin in the service, partly because he thought it valuable for educating the young.

Lutheran church music

In applying Luther's beliefs to local conditions, congregations all over Germany developed a number of usages. Large churches with trained choirs generally kept much of the Latin liturgy and its polyphonic music. Smaller congregations adopted a German Mass (*Deudsche Messe*), first published by Luther in 1526, that followed the main outlines of the Roman Mass but with

German Mass

distinct differences: the Gloria was omitted; the recitation tones were adapted to the inflections of the German language; several parts of the Proper were condensed or omitted; and chorales sung in German replaced the remaining items of the Proper and most of the Ordinary. But Luther did not intend this German Mass to prevail uniformly in Lutheran churches; indeed, Latin Masses and motets were sung in some parts of Germany well into the eighteenth century.

The Lutheran chorale

Just as most Catholic church music developed from the elaboration of plainsong, so Lutheran church music largely expanded from the chorale. As in plainsong, the chorale consisted essentially of only two elements, a text and a tune. The congregation learned the tenets of their faith and celebrated the yearly cycle of religious holidays by singing these easily memorized hymns comprised of simple, metrical tunes and rhyming verses. A large number of chorales were newly composed; Luther himself wrote many texts and some melodies. For example, the words of the well-known *Ein' feste Burg ist unser Gott* (A mighty fortress is our God, 1529) are by Luther and the melody is generally ascribed to him as well. Secular and sacred songs or Latin chants supplied an even larger number of chorale tunes. Thus, the Easter sequence *Victimae paschali laudes* (NAWM 5) provided the model for *Christ lag in Todes Banden* (Christ lay in the bonds of death).

Contrafacta

The *contrafacta*—extant melodies recycled with a new or spiritualized text—made up a particularly important class of chorales. Perhaps the most famous and certainly one of the most beautiful is *O Welt, ich muss dich lassen* (O world, I must leave you), adapted from Isaac's lied *Innsbruck, ich muss dich lassen* (NAWM 35). A later and somewhat startling example uses Hassler's lied *Mein G'müth ist mir verwirret* (My peace of mind is shattered [by a tender maiden's charms]), which, with new sacred words, became the Passion chorale *O Haupt voll Blut und Wunden* (O head, all bloody and wounded). Example 8.1 shows the transformation of the opening phrase from Hassler's original version into one of the settings in Bach's *Passion according to St. Matthew*.

Polyphonic chorale settings

The chorale, like plainsong, could be enriched through harmony and counterpoint, and was often reworked into large musical forms. Lutheran composers soon began to write polyphonic settings for chorales. In 1524 Luther's principal musical collaborator, Johann Walter (1496–1570), published a volume of thirty-eight German chorale settings together with five Latin motets. Georg Rhaw (or Rhau; 1488–1548), the leading music publisher of Lutheran Germany, issued an important collection of 123 polyphonic chorale arrangements and motets in 1544, including pieces by all the leading German and Swiss-German composers of the time. As we might expect, the chorale settings in these and other sixteenth-century collections varied considerably in style. Some composers used the older technique of the German lied, placing the plain chorale tune in long notes in the tenor, and surrounding it with three or more free-flowing parts. Others developed each phrase of the chorale imitatively in all voices in the manner of Franco-Flemish motets. Still

EXAMPLE 8.1

a. Hans Leo Hassler, *Mein G'müth ist mir verwirret*

Mein G'müth ist mir ver-wir-ret, das macht ein Jungk-frau zart, bin
gantz und gar ver-ir-ret, mein Herz das kränkt sich hart

My peace of mind is shattered by a tender maiden's charms, I've lost my way
completely, my heart is deeply sore.

b. J. S. Bach, *Passion according to St. Matthew*

Be - fiehl du dei - ne We - ge und was dein Her - ze kränkt
Der al - ler-treu - sten Pfle - ge dess, der den Him - mel lenkt;

Entrust your ways and whatever grieves your heart to the most faithful care, to
the One who rules heaven.

others wrote in a simple, almost chordal, style, with the tune in the soprano
instead of the tenor; this became the preferred arrangement.

The choir, sometimes doubled by instruments, commonly alternated chorale stanzas with the congregation, who sang in unison without accompaniment. Eventually all parts were played on the organ while the congregation
sang only the tune. More elaborate treatments of the chorale—for example,
for organ solo or for trained choir—also became part of the Lutheran church
music repertory in Germany. By the end of the sixteenth century, some Protestant composers followed the example of Orlando di Lasso, among others,
and created chorale motets or free polyphonic compositions around the traditional melodies, incorporating personal interpretations and pictorial details
in the manner of the Latin motets. Others used chorale tunes as the basis for
organ improvisations. Both traditions culminated more than a hundred years
later in the keyboard chorale preludes and vocal chorale fantasias of J. S. Bach.

Reformation Church Music outside Germany

The Reformation influenced musical developments in France, the Low Countries, and Switzerland quite differently than in Germany. Jean Calvin
(1509–1564) fervently rejected the Catholic liturgy and its trappings, believing
with the English Puritans that the distraction of the senses, however innocent,

MUSIC AS A SYMBOL FOR HUMAN FRAILTY

Paintings that incorporate musical subjects often help us understand the way people thought and felt about music in their society. The great reformers Luther and Calvin regarded music as God's gift, whose highest and only purpose was to honor God. But while Luther considered music on earth as a preview of the heavenly choir, Calvin also warned of its dangers as a source of temptation.

This picture illustrates an entire class of sober still lifes that became very popular in northern countries after the Reformation. Known as *vanitas* (vanity) paintings, they testify to the transience and sometimes the distractions of art and of all earthly pleasures and possessions. Musical instruments, because of their rapidly decaying sound, were well-known *vanitas* symbols and served as favorite props along with other objects, as in this *"Vanitas" Still Life with a Violin* (1629) by Pieter Claeszoon, a Dutch painter who specialized in this theme.

The term "vanitas" as used in this title comes from the opening of the Book of Ecclesiastes (in its Latin translation from the Hebrew): "Vanitas vanitatum, omnia vanitas . . ."; "Vanity of vanities! All things are vanity! What profit has man from all the labor which he toils at under the sun? One generation passes and another comes, but the world forever stays." Literature as well as painting of the time frequently expressed this idea, with its compelling reminder of human mortality.

Every object in Claeszoon's painting contains a symbolic meaning that contributes to the *vanitas* message. The human skull obviously signifies death, and the smoking oil lamp recently extinguished reminds us that life inevitably comes to an end. What good will our accumulated wealth—represented by the ornate empty goblet on the left and the gilded beaker on the right, as well as by the rare and exotic shells—be to us then? Even all our learning, gathered from books or inscribed with the quill pen, will not help us after death. That

might lead people astray (see illustration and window above). Consequently, the only music heard in the Calvinists' worship service was the singing of psalms to monophonic tunes collected in a Psalter. The principal French Psalter was published in 1562, with psalm texts translated by Clément Marot and Théodore de Bèze set to melodies selected or composed by Loys Bourgeois (ca. 1510–ca. 1561). Like Lutherans, Calvinists originally sang

French Psalter

our time on earth runs out is suggested by the watch, whose mechanism lies exposed in its case. The violin and bow, lying at the center of the painting but partly hidden behind the skull, function as emblems of temporality, of the impermanence of music and all the arts, and of the tenuous pleasures associated with them.

The impact of these paintings (and there were hundreds of them made for middle-class consumers) may be compared to that of contemporary commercial art. However, the message was a negative one: worldly goods are a hindrance to leading a virtuous life, music and other pleasures are frivolous, and learning is ephemeral. The visual effect, all the more convincing because of its shocking realism, was no doubt as persuasive for a seventeenth-century Dutch citizen as the symbol of skull-and-crossbones on a package of cigarettes would be for us today.

▲ Pieter Claeszoon, "Vanitas" Still Life with a Violin (1629). (By permission of Art Dealers Hoogsteder & Hoogsteder, The Hague, the Netherlands)

psalms only in unaccompanied unison at church services. For devotional use at home, they availed themselves of settings in four or more parts, with the tune either in the tenor or the soprano, sometimes in simple chordal style and sometimes in fairly elaborate motetlike arrangements. Eventually, some of the simpler four-part settings were also used in public worship.

The most prominent French composers of psalm settings were Claude

C H R O N O L O G Y

1500		1560	
	Henry VIII (1491–1547), king of England (1509–47)		*French Psalter published (1562)
	*Martin Luther (1483–1546), ninety-five theses (1517)		*Death of Jean Calvin (b. 1509) (1564)
1520		1580	Concerto delle donne established in Ferrara
			*Death of Thomas Tallis (b. ca. 1505) (1585)
	Death of Josquin des Prez (b. ca. 1440) (August 27, 1521)		Mary I (Stuart) executed (1587)
	Sack of Rome; Adrian Willaert appointed director of music, St. Mark's, Venice (1527)		Nicholas Yonge (d. 1619) issues Musica transalpina (1588)
	*Henry VIII breaks with the pope (1532)		Gesualdo (d. 1613) marries Leonora d'Este of Ferrara (1593)
	English Bible adopted; Arcadelt's first book of madrigals published (1539)		*Death of Palestrina (b. 1525 or 1526) and Lasso (b. 1532) (1594)
1540			Shakespeare's Romeo and Juliet (1594)
	*Council of Trent meets (1545–63)		Caravaggio (1571–1610), The Lute Player (ca. 1595; see Plate V, facing page 178)
	*Death of John Taverner (b. ca. 1490) (1545)	1600	
	Edward VI (d. 1553) becomes king of England (1547)		Morley issues Triumphes of Oriana (1601)
	Queen Mary I of England restores Latin rite and link to Rome (1553–58)		Monteverdi publishes fifth book of madrigals (1605)
	*Palestrina issues first book of Masses (1554)		*Death of Tomás Luis de Victoria (b. 1548) (1611)
	Zarlino's Istitutioni harmoniche; Elizabeth I (d. 1603) becomes queen of England, restores Church of England (1558)	1620	Pilgrims arrive in Massachusetts
			*Death of William Byrd (b. 1543) (1623)

Goudimel (ca. 1505–1572) and Claude Le Jeune (1528–1600); the leading Netherlands composer was Jan Pieterszoon Sweelinck (1562–1621). Translations of the French Psalter appeared in Germany, Holland, England, and Scotland, and the Reformed churches in those countries took over many of the French tunes. The Germans adapted Psalter melodies for use as chorales (see Example 8.2a). The French model also influenced the most important English Psalter of the sixteenth century; and the Psalter brought by the Pilgrims to New England in 1620 was a combination of the English and the French-Dutch traditions.

The French Psalter melodies are on the whole sweet and somewhat simple in comparison with the forthright, vigorous quality of the German chorales. Since the Reformed churches discouraged musical elaboration, the Psalter tunes were seldom expanded into larger forms of vocal and instrumental music, as the Lutheran chorales were, so they figure less conspicuously in the general history of music. Their melodic lines, which move mostly by step, resemble plainsong, and their phrases demonstrate a rich variety of rhythmic patterns. Surprisingly few of the melodies from the French Psalter (1562) made their way into modern hymnals. The best-known example is the tune sung originally to Psalm 134, used in the English Psalters for Psalm 100 and therefore known as "Old Hundredth" (Example 8.2b).

England   English composers, though aware of developments in Continental music, worked in relative isolation. No Franco-Flemish musicians came to England

EXAMPLE 8.2   Melodies from the French Psalter of 1562, with Some Later Adaptations

a. Psalm 136

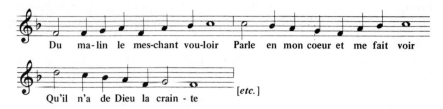

Du ma-lin le mes-chant vou-loir   Parle en mon coeur et me fait voir

Qu'il n'a de Dieu la crain-te   [*etc.*]

The transgression of the wicked saith within my heart that there is no fear of God [before His eyes]

J. S. Bach, Chorale Prelude, *O Mensch, bewein' dein' Sünde gross*, BWV 622

b. Psalm 134

Or sus, ser-vi-teurs du Sei-gneur,   Vous qui de nuit en Son hon-neur

Arise ye servants of the Lord, which by night [stand] in the house of the Lord.

Presbyterian Hymnal

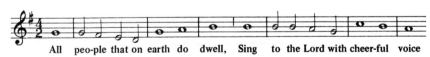

All peo-ple that on earth do dwell, Sing to the Lord with cheer-ful voice

until after 1510, and English composers only gradually adopted the prevailing international style of imitative counterpoint. Meanwhile, native production of secular music continued. Manuscripts from the time of Henry VII and Henry VIII (reigned 1509–47) contain a variety of songs and instrumental pieces in three- and four-part settings, reflecting many facets of court life, including popular elements.

Most of the surviving English polyphonic music from this period is sacred—Masses, Magnificats, and devotional antiphons or motets (in honor of the Blessed Virgin Mary). Many illustrate the English preference for a fuller sonority of five or six voices instead of the more common four-part imitative texture of Continental music. Accordingly, the works display a strong feeling for the harmonic dimension of music and for achieving textural variety through the use of contrasting voice groups. Long melismas executed simultaneously in all voices often resulted in passages of extraordinary beauty and expressiveness.

Taverner

Undoubtedly the greatest English musician of this period was John Taverner (ca. 1490–1545), whose career included four years as director of a large choir at Oxford. Taverner's festal Masses and Magnificats illustrate the full, florid English style of the early part of the century, with occasional sequential passages and some use of imitation. His *Western Wynde* Mass, one of three on this tune by sixteenth-century English composers, treats the cantus firmus as a series of variations, a form that later English keyboard composers favored.

Tallis

Toward the middle of the century, the leading English composer was Thomas Tallis (ca. 1505–1585), whose career reflects the religious upheavals and bewildering political changes that influenced English church music in this period. Under Henry VIII, Tallis wrote Latin Masses (including one imitation Mass) and antiphons. Under Edward VI (reigned 1547–53), he composed music for the Anglican service and motets to English texts. During the reign of Catholic Queen Mary, he wrote a number of Latin hymns, and his large seven-voice Mass *Puer nobis* probably dates to her reign. Under Queen Elizabeth, Tallis set music to both Latin and English words. His late works include two sets of *Lamentations*, among the most eloquent settings of these verses from the Hebrew Scriptures. One remarkable feature of all his compositions (and of much sixteenth-century English music) is the obvious vocal quality of the melodies. They strike the listener not as an interplay of abstract musical lines but as a profusion of human voices—so closely is the melodic curve wedded to the natural inflection of speech, and so imaginatively does it project the content of the words.

The Counter-Reformation

Council of Trent

In the wake of the Protestant Reformation and the capture and sack of Rome (1527), advocates of internal reform came to power in the Catholic Church. Their main tool of change was the Council of Trent, which met intermittently in Trent (a city in northern Italy) between 1545 and 1563 to find ways to purge the church of abuses and laxities. Church music took up only a small part of the Council's time, but it was the subject of serious complaints. Some contended that the Mass was profaned when its music was based on secular cantus firmi or chansons. Others argued that complicated polyphony made it impossible to understand the words, even if they were pronounced correctly—and often they were not. Musicians were accused of using instruments inappropriately, of being careless in their duties, and of having an irreverent

More about Anglican Church Music

The Church in England formally separated from the Roman Catholic communion in 1534 under Henry VIII. English gradually replaced Latin in the church service, and in 1549 the Act of Uniformity made the English Book of Common Prayer the only prayerbook permitted for public use. A brief return of Roman Catholicism occurred under Queen Mary (reigned 1553–58), but Elizabeth I restored the English rites, and during her reign (1558–1603) the Church of England was established essentially in its present-day form.

The subsequent changes in language and liturgy finally gave rise to a new body of English church music. Thomas Tallis, whose major efforts went into Latin church composition, also contributed some English works. William Byrd (see page 167), a Roman Catholic composer of Latin motets and Masses, also wrote five Services and about sixty anthems (motetlike compositions on English texts) for Anglican use. Orlando Gibbons (1583–1625), often called the father of Anglican church music, composed works that are thoroughly English in spirit, even though their technique derives from the Latin tradition. Thomas Weelkes and Thomas Tomkins (1572–1656) also produced English church music of lasting quality.

Leading composers

The principal forms of Anglican music are the *Service* and the *anthem*. A complete Service consists of the music for fixed portions of Morning and Evening Prayer (corresponding to the Catholic Matins and Vespers) and for Holy Communion (which corresponds to the Roman Mass). Music for a *Great Service* is contrapuntal and melismatic, for a *Short Service*, chordal and syllabic—but there is no difference in content between the two. One of the finest examples of Anglican church music remains the *Great Service* of William Byrd.

Service

The English anthem corresponds to the Latin motet. Byrd's energetic *Sing joyfully unto God* (NAWM 52) illustrates one type (full anthem), written in contrapuntal style for unaccompanied chorus throughout. Another type of anthem (verse anthem) employed one or more solo voices with organ or viol accompaniment and had brief alternating passages for chorus. This type, which developed from the consort song, was highly popular in England during the seventeenth century.

Anthem

attitude. Despite these charges, the Council of Trent's final pronouncement on church music was extremely general. Neither polyphony nor the imitation of secular models was specifically forbidden. The Council merely stated that everything "impure or lascivious" must be avoided so that "the House of God may rightly be called a house of prayer" (see vignette, page 160). It directed

Council of Trent, Canon on Music to Be Used in the Mass:

66 All things should indeed be so ordered that the Masses, whether they be celebrated with or without singing, may reach tranquilly into the ears and hearts of those who hear them, when everything is executed clearly and at the right speed. In the case of those Masses which are celebrated with singing and with organ, let nothing profane be intermingled, but only hymns and divine praises. The whole plan of singing in musical modes should be constituted not to give empty pleasure to the ear, but in such a way that the words be clearly understood by all, and thus the hearts of the listeners be drawn to desire of heavenly harmonies, in the contemplation of the joys of the blessed. . . . They shall also banish from church all music that contains, whether in the singing or in the organ playing, things that are lascivious or impure. 99

From A. Theiner, *Acta . . . Concilii tridentini . . .*, 2 (1874):122, trans. in Gustave Reese, *Music in the Renaissance*, p. 449.

the local bishops to implement reform and appointed a special commission of cardinals to oversee its enforcement in Rome.

Palestrina

According to a legend from the late 1590s, Giovanni Pierluigi da Palestrina (1525 or 1526–1594) saved polyphony from the Council's condemnation by composing a six-voice Mass that was reverent in spirit and lucid in presenting the text. The work in question was the *Missa Papae Marcelli* (*Pope Marcellus* Mass, see page 162), published in 1567. Whatever the merits of this legend, Palestrina's name is justifiably linked to the Counter-Reformation chiefly for two, more general reasons: his almost exclusive devotion to sacred music and his lifelong association with Rome.

Career   Born in the small town of Palestrina, the "Prince of Music" (as Palestrina would later be called) served as a choirboy and received his musical education in nearby Rome. After seven years there as a church musician, he became choirmaster of the Cappella Giulia at St. Peter's in 1551. He dedicated his first book of Masses (1554) to his patron, Pope Julius III. In 1555 he served briefly as a singer in the Cappella Sistina, the pope's official chapel, but had to relinquish the honor because he was married. He spent the remaining forty years of his career in Rome as choirmaster at St. John Lateran and Santa Maria Maggiore, as teacher at a newly founded Jesuit Seminary, and once again as choirmaster of the Cappella Giulia, from 1571 until his death in 1594.

➤ Title page of the first published collection of works by Palestrina. (Rome: Valerio and Luigi Dorico, 1554). The composer is shown presenting the music to Pope Julius III. (*Staatsbibliothek zu Berlin, Preussischer Kulturbesitz, Musikabteilung*)

IOANNIS PETRI
Loysij Praeneſtini in baſilica
S. Petri de vrbe capellae
Magiſtri.

MISSARVM LIBER PRIMVS.

Editing of chant books

During the latter part of his life, Palestrina supervised the revision of the official chant books to accord with the changes ordered by the Council of Trent. His task was to purge the chants of "barbarisms, obscurities, contrarieties, and superfluities" acquired, according to Pope Gregory XIII, "as a result of the clumsiness or negligence or even wickedness of the composers, scribes, and printers."[1] This work, not completed during Palestrina's lifetime, was continued by others and remained valid until the definitive Vatican Edition appeared in 1908.

By far the greatest part of Palestrina's work was sacred. He wrote 104 Masses, about 250 motets, many other liturgical compositions, and some 50 spiritual madrigals with Italian texts. His (approximately 100) secular madrigals are technically polished but conservative; even so, Palestrina later confessed that he "blushed and grieved" to have written music for love poems.

Style

Palestrina's style was the first in the history of Western music to have been consciously preserved, isolated, and imitated as a model in later ages. Few composers before Bach are as well known today, and perhaps no other

1. "Brief on the Reform of the Chant," *Source Readings in Music History: The Renaissance* (New York: Norton, 1997), pp. 96–97.

composer's technique has received closer scrutiny. Better than any of his contemporaries, he captured the essence of the sober, conservative, yet elegantly expressive style of the Counter-Reformation. Not long after he died it was common to speak of the "stile da Palestrina," the Palestrina style, as the standard for polyphonic church music.

Masses

Palestrina studied the works of the Franco-Flemish composers and completely mastered their craft. Half of his Masses incorporate polyphonic models, many of them by leading contrapuntists of previous generations. Palestrina used the old-fashioned cantus firmus method for a few of his Masses (including the first of two he wrote on the traditional *L'homme armé* melody), but generally he preferred to paraphrase the chant in all the parts rather than confine it to the tenor voice. Palestrina composed other works reminiscent of the older Flemish tradition, such as the early *Missa ad fugam*, written throughout in double canon, and the Mass *Repleatur os meum* of 1570, which systematically introduces canons at every interval from the octave down to the unison, ending with a double canon in the last Agnus Dei. Canons also occur in Palestrina's later Masses, though seldom carried through so rigorously as in these two. While other composers were writing for five or more voices he continued to produce works for four voices, another indication of his conservative bent.

An almost plainsong-like quality pervades Palestrina's individual voice parts—their curve often describes an arch, and the motion is mostly stepwise, with short, infrequent leaps. In the first Agnus Dei from the famous *Pope Marcellus* Mass (Example 8.3 and NAWM 49b), for example, we observe long, gracefully shaped phrases, easily singable and staying for the most part within the range of a ninth. The few leaps greater than a third are immediately filled

EXAMPLE 8.3   Giovanni Pierluigi da Palestrina, *Pope Marcellus* Mass: Agnus Dei I

in by notes that reverse the direction of the skip and smooth the contour. There are few repeated notes, and the rhythmic units vary in length without ever creating extreme contrasts of motion. This melodic and rhythmic suavity is matched by fidelity to the diatonic modes. Palestrina studiously avoided chromaticism, admitting only those alterations demanded by the conventions of musica ficta (see page 77).

This same Agnus Dei also illustrates how Palestrina unifies a composition by purely musical means. Externally, the movement resembles a typical Franco-Flemish motet. Each phrase of the text has its own musical motive, and the contrapuntal development of each motive overlaps at a cadence with that of the next. But there is more connection between motives than mere succession; Palestrina also achieved organic unity through systematic repetition and cadences, pausing only on those scale degrees that define the mode.

Form

*P*alestrina's counterpoint conforms in most details with the teachings of Willaert's school as transmitted by Zarlino in *Le istitutioni harmoniche*. The music is written almost entirely in the alla breve measure of ₵, which in the original editions (as in Example 8.4) consists of a downbeat and upbeat of one semibreve each (two half-notes in the transcription of Example 8.3). The independent lines are expected to meet in a full triad on each beat. This convention is broken for suspensions—a contrapuntal device in which a voice, consonant with the other parts on the upbeat, is held through the downbeat while one or more of the other parts makes a dissonance against it; then the suspended voice resolves into a consonance by moving downward by step. This alternation of tension and relaxation—strong dissonance on the downbeat and sweet consonance on the upbeat—more than the recurrence of accented syllables, endows the music with a pendulum-like pulse. Dissonances between beats may occur if the voice that is moving does so in stepwise fashion. Palestrina's only exception to this rule is his use of the *cambiata*, as it was later called, in which a voice leaps a third down from a dissonance to a consonance instead of approaching it by step. (The term *cambiata* means "exchanged"—that is, a dissonance is exchanged for a consonance.)

The alternation of consonance and dissonance is clearly evident in Example 8.4, which gives the lowest four voices of Example 8.3, measures 10–15, in their original values. P stands for passing note, S for suspension, and C for cambiata; numbers indicate the dissonant intervals and their resolutions, and arrows mark the down- and upbeats.

EXAMPLE 8.4 Contrapuntal Analysis of Example 8.3, measures 10–15, Tenors I, II, Basses I, II

The smooth diatonic lines and the discreet handling of dissonance give Palestrina's music a consistent serenity and transparency. Another positive quality of his counterpoint lies in the vertical combination of voices. Because the voice groupings and spacings are so varied, the same harmony produces a large number of subtly different shadings and sonorities.

Palestrina composed the *Pope Marcellus* Mass in 1562–63, precisely when the Council of Trent was urging in the *Canon on Music to Be Used in the Mass* that "the words be clearly understood by all" (see vignette, page 160). His attention to text setting is particularly evident in the Credo (NAWM 49a), where the voices often pronounce a given phrase simultaneously rather than in the staggered manner of imitative polyphony. To achieve variety, Palestrina divided the six-voice choir into various smaller groups, each with its particular sonorous color, and reserved the full six voices for climactic or particularly significant words, such as "Et incarnatus est" (and He was made flesh).

Text comprehension

Palestrina's contemporaries

After Palestrina, the most illustrious composers of sacred music at the end of the sixteenth century were the Spanish priest Tomás Luis de Victoria (1548–1611); the cosmopolitan Orlando di Lasso (1532–1594; see also pages 130 and 139); and the Englishman William Byrd (1543–1623), who remained a lifelong Catholic even though he worked for the Anglican Church and monarchy. Their compositions—all products of the international musical language of the late Renaissance—share many characteristics of Palestrina's polished style; yet, each composer is different enough to warrant separate attention here.

A close connection existed between Spanish and Roman composers throughout the sixteenth century. In 1565 Victoria enrolled in the Jesuit Collegio Germanico in Rome and may have studied with Palestrina. Victoria followed him as teacher at the Seminary in 1571 and was later appointed choir director there. Returning to Spain about 1587, he became chaplain to the Empress Maria, for whose funeral services he wrote a famous Requiem Mass in 1603. In the spirit of the Counter-Reformation, he composed sacred music exclusively. Though his style resembles Palestrina's, Victoria infused his music with greater expressive intensity, and he utilized more notes outside the diatonic modes. For example, in his Mass *O magnum mysterium* (O great mystery, NAWM 50), which is in transposed first mode, the sixth degree is often lowered and the seventh raised, as in the later minor mode.

Victoria

Like most of Victoria's Masses, this one is based on his own motet, *O magnum mysterium* (Example 8.5 and NAWM 50a), in which the opening motive, with its stark falling and rising fifth imitated downward throughout the entire musical space, conveys the magnitude, wonder, and mystery of Christ's birth. Although this is a far more dramatic gesture than any Palestrina would have used, Victoria achieved the same melodic and rhythmic smoothness and suave triadic harmonies as his Roman contemporary.

Orlando di Lasso was the last in the long line of sixteenth-century Franco-Flemish composers, and perhaps the most international in terms of his career and his compositions. Unlike Palestrina and Victoria, he wrote many secular works. By the age of twenty-four Lasso had already published books of madrigals, chansons, and motets, and his total production eventually amounted

Lasso

EXAMPLE 8.5   Tomás Luis de Victoria, Motet: *O magnum mysterium*

to over two thousand works. Yet he ranks with Palestrina among the great composers of sacred music in the late sixteenth century. If Palestrina was above all a master of the Mass, Lasso's chief glory resided in his motets. In these works he let both the overall form and the musical details determine a rhetorical, pictorial, and dramatic interpretation of the text. (See Plate VI, facing page 179.)

Lasso's *Tristis est anima mea* (1598; My soul is sad, NAWM 51), one of his most deeply moving and vivid settings, illustrates this approach. The text, a Respond for Maundy Thursday, is based on the words of Jesus before he was crucified as reported by Matthew (26:38) and Mark (14:34). The motet's opening (Example 8.6) is a masterful sound-image of sadness, illustrated by

EXAMPLE 8.6 Orlando di Lasso, Motet: *Tristis est anima mea*

a descending-semitone motive, sung to the word "Tristis," which dominates the first nine measures along with carefully drawn-out suspensions. This use of the suspension to achieve emotional tension rather than to prepare a cadence was common in the madrigal but still rare in sacred music. Later in the motet Lasso wrote a lively contrapuntal section to represent the watchful vigilance Jesus demanded of his disciples. Lasso also depicted the flight of the eleven disciples (as Jesus is attacked by the twelfth disciple, Judas, and the mob) in eleven entrances of a running subject that follow one another in rapid succession. The words of the text stimulated not only the rhythms, accents, and contours of the motives, but the music's every gesture: harmonic effects, textures, constructive devices such as suspensions and fugal imitation, and the weight and placement of cadences.

Under the influence of the Counter-Reformation, Lasso devoted the latter years of his life to setting sacred texts, particularly spiritual madrigals, renouncing the merry and festive songs of his youth. We cannot properly speak of a "Lasso style"; he was too versatile for that. Franco-Flemish counterpoint, Italian harmony, Venetian opulence, French vivacity, German severity—all abound in his work. More fully than any other sixteenth-century composer, he synthesized the achievements of an epoch.

William Byrd, the last of the great Catholic church composers of the sixteenth century, studied music probably under Thomas Tallis and was ap-

Byrd

pointed organist of Lincoln Cathedral in 1563. About ten years later he moved to London to take up duties as a member of the royal chapel, a post he held for the rest of his life even while maintaining his allegiance to Rome. In 1575 he and Tallis were granted a monopoly for music printing in England, which he continued to control after Tallis's death in 1585.

Byrd's works include English polyphonic songs, keyboard pieces (see Chapter 7, page 147), and music for the Anglican Church. Undoubtedly his best vocal compositions remain his Latin Masses and motets. Given the religious situation in England at the time, Byrd understandably wrote only three Masses (one each for three, four, and five voices); yet these are considered the finest Masses by any English composer.

Byrd probably intended his earlier Latin motets for private devotional gatherings, but he designed the later ones, published in two collections (*Gradualia* 1605, 1607), for liturgical use. In the dedication of the first collection he praised the power of scriptural texts to inspire a composer's imagination:

> I have found there is such a power hidden away and stored up in those words [of Scripture] that—I know not how—to one who meditates on divine things, pondering them with detailed concentration, all the most fitting melodies come as it were of themselves, and freely present themselves when the mind is alert and eager.

This passage also serves as an eloquent reminder that many Renaissance composers relied on the text as their starting point for musical invention.

POSTLUDE

Renaissance, Reformation, Counter-Reformation—these terms have been used to suggest different aspects of sixteenth-century musical styles and practices; yet their meanings overlap and more than one term may be applicable to the same composer. Certainly their qualities outlived the chronological boundary of the year 1600, which is the convenient but artificial limit usually assigned at least to the Renaissance period. Although our discussion of Renaissance music officially ends with this chapter, the musical characteristics connoted by the word Renaissance persisted well into the next century, when Palestrina's style continued to be revered by some as the "absolute perfection" of church music. In retrospect, Palestrina's style became known as the *stile antico*, the old style, shared by Victoria, Lasso, Byrd, and earlier Renaissance composers, such as Josquin, Willaert, and Rore.

The new musical practices of the Reformation—especially those involving the chorale—had far-reaching consequences for music history: they resulted ultimately in, among other things, Bach's glorious church cantatas and in his superb harmonizations of the chorales, which still serve as a bible for students of harmony. Finally, the goal of the Counter-Reformation—which had idealized sacred polyphony as a vehicle for drawing "the hearts of the listeners . . . to desire of heavenly harmonies" (see vignette, page 160)—was to reconquer the minds and souls of the faithful, bringing them back into the papal fold. This Counter-Reformation attitude, intent on manipulating the senses and the emotions, influenced the new, Baroque musical aesthetic that we will explore now.

Music of the Early
Baroque Period

In music history, we apply the term *baroque* to describe the period between 1600 and 1750. While the word is sometimes used in its original, rather negative sense—deformed, abnormal, bizarre, exaggerated, grotesque—art critics of the nineteenth century gave it a more positive spin. For them, *baroque* summed up the delightfully flamboyant, decorative, and expressionistic tendencies of seventeenth-century painting and architecture (see Plate VII, facing page 226, and window, pages 196–97). Music historians followed suit and adopted the word to describe the music of an entire era, although we now recognize that a single term cannot adequately embrace the many different styles in use during these years.

As with other epochs, boundary dates for the Baroque era are only approximations. Many **General Characteristics of Baroque Music** appeared before 1600 and many were declining by the 1730s. But within the chronological limits of 1600 to 1750, composers accepted a set of conventions for organizing music and adopted certain ideas about how music should sound. Most important, they believed that music, by acting on emotions, should move the listener.

In the political sphere, wealthy absolute governments ruled Europe between 1600 and 1750—the time of American colonization—and their patronage helped cultivate new genres of music. Many of the European courts were important centers of musical culture. The most imposing of these, the court of Louis XIV of France, who reigned from 1643 to 1715, served as the model for all lesser establishments. Other patrons of music included popes, emperors, kings of England and of Spain, and rulers of smaller Italian and German entities. City-states, such as Venice and many of the north German towns, also maintained musical organizations, both ecclesiastical and secular. The church, of course, continued to support music, though its role diminished during the Baroque era. Aristocratic, civic, and ecclesiastical patronage shared the scene with "academies," private clubs that sponsored musical activities in many cities, but concerts open to the public were still rare.

Italian trends dominated musical fashions during the Baroque era, and by 1750 the international language of European music had acquired a distinct Italian accent. Despite its political fragmentation, Italy remained the most influential region of Europe in musical matters. Several Italian cities loomed disproportionately larger on the musical map than their real size or political power suggested. Florence, for example, hosted a brilliant period of musico-theatrical innovation at the dawn of the seventeenth century that led to the flowering of **Early Opera**. Rome continued to influence sacred music and for a time became an important center of opera, several types of **Vocal Chamber Music**, and instrumental music. Venice, a leading musical city throughout the seventeenth century, nurtured the development of opera, as did Naples in the eighteenth century. **The Venetian School** of composers centered at St. Mark's Church wielded a mighty influence on Baroque choral music. Meanwhile, Bologna and other northern cities witnessed notable developments in instrumental music.

The religious break that had separated northern Protestant Europe from the Catholic south in the sixteenth century continued to reverberate in seventeenth-century music. Several new **Genres of Sacred Music**—such as the sacred vocal concerto and the oratorio—developed, and throughout Europe **Instrumental Music** flourished in both religious and secular circles, expanding on genres that had their beginnings in the sixteenth century. But for the first time in music history, solo and instrumental chamber music achieved a parity with vocal music, both in quantity and quality.

The arts and sciences also flourished in the Baroque era. To realize the magnificence of this age in the history of Western civilization, we need only recall the names of a few great writers and artists of the seventeenth century: in England, Donne and Milton; in Spain, Cervantes; in France, Corneille, Racine, and Molière. The Netherlands, its musical golden age past, produced the painters Rubens and Rembrandt. Spain, somewhat isolated and of secondary importance in music, could boast the painters Velasquez and Murillo. Italy contributed the sculptor Bernini (see Plate VII, facing page 226, and window, pages 196–97) and the architect Borromini. In the seventeenth century, one of the great ages in the history of philosophy and science, Bacon, Descartes, Leibniz, Galileo, Kepler, and Newton established the foundations of modern science, mathematics, and rational thought.

The changes occurring in intellectual and artistic realms profoundly influenced the course of music history. While seventeenth-century thinkers left behind outmoded ways of viewing the world and proposed new explanations, musicians expanded their vocabulary to meet new expressive needs. As philosophers developed new ideas within the frame of older methods, so composers—such as Claudio Monteverdi in his madrigals and Giovanni Gabrieli in his motets—poured more intense and more varied emotions into the musical genres they inherited from the Renaissance. Much early-seventeenth-century music was truly experimental; but by the middle of the century, the new resources of harmony, color, and form had created a common language with a clear vocabulary, grammar, and syntax.

General Characteristics of Baroque Music

Two practices

In 1605, Monteverdi distinguished between a *prima pratica* and a *seconda pratica*, or a first and second "practice." By the first, he meant the style of vocal polyphony codified by Zarlino. By the second, Monteverdi meant the adventurous style of the modern Italians such as Rore, Marenzio, and himself. In the first practice, according to Monteverdi, the musical values prevailed over the words, while in the second practice the text dominated and dictated its musical setting. The seconda pratica, sometimes called the modern style, not only used dissonances more freely but also broke many of the old rules of counterpoint in order to express the words more effectively.

Idiomatic writing

Polyphony tended to homogenize instrumental and vocal writing, to the point where almost any combination of voices and instruments was interchangeable. But even the earliest music for solo lute, organ, or harpsichord maintained a quality peculiar, or idiomatic, to the instrument. In addition, the prominent role of the soloist—whether singer, violinist, or wind player—enticed composers to adapt their writing to a particular medium, such as the violin or the solo voice. Technical improvements in wind instruments made them suitable for exposed solo performance. Famous teachers and practitioners of the art of singing promoted new standards of virtuosity, color, and vocal projection. Instrumental and vocal styles began to diverge, and once they achieved their distinct idioms composers could mimic these styles, writing a violin melody that sighed like a voice, or a vocal melody that blared like a trumpet.

The affections

Vocal and instrumental compositions were united in a common goal: to express or represent a wide range of feelings vividly and vigorously, continuing the efforts begun in the late-sixteenth-century madrigal. Composers sought musical means to express or arouse the *affections*—then considered states of the soul—such as rage, excitement, grandeur, heroism, sorrow, wonder, or joy. Composers were not trying to express their personal feelings;

rather, they wanted to represent, in a generic sense, the range of human emotions. In Baroque architecture, sculpture, and painting, the normal forms of objects were sometimes distorted, so that the images would embody the passionate intensity of the artist's vision. Similarly in music, composers breached the limits of the old order of consonance and dissonance, of regular and even rhythmic flow, exploiting instead harmonic and rhythmic extremes, and contrasts of color and texture, all for the purpose of arousing or moving the affections.

> **Rhythm**

In contrast to the steady rhythmic flow of Renaissance polyphony, music during the Baroque period was either very regular or very free. Regular dance rhythms had characterized a lot of earlier instrumental music, but not until the seventeenth century was most music (as opposed to just dance music) written in measures separated by bar lines, implying regular patterns of strong and weak beats. (Compare the facsimiles reproduced on page 107 and below.) Baroque composers used regular, patterned rhythm to arouse a particular affection, and irregular, flexible rhythm when writing speechlike recitative and improvisatory solo instrumental pieces, such as toccatas and preludes. The two types of rhythm could not, of course, occur simultaneously, but in succession they provided deliberate contrast, as we will discover in the customary pairing of recitative with aria and of toccata or prelude with fugue.

▼ Giulio Caccini's madrigal *Perfidissimo volto,* as printed in *Le nuove musiche* (Florence: Marescotti, 1601/2). The bass is figured with the exact intervals to be sounded in the chords above it, such as the dissonant eleventh resolving to the tenth in the third measure.

Basso continuo

The typical texture of Renaissance music was a polyphony of independent voices; the typical texture of the Baroque period was a firm bass and a florid treble, held together by unobtrusive harmony. A single melody line supported by accompanying parts was not in itself new—something like it had been used in the performance of sixteenth-century songs and madrigals, for example. (See window, Chapter 7.) New was the emphasis on the bass and the highlighting of the treble—the two essential lines of the texture. This polarity between top and bottom resulted in a seeming indifference to the inner parts, evident in the system of notation called *thorough bass* or *basso continuo*. In this system, the composer wrote only the melody and the bass, leaving the players to fill in the rest. Moreover, the notation appeared in score format rather than in parts, which gave music an entirely new look on the page, as we have seen in the illustration on page 173. The bass was played on one or more *continuo* instruments—for example, harpsichord, organ, or lute—usually reinforced by a sustaining instrument such as a bass viola da gamba, violoncello, or bassoon. Above the bass notes, the keyboard or lute player filled in the required chords, which were not written out. If these chords were other than common triads in root position, or if the music required chord tones (such as suspensions) or accidentals beyond those in the key signature, the composer added interval numbers (*figures*) or accidental signs above or below the bass notes to guide the performer.

The *realization*—the actual playing—of such a *figured bass* varied according to the type of piece and the skill and taste of the player, who had a good deal of room to improvise within the given framework. The performer might play only simple chords, introduce passing tones, or incorporate melodic motives that imitated the treble or bass parts. Realizing the basso continuo was not always essential: many pieces with a continuo already provided the full harmony in the notated melodic parts. In motets and madrigals for four or five voices, for example, the continuo instrument merely doubled or supported the voices. But for solos and duets, the continuo was usually necessary to complete the harmonies as well as to produce a fuller sonority. This filling was sometimes called *ripieno*, a term used in Italian cooking to mean "stuffing." (A modern edition of a composition with a figured bass usually indicates in smaller notes the editor's realization: see facsimile, page 173, and its realization, NAWM 54.)

*The new
counterpoint*

The development of basso continuo texture—a firm bass supporting a florid treble—did not lead to the rejection of sixteenth-century counterpoint. Composers continued to write unaccompanied motets and madrigals (though they sometimes conformed with current practice by adding a basso continuo). And in vocal and instrumental ensemble pieces accompanied by continuo, counterpoint remained the basis of composition. This was a new kind of counterpoint, however, because the different melodic lines now had to fit into the pattern of chords set up by the continuo. Such harmonically governed counterpoint, in which individual lines were subordinated to a succession of chords, held sway through the remainder of the Baroque era.

With the chordal structure articulated so clearly, dissonance was recognized less as an interval between two voices than as an individual tone that did not fit into a chord. As a result, dissonances other than stepwise passing tones were tolerated more easily. Many of these dissonances remained ornamental and experimental, but by the middle of the century various conventions governing when and how to introduce and resolve these dissonances had arisen. Eventually, the role of dissonance in defining the tonal direction of a piece became evident—particularly in instrumental music of Arcangelo Corelli (1653–1713) and others (see Chapter 11) where chains of dissonant suspensions led inexorably to a cadence establishing the keynote or tonic.

Dissonance

Chromaticism followed a similar development, from experimental forays on the one hand, to freedom within an orderly scheme on the other. Gesualdo's chromatic harmonies in the early 1600s included expressionistic digressions within a loose structure that respected the confines of a mode. Throughout the seventeenth century composers used chromaticism in improvisatory instrumental pieces, such as the toccatas of Frescobaldi and

Chromaticism

C H R O N O L O G Y

1590	*Giovanni Bardi's Camerata (ca. 1573–90)		*Francesca Caccini (1587–ca. 1640), *La liberazione di Ruggiero dall'isola d'Alcina* in Florence (1625)
	Death of Palestrina and Lasso (1594)		
	*Peri-Corsi-Rinuccini, *Dafne* (1597)		*Schütz, *Symphoniae sacrae I* printed in Venice (1629)
1600	*Emilio de' Cavalieri (ca. 1550–1602), *La rappresentazione di Anima et di Corpo* in Rome		*Biagio Marini (ca. 1587–1663), *Sonate . . .*, Op. 8 (1629)
	*Peri-Caccini-Rinuccini, *Euridice* in Florence for wedding of Henry IV of France and Maria de' Medici (1600)	**1630**	
	*Giulio Caccini (1551–1618), *Le nuove musiche* (1602)		Galileo Galilei (1564–1642), *Dialogue on the Two Chief Systems of the World* (1632)
	William Shakespeare (1564–1616), *Othello* (1604)		*Frescobaldi (1583–1643), *Fiori musicali* (1635)
	Monteverdi publishes fifth book of madrigals; Francis Bacon (1561–1626), *On the Advancement of Learning* (1605)		Founding of Harvard College (1636)
			René Descartes (1596–1650), *Discourse on Method* (1637)
	*Monteverdi, *Orfeo* in Mantua (1607)	**1640**	*The Bay Psalm Book*, first book printed in North America
	Johannes Kepler (1571–1630), *Astronomia nova* (1609)		*Monteverdi, *L'incoronazione di Poppea* in Venice (1642)
1610			*Giovanni Lorenzo Bernini (1598–1680), *The Ecstasy of St. Teresa*, Sta. Maria della Vittoria, Rome (1644; see Plate VII, facing page 226, and window, pages 196–97)
	Monteverdi appointed director of music, St. Mark's, Venice (1613)		
	*Giovanni Gabrieli (ca. 1553–1612), *Symphoniae sacrae II* (1615)		*Luigi Rossi (1597–1653), *Orfeo* in Paris (1647)
	Thirty Years' War in Germany begins (1618)		Treaty of Westphalia: end of the Thirty Years' War (1648)
	*Heinrich Schütz (1585–1672), *Psalmen Davids* printed in Dresden (1619)	**1650**	*Carissimi (1605–1674), *Jephte* in Rome (ca. 1650)
1620	Pilgrims arrive in Massachusetts; Mayflower Compact		

Froberger, and in vocal works to express the most intense passions of a text. But later in the century composers also submitted chromaticism, as they did dissonance, to the control of tonal harmony.

Major-minor tonalities

Tonal harmony operated within the system of major-minor tonalities familiar to us from eighteenth- and nineteenth-century music. All the harmonies of a given composition were organized around a triad on the tonic supported primarily by triads on its dominant and subdominant, and chords leading to these. Temporary modulations to different keys did not diminish the supremacy of the principal key.

Like the medieval modal system, the major-minor system evolved gradually through musical practice. The habitual, long-standing use of certain techniques eventually bred a consistent theory. Just as the repeated use in the early Middle Ages of certain melodic formulas led to the theory of the modes, so the constant use in the seventeenth century of particular harmonic and melodic successions led to the theory of major-minor tonality. The figured basso continuo was important in this theoretical development because its notation drew attention to the succession of chords. Indeed, figured bass became the road over which music traveled from counterpoint to homophony, from a linear-melodic to a chordal-harmonic structure.

Early Opera

Forerunners

Opera, an invention of the early Baroque, is a drama that combines soliloquy, dialogue, scenery, action, and continuous (or nearly continuous) music. Although the earliest works in this genre date from the very end of the sixteenth century, the association of music with drama goes back to ancient times. Choruses and some lyric speeches in plays by Euripides and Sophocles were sung; medieval liturgical dramas were sung; and music figured incidentally in the religious mystery and miracle plays of the late Middle Ages. Renaissance theater, where many tragedies and comedies imitated or were inspired by Greek examples, included sung choruses, especially at the beginning or end of an act. Moreover, between acts of a comedy or tragedy, musical interludes known as *intermedi* or *intermezzi* occupied the stage. On important state occasions, such as princely weddings, these intermedi became spectacular and elaborate musical productions, with choruses, soloists, and large instrumental ensembles.

Greek tragedy as a model

Greek tragedy served as a distant model for the Renaissance theater, although scholars disagreed on how centrally music figured in the Greek drama. One view held that only the choruses were sung. Another, that the entire text, including the actors' parts, was sung—an opinion authoritatively expressed by Girolamo Mei (1519–1594), a learned Florentine scholar who had edited a number of Greek tragedies.

Mei kept up a lively correspondence with many colleagues, including Giovanni Bardi and Vincenzo Galilei (d. 1591). From the early 1570s, Count Bardi hosted an informal academy at his palace in Florence, where scholars and artists discussed literature, science, and the arts, and musicians performed new music. Bardi's protégé, the singer-composer Giulio Caccini (1551–1618), later referred to this gathering as the "Camerata" (circle or coterie) of Bardi. Around 1577, Mei's letters about Greek music often appeared on the agenda. Mei concluded that the ancient Greeks had obtained powerful effects with their music because it consisted of a single melody, whether sung by a soloist with or without accompaniment, or by a chorus. By conveying the message of the text through the natural expressiveness of vocal registers, the rises and falls in pitch, and the changing rhythms and tempo, this single melody succeeded in moving the listener.

> *Florentine Camerata*

In his *Dialogo della musica antica et della moderna* (Dialogue Concerning Ancient and Modern Music, 1581), Vincenzo Galilei, father of the famous astronomer and physicist Galileo, used Mei's doctrines to attack the theory and practice of vocal counterpoint as exemplified in the Italian madrigal: he proposed to revive the ancient style of *monody* (*monodia*—from the Greek *monos*, alone, and *aidein*, to sing). His argument, in brief, held that only a single line of melody, with appropriate pitches and rhythms derived from the inflection and meaning of the text, could truly express the poetry. When several voices simultaneously sang different melodies and words, in different rhythms and registers, as in the sixteenth-century madrigal, music could never deliver the emotional message of the text. If some voices were low and others high, some rising and others descending, some moving in slow notes and others in fast, then the resulting web of contradictory impressions confused the listener and served only to show off the cleverness of the composer and the ability of the performers.

> *V. Galilei*

> *Monody*

It was through such theories that the poet Ottavio Rinuccini (1562–1621) and the composer Jacopo Peri (1561–1633) became convinced that the ancient tragedies were sung in their entirety. They first experimented with Rinuccini's poem *Dafne* but only fragments of the work, produced in Florence in 1597, survive. Jacopo Peri and Giulio Caccini each set to music a second, more ambitious poem by Rinuccini in 1600—*Euridice*—and both scores were published.

> *Earliest operas*

Peri and Caccini had similar approaches to theatrical music. Both were singers by profession, and Caccini became a famous singing teacher. They both aimed for a type of song halfway between spoken recitation and singing. Caccini wrote in a more lyrical style based on the madrigal and on the old improvised air for singing poetry. Peri also used the air for singing in his prologue to *Euridice* (NAWM 55a). But for dialogue he invented a new idiom, which was soon known as *stile recitativo* or recitative style (see page 179). This should not be confused with monody, a term that embraces all the styles of solo singing practiced in the early years of the seventeenth century, including arias, and madrigals and airs for solo voice and basso continuo, as well as operatic recitative.

Solo singing was certainly not new: performers often improvised on melodic formulas (airs) to recite epic and other strophic poems. Many songs were composed for solo voice and lute, and it was common in the sixteenth century to sing one part of a polyphonic madrigal while instruments played the other parts, a practice often followed in the intermedio (for example, NAWM 53; see also window in Chapter 7, page 127). Moreover, many late-sixteenth-century madrigals seem to have been written for a soprano solo with chordal accompaniment.

Caccini

Caccini developed a tuneful style of solo songwriting that did not distort the text. He aimed at clear and flexible declamation of the words, with melodic embellishments at appropriate places. Singers of the sixteenth century had commonly improvised ornaments—scalar figures, turns, runs, passing notes, and the like—when performing polyphonic music, but usually without regard to the character of the text. By contrast, Caccini chose and placed his ornaments carefully, to enhance the message of the text.

Caccini wrote two types of solo song—airs, which were strophic, and madrigals, which were through-composed—some dating from the 1590s; many were published in his 1602 collection *Le nuove musiche* (The New Mu-

➤ A sketch of Jacopo Peri, costumed as the legendary singer Arion, a role he played in the Florentine intermedi of 1589. Arion, returning from concerts in Corinth, sings an echo-aria just before he plunges into the sea to escape his mutinous crew. The music was by Jacopo Peri and Christofano Malvezzi, the costume by Bernardo Buontalenti.

V. *The Lute Player,* one of several paintings on musical subjects by Michelangelo Merisi da Caravaggio (1571—1610). The performer is simultaneously playing and singing an Italian madrigal from the early sixteenth century, rendering it as a solo song with lute accompaniment. Solo singing became newly fashionable toward the end of the Renaissance, when Caravaggio was working in Rome for a patron who was equally important in artistic and musical circles (see window, page 127)   (*PRIVATE COLLECTION. PHOTOGRAPH COURTESY THE METROPOLITAN MUSEUM OF ART, NY*)

VI. Orlando di Lasso at the virginal leading his chamber ensemble in St. George's Hall at the court of Duke Albrecht V in Munich. Shown are three choirboys, about twenty singers, and fifteen instrumentalists. Miniature by Hans Mielich (1516–1573) in a manuscript of Lasso's Penitential Psalms.   (*MUNICH, BAYERISCHE STAATSBIBLIOTHEK*)

sic). Caccini boasted in his foreword that around 1590, Bardi's Camerata greeted his solo madrigal *Perfidissimo volto* (NAWM 54 and facsimile, page 173) "with affectionate applause." At a number of the cadences, Caccini wrote out the ornaments that singers would normally have added in performance, because he did not trust them to invent appropriate ones on their own. Other refinements and embellishments that Caccini considered essential were crescendos and decrescendos, trills (called *gruppi*), rapid repetitions of the same pitch (called *trilli*), "exclamations"—a sforzando at the point of releasing a tone—and departures from strict observance of the printed note values, or what we call *tempo rubato*.

While Caccini built his solo vocal idiom on the improvised, formulaic air (see page 178) and the traditional madrigal, Peri searched for a new, more radical solution to suit the needs of the stage. In his preface to *Euridice* (see vignette, page 180), Peri recalled the distinction made in ancient theory between the continuous or sliding changes of pitch in speech and the intervallic, or "diastematic," motion in song. He wanted to find a type of speech-song that was halfway between them, similar to the style scholars imagined Greeks used for reciting heroic poems. By sustaining the notes of the basso continuo while the voice passed through both consonances and dissonances—thereby imitating the sliding-pitch motion of speech—he liberated the voice from the harmony so that it approached the freedom and flexibility of declamation. For syllables that were emphasized in ordinary speech—in his words "intoned"—he formed consonances with the bass and its harmony, thereby reinforcing the importance of these accented syllables.

Peri and recitative style

In 1600, Peri set to music the pastoral-mythological verse play, *Euridice*, by Ottavio Rinuccini, which was publicly performed in Florence that year at the marriage of Henry IV of France and Maria de' Medici, niece of the reigning grand duke. But Caccini, who wanted to protect his status at court, would not allow his singers to perform music composed by others, so a portion of his own setting was incorporated into the production. Both Peri's and Caccini's versions were published the following year, and these two scores remain the earliest complete operas that survive.

Euridice

In *Euridice*, Peri elaborated the well-known myth of Orpheus and Eurydice, treated in the then-fashionable manner of the pastoral—that is, with the main characters surrounded by nymphs and shepherds singing and dancing in an idyllic setting—and given a happy ending to suit the joyous occasion. Of the two settings, Caccini's sounds more melodious and lyrical, resembling the madrigals and airs of his *Nuove musiche*. Peri's is more dramatic; he not only realized a style that lies between speech and song, but he varied his approach according to the dramatic situation. The speech in which Dafne (the Messenger) tells of Euridice's death (NAWM 55c) exemplifies the new recitative style. In his *Euridice*, Peri devised a musical idiom that met the demands of dramatic poetry—to represent action and emotion on stage. Al-

Peri's Description of His Recitative Style:

❝ Putting aside every other manner of singing heard up to now, I dedicated myself wholly to searching out the imitation that is owed to these poems. And I reflected that the sort of voice assigned by the ancients to song, which they called diastematic (as if to say sustained and suspended), could at times be hurried and take a moderate course between the slow sustained movements of song and the fluent and rapid ones of speech, and thus suit my purpose (just as the ancients, too, adapted the voice to reading poetry and heroic verses), approaching that other [voice] of conversation, which they called continuous and which our moderns (though perhaps for another purpose) also used in their music.

I recognized likewise that in our speech certain sounds are intoned in such a way that a harmony can be built upon them, and in the course of speaking we pass through many that are not so intoned, until we reach another that permits a movement to a new consonance. Keeping in mind those manners and accents that serve us in our grief and joy and similar states, I made the bass move in time with these, faster or slower according to the affections. I held [the bass] fixed through both dissonances and consonances until the voice of the speaker, having run through various notes, arrived at a syllable that, being intoned in ordinary speech, opened the way to a new harmony. I did this not only so that the flow of the speech would not offend the ear (almost tumbling upon the repeated notes with more frequent consonant chords), but also so that the voice would not seem to dance to the movement of the bass, particularly in sad or severe subjects, granted that other more joyful subjects would require more frequent movements. Moreover, the use of dissonances lessened or masked the advantage gained from the necessity of intoning every note, which perhaps for this purpose was less needed in ancient music. **❞**

From Peri, *Le musiche sopra l'Euridice* (Florence, 1600), trans. in Palisca, *Humanism in Italian Renaissance Musical Thought* (New Haven: Yale University Press, 1985), pp. 428–32.

though he and his associates knew they were not reviving Greek music, they claimed to have realized a speech-song that not only resembled what had been used in the ancient theater but was also compatible with modern musical practice.

Monteverdi patterned his *Orfeo* (1607), in its subject matter and its mixture of styles, on the *Euridice* operas. Rinuccini's little pastoral was expanded by the poet Alessandro Striggio into a five-act drama, and Monteverdi, already an experienced composer of madrigals and church music (see Chapter 7), drew on a rich palette of vocal and instrumental resources. His recitative achieves more continuity and a longer line through careful tonal organization, and, at significantly dramatic moments, it reaches a high level of lyricism. In addition, Monteverdi introduced many solo airs, duets, madrigalesque ensembles, and dances, which, taken together, make up a large proportion of the work and furnish a welcome contrast to the recitative. The ritornellos—recurring instrumental sections—and choruses help organize the scenes into schemes of almost ceremonial formality.

Three sections from *Orfeo* are more or less analogous to those from *Euridice* (given as NAWM 55a, b, c)—the Prologue, Orfeo's song, and the Messenger's narration of Euridice's death (NAWM 56a, b, c)—but it becomes clear immediately that the proportions are very much expanded. The ritornello to the Prologue is carefully scored, and although the Prologue itself is patterned on the air for singing poetry, Monteverdi wrote out each strophe, varying the melody while leaving the harmony intact. Orfeo's strophic canzonet, *Vi ricorda o boschi ombrosi* (Do you recall, o shady woods, NAWM 56b), is a simple dance-song; Orfeo is exulting with friends over his impending marriage. Again, the musical idiom is a traditional one: the hemiola rhythm is the same as that in many frottole written a hundred years earlier (see NAWM 36, for example), and the harmonization with root-position chords is also similar.

As in Peri's *Euridice*, the most modern style is reserved for dramatic dialogue and impassioned speeches. The Messenger's narrative, *In un fiorito prato* (In a flowery meadow, NAWM 56c), imitates the recitative style developed by Peri, but the harmonic movement and melodic contour are more broadly conceived. As in Peri's score, too, the chords specified by the basso continuo and its figures have no rhythmic profile or formal plan and are there only to support the voice's recitation, which is free to imitate the inflections and rhythms of speech. While the vocal line often returns to pitches that are consonant with the harmony, it may wander away on syllables that are not sustained in speech. Only some line endings are marked by cadences; others are elided to simulate the continuity of speech.

Orfeo's lament (see Example 9.1) attains a new height of lyricism that leaves the first monodic experiments far behind. In the passage that begins "Tu se' morta" (You are dead), each phrase of music, like each phrase of text, builds on the preceding one, intensifying through pitch and rhythm. The dissonances against the sustained chords not only enhance the illusion of speech but also underscore Orfeo's bleak prospects. The raw passage from an E-major chord to a G-minor chord (measures 3–4) emphasizes his poignant

Monteverdi's Orfeo

EXAMPLE 9.1   Claudio Monteverdi, *Orfeo: Tu se' morta*

You are dead, my life, and I still breathe? You have departed from me, never to return, and I remain? No, for if verses have any power I shall go safely to the most profound abyss . . .

question: why must he continue to live, when his bride—his "life"—is dead? The progress of the melody parallels Orfeo's changing mood—from his initial despair to his resolution to follow and rescue Euridice from the realm of death.

Despite the interest aroused by the first operas, only a few more were written and performed during the next thirty years. The Florentine court continued to prefer ballets, masques, and intermedi for glamorizing state weddings and other events. When a Polish prince visited Florence in 1625, the court staged a combination of ballet and musical scenes (see illustration below)—*La liberazione di Ruggiero dall'isola d'Alcina* (The Freeing of Ruggiero from the Island of Alcina) written by Francesca Caccini (1587–ca. 1640), daughter of Giulio. Known as "La Cecchina," Francesca Caccini had performed frequently as a solo singer as well as with her sister Settimia and her stepmother Margherita (Giulio's wife). Their trio formed a *concerto delle donne* that rivaled the one at Ferrara (see page 126). Francesca composed music for ballets as early as 1607 (*La Stiava*), and *La liberazione* climaxed her brilliant career: she became the highest-paid musician in the duke's service.

Although billed as a ballet, this work contains all the trappings of opera—an opening sinfonia, a prologue, recitatives, arias, choruses, and in-

Francesca Caccini

ISOLA D'ALCINA SECONDA MVTA DELLE SCENE

Alfonso Parigi l et f.

▲ Stage design for the second scene of *La liberazione di Ruggiero*, produced in 1625, with music by Francesca Caccini. The setting is the enchanted island of the sorceress Alcina, who holds the crusader Ruggiero captive there (based on an episode in Ariosto's *Orlando furioso*). Ruggiero proceeds in the next scene to break her spell, burn her castle down, and escape. Engraving by Alfonso Parigi.

strumental ritornellos. In addition, some of the dances may have been performed while the chorus sang.

Rome

For a variety of reasons, opera did not take root in Rome until the 1620s, even though the city was teeming with wealthy prelates who vied with each other, offering lavish entertainment to their guests. Most of the Roman operas treated mythological subjects or episodes from the epic poems of Tasso, Ariosto, and Marino, but some based their stories on the lives of saints. Roman composers also produced a number of pastoral operas; the genre of comic opera also began its independent career in that city.

Luigi Rossi's Orfeo

Let us compare a midcentury *Orfeo* (Paris, 1647) by the Roman composer Luigi Rossi (1597–1653) with its predecessors. On a libretto by Francesco Buti, the opera is based on the same subject as the earlier works of Peri, Caccini, and Monteverdi, but it epitomizes the changes in opera during the first half of the seventeenth century. The simplicity of the ancient myth is almost buried under a mass of incidents and characters, spectacular scenic effects, and comic episodes. Allowing the comic, the grotesque, and the merely sensational to intrude into a serious drama was common among Italian librettists of the seventeenth century. The practice suggests that composers no longer put the integrity of the drama first, as Monteverdi and the earlier Florentines had done. The ancient Greek and Roman myths were now mere conventions on which to elaborate in any way that promised good entertainment and provided ample opportunities to the composer and singers. The music fell more neatly into two clearly defined styles, recitative and aria. The recitative was more speechlike than Peri's or Monteverdi's, while the arias were melodious and mainly strophic. Rossi's *Orfeo*, a succession of beautiful arias and ensembles, beguiles the listener into overlooking its faults as a drama.

Venetian opera

A troupe from Rome brought opera to Venice. The librettist, composer, and theorbo-player Benedetto Ferrari (ca. 1603–1681) and the composer Francesco Manelli (after 1594–1667) inaugurated opera in Venice with a 1637 production of *Andromeda* in the Teatro San Cassiano. This theater admitted the paying public, a decisive step in the history of opera, since until then musical theater depended on wealthy or aristocratic patrons. Although *Andromeda* was a low-budget operation, the producers tried to duplicate on a small scale the mechanical stage marvels for which the Florentine and Roman extravaganzas were famous.

Monteverdi's Poppea

Claudio Monteverdi, in his seventies, but still very much up on the latest musical trends, composed his last two operas for Venice: *Il ritorno d'Ulisse* (The Return of Ulysses, 1641) and *L'incoronazione di Poppea* (The Coronation of Poppea, 1642). *Poppea*, Monteverdi's operatic masterpiece, lacks the varied orchestral colors and large instrumental and scenic apparatus of *Orfeo* but surpasses the earlier work in its musical depiction of human character and passions.

Despite the contemporary preference for separating recitative and aria, Monteverdi continued to write in a fluid mixture of speechlike recitative and

Opera in Seventeenth-Century Venice

*V*enice was an ideal place for opera to flourish. The city's reputation for religious and social freedoms made it a mecca for revelers who wanted to indulge themselves during Carnival in masked balls and other delightful pastimes. The population of Venice swelled with visitors from the day after Christmas, when Carnival officially began, to Shrove Tuesday, the day before Lent (a penitential period of forty days during which public entertainments were discouraged). The Venetian Carnival brought together a diverse audience, and producers sought to lure them to the opera.

Rich merchants built and supported theaters. Less wealthy families could lease boxes, and anyone could rent a seat in the ground-level stalls for a single performance. Everyone, including box holders, had to buy admission tickets. With steady financing and a guaranteed audience for at least part of the year, librettists, composers, producers, designers, and companies of singers and musicians could count on multiple performances of a work during a season. Between 1637, when San Cassiano opened, and 1678, when San Giovanni Grisostomo, the last new theater of the century, was completed, more than 150 operas were produced in nine Venetian theaters.

Mythological themes continued to inspire the librettos, populated by figures such as Venus, Adonis, Apollo, Orpheus, Jason, Andromeda, and Hercules. Around the middle of the century, librettists drew on episodes concerning the heroes of the Crusades from the epic poems of Tasso and Ariosto. Similarly, the Trojan wars provided adventurous tales of Ulysses, Paris, Helen, Dido, Aeneas, Aegisthus, and Achilles. The poets and librettists eventually mined Roman history for its military heroes and rulers—Alexander, Scipio, Pompey, Hannibal, Caesar, and Nero. The plots were chosen with an eye for stunning stage effects—clouds bearing flocks of singers, enchanted gardens, magical transformations—and for dramatic personal relationships and conflicts.

more lyrical and formal monody. For example, the love scene between Nero and Poppea in Act I, Scene 3 (NAWM 57) passes through various levels of recitative: unmeasured, speechlike passages with few cadences; airs for singing poetry, as in the Prologue of *Orfeo*; and measured arioso (a style that shares characteristics of both recitative and aria, but falls somewhere between the two). The aria passages are similarly varied. Even when the poet, Giovanni Francesco Busenello, did not provide strophic or other formally structured verse, the composer sometimes turned to aria style. Content rather than poetic form, and heightened emotional expression rather than the wish to charm and dazzle, determined the shifts from recitative to aria and back, and from one level of speech-song to another. Monteverdi's music, therefore, expresses every nuance of emotion in the dialogue and the results are dramatically convincing.

Cavalli and Cesti

Among Monteverdi's pupils and successors in Venice were Pier Francesco Cavalli (1602–1676) and Antonio Cesti (1623–1669). Cavalli wrote forty-one operas, the most famous of which was *Giasone* (1649), a full-blown score in which arias and recitatives alternate, the two styles always clearly differentiated. Cesti's opera *Orontea*, from approximately the same year (1649), became one of the most frequently performed in the seventeenth century, not only in Venice but also in Rome, Florence, Milan, Naples, Innsbruck, and elsewhere. Orontea's Act II aria, *Intorno all'idol mio* (Around my idol, NAWM 58), shows how developed the aria was by midcentury. The form is strophic, with some musical adjustments to the new text of the second stanza. A new vocal idiom reigns, one that became known as *bel canto*—smooth, mainly diatonic lines and flowing rhythm gratifying to the singer. The two violins, no longer restricted to ritornellos before and after the singer's strophes, play throughout the aria.

Characteristics of opera

By the middle of the seventeenth century, Italian opera had acquired the main features it would maintain without essential change for the next two hundred years: (1) concentration on solo singing to the detriment of ensembles and instrumental music; (2) the stylistic separation of recitative and aria; and (3) the introduction of distinctive styles and patterns for the arias. One additional feature concerned the relation of text and music. The Florentines had considered music accessory to poetry; in contrast, the Venetians treated the libretto as hardly more than a scaffolding for the musical structure.

Vocal Chamber Music

Except in Venice, where it became the focus of musical life, opera was an uncommon event. Chamber music, most of it involving voices, remained the standard fare. The new monodic idioms and the basso-continuo texture permeated this genre as well. But since dramatic dialogue and the representation of actions were outside the scope of chamber music, composers felt free—indeed compelled—to find new ways of organizing their musical thoughts.

Strophic aria

The strophic aria, neglected in the polyphonic madrigal but kept alive in the canzonet and other popular forms, now offered the best framework for setting poetry without interfering with the poem's continuity. Using the strophic method, the composer could repeat the same melody, perhaps with minor rhythmic modifications, for each stanza of poetry; write new music for each strophe; or keep the same harmonic and melodic plan for all the strophes—the favored technique, known as *strophic variation*.

Baroque Ostinato Patterns

Composing a strophic song on a standard formula, such as the *romanesca*, became popular during the Baroque period. The *romanesca*, an air for singing *ottave rime* (poems organized in eight-line stanzas, each having a rhyme scheme of abababcc), consisted of a treble formula with a standard harmonization and bass. Example 9.2 gives the formula, reduced to its essentials. In some compositions built on the romanesca formula, only the bass is recognizable, so it is often referred to as a *ground bass*, or *basso ostinato*, a bass that is repeated intact while the melody above it changes. Monteverdi wrote his setting of the ottava rima *Ohimè dov'è il mio ben* (Alas, where is my love, NAWM 59) as a strophic duet on the romanesca air.

Romanesca

EXAMPLE 9.2   Outline of the Romanesca Aria

Some short ground-bass patterns, such as the *chaconne* (Spanish: *chacona*; Italian: *ciaccona*) and *passacaglia* (Spanish: *passecalle*; French: *passecaille*) were not associated with any particular poetic form. The chacona, a dance-song with a refrain that followed a simple pattern of guitar chords, probably came into Spain from Latin America. The Italian ciaccona reduced the harmonic pattern to a bass line. The passacaglia originated in Spain as a ritornello—that is, music played before and between the strophes of a song. It too evolved into a variety of bass formulas, usually in triple meter and minor mode, that were suitable for supporting instrumental or vocal variations. Characteristic of both the chaconne and passacaglia in the seventeenth century is the continuous repetition of a four-bar formula in triple meter and slow tempo. Examples from the eighteenth century, when the two terms became confused, appear in Example 9.3.

Chaconne and passacaglia

EXAMPLE 9.3   Bass Patterns

a. Buxtehude (ca. 1637–1707), *Ciaccona*

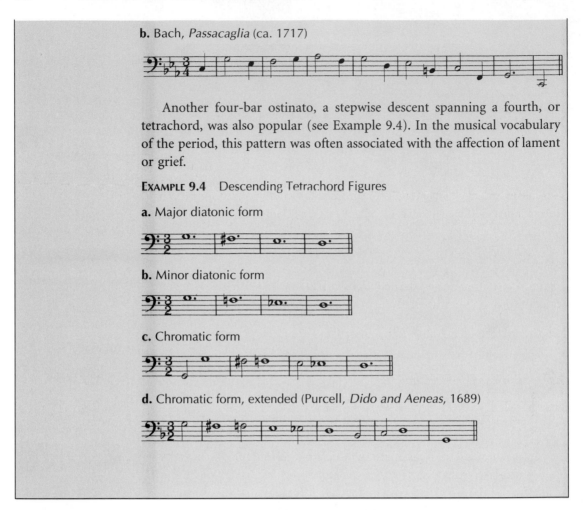

b. Bach, *Passacaglia* (ca. 1717)

Another four-bar ostinato, a stepwise descent spanning a fourth, or tetrachord, was also popular (see Example 9.4). In the musical vocabulary of the period, this pattern was often associated with the affection of lament or grief.

EXAMPLE 9.4   Descending Tetrachord Figures

a. Major diatonic form

b. Minor diatonic form

c. Chromatic form

d. Chromatic form, extended (Purcell, *Dido and Aeneas*, 1689)

The concertato medium

The practice of writing out separate parts for voices and instruments, or different groups of voices and instruments, gave rise to the *concertato* medium. (The adjective *concertato* comes from the Italian verb *concertare*, meaning to reach agreement; the English *consort* and the verb *concert* are derived from the same root.) In a musical *concerto*, diverse and sometimes contrasting forces come together in a harmonious ensemble. *Concertato madrigal* describes a work in which instruments and voices are joined together as equals. *Sacred concerto* means a sacred vocal work with instruments. *Instrumental concerto* defines a piece for various instruments, sometimes including one or more soloists and an orchestra with several players to a part. Today we think of a concerto as a piece for soloists and orchestra, but the older sense was more inclusive. The seventeenth-century concertato medium, then, is not a style but a mingling of voices with instruments that are playing independent parts.

Monteverdi's Eighth Book of Madrigals

*B*ook 8, *Madrigali guerrieri et amorosi* (Madrigals of War and Love), contains a variety of concertato forms and types, including madrigals for five voices; solos, duets, and trios with continuo; and large works for chorus, soloists, and orchestra. The eighth book also contains two *balli* (semidramatic ballets) and the *Combattimento di Tancredi e Clorinda* (The Combat of Tancred and Clorinda), a work in the *genere rappresentativo* (theatrical medium), first performed in 1624. Here Monteverdi set a portion of the twelfth canto of Tasso's *Jerusalem Delivered* describing the combat between the crusader knight Tancred and the armed pagan heroine Clorinda, ending with her death. The bulk of Tasso's text is straight narrative, which Monteverdi assigned to a tenor soloist in recitative. The few short speeches of Tancred and Clorinda are sung by a tenor and soprano, who also mime the actions while the narrative is sung. The instruments (string quartet with bass gamba and continuo), in addition to accompanying the voices, play interludes that suggest the action—the galloping of horses, the clash of swords, the excitement of combat. For such purposes, Monteverdi used what he called the *stile concitato* ("excited style"). One of the most striking devices of this style, often meant for warlike affections and actions, is the prolonged rapid reiteration of a single note or series of them, either with quickly spoken syllables in the voice or instrumentally as a measured string tremolo.

Stile concitato

We can trace the changing patterns of instrumental participation, strophic variation, and other novel devices in Monteverdi's fifth through eighth books of madrigals (1605, 1614, 1619, 1638). Beginning with the last six madrigals of Book 5, all include a basso continuo, and many call for other instruments as well. Solos, duets, and trios are set off against the full vocal ensemble, and there are instrumental introductions and recurring instrumental interludes (ritornellos). The seventh book, titled *Concerto*, is described as consisting of "madrigals and other kinds of songs."

Monteverdi's concertato madrigals

From the beginning of the century, Italian composers turned out thousands of monodies—solo madrigals, strophic arias, and canzonets. These pieces were more widely known than any of the operas, performed only a few times for restricted audiences. Monodies and music for small ensembles were sung everywhere, and they appeared in copious collections of madrigals, arias, dialogues, duets, and the like. As we have seen, Caccini's *Nuove musiche*

Genres of vocal solo music

| Window |

BARBARA STROZZI, RENAISSANCE WOMAN

Barbara Strozzi (1619–after 1664) was the adopted heir, and probably the illegitimate daughter, of Giulio Strozzi, a prominent figure in seventeenth-century intellectual and musical circles in Venice. Largely with her father's encouragement and support, she achieved some notoriety as a singer and as the composer of secular vocal works—just over one hundred pieces—published between 1644 and 1664, in eight volumes.

As a musician, Strozzi herself became the central figure in the *Accademia degli Unisoni*, an academy evidently created by her parent/patron to exhibit her talents. Members met regularly, discoursing and engaging in debates about subjects that invariably dealt with love. Barbara Strozzi acted as mistress of ceremonies—setting the topics, choosing the winners, and performing her music. We may compare her role to that of a Renaissance courtesan, whose activities in the Venetian academies of the sixteenth century are well documented. Certainly, the traditional association in Renaissance life and art between music making and sexual license strongly suggests that Strozzi's songs were also intended to inspire love.

An intriguing portrait of a *Female Musician*, very possibly Barbara Strozzi, confirms this association. The painting, by Bernardo Strozzi (apparently no relation despite the surname), is traced back to about 1637 in Venice, and was likely commissioned by Giulio himself to help launch Barbara's musical career. It shows a handsome young woman, with a somewhat melancholy expression, holding a viola da gamba. The seductive costume, which allows

(1602) was the first important collection of monodies. The solo songs of Sigismondo d'India (ca. 1582–before 1629), as well as his polyphonic madrigals and motets, mark him as another outstanding musical personality of the time.

Cantata

The *cantata* (literally, a piece that was "sung") eventually engaged most Italian composers. By the middle of the century *cantata* came to mean a composition with continuo, usually for solo voice, on a lyrical or quasi-dramatic text; it consisted of several sections that included both recitatives and arias. The Roman Luigi Rossi was the first eminent master of this type of cantata. Other leading Italian cantata composers of the mid–seventeenth century were Giacomo Carissimi (1605–1674)—who is remembered chiefly for his sacred oratorios—the opera composer Antonio Cesti, and the singer us to observe her ample bosom, and the flowers in her hair refer directly to her role as courtesan. The painting's musical objects also betoken her invitation to love: in addition to the instrument she holds, a violin lies on the table in the lower left corner, as though awaiting the arrival of its player; and the music shown in the songbook is in fact a duet, requiring the participation of another.

Whatever the social position of Barbara Strozzi and whatever the function of her art, we can say that her surviving compositions—mostly cantatas and arias for solo voice and basso continuo—were intended for intimate, private gatherings rather than for the large, public audiences of opera, and that her music speaks movingly, and often tearfully, of love (see *Lagrime mie*, NAWM 60, and Example 9.5).

➤ Bernardo Strozzi, *Female Musician with Viola da Gamba*. (Dresden, Staatliche Kunstsammlungen)

The information in this discussion is based on an essay by Ellen Rosand, "The Voice of Barbara Strozzi," in *Women Making Music: The Western Art Tradition, 1150–1950*, eds. Jane Bowers and Judith Tick (Chicago and Urbana: University of Illinois, 1986), pp. 168–90.

Barbara Strozzi (1619–after 1664), composer of eight published collections of motets, madrigals, arias, and cantatas.

Barbara Strozzi's *Lagrime mie* (My tears, NAWM 60), with its successive sections of recitative, arioso, and aria, exemplifies the solo cantata. The poet is unknown, but, like many of the verses Barbara Strozzi set, it may be by Giulio Strozzi with whom she lived from childhood and who was probably her father (see illustration and window above). In the opening recitative (Example 9.5), Barbara Strozzi artfully exploits rhetorical devices that Roman composers first introduced into the cantata. The hesitations on the dissonant $D\sharp$, A, and $F\sharp$ over the opening E-minor harmony, together with the $C\natural$ of the harmonic-minor scale, make this one of the most moving and vivid projections of the lamenting lover's sobs and tears.

EXAMPLE 9.5   Barbara Strozzi, Cantata: *Lagrime mie*

My tears, [what holds you back] . . . ?

Church music   The innovations of the late sixteenth and early seventeenth centuries strongly affected the normally conservative category of sacred music. Monody, the basso continuo, and the concertato medium were all soon applied to sacred texts. Opposition to the new styles did arise in the Roman Catholic Church, which never completely abandoned polyphony. Indeed, Palestrina's style, called *stile antico*, became the supreme model for church music. Composers were routinely trained to write in this style of counterpoint, which coexisted with the *stile moderno* throughout the seventeenth century. A composer might utilize both styles, sometimes in a single piece; Monteverdi, for example, wrote with equal mastery in both. In the course of time, the old style grew more modern: a basso continuo was often added, rhythms became more regular, and the older modes gave way to the major-minor system.

The Venetian School

The heart and center of Venetian musical culture was the great eleventh-century Church of Saint Mark, with its Byzantine domes, bright gold mosaics, and spacious interior suffused with dim, greenish golden light. Like Venice itself, Saint Mark's was independent. Its clergy and musicians responded more directly to the reigning doge than to any outside ecclesiastical authority. Most of the exalted civic ceremonies took place in this church and in its vast piazza. Venetian music glorified the majesty of state and church on solemn and festive occasions in magnificent displays of sound and pageantry. Life in Venice had little of the ascetic quality associated with Roman devotions. Venetians took their religion less seriously. The city's wide commercial interests, especially the centuries-old trade with the East, gave it a peculiarly cosmopolitan, flamboyant atmosphere. Painters such as Titian, Tintoretto, and Veronese (see Plate III, facing page 130) had pioneered new techniques in oils exploiting color and form in dramatic ways.

Music in Saint Mark's was supervised by officials of the state who spared no pains or expense. The position of choirmaster, the most coveted musical post in all Italy, had been held by Willaert, Rore, and Zarlino in the sixteenth century, and by Monteverdi in the early seventeenth.

Many Venetian composers contributed notably to the madrigal, and Venice produced the best Italian organ music. Venetian music was characteristically full and rich in texture, homophonic rather than contrapuntal, varied and colorful in sonority. Massive chordal harmonies replaced the intricate polyphonic lines of the Franco-Flemish composers.

From before the time of Willaert, composers in the Venetian region often wrote for double chorus that sometimes echoed one another in antiphony, a style particularly suited to psalm settings. The medium of divided choirs (*cori spezzati*), which encouraged homophonic choral writing and broad rhythmic organization, did not originate in Venice but found a congenial home there. In the polychoral music of Giovanni Gabrieli (ca. 1553–1612)—who served as organist at St. Mark's—the performance forces grew to unheard-of proportions. Two, three, four, even five choruses, each with a different combination of high and low voices, mingled with instruments of diverse timbres, answered one another antiphonally, alternated with solo voices, and joined together in massive sonorous climaxes. Gabrieli's motet *In ecclesiis* (In churches, NAWM 61) explored these new resources.

Venetian polychoral motets

The Venetian school exercised broad influence during the late sixteenth and early seventeenth centuries. Gabrieli's students and admirers spread his style throughout northern Italy, Germany, Austria, Scandinavia, and Poland. His most famous pupil was Heinrich Schütz, the greatest German composer of the mid–seventeenth century (see pages 195–98).

Venetian influence

Genres of Sacred Music: Catholic and Lutheran

The grand concerto was inspired by the works of Gabrieli and the Venetian school. Sometimes these sacred works, for huge groups of singers and players, reached colossal proportions. One festival Mass, probably written by Andreas Hofer (1629–1684) for Salzburg Cathedral, called for two eight-part choruses with soloists. Each chorus joined with three different instrumental combinations and had its own basso continuo; a third basso continuo served the whole ensemble. A single page of score for this formidable composition requires fifty-three staves. The undisputed master of the grand concerto and a major figure in seventeenth-century Catholic church music was Orazio Benevoli (1605–1672). His later works, written mostly for St. Peter's during the 1640s, include psalms, motets, and Masses for three or more choruses with a figured bass for the organ, but they could be sung equally well unaccompa-

Grand concerto

nied. The choruses, stationed at separate places on different levels within the ample basilica of St. Peter's, literally surrounded the listeners. Benevoli combined and controlled the sonorities with utmost skill, producing antiphonal effects alternating with massive climaxes.

Concerto for few voices

The concerto for few voices, in which one, two, or three solo voices sang to the accompaniment of an organ continuo, was much more familiar to the average parishioner than the grand concerto. One of the first composers to exploit this medium for church music was Lodovico Viadana (1560–1627), who in 1602 published a collection, *Cento concerti ecclesiastici* (One Hundred Sacred Concertos; see, for example, NAWM 62).

Where resources permitted, the grand concerto was combined with the concerto for few voices, as in Monteverdi's pioneering *Vespers* of 1610, which include all varieties of solo, choral, and instrumental groupings. In these settings for the liturgical Office, Monteverdi also incorporated the traditional psalm tones while exploiting the new musical resources of the time—recitative, aria, and concerto. Alessandro Grandi (ca. 1575/80–1630), who greatly impressed the German composer Heinrich Schütz, received recognition for his sacred compositions in the new style. His solo motet *O quam tu pulchra es* (O how beautiful you are, NAWM 63), on a text from the *Song of Songs*, illustrates the smooth mingling of elements from theatrical recitative, solo madrigal, and bel canto aria into a single composition.

A sacred opera

Monody, the concertato medium, and even the apparatus of the theater were all turned to sacred uses. In February 1600, even before the first surviving opera was performed in Florence, Emilio de' Cavalieri (ca. 1550–1602) produced a morality play with music on a stage in Rome. Titled *La rappresentazione di Anima et di Corpo* (The Representation of the Soul and Body), it was, in effect, a sacred opera with allegorical characters, intended for an informal devotional service. Although the work did not establish a genre, it probably whet the appetite of the Roman curia, with its rich mixture of monody, choral declamation, dancelike instrumental music, and tuneful airs.

Oratorio

The dramatic impulse in Rome found an outlet in the sacred dialogues, which combined elements of narrative, dialogue, and meditation or exhortation, but were not usually intended for stage performance. Toward the middle of the century, works of this kind began to be called *oratorios*, because they were most often performed in the oratory, the part of a church where groups of the faithful met to hear sermons and sing devotional songs. The libretto of an oratorio might be in Latin (*oratorio latino*) or Italian (*oratorio volgare* [vernacular]). The principal master of the Latin oratorio at this time was Giacomo Carissimi (1605–1674).

Carissimi's Jephte

A synopsis of Carissimi's *Jephte* exemplifies a typical midcentury oratorio. The Latin libretto comes from the Book of Judges 11:29–40, with some paraphrasing and added material. The narrator, called the *storicus* or *testo*, introduces the story. Jephtha, leader of the Israelites, vows that if the Lord gives him a victory over the Ammonites in the impending battle, he will sacrifice the first person to greet him on his return home. That person is his own daughter, who, along with her friends, welcomes Jephtha with songs of rejoicing (solo arias, duets, choruses). After a section of dialogue, in recitative, between father and daughter, the chorus relates how the daughter, still a virgin, goes away to the mountains with her companions to bewail her approaching untimely death. She then sings a lament, to which the chorus responds, as in the *kommos* of the Greek tragedy (this final scene is in NAWM 64). The lament is a long, affecting recitative, sweetened, as was customary in sacred music, with moments of florid song and with arioso passages built on sequences. Two sopranos, representing the daughter's companions, echo some of her cadential phrases. The choral response, a magnificent six-voice lamentation, employs both polychoral and madrigalistic effects.

Both oratorios and operas used recitative, arias, duets, and instrumental preludes and ritornellos, but oratorios had numerous differences: their subject matter was always sacred; narration was included; the chorus was used for dramatic, narrative, and meditative purposes; and they were seldom if ever meant to be staged. Action was described or suggested, not played out.

In the German-speaking regions, both the Catholic and Lutheran churches took up the new monodic and concertato techniques. Sacred music in Austria and the Catholic southern cities of Germany remained wholly under Italian influence, with Italian composers particularly active in Munich, Salzburg, Prague, and Vienna. Composers in the Lutheran central and northern regions began, early in the seventeenth century, to employ the new media, sometimes using chorale tunes as melodic material. Along with these compositions in *stile moderno*, the Lutheran composers continued to write polyphonic chorale motets as well as biblical motets that did not use chorale melodies. Many were in the grand concerto medium, testifying to German musicians' admiration for the Venetian school.

> *Lutheran church music*

The concerto for few voices also attracted German composers. An important collection of such pieces was published in 1618 and 1626 at Leipzig by Johann Hermann Schein (1586–1630), entitled *Opella nova* (New Little Works), and subtitled *Geistliche Konzerte . . . auff ietzo gebräuchliche italiänische Invention* (Sacred Concertos in the Nowadays Customary Italian Manner). In many respects the pieces are Lutheran counterparts of some of Monteverdi's concertato madrigals. The collection consists chiefly of duets and a few solos on chorale texts; they set a precedent for a long series of similar works by Lutheran composers of the seventeenth century.

> *Sacred concerto in Germany*

The great German composer Heinrich Schütz (1585–1672), like many of his countrymen for centuries to come, completed his musical education in Italy. He studied in Venice with Giovanni Gabrieli from 1609 to 1612 and there brought out his first published work, a collection of five-part Italian madrigals. From 1617 to the end of his life, Schütz was master of the chapel

> *Heinrich Schütz*

Window

THE ECSTASY OF SAINT TERESA

Baroque art is essentially theatrical. Whether in opera, painting, sculpture, or other media, its principal concern is the representation of action and reaction, the evocation of motion and emotion. These forces and tensions underlie the basic premise of the Baroque and help explain its aesthetic goal: to move our emotions and to stir the passions in our soul.

By the mid–seventeenth century the dramatic gestures and attitudes of the stage permeated the style of sacred works too, as we have seen in the music of Schütz and Carissimi. Nowhere is this more evident than in the church of Santa Maria della Vittoria in Rome, where Giovanni Lorenzo Bernini's marble sculpture, *The Ecstasy of Saint Teresa*, dominates the Cornaro chapel. The Cornaro family commissioned Bernini, a contemporary of Carissimi working in Rome, to design a side chapel within the church as their final resting place. The commission gave Bernini the opportunity not only to create a sculptural group for the chapel's altarpiece, but also to plan and decorate its entire setting. Perhaps at the family's request, he chose as his subject the popular Saint Teresa of Avila (see Plate VII, facing page 226).

Saint Teresa (1515–1582) was a Spanish nun and one of the greatest mystics of the Catholic Church. In her autobiography she describes how, in one of her many visions, an angel repeatedly pierces her heart with a golden arrow, her pain made bearable by the sweet sensation of her soul being caressed by God. With consummate skill Bernini transformed Saint Teresa's

of the elector of Saxony at Dresden, although during the Thirty Years' War he spent several years as court conductor in Copenhagen. Schütz renewed his acquaintance with Italian music on a trip to Venice in 1628. As far as we know, Schütz, like Monteverdi, did not write any independent instrumental music. He is reputed to have composed the first German opera, as well as several ballets and other stage works, but no such music survives. What remains is a great quantity and variety of church music dating from 1619 to the final years of his life.

Venetian magnificence and color appear frequently in Schütz's music. The *Psalmen Davids* (1619) for multiple choruses, soloists, and concertato instruments, combines the massive colorful sonority of the grand concerto with sensitive treatment of the German text. His works lack only one significant words into action and reaction: the angel is frozen *in the act* of plunging the arrow into the saint's breast, bringing about her mystical union with Christ, the heavenly bridegroom. Saint Teresa *reacts* by swooning in an ecstatic trance, her limbs dangling, her head tipped back, her eyes half closed, and her mouth forming an almost audible moan. The pair is bathed in a warm and mysterious glow coming through the chapel's hidden window of yellow glass, architecturally contrived to throw a spotlight on the scene.

Bernini stunningly reinforces the theatricality of it all by his treatment of the chapel's side walls: there, in pews that resemble theater boxes, he depicts the members of the Cornaro family in almost three-dimensional relief, as though they are witnessing the enactment of this dramatic mystery (see illustration). Because Bernini created the illusion of the Cornaro family sitting in the same space in which we are moving, we feel as if they are alive. In this way we too are drawn in, both physically and emotionally, to the Baroque world of Saint Teresa's vision; we become the audience at a command performance of this silent, sacred opera.

➤ Detail from Bernini's *Ecstasy of St. Teresa*, sculpted 1645–52. (*Scala/Art Resource, NY*)

Discussion about the chapel and its sculpture is based on Rudolf Wittkower, *Gian Lorenzo Bernini, the Sculptor of the Roman Baroque* (London: The Phaidon Press, 1966), pp. 24–26.

element of the fully developed Lutheran style: he seldom made use of traditional chorale melodies, although he set many chorale texts.

In 1636 and 1639, when war had sadly reduced the electoral chapel, Schütz published his *Kleine geistliche Konzerte* (Little Sacred Concertos), motets for one to five solo voices with organ accompaniment. The year 1636 also saw the publication of the *Musikalische Exequien* (funeral music for Schütz's friend and patron Prince Heinrich Posthumus von Reuss), for soloists and choruses in various combinations with basso continuo accompaniment. Another collection of German motets, written in a severe contrapuntal style, was the *Geistliche Chormusik* (Spiritual Choral Music, 1648). Most important among Schütz's concertato motets are his *Symphoniae sacrae* (Sacred Symphonies), published in three series (1629, 1647, and 1650). The first two use various

Schütz's Symphoniae sacrae

small combinations of voices and instruments, up to a total of five or six parts with continuo. The *Symphoniae sacrae* of 1629 betray the strong influence of Monteverdi and Grandi.

The last installment of the *Symphoniae sacrae* (1650) was published after the end of the Thirty Years' War, when the full musical resources of the Dresden chapel were again available. It calls for as many as six solo voices and two solo instrumental parts with continuo, supplemented by a full choral and instrumental ensemble. Many of these works are laid out as dramatically conceived "scenes," sometimes with a closing chorus of pious reflection or exhortation, foreshadowing the design of the later church cantata.

One of the most dramatic scenes, the evocation of the conversion of St. Paul (Acts 26:12–18; *Saul, was verfolgst du mich*, NAWM 65), brings to life the moment when Saul, a Jew on the way to Damascus to fetch Christian prisoners, is stopped by a blinding flash of light and the voice of Christ calling to him: "Saul, why do you persecute me?" The experience led to his conversion and to his new career as the Apostle Paul, spreading the Gospel. The concerto is set for six solo voices (the ensemble Schütz called *favoriti*), two violins, two four-voice choirs, and, we may assume, an orchestra that doubles the choral parts. Paired solo voices rising from the depths of the basses through the tenors to the sopranos and violins represent the flash of light and the voice leaping from the desert. Christ's question "Why do you persecute me?" is a mesh of dissonant anticipations and suspensions. Then the grand concerto takes over as the choruses and soloists together reverberate with echoes, suggesting the effect of Christ's voice bouncing off rocky projections in the desert.

Instrumental Music

Instrumental music did not escape the spell of the recitative and aria styles (although these had less impact than the basso continuo). The sonata for solo instruments, especially, surrendered to vocal influences. The violin, which rose to prominence in the seventeenth century, tended naturally to emulate solo singing, and it absorbed many vocal techniques.

Instrumental music in the first half of the seventeenth century gradually became the equal, both in quantity and content, of vocal music. Certain basic compositional procedures resulted in five broad categories of instrumental music—dance music, improvisatory compositions, contrapuntal genres, canzona or sonata, and variations—which correspond to the emerging categories first described in Chapter 7. While these classifications are useful as an introduction to a complex field they are neither exhaustive nor mutually exclusive. Various types overlap and intertwine.

1. Dance Music

Dance music was important not only for its own sake but also because its rhythms permeated vocal and instrumental music, both sacred and secular. The characteristic rhythm of the sarabande and the lively movement of the gigue, for example, appear in many compositions that are not called dances at all (see page 209).

The suite, as a composition in several movements rather than a mere succession of short pieces each in a certain mood and rhythm, was a German phenomenon. The technique of thematic variation—already established in the pavane-galliard, Tanz-Nachtanz, and passamezzo-saltarello combinations of the sixteenth century—was now extended to all the dances of a suite. This organic musical connection exists among dances in all the suites in Johann Hermann Schein's *Banchetto musicale* (Musical Banquet, 1617). The movements "finely correspond both in key and invention," Schein claimed in his foreword. Some of the suites build on one melodic idea that recurs in varied form in every dance. In other suites, subtle melodic reminiscence rather than outright variation provides the connection. The *Banchetto* contains twenty suites in five parts, each suite having the sequence paduana (pavane), gagliarda, courante, and allemande with a *tripla* (a variation in triple meter of the allemande). The music is dignified, aristocratic, vigorously rhythmic, and melodically inventive, with that union of richness and decorum, of Italianate charm and Teutonic gravity, so characteristic of this moment in Germany.

Suites

Schein

Composers in France established a characteristic idiom for the individual dances through their arrangements of actual ballet music. These arrangements were written not for an ensemble but for a solo instrument—first the lute and later the *clavecin* (the French term for harpsichord) or the *viole* (the French term for viola da gamba). Such a version for lute is *La Poste* (NAWM 66a) by Ennemond Gaultier (1575–1651). Lute arrangements were sometimes transcribed for the harpsichord, as in the gigue drawn from this piece (NAWM 66b), in the process transferring ornaments and textures that are idiomatic, or peculiar to the lute.

French lute and keyboard music

Since lutenists normally struck only one note at a time, it was necessary to sketch in the melody, bass, and harmony by sounding the appropriate tones in succession—now in one register, now in another—creating the illusion of a contrapuntal texture while relying on the hearer's imagination to supply the continuity of the various lines. This technique, the *style brisé* (broken style), was adapted by other French composers to the harpsichord. Lutenists also developed systematically the use of little ornaments (*agréments*), either indicated on the page or left to the discretion of the player. The French lute style was the basis for important developments in keyboard music and, indeed, for the entire French style of composition in the late 1600s and early 1700s.

Influence of lute technique

Lute music flourished in France during the early seventeenth century, culminating in the work of Denis Gaultier (1603–1672). A manuscript col-

Denis Gaultier

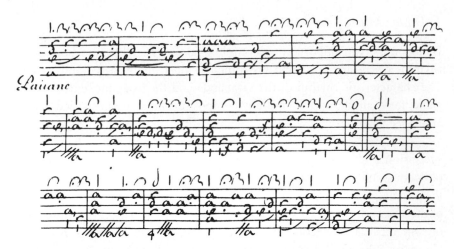

▲ A pavane in Denis Gaultier's collection of lute pieces, *La Rhétorique des dieux* (Paris, ca. 1652), arranged according to mode. The horizontal lines in this French tablature represent the strings, with the lowest at the bottom; the frets are indicated by letters, a, b, c, etc.

lection of Gaultier's compositions titled *La Rhétorique des dieux* (The Rhetoric of the Gods) contains twelve sets (one in each mode) of highly stylized dances. Each set includes an allemande, a courante, and a sarabande, with other dances added apparently at random. Each suite is thus a little anthology of short character pieces, many of which were given fanciful titles.

The earliest important composer in the new keyboard idiom was Jacques Champion de Chambonnières (1601 or 1602–1672), the first of a long and brilliant line of French clavecinists that included Louis Couperin (1626–1661), Jean Henri d'Anglebert (1635–1691), Elisabeth-Claude Jacquet de la Guerre, and François Couperin (concerning the last two composers, see Chapter 11).

Froberger

Johann Jakob Froberger (1616–1667), who established the allemande, courante, sarabande, and gigue as standard components of dance suites, carried the French style to Germany. He was also one of the first to imitate lute music on the harpsichord. The fusion of genre pieces and dance rhythms in the mid-seventeenth-century keyboard suite is well illustrated in one of Froberger's most famous compositions, a lament (*tombeau*) on the death of the Emperor Ferdinand III in 1657 (NAWM 67), written in the pattern and rhythm of a slow allemande. The style brisé dominates the texture. Not only the rare key of F minor but also the prominent threefold *F* at the end allude to the emperor's name. Another programmatic touch is the use of an arpeggio, which stretches from deep in the bass to the high treble, representing the ascent of the emperor's soul.

2. Improvisatory Compositions

The toccata had been established in the sixteenth century as a kind of "warm-up" piece, full of scalar and other florid passages that burst forth from the player's fingers at irregular intervals. The toccatas of Girolamo Frescobaldi (1583–1643), organist at St. Peter's in Rome from 1608 until his death, are unusual because they restrain virtuosity in favor of quiet contemplation. In contrast to the imposing objective grandeur and virtuosity of Merulo (see Chapter 7, page 145) and other Venetians, Frescobaldi's toccatas are often reserved, subjective, and mystical, with sustained harmonies and extraordinary, original chord progressions.

Frescobaldi's toccatas

Others of his keyboard toccatas are related to the Venetian type. Long series of loosely connected sections with a great luxuriance of musical ideas allow for virtuosity, as in the third toccata of Book One (1637; NAWM 68). This toccata, like so many others of Frescobaldi, has a restless character. As the music approaches a cadence on either the dominant or tonic, the goal is always evaded or weakened—harmonically, rhythmically, or through continued voice-movement—until the very end. According to the composer's preface, the performer may play the various sections of these toccatas separately and may end the piece at any appropriate cadence. Frescobaldi also indicated that the tempo is not subject to a regular beat but may be modified according to the sense of the music, especially by retarding at cadences.

Froberger wrote more solidly constructed though less exuberant toccatas. His free improvisatory passages provide a framework for systematically developed sections in the contrapuntal style of the fantasia. Froberger's pieces were the model for the later merging of toccata and fugue, as in the works of Buxtehude (see Chapter 11, page 230), or their coupling, as in the works of Bach.

Froberger's toccatas

3. Contrapuntal or Fugal Genres (in Continuous or Nonsectional Imitative Counterpoint)

The typical seventeenth-century *ricercare*, a brief, serious, contrapuntal composition for organ or keyboard, continuously develops one theme through imitation, as in Frescobaldi's *Ricercar dopo il Credo* ("after the Credo"). This particular ricercare is from his *Fiori musicali* (Musical Flowers, 1635), a collection of organ pieces intended for use in the church service. Frescobaldi's remarkably skillful handling of chromatic lines and subtly shifting harmonies and dissonances characterizes much of his organ music, which exudes a quiet intensity (see Example 9.6).

Ricercare

EXAMPLE 9.6   Girolamo Frescobaldi, *Ricercar dopo il Credo*

Fantasia

The keyboard *fantasia* is usually constructed on a larger scale than the simple ricercare and has a more complex formal organization. The leading fantasia composers in this period were the Amsterdam organist Jan Pieterszoon Sweelinck (see page 156) and his German pupils Samuel Scheidt (1587–1654) of Halle and Heinrich Scheidemann (ca. 1596–1663) of Hamburg. In Sweelinck's fantasias, a fugal exposition usually leads to successive sections with different countersubjects and toccata-like figurations. Such pieces must have been intended to set and explore a mode or key in preparation for some other music.

In general the ricercare and fantasia were built on a theme or themes of sustained legato character. The fantasia used borrowed themes and learned devices more frequently to develop a continuously imitative counterpoint, thereby creating a series of fugues. Indeed, *fuga* was the name used in Germany for pieces of this sort from the earliest years of the seventeenth century.

English consort music

Consort (ensemble) music for viols flourished in England beginning in the early decades of the seventeenth century, when the works of Alfonso Ferrabosco the Younger (before 1578–1628) and John Coprario (Cooper; d. 1626) were popular. The fancies of John Jenkins (1592–1678), the leading composer of viol consort music in the mid–seventeenth century, exhibit a variety of procedures, with and without continuo, some strictly contrapuntal and some less so.

The contrapuntal fantasia for strings without basso continuo, the leading form of early-seventeenth-century English chamber music, was cultivated even after the Restoration (1660). The principal later composers were Matthew Locke (1621–1677) and Henry Purcell (1659–1695), whose fantasias for viols, written about 1680, are the last important examples of the species.

4. Canzona or Sonata

Canzona

In contrast to the contrapuntal genres, the canzona had livelier, more markedly rhythmic melodic material, with emphasis on the division of the piece into sections, betraying its origins in the French chanson. Composers approached the canzona in a variety of ways. One was to build several contrasting sections, each on a different theme in fugal imitation (much like a vocal chanson), rounding off the whole with a cadenza-like flourish. In another type, called the *variation canzona*, the composer used transformations of a single theme in successive sections, as in the keyboard canzona of Giovanni Maria Trabaci (ca. 1575–1647) illustrated in Example 9.7. Some keyboard canzonas, however, and most ensemble canzonas are a patchwork of short, thematically unrelated sections that might be repeated literally or in varied form later in the work.

A later composer would probably have called Trabaci's canzona a *sonata*. This term, the vaguest of all designations for instrumental pieces in the early 1600s, gradually came to mean a composition that resembled a canzona in form but that also had special features. Early-seventeenth-century sonatas were often scored for one or two melody instruments, usually violins, with a

Sonata

EXAMPLE 9.7   G. M. Trabaci, Keyboard Canzona

basso continuo, while the ensemble canzona was traditionally written in four parts that could be played just as well without a continuo. Moreover, sonatas often took advantage of the idiomatic possibilities offered by a particular instrument. They had a somewhat free and expressive character, while the typical canzona displayed more of the formal, abstract quality of instrumental polyphony in the Renaissance tradition.

Biagio Marini

The differences, as well as the similarities, will be most evident if we compare one of the earliest sonatas for solo violin and continuo, by Biagio Marini (ca. 1587–1663), with the canzonas described above. Marini's *Sonata per il violino per sonar con due corde*, Op. 8, published in 1629, is an early example of what may be called "instrumental monody." Like the canzona, it has contrasting sections, the last of which is particularly canzona-like in spirit. The sonata opens with a sentimental melody reminiscent of a Caccini solo madrigal, but it turns almost immediately to violinistic sequential figures (see Example 9.8). There are no literal repetitions, although the recurring cadences on *A* and the alternation of rhapsodic with regularly metrical sections give coherence to the piece. Most notable is the idiomatic violin style, which makes use of sustained tones, runs, trills, double stops, and improvised embellishments called *affetti*.

EXAMPLE 9.8   Biagio Marini, Sonata

By the middle of the seventeenth century the canzona and the sonata had thoroughly merged, and the term *sonata* came to stand for both. Sometimes the name was qualified, as sonata da chiesa, since many such pieces were intended for use "in church." Sonatas used many different combinations of instruments, a common medium being two violins with continuo. The texture of two treble melodic parts, vocal or instrumental, above a basso continuo attracted composers throughout the seventeenth century: instrumental combinations of this sort were usually called *trio sonatas*.

5. Variations

The variation principle permeated many of the instrumental genres of the seventeenth century, and the theme-and-variations form itself, a favorite type of late-Renaissance keyboard composition, underwent further development. Pieces using this method were called "Aria con variazioni," "Variationes super [or 'on'] . . . ," and "Diferencias" (Spanish for "variations"). But just as often, the term *variation* did not appear in the title. Composers of the early seventeenth century often used the term *partite* (divisions or parts) for sets of variations; only later was it applied to sets, or suites, of dances. Composers favored a number of techniques in such pieces, the most common being the following:

• The melody could be repeated with little or no change, although it might wander from one voice to another amidst different contrapuntal material in each variation. This type is sometimes called the *cantus firmus variation.*

• The melody itself could receive different embellishment in each variation. Most often melodic variations occurred in the topmost voice, with the underlying harmonies remaining essentially unchanged.

• The bass or the harmonic structure, rather than the melody, could supply the constant factor. Often, as in the case of the romanesca, a treble tune or melodic outline is associated with the bass, but it is usually obscured by figuration.

Frescobaldi's partite

The set of partite by Frescobaldi on the *Aria di Ruggiero* (Example 9.9a) represents an early example of the third type. Like the romanesca, *Ruggiero* was an air or tune for singing ottave rime, a verse scheme employed in epic poems (see page 187). The bass and harmony of the air are clearly the fixed elements in Frescobaldi's twelve partite, and only in the sixth *parte* or variation is the melody at all prominent. Perhaps recalling the *Ruggiero*'s original function as a poetic recitation formula, Frescobaldi made the first variation very rhapsodic and free, like a recitative. The tenth *parte* falls into a syncopated mode similar to that used later by Buxtehude and Bach in their passacaglias (Example 9.9b).

EXAMPLE 9.9

a. The Ruggiero theme

[Rug - gier, qual sem-pre fui,   tal es-ser vo - glio Fin al-la mor-te, e più, se più si puo-te.]

b. Frescobaldi, *Partite 12 sopra l'Aria di Ruggiero, Decima parte*

An important class of organ compositions from middle and northern Germany comprised works based on chorale melodies. These pieces were produced in large numbers and in a great variety of forms after the middle of the seventeenth century, but examples already appear in the works of Swee-linck and Scheidt. In 1624, Scheidt published a large collection of compositions for the organ under the title *Tabulatura nova*. He called it new, because instead of the old-fashioned German organ tablature, Scheidt adopted the modern Italian practice of writing out each voice on a separate staff. Notable among the collection's chorale pieces are several sets of variations on chorale tunes. There are also shorter organ settings of plainsong melodies, many variations on secular songs, and several monumental fantasias. The works of Scheidt, and his influence as a teacher, were the foundation of a remarkable development of North German organ music in the Baroque era.

Chorale variations

Scheidt

POSTLUDE

During the period 1600–1750, called by music historians the Baroque era and dominated largely by Italian tastes and fashions, composers shared a penchant for dramatic expression; collectively, they devised a music vocabulary that aimed at representing human passions and moving the affections, whether their music was intended for theater, church, or private quarters. In the early Baroque (until approximately the mid–seventeenth century) the musical style of Monteverdi and his contemporaries comprised diverse elements, some dating back to the sixteenth century, others new. Monody and madrigal were combined; form was achieved via the organization of the bass and the harmonies it supported and through the systematic introduction of ritornellos; and the typical basso-continuo texture—a florid treble supported by a firm bass—was varied by the use of the concertato medium. By these means, composers enlarged and enriched the representational and emotional resources of music.

New types of composition—solo song, opera, oratorio, sacred vocal concerto, cantata—incorporated novel styles of writing, such as recitative and aria. Choral and instrumental textures also assimilated the new dramatic aesthetic. Staying within the same basic categories that had emerged in the sixteenth century, instrumental music not only expanded but also achieved independence from vocal music through the exploitation of styles idiomatic to instruments such as the lute, violin, and keyboard. By about midcentury, the bel canto style of vocal writing, a creation of Italian composers, was imitated all over Europe and influenced both vocal and instrumental music throughout the Baroque period and beyond.

10

OPERA AND VOCAL MUSIC IN THE
LATE SEVENTEENTH CENTURY

Opera spread throughout Italy as well as to other countries during the second half of the seventeenth century. The principal Italian center remained Venice, whose opera houses were famous all over Europe. But Naples also became important, particularly in the transition to the new, simpler style that emerged at the end of the century. Germany imported Venetian opera, which then fused with native styles into a national German opera. France resisted Italian influence and eventually developed its own operatic idiom—one that was largely determined by the court's penchant for ballet and the tastes of Louis XIV, who acquired his nickname *le Roi Soleil* (the Sun-King) after dancing in a court ballet costumed as Apollo (see illustration, page 213). The reception of opera in England, however, was different: there King Charles I was beheaded in 1649 and during the ensuing Commonwealth period the puritanical climate was hardly friendly to the cultivation of such an extravagant art form. Even after the restoration of the English king in 1660, the monarchy was too weak and its treasury too depleted to support opera on the grand scale of the French or the Italians.

Vocal Music for Chamber and Church also flourished during this period. The Italian chamber cantata, the Lutheran church cantata, the oratorio, and Passion settings were all influenced by the language of opera—especially recitative and aria—and by its musical vocabulary of the affections. Older types of church music, however, such as Mass and motet, persisted in the more conservative idioms of *stile antico* counterpoint and the concerted, sometimes polychoral styles of the early Baroque.

Opera

Venice

Venetian theaters continued to vie with one another in luring audiences to their opera productions. More than the drama or spectacle, it was the singers and arias attracting the public. Impresarios competed for the most popular singers, who sometimes earned more than twice as much as composers, by paying high fees. The famous Anna Renzi inaugurated the vogue of the operatic diva when she created the role of the spurned empress Ottavia in Monteverdi's *Poppea*, and composers wrote parts expressly for her special talents.

Singers

The singers' vehicle was the aria. While it was common in midcentury for an opera to include twenty-four arias, sixty became the norm by the 1670s. The favorite form was the strophic song, in which several stanzas were performed to the same music. Other favorites were short two-part arias in AB form, and three-part, ABB′ and ABA or ABA′ forms. Many had refrains. Typical arias used characteristic rhythms from the march, gigue, sarabande, or minuet. Others relied on ostinato basses, perhaps in combination with dance rhythms. Musical motives in both the vocal part and the accompaniment reflected the content of the text. For example, a composer might imitate trumpet figures to portray martial or aggressive moods.

Aria types

Germany as well as other Italian cities imported Venetian opera. Among

Intima si cantum simulat præcordia mulcet,
Ipsam animam sensim si canit Anna rapit.
Jacobus Piccinus Venetus faciebat Ven:

◄ The famous opera singer Anna Renzi, about whom Giulio Strozzi wrote in *La glorie della signora Anna Renzi romana* (Venice, 1644): "Our Signora Anna is endowed with such lifelike expression that her responses and speeches seem not memorized but born at the very moment. In sum, she transforms herself completely into the person she represents, and seems now a Thalia full of gaiety, now a Melpomene rich in tragic majesty." (Quoted from Ellen Rosand, *Opera in Seventeenth-Century Venice*, p. 232) the many Italian composers who brought Italian opera to the eagerly receptive German courts were Carlo Pallavicino (1630–1688) and Agostino Steffani (1654–1728). Steffani, one of the best Italian opera composers of his time, created works that are important both in themselves and for their decisive influence on eighteenth-century composers, especially Handel.

An Aria by Agostino Steffani

*S*teffani's aria *Un balen d'incerta speme* (A flash of uncertain hope) from the opera *Enrico detto il Leone* (Henry the Lion; Hanover, 1689) illustrates his early style. The dimensions of the aria, in ABA form, are modest. The coloratura passages, which are prominent though not excessive, occur on the pictorial words *balen* (flash) and *raggio* (ray), while the passage on *dolor* (pain) expresses the word in typical fashion with chromatic melody and harmonic cross-relations (Example 10.1). Two features of this aria occur fairly often in other examples from the period: (1) a *motto beginning*, in which the voice announces a short musical subject developed later in the aria, but which continues only after an instrumental interruption; and (2) a walking-bass accompaniment.

EXAMPLE 10.1   Agostino Steffani, Aria: *Un balen*, from *Enrico detto il Leone*

. . . is the only ray [of hope] that sustains me amidst the clouds of pain.

Naples

Italian opera in the late seventeenth century tended toward stylized musical language and simple textures that concentrated on the solo melodic line, supporting it with ingratiating harmonies. From this combination an operatic style evolved that was more concerned with musical elegance and effect than with dramatic force and truth. Developed principally in Naples, this new style dominated the eighteenth century. Alessandro Scarlatti (1660–1725) made the transition from the older seventeenth-century opera to this newer, Neapolitan style just described. In many of his later works, notably *Griselda* (Rome, 1721), Scarlatti's shrewdly dramatic conception of the arias and his detailed attention to the orchestral parts demonstrated his commitment to the genre.

A. Scarlatti

Scarlatti and other composers carefully fashioned their recitatives so that the harmonic progressions reflected the quick changes of feeling and ideas in the text. Two distinct kinds of recitative emerged. One type, accompanied by a basso continuo, presented stretches of dialogue or monologue in as speechlike a manner as possible. It would later be called *recitativo semplice* (simple recitative) and eventually *recitativo secco* (dry recitative). The other type, accompanied by an orchestra, was used for tense dramatic situations. The orchestra reinforced the rapidly changing emotions in the dialogue and punctuated the singer's phrases with brief instrumental outbursts. This was called *recitativo obbligato* (because the instruments were "obliged" to play) and later *recitativo accompagnato* or *stromentato*. Meanwhile, a further category of sung monody evolved: the *recitativo arioso* ("arialike recitative") or *arioso*, which occupied a place somewhere between the free recitative and the rhythmically regular aria.

Kinds of recitative

The form that eventually reigned supreme in the early eighteenth century was the *da capo aria*. Its name comes from "Da capo" (from the head), words inserted at the close of the second section of a two-section form; these words instruct the performers to return to the beginning (the "head") of the aria and repeat the first section. The da capo aria was the perfect vehicle for sustaining a lyrical mood through a musical design that expressed a single sentiment, sometimes joined with an opposing or related one. Scarlatti's *Mi rivedi, o selva ombrosa* (You see me again, O shady wood, NAWM 69), the aria that opens Act II of *Griselda*, exemplifies the use of the da capo aria to bring out conflicting reactions. A queen for fifteen years, Griselda has been repudiated by her husband the king and must return to her humble origins. The melody of the first line, out of which the rest of the main A section develops through extension, sequence, and combinatorial methods, captures Griselda's feelings of subjection (Example 10.2a). The subordinate B section, linked to the A section rhythmically, presents the bright side for a moment—her pleasure at being home (Example 10.2b). Having completed the B section, the singer follows the direction "Dal segno," to return to the *segno*

Da capo aria

or sign placed above her first entrance, skipping the opening ritornello. This results in an abbreviated da capo form, as follows:

		§		Fine		Dal segno
Section:	Ritornello	A	Transitional Rit.	B		
Key:	C minor			Modulation to E♭		
Measure:	1	4	16	18 19	26	(27=)4–18

The A section, in C minor, occupies eighteen measures; the B section, eight measures in length, modulates from the C-minor cadence at the end of A to E♭. Then the A section follows immediately, in C minor, closing the aria on the fermata at the end of the transitional ritornello.

EXAMPLE 10.2   Alessandro Scarlatti, *Griselda*, Aria: *Mi rivedi, o selva ombrosa*

You see me again, o shady forest, but no longer queen and bride; unfortunate, disdained, a shepherdess.

France

By around 1700, Italian opera was flourishing in every corner of western Europe except France. Although the French long resisted Italian opera, they finally established a national French opera in the 1670s, under the august patronage of Louis XIV, with special features that persisted for a century. Two powerful traditions influenced French opera: the sumptuous and colorful ballet, which had flourished at the royal court ever since the late sixteenth century; and the classical French tragedy, represented best by the works of Pierre Corneille (1606–1684) and Jean Racine (1639–1699). France's literary and theatrical culture insisted that poetry and drama be given priority on the stage. The composer who succeeded in reconciling the demands of drama, music, and ballet was Jean-Baptiste Lully. His new amalgam, *tragédie en musique*, was later renamed *tragédie lyrique*.

Tragédie lyrique

Jean-Baptiste Lully (1632–1687), an Italian musician, came to Paris at an early age. From 1653, as a member of King Louis XIV's string orchestra (*vingt-quatre violons du roy*, or the king's twenty-four "violins"), he composed instrumental music and dance pieces that were added to productions of Italian operas. He also provided overtures, dances, and vocal numbers in both the Italian and French styles for court ballets. Lully became the virtual musical dictator of France when a 1672 royal privilege gave his Académie Royale de Musique a monopoly in the medium of sung drama.

Lully

Lully's librettist, the esteemed playwright Jean-Philippe Quinault, provided the composer with mythological plots adorned by frequent long inter-

Quinault

◄ Louis XIV got his nickname *le Roi Soleil* (the Sun-King) after having danced in a court ballet dressed in the golden-rayed costume of Apollo, shown here. (*The Lebrecht Collection, London*)

ludes (called *divertissements*) of dancing and choral singing. Quinault's texts cleverly combined adulation of the king, glorification of the French nation, and moral lessons with episodes of romance and adventure. For these librettos Lully composed music that was appropriately pompous or gracious and that projected the highly formal splendor of the French royal court, still given to admiring the conventions of courtly love and knightly conduct. The public found Lully's spectacular choruses and lively ballet scenes especially appealing. Dances from Lully's stage works became so popular that they were arranged as independent instrumental suites; many new suites also appeared in imitation of Lully's divertissements.

Lully's recitative

Lully adopted the style of Italian recitative to the French language and French poetry—no simple task, since neither the rapid *recitativo secco* nor the quasi-melodic *arioso* of Italian opera suited the rhythms and accents of the French language. It is said that Lully arrived at his solution by listening to celebrated French actors and actresses and closely imitating their declamation. Certainly the timing, pauses, and inflections of his recitatives resemble stage speech, but the rhythmic bass and the often tuneful melody hampered Lully's ability to create the same illusion of speech that Italian recitative achieved.

Récitatif simple *and* mesuré

In what would later be called *récitatif simple*, Lully shifted the meter between duple and triple to accommodate the accented syllables of the verse. This recitative was frequently interrupted by a more songlike, uniformly measured style, *récitatif mesuré*, whose accompaniment has more deliberate motion. Discrete sections of *récitatif mesuré* are sometimes marked "Air" in the scores, but they lack the closed form or the rhyme schemes of a true air, which usually has the meter and form of a dance. Armide's monologue in *Armide* (1686; NAWM 70b) illustrates this mixture of styles (Example 10.3). The scene begins in the unmeasured *récitatif simple* until a six-measure transition in the measured style (not shown) leads to an air in minuet meter. Armide, dagger in hand, stands over her captive warrior, the sleeping Renaud, but because of her deep love for him, she cannot bring herself to kill him. She sings in an unmetrical rhythm, punctuated by rests that not only complete each line but are also used dramatically, as in the passage where Armide hesitates between uncertainty and resolve (measures 36–42).

EXAMPLE 10.3　Jean-Baptiste Lully, Monologue: *Enfin il est en ma puissance,* from *Armide*

What in his favor does pity want to tell me? Let us strike. . . . Heavens! Who can stop me? Let us get on with it. . . . I tremble! . . . let us avenge. . . . I sigh!

Even before he composed operas, Lully had established a two-part *ouverture*—the "French overture"—for the ballets. Typically, the first section is homophonic, slow, and majestic, marked by persistent dotted rhythms and by anacrustic (upbeat) figures rushing toward the downbeats. The second section begins with a flurry of fugal imitation and is comparatively fast-moving without sacrificing its grave and serious character. The slow section, or one like it, sometimes returns at the end. Throughout the remainder of the Baroque era, composers used *ouvertures* to introduce ballets, operas, oratorios, and instrumental works such as suites, sonatas, and concertos. Originally intended to create a festive atmosphere for the ballet or opera that followed, and to welcome the king to a dance or performance, *ouvertures* also appeared as independent pieces. The overture to *Armide* (NAWM 70a) typifies the genre.

Ouverture

Lully's influence extended beyond the arena of opera and ballet. Elsewhere in France and in Germany, composers and musicians admired and imitated the discipline with which he directed his orchestra and his methods of scoring. Lully himself conducted by beating time on the floor with a long cane. The core of Lully's twenty-four-piece string orchestra, the *vingt-quatre violons du roy*, contained six soprano violins, tuned like the modern violin; twelve alto and tenor violins of various sizes, tuned like the modern viola but playing three separate parts; and six bass violins, tuned like the modern cello but a tone lower. This rich, five-part texture was augmented by woodwinds, which both supported the strings and played contrasting passages, often for a trio of solo wind instruments (usually two oboes and bassoon).

Orchestra

England

Masque

Opera in England—or what was known there as opera—had a short career during the second half of the seventeenth century. The *masque*, an aristocratic entertainment similar to the French court ballet, had flourished in England for years. Best known is Milton's *Comus*, produced in 1634 with music by Henry Lawes (1596–1662), consisting of dances and other instrumental pieces, songs of various types, recitatives, and choruses.

Meanwhile, English opera had a modest beginning under the Commonwealth (1649–60), although the English composers and public did not especially like the genre. Stage plays were prohibited, but a play set to music could be called a "concert," thereby avoiding the ban. Although this pretext was no longer necessary during the Restoration (1660–85), the trend continued, so that nearly all the English "semi-operas" of the seventeenth century were actually plays with a large number of vocal solos and ensembles, choruses, and instrumental music. The only important exceptions were John Blow's *Venus and Adonis* (1684 or 1685) and Henry Purcell's *Dido and Aeneas* (1689), both of which were sung throughout.

Purcell

Henry Purcell (1659–1695), a pupil of Blow, served as organist of Westminster Abbey and held other musical posts in London. In addition to his many odes for chorus and orchestra, cantatas, songs, catches (see page 220), anthems, Services, fancies, chamber sonatas, and keyboard works, he also wrote incidental music for forty-nine plays, mostly during the last five years of his life.

Dido and Aeneas

Purcell composed *Dido and Aeneas* for a girls' boarding school at Chelsea. The libretto by Nahum Tate, although crude as poetry, dramatized the familiar story from Vergil's *Aeneid* in a way that proved conducive to musical setting. Purcell's score remains a masterpiece of opera in miniature: there are only four principal roles; the orchestra consists of strings and continuo; and the three acts, including dances and choruses, take only about an hour to perform. Purcell's style incorporated both the achievements of earlier English theater music and its Continental influences. The French overture and the homophonic choruses in dance rhythms resemble Lully's choruses, as in *Fear no danger to ensue*, with its minuet rhythms alternating iambs (∪—) and trochees (—∪).

Thoroughly English, however, is Purcell's inimitable tune *Pursue thy conquest, Love* from *Dido* as well as the melody from the chorus *Come away, fellow sailors*, with its fascinating phrasing of 3 + 5, 4 + 4 + 4, and 4 + 5 measures. The choruses, which freely alternate with the solos, are an important part of the work. The recitatives approach neither the rapid chatter of the Italian *recitativo secco* nor the stylized rhythms of French operatic recitative, but display supple melodies cleverly molded to the accents, pace, and emotions of the English text.

The most Italianate parts of the work are the arias, three of which build over a different *basso ostinato*, or ground bass; the last of these—and one of the most moving in all opera—is Dido's lament *When I am laid in earth* (NAWM 71). It is preceded by a recitative that does more than serve as a vehicle for the text: by its slow, stepwise descent of a seventh, the recitative portrays the deathly mood that overcomes Dido as she contemplates suicide. The lament itself follows the Italian tradition of setting such songs over a ground bass, which creates a sense of utter despair through its relentless repetition. The bass grows out of the descending tetrachord, or fourth, common in such pieces, but it is extended by a two-measure cadence formula, adding up to a five-measure pattern repeated nine times (see Chapter 9, pages 187–88). Purcell creates great tension and forward thrust by re-attacking suspended notes on the strong beat, intensifying the dissonance.

The closing chorus, *With drooping wings* (NAWM 71), was certainly suggested to Purcell by the final chorus of Blow's *Venus and Adonis*. Equally perfect in workmanship, it proceeds on a larger scale and conveys a more profound depth of sorrow. Descending minor-scale figures portray the cupids' "drooping wings," and arresting pauses mark the words "never part."

Unfortunately for English music, no composer in the next two centuries would develop and maintain a national tradition in the face of Italian opera's popularity. Instead, English audiences lavished their enthusiasm on productions of Italian, French, or German composers.

Germany

Despite the taste for Italian opera at seventeenth-century German courts, a few cities supported companies that performed operas by native Germans. The German version of opera was the *Singspiel* ("sing-play"), a play that interspersed songs with spoken dialogue. When German composers replaced the spoken dialogue with recitative, they adopted the Italian recitative style almost without alteration. The most important center of German opera was

C H R O N O L O G Y

1640		Royal Academy of Music founded in Paris (1669)
	Giovanni Lorenzo Bernini (1598–1680), *The Ecstasy of St. Teresa* (1644; see Plate VII, facing page 226, and window, pages 196–97)	1670 Jean Molière (1622–1673), *Le Bourgeois Gentilhomme*
		Jean Racine (1639–1699), *Phèdre* (1677)
	Luigi Rossi (1597–1653), *Orfeo* in Paris (1647)	1680
	Treaty of Westphalia: end of the Thirty Years' War (1648)	James II of England crowned (1685)
		*Lully, *Armide* (1686)
1650	Carissimi, *Jephte* (ca. 1650)	Isaac Newton (1642–1727), *Principia mathematica* (1687)
	Oliver Cromwell dissolves Parliament (1653)	*Purcell, *Dido and Aeneas* (1689)
		1690 John Locke (1632–1704), *An Essay Concerning Human Understanding*
1660	Restoration of Charles II in England	
	Louis XIV (1638–1715) assumes French throne (1661)	*Alessandro Scarlatti (1660–1725) dominates opera in Naples (1690s)
		1700

R. Keiser

the northern free city of Hamburg, where the first public opera house outside Venice opened in 1678, and closed its doors in 1738. During those sixty years a national opera emerged, whose leading and most prolific representative was Reinhard Keiser (1674–1739). At their best, Keiser's operas bring together Italian and German qualities. The subject matter and general plan of the librettos follow those of Venetian opera, and the virtuoso arias even surpass their Italian counterparts in vigor and brilliance. The slower melodies, though lacking the suave flow of the Italian bel canto, can be profoundly expressive, and the harmonies are well organized in broad, clear structures. Keiser wrote more than a hundred works for the Hamburg stage between 1696 and 1734.

Vocal Music for Chamber and Church

Italian cantata

The Italian cantata evolved from the early-seventeenth-century monodic strophic variations and developed into a genre with many short, contrasting sections. By the second half of the century, it had settled into a clearly defined pattern of alternating recitatives and arias—normally two or three of each—for solo voice with continuo accompaniment. The text, usually about love, took the form of a dramatic narrative or soliloquy. The work might be ten to fifteen minutes long. So, in both its literary and musical aspects, the cantata resembled a scene detached from an opera, although its poetry and music were on a more intimate scale. In addition, because composers designed the cantata for performance before a small, discriminating audience in a room without a stage, scenery, or costumes, it attained an elegance and refinement that would have been lost in an opera house. Finally, the cantata offered a better opportunity to experiment than opera did, and many Italian composers produced quantities of cantatas, notably Carissimi (see page 194), Luigi Rossi (see page 184), Cesti (see page 186), Alessandro Stradella (1644–1682), and Alessandro Scarlatti (see page 211, and window, pages 244–45).

A. Scarlatti

The more than six hundred cantatas of Alessandro Scarlatti mark a high point in this repertory; his *Lascia, deh lascia* (Cease, O cease) is typical of the genre. It begins with a short arioso section (Example 10.4a). The recitative that follows (Example 10.4b) exemplifies Scarlatti's mature style in its wide harmonic range—there is a noteworthy modulation to the remote key of E♭ minor at the words "inganni mortali." The next movement, a full da capo aria (Example 10.4c) with long, supple melodic phrases over a bass in stately eighth-note rhythm, displays unusual harmonic progressions and chromatics underscoring the word "tormentar." In many of Scarlatti's modulations, the unprepared diminished-seventh chord—rare for the time—serves as a pivot chord. Scarlatti sometimes exploited the enharmonic ambiguity of the diminished-seventh chord, but more often he used it to add bite to a cadence. Numerous instances of this chord, in both melodic and harmonic form, occur in the brief passage reproduced in Example 10.4c.

EXAMPLE 10.4   Alessandro Scarlatti, Cantata: *Lascia, deh lascia*

a.

Cease, O cease to torment me.

b.

[... bitterness] of an adored one too ungrateful, among the deceptions of mortal
life; if it is the purpose of the wrath of adverse fate [only to make me die ...]

c.

Enough, cruel love; torment me no more, because I want to die.

**France and
Germany**

Composers across Europe imitated or adapted the Italian chamber cantata, though to a lesser extent than Italian opera. In France, Marc-Antoine Charpentier (1634–1704), a pupil of Carissimi, wrote both secular cantatas and sacred oratorios in the Italian style. Throughout the early eighteenth century, Italian influence remained strong on most of the French cantata composers. In Germany, Keiser and his contemporaries wrote songs and arias with sacred texts, as well as cantatas in both Italian and German. Unlike France and Germany, England withstood Italian influence for much of the seventeenth century. During the Commonwealth, some attempts to imitate the new monodic recitative occurred, and after the Restoration English musicians became acquainted with the work of Carissimi and Stradella. But the best songs, from the pens of Henry Purcell and John Blow, owed little to foreign models. In addition to many theater songs, Purcell wrote a large number of vocal solos, duets, and trios, many of which appeared in *Orpheus Britannicus* (Vol. 1, 1698). John Blow issued a similar collection of songs under the title *Amphion Anglicus* (1700). A specialty of English composers in this period was the *catch*, a round or canon with often humorous, ribald texts that were sung unaccompanied by a convivial group.

England

The restoration of the English monarchy in 1660 encouraged the creation of large works for chorus, soloists, and orchestra for ceremonial or state occasions, such as royal birthdays, the king's return to London, or holidays. Purcell's magnificent *Ode for St. Cecilia's Day* (1692) was a direct ancestor of Handel's English oratorios (see Chapter 12).

Church music

A mixture of old and new styles characterized Catholic church music throughout the Baroque era. Bologna and its basilica of San Petronio continued as a thriving center of church music in both the old and concerted forms. In the Catholic centers of southern Germany—Munich, Salzburg, and especially Vienna, the seat of the imperial chapel—modern church music united Italian and German characteristics. The style of Masses and motets by composers such as Maurizio Cazzati (ca. 1620–1677) and Antonio Caldara (1670–1736) varied from one extreme to another—from the sober, a cappella, *stile antico*, emulating Palestrina-style counterpoint, to the most modern succession of operatic-style arias, duets, and choruses, all with orchestral ritornellos.

Oratorio

Although oratorios were still performed in churches, they were also presented in the palaces of princes and cardinals, in the academies, and in other institutions as a substitute for opera during Lent or special seasons when the theaters were closed. Most oratorios came in two parts, usually divided by a sermon, or, in private entertainments, by an intermission with refreshments. Whether or not on a biblical subject, the oratorio had a verse libretto and so followed the conventions of opera rather than of liturgical music (see vignette on facing page).

**French
church music**

Like French opera, church music in France deviated from the patterns of Italian and southern German music. Carissimi's disciple Marc-Antoine Charpentier (1634–1704) introduced the Latin oratorio into France, combining

André Maugars on the Italian Oratorio, 1639:

❝ There is another kind of music that is not used at all in France and for that reason merits separate treatment. It is called *recitative style*. The best that I have heard was in the Oratory of San Marcello, where there is a Congregation of the Brothers of the Holy Crucifix, made up of the grandest lords of Rome, who consequently have the power to assemble all the rarest resources that Italy produces. In fact, the most excellent musicians compete to appear, and the most consummate composers covet the honor of having their compositions heard there and strive to exhibit all the learning that they possess.

They do this admirable and ravishing music only on Fridays of Lent, from three to six. The church is not as big as the Sainte-Chapelle of Paris. At its end there is a spacious jube [a gallery between the nave and the choir] with a modest organ that is very sweet and suits voices very well. On the sides of the church there are two other little galleries, in which some of the most excellent instrumentalists were placed. The voices would begin with a psalm in the form of a motet, and then all the instruments would play a very good symphony. The voices would then sing a story from the Old Testament in the form of a spiritual play, for example that of Susanna, of Judith and Holofernes, or of David and Goliath. Each singer represented one person in the story and expressed the force of the words perfectly. Then one of the most famous preachers made the exhortation. When this was done, the choir recited the Gospel of the day, such as the history of the good Samaritan, of Canaan, of Lazarus, or of Magdalen, and the Passion of our Lord, the singers imitating perfectly well the different characters that the evangelist spoke about. I cannot praise this recitative music enough; you have to hear it on the spot to judge its merits. ❞

Maugars, *Response faite à un curieux sur le sentiment de la musique d'Italie, escrite à Rome le premier octobre 1639*, ed. Ernest Thoinan (pseud. for Antoine Ernest Roquet) in *Maugars, sa biographie* (Paris: A. Claudin, 1865; facs. London: H. Baron, 1965), p. 29.

Italian and French recitative and air styles. He usually assigned a prominent role to the chorus, often a double chorus, in his thirty-four works in this genre. Charpentier loved dramatic contrasts, and his music brought details of the text to life.

Motets on biblical texts were principally cultivated in the royal chapel of Louis XIV, where composers produced a large number of motets for solo voices with continuo, much in the style of the currently fashionable secular

Motet

cantata. They also created more elaborate motets and similar works for soloists, double choruses, and full orchestra. These larger pieces were called *grands motets* because the forces assembled to perform them were truly grand. Louis XIV's favorite composer of sacred music was Michel-Richard de Lalande (1657–1726), whose more than seventy motets reveal a masterly command of the grand motet style: syllabic *récits*, sweeping homophonic choruses, double fugues, and florid opera-like airs and duets. His style features rich harmonies—spiced, when expression demanded, with dissonances—and surprising contrasts of texture and mood.

F. Couperin

The French version of the sacred concerto for few voices was the *petit motet*. François Couperin (1668–1733) made an important contribution in this arena with his *Leçons de ténèbres* (1714), on texts from the Matins and Lauds for Holy Week, for one or two solo voices with accompaniment in a spare concertato style.

Lutheran church music

The golden age of Lutheran music took place between 1650 and 1750. After the ravages of the Thirty Years' War, church establishments in the Lutheran territories of Germany were quickly restored. Composers such as Dietrich Buxtehude (ca. 1637–1707) and Johann Pachelbel (1653–1706) followed in Schütz's footsteps by writing sacred concertos for chorus, solo voices, and orchestra, with or without the use of chorale texts and melodies. The most famous of a long line of composers working in or near Nuremberg, Pachelbel frequently wrote for double chorus, like many composers in southern Germany, where Venetian influence remained powerful.

Buxtehude

Buxtehude was organist at the Marienkirche in Lübeck, where he composed and played much of his church music for the *Abendmusiken*, public concerts following the afternoon church services in Lübeck during the Advent season. These concerts were long, varied, quasi-dramatic affairs, on the order of loosely organized oratorios, incorporating recitatives, strophic arias, chorale settings, and polyphonic choruses, as well as organ and orchestral music. The Abendmusiken attracted musicians from all over Germany, including the twenty-year-old J. S. Bach, who made a kind of pilgrimage during the autumn of 1705 to Lübeck, traveling all the way on foot.

Although this period was known as the golden age of Lutheran church music, deep conflicts existed within the church itself that inevitably affected musical composition. On the one hand, the Orthodox party, holding to established dogma and public institutional forms of worship, favored using all available resources of choral and instrumental music in the services. On the other, a widespread movement known as Pietism emphasized the freedom of the individual believer. Pietists distrusted formality and high art in worship and preferred music of simpler character that expressed personal feelings of devotion.

The common musical heritage of all Lutheran composers was the chorale, the congregational hymn established during the earliest days of the Refor-

◄ A singer rehearsing to the accompaniment of a positive organ. Engraving by Martin Englebrecht (1684–1765). "The Organ," a poem inscribed below the illustration, reads in translation: "The organ may be called the foundation of music, because through its ranks of pipes much wisdom may be imparted. All voices must conform to its sound and cadence. One need only pull the stops, and it resonates strong, dulcet, low, or mild. It leads a variety of instruments in sweet harmonies and lets itself be heard most delightfully in churches to praise the Supreme One."

mation and continued during the seventeenth century. But with the increased number of devotional songs written in the late 1600s came a general decline in both poetic and musical quality. Many of the Pietistic texts expressed self-centered and sentimental religious attitudes in extravagantly emotional language, while attempts to give the music a simple folklike quality too often resulted in banality.

Not until after 1700 did the opposing currents of Pietism and Orthodoxy come together in a new type of cantata introduced by Erdmann Neumeister (1671–1756). Neumeister was an Orthodox theologian but a poet of decidedly Pietist leanings who, in 1700 in Hamburg, introduced a new kind of sacred poetry for musical setting, which he called by the Italian term "cantata" (see

Lutheran church cantata

vignette below). Throughout the seventeenth century, the texts of Lutheran compositions were chiefly drawn from the Bible or the church liturgy, together with verses taken from or modeled on chorales. Neumeister, however, added poetry that concentrated on the day's scriptural reading and brought its meaning home to the individual worshiper through meditation. Furthermore, he specifically designed these poetic texts to be set as ariosos or arias, the latter usually in da capo form and often including an introductory recitative. Neumeister—and several later Lutheran poets—wrote cycles of cantata texts, intended to fit each slot in the church calendar.

The widespread acceptance by Lutherans of this new type of cantata brought the Orthodox and Pietistic tendencies together. Its poetry blended objective and subjective, formal and emotional elements. Its musical scheme incorporated all the great traditions of the past—the chorale, the solo song, the concerted style—while adding the dramatically powerful elements of operatic recitative and aria. J. S. Bach would become the greatest master of the church cantata, but several composers preceded him in defining its form: Johann Philipp Krieger of Weissenfels (1649–1725), who also composed operas; Johann Kuhnau (1660–1722), Bach's predecessor at Leipzig; and Friedrich Wilhelm Zachow (1663–1712) of Halle.

Erdmann Neumeister on the Sacred Cantata, 1704:

❝ If I may express myself succinctly, a cantata appears to be nothing but a piece out of an opera, put together from recitative style and arias. Whoever understands what these two demand will find this genre of song not difficult to work with. Just the same, let me say a little about each of them as a service to beginners in poetry. For a recitative choose an iambic verse. The shorter it is, the more pleasing and comfortable will it be to compose, although in an affective period now and then one or a pair of trochaic lines—and no less a dactylic—may be inserted nicely and expressively.

As far as arias are concerned, they may consist mainly of two, seldom three, strophes and always contain some affection or moral or something special. You should choose a suitable genre according to your pleasure. In an aria the so-called *capo*, or beginning, may be repeated at the end in its entirety, which in music is altogether welcome. ❞

Erdmann Neumeister, *Geistliche Cantaten statt einer Kirchen-Musik*, 1704, quoted in Max Seiffert, ed., J. P. Krieger, *21 Ausgewählte Kirchen Kompositionen*, DdT 52/53 (Leipzig, 1916), p. lxxvii.

The Passion

*I*n Lutheran Germany, the *historia*, a musical setting based on some biblical narrative, such as the Christmas story, was favored over the oratorio, and the most important type of *historia* was the *Passion*. Plainsong settings of the suffering and death of Christ according to the Gospel accounts had existed since early medieval times. After the twelfth century it was customary to recite the story in a semidramatic mode, one priest singing the narrative portions, another the words of Christ, and a third the words of the crowd or *turba*, all with appropriate contrasts of range and tempo. After the late fifteenth century, composers wrote polyphonic settings of the turba portions in motet style, contrasting with the plainsong solo parts; this type of setting became known as the *dramatic* or *scenic Passion*. Many Lutheran composers, including Heinrich Schütz, adapted the dramatic Passion with a German text to Lutheran use.

The rise of the concerted medium led, in the late seventeenth century, to a new type of Passion derived from the oratorio. Called the *oratorio Passion*, this setting employs recitatives, arias, ensembles, choruses, and instrumental pieces, all of which lend themselves to a dramatic, almost operatic presentation. Poetic meditations on the Gospel story were inserted at appropriate points in the Passion text and typically set as solo arias, sometimes with preceding recitatives. At other points, the choir or congregation sang chorales traditionally associated with the Passion story.

POSTLUDE

Recitative and aria became the most characteristic styles of vocal music in the seventeenth century. While Italian recitative spawned several different varieties, French recitative took another path, responding to the sonic patterns of the French language. Among the aria types common in this period—strophic, ostinato, and da capo—perhaps the most important, and certainly the most ubiquitous, was the da capo aria. Its function in opera was to epitomize and explore a particular affection, to portray and project a psychological state, in much the same way a film director is sometimes compelled to dwell on the close-up or slow-motion camera shot in order to convey the emotional values of a particular scene. Not confined to amorous or heroic sentiments, the da capo aria was also suited to the expression of religious piety or fervor, and so was adopted by composers of Lutheran church cantatas, oratorios, or of any work having dramatic elements.

Whereas Alessandro Scarlatti, among a host of competing Italian composers, represented the most forward-looking trends in Italy, Lully exercised a virtual monopoly over the musical stage in France. His *tragédies lyriques* were stylistically conservative and continued to be performed unchanged even after the death of Louis XIV in 1715. Across the Channel, Purcell synthesized French and Italian elements with native styles into a unique English operatic style which, however, did not survive into the eighteenth century.

Italy, France, and southern Germany continued to cultivate Catholic church music of the traditional Venetian and Roman types: vocal concertos for larger or smaller forces and strict counterpoint *à la* Palestrina. The most important new vocal genre in northern Germany was the Lutheran church cantata. It eventually combined operatic styles and genres, such as recitative and aria, suitable for the representation of personal sentiments, with those capable of expressing collective feelings, such as the congregational hymn (hymn-chorale) and the concerted motet for chorus and instruments.

Although we did not discuss the basso continuo in this chapter, we should keep in mind that most types of music described here were supported by that firm bass so characteristic of Baroque texture. Indeed, in every country, court, and church of Europe the Baroque sound was in full swing.

VII. *The Ecstasy of Saint Teresa,* sculpted by Giovanni Lorenzo Bernini (1598–1680) for the Cornaro chapel in the church of Santa Maria della Vittoria in Rome. Saint Teresa of Avila was a sixteenth-century Spanish mystic, and this depiction of one of her famous visions (as though it were being "enacted" for us in marble) illustrates how the theatricality of Baroque art permeated even the representation of sacred themes by the mid–seventeenth century (see window, pages 196–97). (*ROME, CORNARO CHAPEL, S. MARIA DELLA VITTORIA. SCALA / ART RESOURCE, NY*)

VIII. Jean Antoine Watteau (1684–1721) painted several versions of this scene, of which *The Shepherds*, from 1716–17, is the most recent. Although the activities and manners are those of peasants, the figures are in courtly dress. At the center is a musette (bagpipe) player, getting ready to accompany the dancers. While one couple looks toward the dancers, the woman at the left acquiesces to a rude embrace from the youth with the shepherd's staff. In the background an elegant lady is in mid-swing, not sure how to respond to her courtier; in the foreground a man and his dog wistfully observe the dancers, but no one attends to the sheep. The painting expresses the longing for an idyllic pastoral innocence free of the constraints of middle-class and courtly polite society.   (*BERLIN, SCHLOSS CHARLOTTENBURG / GIRAUDON, ART RESOURCE, NY*)

11

INSTRUMENTAL MUSIC IN THE LATE BAROQUE PERIOD

PRELUDE

Once instrumental music had come into its own, decisions about what instrument to use rather than simply what kind of piece to write challenged the creative imaginations of composers. During the second half of the seventeenth century, the possibilities offered by the modern organs, by the two-manual harpsichord (an instrument with two keyboards and different registers), and particularly by the violin family, inspired new idioms, genres, and formal structures. A sixth instrumental category, the *concerto*, was added to the five outlined in Chapters 7 and 9. But, because of the new importance to composers of the sound and idiom of instruments, it is more appropriate to organize this chapter around the two main types of instrumentation used: solo keyboard music, which is divided between **Music for Organ** and **Music for Harpsichord and Clavichord**; and **Ensemble Music**, which includes *chamber* and *orchestral* music for a variety of instrumental combinations, all employing the ever-present keyboard as a supporting, or continuo, instrument.

The principal categories of composition associated with each of the two major instrumental groups are:

For Keyboard: toccata (or prelude, fantasia) and fugue; arrangements of Lutheran chorales or other liturgical material (chorale prelude, chorale partita, etc.); variations; passacaglia and chaconne; suite; and sonata (after 1700). These types of pieces, taken together, account for all five categories enumerated earlier.

For Ensemble: sonata (sonata da chiesa), sinfonia, and related genres; suite (sonata da camera) and related genres; and concerto. These genres essentially grow out of two of the earlier categories (dance and canzona-sonata), although elements of the other three (improvisatory, contrapuntal, and variation) were often incorporated; and the new, sixth category (concerto) belongs exclusively to this group.

Among the keyboard instruments, the so-called Baroque organ is familiar to us from the many copies of early-eighteenth-century instruments that exist today, modeled especially on instruments originally built by Arp Schnitger (1648–1718) and Gottfried Silbermann (1683–1753). Silbermann was trained in France and Alsace, and, like other German organ builders, was influenced by the French full organ sound and by the musical colors of the different stops or registers used in France to play solos and contrapuntal lines. The German builders also learned from the highly developed instruments constructed in Antwerp and Amsterdam. Organ building and organ music reached a golden age in Germany between about 1650 and 1750.

While organs were constructed mainly in churches, the keyboard instrument of choice for princely chambers and household use was the harpsichord (see Chapter 7, page 142), which was easily adapted to solo or ensemble playing. The clavichord, on the other hand, had a much more delicate sound and could be appreciated only in the most intimate settings. Although French builders and composers did not have a monopoly on the harpsichord, they certainly excelled in producing the instrument and its music.

By about 1700, Italian musical preeminence had been challenged by the French clavecinists and the North German organists. But in the realm of instrumental chamber music, as in the opera and cantata, Italians reigned as the undisputed masters and teachers. The early eighteenth century was the age of the great violin makers of Cremona—Niccolò Amati (1596–1684), Antonio Stradivari (1644–1737), and Giuseppe Bartolomeo Guarneri (1698–1744). It was also the age of great string music in Italy, as we will see.

Music for Organ

Most organ music written for Protestant churches served as a prelude to something else—a hymn, a scriptural reading, or a larger work. In northern Germany these preludes were often organ arrangements of chorales, or toccatas or praeludia that either contained fugues or culminated in them.

Toccata

The typical German toccata consists of contrapuntal and free sections in succession. One type of section is fugal in design and content. Another sim-

▲ Map of Italy, marked with important music centers in the sixteenth and seventeenth centuries.

ulates improvisation in a number of ways: by contrasting irregular or free rhythm with a steady stream of sixteenth notes; by using phrases that are deliberately irregular or have unclear endings; and by presenting sudden and unexpected changes in texture. The improvisatory effect maintains itself most often through a contrived ambiguity in the harmonic flow and through sudden, erratic shifts of musical direction. At the opposite extreme a slow-paced section might consist of long, harmonically static stretches that usually include extended pedal points. The capricious, exuberant character of toccatas was intensified once they became vehicles for virtuosic display at the keyboard and on the organ pedals. (Most organ music was performed simultaneously by both the hands and feet.)

Fugal sections

Toccatas began early to incorporate well-defined sections of imitative counterpoint. Out of these segments emerged the fugue, later conceived as a separate piece to follow the toccata proper. Buxtehude's toccatas, for example, consist of shorter sections in free style that alternate with longer ones in imitative counterpoint. His toccatas are filled with movement and climax; they display a great variety of figuration and take full advantage of the idiomatic qualities of the organ. The opening, a free improvisatory section ending with a solid cadence, is followed by a fugue, on a catchy subject with well-marked rhythm. The fugue eventually merges into a second toccata section, shorter than the first, again leading to a cadence. At this point the composition may close, but as a rule Buxtehude continued to a second and sometimes a third fugue, with brief interludes and a closing climactic section in toccata style. When there is more than one fugue, the subjects are usually variants of a single musical idea (see Example 11.1).

EXAMPLE 11.1   Varied Forms of a Fugal Subject in Dietrich Buxtehude, Praeludium in E

In the seventeenth century, such keyboard pieces were called "toccata," "prelude," "praeludium," "preambulum," or by some similar name, even though they included fugal sections. Buxtehude's Praeludium in E (NAWM 73), which is designated in the manuscripts simply as "Praeludium," has all the earmarks of a toccata, as discussed above.

Fugue

Composers wrote fugues both as independent pieces and as sections within preludes or toccatas. By the end of the seventeenth century, the fugue had almost entirely replaced the old ricercare. Fugue subjects have a more clearly defined melodic character and a livelier rhythm than ricercare themes. As in the ricercare, independent voices enter with the theme in turn. In the fugue these entries are called the *exposition*. Normally the *subject* is stated in the tonic and *answered* in the dominant. The voices then alternate *subject* and *answer*. Further full or partial expositions are usually separated by short *episodes* (passages in which the subject does not appear) that are sometimes set off by a lighter texture or by sequences. These episodes may modulate to various keys before the final statement of the subject returns in the tonic. The return is often intensified by devices such as pedal point, *stretto* (in which statements of the subject pile up in quick succession), or *augmentation* (in which the rhythmic values of the subject are doubled).

While toccatas, preludes, and fugues remained independent of vocal music, chorale-inspired compositions for organ were linked both by function and subject to the repertory of Lutheran hymns. Organ composers in the seventeenth century used chorale melodies in four fundamental ways: as independent presentations of the chorale melody enhanced by harmony or counterpoint; as themes for variations; as subjects for fantasias; and as melodies requiring embellishment and accompaniment.

Chorale compositions

The simplest organ chorales were essentially harmonizations with contrapuntal activity in the accompanying parts. These chorales were probably used when the organist and the congregation alternated in playing and singing strophes of the chorale. Sometimes each melodic phrase of the chorale served

Organ chorales

Key Cycles and Equal Temperament

Although preludes and fugues were performed as meditative interludes in church, they also proved useful for training students in composition and performance. To this end, J. K. F. Fischer (ca. 1665–1746) compiled a collection of keyboard preludes and fugues, *Ariadne musica* (1715), written in nineteen different major and minor keys. This was not the first nor the most complete published tour around the keys. As early as 1567 the lutenist Giacomo Gorzanis published a cycle of twenty-four passamezzo-saltarello pairs, one in each of the major and minor keys, and Vincenzo Galilei left a manuscript dated 1584, also for lute, of a similar cycle of twenty-four sets in major and minor.

The lute was a natural instrument for such cycles, because its frets marked off twelve equal semitones in the octave. Keyboard octaves were not so equally divided, and keyboard players were reluctant to give up the sweeter imperfect consonances and truer perfect consonances possible in such nonequal divisions. But unequal half-steps made it impossible to play in tune in every key or to modulate through the entire cycle of fifths. The remedy—*equal temperament*, in which all semitones are equal and all other intervals are not quite correct but acceptable—was proposed as early as the sixteenth century and was eventually embraced by many keyboard players, composers, and organ builders of the Baroque era. The title J. S. Bach gave to his first set of preludes and fugues in all twenty-four keys, *Das wohltemperirte Clavier* (The Well-Tempered Keyboard, Part I, 1722), suggests that he had equal, or at least adequate, temperament in mind.

➤ The organ built by Andreas Silbermann (1678–1734) at the Abbey Church in Marmoutier (Alsace), France, 1708–10, and enlarged by his son Johann Andreas in 1746. In the foreground is the *Rückpositiv*, above the hidden console the *Hauptwerk*. The tall pipes are for the pedals.

as a subject for imitation, which resulted in a more contrapuntally elaborate setting resembling the motet.

Chorale variation

In the *chorale variation*, also called *chorale partita*, the chorale tune served as the theme for a set of variations. This genre emerged early in the seventeenth century in the works of Sweelinck and Scheidt. Later composers, up to the time of Bach and beyond, modified the technique. Buxtehude's *Danket dem Herrn, denn er ist sehr freundlich* (Thank the Lord, for He is very kind, NAWM 74) is an example of a late-seventeenth-century chorale variation. Here, Buxtehude treats the chorale as a cantus firmus, placing it in a different voice in each variation.

Chorale fantasia

In a *chorale fantasia* the composer fragments the chorale melody and develops the resultant motives through virtuoso fingerwork, echoes, imitative counterpoint, and ornamentation. The severe contrapuntal style of Scheidt's fantasias gradually gave way to the free, loquacious compositions of Buxtehude and other North German composers.

Chorale prelude

Chorale prelude, a term often applied to any chorale-based organ work, is used here to denote a short piece where the entire melody is presented just once in readily recognizable form. This type of chorale prelude did not appear until the 1650s. The name suggests a liturgical practice in which the organist played through the tune, improvising the accompaniment and ornaments, as a prelude to the congregation's or choir's singing of the chorale. Later, these pieces were called chorale preludes even if they did not serve the original purpose. Such a work was, in effect, a single variation on a chorale, and it used any one of a number of different variation techniques.

Music for Harpsichord and Clavichord

In the Baroque period, especially in Germany, it is not always clear whether a given piece was intended for the harpsichord or clavichord, or indeed for the organ. The most important genres were the *theme and variations* and the *suite*; many works of either genre were suitable for any keyboard instrument.

The statement of a theme (air, dance, chorale, or the like) followed by a series of variations goes back to the early history of instrumental music. Composers after 1650 preferred to write an original songlike theme (often called an *aria*) rather than follow the earlier practice of borrowing a familiar tune.

Theme and variations

Suites comprised a large proportion of later Baroque keyboard music. Two distinct kinds emerged: the amorphous collections produced by the French clavecinists, and the German variety clustered around four standard dances. By 1700, the clavier suite (or *partita*) in Germany had assumed a definite order of four dances: allemande, courante, sarabande, and gigue. To these might be added an introductory movement or one or more optional dances placed either after the gigue or before or after the sarabande. The international character of the suite is striking: the allemande is probably of German origin, the courante French, the sarabande Spanish (imported from Mexico), and the gigue Anglo-Irish. The four standard dance movements are all in different meters but have the same key and the same two-section, or binary, form.

Suite

◄ Double-manual harpsichord built by Michel Richard, Paris, 1688. (*New Haven, Yale University, Collection of Musical Instruments, The Albert Steinert Collection. Photo copyright 1995 by Thomas A. Brown*)

**Jacquet
de la Guerre**

Two representative composers of suites in France were Elisabeth-Claude Jacquet de la Guerre (1665–1729), and François Couperin (1668–1733). Jacquet de la Guerre earned an enviable reputation as a singer and harpsichordist and as a composer of cantatas, church music, and works for harpsichord and chamber ensembles. A Parisian critic hailed her as "the marvel of our century." Couperin, who wrote in all of these media and for the organ as well, published twenty-seven groups of clavecin pieces, which he called *ordres* (ironic given that they were not as "ordered" as their German counterparts).

Characteristic Dances of the German Suite

The *allemande* is usually in a moderately fast duple meter; it begins with a short upbeat and presents a smooth, continuous movement of eighth and/or sixteenth notes in which all the voices participate (see Froberger's *Lamentation*, NAWM 67).

The typical *courante* is in a moderate compound duple or compound triple meter ($^6_4$ or $^3_2$) or shifts between the two (see Example 11.2). The hemiola resulting from such shifting is particularly effective at cadences. Sometimes the French courante is replaced in suites by the Italian *corrente*, a faster dance in $^3_4$ time with a more homophonic texture.

EXAMPLE 11.2 Elisabeth-Claude Jacquet de la Guerre, Courante, from *Pièces de clavecin*, 1687

The *sarabande* is a slow movement in $\frac{3}{2}$ or $\frac{6}{4}$ meter, often with the rhythmic pattern ♩ ♩. ♩ | ♩ 𝅝 or ♩ ♩ ♩ | ♩. ♪ ♩, with emphasis on the second beat (Example 11.3). It is generally more homophonic than the allemande and courante. A *double*, an ornamented variation of the original dance, sometimes follows the sarabande.

EXAMPLE 11.3   Elisabeth-Claude Jacquet de la Guerre, Sarabande, from *Pièces de clavecin*, 1687

The *gigue*, usually the final number of the suite, may be in $\frac{12}{8}$, $\frac{6}{8}$, or $\frac{6}{4}$ (sometimes, $\frac{3}{8}$, $\frac{3}{4}$, or even $\frac{4}{4}$), with wide melodic skips and continuous lively triplets. Quite often the style is fugal or quasi-fugal (Example 11.4). The second section may use an inversion of the first section's theme.

EXAMPLE 11.4   Elisabeth-Claude Jacquet de la Guerre, Gigue, from *Pièces de clavecin*, 1687

Source of examples: Carol Henry Bates, ed., *Pièces de clavecin* (Paris: Heugel, HE 32629), pp. 32, 34, 35.

The *ordres* of François Couperin each comprise a loose aggregation of as many as twenty or more miniature pieces. Most are in dance rhythms, such as courante, sarabande, gigue, and the like, and are highly stylized and refined. Their transparent texture, their delicate melodic lines decorated with many embellishments, and their conciseness and humor are typical of French music

Couperin's **ordres**

from the Regency period. Most of them carry fanciful titles, as in Couperin's *Vingt-cinquième ordre* from his fourth book for clavecin, 1730 (Twenty-fifth Ordre, NAWM 75): *La Visionaire* (The Dreamer), *La Misterieuse* (The Mysterious One), and *La Monflambert* (probably named after Anne Darboulin, who married Monflambert, the king's wine merchant). *La Visionaire*, the first movement of this set, is a whimsical French overture. *La Misterieuse* is a more proper allemande in $\frac{4}{4}$, with mainly steady sixteenth-note motion. It takes the typical binary dance form, the first half modulating to the dominant. All these pieces were intended as recreation for amateur performers.

Passacaglia and chaconne

Another element that made its way into the suite is the *passacaglia* or *chaconne*, a type of variation form. The chaconne, a stately movement in triple rhythm, was made popular by Lully's stage music (see Chapter 10). As in the ground, it uses a repeating bass line and harmonic pattern. All sorts of refinements could be imposed on the basic scheme. Often no distinction was made between the chaconne and passacaglia, as in the *Passacaille ou Chaconne* from Couperin's first Suite for Viols (1728), which maintains the regular phrasing of 4 + 4 measures for 199 measures (see Example 11.5a), but with numerous variations and alterations in the pattern.

EXAMPLE 11.5   François Couperin, *Passacaille ou Chaconne* from Suite No. 1 for Viols

a. (m. 1)

The lower line of music is for the second viol, together with the harpsichord realizing the basso continuo.

b. Some of Couperin's *agréments;* according to his *Explication,* they are to be interpreted as follows:

c. Since each ornament begins on the beat and takes its time value from the note to which it is attached, the upper line of part a of this example would be played approximately as shown here.

C H R O N O L O G Y

1680	1710
*Arcangelo Corelli, publication of Op. 1, Twelve trio *sonate da chiesa* (1681)	*Death of Corelli (b. 1653) (1713)
Birth of Johann Sebastian Bach (d. 1750) and George Frideric Handel (d. 1759) (1685)	*Construction of Freiburg organ by Gottfried Silbermann (1683–1753) (1714)
Lully, *Armide* (1686)	Death of Louis XIV; crowning of Louis XV and beginning of Regency (until 1723) of Philippe II, duc d'Orleans (1715)
*Elisabeth Jacquet de la Guerre (1665–1729), *Pièces de clavecin* (1687)	Jean Antoine Watteau, *The Shepherds* (see Plate VIII, facing page 227) (ca. 1717)
1690	**1720**
Salem witchcraft trials in Massachusetts (1692)	*J. S. Bach, *The Well-Tempered Keyboard*, Part I (1722)
Death of Henry Purcell (b. 1659) (1695)	Death of Alessandro Scarlatti (b. 1660) (1725)
1700	
*Death of Dietrich Buxtehude (b. ca. 1637) (1707)	**1730**
*Giuseppe Torelli (1658–1709), Op. 8, Twelve concertos (1709)	*Death of Antonio Stradivari (b. 1644) (1737)

The characteristic ornaments or agréments of both the keyboard and ensemble music from this period are indicated in the scores by certain signs that the performer must interpret. Example 11.5b and c illustrate some of these signs and how they might be played. In his *L'Art de toucher le clavecin* (The Art of Playing the Harpsichord, 1716), one of the most important practical musical treatises of the eighteenth century, Couperin gave precise and detailed instructions for fingering and executing the agréments and discussed other aspects of clavecin performance as well.

Ensemble Music

Ensemble sonatas

The word *sonata* appears regularly on Italian title pages throughout the seventeenth century. In the earlier decades the term (like the parallel word, *sinfonia*) chiefly denoted instrumental preludes or interludes in predominantly vocal works. After 1630 the two terms were used more and more often to designate separate instrumental compositions. The early stages of the sonata's emergence from the canzona have been sketched in Chapter 9.

The typical instrumental sonata is a composition with several sections or movements in contrasting tempos and textures, and scored for two to four solo instruments and basso continuo. Within this general scheme, we can distinguish two main types after about 1660. The *sonata da chiesa*, or church sonata, had a mixture of abstract movements and dancelike movements. The *sonata da camera*, or chamber sonata, was essentially a suite of stylized dances, though the opening movement was not always a dance. After 1670 both

Emergence of the Baroque Sonata

*I*n the seventeenth-century canzona/sonata, movements increased in length and decreased in number. Traces of the old cyclical variation-canzona survived for many years, and the order of the movements did not become standardized until the end of the century. Giovanni Battista Vitali (ca. 1644–1692) preserved thematic similarity between the movements of many of his sonatas, as did his son Tommaso Antonio Vitali (ca. 1665–1747). However, complete thematic independence of the various movements increasingly became the rule in the late seventeenth century; the principle is illustrated in Giovanni Legrenzi's sonata *La Raspona* (NAWM 76). It consists of two movements, Allegro and Adaggio [*sic*], each of which has a canzona-like structure and a combination of fugal and nonfugal textures.

Trio sonatas

church and chamber sonatas were typically scored for two treble instruments (usually violins) and bass; the harmonies were realized by the continuo player reading the bass part. This type of sonata was called a *trio sonata*, even though it required four players (since the basso continuo line was performed on a cello or other bass instrument while the harpsichordist or organist filled in the implied harmonies). The texture described for the trio sonata—two high melody lines over a bass—remained standard in many other types of chamber music, both vocal and instrumental.

Solo sonatas

Solo sonatas, for solo violin (or flute or viola da gamba) with continuo, were at first less numerous than trio sonatas but gained in popularity after 1700. Composers also began writing sonatas for larger groups—up to eight instrumental parts with continuo—as well as a few for unaccompanied stringed or wind instruments.

Arcangelo Corelli

The violin sonatas of Arcangelo Corelli (1653–1713) are perfect examples of the serene, classical phase of seventeenth-century musical style. Corelli, a well-known performer as well as composer, studied for four years at Bologna and thoroughly assimilated the craft of the Bolognese masters. After 1671 he spent most of his life tranquilly in Rome, in the artistic circle of Queen Christina of Sweden (see window, pages 244–45). His published works consist entirely of ensemble music for the violin:

   Opus 1. Twelve trio sonatas (sonate da chiesa), 1681;
   Opus 2. Eleven trio sonate da camera and a chaconne, 1685;
   Opus 3. Twelve trio sonate da chiesa, 1689;

Opus 4. Twelve trio sonate da camera, 1695;

Opus 5. Twelve solo sonatas (six da chiesa, five da camera, and one set of variations), 1700; and

Opus 6. Twelve concerti grossi, 1714 (composed before 1700, some probably as early as 1682).

Corelli's trio sonatas were the crowning achievement of Italian chamber music in the late seventeenth century. Moreover, his solo sonatas and concertos served as models that composers followed for the next half century. Unlike his compatriots, he apparently wrote no vocal music at all but sang through the violin, the instrument that most nearly approaches the lyric quality of the human voice. As if acknowledging this relationship, Corelli deliberately kept the two violins in his trio sonatas from virtuosic displays. He never required a player to reach beyond the third position and seldom called for extremely low notes, fast runs, or difficult double stops. The two violins, treated exactly alike, constantly cross and exchange ideas, often involving interlocking suspensions that give his works a decisive forward momentum.

Trio sonatas

Corelli relied on sequences to achieve clear tonal organization. Whether constructed diatonically within one key or modulating downward in the circle of fifths, the sequence is a powerful agent for establishing tonality. Corelli's modulations within a movement—most often to the dominant and (in minor keys) the relative major—are always logical and straightforward. The principles of tonal architecture that he developed were further elaborated and extended by Handel, Vivaldi, Bach, and other composers of the next generation. Corelli's music is almost completely diatonic: chromaticism is limited to the rare diminished seventh or the occasional flatted (Neapolitan) sixth at a cadence.

Harmonic sequences

Many of Corelli's church trio sonatas consist of four movements in the same slow-fast-slow-fast order favored by other composers of the late Baroque. But this pattern has many exceptions and should not be taken as a standard. The first slow movement of a typical church sonata has a contrapuntal texture and a majestic, solemn character. The Allegro that follows is usually a fugue. This movement is the musical center of gravity for the church sonata, and it most obviously retains traits of the canzona—in its imitative style, its rhythmic character of the subject, and its modification of the subject after the exposition. (In some of Purcell's sonatas, for instance, a movement like this is actually called "canzona.") The middle slow movement most often resembles a triple-time operatic aria or duet. The last movement is usually a carefree dance in binary form.

Church sonatas

Corelli's chamber sonatas, both trio and solo, typically begin with a *preludio*, after which two or three dances follow in the normal suite order, with a gavotte sometimes replacing the final gigue. In many of Corelli's chamber sonatas, the first two movements retain the serious character of the church sonata as well as its outward forms. They also remind us of the French overture: a slow introduction with persistent dotted rhythms, followed by an imitative, canzona-like Allegro. The combination of slow introduction and fugal

Chamber sonatas

Allegro followed by a series of dances was common in this genre. The dance movements are almost always in binary form, the first section (played twice) closing on the dominant or relative major and the second section (also repeated) making its way back to the tonic.

Unity of key

Like his contemporaries, Corelli kept all the movements of a trio sonata in the same key, but in all his later major-key solo sonatas, he cast one slow movement in the relative minor. Similarly, every concerto grosso has a slow movement in a contrasting key.

Unity of theme

In general, Corelli's movements are thematically independent; there are no contrasting or "secondary" themes within a movement. He states the subject of the whole musical discourse at the outset in a complete sentence with a definite—often Phrygian—cadence. The music then unfolds in a continuous expansion of this subject, with sequential treatment, brief modulations closing in nearby keys, and fascinating subtleties of phrasing. This steady spinning-out of a single theme is highly characteristic of the late Baroque. Unlike the procedures used by later composers for developing motives from a theme, the original idea seems to generate a spontaneous flow of musical thoughts. Corelli often stated the last phrase of a movement twice, as though avoiding too abrupt an ending.

Corelli's Trio Sonata (da chiesa), Op. 3, No. 2 (NAWM 77) illustrates some of these points. In the first movement, marked Grave, the two violins imitate each other, meet repeatedly in suspensions, separate, and cross each other over a walking bass. The following Allegro has a lively fugue subject that soon dissolves in a continuous stream of counterpoint. The middle slow movement is like a sarabande in which the two violins hold an intense dialogue. The final movement, simply labeled Allegro, is a gigue in binary form. Like the first Allegro, it is fugal in conception, and the subject of the second half is an inversion of the opening of the first half.

Solo sonatas

The movements of Corelli's solo sonatas correspond to those of the church and chamber trio sonatas. In the first Allegro, the solo violin employs double and triple stops to simulate the rich three-part sonority of the trio sonata. In general, the solo violin part demands some virtuosity to execute fast runs, arpeggios, cadenzas, and extended perpetual-motion passages.

Improvisation in musical performance

Performers in the Baroque era were always expected to add to, or improvise over, what the composer had written. For example, keyboard players realized figured basses by improvising chords, arpeggios, and even counterpoints. Vocal and instrumental solo performers applied skill, taste, and experience to achieve the full effect of the music by means of ornaments and embellishments. Such impromptu additions varied from country to country and from one generation to another. Modern scholars, conductors, and performers who have tried to reconstruct these performance practices have found the task complex, delicate, and controversial.

Influence outside Italy

Composers all over Europe, especially the English composer Henry Purcell, were greatly influenced by Italian trio sonatas and freely imitated or adapted them. Handel's trio sonatas, for example, resemble Corelli's in their

Baroque Ornamentation

Ornaments usually originated in improvisation. Even though they might be written out later or at least indicated by special symbols (as in Example 11.5), ornaments still retained a certain spontaneity. For us the word *ornamentation* suggests an unessential or superfluous process, but Baroque musicians saw it differently. In their view, ornaments were not merely decorative; they were an important means for moving the affections. Also, some of the dissonant ornaments—especially the trill and the appoggiatura—added a certain spice that the notated music lacked.

Musicians recognized two principal ways of ornamenting a given melodic line: (1) Small melodic formulas, such as trills, turns, appoggiaturas, and mordents, were attached to one or two written notes. Special signs sometimes, though not always, indicated their placement. (2) More extended embellishments, such as scales, runs, leaps, arpeggios, and the like were added to make up a free and elaborate paraphrase of the written line. This process, sometimes called *division, diminution,* or *figuration,* was most appropriate for melodies in slow tempo. Embellished versions of slow movements from Corelli's solo sonatas have been preserved in a 1710 edition by Estienne Roger of Amsterdam (see facsimile). Roger claimed that his edition represented the way the composer himself played the sonatas. Whether or not these ornamented versions were Corelli's own, they surely reflected embellishment practices of his time.

◄ The Adagio of Corelli's Sonata Op. 5, No. 3 in the edition printed about 1711 for John Walsh, London, and based on a 1710 edition by Estienne Roger, Amsterdam. The violin part is given both as originally published and in an embellished version said to represent the way Corelli himself performed it. (*Yale University Music Library. Used by permission*)

Performers thus had the liberty to add to the composer's written score; they were equally free to subtract from it or change it in various other ways. Arias were omitted from operas, or different arias substituted, almost at the whim of the singers. Frescobaldi permitted organists to end his toccatas at any appropriate point they pleased. Composers of variations, suites, and sonatas took it for granted that movements would be omitted *ad libitum*. Title pages of ensemble collections encouraged players to choose which instruments and even how many to use for a performance. For example, sonatas were issued for violin and basso continuo with an additional violin or two "if desired," and string concertos could be played as trio sonatas.

F. Couperin

four-movement form and compositional approach. Some of the earliest and the most important trio sonatas in France were by François Couperin, probably dating from 1692, although not published until many years later. His collection *Les Nations: Sonades et suites de simphonies en trio* (1726) contains four ordres, each consisting of a multi-movement sonata da chiesa (the *sonade* of the title) followed by a suite of dances (the *suite de simphonies*). The style, though obviously influenced by Corelli and other Italians, is distinguished throughout by the refined melody and exquisite taste in ornaments that mark Couperin's clavecin pieces.

Couperin on the Union of the Italian and French Styles:

❝ The Italian and French styles have long divided up the Republic of Music in France. As for me, I have always esteemed the things that deserved to be, without regard to the composer or nation. The first Italian sonatas that appeared in Paris more than thirty years ago and encouraged me to start composing some myself, to my mind wronged neither the works of Monsieur de Lully nor those of my ancestors, who will always be more admirable than imitable. Thus, by a right that my neutrality confers upon me, I sail under the happy star that has guided me until now.

Since Italian music has the right of seniority over ours, at the end of this volume you will find a grand trio sonata titled *L'Apothéose de Corelli*. A feeble spark of self-love persuaded me to present it in score. If some day my muse outdoes itself, I shall dare to undertake likewise something in the style of the incomparable Lully, although his works alone ought to suffice to immortalize him. ❞

From François Couperin, Preface, *Les Goûts-réünis* (Paris, 1724). The original French is in *Oeuvres complètes*, Vol. 8, ed. André Schaeffner.

Couperin admired the works of both Lully and Corelli, and he maintained a neutral position in the raging controversy over the respective merits of French versus Italian music. Through the titles, prefaces, and choice of contents for his published collections he demonstrated his belief that the perfect music would be a union of the two national styles (see vignette, page 242). Two other trio suites hold to this ideal: *Parnassus, or the Apotheosis of Corelli*, and *The Apotheosis of Lully*. In the second, Lully is represented as joining Corelli on Parnassus, where they play the first and second violins in a French overture and in the trio sonata that follows. To another set of suites intended for harpsichord and various combinations of instruments Couperin gave the collective title *Les Goûts-réünis*, signifying that these works united the two principal styles (*goûts*), the French and Italian.

Larger Ensembles

From the days of Giovanni Gabrieli through about 1650, Italy produced a steady stream of canzonas, dance suites, sonatas, and sinfonias for groups of three or more melody instruments plus basso continuo. Many Venetian sonatas of this period resemble the contemporary Venetian opera overtures. The Bolognese composers in the late seventeenth century also wrote works for larger groups which in form and style resembled either the trio sonata or the concerto.

The ensemble sonata and, more especially, the instrumental suite had a particularly long life in Germany, where musical traditions frequently became part of everyday life. German composers preferred relatively large ensembles and liked the sound of wind instruments as well as strings. *Collegia musica* (associations of performers) in many German towns offered citizens the opportunity to play and sing together for their own pleasure. Town bands (*Stadtpfeifer*) and, in Lutheran regions, church musicians enriched the ordinary lives of the people. In some places, chorales or sonatas called *Turmsonaten* (tower sonatas) were played daily on wind instruments from the tower of a Rathaus (town hall) or church.

Ensemble music in Germany

Toward the end of the seventeenth century, a generally recognized distinction arose between *chamber* music—ensemble music with only one instrument to a part—and *orchestral* music. Prior to that composers did not express their preferences, and the choice depended on circumstances. For instance, an orchestral ensemble might play a trio sonata da chiesa scored for two solo violins if the size of the auditorium made it desirable or if the occasion were festive. But neither the designation "sinfonia" or "concerto" nor the presence of three, four, or more melodic parts above the bass *necessarily* called for an orchestra rather than a chamber group of players. Beyond the use of basso continuo and the predominance of stringed instruments, no common standard regulated either the makeup of an ensemble or the number of instruments to a part.

Orchestral music

Opera houses, of course, maintained orchestras, so opera overtures in

QUEEN CHRISTINA OF SWEDEN AND HER CIRCLE

In 1681 Arcangelo Corelli dedicated his first opus, twelve trio sonatas (da chiesa), to Queen Christina of Sweden (1626–1689):

If Your Majesty will have the generosity, as I hope, to both receive with favor and support these first fruits of my studies, it will renew my strength to continue with my other works, which are already in draft; and to make known to the world that perhaps I am not wrong to aspire to the glorious position of Your Majesty's servant. . . .

Who was this eminence whom Corelli hoped would become his patron?

Nearly thirty years earlier, Christina had abdicated her throne, left Sweden dressed as a man, converted to Catholicism, and in 1655 established her court-in-exile in Rome where, until her death in 1689, she presided as an independent thinker, avid book collector, and beneficent patron. In Rome, Christina founded at least two academies that attracted scholars and poets, theologians and philosophers, librettists and composers, as well as members of the Roman aristocracy. She encouraged open discussion of ethical and scientific questions at a time when Galileo's theories were still taboo. She supported theatrical and operatic performances around the city, right under the nose of the reigning Pope Innocent XI, who was oppressively hostile to the stage. And she regularly sponsored concerts at her palace, which became an important center in the city's musical life. Among others, Alessandro Scarlatti, who had just begun his long career as a composer of operas and cantatas (see pages 211 and 218), was employed by Christina. He described himself in 1680 as her *maestro di cappella*, a position he held until his departure for Naples in 1684.

One of the foremost violinists in Rome, Arcangelo Corelli (see pages 238 ff.) also became a protégé of Christina, as he had hoped in the dedication to his Opus 1 quoted above. After entering her service as a chamber musician, he attracted her attention by composing and performing sonatas for her acad-

both Italy and France, as well as the numerous dances that formed an indispensable part of French opera, were always written specifically for orchestral performance. Lully brought the Paris orchestra, the most famous in Europe, to a height of technical perfection that was previously unknown for so large a group of instrumental performers.

Lully's German disciples introduced French standards of playing, along emy. When Christina organized a huge concert at her palace in honor of the new English ambassador to the Holy See, she asked Corelli to conduct an orchestra of 150 string players and an ensemble of more than 100 singers and soloists lent by the pope. On this magnificent occasion, there were seats for 150 ladies, and the number of gentlemen who were left standing was even greater. In 1689 Corelli again directed a large group of performers in two solemn Masses to celebrate Christina's apparent recovery from illness. Unfortunately, she died one month later.

Christina was among the most prominent intellectuals of her day, as suggested by the painting in which, surrounded by scholars and clerics, she engages the philosopher René Descartes (1596–1650) in animated discussion (see illustration).

➤ This detail, from a seventeenth-century painting by Pierre Dumesnil, shows a youthful Queen Christina of Sweden (seated to the left of the table) presiding in the company of scholars, clerics, and others in her circle. Standing opposite her is René Descartes. (*Courtesy of Giraudon/ Art Resource, NY*)

with the French musical style, into their own country. One result was a new type of *orchestral suite* that flourished in Germany from about 1690 to 1740. The dances of these suites, patterned after those of Lully's ballets and operas, did not appear in any standard number or order. Because they were always introduced by a pair of movements in the form of a French overture, the word *ouverture* soon came to designate the suite itself. Among the early col-

The orchestral suite

lections of orchestral suites was Georg Muffat's *Florilegium* (1695 and 1698), which includes an essay with musical examples about the French system of bowing, the playing of agréments, and similar matters. A host of other German composers, including J. S. Bach, wrote overture suites.

The concerto

The concerto, a new kind of orchestral composition that appeared in the 1680s and 1690s, soon became the most important type of Baroque orchestral music. It afforded composers the chance to combine in one work several favorite traits: the contrasts of the *concertato* medium; the texture of a firm bass and a florid treble; the musical organization based on the major-minor key system; and the construction of a longer work from several separate movements.

Composers wrote several kinds of orchestral concertos around 1700, the most numerous and important of which were the *concerto grosso* and the *solo concerto*. Both types systematically exploited the contrast in sonority between many instruments and one or only a few. The concerto grosso set a small ensemble of solo instruments, the *concertino*, against a large ensemble, the *concerto grosso*. In the solo concerto a single instrument contrasted with the large ensemble. The large group was almost always a string orchestra, usually divided into first and second violins, violas, cellos, and bass viols, with basso continuo. The solo instruments were also usually strings: in the solo concerto, a violin; in the concerto grosso, most often two violins and continuo, though other solo string or wind instruments might be added or substituted. In both the solo concerto and the concerto grosso, the full orchestra was designated *tutti* (all) or *ripieno* (full).

Corelli's concertos

The concerti grossi of Corelli, among the earliest examples of the genre, employ soli-tutti contrasts in a special way: his concertos are in effect church sonatas or chamber sonatas divided between soli and tutti, in which the larger group echoes the smaller, fortifies cadential passages, or otherwise punctuates the structure. The relative prominence of the first violin part occasionally suggests the texture of the later solo concerto.

Concerto in Germany

German composers similarly adopted the form and style of the sonata in their earliest concerti grossi. Georg Muffat wrote in 1701 that he first encountered this new genre in Rome and decided to try his hand at it. Well into the eighteenth century, many concertos continued to exhibit at least one characteristic of the sonata: the fugal or quasi-fugal Allegro. Concerti grossi tended to be conservative, and many composers shared Corelli's conception of them as sonatas with the musical substance divided between concertino (soli) and ripieno (tutti). But in the solo concerto, composers experimented with new rhythmic ideas, textures, and formal schemes.

G. Torelli

Giuseppe Torelli (1658–1709), a leading figure in the Bologna school, contributed most to the development of the concerto around the turn of the century. The six violin concertos of Torelli's Opus 8 (1709), which also includes six concerti grossi, represent a significant stage in the evolution of a new type of concerto that departs from Corelli's model. Most of Torelli's are in three movements in the order fast-slow-fast, a succession adopted by later concerto composers. Each of the Allegro movements begins with a ritornello that develops one or more motives in the full orchestra. This leads to a solo episode that presents entirely new material, after which the tutti recalls some part of the ritornello in a different key. This alternation may recur several times before the movement is rounded off and brought to a close with a final tutti in the tonic almost identical to the opening ritornello.

The term *ritornello* is derived from vocal music, where it meant refrain. Indeed, Torelli's scheme is reminiscent of the da capo aria, with the important exception that the solo instrument or concertino replaces the voice. This ritornello structure provided the master plan for the first and last movements of the concertos of Torelli, Vivaldi, and some of their contemporaries. A typical scheme is illustrated by the diagram below, which sketches a movement consisting of an opening ritornello, two modulating solo sections separated by an abbreviated statement of the ritornello in the relative major, and a repetition of the opening ritornello to close the movement:

Ritornello

Tutti		Soli	Tutti		Soli		Tutti	
Ritornello I		Solo I	Ritornello II		Solo II		Ritornello III	
Motives: a	b		a	b			a b	
Key: i	i	v	III		iv	v$_7$	i	i

The achievements of Torelli in the realm of the concerto were matched and extended by other Italian composers, especially the Venetian Tomaso Albinoni (1671–1750) and the Italian-German Evaristo Felice dall'Abaco (1675–1742). The greatest master of the Italian concerto of the late Baroque period was Antonio Vivaldi, whose works we will study in the next chapter.

Other composers of concerti

POSTLUDE

Two types of instrumental music became prominent during the second half of the seventeenth century: (1) solo keyboard music, especially that written for the great Baroque organs built in Germany; and (2) ensemble music, dominated by the violin, whose famous Italian makers also flourished during this period. Important genres of keyboard music included toccata and fugue, a variety of chorale-based compositions cultivated by Lutheran composers, stylized dance suites, and all sorts of variations, especially chaconne and passacaglia. Influential composers were Dietrich Buxtehude in Germany and François Couperin in France. Ensemble forms—sonatas for church and chamber, and concertos—emerged in Italian centers, such as Bologna and Rome, and from there spread throughout Europe. Pioneers in these genres were Arcangelo Corelli and Giuseppe Torelli. Although trio texture predominated, orchestral music began to have a life of its own in the opera overture and concerto, while soloists refined the art of ornamentation for expressive purposes as well as for virtuosic display.

Even though instrumental music explored and exploited the independent idioms of organ, harpsichord, and violin, composers still aimed to move the affections. How was this possible in the absence of words? They borrowed and adapted the already rich harmonic, melodic, and rhythmic vocabulary of vocal music, dance, and theatrical music, with all of its affective associations. With this essentially international, Baroque language, Corelli on the violin could lament as effectively as any operatic heroine; Couperin on the harpsichord could charm his listeners as elegantly as any ballet dancer; and Buxtehude on the organ could inspire awe as convincingly as a massive church choir.

12

MUSIC IN THE EARLY EIGHTEENTH CENTURY

The early eighteenth century, particularly the decades between 1720 and 1750, represents a period of stylistic turmoil in music. Rivalry between French and Italian music, as suggested in Chapter 11, was rife. At the same time, a new style of music was emerging that competed with the older, Baroque styles. This newer music—eventually described as *galant*—sounded more songful and less contrapuntal, more natural and less artificial, more sentimental and less intensely emotional than its Baroque counterpart. We will explore the *galant* style, an early stage of the Classical era, in the next chapter but its influence is already apparent in some of the later works by Vivaldi, Rameau, Bach, and Handel, the four masterful composers discussed in this chapter. Together, these four summarize and, to some extent, synthesize all the Baroque musical qualities and trends we have studied so far in Italy, France, Germany, and England.

All four composers were successful and eminent during their own time. All were aware of new currents in musical thought, and each found his own solution to the conflicts between contrapuntal and homophonic, older and more recent styles. All worked within the established genres of the late Baroque. **Antonio Vivaldi** excelled as a composer of concertos and operas. **Jean-Philippe Rameau** wrote opera and instrumental music in France and, in his theoretical writings, developed new ideas about harmony and tonality, some aspects of which were incorporated into later theory. **Johann Sebastian Bach**, somewhat isolated in Germany from the main European cultural centers, brought to consummation all forms of late Baroque music except opera. And **George Frideric Handel**, who also excelled in composing Italian opera, recognized the social changes in England that created the perfect climate for a new kind of oratorio—one that long outlived the audiences for which it was intended.

Antonio Vivaldi

Venice

At the beginning of the eighteenth century, Venice, though declining in political power and headed for economic ruin, still remained the most glamorous city in Europe. It was full of tourists, tradespeople, intellectuals, prostitutes, artists, and musicians—all attracted to its colorful, exuberant life. People sang on the streets and on the lagoons; gondoliers had their own repertory of songs (among them verses of Tasso declaimed to traditional melodies or airs); patrician families who owned opera theaters recognized and rewarded fine musicians and composers, and they themselves played and sang at private gatherings.

Public festivals, more numerous in Venice than elsewhere, remained occasions of musical splendor, and the musical establishment of St. Mark's was still famous. The city had always taken pride in its musical greatness—as a center of music printing, of church music, of instrumental composition, and of opera. Even in the eighteenth century, Venice never had fewer than six opera companies, which together played a total of thirty-four weeks in the year. Between 1700 and 1750 the Venetian public heard ten new operas annually (and the count was even higher in the second half-century). Outside the theaters private individuals, religious confraternities called *scuole*, and academies frequently sponsored musical programs. Services in the churches on festival days resembled great instrumental and vocal concerts more than they did religious ceremonies.

The Pietà

In addition to these musical establishments, Venice nurtured an unusual group of charitable institutions that specialized in musical training for orphaned, illegitimate, or abandoned children. Vivaldi was employed by one of these institutions, the Pio Ospedale della Pietà, a boarding school and conservatory for girls. Run like a convent, it provided excellent musical training for its young students and a first-class musical laboratory for the composer. Such institutions, through their teaching, had a notable impact on the musical life of the entire country. The concerts at the Pietà and other places of worship in Venice attracted large audiences. Travelers wrote of these occasions with enthusiasm and even amusement at the spectacle of a choir and orchestra comprised mainly of teenage girls (see Plate IX, facing page 274, and vignette below).

Vivaldi's life

Antonio Vivaldi (1678–1741), son of one of the leading violinists of St.

Charles de Brosses on the Concerts in Venice:

❝ A transcending music here is that of the hospitals [orphanages]. There are four, all made up of bastard or orphaned girls or whose parents are not in a condition to raise them. They are reared at public expense and trained solely to excel in music. So they sing like angels and play the violin, the flute, the organ, the violoncello, the bassoon. In short no instrument is large enough to frighten them. They are cloistered in the manner of nuns. They alone perform, and each concert is given by about forty girls. I swear to you that there is nothing so charming as to see a young and pretty nun in her white robe, with a bouquet of pomegranate flowers over her ear, leading the orchestra and beating time with all the grace and precision imaginable. Their voices are adorable for their quality and lightness, because here they don't know about roundness or a sound drawn out like a thread in the French manner. . . .

The hospital I go to most often is that of the Pietà, where one is best entertained. It is also first for the perfection of the symphonies. What an upright performance! It is only there that you hear the first stroke of the bow (*le premier coup d'archet*—the first chord of a piece attacked as one by the strings), of which the Opéra in Paris falsely boasts. ❞

Charles de Brosses, *L'Italie il y a cent ans ou Lettres écrites d'Italie à quelques amis en 1739 et 1740*, ed. M. R. Colomb (Paris: Alphonse Levavasseur, 1836), 1:213–14.

Mark's, was educated both for the priesthood and for music (under Legrenzi), not an unusual combination in those days. He was known as *il prete rosso* (the red[-headed] priest)—the sort of nickname that the Italian public often bestows on its favorite artists. From 1703 to 1740, Vivaldi was employed on and off as conductor, composer, teacher, and general superintendent of music at the Pio Ospedale della Pietà. He also traveled extensively, composing and conducting operas and concerts throughout Italy and Europe.

The eighteenth-century public constantly demanded new music; there were no "classics," and few works of any kind survived more than two or three seasons. Such relentless pressure accounts both for the vast output of many eighteenth-century composers and for the phenomenal speed at which they worked. Vivaldi was expected to furnish new oratorios and concertos for every church feast day at the Pietà and prided himself on being able to compose a concerto faster than a copyist could write out the parts. Like his contemporaries, Vivaldi composed every work for a definite occasion and for a particular company of performers. He fulfilled forty-nine opera commis-

Vivaldi's works

◄ Antonio Vivaldi (1678–1741), the red priest, drawn in Rome in 1723 by P. L. Ghezzi. It is the only authenticated portrait of the composer. (*The Lebrecht Collection, London*)

sions, most of them for Venice, and a few for Florence, Ferrara, Verona, Rome, Vienna, and elsewhere. Vivaldi also composed many concertos, a genre commonly used at church festival services, for the Pietà, but he dedicated a large number of them to foreign patrons. In addition to his operas, five hundred concertos and sinfonias survive, as well as ninety solo and trio sonatas, and many cantatas, motets, and oratorios.

Vocal works

Vivaldi is known today mainly for his orchestral music; the only works printed during his lifetime (mostly in Amsterdam) were about forty sonatas and a hundred concertos. It would be a mistake, however, to ignore his achievements in opera, cantata, motet, and oratorio. We know too little about Italian opera in the early eighteenth century to compare Vivaldi with others whose operas were produced in Venice at that time. But Vivaldi was certainly successful in his day: between 1713 and 1719, Venetian theaters staged more works by him than by any other composer, and his fame was not limited to his own city and country.

Concertos

Vivaldi's instrumental works, and especially the concertos, have a freshness of melody, a rhythmic drive, a skillful treatment of solo and orchestral color, and a clarity of form that have made them perennial favorites. Many of the sonatas, as well as some of the early concertos, betray their debt to Corelli. However, in his first published collection of concertos (Opus 3, ca. 1712) Vivaldi already showed that he was fully aware of the modern preference for the more distinct musical form, vigorous rhythm, and idiomatic solo writing that characterized the music of Torelli.

About two-thirds of Vivaldi's concertos are scored for one solo instrument with orchestra—most for violin, but a considerable number also for cello, flute, or bassoon. The concertos for two violins give the soloists equal prominence, producing the texture of a duet for two high voices. But many works that call for several solo instruments are, in effect, solo or duo concertos rather than genuine concerti grossi: Vivaldi singled out from the concertino one or two instruments and gave them particularly virtuosic passages.

Solo concertos

Vivaldi's orchestra at the Pietà consisted of some twenty to twenty-five stringed instruments, with harpsichord or organ for the continuo. This was always the basic group, though in many concertos he also called for flutes, oboes, bassoons, or horns, any of which might be used either as solo instruments or in ensemble combinations. The exact size and makeup of the orchestra depended on what players were available for a particular occasion. Vivaldi achieved a remarkable variety of color with different groupings of solo and orchestral strings. The familiar *Primavera* (Spring) concerto—the first of a group of four concertos in Opus 8 (1725) representing the four seasons—displays his extraordinary instinct for sonorities.

Instrumentation of the concertos

Most of Vivaldi's concertos follow the usual pattern of three movements: an Allegro; a slow movement in the same key or a closely related one (relative minor, dominant, or subdominant); and a final Allegro somewhat shorter and sprightlier than the first. Vivaldi abandoned the older fugal style in favor of a more homophonic rather than contrapuntal texture, emphasizing the two outer voices. In the fast movements, as in Torelli's, ritornellos for the full orchestra alternate with episodes for the soloist (or soloists). Vivaldi distinguished himself in the spontaneity of his musical ideas, his clear formal structures, assertive harmonies, varied textures, and forceful rhythms. He established a certain dramatic tension between solo and tutti, not only by giving the soloist contrasting figuration (as Torelli had already done), but also by letting the soloist prevail as a dominating musical personality. Vivaldi transferred the musical dialogue of the operatic ritornello, or da capo, aria—the exchange between singer and orchestra described in Chapter 10 (see page 211)—to the instrumental concerto.

Form of the concertos

Vivaldi's approach to the first Allegro is illustrated in the second movement (the first is an introductory Adagio) of the Concerto grosso in G minor, Op. 3, No. 2, RV 578[1] (NAWM 78b). The concertino consists of two violins

Form of the Allegro

---

1. There are several catalogues of Vivaldi's works, the most recent and reliable of which, known as "RV," is Peter Ryom, *Verzeichnis der Werke Antonio Vivaldis: kleine Ausgabe* (Leipzig, 1974; suppl., Poitiers, 1979).

and a cello. The opening ritornello has three distinct motivic sections (marked a, b, and c in Example 12.1), the last of which is an inverted counterpoint of the second. The solo sections contain mostly harmonic-melodic figuration, but the second solo section makes a veiled reference to the opening tutti motive. An unusual feature is that the closing ritornello reverses the order of the themes, with the concertino playing the opening one. This movement is also unusual because only one of the four main tutti is in a foreign key, D minor. Far from following a textbook plan, Vivaldi's Allegro structures show an almost infinite variety of invention.

EXAMPLE 12.1   Antonio Vivaldi, Concerto grosso Op. 3, No. 2, RV 578, Allegro (inner parts omitted)

By kind permission of Casa Ricordi, Milan.

Slow movements

Vivaldi became the first composer to make the slow movement as important as the two Allegros. His slow movement is typically a long-breathed, expressive, cantabile melody, like an adagio operatic aria or arioso, to which the performer was expected to add embellishments. The slow movements of the later concertos are particularly forward-looking. The Largo (NAWM 79) from the Concerto for Violin, Op. 9, No. 2 (1728), exhibits many features of the early Classic style: trills, triplets, balanced phrases, frequent half cadences clarifying the structure, and cadences softened by appoggiaturas.

Changing style

Vivaldi's music parallels the stylistic changes of the first half of the eighteenth century. At the conservative extreme are some of the sonatas and concertos in the style of Corelli; at the progressive extreme are the solo concerto finales, the orchestral concertos (those without solo instruments), and

▲ A page from one of Vivaldi's manuscripts—a tutti section from the finale of the Concerto in A for solo violin and four-part string ensemble.

most of the twenty-three *sinfonias*—works that establish Vivaldi as a founder of the Classic symphony. The concise form, the markedly homophonic texture, the melodically simple themes, the minuet finale—all these traits thought to have been invented by German composers of the Mannheim school in the next generation—had already appeared in Vivaldi's works.

Jean-Philippe Rameau

Despite the stultifying influence of Louis XIV's absolute rule, Paris in the early eighteenth century was a musical crossroads where the public could enjoy the latest from Italy as well as from native composers. Besides the royal court, the leading patron of the arts, and especially of music, was Alexandre Jean-Joseph Le Riche de la Pouplinière (1693–1762), who supported an orchestra, sponsored concerts for the wealthy, and took pleasure in promoting the careers of obscure musicians. One of his biggest successes was Jean-Philippe Rameau (1683–1764), who subsequently became the foremost French musician of the century. Descendant of an ancient and noble French

La Pouplinière

C H R O N O L O G Y	
1700	**1720**
*George Frideric Handel (1685–1759) in Hamburg (1703) *Johann Sebastian Bach (1685–1750) travels to Lübeck to hear Buxtehude (1705) *J. S. Bach in Weimar (1708)	*J. S. Bach, *The Well-Tempered Keyboard,* Part I (1722) *Jean-Philippe Rameau (1683–1764), *Traité de l'harmonie* (1722) *J. S. Bach in Leipzig (1723) *Handel, *Giulio Cesare* (1724)
1710	*Vivaldi, *The Seasons;* Jonathan Swift (1667–1745), *Gulliver's Travels* (1726)
*Handel, *Rinaldo* in London; Charles VI crowned Holy Roman Emperor (1711) *Antonio Vivaldi (1678–1741) Concertos, Op. 3 (1712) The elector of Hanover (Handel's patron) crowned George I of England (1714) *J. S. Bach in Cöthen (1717) Jean Watteau (1684–1721), *The Shepherds* (Plate VIII, facing page 227) (ca. 1717)	George II of England crowned (1727) John Gay (1685–1732), *Beggar's Opera* (1728) *J. S. Bach, *St. Matthew Passion* (1729)
1730	
1740	*Rameau, *Hippolyte et Aricie* (1733) Frederick the Great of Prussia crowned *Handel, *Messiah* (1742) *J. S. Bach, *The Art of Fugue* (1749)

family, La Pouplinière had inherited an immense fortune that he increased by speculation. He maintained several residences in Paris as well as houses in the country nearby. His salon attracted a motley company of aristocrats, writers (Voltaire and J.-J. Rousseau), painters (Van Loo and La Tour), adventurers (Casanova), and above all, musicians.

Rameau's life

Rameau entered this circle fairly late in life. He was practically unknown before the age of forty, first attracting attention as a theorist and only afterward as a composer. In fact, Rameau composed most of his famous musical works between the ages of fifty and fifty-six. Attacked then as a radical, he was assailed twenty years later even more severely as a reactionary. He enjoyed the favor of the French court and was reasonably prosperous during the later years of his life, always remaining a solitary, argumentative, and unsociable person but a conscientious and intelligent artist.

From his father, an organist in Dijon, Rameau received his first and, as far as we know, only formal musical instruction. After holding provincial posts for two decades, he published his famous *Traité de l'harmonie* (Treatise on Harmony) in 1722 and then returned to Paris. Only there could a composer achieve true success and reputation, and the high road for a composer—indeed the only road to real fame—was the opera. Rameau's prospects were poor: he had neither money nor influential friends, nor the disposition of a good courtier. Seeking better opportunities, he wrote airs and dances for three or four little musical comedies, pieces with spoken dialogue performed at the popular theaters of Paris. He published some cantatas and several books of clavecin pieces. Meanwhile, his reputation as a teacher and organist began to attract students. Finally, Rameau's luck changed when in 1731 he was appointed La Pouplinière's organist, conductor, and composer-in-residence, a position he held until 1753.

La Pouplinière helped Rameau make his name as an opera composer. He funded a production of *Hippolyte et Aricie*, which was performed privately in 1733 before being produced in Paris later the same year. A more distinct success came in 1735 with Rameau's opera-ballet *Les Indes galantes* (The Gallant Indies). Two years later Rameau composed *Castor et Pollux*, the opera that is usually regarded as his masterpiece. From the first, his operas stirred up a storm of critical controversy. The Paris intelligentsia, always eager for a battle of words, divided into two noisy camps, one supporting Rameau and the other attacking him as a subverter of the good old French opera tradition of Lully. The Lullists found Rameau's music difficult, forced, grotesque, thick, mechanical, and unnatural—in a word, baroque. Rameau protested, in a foreword to *Les Indes galantes*, that he had "sought to imitate Lully, not as a servile copyist but in taking, like him, nature herself—so beautiful and so simple—as a model."

Rameau's operas

Polemical writings and further theoretical essays occupied Rameau's closing years. He died in Paris in 1764; feisty to the end, he found strength even on his deathbed to reproach the priest, who came to administer the last rites, for poor chanting.

◄ Jean-Philippe Rameau, in a copy by Jacques Aved of the portrait by Chardin. (*The Lebrecht Collection, London*)

Rameau's
theoretical works

Throughout his life, Rameau was interested in the theory or, as it was called at the time, the "science" of music. In his various writings he sought to derive the basic principles of harmony from the laws of acoustics. He not only clarified the musical practice of his time but also influenced music theory for the next two hundred years.

Characteristics
of French opera

French opera after Lully acquired an ever larger proportion of decorative elements: scenic spectacle, descriptive orchestral music, dances, choruses, and songs. The dramatic element, even in works called *tragédies lyriques*, had deteriorated in both importance and quality, and eventually opera-ballet lost all but the thinnest thread of continuity between dramatic scenes. For example, Rameau's *Les Indes galantes*, one of his most frequently performed works in modern times, had four *entrées* or acts, each with a self-contained plot located in a different quarter of the globe. It presented a variety of decorations and dances that gratified the early-eighteenth-century French public's interest in exotic scenes and peoples. The entrée "The Generous Turk," set in "an island of the Indian Ocean," has a plot outline later used by Mozart for his *Abduction from the Seraglio*. The other entrées were "The Incas of Peru," "The Flowers, a Persian Festival," and "The Savages," which takes place in "a forest of

A Synopsis of Rameau's Most Important Musical Theories

(1) A chord is the primal element in music. When a string is divided into two, three, four, and five equal parts, the tones of a major triad are generated. (Later, Rameau realized that the overtone series supported his beliefs. He had more difficulty using "natural principles" to account for the minor triad, though he did establish the so-called melodic minor scale.)

(2) Chords are built up by thirds within the octave, so that triads can be expanded to seventh chords, and beyond the octave to ninth and eleventh chords.

(3) The *basse fondamentale*, or root-progression, controls a succession of harmonies. (Rameau also recognized the identity of a chord through all its inversions.)

(4) The tonic, dominant, and subdominant chords are pillars of tonality. By relating other chords to these, Rameau established the hierarchies of functional harmony.

(5) Modulation results from the change of function of a chord (in modern terminology, a pivot chord).

America" and introduces Spanish and French characters as well as native people. Rameau's music, however, is far more dramatic than the libretto would suggest.

The musical features of Rameau's theater works resemble Lully's in several ways: both exhibit realistic declamation and precise rhythmic notation in the recitatives; both mix recitative with more tuneful, formally organized airs, choruses, and instrumental interludes; and both include frequent long scenes of divertissement. In addition, the form of the overture in Rameau's early operas is the same as Lully's. But within this general framework, Rameau introduced many changes, so that the resemblance between his music and Lully's is largely superficial.

Rameau's musical style

Perhaps the most notable contrast lies in the nature of the melodic lines. Rameau the composer constantly practiced the doctrines of Rameau the theorist, one of which was that all melody is rooted in harmony. Many of his melodic phrases, therefore, delineate triads and so leave no uncertainty as to the harmonic progressions that must support them. Also, orderly relationships within the major-minor tonal system of dominants, subdominants, and secondary chords, and logical modulations govern the harmony. Rameau drew from a richer palette than Lully of consonant and dissonant chords: he employed both more direct and more contrived progressions, and used modulation for expressive purposes. His harmonies are for the most part diatonic, but on occasion he uses chromatic and enharmonic modulations very effectively. For example, in the trio of the Fates in Act II of *Hippolyte et Aricie* (Example 12.2), a descending chromatic sequence modulates rapidly through five keys in as many measures, underlining the words "Où cours-tu, malheureux? Tremble, frémis d'effroi!" (Where do you flee, wretch? Tremble, shudder with terror!).

Melodic style

Harmonic style

EXAMPLE 12.2 Jean-Philippe Rameau, Modulations in *Hippolyte et Aricie*

(g: V =) D: f♯:   f: e: e♭:   d:

Compared to Italian opera composers, Rameau—like Lully and other French composers—minimized the contrast between recitative and air. Rameau's vocal airs, in all their variety of dimensions and types, fall into two basic patterns: the relatively short two-part form AB; and the longer form with repetition after contrast, either ABA or a rondo-like pattern. His airs preserve a certain coolness and restraint, lacking the intensity and abandon of the Italian opera arias. Their outstanding traits are elegance, catchy

Airs

rhythms, fullness of harmony, and melodic ornamentation through the use of agréments.

Rameau's music achieved dramatic force by other means. The opening scenes of *Castor et Pollux*, for example, and the monologue, *Ah! faut-il*, in Act IV of *Hippolyte et Aricie* (NAWM 80) have a grandeur that is unsurpassed in eighteenth-century French opera. Hippolyte's anguish is expressed with highly charged dissonances that propel the harmony forward, as we see from the number of sevenths, ninths, diminished fifths, and augmented fourths required by the bass figures, and from the obligatory appoggiaturas and other notated ornaments. However, the most powerful effects in these operas are

Choruses

achieved by the joint use of solo and chorus. Choruses, which remained prominent in French opera long after they had passed out of use in Italy, are numerous throughout Rameau's works. The chorus that describes and mourns Hippolyte's death at the hands of the sea monster in Act IV provides a stunning example of his highly effective homophonic choral writing.

Instrumental music

Rameau made his most original contribution in the instrumental components of his operas—the overtures, the dances, and the descriptive symphonies that accompany the stage action. In all these his invention was inexhaustible. Themes, rhythms, and harmonies have a marked individuality and a decisive pictorial quality. The French valued music for its powers of depiction, and Rameau was their champion tone-painter. His musical illustrations range from graceful miniatures to broad representations of thunder (*Hippolyte*, Act I), tempest (*Les Surprises de l'Amour* [1757], Act III), or earthquake (*Les Indes galantes*, Act II). Novel orchestration often enhances the imagistic quality of his music. Rameau's use of the bassoons and horns, and the independence of the woodwinds in his later scores, rivaled the most advanced orchestral practices of his time.

Clavecin pieces

Rameau's clavecin pieces have the fine texture, rhythmic vivacity, elegance of detail, and humor that we associate with the works of Couperin. In his third and last collection (*Nouvelles suites de pièces de clavecin*, ca. 1728), Rameau experimented with virtuoso effects in somewhat the same manner as the contemporary Italian keyboard composer, Domenico Scarlatti (see Chapter 13).

Johann Sebastian Bach

Compared to the exciting cosmopolitan centers like Venice and Paris, an eighteenth-century traveler would have found the world of Lutheran Germany—where Johann Sebastian Bach (1685–1750) spent his entire career—very ordinary indeed. For example, one of its principal cities, Leipzig, had several prominent churches and one of Europe's oldest universities, but not one opera house after 1729, nor any princes or bishops in residence. For the last twenty-five years of his life, Bach lived and worked in Leipzig, where he was forced to confront apathy and to engage in petty disputes with town and university officials. Although he enjoyed a reputation in Protestant Germany as an organ virtuoso and writer of learned contrapuntal works, he remained unknown in wider circles. Unlike Vivaldi, who traveled and was recognized throughout Europe, or Rameau, who rubbed shoulders with Parisian high society, Bach saw himself as a conscientious craftsman doing a job to the best of his ability in order to satisfy his superiors, to please and edify his fellow citizens, and to glorify God.

Johann Sebastian was one of a large family of Bachs that came from the German region of Thuringia. In the course of six generations, from around 1560 to the nineteenth century, the Bach family produced an extraordinary number of good musicians and several outstanding ones. Our Bach received his earliest training from his father, a town musician of Eisenach, and from his elder brother Johann Christoph, an organist who was a pupil of Pachelbel. He studied the music of other composers by copying or arranging their scores, a habit he retained throughout his life. In this way he became familiar with the methods of the foremost composers in France, Germany, Austria, and Italy, assimilating the best traits of each.

Bach's life and works

Bach composed in all the genres practiced in his time with the exception of opera. He wrote primarily to meet the demands of the positions he held, and his works may be grouped accordingly. Thus at Arnstadt (1703–7), Mühlhausen (1707–8), and the court and chapel of the duke of Weimar (1708–

➤ Johann Sebastian Bach. Detail from Bach monument at Leipzig. (*Courtesy Corbis-Bettmann*)

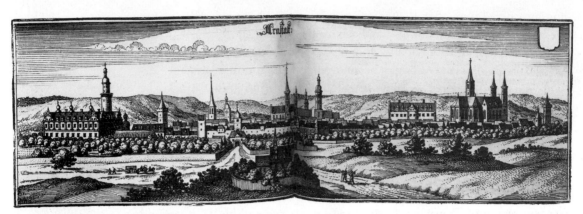

▲ A view of Arnstadt, engraved by Matthaeus Merian. From Martin Zeiller, *Topographia Superioris Saxoniae Thuringiae Misniae Lusatiae &c.,* Frankfurt, 1650. (*Rare Books Division, The New York Public Library, Astor, Lenox, and Tilden Foundations*)

17), where he was employed to play the organ, most of his compositions were for that instrument. At Cöthen (1717–23), where he worked as music director for a princely court, his duties did not include church music, so he mostly composed works for keyboard or instrumental ensembles, as well as music for instruction and for domestic or court entertainment. He produced most of his cantatas and other church music during his years in Leipzig (1723–50), where his final position as cantor of St. Thomas's School and music director at St. Thomas's and St. Nicholas's churches carried considerable prestige in the Lutheran world. Some of his most important mature compositions for organ and other keyboard instruments also date from the Leipzig period. Consequently, our survey of Bach's compositions follows the order that corresponds to his places of employment.

Organ Works

Bach was trained as a violinist and organist, but it was organ music that first attracted his interest as a composer. As a youth he visited Hamburg to hear the organists there, and while working in Arnstadt he made a journey on foot to Lübeck—a distance of about two hundred miles—to hear the famous Buxtehude, who was then almost seventy. There the music of the older composer so fascinated him that he overstayed his leave and got into trouble with his employers.

Bach's earliest organ compositions include chorale preludes, several sets of variations on chorales (partitas), and some toccatas and fantasias that recall the toccatas of Buxtehude in their length and exuberance. While at the court of Weimar, Bach became interested in the music of Italian composers, and with his usual diligence set about copying their scores and arranging their works. He reduced several of Vivaldi's string concertos in order to play them on organ or harpsichord—writing out the ornaments, occasionally reinforcing the counterpoint, and sometimes adding inner voices. He also composed fugues on subjects by Corelli and Legrenzi. These studies naturally resulted in important changes in Bach's own style. From the Italians, especially Vivaldi, he learned to write concise themes and to clarify and tighten the harmonic scheme. Above all, he learned to develop subjects into grandly proportioned formal structures, particularly concerto-ritornello movements. He enhanced these qualities with his own prolific imagination and his profound mastery of contrapuntal technique. In addition, he was able to merge characteristics of Italian, French, and German music to forge a personalized and highly distinctive style all his own.

One of the favorite larger musical structures in this period was the combination of prelude (or toccata or fantasia) and fugue. Most of Bach's im-

Toccatas and fugues

▲ Cities that figured in J. S. Bach's career are indicated in color on this map of modern Germany. In Bach's time, Germany comprised a number of duchies, bishoprics, principalities, and electorates of the Holy Roman Empire. For example, Leipzig and Dresden were in the electorate of Saxony, Lüneburg in that of Hanover, Berlin in that of Brandenburg. Hamburg and Lübeck belonged to the duchy of Holstein, and Anhalt-Cöthen and Weimar were themselves tiny dukedoms.

portant compositions in this form date from the Weimar period, though a few were written at Cöthen and Leipzig. While they are idiomatic for the organ and technically difficult, these works never parade empty virtuosity, and their well-defined fugue subjects show remarkable inventiveness. The Toccata in D minor, BWV 565 (before 1708?),[2] exemplifies the form established by Buxtehude, in which a fugue is interspersed with sections of free fantasia. Some of Bach's preludes are extended compositions in two or three movements: for example, the Fantasia and Fugue in G minor, BWV 542, is a passionately expressive fantasia/toccata with contrapuntal interludes.

Elements of the Italian concerto appear in several toccatas and fugues, particularly in the Prelude and Fugue in A minor, BWV 543 (NAWM 81). In the prelude, violinistic figuration resembling that of concerto solos alternates with toccata-like sections, including a pedal solo and chains of suspensions in the manner of Corelli. The fugue's structure resembles a concerto Allegro: the expositions of the violinistic subject appear, like tutti, in related keys as well as in the tonic, and the more free-flowing, modulatory episodes have the character of solo sections.

From the later years of Bach's life comes the gigantic Prelude and Fugue ("St. Anne's") in E♭ major, BWV 552, published in 1739. They appear as the opening and closing sections of Part III of the *Clavier-Übung* (literally, "Keyboard Practice," a catchall title that Bach used for four different collections of keyboard pieces). Part III comprises a series of chorale preludes on the hymns of the Lutheran Catechism and Mass (Kyrie and Gloria, the so-called *Missa brevis*). In symbolic recognition of the Trinity, the conclusion is a triple fugue in three sections with a key signature of three flats. Each section of the fugue has its own subject, and the first subject is combined contrapuntally with each of the other two.

As an organist and a devout Lutheran, Bach cared deeply about the chorale. In writing some 170 organ chorales, he exhausted all known types in a **Orgelbüchlein** constant search for artistic perfection. Bach's *Orgelbüchlein* (Little Organ Book) contains short chorale preludes, compiled at Weimar and Cöthen with his pupils in mind. So we read on the title page, "Little organ book, in which a beginning organist is given guidance in all sorts of ways of developing a chorale, and also for improving his pedal technique, since in these chorales the pedal is treated as completely *obbligato* [essential, not optional]." He added a rhymed couplet, "To honor the Most High God alone, and for the instruction of my fellow-men." It seems plausible that Bach, a humble and **Pedagogic aims** diligent student all his life, was also a wise and kindly teacher. He compiled two "Little Notebooks"—collections of short keyboard pieces that taught technique and musicianship—for his talented son Wilhelm Friedemann and

2. BWV (abbreviation for "Bach Werke-Verzeichnis") stands for *Thematisch-systematisches Verzeichnis der musikalischen Werke von Johann Sebastian Bach* (Thematic-Systematic Index of the Musical Works of J. S. Bach), ed. Wolfgang Schmieder (Leipzig, 1950). The abbreviation S. (for Schmieder) is sometimes used instead of BWV for referring to Bach's works.

for his second wife Anna Magdalena. His two-part *Inventions* and three-part *Sinfonie* are also pedagogical works, as is the first book of *The Well-Tempered Keyboard*.

In each of the *Orgelbüchlein*'s chorale preludes, the tune is heard once through in a readily recognizable form. The melody is sometimes treated in canon and sometimes presented with fairly elaborate ornaments. The accompanying voices are not necessarily derived from the chorale melody and, in some instances, symbolize the visual images or underlying ideas of the chorale text through pictorial or graphic motives. One of Bach's most striking organ representations is *Durch Adams Fall ist ganz verderbt* (Through Adam's fall, all is spoiled, NAWM 82). A jagged series of dissonant leaps in the pedals depicts the idea of "fall," departing from a consonant chord and falling into a dissonant one—as if from innocence into sin—while the twisting chromatic lines in the inner voices suggest at once temptation, sorrow, and the sinuous writhing of the serpent in the Garden of Eden (Example 12.3).

EXAMPLE 12.3   J. S. Bach, Chorale Prelude: *Durch Adams Fall*

Harpsichord and Clavichord Music

Bach's music for these two keyboard instruments includes masterpieces in every contemporary genre: preludes, fantasies, and toccatas; fugues and other pieces in fugal style; dance suites; and sets of variations. In addition there are early sonatas and capriccios, miscellaneous short works (including many teaching pieces), and concertos with orchestra. Bach composed a large proportion of this music while in Cöthen, although many important works were also written in Leipzig. The keyboard compositions, which were not bound to a local German tradition or liturgy, as organ works were, reveal the international features of Bach's style—the intermingling of Italian, French, and German characteristics.

Undoubtedly the best known of Bach's works for keyboard is the double cycle of preludes and fugues that he titled *Das wohltemperirte Clavier* (The Well-Tempered Keyboard, I and II, 1722 and ca. 1740). Each of the two cycles consists of twenty-four preludes and fugues, one set in each of the twelve major and minor keys. Part I is more unified in style and purpose than Part II, which includes compositions from many different periods of Bach's life. In addition to demonstrating the possibility of using all the keys, with the novel equal- or nearly equal-tempered tuning (see Chapter 11, page 231), Bach had particular pedagogic intentions in Part I.

Preludes

In the typical prelude, Bach assigned the player a specific technical task, so that the piece functioned as a kind of étude. But the teaching aims of *The Well-Tempered Keyboard* go beyond mere technique because the preludes also illustrate different types of keyboard composition. For example, Nos. 2, 7, and 21 of Part I are toccatas, No. 8 is a trio-sonata Grave, and No. 17 a concerto Allegro.

Fugues

The fugues are wonderfully varied in subjects, texture, form, and treatment; as a set, they constitute a compendium of all the possibilities for monothematic fugal writing. The ancient ricercare is represented (Part I, No.

Mm. 21 (2nd half)–24 (1st half), in Bach's autograph

Mm. 21–26, in Carl Czerny's edition

Mm. 22–24, in Hans Bischoff's edition

▲ This passage from the first prelude in Part I of *The Well-Tempered Keyboard* is shown in Bach's autograph manuscript and in two publications. Carl Czerny's edition (first published in the 1830s), evidently based on a copy made after Bach's death, incorporates an inauthentic extra measure after measure 22; elsewhere, Czerny adds phrasings, tempo markings, and dynamics not present in Bach's manuscript (e.g., the *dimin.* in measure 21). In his edition of 1883, Hans Bischoff tries to present as accurate a reproduction of the source as possible. This aim, while not without its problems in practice, is generally adhered to by modern scholars.

4 in C♯ minor), as well as are the techniques of inversion, canon, and augmentation (No. 8, E♭ minor), a da capo ending (No. 3, C♯ major), and much more. In Part II, the Fugue in D major (No. 5) offers a superb example of a concentrated abstract musical structure using the simplest materials, while the Prelude and Fugue in F♯ minor (No. 14) stands out for the beauty of its themes and its proportions. As in the organ fugues, each subject has a clearly defined musical personality that unfolds throughout the entire fugue.

Bach's keyboard suites show the influence of French and Italian as well as German models. He wrote three sets of six: the "English" suites, BWV 806–11 (1715), the "French" suites, BWV 812–17, and the six Partitas, BWV 825–30, which were first published separately and then collected in 1731 to form Part I of the *Clavier-Übung* (1731). The designations "French" and "English" for the suites are not Bach's own, and both collections blend French and Italian qualities in a highly personal style. Each set consists of the standard four dance movements—allemande, courante, sarabande, and gigue—with additional short movements following the sarabande; each of the "English" suites opens with a prelude. In the preludes we can see very clearly the skill with which Bach transferred the Italian ensemble idiom to the keyboard. The prelude of the third suite, for example, simulates a concerto Allegro movement with alternating tutti and solo. The dances in the "English" suites are based on French models and include several examples of the *double* or ornamented repetition of a movement. In the "French" suites, the second movement is more often an Italian corrente than a French courante.

Suites

Bach raised the keyboard theme-and-variations genre to a new high point in his *Aria mit verschiedenen Veränderungen* (Aria with Sundry Variations), BWV 988, published in 1741 or 1742 as Part IV of the *Clavier-Übung* and generally known as the *Goldberg Variations*. All thirty variations preserve the bass and the harmonic structure of the theme, which is a sarabande in two balanced sections. Every third variation is a canon, the first at the interval of a unison, the second at a second, and so on through the ninth. For the thirtieth and last variation, Bach wrote a *quodlibet*, a mixture of two popular song melodies combined in counterpoint above the bass of the theme. To end the work, the original theme is repeated da capo. The noncanonic variations take many different forms: invention, fugue, French overture, ornamental slow aria, and, at regular intervals, a sparkling bravura piece for two manuals. The whole is a structure of magnificent proportions.

Goldberg Variations

Solo and Ensemble Music

Bach wrote sonatas, partitas, and suites for unaccompanied violin, cello, and flute, in which he created the illusion of a harmonic and contrapuntal texture. By means of multiple stops and even single melodic lines that leap from one register to another and back, he suggested an interplay of independent voices—a technique going back to the Renaissance lute composers. The chaconne from Bach's solo violin Partita in D minor is one of the most famous pieces of this kind. The chief compositions for chamber ensemble are his sonatas for violin, viola da gamba, or flute and harpsichord. Most of these works have four movements in slow-fast-slow-fast order, like the sonata da chiesa. Indeed, most of them are virtual trio sonatas, since often the right-hand harpsichord part is written as a melodic line in counterpoint with the other instrument.

Brandenburg Concertos

In the six Brandenburg Concertos, BWV 1046–51, composed in 1721 and dedicated to the Margrave of Brandenburg, we see how fully Bach combined the Italian and German styles. He adopted the three-movement, fast-slow-fast order of the Italian concerto, as well as its triadic themes, steadily driving rhythms, and the ritornello form of the Allegro movements. At the same time, he stamped these concertos with many characteristic traits of his own. For example, he introduced tutti material into the soli, and he expanded the form with such devices as the long cadenza of the Fifth Brandenburg Concerto and elaborately developed fugues, as the one in da capo form in this same concerto. The Third and Sixth are ripieno concertos without featured solo instruments. The others are concerti grossi, pitting solo instruments in various combinations against the body of strings and continuo.

Harpsichord concertos

Bach was one of the first to write (or arrange) concertos for harpsichord. He composed seven for solo harpsichord with orchestra, three for two harpsichords, two for three harpsichords, and one for four harpsichords, this last an arrangement of a Vivaldi concerto for four violins. Most, and possibly all, of the harpsichord concertos are, in fact, arrangements of violin compositions by Bach or by other composers.

Orchestral suites

The four *Ouvertures*, or orchestral suites, BWV 1066–69, contain some of Bach's most exuberant and attractive music. The Third and Fourth Suites (ca. 1729–31), which have trumpets and timpani added to the strings and winds, were intended for performance out-of-doors.

Other instrumental works

Two of Bach's late instrumental works form a class in themselves. *Musikalisches Opfer* (A Musical Offering), BWV 1079, is a collection of various kinds of pieces, all based on a theme proposed by Frederick the Great of Prussia. Bach had improvised on the theme while visiting the monarch at Potsdam in 1747, subsequently writing them out and later revising his own improvisations. He then added a trio sonata in four movements for flute (King Frederick's instrument), violin, and continuo, in which the theme also appears, had the set printed, and dedicated it to the king. *Die Kunst der Fuge* (The Art of Fugue), BWV 1080, composed in 1749–50 and apparently left unfinished at Bach's death, systematically demonstrates all types of fugal writing. It consists of eighteen canons and fugues in the strictest style, all based on the same subject or one of its transformations, and arranged in a general order of increasing complexity. In this work, even the most difficult and abstruse contrapuntal devices are handled with masterful ease.

▲ The Thomaskirche, Leipzig, where J. S. Bach was cantor and *director musices* (1723–50). The building at the far end of the square, beyond the fountain, is the Thomasschule (after it was enlarged in 1732), where Bach taught. (*Copper engraving by Johann Georg Schreiber, 1735. Photo © AKG London*)

Bach at Leipzig: Vocal Music

In 1723, when Bach was appointed cantor of St. Thomas's School and Leipzig's director of music, he was not the first choice of the city council members, who had hopes of hiring a more "modern" musician. That was Georg Philipp Telemann (1681–1767), who was then regarded as the greatest living composer besides Handel. (Telemann turned the job down after using the offer to wangle a salary raise from his employer in Hamburg.) The Thomasschule was a long-established foundation that took in both day and boarding pupils. It provided fifty-five scholarships for boys and young men chosen on the basis of their musical and general scholastic abilities. In return, they had to sing or play in the services of four Leipzig churches and to fulfill other musical duties. As cantor of St. Thomas's School, Bach was obliged to teach four hours each day (Latin as well as music) and also to prepare music for the services at St. Thomas's and St. Nicholas's churches. In addition, he had to promise to lead an exemplary Christian life and not to leave town without permission from the mayor. He and his family lived in an apartment in one wing of the school, where his study was separated by a thin partition from the home room of the second-year schoolboys.

The citizens of Leipzig spent a great deal of time in their churches —daily services, special celebrations at festival times, and regular Sunday programs beginning at seven in the morning and lasting until about noon. At the Sunday services the choir (comprised of a minimum of twelve singers) sang a motet, a Lutheran Mass (Kyrie and Gloria only), hymns, and a multi-movement cantata. Bach knew exactly how much work was involved before he took the job: when he visited Leipzig in 1714, he carefully wrote down the order of events on the back of a cantata (see vignette below).

The sacred cantata figured prominently in the Lutheran liturgy of Leipzig. The subject matter was often linked to the content of the Gospel reading, which immediately preceded it. This suggests that Bach's role was like a musical preacher whose responsibility was to interpret and comment on the Gospel reading in the cantata, and to bring its message vividly before the congregation. Singers and instrumentalists, however inadequate they may have been at times, were always at his disposal. Altogether, the Leipzig churches required fifty-eight cantatas each year, in addition to Passion music for Good Friday, Magnificats at Vespers for three festivals, an annual cantata for the installation of the city council, and occasional music such as funeral motets and wedding cantatas (for which the cantor received an extra fee). Between

Bach's Summary of the Order of Service in Leipzig, 1714:

1) Preluding
2) *Motetta*
3) Preluding on the Kyrie, which is performed throughout in concerted music
4) Intoning before the altar
5) Reading of the Epistle
6) Singing of the Litany
7) Preluding on [and performance of] the Chorale
8) Reading of the Gospel
9) Preluding on [and performance of] the principal composition [cantata]
10) Singing of the Creed
11) The Sermon
12) After the Sermon, as usual, singing of several verses of a hymn
13) Words of Institution [of the Sacrament]
14) Preluding on [and performance of] the composition [probably the second part of the cantata]

After the same, alternate preluding and singing of chorales until the end of the Communion, *et sic porrò* [and so on].

Adapted from *The Bach Reader*, ed. Hans T. David and Arthur Mendel (New York: Norton, 1945), p. 70.

1723 and 1729 Bach composed four complete annual cycles, each with about sixty cantatas. He apparently composed a fifth cycle during the 1730s and early 1740s, but many of these and of the fourth cycle have not survived.

We have, then, approximately two hundred cantatas by Bach, some newly written for Leipzig, others refashioned from earlier works. Under tremendous time pressure to produce this repertory, Bach sometimes reworked movements from his chamber and orchestral compositions and inserted them into his Leipzig cantatas. For example, a movement from one of the Brandenburg Concertos and no fewer than five movements from the solo harpsichord concertos found a niche in the cantatas. But given Bach's religious outlook, which offered even his secular art "to the glory of God," there is nothing incongruous or surprising about this accommodation. In the early cantatas the composer responded to the changing affections and images of the text with music of intense dramatic expression and unexpectedly varied forms. By comparison, the later Leipzig cantatas are less subjective in feeling and more regular in structure. However, no generalized description can possibly suggest the infinite variety and wealth of musical invention, technical mastery, and religious devotion in Bach's cantatas. Two or three examples will serve as an introduction to this vast treasure of music.

Church cantatas

Erdmann Neumeister's innovative idea—to introduce opera-like recitatives and arias into the cantata (see Chapter 10, page 223)—deeply affected Bach, even though he set only five of the pastor's texts. In the text for *Nun komm, der Heiden Heiland* (Come, Savior of the Gentiles, 1714), BWV 61, Neumeister combined chorale verses, newly invented metrical poetry, and prose from the Bible. For the opening choral movement, based on the text and melody of the chorale *Nun komm, der Heiden Heiland*, Bach wrote an elaborate variation in the style and form of a French overture. The choice of this genre is significant, not only because Bach was preoccupied at the time with assimilating foreign styles but also because it was written for the opening (ouverture) of the church year, the first Sunday of Advent. The cantata also includes operatic movements: a simple recitative, an accompanied recitative, two da capo arias, one of which is a *siciliano* (based on a folk dance and associated with pastoral subjects), and a final chorus on a different chorale. Thus Bach combined secular genres and Lutheran hymn settings in a composition full of youthful ingenuity, yet completely convincing as a work of art.

Neumeister cantatas

Bach treated chorale texts and melodies in a multitude of different ways. In the well-known *Christ lag in Todes Banden* (Christ lay in the bonds of death), BWV 4, which dates from around 1708, the seven strophes of the chorale are set as variations on the hymn tune. Following the opening sinfonia, the performing resources are arranged symmetrically around the quartet of soloists in the center: Chorus—Duet—Solo—Quartet—Solo—Duet—Chorus. This order is thought to symbolize the cross.

Chorale cantatas

More typically, Bach based the opening chorus on a chorale melody and ended the work with a simple or embellished statement of the same chorale. The texts of the interior solos and duets often paraphrased strophes of the chorale, but the music referred back to the hymn tune only rarely. For example, in *Wachet auf, ruft uns die Stimme* ("Wake up," the voice calls to us; NAWM 83), BWV 140, the enchanting middle movement is constructed like a chorale prelude. Each phrase of the chorale, sung plainly by the tenor, is preceded and accompanied by a musical commentary in unison strings. The opening chorus imaginatively combines concerto form with cantus firmus technique. The sixteen-measure ritornello for orchestra is heard four times (once abbreviated), to frame the different sections of the chorale melody. With its repeated dotted-note chords and halting syncopations, it sets a mood of anticipation as the wise and foolish virgins wait for the bridegroom mentioned in the first stanza of the chorale. (The parable is told in Matt. 25:1–23, the Gospel reading for the twenty-seventh Sunday after Trinity, also the occasion for which Bach wrote the cantata in 1731.) A violino piccolo and the first oboe, as if paired in a concertino, exchange running figures that elaborate upon motives from the chorale melody. The sopranos, supported by a "corno"—perhaps a hunting horn—sing the phrases of the hymn in long notes, while motives derived from the same phrases are developed imitatively in the three other parts (Example 12.4). Bach wrote "Aria" at the head of two of the other movements and introduced each with a recitative, one *secco* and one *accompagnato*. The arias are actually duets modeled on operatic love duets, but here the dialogues are between Jesus and a soul searching for salvation.

EXAMPLE 12.4   J. S. Bach, *Wachet auf*: Chorus, *Wachet auf*

Wake up, the voice calls to us.

Bach customarily gave the title "dramma per musica" to cantatas that he composed for secular occasions. Among the best of the "musical dramas" are *Der Streit zwischen Phoebus und Pan* (The Quarrel between Phoebus and Pan), BWV 201, and *Schleicht, spielende Wellen* (Glide gently, playful waves), BWV 206, written to celebrate the birthday of Augustus III in 1733. The *Coffee Cantata* (ca. 1734–35), BWV 211, and the burlesque *Peasant Cantata* (1742), BWV 212, are delightful examples of Bach's lighter music. In some of these cantatas from the 1730s Bach experimented with the new *galant* style. He reined in his tendency to write elaborate accompaniments and allowed the vocal line to dominate. He also invented melodies that divide symmetrically into antecedent and consequent phrases, and indulged in other mannerisms of the new operatic style.

Bach's two surviving Passions, the story of Christ's suffering and death according to the Gospels of St. John and St. Matthew, remain the crowning achievement of the North German tradition of Passion settings in oratorio style (see Chapter 10, page 225). The *St. Matthew Passion*, BWV 244, for double chorus, soloists, double orchestra, and two organs, is a drama of epic grandeur, the most noble and inspired treatment of its subject in the whole repertory. First performed in an early version on Good Friday 1727, the work dramatizes the text from Matthew, chapters 26 and 27, narrated by a tenor in recitative with the help of the chorus. Chorales, a duet, and numerous arias, most of which are preceded by arioso recitatives, complement the narration. The "Passion Chorale" (see Example 8.1) appears five times, in different keys and different four-part harmonizations. The author of the text for the added recitatives and arias, Christian Friedrich Henrici (1700–1764), writing under the pseudonym Picander, was a Leipzig poet who also provided many of Bach's cantata texts. As in the *St. John Passion*, the chorus sometimes participates in the action and sometimes, like a Greek chorus, introduces or reflects on the narrative. The magnificent opening and closing choruses of Part I are huge chorale fantasias; in the first, the chorale melody is sung by a special choir of boy sopranos.

In the *St. Matthew Passion*, the chorale, concertato medium, recitative, arioso, and da capo aria are united under the ruling majesty of a central religious theme. Except for the chorale, all these elements are equally characteristic of late Baroque opera. Although Bach never wrote one, the language, the forms, and the very spirit of opera pervade the Passions.

Bach's ambitions as a composer were often encyclopedic. Not only did he write in every genre, but he also arranged many of his mature compositions according to some large, unified design—for example, the Preludes and Fugues in all the major and minor keys in *The Well-Tempered Keyboard*, the cycle of chorales in the *Clavier-Übung*, the canons at increasing intervals in the *Goldberg Variations*, the exhaustive treatment of a single subject in *A Musical Offering*, and the comprehensive collection of fugue types in *The Art of Fugue*.

Mass in B minor

Similarly monumental in design is Bach's Mass in B minor, compiled between 1747 and 1749 mostly from earlier composed music. He had already presented the Kyrie and Gloria in 1733 to Friedrich August II, the Catholic king of Poland, in hopes of getting an honorary appointment to the electoral chapel, which he did three years later. The Sanctus was first performed on Christmas Day 1724. He adapted some of the other movements from choruses of cantatas, replacing the German text with the Latin words of the Mass and sometimes reworking the music. Of the newly composed sections, the opening of the Credo and the Confiteor (NAWM 84b) are in *stile antico*, while the *Et in unum Dominum*, the *Et in spiritum sanctum* (NAWM 84a), and the *Benedictus* are in a modern style that contrasts sharply with the more conservative sections. Bach never heard the work performed as a whole, though parts were sung at Leipzig, where an abbreviated Latin Mass still had a place in the liturgy. Although Bach's habit of reworking his earlier compositions for new situations most often resulted from the pressures of his job, in this case Bach evidently wanted to create a universal religious statement in the traditional and solemn medium of the Catholic Mass. In so doing, he was able to endow some of his best movements with a permanence they surely deserved.

Reception History

The history of Bach's music tells a story of burial and resurrection. Compositions published or prepared by Bach for publication during his lifetime include only *A Musical Offering*, *The Art of Fugue*, and a few more. The rest are preserved in handwritten copies. Bach's work was quickly forgotten after his death because musical tastes changed radically in the middle of the eighteenth century. The new style that emerged from the opera houses of Italy to invade Germany and the rest of Europe made Bach's music sound

IX. Women singers and string players (upper left), thought to be from the Pio Ospedale della Pietà, give a concert in Venice honoring Archduke Paul and Mary Fedorov of Russia. Painting by Francesco Guardi (1712–1793). (*MUNICH, ALTE PINAKOTHEK / PHOTOGRAPH BY JOACHIM BAUEL-ARTOTHEK*)

X. John Henry Fuseli (1741–1825), *The Nightmare* (1785–90). Fuseli rejected the elegance of the *style galant* and turned his attention to the macabre and fantastic subjects that character-ized the *Sturm und Drang* in art.   (*FRANKFURT, GOETHE-MUSEUM*)

old-fashioned. The composer-critic Johann Adolph Scheibe (1708–1776) considered Bach unsurpassable as an organist and keyboard composer, but he found the rest of his music overly elaborate and confused (see vignette below), preferring the more tuneful and straightforward style of younger German composers, such as Johann Adolph Hasse (1699–1783).

Bach's eclipse in the mid–eighteenth century was not total. In the second half of the century, some of the preludes and fugues from *The Well-Tempered Keyboard* appeared in print, and the whole collection circulated in innumerable manuscript copies. Haydn owned a copy of the Mass in B minor; Mozart knew *The Art of Fugue* and studied the motets on a visit to Leipzig in 1789. Citations from Bach's works appeared frequently in the musical literature of the time, and the important periodical, the *Allgemeine musikalische Zeitung*, opened its first issue (1798) with a Bach portrait. A full rediscovery of Bach finally began in the nineteenth century, with the publication of the biography by Johann Nikolaus Forkel in 1802 marking an important step. The revival of the *St. Matthew Passion* by composer-conductor Carl Friedrich Zelter (1758–1832) and its 1829 performance at Berlin under Felix Mendelssohn

Johann Adolph Scheibe's Critique of Bach's Style, 1737:

❝ This great man would be the admiration of whole nations if he had more amenity, if he did not take away the natural element in his pieces by giving them a turgid and confused style, and if he did not darken their beauty by an excess of art. Since he judges according to his own fingers, his pieces are extremely difficult to play; for he demands that singers and instrumentalists should be able to do with their throats and instruments whatever he can play on the clavier. But this is impossible. Every ornament, every little grace, and everything that one thinks of as belonging to the method of playing, he expresses completely in notes; and this not only takes away from his pieces the beauty of harmony but completely covers the melody throughout. All the voices must work with each other and be of equal difficulty, and none of them can be recognized as the principal voice. In short, he is in music what Mr. von Lohenstein was in poetry. Turgidity has led them both from the natural to the artificial, and from the lofty to the somber; and in both one admires the onerous labor and uncommon effort—which, however, are vainly employed, since they conflict with Nature. ❞

From an anonymous letter by "an able traveling musician" published in Scheibe's periodical review, *Der critische Musikus*, May 1737, translated in *The Bach Reader*, ed. Hans T. David and Arthur Mendel (New York: Norton, 1945), p. 238.

did much to inspire interest in Bach's music. Finally, the establishment of the *Bach Gesellschaft* (Bach Society) in 1850 led to the first collected edition of Bach's works, completed by 1900.

George Frideric Handel

Compared to Vivaldi, Rameau, and Bach—each absorbed in his own national tradition—George Frideric Handel (1685–1759) was a completely international composer. After being educated in Germany and Italy, he matured as a composer in England, the country then most hospitable to a cosmopolitan style.

London

Italian opera was all the rage in London during the early eighteenth century. To take advantage of this fashion, about sixty wealthy gentlemen organized a joint stock company, the Royal Academy of Music, in 1718–19, and engaged Handel and two Italian composers to present operas to the London public. Even when the popularity of Italian opera waned, as it did in the following decades, London's prosperous middle-class audiences quickly warmed to Handel's English oratorios, some of which were based on the military exploits of biblical heroes—Saul, Judas Maccabaeus, Joshua, and others—and therefore appealed to their British imperial pride. Moreover, the English taste for choral music fostered the success of these new English oratorios—dramatic works in which choruses played a large role, representing ordinary solid citizens with whom Londoners could identify, in contrast to the sometimes effete and affected characters of the operatic stage. The court also became a factor in Handel's ascendancy: he enjoyed the patronage of the newly crowned King George I, who also came from Germany, where he had been Handel's employer as elector of Hanover.

Handel's life

Handel was born in Halle, where he studied music with Friedrich Wilhelm Zachow, the local organist and Kapellmeister. Under Zachow's teaching, Handel became an accomplished organist and harpsichordist, studied violin and oboe, received a thorough grounding in counterpoint, and learned the music of German and Italian composers by copying their scores. He matriculated at the University of Halle in 1702 and at eighteen was appointed cathedral organist. But almost as soon as he landed this first job, Handel decided to give up his career as a church musician to try his hand at writing opera. In 1703 he moved to Hamburg—then the principal center of German opera—and at the age of nineteen composed his first opera, *Almira*, which was performed there in 1705. The next step for the aspiring opera composer, obviously, was Italy, where he lived from 1706 until the middle of 1710. Soon recognized as one of the coming young composers, Handel began associating with the leading patrons and musicians of Rome, Florence, Naples, and Venice. He made the acquaintance of many Italian composers, including Corelli and Alessandro Scarlatti (whose musical styles exerted an important influence

➤ Statue of George Frideric Handel by the French sculptor Roubiliac, made for Vauxhall pleasure gardens in London in 1737. The work established Roubiliac's reputation in England, and he was later commissioned to design the composer's funerary monument in Westminster Abbey. (*Victoria & Abert Museum, London/Art Resource, NY*)

on him), and returned to Germany at the age of twenty-five to become music director at the electoral court of Hanover. But almost immediately he took a long leave of absence to visit London. There, during the 1710–11 season, he made a tremendous hit with his opera *Rinaldo*. Instead of going back to Germany, Handel then settled down to a long and prosperous career in London.

For the Royal Academy of Music, which flourished from 1720 to 1728, Handel composed some of his best operas, including *Radamisto* (1720), *Ottone* (1723), *Giulio Cesare* (1724), *Rodelinda* (1725), and *Admeto* (1727). The popular success of Gay's *The Beggar's Opera* in 1728 (see Chapter 13, page 297) proved that the English public was growing tired of Italian opera; in addition, the Academy began experiencing financial difficulties. In 1729, when it stopped producing operas, Handel and a partner took over the theater. But during the next decade a competing organization, the Opera of the Nobility, so completely divided the London public that both companies nearly went bankrupt. The Opera of the Nobility featured the Neapolitan composer Nicola Porpora (1686–1768) and the highest-priced singers in Europe, among them the legendary castrato Farinelli (1705–1782; see illustration and window, pages 280–81). Despite repeated failures, Handel clung to the opera tradition. Only when subscriptions to the 1738–39 season were insufficient did he begin to compose his first (*Saul*) of twenty-six oratorios, which were much less expensive to mount than operas. The work was well received and the following year he was invited to write another for Dublin, where *Messiah* was first performed in 1742. After that success, and despite his failing eyesight, Handel leased a theater to present oratorios every year during Lent. As an added attraction at these performances, the composer himself improvised at the organ during intermissions. The public's enthusiastic response to these concerts allowed Handel's music to become the prevailing influence in British musical life for more than a century. His imperious, independent nature made him a formidable presence—he was satirized as a glutton and a tyrant—but the rougher aspects of Handel's personality were balanced by a sense of humor and redeemed by a generous, honorable, and fundamentally pious nature (see vignette below). He was buried in London, in Westminster Abbey, alongside British royalty and national heroes—a clear indication of the affection and respect Handel earned during his lifetime.

Instrumental music

Although Handel wrote some fine keyboard music, including three sets of concertos for harpsichord or organ, and some sophisticated solo and trio sonatas, the most significant remain his instrumental works for full orchestra. These include the overtures to his operas and oratorios, the two suites known as *Water Music* (1717) and *Music for the Royal Fireworks* (1749), and, above all, his six concertos for woodwinds and strings (usually called the oboe concertos) and twelve *Grand Concertos*, Op. 6, composed in 1739.

The concerti grossi of Opus 6 combine modern traits with retrospective

Charles Burney on Handel's Personality:

❝ The figure of Handel was large, and he was somewhat corpulent, and unwieldy in his motions; but his countenance, which I remember as perfectly as that of any man I saw but yesterday, was full of fire and dignity; and such as impressed ideas of superiority and genius.

He was impetuous, rough, and peremptory in his manners and conversation, but totally devoid of ill-nature or malevolence; indeed, there was an original humour and pleasantry in his most lively sallies of anger or impatience, which, with his broken English, were extremely risible. His natural propensity to wit and humour, and happy manner of relating common occurrences, in an uncommon way, enabled him to throw persons and things into very ridiculous attitudes. . . .

He knew the value of time too well to spend it in frivolous pursuits, or with futile companions, however high in rank. Fond of his art, and diligent in its cultivation, and the exercise of it, as a profession, he spent so studious and sedentary a life, as seldom allowed him to mix in society, or partake of public amusements. . . . Handel's general look was somewhat heavy and sour, but when he *did* smile, it was his sire the sun, bursting out of a black cloud. There was a sudden flash of intelligence, wit, and good humour, beaming in his countenance, which I hardly ever saw in any other. ❞

From Charles Burney, *An Account of the Musical Performances in Westminster Abbey and the Pantheon . . . 1784 in Commemoration of Handel* (London, 1785), pp. 31–37.

elements, which predominate. Handel adopted Corelli's conception of a
sonata da chiesa for full orchestra and the conventional slow-fast-slow-fast
scheme of movements including one fugal Allegro, but he often added a
movement or two. The solo parts are not very different in character from the
tuttis; in fact, the concertino strings generally play throughout in unison with
the ripieno or else appear by themselves only for brief trio-like interludes.
Rarely does Handel follow Vivaldi in giving decorative figuration to a solo
violin (as he does in Concertos Nos. 3, 6, and 11). The serious, dignified
bearing and the prevailing full contrapuntal texture of this music hark back
to the earlier part of the century, when Handel was forming his style in Italy.
Yet the variety in these concertos, the individual quality of the themes, the
inexhaustible flow of invention, and the grand proportions of the works have
assured the Opus 6 concertos a permanent place in the repertory.

The English-speaking public has long thought of Handel almost exclu-

Concertos

▲ Johann Zoffany: The Sharp Family's Boating Party on the Thames, ca. 1781. The Sharps
regularly gave outdoor concerts on their barge, named the "Apollo," in which Handel's
music was prominently featured. (*By courtesy of the National Portrait Gallery, London, and
the Lloyd-Baker Trustees*)

Window

FARINELLI, THE ADORED CASTRATO

Singing was so prized as an art form in the late Renaissance and Baroque eras that many choirboys were castrated before puberty in order to preserve the soprano or contralto range of their voices. The musical needs of the church (which did not admit women into the prestigious Sistine Chapel choir, for example) and the promise of a potentially glorious operatic career as an adult made this practice tolerable to poor families who wished to provide an education for their talented offspring, and who often received clandestine payments in exchange for their consent. The operation left the male infertile but still able to have sexual intercourse, making him extremely desirable as a lover. It also resulted in androgyny, since secondary male sex characteristics, such as muscular development and facial hair, were suppressed along with the change in voice. Castrati often appeared more fleshy, especially around the hips and thighs, and in the face as well. As to musical accomplishments, the castrato voice was valued for its greater power and endurance compared with a woman's voice, and praised for its agility, range, breath control, and ability to thrill the listener. The most successful castrati were adored by audiences, swarmed by fans, coddled by composers, paid huge sums by producers—in short, treated very much like modern rock stars.

Carlo Broschi (1705–1782), known as Farinelli, was the most famous castrato soprano of all time. His career took him from triumph to triumph in all the operatic capitals of Europe: Venice, Naples, Rome, Vienna, Paris, London, and Madrid. The painting shown here depicts him as he appeared in 1734, the year he made his debut in London for the Opera of the Nobility—the company that rivaled Handel's own (see page 277)—led by Nicola Porpora, who had been Farinelli's teacher in Naples. The portrait presents the virtuoso, exquisitely outfitted in brocade, fur-trimmed velvet, and lace, standing next to a harpsichord. We can assume from his authoritative, if not arrogant, pose that he had already reached the height of his powers. In fact, he retired from the stage only three years later, at age thirty-two, and spent the next two decades in the service of Philip V and Ferdinand VI of Spain.

Operas

sively as an oratorio composer. But he devoted thirty-five years to composing and directing operas, which contain as much memorable music as do his oratorios. In an age when opera was the main concern of ambitious musicians, Handel excelled among his contemporaries. During his lifetime, his operas were heard not only in London but in Germany and Italy as well.

London audiences were ecstatic about Farinelli. One letter, written shortly after his London debut, says it all:

I must have you know—for it deserves to be known—that Farinelli was a revelation to me, for I realized that till I had heard him I had heard only a small part of what human song can achieve, whereas I now conceive that I have heard all there is to hear.

An interesting if somewhat melodramatic film (*Farinelli*, 1994) tells the obviously embroidered story of Farinelli's rise to fame and fortune, his relationship with his brother (the composer Riccardo Broschi), and his dealings with Porpora, Handel, and his adoring public. The film also manages to give a reasonably authentic idea of the music and staging of Baroque opera. Because it is nowadays impossible to reproduce naturally the enormous vocal range and unique timbre of the castrato voice, with its peculiar combination of power and sweetness, recording the ornate and difficult eighteenth-century arias on the film's soundtrack involved "reinventing" Farinelli's voice from studio performances of two fine modern singers—a male countertenor and a female soprano. The resulting tape includes no fewer than 3,000 edit points!

➤ Bartolommeo Nazari: portrait in oils of Farinelli, 1734. (*London, Royal College of Music*)

Because Handel's London audiences did not understand Italian, they cared more about hearing their favorite singers than following the story. Nevertheless, the plots are the usual ones of the time: tales of magic and marvelous adventure, such as those by Ariosto and Tasso revolving around the Crusades (*Rinaldo, Orlando, Alcina,* for example) or, more often, episodes from the lives of Roman heroes (*Giulio Cesare, Scipione*, among others) freely adapted to include the maximum number of intense dramatic situations. The action develops through dialogue set as *recitativo secco*, accompanied by harpsichord. Particularly stirring moments, such as soliloquies, are enhanced through *recitativo obbligato*, that is, accompanied by the orchestra. For these accompanied recitatives—as indeed for many other features of his operas—Handel found impressive models in the works of Alessandro Scarlatti and others. Solo da capo arias allow the characters to respond lyrically to their situations. Each aria represents a single specific mood or affection, sometimes even two contrasting but related affections. The two types of recitative are sometimes freely combined with short arias or ariosos to make large scene-complexes that recall the freedom of early-seventeenth-century Venetian opera and at the same time foreshadow the methods of later composers, such as Gluck. Examples of such scene-complexes occur in *Orlando* (end of Act II) and, on a smaller scale, in *Giulio Cesare* (Act III, Scene 4: *Da l'ondoso periglio* [From the perilous waves]), in which the da capo structure is interrupted by an accompanied recitative (NAWM 85). Instrumental symphonies mark key moments in the plot, such as battles, ceremonies, or incantations, and a few operas include ballets. Ensembles larger than duets are rare, and there are almost no choruses at all.

Arias

The arias, traditionally allocated according to the importance of each member of the cast, had to display the scope of the singers' vocal and dramatic powers. These constraints still left the composer plenty of freedom. Like most of his contemporaries, Handel could easily turn out an opera that enjoyed the usual brief success, but he could also on occasion create a masterpiece like *Ottone* or *Giulio Cesare*, scores that are remarkable for their variety of aria types. These range from brilliant coloratura displays to sustained, sublimely expressive pathetic songs, such as *Cara sposa* in *Rinaldo* or *Se pietà* in *Giulio Cesare*. Arias of regal grandeur with rich contrapuntal and concertato accompaniments alternate with simple, folklike melodies or arias in which the strings play in unison with the voice throughout. The pastoral scenes are especially noteworthy examples of eighteenth-century nature painting. Not all of Handel's arias are in da capo form; those composed in the 1730s, particularly, favor simpler, abbreviated forms.

Toward the end of his operatic career, Handel turned more and more to the fashionable light melodic manner of the modern Italian composers, especially in *Serse* (1738) and *Deidamia* (1741). It is ironic that one of Handel's best-known pieces, the "Largo from *Xerxes*," with its clearly articulated phrases and simple accompaniment, is stylistically worlds apart from the typical Baroque da capo aria.

Oratorios

Handel's English oratorios constituted a new genre that differs from both the Italian oratorio and his own London operas. Hardly more than an opera on a sacred subject, the eighteenth-century Italian oratorio was presented in concert instead of on stage. Handel had written such a work, *La resurrezione*

(1708), during his stay in Rome. In his English oratorios, he retained some aspects of this tradition by setting dialogue as recitative and lyrical verses as arias. Most of these arias resemble his opera arias in form, musical style, the nature of musical ideas, and the technique of expressing the affections. As in the operas too, recitative prepares the mood of each aria. But Handel and his librettists brought elements to their oratorios that were foreign to Italian opera: from the English masque, the choral anthem, French classical drama, ancient Greek drama, and the German historia. Everything, of course, was adapted for the London environment, with the result that Handel's oratorios became a genre in themselves.

Oratorios were intended for the concert hall and were much closer to theatrical performances than to church services. Although not all of Handel's oratorios deal with sacred subjects, many of his most popular are based on Old Testament stories; even *Messiah* has more text from the Old than from the New Testament. The Hebrew Scriptures were a storehouse of both history and mythology well known to middle-class Protestant England in the eighteenth century. Moreover, for reasons mentioned earlier, many of Handel's oratorio subjects struck a responsive patriotic note with the British public. Most of the biblical oratorios stayed close to the original narrative, but the biblical text was rewritten in recitatives (sometimes prose, sometimes rhymed verse), arias, and choruses—although *Israel in Egypt* tells the story of Exodus entirely in the words of Scripture. *Messiah* also has a purely scriptural text but is the least typical of all Handel's oratorios. Instead of telling a story, *Messiah* unfolds as a series of contemplations on the Christian idea of redemption, beginning with Old Testament prophecies and going through the life of Christ to His final triumph over death.

Beyond question Handel's most important innovation in the oratorios was his use of the chorus. To be sure, the chorus had its place in the Latin and Italian oratorios of Carissimi, but later oratorios had at most a few "madrigals" and ensembles sometimes marked "coro." Handel's early training made him familiar with Lutheran choral music and with the southern German combination of the chorus with orchestra and soloists. But the English choral tradition impressed him most profoundly. He fully captured this English musical idiom in the *Chandos* anthems, written for the duke of Chandos between 1718 and 1720—masterpieces of Anglican church music from which the composer frequently borrowed in his later works.

Role and style of the choruses

The monumental character of Handel's choral style fits the oratorio's emphasis on communal rather than individual expression. Where an opera had an aria Handel often inserted a chorus to comment on the action, as in the choruses of Greek drama. The chorus *How dark, O Lord, are Thy decrees* (NAWM 86) from *Jephtha* is an outstanding example of this. Here, the chorus expresses the sorrow and dismay of the Israelites—and by extension, of the spectators—over Jephtha's having to sacrifice his own daughter. Handel's oratorio choruses also participate in the action, as in *Judas Maccabaeus*, and they figure in incidental scenes, as in *Solomon*. The chorus may even narrate, as in *Israel in Egypt*, where the choral recitative *He sent a thick darkness* is remarkable for its unusual form, its strange modulations, and its pictorial writing.

Musical symbolism is a conspicuous and endearing feature of Handel's choral writing. Word painting and descriptive figures were universal at the time, but Handel often used these devices in especially felicitous ways. The *larghetto* section of *How dark, O Lord, are Thy decrees* sets the text "All our joys to sorrow turning" to a canonic treatment of a theme full of wide skips and reversals of direction (see Example 12.5). Many other descriptive passages are found, for example, in *Israel in Egypt*: the somewhat literal representation of frogs, flies, lice, hail, and the other plagues in Egypt is amusing, but the profound and moving portrayal of *The people shall hear* lifts this chorus to a height hardly equaled elsewhere. Passages such as these also reveal Handel the dramatist, the unerring master of grandiose effects.

EXAMPLE 12.5   George Frideric Handel, *Jephtha*: Act II, Chorus, "How dark, O Lord, are Thy decrees!"

Handel's borrowings

Handel often borrowed extensively from his own earlier works and—following the practice of his day—from other composers, living or dead. Three duets and eleven of the twenty-eight choruses of *Israel in Egypt*, for example, were taken in whole or in part from the music of others, while four choruses were arrangements from earlier works by Handel himself. Some scholars conjecture that Handel resorted to borrowing in order to overcome

▲ Autograph manuscript page from the chorus *How dark, O Lord, are Thy decrees*, from Handel's oratorio *Jephtha* (see NAWM 86, measures 16–25). At the foot of the page Handel noted on February 13, 1751 that his weakening eyesight forced him to stop composing temporarily. (*London, British Library. By permission of the British Library*)

the inertia that sometimes afflicted him when beginning a new work, especially after he suffered a paralytic stroke and nervous collapse in 1737. However that may be, Handel cannot be charged with plagiarism because borrowing, transcribing, adapting, rearranging, and parodying were universal and accepted practices. Besides, when Handel borrowed from others, he more often than not repaid with interest, clothing the borrowed material with new beauty and preserving it for generations that would otherwise scarcely have known of its existence.

POSTLUDE

In this, the last chapter about the Baroque era, we have studied the lives and works of the four composers who represent, in many respects, both the efflorescence and the afterglow of the musical Baroque in Italy, France, Germany, and England. Each made lasting contributions.

Although Vivaldi was a consummate master of opera, he is best remembered for his influence on instrumental music of the middle and later eighteenth century. His impact equaled Corelli's on an earlier generation. Composers of the Classic concerto adopted and developed Vivaldi's dramatic conception of the soloist. His successors admired and emulated his concise themes, clarity of form, rhythmic vitality, and logical flow of musical ideas. These qualities, so characteristic of Vivaldi's music, directly influenced J. S. Bach—who made keyboard arrangements of at least nine of his concertos—and many younger composers as well.

Rameau's work, dominated by his operas and noted especially for their novel instrumental music, is characterized by the French traits of clarity, grace, moderation, and elegance, and a constant striving for pictorialism. In these respects he may be compared with his contemporary, the painter Jean Watteau. Equally typical of his countrymen, Rameau thought of himself as a *philosophe* as well as a composer, an analyst as well as a creator. In short, he was one of the most complex and productive musical personalities of the eighteenth century.

We realize the central position Bach occupies in the history of music when we consider that he absorbed into his works all the genres, styles, and forms of his time and developed their potential to a degree never even imagined by others. In his music the often conflicting demands of harmony and counterpoint, of melody and polyphony, reached a tense but satisfying balance. The continuing vitality of his music cannot be explained in a few words, but among the qualities that stand out are his concentrated and distinctive themes, his ingenious counterpoint, his copious musical invention, the majestic formal proportions of his works, his imaginative musical representation of pictorial and symbolic ideas, and the technical perfection of every detail.

Handel's greatness and historical significance rests largely on the fact that his compositions, especially the choral works, still command an eager audience. His music aged well because he embraced devices that became important in the new style of the mid–eighteenth century. Handel's emphasis on melody and harmony, as compared to the more strictly contrapuntal procedures of Bach, allied him with the fashions of his time. As a choral composer in the grand style he had no peer. He was a consummate master of contrast, not only in choral music but also in all types of composition. And in the oratorios he deliberately appealed to a middle-class audience, recognizing social changes that had far-reaching effects on music.

13

THE EARLY CLASSIC PERIOD: OPERA AND INSTRUMENTAL MUSIC IN THE EIGHTEENTH CENTURY

The word *classic* has been applied both to the mature styles of the later eighteenth-century composers Haydn and Mozart as well as to music written between the 1720s and 1800. We call this music "classic," an adjective that refers to the ancient Greeks and Romans, because it shares many attributes of the art and architecture of antiquity. At its best, classic music reached a consistently high standard and possessed the qualities of noble simplicity, balance, perfection of form, diversity within unity, seriousness of purpose, and restrained use of ornamentation. We find these characteristics most evident in the music of Gluck, Haydn, and Mozart, but we should not make the mistake of viewing the mid-eighteenth century composers who preceded them as merely lesser forerunners.

Many different personal and regional styles thrived, and a wealth of stylistic diversity existed among the various musical genres, such as opera and church music. Nevertheless, it is convenient and appropriate to call the years from approximately 1720 to 1800 the Classic period, even though its boundaries overlap with the preceding Baroque and subsequent Romantic periods. For, while Baroque musical styles were dying out in Italy during the 1720s (as we have seen in the works of Vivaldi, for example), they remained very much alive in France, England, and some parts of Germany.

Other terms have also been applied to characterize this period, among them *rococo*, *galant*, and *empfindsam*. *Rococo* originally described a style of architecture that softened the heavier, more monumental angular forms of the post-Renaissance period with curved arabesques (*rocaille* or "rock-work"), especially in France at the end of the seventeenth century. We might see the pieces of François Couperin, with their refined ornamentation, as counterparts to the movement in architecture, but a broader application of the term has lost favor. The French word *galant* was widely used in the eighteenth century to describe the courtly manner in literature and the subjects of paintings depicting courtly flirtation. It was a catchword for everything that was considered modern, smart, chic, smooth, easy, and sophisticated. Contemporary theorists distinguished between the learned or strict style of contrapuntal writing and the freer, more chordal, *galant* style. The latter was characterized by an emphasis on melody made up of short-breathed, often repeated motives, organized in two-, three-, and four-bar phrases, as we have seen in some of Handel's late works (Chapter 12). These and other **General Characteristics of the New Style** are discussed below.

The German word associated with the music of the mid–eighteenth century, *Empfindsamkeit* (noun) or *empfindsam* (adjective), derives from the verb *empfinden*, to feel. *Empfindsamkeit*, which translates as "sentimentality" or "sensibility," is a quality associated with the restrained passion and melancholy that typifies some slow movements and obbligato recitatives in particular. Characterized by surprising turns of harmony, chromaticism, nervous rhythmic figures, and rhapsodically free, speechlike melody, it is found, for example, in certain late concertos of Vivaldi (see NAWM 79) and, allied with the *galant* idiom, in C. P. E. Bach's keyboard sonatas (see NAWM 94), discussed below.

Of course, styles change as new systems of thought and behavior challenge old beliefs. The eighteenth-century movement known as the Enlightenment posed such a challenge. In the sphere of religion, the movement valued individual faith and practical morality more than the supernatural and the church. In philosophy and science, the emphasis on reasoning from experience and from careful observation assigned more importance to the examination of the human mind, the emotions, social relations, and established institutions. This attitude affected the arts as well: Rameau, for example, based his theories of harmony and tuning on observed natural phenomena rather than on abstract mathematical laws. In social behavior, naturalness was preferred to artificiality and formality. Most important, the Enlightenment stood for the conviction that reason and knowledge could solve social and practical problems as well as advance scientific discovery.

Musical life reflected the international culture that spread throughout Europe during the Enlightenment. German symphony composers were active in Paris; Italian opera composers and singers worked in what are now Austria and Germany, in Spain, England, Russia, and France. The flutist Johann Joachim Quantz (1697–1773), writing from Berlin in 1752, pro-

Cosmopolitan Vienna

*E*ighteenth-century Vienna is a striking example of a cosmopolitan cultural center. Between 1745 and 1765, the emperor was a Frenchman, Francis Stephen of Lorraine. The imperial court poet was the Italian Pietro Metastasio. A German, Johann Adolph Hasse, composed operas in Italian set to Metastasio's librettos, sometimes for state occasions. The manager of the court theaters was Count Giacomo Durazzo, a diplomat from Italy. An imported French company mounted a regular season of French comic operas. French-style ballets were also popular, though the music tended to be by local composers, among them Gluck, whose partner in operatic reform was Raniero de Calzabigi, another Italian. The composer Giuseppe Bonno, born in Vienna but trained in Naples, became imperial Kapellmeister in 1774. His weekly concerts conducted at the Palais Rofrano featured soloists such as the soprano Caterina Gabrielli and the violinist Gaetano Pugnani, both Italians, and the Belgian Pierre van Maldere. The most influential musician in Vienna during the last quarter of the century was Antonio Salieri (1750–1825), who had been brought there from Venice at the age of fifteen. He eventually succeeded Florian Gassmann as imperial court composer and conductor of Italian opera, a post he held for thirty-six years. This mix of cultures underlay the phenomenon that has been called, not altogether appropriately, the "Viennese" Classical style.

posed that the ideal musical style was made up of the best features of music from all nations (see vignette, page 290).

The age of Enlightenment was humanitarian as well as cosmopolitan. Enlightened despots, such as Catherine the Great of Russia, not only patronized arts and letters, they also promoted social reform. Freemasonry, built on humanitarian ideals and a longing for universal brotherhood, spread rapidly throughout Europe and numbered among its adherents kings (Frederick the Great and Joseph II), poets (Goethe), and composers (Haydn and Mozart). Mozart's opera *Die Zauberflöte* (The Magic Flute) and Schiller's *Ode to Joy* (set by Beethoven in his Ninth Symphony) reflect the eighteenth-century humanitarian movement.

The pursuit of learning and the love of art became more widespread, particularly among the expanding middle class. This growing interest made new demands of writers and artists that affected both the subject matter and its manner of presentation. Philosophy, science, literature, and the fine arts all began to address a general public beyond the select group of ex-

J. J. Quantz on the Superiority of a Nationally Mixed Style:

❝ In a style that consists, like the present German one, of a mix of the styles of different peoples, every nation finds something familiar and unfailingly pleasing. Considering all that has been discussed about the differences among styles, we must vote for the pure Italian style over the pure French. The first is no longer as solidly grounded as it used to be, having become brash and bizarre, and the second has remained too simple. Everyone will therefore agree that a style blending the good elements of both will certainly be more universal and more pleasing. For a music that is accepted and favored by many peoples, and not just by a single land, a single province, or a particular nation, must be the very best, provided it is founded on sound judgment and a healthy attitude. **❞**

Johann Joachim Quantz, *Versuch einer Anweisung, die Flöte traversiere zu spielen* (Berlin: J. F. Voss, 1752), Ch. 18, § 89.

perts and connoisseurs. Popular treatises were written with an eye to bringing culture within the reach of all, while novelists and playwrights began depicting everyday people with everyday emotions. This had far-reaching effects in the world of opera, where comic opera or **Opera buffa** began to rival and even eclipse the more staid **Opera seria**; eventually the stage was set for **Opera Reform**, both musically and dramatically.

As private patronage declined, a modern audience for music emerged. Public concerts competed with the older-style private concerts and academies. In Paris, the composer and oboist Anne Danican Philidor founded the *Concert spirituel* series in 1725, which lasted until 1790; he also started the more secular but short-lived *Concerts français* in 1727. J. A. Hiller began a concert series in Leipzig in 1763, which continued after 1781 as the famous *Gewandhaus* concerts. Similar organizations were founded in Vienna (1771) and in Berlin (1790). Concert societies had flourished in London sporadically since 1672.

All of this concert activity created a favorable climate for **Instrumental Music**, which ultimately triumphed over opera in popularity by the end of the century. Chamber or solo **Sonatas**, orchestral **Symphonies**, and solo **Concertos** for pianoforte and other instruments became the new vehicles to fame for composers of the Classic period.

What educated people in the middle and later eighteenth century wanted, according to leading critics of the time, might be summarized as follows: the language of music should be universal, that is, not limited by

▲ Concert at Vauxhall pleasure gardens, where for a fee the public could enjoy music and other entertainment outdoors. Here Mrs. Weischel sings from the "Moorish-Gothick" temple, accompanied by the orchestra behind her, while Dr. Johnson, Boswell, and others eat in the supper box below. Watercolor (ca. 1784) by Thomas Rowlandson. (*Print Collection, Miriam and Ira D. Wallach Division of Arts, Prints & Photographs, The New York Public Library, Astor, Lenox, and Tilden Foundations*)

national boundaries; music should be noble as well as entertaining; it should be expressive within the bounds of decorum; and it should be "natural"—free of needless technical complications and capable of immediately pleasing any sensitive listener.

General Characteristics of the New Style

The focus on melody in the new eighteenth-century style led to a more linear construction that contrasted sharply with the motivic variation and thorough-bass accompaniment characteristic of earlier styles. J. S. Bach, for example, would announce the musical idea of a movement—a melodic-rhythmic subject embodying the basic affection—at the outset. He then spun out his material with relatively infrequent and inconspicuous cadences, and with sequential repetition of phrases within periods as a principal constructive device. The result was either a highly integrated movement without sharp contrasts, or (as in many Vivaldi concertos) a formal pattern of contrasts between thematic tutti and nonthematic solo sections. In either case, the phrase structure was usually so irregular that no pronounced feeling of musical *periodicity* existed.

Melody

C H R O N O L O G Y

1720			*Gluck, Orfeo ed Euridice in Vienna; Jean-Jacques Rousseau, Le Contrat social (1762)
	*The Beggar's Opera in London (1728)		Mozart in London as a child prodigy (1764)
	*Metastasio appointed court poet in Vienna (1729)		Joseph II becomes Holy Roman Emperor and co-ruler with his mother, Maria
1730			Theresa (1765)
	*Johann Adolph Hasse, Cleofide in Dresden (1731)	**1770**	*J. C. Bach, Sei concerti for pianoforte, Op. 7 (ca. 1770)
	Birth of Franz Joseph Haydn (1732)		*Gluck, Orphée et Euridice in Paris; first
	*G. B. Pergolesi, La serva padrona in Naples; Rameau, Hippolyte et Aricie in Paris (1733)		Continental Congress in Philadelphia; Louis XVI, king of France (reigned until 1792) (1774)
	*Domenico Scarlatti, first collection of harpsichord sonatas published (1738)		American Revolution (until 1783) (1775)
1740	Frederick the Great of Prussia crowned (reigned until 1786)		General histories of music by Sir John Hawkins and Charles Burney; Declaration of Independence
	Handel, Messiah in Dublin (1742)		
	*C. P. E. Bach, "Prussian" sonatas for keyboard (1742)	**1780**	Death of Maria Theresa: Joseph II sole Habsburg ruler
	*Sammartini, Symphony in F major (ca. 1744)		Immanuel Kant (1724–1804), Critique of Pure Reason (1781)
1750	J. S. Bach dies		
	*Pergolesi, La serva padrona in Paris; outbreak of Querelle des bouffons (1752)		Edward Gibbon (1737–1794), The History of the Decline and Fall of the Roman Empire (1788)
	Voltaire, Candide (1759)		
	*Mannheim orchestra thrives under Johann Stamitz (1750s)		John Henry Fuseli (1741–1825), The Nightmare (ca. 1790) (see Plate X, facing page
1760	George III of England crowned (reigned until 1820)		275)
			French Revolution (until 1794) (1789)

Melodic periodicity

Such periodicity, however, does characterize the newer styles, in which the melodic flow is disrupted by resting points that divide the line into, for example, antecedent and consequent phrases. Instead of persistently spinning out musical ideas, the composer articulates them through distinct phrases, typically two or four measures in length (but also frequently three, five, or six measures). This technique creates a structure marked by frequent full and half cadences and integrated through motivic correspondences. By analogy with verbal composition, a musical unit made up of shorter phrases was considered a period, and a composition as a succession of such periods. It was natural, then, to compare a melody to a sentence or paragraph, to think of a musical composition as equivalent to a piece of prose writing or speech. (See the revealing parallels between oratory and music drawn by Johann Nikolaus Forkel [1749–1818] in the vignette, page 294.)

Harmonic periodicity

As with melody, the continuously driving harmonic motion typical of the older styles was also divided into a series of stable or even static moments. Consequently, harmonic change slowed down and modulations sounded less adventuresome. However, a lot of bustling activity occurs during these relatively slow-moving and conventional harmonies. For example, the *Alberti bass*, one of the most widely used devices of mid-eighteenth-century keyboard music, frequently animated the simple harmonies that accompany the new, *galant*-style melody. Named for the Italian composer Domenico Alberti (ca. 1710–1740), this device broke each of the underlying chords into a simple pattern of short, repeating notes that produced a discreet chordal background, thereby setting off the melody to advantage (Example 13.1). Haydn, Mozart, and Beethoven employed the handy Alberti bass, and its use lasted well into the nineteenth century.

Alberti bass

EXAMPLE 13.1   Domenico Alberti, *VIII sonate per cembalo*, Op. 1 (London, 1748), Sonata III, Allegro ma non tanto

Composers of the new eighteenth-century style still constructed a movement based on related keys but abandoned the older idea of expressing just one basic affection. Instead, they began to introduce contrasts between the various parts of a movement or even within the themes themselves. At the same time, natural philosophers also changed their perceptions about the emotional life of an individual. No longer believing that a person once aroused to a certain state of mind, like anger or fear, remained in that affection until moved by some stimulus to a different state, they now observed that feelings were in a constant state of flux, jostled by associations that might take unpredictable turns. Daniel Webb wrote of the pleasure a person experiences "not, as some have imagined, the result of any fixed or permanent condition of the nerves and spirits, but from a succession of impressions, and greatly augmented by sudden or gradual transitions from one kind of strain of vibrations to another."[1] Composers no longer tried to arouse listeners into a trancelike state of religious fervor or sympathetic identification with a char-

Emotional contrasts

1. Daniel Webb, *Observations on the Correspondence between Poetry and Music* (London: J. Dodsley, 1769), p. 47.

Johann Nikolaus Forkel on Oratory and Music:

❝An orator would behave unnaturally and contrary to the goals of edifying, persuading, and moving [an audience] by giving a speech without first determining what is to be the main idea [*Hauptsatz*], the secondary ideas [*Nebensätze*], the objections and refutations of the same, and the proofs. . . .

As musical works of any substantial length are nothing other than speeches by which one seeks to move the listener to a certain empathy and to certain emotions, the rules for the ordering and arrangement of ideas are the same as in an actual oration. And so one has, in both, a main idea, supporting secondary ideas, dissections of the main idea, refutations, doubts, proofs, and reiterations. Similar means to our end (in the musical sense) must be used. This order and sequence of the individual sections is called the aesthetic ordering of the ideas. A musical work in which this ordering is so arranged that all thoughts mutually support and reinforce one another in the most advantageous way possible, is well ordered. ❞

From *Allgemeine Geschichte der Musik* (Leipzig: Schwickert, 1788–1801), I, 50, adapted from the translation in Mark Evan Bonds, *Wordless Rhetoric: Musical Form and the Metaphor of the Oration* (Cambridge, Mass.: Harvard University Press, 1991), p. 123.

acter on stage. Instead, they now expected listeners to follow a series of musical thoughts like verbal discourse and understand their logic. Listening to a piece of music could thus be a daring exploration of different related or even opposed feelings.

Opera buffa

Many of the stylistic traits associated with the Classic period had their origins in the first decades of eighteenth-century Italian musical theater. Because tradition weighed less heavily on comic opera, it was more hospitable to innovations than serious opera. An Italian *opera buffa* was a full-length work with six or more singing characters and, unlike comic opera in other countries, was sung throughout. It served a moral purpose by caricaturing the foibles of both aristocrats and commoners, vain ladies, miserly old men, awkward and clever servants, deceitful husbands and wives, pedantic lawyers and notaries, bungling physicians, and pompous military commanders. These generally resemble the stock characters of the *commedia dell'arte*, the improvised comedy popular in Italy since the sixteenth century. The comic characters often spoke or sang in a dialect, as they did in some of the Venetian comedies, or the entire play might be in the local dialect, as in Naples. The comic cast was usually complemented by a number of serious characters who interacted with the comic characters, particularly in amorous intrigues, and were central to the main plot. The dialogue was set in rapidly delivered recitative and accompanied by keyboard only. The arias presented short tuneful phrases, often repeated, accompanied by simple harmonies, and organized into tidy periods.

Another important type of Italian comic opera, the *intermezzo*, originated in the custom of presenting short comic musical interludes between the acts of a serious opera or play. These intermezzi contrasted sharply with the grand and heroic manners of the principal drama, sometimes even parodying its excesses. The plots were mostly situation comedies involving a few ordinary people, who sang, as in serious opera, recitatives and arias.

Giovanni Battista Pergolesi (1710–1736) was an early master of the intermezzo. One of the most original composers in the early Classic style, he also wrote important *opere serie*. Pergolesi's *La serva padrona* (The Maid as Mistress), for soprano, bass, a third character who is mute, strings, and continuo, was written as an interlude to one of his own serious operas in 1733 in Naples. Its performance in Paris twenty years later set off the *querelle des bouffons* (see page 305).

> **Intermezzo**

> **Pergolesi, La serva padrona**

◄ Performance of an *intermezzo*, a short comic work given between the acts of an opera seria. Painting, Venetian School, eighteenth century. (*Milan, Museo Teatrale alla Scala*)

A scene in which Serpina, the maid, warns her grumpy boss and would-be lover, Uberto, that she is about to marry the mute character, Vespone, displays the extraordinary aptness and nimbleness of Pergolesi's music (see NAWM 87). Serpina delivers the news in simple recitative, to which Uberto reacts first in an agitated *obbligato* recitative, then in a da capo aria. Neither the main nor the middle section develops a single musical motive; rather, there are as many melodic ideas as there are thoughts and moods in the text. The first line, in which Uberto exclaims in a patter style how confused he is, repeats the same music three times, reinforcing it for the listener but also suggesting Uberto's mental paralysis (Example 13.2a). Then Uberto, realizing that something mysterious is stirring his heart (measure 15), waxes lyrical as he asks himself whether he is in love. But a sober voice within checks his ardor—he should think of himself, guard his independence and interests—and now the melody shifts to deliberate, brooding, drawn-out notes (Example 13.2b). The middle section, instead of presenting contrasting music, develops earlier material, converting some of the musical motives of the first section into the minor mode.

EXAMPLE 13.2   Giovanni Battista Pergolesi, *La serva padrona: Son imbrogliato io già*

I am all mixed up. I have a certain something in my heart. Truly I cannot tell whether it's love or pity. I hear a voice that tells me: "Uberto, think of yourself."

Unlike opera seria, which maintained its character across national boundaries, comic opera took different forms in different countries. It usually represented everyday people in familiar situations and required relatively modest performing resources. Comic opera librettos were always written in the national tongue, and the music itself tended to accentuate the national musical idiom. From humble beginnings the comic opera grew steadily in importance after 1760, and before the end of the century many of its characteristic features were absorbed into the mainstream of operatic composition. The historical significance of comic opera was twofold: it responded to the widespread demand for naturalness during the latter half of the eighteenth century, and it represented the earliest conduit toward musical nationalism, which became prominent during the Romantic period.

The French version of opera buffa, known as *opéra comique*, began around 1710 as a lowly form of popular entertainment performed at parish fairs. Until the middle of the century, the music consisted almost entirely of popular tunes (*vaudevilles*) or simple melodies imitating such tunes. The visit of an Italian comic opera troupe to Paris in 1752 stimulated the production of opéras comiques in which original airs (called *ariettes*) in a mixed Italian-French style were introduced along with the old vaudevilles. Ariettes gradually replaced the vaudevilles until, by the end of the 1760s, they, too, were completely discarded and all the music was freshly composed. Christoph Willibald Gluck (see pages 303–5), one of the composers exposed to the French opéra comique during this transitional decade, arranged and composed a number of opéras comiques for the entertainment of the Vienna court. Jean-Jacques Rousseau (1712–1778) wrote a charming little comic opera in 1752 with airs and recitatives, *Le Devin du village* (The Village Soothsayer). The air "J'ai perdu tout mon bonheur" (I have lost all my happiness, NAWM 89), inspired by the new Italian melodic style, is neatly phrased in groups of two measures, naïvely harmonized, and simply accompanied. The air is interrupted by a passage that imitates Italian recitative in its speechlike delivery but somewhat incongruously introduces French-style ornaments.

> *French* **opéra**
> **comique**

> *Rousseau*

The French opéra comique, like all the national variants of light opera except the Italian, used spoken dialogue instead of recitative. Following the European trend in the second half of the century, opéra comique dealt boldly with the social issues that were agitating France during the pre-Revolutionary years. François André Danican Philidor (1726–1795; also a famous chess master), Pierre-Alexandre Monsigny (1729–1817), and above all the Belgian-born André Ernest Modeste Grétry (1741–1813) were the principal composers of the time.

Ballad opera rose to popularity after the extraordinary success of *The Beggar's Opera* in London in 1728. This piece broadly satirizes the fashionable Italian opera; its music, like that of the early opéra comique, consists for the most part of popular tunes—ballads—with a few numbers that parody familiar operatic airs (see excerpts in NAWM 90). The immense popularity of ballad operas in the 1730s signaled a general reaction in England against foreign opera—that "exotic and irrational entertainment," as Dr. Samuel Johnson called it. As we have already seen, Handel turned his energies from opera to oratorio in the latter part of his life, partly in reaction to the success of ballad opera (see pages 277–78).

> *English ballad*
> *opera*

Although Singspiel existed in Germany since the sixteenth century, the success of the ballad opera in the eighteenth century inspired its revival. At

> *German Singspiel*

first librettists adapted English ballad operas, but they soon turned to translating or arranging French comic operas, for which the German composers provided new music in a familiar and appealing melodic vein. Many of the eighteenth-century Singspiel tunes found their way into German song collections and in the course of time have virtually become folksongs. The principal composer of Singspiel music during this period was Johann Adam Hiller (1728–1804) of Leipzig. In northern Germany, the Singspiel eventually merged with early-nineteenth-century native opera. In the south, particularly in Vienna, farcical subjects and treatment became fashionable, with lively music in a popular vein influenced by Italian comic opera.

Opera seria

The light and charming style of opera buffa soon invaded serious opera. Opera seria was based on Italian librettos treating serious subjects and purged of comic scenes and characters. Its standard form came from the Italian poet Pietro Metastasio (1698–1782), whose dramas many eighteenth-century composers (including Mozart) set to music hundreds of times. Metastasio's success with librettos for Naples, Rome, and Venice, most notably *Didone abbandonata* (Dido Abandoned) in 1724, led to his appointment in 1729 as court poet in Vienna. He remained in Vienna for the rest of his life, turning out a profusion of Italian librettos and many works for special occasions at the imperial court. His heroic operas present a conflict of human passions, often pitting love against duty, in stories based on ancient Greek or Latin tales. They were intended to promote morality through entertainment and to present models of merciful and enlightened rulers. The magnanimous tyrant—for example, Alexander the Great in *Alessandro nell'Indie*, or Titus in *La clemenza di Tito*—is a favorite character. The librettos employ the conventional cast of two pairs of lovers and subordinate personages. The action provides opportunities for introducing varied scenes—pastoral or martial episodes, solemn ceremonies, and the like. The resolution of the drama, which rarely has a tragic ending, often turns on a deed of heroism or sublime renunciation by one of the principal characters.

Metastasio

The three acts of an opera seria consist almost invariably of alternating recitatives and arias; recitatives develop the action through dialogue, while each aria is a virtual dramatic soliloquy in which a principal actor expresses feelings or reacts to the preceding scene. Occasional duets or larger ensembles do occur, and rarely choruses in a simple style, but the main musical interest of the Italian opera seria is centered in the arias, which eighteenth-century composers created in astounding profusion and variety.

Musical structure

The most frequently used form in the first half of the century was the
da capo aria, a basic scheme that permitted enormous variation in detail.
Metastasio's two-stanza aria texts set the standard for the full-blown da capo
aria from the 1720s through the 1740s. The form, originally presented in
Chapter 10 (see page 212), is now somewhat expanded and may be represented by the following outline (in which the keys, indicated by Roman numerals, are hypothetical):

The aria

							Fine		Da capo al fine
Music:	Ritornello	A1		Rit.	A2		Rit.	B	
Text:		lines 1–4			lines 1–4 developed			lines 5–8	
Key:	I	I	→ V	V	V	→	I∥I	vi	

(For an example and discussion of an aria that conforms to this outline see
NAWM 88.)

After about the middle of the century, composers explored ways to
shorten the repetitious and long-winded A sections with their full da capo
reiteration. They invented various schemes that abbreviated the return of the
ritornello and the primary section, often by altering the instruction "da capo"
(from the beginning) to "dal segno" (from the sign), indicating that only a
portion of the A section is repeated, or writing out an abridged return (see
the aria by Pergolesi, NAWM 87, for an example). It also became more common to write arias in a single movement—usually an expanded version of a
da capo-aria A section using a typical key scheme of the sonata, and orchestral
ritornellos as in a concerto.

Abbreviated da capo

Turning the aria into virtually the only significant musical ingredient in
opera opened the way to abuses. Singers, including the famed Italian *castrati*
(male sopranos and altos who were castrated before their voices changed; see
window, pages 280–81), made arbitrary demands on the poets and composers, compelling them to alter, add, and substitute arias without respect for
dramatic or musical appropriateness. Moreover, the melodic embellishments
and cadenzas that singers added at will were often mere displays of vocal
acrobatics. Some of the excesses were enumerated in *Il teatro alla moda* (The
Fashionable Theater), a famous satire on the opera and everything connected with it, published anonymously in 1720 by the composer Benedetto
Marcello.

Reign of the singers

Despite these criticisms, the da capo aria continued to grow and evolve.
Arias written in the first decades of the century usually projected a single
affection through the development of a single motive. Now composers started
to express a succession of moods, using a variety of musical material that
ranged from lighthearted to tragic. Often two keys are contrasted in the first

New features of da capo arias

main period (the A1 section); then the material in the second key is recapitulated in the tonic at the close of the second main period (the A2 section). The aria's ritornello may introduce both the material sung later in the primary key and that in the secondary key, thus resembling the orchestral exposition of a concerto (see page 313). In this way vocal music began incorporating structural methods of instrumental music—the sonata and concerto—something that remained true throughout the eighteenth century. But the vocal melody still dominated the music and carried it forward, and the orchestra provided harmonic support to the singer rather than adding independent contrapuntal lines. The melodies were usually presented in four-measure units, consisting of two-measure antecedent and consequent phrases. When a composer deviated from this formula, it was usually for a deliberately unbalancing effect.

Handel employed this new idiom in his late operas, such as *Alcina* (1735) and *Serse* (1738), as did Pergolesi (see page 296) and Handel's rivals in London, Giovanni Bononcini and Nicola Porpora, and a German, Johann Adolph Hasse (1699–1783).

Hasse

Hasse was acknowledged by most of his contemporaries as the great master of the opera seria. For most of his life he directed music and opera at the court of the elector of Saxony in Dresden, but he spent many years in Italy, married the celebrated Italian soprano Faustina Bordoni, and became so thoroughly Italian in his musical style that the Italians nicknamed him "il caro Sassone" (the dear Saxon). His music is the perfect complement to Metastasio's poetry; the great majority of his eighty operas use Metastasio librettos, some of which he set two and even three times. Hasse was the most popular and successful opera composer in Europe around the middle of the century, and the contemporary English music historian Charles Burney reveals the qualities that endeared him to the connoisseurs:

Burney on Hasse

> . . . the most natural, elegant, and judicious composer of vocal music . . . now alive; equally a friend to poetry and the voice, he discovers as much judgment as genius, in expressing words, as well as in accompanying those sweet and tender melodies, which he gives to the singer.[2]

The famous aria "Digli ch'io son fedele" (Tell him that I am faithful; NAWM 88) from Hasse's *Cleofide* (1731), his first opera for Dresden, illustrates the qualities that Burney admired.

Faustina Bordoni

The title role of Cleofide in 1731 was created by Hasse's bride, Faustina Bordoni (1700–1781). Bordoni, who established her reputation in Venice while still in her teens, made her German debut in Munich at the age of twenty-three. Like other opera singers, she embellished the written vocal line

---

2. Burney, *The Present State of Music in Germany* (2nd ed., London, 1775), 1:238–39.

when she performed an aria. An elaborated version of this aria survives in the hand of Frederick II, king of Prussia (reigned 1740–86), an amateur flutist and composer, as sung by the castrato Antonio Uberti, known as Porporino. This version, written out above Hasse's melody in Example 13.3, is ablaze

EXAMPLE 13.3   J. A. Hasse, *Cleofide*, Act II, Scene 9: Digli ch'io son fedele

Tell him that I am faithful, tell him that he's my darling; to love me; that I adore him; that he not yet despair.

▲ Faustina Bordoni (1700–1781), universally admired as one of the great singer-actresses of her age. She married Johann Adolph Hasse in 1730 and enjoyed her first success in Germany in the title role of his *Cleofide* (Dresden, 1731; see NAWM 88). She created several roles in Handel's London operas in the 1720s. Burney praised her fluent articulation, trills, improvised embellishments, and expressive power. She is shown here as Attilia in Hasse's *Attilio Regolo* in a costume designed for the original production at the Dresden Hoftheater, January 12, 1750. (*Sächsische Landesbibliothek, Dezernat Deutsche Fotothek, Dresden*)

Vocal embellishment ▶ with trills, mordents, rapid turns, appoggiaturas, scales, triplets, and arpeggios. Scholars believe that such embellishments were added especially in the da capo repetition.

Opera Reform

Certain Italian composers wanted to bring opera into harmony with the changing ideals of music and drama. They sought to make the entire design more "natural"—that is, more flexible in structure, more deeply expressive, less laden with coloratura, and more varied in other musical resources. They did not abandon the da capo aria but modified it and introduced other forms as well; they alternated arias and recitatives less predictably so as to move the action forward more rapidly and realistically; they made greater use of obbligato recitative and ensembles, such as trios; they made the orchestra more important, both for its own sake and for adding harmonic depth to accompaniments; they reinstated choruses, long absent in Italian opera; and they stiffened their resistance to the arbitrary demands of the solo singers.

Two of the most important figures in the movement of reform were Nicolò Jommelli (1714–1774) and Tommaso Traetta (1727–1779). That both these Italian composers worked at courts where French taste predominated—Jommelli at Stuttgart and Traetta in Parma—naturally influenced them toward a cosmopolitan type of opera. As the composer of some one hundred stage works, Jommelli enjoyed great popularity; his arias permeate the many collections of Italian vocal music that circulated in manuscripts copied during the second half of the eighteenth century. Traetta aimed to combine the best of French *tragédie lyrique* and Italian opera seria in his *Ippolito ed Aricia* (1759), adapted from the same libretto that Rameau had set. He even utilized some of Rameau's dance music and descriptive symphonies, and, unusual for this time in Italy, included a number of choruses. For the solo roles, Traetta relied on the conventional genres of recitative and aria. In his own way Traetta reconciled the two types of music drama—Italian and French—years before Gluck set out to do so.

Christoph Willibald Gluck (1714–1787) achieved a synthesis of French and Italian opera that made him the man of the hour. Born in what is now Bavaria of Bohemian parents, Gluck studied with Sammartini in Italy (see page 308), visited London, toured in Germany as conductor of an opera troupe, became court composer to the Emperor Charles VI at Vienna, and triumphed in Paris under the patronage of Marie Antoinette. Initially, he composed operas in the conventional Italian style but was strongly affected by the reform movement in the 1750s. Spurred on by the forward-looking impresario Giacomo Durazzo, he collaborated with the poet Raniero de Calzabigi (1714–1795) to produce at Vienna *Orfeo ed Euridice* (1762) and *Alceste* (1767). In a dedicatory preface to *Orfeo*, Gluck expressed his resolve to remove the abuses that had deformed Italian opera (see vignette, page 304) and to confine music to its proper function—to serve the poetry and advance the plot. This he wanted to accomplish without regard either to the outworn conventions of the da capo aria or the desire of singers to show off their skill in ornamental variation. He further aimed to make the overture an integral part of the opera, to adapt the orchestra to dramatic requirements, and to lessen the contrast between aria and recitative.

Gluck

As an opera composer Gluck aspired to "a beautiful simplicity," which he realized in the celebrated aria *Che farò senza Euridice?* (What shall I do without Euridice?) from *Orfeo*, and in other airs, choruses, and dances from the same work. *Alceste* is more dramatic and monumental, in contrast to the prevailingly pastoral and elegiac tone of *Orfeo*. In both, Gluck molded the

Gluck on the Reform of Opera:

❝ I sought to confine music to its true function of serving the poetry by expressing feelings and the situations of the story without interrupting and cooling off the action through useless and superfluous ornaments. I believed that music should join to poetry what the vividness of colors and well disposed lights and shadows contribute to a correct and well composed design, animating the figures without altering their contours.

I further believed that the greater part of my task was to seek a beautiful simplicity, and I have avoided a display of difficulty at the expense of clarity. I assigned no value to the discovery of some novelty, unless it were naturally suggested by the situation and the expression. And there is no rule that I did not willingly consider sacrificing for the sake of an effect. ❞

From Gluck's dedication, in Italian, to *Alceste* (Vienna, 1769). For a facsimile, see *New Grove Dictionary* 7:466.

music to the drama, intermingling recitatives, arias, and choruses in large unified scenes. He also assigned an important role to the chorus. Compared to the final choruses Jommelli had employed in his Viennese operas in the early 1750s, Gluck's chorus of Furies in Act II (NAWM 91) is more integral to the action. In this scene Orfeo, accompanied by harp and strings to simulate a lyre, pleads for the liberation of Euridice, which the Furies resist, provoking and challenging Orfeo.

Gluck achieved his mature style in *Orfeo* and *Alceste*, amalgamating Italian melodic grace, German seriousness, and the stately magnificence of the French *tragédie lyrique*. After the success of those two works, he was ready for the climax of his career, which was ushered in with the Paris production of *Iphigénie en Aulide* (Iphigenia in Aulis) in 1774.

With a libretto adapted from Racine's tragedy, this work too was a tremendous success. Revised versions of *Orfeo* and *Alceste* (both with French texts) swiftly followed, and a new setting of Quinault's *Armide* (1777) to the same libretto that Lully had used in 1686. Gluck's next masterpiece, *Iphigénie en Tauride* (Iphigenia in Tauris, 1779) is a work of large proportions that displays an excellent balance of dramatic and musical interest and utilizes all the resources of opera—orchestra, ballet, solo and choral singing—to produce a total effect of classical tragic grandeur.

Gluck's operas became models for the works of his immediate followers in Paris. His influence on the form and spirit of opera was transmitted to the nineteenth century through such composers as Niccolò Piccinni (1728–1800), Luigi Cherubini (1760–1842), Gasparo Spontini (1774–1851), and Hector Berlioz (1803–1869).

Instrumental Music: Sonata, Symphony, and Concerto

Sonata

In the Baroque era, sonata generally meant a multi-movement work for a small group of instruments, most often in trio texture. In the Classic period, the word had different meanings for different composers, two of whom we

The *Querelle des bouffons*

The musical atmosphere of the French capital was so charged that Gluck's *Iphigénie en Aulide* awakened extraordinary interest. Long-simmering critical opposition to the old-fashioned, state-subsidized French opera erupted in 1752 in a pamphlet war known as the *querelle des bouffons* ("quarrel of the comic actors"). The immediate occasion for the dispute was the presence in Paris of an Italian opera company that for two seasons had enjoyed sensational success with its performances of Italian comic operas and intermezzi, particularly Pergolesi's *La serva padrona*. Practically every intellectual and would-be intellectual in France took part in the quarrel—partisans of Italian opera on one side and friends of French opera on the other. Rousseau, one of the leaders of the "Italian" faction, published an article in which he argued that the French language was inherently unsuitable for singing. Rousseau and his friends, despite the foolish extremes to which they occasionally strayed in the heat of argument, represented enlightened opinion in Paris. As a result of their campaign, the traditional French opera of Lully and Rameau soon lost favor; but nothing appeared to take its place until Gluck arrived on the scene. Gluck cleverly represented himself—or was represented by his supporters—as wanting to prove that a good opera could be written to French words; he professed a desire for Rousseau's aid in creating "a noble, sensitive, and natural melody . . . music suited to all nations, so as to abolish these ridiculous distinctions of national styles."* He thus appealed at the same time to the patriotism and to the curiosity of the French public.

* Gluck, Letter to the Editor of *Mercure de France*, February 1773.

will study here—Domenico Scarlatti and C. P. E. Bach; it also connoted a compositional procedure or form, first articulated by the German theorist Heinrich Christoph Koch (1749–1816).

D. Scarlatti

Domenico Scarlatti (1685–1757), born to Alessandro Scarlatti in the same year as Bach and Handel, would become the chief Italian keyboard composer of the eighteenth century and one of the most original creative artists in the history of music. He left Italy in 1720 or 1721 to work as a musician for the king of Portugal. When his pupil, the infanta of Portugal, was married to Prince Ferdinand of Spain in 1729, Scarlatti followed her to Madrid, where he remained for the rest of his life in the service of the Spanish court. He published his first collection of harpsichord sonatas (called on the title page *essercizi*—exercises) in 1738, but most of his 555 sonatas are known to us through scribal copies from his time.

Scarlatti's sonatas are organized by means of tonal relationships into the standard late-Baroque and early-Classic binary pattern used for dance pieces and other types of composition. They have two sections, each repeated, the first closing in the dominant or relative major (rarely some other key), the second modulating further afield and then returning to the tonic. This basic scheme underlies much instrumental and solo vocal music in the eighteenth century. In Scarlatti's sonatas the closing part of the first section invariably returns at the end of the second section, but in the tonic key.

The one-movement sonata written around 1749 identified as K. 119 or Longo 415[3] (NAWM 92) exhibits many of the genre's traits. It has two sections, each repeated. After a brilliant opening, several ideas are announced, each immediately restated. The ideas are not all of the same importance or function. The first, a broken-chord motive spanning two octaves, is introductory. The next bold theme (Example 13.4a), immediately repeated, never returns. The third (Example 13.4b) is purely cadential; the fourth (Example 13.4c), imitating the rhythm and effect of castanets, has a modulatory function here but comes back again to close each half of the sonata. Then the central idea arrives, in the dominant minor (Example 13.4d). It is inspired by Spanish guitar music, with an almost constant a' sounding like an open string being strummed alongside those being fingered. This thematic element is most developed throughout the piece; in the second section it rises to a vigorous climax in which all the notes of the key but one are sounded together (Example 13.4e).

The majority of Scarlatti's sonatas after 1745 appear in the manuscripts in pairs, each pair comprising, in effect, a sonata of two movements, always in the same key (though one may be major and the other minor), sometimes similar in mood, sometimes contrasted. Many eighteenth-century composers, from Alberti to Mozart, wrote sonatas in two movements, possibly under

---

3. The sonatas are identified by K. numbers in Ralph Kirkpatrick's index of the sonatas or by a different set of numbers in A. Longo's complete edition of the sonatas.

EXAMPLE 13.4   Domenico Scarlatti, Motives from Sonata K. 119

Italian influence, although there is no evidence that they took the idea from Scarlatti. In fact, just as Scarlatti seems to have created his own keyboard idiom virtually without models, so too he had no successors, with the exception of a few Iberian composers, notably the Catalan Antonio Soler (1729–1783).

Italian composers of the middle and late eighteenth century produced a large amount of music for harpsichord that remains less familiar than the works of C. P. E. Bach and other German composers. Yet Italians and Germans were equally active in experimenting with formal organization in the keyboard sonatas of the eighteenth century.

The Italian opera overture (*sinfonia*) influenced keyboard sonatas and orchestral compositions of similar form during the early part of the eighteenth century. About 1700, the overture assumed a three-movement structure in the order fast-slow-fast: an Allegro, a short lyrical Andante, and a finale in the rhythm of some dance, such as a minuet or a gigue. These overtures, as a rule, had no musical connection with the opera they introduce and could be played as independent pieces in concerts. It was a natural step, then, for Italian composers to begin writing concert symphonies using the general plan of opera overtures. The earliest of these, dating from around 1730, are equally

Early symphonies

indebted to the tradition of the late Baroque concerto and of the trio sonata in details of structure, texture, and thematic style. One of the early works in this genre, the Symphony in F major (ca. 1744) by Giovanni Battista Sammartini (1701–1775) of Milan, is scored for two violins, viola, and bass. The opening Presto (NAWM 93) presents a variety of ideas in rapid succession, much like a Scarlatti keyboard sonata. The binary form, with full recapitulation of the opening tonic and closing dominant sections, fits the scheme of a sonata-form movement.

Most instrumental music by Haydn, Mozart, Beethoven, and their contemporaries, whether called sonata, trio, string quartet, or symphony, is written in three or four movements of contrasting mood and tempo. The first movement is usually in sonata form, which expands and divides the original binary form into three sections:

> **Sonata form**

(1) An *exposition* (usually repeated), incorporating a first theme or group of themes in the tonic; a second, often more lyrical, theme or group in the dominant, or in the relative major if the movement is in a minor key; and a closing, often cadential, theme also in the dominant or relative major—the different themes being connected by appropriate transitions or bridge passages.

(2) A *development* section in which motives or themes from the exposition are presented in new aspects or combinations and in the course of which modulations may be made to relatively remote keys.

(3) A *recapitulation*, where the material of the exposition is restated in the original order but with all themes in the tonic; following the recapitulation there may be a *coda*.

: Exposition :	Development	Recapitulation	(Coda)
: (1) :	(2)	(3)	

This description of sonata form is obviously an abstraction, dwelling particularly on the key scheme and the melodic-thematic ideas. So understood, it fits a good many sonata movements of the late Classic period and the nineteenth century, but there are many that depart from it in creative ways.

The Empfindsam *Style*

German composers, though not the originators of the sentimental style (*empfindsamer Stil*, see page 288), began introducing it into their instrumental music toward the middle of the century. Two of J. S. Bach's sons are important in this connection. The eldest, Wilhelm Friedemann (1710–1784), was a gifted organist and composer whose life ended in disappointment and poverty

> **W. F. Bach**

◀ Frederick the Great playing the flute, accompanied by a small orchestra, with C. P. E. Bach at the harpsichord. Painting by Adolph von Menzel, 1852. (*Staatliche Museen zu Berlin, Preussicher Kulturbesitz: National-Galerie*)

because he could not adjust to the requirements for a successful musical career. Carl Philipp Emanuel Bach (1714–1788) was one of the most influential composers of his generation. Trained in music by his father, he served at the court of Frederick the Great in Berlin from 1740 to 1768 and then became music director of the five principal churches in Hamburg. His compositions include oratorios, songs, symphonies, concertos, and chamber music, but most numerous and important are his works for keyboard. In 1742 he published a set of six sonatas (the *Prussian sonatas*) and in 1744 another set of six (the *Württemberg sonatas*). These sonatas were new in style and exerted a strong influence on later composers. His favorite keyboard instrument was not the harpsichord but the softer, more intimate, clavichord, which had a capacity for delicate dynamic shadings. The clavichord enjoyed a spell of renewed popularity in Germany around the middle of the eighteenth century before both it and the harpsichord were gradually supplanted by the pianoforte. The last five sets of C. P. E. Bach's sonatas (1780–87) were evidently written with the pianoforte chiefly in mind, as were many of the later keyboard pieces of W. F. Bach. This instrument, ancestor of the modern piano and now commonly called the "fortepiano," permitted the player to vary the loudness from *piano* to *forte* by striking the keys more heavily.

C. P. E. Bach

The main technical characteristics of the *empfindsam* style, of which C. P. E. Bach was a leading exponent, are apparent in the second movement, Poco Adagio (NAWM 94), of the fourth sonata from his *Sonaten für Kenner und Liebhaber* (Sonatas for Connoisseurs and Amateurs; composed in 1765 but not published until 1779). It begins with a kind of melodic sigh, a singing motive ending in an appoggiatura that resolves on a weak beat, followed by

Main characteristics of **empfindsam** *style*

a rest (Example 13.5). This opening is decorated with a turn, Scotch snaps, and a trill. The multiplicity of rhythmic patterns, nervously and constantly changing—short dotted figures, triplets, asymmetrical flourishes of five and thirteen notes—gives the music a restless, effervescent quality.

EXAMPLE 13.5   C. P. E. Bach, Sonata: Poco Adagio

The expressive style of C. P. E. Bach and his contemporaries often exploited the element of surprise, with abrupt shifts of harmony, strange modulations, unusual turns of melody, suspenseful pauses, changes of texture, sudden *sforzando* accents, and the like. The subjective, emotional qualities of this *Empfindsamkeit* reached a climax during the 1760s and 1770s; the trend

Sturm und Drang   is sometimes described by the expression *Sturm und Drang*—storm and stress—a movement in German literature that relished tormented, gloomy, terrified, irrational feelings. Later, composers brought this emotionalism under control, but its relevance will be discussed in the next chapter.

German Symphonic Composers

Mannheim, Vienna, and Berlin were the principal German centers of symphonic composition after 1740. Under the leadership of Johann Stamitz (1717–1757), the Mannheim orchestra became renowned all over Europe for its virtuosity (Burney called it "an army of generals"), for its astonishing and novel dynamic range—from the softest *pianissimo* to the loudest *fortissimo*—and for the thrilling sound of its crescendo, though many of the striking dynamic effects and the dramatic contrasts were adapted from the Italian opera overture. The first movement (NAWM 95) of Johann Stamitz's Sinfonia in E♭ from the mid-1750s provides a good example of the Mannheim symphony.

Mannheim and Stamitz

Another center of symphonic writing in the 1740s was Vienna, home to Georg Matthias Monn (1717–1750) and Christoph Wagenseil (1715–1777). In Wagenseil's music we find the pleasant, typically Viennese lyricism and good humor that is such an important feature of Mozart's work. The Viennese composers for the most part favored contrasting theme groups in their sonata-form movements.

Vienna

The Eighteenth-Century Orchestra

The eighteenth-century concert orchestra was much smaller than today's. Haydn's orchestra from 1760 to 1785 rarely had more than twenty-five players, comprising strings, flute, two oboes, two bassoons, two horns, and a harpsichord, with trumpets and kettledrums occasionally added. Even in the 1790s the Viennese orchestras did not usually number more than thirty-five players. After 1775 the basso continuo was gradually abandoned in the symphony, and in other forms of ensemble music, as all the essential voices were taken over by the melody instruments. Responsibility for conducting the group fell to the leader of the violins. Typical orchestration at midcentury gave all the essential musical material to the strings and used the winds only for doubling, reinforcing, and filling in the harmonies. Sometimes in performance woodwinds and brasses might be added to the orchestra even though the composer had not written any parts specifically for them. Later in the century the wind instruments were entrusted with more important and more independent material.

▲ Surrounding a harpsichord and a seated cellist is a chamber ensemble consisting of three violins, four woodwinds, two trumpets, and three singers. The instrumentalists read from music desks, while the singers hold their parts. The man at the end seems to be conducting with a scroll, but the folio in his left hand contains a Christian motto or perhaps the title of a cantata, rather than music notation. Anonymous eighteenth-century painting. (*Germanisches Nationalmuseum, Nuremberg, Courtesy RCMI*)

Berlin   The principal symphonists of the Berlin, or North German, school clustered around Frederick the Great, who was himself a composer; Johann Gottlieb Graun (1702 or 1703–1771) and C. P. E. Bach became two of its chief members. The North Germans were conservative in holding to the three-movement structure for the symphony and in their reluctance to introduce sharp thematic contrasts within a movement. But they were also forward-looking, often utilizing thematic development within a dynamic, organically unified, serious, and quasi-dramatic style, as well as enriching the symphonic texture with contrapuntal elements.

J. C. Bach's Concertos

Johann Christian Bach (1735–1782), J. S. Bach's youngest son, created a great stir in London with some of the earliest concertos for the pianoforte. He was also an important composer of symphonies, as well as of chamber music, keyboard music, and operas. Trained in music by his father and his elder brother C. P. E. Bach, Johann Christian made his way to Milan at the age of twenty. He studied with the celebrated theorist, teacher, and composer Padre

Giovanni Battista Martini (1706–1784) of Bologna. Bach was appointed organist of the cathedral at Milan in 1760, by which time he had converted to the Roman Catholic faith. Two years later, after two of his operas had been successfully produced in Naples, he moved to London, where he enjoyed a long career as composer, performer, teacher, and impresario. He had great success there with some forty keyboard concertos, written between 1763 and 1777. The title of his Opus 7 (ca. 1770), *Sei concerti per il cembalo o piano e forte* (Six Concertos for Harpsichord or Pianoforte), bears witness to his early adoption of the pianoforte for public performance. The eight-year-old Mozart spent a year in London (1764–65), during which he met Bach and was very much impressed with his music. Mozart converted three of Bach's keyboard sonatas into concertos (K. 107/21b) and must have had Bach's models in mind when he wrote his first complete piano concerto, K. 175, in 1773.

The first movement of Bach's Concerto for Harpsichord or Piano and Strings in E♭, Op. 7, No. 5 (NAWM 96), illustrates many features typical of the concerto at this time. By 1770 the main outlines of the solo concerto's first-movement form were well established. It retains elements of the ritornello structure of the Baroque period but is imbued with the contrasts of key and thematic material characteristic of the sonata. The first movement usually exhibits the following succession of events:

Section:	Exposition							
Key:	Tonic					Dominant		
Instruments:	Orchestra				Solo with Orchestra			Orchestra
Themes:	P	TT	K	KT	P TT	S	K KT	

Development		Recapitulation			
Foreign Keys to Dominant		Tonic			
Solo with Orchestra	Solo	Solo with Orchestra		Solo	Orchestra
New material	Short cad.	P TT (S)	K	Cadenza	KT

In this diagram, P = primary-theme section, S = secondary-theme section, K = closing-theme section, TT = transitional tutti, and KT = closing tutti.

The parallels to the Baroque concerto evident in this design will be discussed in relation to Mozart's K. 488 (see Chapter 14), where they stand out even more in the context of his symphonic style.

POSTLUDE

The early Classic period explored a wealth of new genres, forms, and expressive means. Much of its innovation found outlets in opera, particularly comic opera. There, the urge to entertain and reach a wider audience led to a simplification of means and a striving for naturalness of expression. From the Italian theaters the new styles spread through the cosmopolitan network of musicians, composers, and directors to such centers as Paris, Mannheim, and Vienna. Many practices spilled out of the theaters into the concert halls and private chambers. In the process of conversion the excesses of the Italian opera were purged, resulting in a spare, transparent, logical—almost proselike—flow of musical ideas that could be grasped on first hearing. Instrumental music in particular profited from these developments, because it was now intelligible even without a text or a title. These developments laid the foundations for the eventual complete domination of instrumental music in the Classic period.

14

THE LATE EIGHTEENTH CENTURY:

HAYDN AND MOZART

PRELUDE

Haydn and Mozart, the two outstanding composers of the late eighteenth century, had a great deal in common: even though Haydn was the elder by twenty-four years, they were personal friends; each admired and was influenced by the music of the other; they were both practicing musicians—Mozart a virtuoso pianist, Haydn a fine violinist who also conducted from the harpsichord—and they both composed prolifically and with careful attention to detail.

Their lives and careers also differed in many ways. Haydn, born during J. S. Bach's lifetime, lived to the ripe old age of seventy-seven. Mozart, born in 1756, died in the prime of his life, at the age of thirty-five. Haydn's growth to artistic maturity was much slower than that of Mozart, a child prodigy whose star rose quickly and burned brightly for only a few decades. Haydn worked contentedly during most of his career in the service of a noble Hungarian family. Mozart gave up a steady job in his hometown of Salzburg to become a free agent in Vienna. Most important, Mozart traveled a great deal in his early years—to England, Italy, Germany, and France—and absorbed the many styles and practices current in these countries, whereas Haydn found his models within local traditions around Vienna.

Because **Franz Joseph Haydn** remained in the same job for so long, his career does not easily divide into distinct periods. We will therefore discuss his works chronologically according to genre: first **Haydn's Instru-**

mental Music, where he made his most original contribution, and then Haydn's Vocal Works, which include operas, oratorios, and Masses. By contrast, Wolfgang Amadeus Mozart moved around a lot, and each new location brought new opportunities for composition. Therefore, we will discuss his works chronologically according to place, grouping them generally into Mozart's Years in Salzburg and Mozart's Vienna Years, even though he did not confine his activities solely to these cities.

Franz Joseph Haydn (1732–1809)

Early life

Haydn was born in Rohrau, a little town near the Hungarian border in what is now Austria. He received his first musical training from an uncle with whom he went to live at the age of five. Two years later he became a choirboy at St. Stephen's Cathedral in Vienna, where he acquired a great deal of practical experience but received no systematic instruction in music theory. Dismissed when his voice changed, the youth supported himself precariously as a freelance musician and teacher. He mastered counterpoint by studying J. J. Fux's *Gradus ad Parnassum* (Steps to Parnassus), an important textbook published in 1725 that codified the *stile antico* of Palestrina. Meanwhile he made himself known to influential people in Vienna and took lessons in composition from Nicola Porpora, a famous Italian composer and singing teacher who had been Handel's rival in London. In 1758 or 1759, he became music director for a Count Morzin and probably wrote his first symphony for the

Esterházy service

count's orchestra. The year 1761 was momentous in Haydn's life: he entered the service of Prince Paul Anton Esterházy, head of one of the wealthiest and most powerful Hungarian families, a man devoted to music and a bountiful patron. Haydn remained in the family's employ off and on for the rest of his days.

Haydn's Instrumental Music

Although Haydn's music responded to changing tastes and to a variety of genres, certain enduring traits stand out, especially in the symphonies.

Symphonic Form

Many of Haydn's earliest symphonies are in the early Classic three-movement form derived from the Italian opera overture (sinfonia). They typically consist of an Allegro, an Andante in the parallel minor or subdominant key, and a Minuet or a rapid gigue-like movement in $\frac{3}{8}$ or $\frac{6}{8}$ (for example, Symphonies

▲ Eszterháza Palace, built 1762–66 as a summer residence on the Neusiedler Sea by the Hungarian prince Nicholas Esterházy, whom Haydn served for almost thirty years. The palace opera house opened in 1768 with a performance of Haydn's *Lo speziale*. Engraving, 1791, by János Berkeny after Szabó and Karl Schütz. (*Budapest, Hungarian National Museum*)

Nos. 9 and 19). Other symphonies from the early period (for example, Nos. 21 and 22) are in four movements, all in the same key, usually Andante-Allegro-Minuet-Presto, recalling the slow-fast-slow-fast sequence of the sonata da chiesa. Soon after composing these early symphonies, Haydn established the four-movement pattern as the standard for the Classic era: I. Allegro; II. Andante moderato; III. Minuet and Trio; IV. Allegro.

A typical first-movement Allegro alternates stable and unstable periods. The stable periods are not tension-free, but their tonality as well as their rhythmic and melodic profiles remain consistent. These passages—the statements of the primary, secondary, and closing material—are usually presented symmetrically, most often in balanced four-measure phrases, and are clearly delimited by cadences, at least in the early symphonies. A combination of string and wind ensembles, with some tutti punctuations, presents the ideas. The unstable passages, mainly transitions and developments, are often tutti or culminate in tutti. They are characterized by nervous rhythmic energy, sequences, modulatory thrusts, asymmetrical phrasing, powerful harmonic drive, and avoidance of cadences. Slow introductions, when they occur, are usually unstable from the very outset.

First-movement form

In a typical Allegro movement, Haydn reiterates the opening statement immediately, but with some destabilizing turns of harmony or rhythm that steer the music in a new direction. A transition or bridge passage to the dominant or relative major or minor follows. The transition is usually a loud

Exposition

Music at Eszterháza and Haydn's Career

*A*t the court of Prince Paul Anton and his brother Nicholas, called the "Magnificent," who succeeded to the title in 1762, Haydn spent nearly thirty years under circumstances that were ideal for his development as a composer. Beginning in 1766, Prince Nicholas lived for most of the year at his remote country estate of Eszterháza. Designed to rival the splendor of the French court at Versailles, the palace and grounds boasted two theaters, one for opera and one for puppet plays, as well as two large and sumptuously appointed music rooms in the palace itself. Haydn was required to compose whatever music the prince demanded, to conduct the performances, to train and supervise all the musical personnel, and to keep the instruments in repair. He built up the orchestra to about twenty-five players. Operas and concerts became weekly events; almost every day in the prince's private apartments chamber music was also heard. The prince himself usually played the baryton, an instrument resembling a large viola da gamba with an extra set of resonating metal strings that could be plucked like a harp. Haydn wrote some 165 pieces for the baryton, mostly trios with viola and cello.

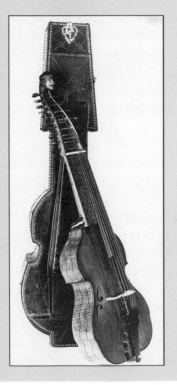

◄ This baryton, shown leaning against its case, was owned by Prince Nicholas Esterházy; it was made in Vienna by Johann Joseph Stalmann in 1750. The instrument, a favorite of the prince's, resembled a bass viol but had a set of sympathetic strings that could be plucked and that added to its resonance. Haydn created a baryton repertory of some 165 pieces so that the prince could participate in chamber music. (*Budapest, Hungarian National Museum*)

Although Eszterháza was isolated, Haydn kept abreast of current developments in the world of music through the constant stream of distinguished guests and artists and through occasional trips to Vienna. He had the double advantage of a devoted, highly skilled troupe of singers and players and an intelligent patron, whose requirements may have been burdensome but whose understanding and enthusiasm were inspiring. As Haydn once wrote, "My prince was pleased with all my work, I was commended, and as conductor of an orchestra I could make experiments, observe what strengthened and what weakened an effect and thereupon improve, substitute, omit, and try new things; I was cut off from the world, there was no one around to mislead and harass me, and so I was forced to become original."

As Haydn's fame spread in the 1770s and 1780s, he filled many commissions from publishers and individuals all over Europe, but he remained at Eszterháza until Prince Nicholas's death in 1790. Nicholas's son Anton became the next Prince Esterházy and immediately disbanded his father's orchestra. Haydn was given a pension and went to live in his own house in Vienna, but not for long. Two strenuous but highly productive and profitable seasons in London followed (January 1791 to July 1792, and February 1794 to August 1795), mostly under the management of the impresario and violinist Johann Peter Salomon. Here Haydn conducted concerts and wrote a multitude of new works, including the *London* symphonies (Nos. 93 to 104), his last twelve works in this genre.

London visits

Anton Esterházy died while Haydn was in London and was succeeded by Nicholas II, who cared less about Haydn's music than about the glory he could claim for having such a famous person in his employ. He persuaded Haydn to resume directing music for the court, which now resided almost all year in Vienna. Haydn's duties were light, the principal obligation being to compose a Mass every year between 1796 and 1802 for the princess's name day. He could devote himself to composing quartets, trios, and his last two oratorios, *Die Schöpfung* (The Creation, completed 1798), and *Die Jahreszeiten* (The Seasons, completed 1801), both performed in Vienna with resounding success.

Last years in Vienna

tutti with dramatic, rushing figures, a perfect foil for the second thematic section, which is more lightly scored, melodically distinctive, and harmonically stable. In most of the symphonies of the 1770s and 1780s, Haydn clearly contrasted the secondary material with the opening idea. But in some, as in the later *London* symphonies, Haydn built the second thematic section on the opening material. The exposition usually ends with a closing tutti based on a cadential, repetitive, vigorous figure, sometimes harking back to the opening but usually distinct from the primary and secondary subjects. In some of the movements, the section in the secondary key is devoted entirely to the closing subject.

Development

Haydn rarely introduced new thematic ideas after the exposition's closing double bar. The development often begins with a restatement of the opening subject, or sometimes with transition material or with one of the other subjects. Motives from the exposition are combined, superimposed, and extended; manipulated through sequences, fugue-like counterpoints, and strettos; or turned into rushing figurations for busy passages. Abrupt changes of subject, digressions, and silences are Haydn's particular signatures. In the course of his career, Haydn endowed the development section with increasing length and weight until it achieved parity with the other two sections.

Recapitulation

We are usually well prepared for the arrival of the recapitulation, but its actual onset is sometimes disguised or played down and not even recognized until after the fact. The section recapitulates all of the material in the tonic, though sometimes a theme originally in the major mode may return in the minor, or vice versa. Only in some early symphonies did Haydn cling to the older procedure of recapitulating only the secondary or closing section in the tonic. He almost always began the reprise with the opening subject, sometimes rescoring and extending it in new ways. Rather than curtailing the transitions because he did not need to modulate, he often intensified and animated them with a simulated modulation. He also occasionally altered the comparative weight given to the secondary and closing subjects. Haydn did not usually write a coda but instead amplified the closing section.

This model of a Haydn symphonic sonata-form movement is only an abstract template that matches any specific movement more or less well. The procedures described here may be observed by studying the first movement of Symphony No. 56 (see NAWM 97 with its commentary).

Minuet and Trio

A Minuet-and-Trio movement appears in most Classic symphonies. The Minuet itself is always in a two-part form: ‖: a :‖: b (a′) :‖. The Trio is built along similar lines; it is usually in the same key as the Minuet (possibly with a change of mode), but it is shorter with lighter orchestration. After the Trio, the Minuet returns da capo, resulting in a three-part ABA form for the movement as a whole. Haydn's Minuets with their Trios contain some of his most charming music, remarkable for its wealth of ideas and happy traits of harmonic invention and instrumental color in such a modest medium. He said once he wished someone would write "a really new minuet," but Haydn himself succeeded admirably in doing so nearly every time he wrote one.

The Classic symphony generally demanded the most attention from its audience in its first movement. The second movement offered an oasis of calm and gentle melody after the complexity and contrasts of the first movement. The Minuet provided relaxation, since it was shorter than either of the two preceding movements; it was written in a more popular style, and its form was easy for the listener to follow. But the Minuet does not make a satisfactory closing movement. It is too short to balance the preceding two, and the spirit of relaxation it induces must be dispelled by a further build-up of tension, climax, and release. Haydn soon came to realize that the $\frac{3}{8}$ or

$^6_8$ Presto finales of his earliest symphonies were inadequate to accomplish this: they were too light in form and content to produce a satisfying effect in the symphony as a whole. He therefore developed a new type of closing movement, which first appeared in the late 1760s: an Allegro or Presto in $^2_4$ or ¢, usually shorter than the first movement, compact, swiftly moving, overflowing with high spirits and nimble gaiety, and abounding in little whimsical tricks of silence and all sorts of impish surprises.

Finale

Of Haydn's more than 104 symphonies, at least ninety-two were completed by 1789, most of them for Prince Esterházy's orchestra. He composed Nos. 82–87, now known as the *Paris* symphonies, on commission in 1785–86 for a concert series in the French capital. Nos. 88–92 were privately commissioned. No. 92, now called the *Oxford* symphony, was played when Haydn received an honorary Doctor of Music degree from Oxford University in 1791. His last twelve, the *London* symphonies, were completed in 1795 for a concert series organized by Salomon in that city. Many of the other symphonies (as well as many of the quartets) have acquired nicknames for one reason or another, few of them from the composer himself.

The Symphonies of 1768–74

The symphonies of 1768–74 (Nos. 38–60) show Haydn as a composer with a mature technique and fertile imagination. No longer viewing it as light entertainment or as a delightful overture to an opera, Haydn now regarded the symphony as a serious work that demanded close listening. The deeply emotional and agitated character of these symphonies, particularly those in minor keys, has been associated with the movement in literature known as *Sturm und Drang* (Storm and Stress). But some of Haydn's symphonies in this group antedate the literary movement, which received its name from a 1776 play by Friedrich Maximilian Klinger (see pages 310–11, and Plate X, facing page 275).

Sturm und Drang

Many are on a larger scale than the symphonies of the previous decade. Themes are more broadly laid out, those of the fast movements often beginning with a bold unison proclamation followed immediately by a contrasting idea, with the whole theme then restated. Development sections, limited to motives from the exposition, have become more propulsive and dramatic. The changes from *forte* to *piano* and the crescendos and *sforzati* that entered Haydn's writing at this time are also startling. The harmonic palette is richer than in the early symphonies; modulations range more widely, the harmonic arches are broader, and counterpoint is integral to the musical ideas.

The slow movements have a romantically expressive warmth. Most of the slow movements are in sonata form, but with such a leisurely flow of musical ideas that a listener is hardly conscious of the structure. In Symphony No. 44 in E minor, known as the *Trauersinfonie* (Symphony of Mourning), we find one of the most beautiful Adagios in all of Haydn's works. The slow move-

Slow movements

ment of No. 47 is a theme with variations, a favorite form for slow movements in Haydn's later works.

Farewell Symphony

According to a well-known story, Haydn wrote the *Farewell* Symphony (No. 45) as a hint to Prince Esterházy that it was time to move back into town from his summer palace and give the musicians a chance to see their families again. The final Presto breaks off into an Adagio, in the course of which one group of instruments after another concludes its part and the players get up and leave; only two first violins remain to play the closing measures.

The Symphonies of 1774–88

The symphonies of 1774–88 exhibit a striking change, most evident in Nos. 54 and 57, both composed in 1774. The minor keys of the preceding period, the passionate accents, and the experiments in form and expression now give way to a smooth and assured exploitation of orchestral resources in works that are cheerful and robust. Indeed, once the composer had resolved to write "not so much for learned ears," he allowed his comic-opera style to affect his symphonic writing.

Symphony No. 56

Symphony No. 56 (1774; see NAWM 97 for first movement) is one of twenty symphonies set in C major. These constitute a special group, many of them composed for particular celebrations at Eszterháza. Like his five previous C-major symphonies, No. 56 is festive and brilliant, with high trumpets (labeled clarini in the score), high French horns, two oboes, a bassoon, and timpani (but no flutes, which Haydn used then only rarely). The work reflects the esteem with which the genre was regarded in the 1770s. Audiences expected symphonies that were serious, ambitious, stirring, and impressive, yet immediately intelligible and appealing.

Paris *symphonies*

The six *Paris* symphonies of 1785–86 (Nos. 82–87) were commissioned for the large orchestra of the *Concerts de la Loge Olympique*. Queen Marie Antoinette, who frequently attended these concerts, is said to have especially loved No. 85, called *La Reine*. After the six symphonies were performed again in 1787, this time at the *Concert spirituel*, a reviewer of the *Mercure de France* noted how "this great genius could draw such rich and varied developments from a single subject, so different from the sterile composers who pass continually from one idea to another."

Symphonies Nos. 88 to 92

Symphonies Nos. 88 to 92 of 1787–88 foreshadow the *London* symphonies. Four of these symphonies begin with a slow introduction, whose themes are sometimes related to the following Allegro. Contrasting subjects in sonata-form movements now appear more infrequently. Rather, a set of ideas announced at the beginning pervades and then is developed continuously throughout the movement. Many of the slow movements close with a quiet, introspective coda that features woodwind instruments and employs colorful chromatic harmonies (as in No. 92, NAWM 98). The wind instruments are prominent also in the Trios of the Minuets. In the finales, Haydn made considerable use of contrapuntal devices and texture—for example he included a canon in the last movement of No. 88. By such means he endowed closing movements with both popular appeal and sufficient weight to balance the rest of the symphony.

London *Symphonies*

Like other composers of his time, Haydn mostly wrote music for specific occasions and for players and singers he knew. When he accepted a commission from outside Eszterháza, he found out as much as he could about the performers, the concert hall, and related matters so that he could adapt the music to the particular circumstances of the performance. The invitation from Salomon in 1790 to compose and conduct six, and later six more, symphonies for the cosmopolitan and exacting audiences of London spurred him to supreme efforts. Hailed by the British as "the greatest composer in the world," he was determined to live up to what was expected of him, and the *London* symphonies are indeed his crowning achievements. Everything Haydn

Haydn on His Rivalry with His Pupil Pleyel:

66 There isn't a day, not a single day, in which I am free from work, and I shall thank the dear Lord when I can leave London—the sooner the better. My labours have been augmented by the arrival of my pupil Pleyel, whom the Professional Concert have brought here. He arrived here with a lot of new compositions, but they had been composed long ago; he therefore promised to present a new work every evening. As soon as I saw this, I realized at once that a lot of people were dead set against me, and so I announced publicly that I would likewise produce 12 different new pieces. In order to keep my word, and to support poor Salomon, I must be the victim and work the whole time. But I really do feel it. My eyes suffer the most, and I have many sleepless nights, though with God's help I shall overcome it all. The people of the Professional Concert wanted to put a spoke in my wheel, because I would not go over to them; but the public is just. I enjoyed a great deal of success last year, but still more this year. Pleyel's presumption is sharply criticized, but I love him just the same. I always go to his concerts and am the first to applaud him. 99

Haydn in London, writing to Marianne von Genzinger in Vienna, March 2, 1792. Translated from the German in H. C. Robbins Landon, *The Collected Correspondence and London Notebooks of Joseph Haydn* (London: Barrie & Rockliff, 1959), p. 132.

had learned in forty years of experience went into them. While he did not depart radically from his previous works, he brought all the elements together on a grander scale, with more brilliant orchestration, more daring harmonic conceptions, more intense rhythmic drive, and, especially, more memorable thematic inventions.

Special effects

Haydn's shrewd appraisal of London's musical tastes is evident in little things as well as great ones. The sudden *fortissimo* crash on a weak beat in the slow movement of Symphony No. 94 that has given this work its nickname *Surprise* was put there because, as he later acknowledged, he wanted something novel and startling to take people's minds off the concerts of his pupil and rival Ignaz Pleyel (1757–1831; see vignette, page 323). The greater tunefulness may also have been prompted by this competition, since Pleyel's strong suit was melody. In response, Haydn turned to Slovenian, Croatian, and other peasant tunes he remembered from his youth. The first, second, and fourth movements of Symphony No. 103 display characteristic instances of folklike melodies. The finale of No. 104 (NAWM 99), with its imitation of the bagpipe, is particularly suggestive of a peasant dance (Example 14.1). Similar allusions are the "Turkish" band effect (triangle, cymbals, bass drum) and the trumpet fanfare in the Allegretto of the *Military* Symphony (No. 100), and the ticking accompaniment in the Andante of No. 101 (the *Clock*). Haydn always aimed to please both the music lover and the expert, and it is a measure of his greatness that he succeeded.

EXAMPLE 14.1   Haydn, Symphony No. 104: Finale, Allegro spiritoso

Orchestration

The orchestra of the *London* symphonies includes trumpets and timpani, which (contrary to Haydn's earlier practice) are used in most of the slow movements as well as in the others. Clarinets appear in all of the second set of *London* symphonies except No. 102. Trumpets sometimes maintain independent parts instead of doubling the horns as they had previously, and the cellos are now more often independent of the basses. In several of the symphonies, Haydn featured solo strings against full orchestra. He treated woodwinds even more independently than before, and the whole sound of the orchestra achieves a new spaciousness and brilliance.

Harmonic imagination plays an important part in the slow introductions of the *London* symphonies. These opening sections have a portentous quality, a deliberate dramatic suspense that grips the listener awaiting the Allegro. They are set either in the tonic minor of the Allegro (as in Symphonies Nos. 101 and 104) or they gravitate toward the minor mode as a foil for the major mode of the ensuing fast movement (as in No. 94).

Harmony

The movements in sonata form tend to revolve around the primary subject. This subject often pervades the section in the dominant, which in Haydn's earlier work usually presented a light, graceful contrast to the dynamic opening. The slow movements take either the form of a theme with variations (Nos. 94, 95, 97, 103) or a free adaptation of sonata form; one feature common to both is a contrasting minor section. The minuets, no longer courtly dances, are allegro movements in Minuet-and-Trio pattern. Like the corresponding movements of the late quartets (see page 329), they are already scherzos in everything but name and tempo.

Sonata-form movements

Some of the finales are in sonata form, but Haydn's favored pattern is the rondo or sonata-rondo, a form in which an opening A section returns following each of several contrasting sections—ABACABA is typical for Haydn. Some of his rondos, however, are infused with sonata-form elements. A brilliant sonata-rondo is the finale of the *Drumroll* Symphony, No. 103 in E♭, in which the A and B sections serve as the first and second themes in the exposition and recapitulation. The first return of A is a tonic interlude in the development section, C is a modulatory passage in the development, and the final return of A acts as a closing section before the coda. The entire movement grows out of two opening ideas, a fanfare for two horns and a sprightly theme that is heard against it (Example 14.2).

Finales

EXAMPLE 14.2   Haydn, Symphony No. 103: Allegro con spirito

The String Quartets

By the time Haydn was forty, his reputation as the first great master of the string quartet was confirmed by the publication of Opp. 17 (1771) and 20 (1772). In these works, all four movement-types—sonata-allegro, minuet, slow movement, and fast finale—are treated with assurance and finesse, although the positions of the second and third movements are often reversed from their usual place in the symphonies. The four instruments make their individual contributions: the first violin plays the most virtuosic part, but the

Quartets through 1781

Fugues

Sonata-form movements

cello shares increasingly in carrying the melodic line; the texture is free of any dependence on a basso continuo. At the same time, counterpoint contributes tension and excitement. Three of the finales in Opus 20 are labeled "fuga," which was not unusual for the time, and suggests that Haydn and his contemporaries were attempting to raise this medium from the lighter, more *galant* chamber works for strings that had been fashionable in Paris during the 1760s.

In the sonata-form movements, Haydn adopted strategies peculiar to his quartets. After the exposition of a primary subject, almost always dominated by the first violin, he usually chose a looser texture in which the primary motives pass from one instrument to another. In place of the orchestral tutti that typically announce the bridge and other transitions in the symphonies, Haydn favored loud unisons or stark modulatory gestures. The arrival of landmark moments, such as the secondary thematic section in the recapitulation, may be marked not by a cadence but by subtler means. For example, in Op. 20, No. 4 in D major, the second theme at measure 84 is preceded by a *fortissimo* broken-chord unison spelling out the dominant seventh of the tonic, D (Example 14.3). The tonality remains ambiguous for several more measures, and the first emphatic cadence does not arrive until measure 99, when a short closing section begins. The development sections of the Opus 20 quartets are nearly equal in length to the exposition and recapitulation. Moreover, motives first presented in the exposition are developed over the entire movement, a procedure that Haydn followed throughout his career.

EXAMPLE 14.3   Haydn, String Quartet Op. 20, No. 4: Allegro di molto

Ten years went by before Haydn composed the six quartets of Opus 33 (1781) and proclaimed to two admirers that they were written in a "quite new and special way." Opus 33 is lighthearted, witty, and tuneful, perhaps influenced by Mozart's six quartets K. 168–173, which were published a few years earlier. Haydn's quartets are very much addressed to the players, who are all invited to share in the fun. Only the first movements are in sonata form; the finales (except that of No. 1) are either rondos or variations. The Minuets, here titled "scherzo" (Italian for jest) or "scherzando" (playful), do literally play tricks on the courtly dance by occasionally breaking the normal metrical pattern of the minuet.

Opus 33

Even apart from the Scherzos, Opus 33 contains some of Haydn's happiest strokes of wit and humor. Near the opening of Op. 33, No. 4 (Example 14.4), in the midst of a serious exposition, Haydn's rhythmic displacements and unexpected rests mock the normal logic of melodic succession. Haydn also

Humor in Opus 33

EXAMPLE 14.4 Haydn, String Quartet Op. 33, No. 4: Allegro moderato

indulged in a lot of playfulness in the themes themselves and in the dialogue between players, thereby adding merriment to the amateur quartet evenings that were held in cities, such as London, Paris, and Vienna, in country estates of the nobility, and even in monasteries.

The quartets of 1785–90

The quartets written between 1785 and 1790 include Opp. 42, 50 (the six *Prussian* quartets, 1787), 54 and 55 (1788), and Op. 64 (six quartets, 1790). Opus 50 stands out because of Haydn's increasingly frequent use of mono-thematic first movements. This unifying technique affects some of the finales also. For example, the finale of Op. 64, No. 5 is a monothematic rondo (NAWM 100). All that distinguishes the *couplets*, or contrasting sections, from the refrains in this movement are their foreign keys and their new applications of counterpoint.

The last quartets

The quartets of Haydn's last period include Opp. 71 and 74 (three works each, 1793), 76 (a set of six, 1797), 77 (two quartets, of which the second is probably Haydn's greatest work in this genre), and the two-movement Op. 103 (1803). In these quartets, Haydn frequently based his second thematic section on the first, and used the closing section to inject contrast. He also expanded the harmonic frontiers, foreshadowing Romantic harmony in his chromatic progressions, in his novel uses of the augmented sixth chords, in his enharmonic changes, and in his fanciful tonal shifts. The powerfully emotional outpouring in the Largo assai of Op. 74, No. 3 reaches a climax with double stops in three of the instruments at a "German" sixth (Example 14.5, measure 8) en route to the dominant.

EXAMPLE 14.5   Haydn, String Quartet Op. 74, No. 3: Largo assai

Another characteristic of Haydn's late quartets, as in his symphonies of this period, is the juxtaposition of the serious and jocular, the artful and the folksy, the enigmatic and the simpleminded. Opus 76, No. 1 opens with three majestic chords before the cello solemnly unfolds its beautiful main theme. By contrast, the second theme simulates a peasant bagpipe tune with a double drone (*D* and *A*; see Example 14.6).

EXAMPLE 14.6   Haydn, String Quartet Op. 76, No. 1: Allegro con spirito

Haydn's use of the slow-movement variations form decreased in the late quartets, but one outstanding example occurs in Op. 76, No. 3 (NAWM 101). Haydn composed the melody as a birthday hymn for Kaiser Franz Joseph I (Example 14.7). (It later became the national anthem of the Austro-Hungarian Empire and serves to this day as the German national anthem.) The variations, which pass the hymn tune from instrument to instrument, are a study in nonharmonic tones: appoggiaturas, suspensions, and changing notes.

Opus 76, No. 3

EXAMPLE 14.7   Haydn, Hymn: *Gott erhalte Franz den Kaiser*

May God preserve Franz, the Kaiser / Our good Kaiser Franz! / Long may he live / in fortune's bright light! / The climbing laurel blooms for him / Bestowing him with wreaths of honor wherever he goes. / May God preserve Franz, the Kaiser / Our good Kaiser Franz!

The Minuets, though less playful than those of Opus 33, are full of offbeat accents, interpolated "extra" measures, exaggerated leaps, and other spoofs of artificial formality. One of the cleverest of Haydn's Minuets appears in Op.

Opus 76 Minuets

76, No. 2 in the form of a canon (Example 14.8), the only complete one in the quartets. Far from being pedantic, it is satirical, as if it represented two drunken courtiers trying vainly to execute this dignified dance with grace to a strain made up of five- and six-bar phrases. The octave doubling of the two voices lays bare the harshness of the dissonances and open fifths. The Trio, as an antidote, is entirely homophonic and is set in the parallel major mode.

EXAMPLE 14.8 Haydn, String Quartet Op. 76, No. 2: Menuetto

Keyboard Sonatas

Haydn's early keyboard sonatas can be performed on a harpsichord, which allows for only certain changes in dynamics. His later sonatas, however, call for the performer to realize dynamic markings such as *sforzando* and *crescendo*, sudden accents, and other variations of touch that require a pianoforte. Haydn used a clavichord in his early years, but by 1780 he had a piano available. The authorized contemporary printed editions of the sonatas after 1780 give "fortepiano" or "pianoforte" as the first option, along with "clavicembalo" (usually meaning harpsichord).

Haydn's piano sonatas follow the same lines of development observed in the symphonies and quartets. Notable among the sonatas of the late 1760s and early 1770s is No. 44 in G minor. In the first movement Haydn skillfully exploited the opening ideas in the transitions and in the secondary and closing sections of the exposition. At the same time, the great rhythmic and textural variety and the delicate chromaticism in the movement betray *empfindsam* tendencies. Sonata No. 20 in C minor, begun in 1771 but not published until 1780, is a tempestuous work that characterizes this expressionistic period in the composer's career.

Haydn's last sonatas demonstrate how much in touch he was with the latest musical fashions and developments. Among them, No. 52 in E♭ merits special attention. Long a favorite of recitalists, it was written in 1794 for the virtuoso Therese Jansen Bartolozzi and published in England around 1800 as a "Grand Sonata for the Piano Forte"—and grand it is in every way. The sonata begins in the manner of the French overture, with full chords in dotted rhythm, and thoroughly exploits the power and scope of the new pianos. In the development section of the first movement Haydn lingered for a while in the Neapolitan-related key of E major, which is also the key of the Adagio that follows.

Haydn's Vocal Works

In a modest autobiographical sketch of 1776 written for an Austrian encyclopedia, Haydn named his most successful works: three operas, an Italian oratorio (*The Return of Tobias*, 1774–75), and his setting of the *Stabat Mater* (1767)—a work that was famous in Europe in the 1780s. He made no

◀ Eighteenth-century opera performance, perhaps at the Eszterháza opera house. (*Munich, Theater-Museum*)

mention of the sixty-odd symphonies he had written by then and referred to his chamber music only to complain that the Berlin critics dealt with it too harshly. Haydn may have been reticent about the symphonies because they were little known outside Eszterháza. Also, he may not have realized their significance and that of the string quartets until their enthusiastic reception in Paris and London showed him how highly regarded they were. Posterity has concurred with this endorsement.

Operas

In contrast, Haydn's operas were very successful in their day, but they were soon dropped from the repertory and are rarely heard even now. Opera occupied a large part of Haydn's time and energy at Eszterháza where, between 1769 and 1790, he arranged, prepared, and conducted some seventy-five operas by other composers; Eszterháza was, despite its remote situation, an international center for opera. Besides six little German operas for the puppet theater, Haydn wrote at least fifteen Italian operas. Most of these were of the opera buffa type, with music abounding in the humor and high spirits that came naturally to the composer. Haydn also composed three serious operas; the most famous was the "heroic drama" *Armida* (1784), remarkable for its dramatic accompanied recitatives and grand-scale arias.

Church music

Haydn was occasionally criticized for writing sacred music that was too cheerful. He replied that at the thought of God his heart "leaped for joy" and he did not think God would reproach him for praising the Lord "with a

Masses

cheerful heart." Among Haydn's most important Masses were the six he composed for Prince Nicholas II Esterházy between 1796 and 1802. All are large-scale festive Masses, using orchestra, chorus, and four solo vocalists. Like those of Mozart and his other South German contemporaries, Haydn's Masses have a flamboyance that also characterizes the architecture of the Austrian Baroque churches in which they were performed. These works, which employ a full orchestra, including timpani and trumpets, are written in a musical idiom similar to that of the opera and the symphony. The best known are the *Missa in angustiis* (Mass for Troubled Times) in D minor,

C H R O N O L O G Y			
1750	Death of J. S. Bach	**1780**	
	Pergolesi, *La serva padrona* in Paris (1752)		*Haydn, Op. 33 quartets (1781)
	Death of Handel (1759)		*Mozart, Haydn quartets published (1785)
1760	*Haydn becomes music director at Eszter-		*Mozart, *Don Giovanni* in Prague (1787)
	háza (1761)		*John Henry Fuseli (1741–1825), *The Night-*
	Gluck, *Orfeo ed Euridice* in Vienna (1762)		*mare* (ca. 1790) (see Plate X, facing page
	*Mozart in London as a child prodigy (1764)		275)
1770	Beethoven born in Bonn (d. 1827)		French Revolution (until 1794) (1789)
	Gluck, *Orphée et Euridice* in Paris (1774)	**1790**	
	American Declaration of Independence		*Death of Mozart; Haydn, first *London* sym-
	(1776)		phonies (1791)
		1800	
			*Haydn, *The Seasons* (1801)

▲ Performance of Haydn's *The Creation* on March 27, 1808, in the banquet hall of the University of Vienna. Engraving after the watercolor by Balthasar Wigand. (*Vienna, Historisches Museum der Stadt Wien*)

known as the Lord Nelson or Imperial Mass; and the *Missa in tempore belli* (Mass in Time of War), also known as the *Paukenmesse*, or Kettledrum Mass.

During his stay in London Haydn became acquainted with Handel's oratorios. At Westminster Abbey in 1791, he was so deeply moved by the Hallelujah Chorus in a performance of *Messiah* that he burst into tears and exclaimed, "He is the master of us all." Haydn's appreciation for Handel is apparent in all the choral parts of his late Masses, and above all in his oratorios *Die Schöpfung* (The Creation, completed 1798) and *Die Jahreszeiten* (The Seasons, completed 1801). The text of *Die Schöpfung*, by Baron Gottfried van Swieten, is based on the Book of Genesis and Milton's *Paradise Lost*. That of *Die Jahreszeiten*, also by van Swieten, is distantly related to James Thomson's poem "The Seasons," which had been published some seventy years earlier.

The charm of both works rests largely in their naïve and loving depiction of nature and of innocent joy in the simple life. Haydn's instrumental introductions and interludes are among the finest examples of late-eighteenth-century program music. His "Depiction of Chaos" at the beginning of *Die Schöpfung* introduces confusing and disturbingly dissonant harmonies. The transition in the following recitative and chorus, with its awesome choral

Oratorios

Creation *and* Seasons

outburst on the C-major chord at the words "Es werde Licht, und es ward Licht" (Let there be Light, and there was Light) was justifiably extolled by contemporary writers as the supreme example of the sublime in music (Example 14.9).

EXAMPLE 14.9   Haydn, *Die Schöpfung*, Part I: "Und Gott sprach"

Wolfgang Amadeus Mozart (1756–1791)

Early life

Wolfgang Amadeus Mozart was born in Salzburg, then a Bavarian city with a long musical tradition. A lively provincial center of the arts, it was the seat of an archbishop, and one of the numerous quasi-independent political units within the German Empire. Mozart's father, Leopold, served in the archbishop's chapel and later became its assistant director. He was a composer of some ability and reputation and the author of a celebrated treatise on violin playing. From earliest childhood Wolfgang showed such a prodigious talent for music that his father dropped all other ambitions and devoted himself to educating the boy (see window, pages 346–47)—and to exhibiting his and his sister Marianne's ("Nannerl") accomplishments in a series of tours that took them to France, England, Holland, and Italy, as well as to Vienna and the principal cities of Germany.

Already a keyboard virtuoso at age six, Mozart soon became a good or-

◄ Three Mozarts making music: Leopold, violin; Amadeus, age 7, piano; and Marianne (Nannerl), age 11, singing from a score. Engraving by Jean Baptiste Delafosse based on a watercolor of about 1764 by Louis Carrogis de Carmonetelle.

ganist and violinist as well. He spent over half his time from 1762 to 1771 touring and displaying his talents. Meanwhile he was composing: he produced his first minuets at the age of five, his first symphony just before his ninth birthday, his first oratorio at eleven, and his first opera at twelve. His more than six hundred compositions are listed and numbered chronologically in a thematic catalogue compiled by Ludwig von Köchel in 1862 and updated by Alfred Einstein and others; the Köchel or "K." numbers are universally used to identify Mozart's compositions.[1]

Mozart's Years in Salzburg

From 1774 to 1781 Mozart lived chiefly in Salzburg, complaining frequently about the narrow provincial life and the lack of opportunities. In a fruitless attempt to improve his situation, he undertook another journey in September 1777, this time with his mother, to Munich, Augsburg, Mannheim, and Paris. All his hopes for a good position in Germany or France came to nothing. His stay in Paris was further saddened by his mother's death in July 1778. He returned to Salzburg early the following year, more disconsolate than ever.

1. New Köchel numbers that have been assigned to reflect modern research are given in this book in parentheses.

Mozart's Teachers

*D*uring his apprentice years until around 1773, Mozart was completely under the tutelage of his father in practical affairs and in most musical matters as well. Thanks to his father's excellent teaching and to the many trips he took during his formative years, young Mozart was exposed to every kind of music written or heard in contemporary western Europe. In Paris he became interested in the keyboard works of Johann Schobert (d. 1767). In London he met J. C. Bach, whose music had a lasting influence on him. In Italy he assimilated the traditions of opera seria, the influence of Sammartini and other Italian symphonists, and studied counterpoint with Padre Giovanni Battista Martini. And in Vienna he came into contact with Haydn's music, which then became increasingly important in the young composer's creative life. He absorbed it all with uncanny aptitude, imitating others' works while improving on them. The ideas that influenced him not only echoed in his youthful compositions but also continued to grow in his mind, sometimes bearing fruit many years later. In this way, his work became a synthesis of national styles, a mirror that reflected the music of a whole age, illuminated by his own genius.

Nevertheless, he was steadily growing in stature as a composer, and he received a commission to compose an opera for Munich. *Idomeneo*, performed there in January 1781, is the best of Mozart's opere serie, despite its rather clumsy libretto. The music is dramatic and pictorial; in its numerous accompanied recitatives, its conspicuous use of the chorus, and its inclusion of the spectacular, *Idomeneo* reveals the influence of Traetta, Gluck, and the French *tragédie lyrique*.

Piano sonatas   Among the important works of this period are thirteen piano sonatas and several sets of variations for piano, including those on the French air *Ah, vous dirais-je maman*, K. 265 (=300e), better known as *Twinkle, twinkle, little star*. The variations were probably intended for pupils, but the sonatas were part of Mozart's concert repertory. Before that time he had improvised such pieces as needed, so that few solo piano compositions from the early years have survived.

The sonatas K. 279–284 were undoubtedly meant to be published together: there is one in each of the major tonalities in the circle of fifths from D down to E♭, and the six works show a wide variety of form and content. Köchel 310 (=300d), Mozart's first minor-key sonata, betrays the influence of Schobert (see above) in its full chordal accompaniments and stringlike tremolos (Example 14.10).

EXAMPLE 14.10 Mozart, Sonata K. 310 (=300d): Allegro maestoso

Sonata K. 331 (=300i) is notable among the sonatas from the early 1780s for its first movement, in variation form, and its finale. The latter, marked *Rondo alla turca*, imitates the Janissary music of the Turkish military bands—then popular in Vienna—with their cymbals and triangles and exaggerated first beats. (Mozart also included "Turkish music" in his comic Singspiel.)

Mozart's themes, more than Haydn's, have a distinct melodic profile. Although seeming to unfold naturally and spontaneously, often in the fluent manner of the Italian Allegro movements, they give evidence of careful shaping and grooming. The phrases of a statement are usually balanced between antecedent and consequent, but the second phrase is often extended, as in the Sonata in B♭, K. 333 (=315c), shown in Example 14.11. The entire theme develops from the opening gesture of a stepwise descent to an appoggiatura, which marks the end of every phrase, subphrase, and smaller unit in measures 1 to 5.

Themes

EXAMPLE 14.11 Mozart, Piano Sonata in B♭, K. 333 (=315c): Allegro

Mozart's piano sonatas are closely related to his sonatas for piano and violin. In his early years these duos were really piano pieces with optional violin accompaniment. Mozart also composed serenades and divertimentos in the 1770s and early 1780s for garden parties or actual outdoor performances, for weddings and birthdays, or for concerts at the homes of friends and patrons. The most familiar of Mozart's serenades is *Eine kleine Nachtmusik* (A Little Night-Music, K. 525; 1787), a work in four movements for string quintet but now usually played by a small string ensemble. Among the most notable compositions of Mozart's Salzburg period are the violin concertos K. 216, 218, and 219, in G, D, and A respectively (all 1775), and the

Other instrumental music

piano concerto in E♭, K. 271 (1777), with its romantic slow movement in C minor. The three violin concertos are the last of Mozart's compositions in this genre. The piano concerto K. 271, however, is but the first of a long series of great works that he wrote in hopes of captivating the Viennese public.

Mozart's Vienna Years

In 1781 Mozart decided, against his father's advice, to quit the service of the archbishop of Salzburg and settle in Vienna. He was optimistic about his prospects there. Indeed, his first years in the imperial capital went well. His Singspiel, *Die Entführung aus dem Serail* (The Abduction from the Harem, 1782), was performed repeatedly. He had all the distinguished pupils he was willing to take, he was idolized by the Viennese public both as pianist and composer, and he led the bustling life of a successful freelance musician. But after four or five seasons the fickle public deserted him, pupils fell off, commissions were few, family expenses mounted, and his health declined. Worst of all, no permanent position with a steady income came his way, except for an appointment in 1787 as chamber music composer to the emperor at less than half the salary that Gluck, his predecessor, had received. The most pathetic pages in Mozart's correspondence are the begging letters written between 1788 and 1791 to his friend and brother Freemason, the merchant Michael Puchberg of Vienna. To Puchberg's credit, he always responded generously to Mozart's appeals.

Most of the works that immortalized Mozart's name he composed in Vienna between the ages of twenty-five and thirty-five, when the promise of his childhood and early youth came to fulfillment. In every kind of composition he achieved a perfect synthesis of form and content, of the *galant* and the learned styles, of polish and charm on the one hand and textural and emotional depth on the other. The principal influences on Mozart during these last ten years of his life came from his continuing study of Haydn and his discovery of J. S. Bach. He was introduced to Bach's music by Baron

van Swieten

Gottfried van Swieten, who during his years as Austrian ambassador to Berlin (1771–78) had become an enthusiast for the music of North German composers. Van Swieten was the imperial court librarian and a busy musical and literary amateur; he later wrote the librettos of Haydn's last two oratorios. In weekly reading sessions during 1782 at van Swieten's home, Mozart became acquainted with Bach's *Art of Fugue, Well-Tempered Keyboard*, and other works. Bach's influence was deep and lasting and may be seen in the increased contrapuntal texture of Mozart's later works (for example, his last piano sonata, K. 576). It was probably also through van Swieten that Mozart became interested in Handel, whose *Messiah* Mozart reorchestrated.

Among the solo piano compositions of the Vienna period, the most important are the Fantasia and Sonata in C minor (K. 475 and 457). The Fantasia foreshadows Schubert's piano sonatas in its melodies and modulations, while the Sonata would serve as the model for Beethoven's *Sonate pathétique*.

Solo piano works

In 1785, Mozart published six string quartets dedicated to Joseph Haydn as a token of his gratitude for all that he had learned from the older composer. These quartets (K. 387, 421=417b, 428=421b, 458, 464, 465) were, as Mozart said in his dedicatory letter, "the fruit of a long and laborious effort"; indeed, the manuscript shows an unusually large number of corrections and revisions for a Mozart autograph. As we have seen, Haydn's Opus 33 quartets (1781) had fully established the technique of pervasive thematic development with complete equality of the four instruments.

The Haydn quartets

Quartet K. 421 (=417b) in D minor stands out because of its relentlessly tragic mood. The old descending tetrachord of the Baroque lament appears in the bass, accompanying a restatement of the opening theme; and although the piece has barely begun, the first violin strains for the highest note heard in the entire movement (Example 14.12). When, following contrasting yet stern secondary and closing groups, the theme returns in E♭ major after the double bar, the same descending bass line immediately darkens the optimistic reawakening.

EXAMPLE 14.12   Mozart, String Quartet K. 421 (=417b): Allegro moderato

Quintets

For all the excellence of his quartets, Mozart's genius reveals itself most fully in his quintets for two violins, two violas, and cello. The String Quintets in C major (K. 515) and G minor (K. 516), composed in the spring of 1787, are comparable to the last two symphonies in the same keys. Another masterpiece, the Clarinet Quintet in A (K. 581), was composed at about the same time as the opera buffa, *Così fan tutte*, and captured some of the same comic spirit.

Symphonies

Like Haydn, Mozart approached the symphony in his mature years with great seriousness. He wrote only six in the last ten years of his life—having earlier produced nearly sixty—and devoted much time and thought to their composition. The symphonies written before 1782 served most often as concert or theatrical "curtain raisers"; those composed after he settled in Vienna constituted the main feature on concert programs or at least shared billing with concertos and arias. The *Haffner* Symphony, K. 385, written in 1782 for the elevation to nobility of Mozart's childhood friend Sigmund Haffner, and the *Linz* Symphony, K. 425, written in 1783 for a performance in that city, typify the late symphonies in their ambitious dimensions, greater demands on performers (particularly wind players), harmonic and contrapuntal complexity and chromaticism, and final movements that are climactic rather than light. These symphonies are in every way as artful as the *London* symphonies of Haydn, and some may indeed have served as models for the older composer. The others of this group—recognized as his greatest—are the *Prague* Symphony in D major (K. 504) and the Symphonies in E♭ (K. 543), G minor (K. 550), and C major (K. 551, named the *Jupiter* by an English publisher). The last three were composed within six weeks in the summer of 1788.

Each of the six symphonies is a masterpiece with its own special character, in some cases influenced by other music that Mozart was working on at the time. Their opening gestures leave an indelible impression. Both the *Haffner* and the *Jupiter* begin with loud, forceful, unison statements followed by delicate ensemble responses (Example 14.13a, c). In both works, the disparate elements of the theme are immediately wedded through counterpoint (Example 14.13b, d).

EXAMPLE 14.13   Mozart, Symphony K. 385 (*Haffner*): Allegro con spirito

a.

b.

EXAMPLE 14.13 Mozart, Symphony K. 551 (*Jupiter*): Allegro vivace

c.

d.

Some of Mozart's symphonies are imbued with the spirit of his operas, for example, the comical element in the otherwise heroic *Jupiter* Symphony. For the closing section of the first movement, Mozart borrowed the melody of a comic aria he had written (Example 14.14). The repeated cadences in the symphony that follow this quotation are also from the world of comic opera.

EXAMPLE 14.14 Mozart's comic aria, *Un bacio di mano*, K. 541

You are a simpleton, my dear Pompeo / You'd better go study the ways of the world.

The three introductions to Symphonies K. 425, 504, and 543 are animated by the energy of the French overture, its majestic double-dotted rhythms, intense chordal harmony, and anacrusis figures. Rather than intimating subtly what is to come, as Haydn sometimes did, Mozart created suspense, tantalizingly wandering away from the key and making its return an important event.

As in Haydn's late symphonies, the finales do more than send an audience away in a cheerful frame of mind. They balance the serious and important opening movement with a highly crafted counterweight fashioned with

Introductions

Finales

whimsy and humor. In the Allegro assai of the G-minor Symphony, the acrobatic transformation of the main theme at once startles and pokes fun, with
its wild leaps and pregnant silences (Example 14.15). There is also a touch of

EXAMPLE 14.15   Mozart, Symphony K. 550: Allegro assai

whimsy in the finale of the *Jupiter* Symphony, which takes its first theme from
a fugue example in Fux's *Gradus ad Parnassum* and combines it in simple
and double counterpoint with five other motives: a countersubject, two bridge
figures, and both of the two motives that make up the second subject of the
sonata scheme. The coda weaves all these together in an unsurpassed triumph
of *ars combinatoria*, the art of combination and permutation derived from
mathematics that was taught by eighteenth-century music theorists as a means
of achieving melodic variety in composition. (See Example 14.16, in which

EXAMPLE 14.16   Mozart, Symphony K. 551: Allegro molto

P, S, and T stand respectively for primary theme, secondary theme, and transitional motives.)

Piano Concertos

Seventeen concertos for piano occupy a central place in Mozart's output during the Vienna years. He wrote many of them as vehicles for his own concerts, and we can gauge the rise and fall of his popularity in Vienna by the number he composed each year: three in 1782–83, four in each of the next two seasons, three again in 1785–86, and only one for each of the next two seasons; after that no more until the last year of his life, when he wrote K. 595 to play at a local concert. The first three Vienna concertos, K. 414 (=385p), 413 (=387a), and 415 (=387b), were, as Mozart wrote to his father,

> a happy medium between what is too easy and too difficult ... very brilliant, pleasing to the ear, and natural, without being vapid. There are passages here and there from which connoisseurs alone can derive satisfaction; but these passages are written in such a way that the less learned cannot fail to be pleased, though without knowing why.[2]

Among the rest are works in a great variety of moods, ranging from the concerto K. 488 in A, in a comparatively light vein (see NAWM 102, first movement) to K. 491 in C minor, one of Mozart's great tragic creations.

Form

The Classic piano concerto by Mozart and his contemporaries preserves certain formal features of the Baroque concerto. It follows the three-movement sequence fast-slow-fast. The first movement is in a modified concerto-ritornello form—indeed, the contemporary theorist Heinrich Christoph Koch described the form of the first Allegro as containing "three main periods performed by the soloist, which are enclosed by four subsidiary periods performed by the orchestra as ritornellos."[3] The second movement is a kind of aria, and the finale is generally dancelike or popular in character. A close look at a typical first movement, such as the Allegro from K. 488 in A major (discussed in detail in NAWM 102), will show how the ritornello of the Baroque concerto permeates the sonata form.

Baroque elements

The opening orchestral section displays both the thematic variety of a sonata-form exposition and several elements of the Baroque concerto ritornello: it is in a single key and it contains a transitional tutti that reappears in various keys throughout the movement. Maintaining the ritornello results in a version of sonata form that actually has two expositions, one orchestral and one solo with orchestra. (J. C. Bach had employed a similar procedure in his

2. Letter dated December 23, 1782, trans. in Emily Anderson, ed., *The Letters of Mozart and His Family* (New York: Norton, 1989).

3. Heinrich Christoph Koch, *Introductory Essay on Composition*, trans. Nancy K. Baker (New Haven: Yale University Press, 1983), p. 210.

Concerto for Harpsichord or Piano and Strings, Op. 7, No. 5, NAWM 96; see page 313). The exposition may be schematized as follows:

Section:	Exposition								
Tonal center:	Tonic				Dominant				
Instruments:	Orchestra				Solo with Orchestra				
Themes:	P	TT	S	KT	P	TT	S	K	TT
Measure:	1	18	30	46	67	82	98	114	137

In this diagram, P = primary group; S – secondary group; KT = closing tutti; TT = transitional tutti; K = closing group.

Typical second movement

The second movement of a Mozart concerto is like a lyrical aria, with a tempo of andante, larghetto, or allegretto. It is in the subdominant of the principal key, or, less often, in the dominant or the relative minor. Its form, although greatly variable in details, is most often a kind of modified sonata scheme without development or, like the *Romance* of K. 466, an ABACA rondo.

Typical finale

The finale is typically a rondo or sonata-rondo on themes with a popular character; these are treated in scintillating virtuoso style with opportunities for one or more cadenzas. Although the concertos were show pieces intended to dazzle an audience, Mozart never allowed display to gain the upper hand. He always maintained a healthy balance of musical interest between the orchestral and solo portions, and his infallible ear regulated the myriad combinations of colors and textures he drew from the interplay between the piano and orchestral instruments, especially the winds. Moreover, the goal of composing for an immediate public response did not keep him from expressing the most profound musical ideas.

Cadenzas

That Mozart put substance before fireworks may be seen in the cadenzas he sketched or fully notated for his own concertos. The cadenza had developed from the trills and runs that singers inserted, particularly before the return of the opening section in the da capo aria. Mozart's early cadenzas were similarly flourishes without thematic links to the movement, but after the 1780s they served to balance the longer modulatory or development sections. These cadenzas, virtually renewed development sections, cast new light on familiar material in daring flights of technical wizardry. In K. 488 Mozart wrote the cadenza into the score, perhaps to make up for the lack of true development earlier.

Operas

After *Idomeneo* Mozart wrote only one more opera seria, *La clemenza di Tito* (The Clemency of Titus), composed in haste during the summer of 1791 for the coronation of Leopold II as king of Bohemia in Prague. The chief dramatic works of the Vienna period were the Singspiel, *Die Entführung aus dem Serail* (The Abduction from the Harem, 1782), three Italian operas, *Le nozze di Figaro* (The Marriage of Figaro, 1786), *Don Giovanni* (Prague, 1787), and *Così fan tutte* (All Women Behave That Way, 1790)—all three on librettos by Lorenzo Da Ponte (1749–1838)—and the German opera *Die Zauberflöte* (The Magic Flute, 1791). Mozart early expressed his preference for librettos that were not ambitiously poetic. Unlike Gluck, he believed poetry should serve the music rather than the contrary (see vignette below).

Figaro followed the conventions of Italian eighteenth-century comic opera (see Chapter 13, pages 294–95). But Da Ponte lifted the opera buffa to a higher level of literature by giving greater depth to the characters, intensifying the social tensions between classes, and introducing moral issues. Mozart's psychological penetration and his genius for musical characterization similarly elevated the genre. Delineation of character occurs not only in solo arias but especially in duets, trios, and larger ensembles. The ensemble finales allow these characters to clash, combining realism with ongoing dramatic action and superbly unified musical form. Mozart's orchestration, and particularly

Figaro

Mozart on Opera Librettos:

❝ In an opera the poetry must be altogether the obedient daughter of the music. Why do Italian comic operas please everywhere—in spite of their miserable libretti—even in Paris, where I myself witnessed their success? Just because there the music reigns supreme and when one listens to it all else is forgotten. Why, an opera is sure of success when the plot is well worked out, the words written solely for the music and not shoved in here and there to suit some miserable rhyme (which God knows never enhances the value of any theatrical performance, be it what it may, but rather detracts from it)—I mean, words or even entire verses which ruin the composer's whole idea. Verses are indeed the most indispensable element for music—but rhymes—solely for the sake of rhyming—the most detrimental. Those high and mighty people who set to work in this pedantic fashion will always come to grief, both they and their music. The best thing of all is when a good composer, who understands the stage and is talented enough to make sound suggestions, meets an able poet, that true phoenix; in that case no fears need be entertained as to the applause even of the ignorant. Poets almost remind me of trumpeters with their professional tricks! If we composers were always to stick so faithfully to our rules (which were very good at a time when no one knew better), we should be concocting music as unpalatable as their libretti. ❞

W. A. Mozart in Vienna in the midst of composing *Die Entführung*, writing to his father, Leopold, in Salzburg, October 13, 1781. Emily Anderson, ed., *The Letters of Mozart and His Family* (New York: Norton, 1989), p. 773.

$$Window$$

MOZART AND HIS FATHER

The relationship between Leopold Mozart and his son was interesting and complex. Leopold recognized and respected the boy's genius; he expended major efforts in furthering young Wolfgang's career, trying—vainly, as it turned out—to secure him a worthy permanent position. Leopold was his son's devoted mentor and friend, who saved Wolfgang's every jotting for posterity and remained by most accounts free from selfish motives. Yet, as happens in most father-son relationships at some point, a strain developed between them—in this case, one that worsened over the years, and (according to one of Mozart's recent biographers)* profoundly influenced the composer's emotional life and creativity.

As a child prodigy, Mozart seemed happy to please his parents. But difficulties began to appear when he reached adolescence and felt that his father was attempting to undermine his independence. After Mozart left Salzburg for Vienna, and married Constanze Weber in 1782 (at the age of twenty-six)—a union that Leopold opposed—the rupture between them became permanent. Leopold rejected Wolfgang's and Constanze's children, and the bitterness between father and son contributed to Mozart's estrangement from his only sibling, the sister with whom he had been so close as a child. When

---

*Maynard Solomon, *Mozart: A Life* (New York: Harper Collins, 1995).

his use of winds, played an important role in defining the characters and situations.

Don Giovanni

Figaro enjoyed only moderate success in Vienna, but its enthusiastic reception in Prague led to the commission for *Don Giovanni*, which was performed there the following year. *Don Giovanni* is a *dramma giocoso* of a very special sort. The medieval legend on which the plot is based had been treated often in literature and music since the early seventeenth century. But Mozart, for the first time in opera, took the character of Don Juan seriously—not as an incongruous mixture of farcical figure and horrible blasphemer, but as a romantic hero, a rebel against authority, a scorner of common morality, and a supreme individualist, bold and unrepentant to the last. It was Mozart's music rather than Da Ponte's libretto that raised the Don to this stature and at the same time paraded his gluttony and selfishness (see window above). The Romantic musical imagination of the nineteenth century relished the demonic quality of the opening measures of the overture, intensified by the

Leopold died in 1787, he was proud of Wolfgang's achievements as a composer but apparently still resentful and unforgiving about what he considered to be his son's irresponsible career choices and dissolute lifestyle. Mozart in turn, after his father's death, fell into increasing financial and emotional difficulty and gradually succumbed to the depression and anxiety that beset him during the years before his own untimely death at the age of thirty-five.

The year 1787 also saw the completion of Mozart's *Don Giovanni*, which received its premiere five months after Leopold's funeral (see below) and may bear the marks of Mozart's tortured relationship with his father. There is no doubt that his music reinforces some troubling aspects of Da Ponte's libretto: on the one hand, we admire Don Giovanni for his grace, charm, and bravery; on the other hand, we deplore his depraved behavior toward women and his thoughtless murder of Donna Anna's father, the Commendatore, at the beginning of the opera. When the Commendatore's ghostly statue reappears in the finale to claim his revenge, we are torn between wanting Don Giovanni to repent his ways and save himself, or wanting him to accept his fate and be punished. In the most powerful, terror-inspiring moments of the opera, Mozart's music makes us understand that through the Don's refusal to repent, he seals his own doom while at the same time freely choosing his fate. Could it be that in those moments Mozart was playing out his own family drama by accepting his father's poor appraisal of his character, blaming himself for failing to live up to an implacable parent's expectations, and therefore identifying with Don Giovanni's simultaneous resistance to authority and surrender to punishment?

sound of the trombones in the cemetery scene and at the apparition of the statue in the finale. Some of the other characters, though they are subtly ridiculed, must also be taken seriously: the tragic Donna Elvira, jilted by the Don but still attempting to reform him, and Leporello, more than a *commedia dell'arte* servant-buffoon, revealing deep sensitivity and intuition.

The fifth scene of Act I (NAWM 103a) musically sketches three personalities. Donna Elvira's melody is in the style of a Baroque "rage aria," with its angry wide leaps and sudden pauses, abetted by the syncopations, agitated runs, and tremolos in the strings. This contrasts sharply with the casual, light-hearted, mocking tone of Don Giovanni and the seemingly idle patter of Leporello, playing down his role as healer of the bruised souls of abandoned women. The famous "catalogue" aria that follows (NAWM 103b), in which Leporello enumerates his master's conquests by country and describes the kinds of women he likes, shows another serious side of Mozart's comic art. Awed as we are by the details of his characterization, by his text animation,

▲ Don Giovanni about to meet his punishment at the hands of the Commendatore, or stone guest, whom the Don had boldly invited to dinner in the final scene of *Don Giovanni*. Title page of an early edition. (*Leipzig: Breitkopf & Härtel, 1801*)

harmonic shadings, and orchestration, we are compelled to take seriously this most entertaining portion of the opera.

Così fan tutte

Così fan tutte is an opera buffa in the best Italian tradition, with a brilliant libretto glorified by some of Mozart's most melodious music. It is also a very moving drama about human frailty, exploring the themes of temptation, betrayal, and reconciliation.

Die Entführung

Die Entführung is a romantic-comic story of adventure and rescue, set against the popular eighteenth-century "oriental" background, a subject that had been treated earlier by Rameau, Gluck, Haydn, and others. But here, in one stroke, Mozart raised the German Singspiel to the realm of great art without altering any of its established features.

Die Zauberflöte

Die Zauberflöte is a different matter. Though outwardly a Singspiel—with spoken dialogue instead of recitative, and with some characters and scenes appropriate to popular comedy—its action is filled with symbolic meaning and its music is so rich and profound that it ranks as the first great German opera. The largely solemn mood of the score reflects the relationship between the opera and the teachings and ceremonies of Freemasonry. We know that Mozart valued his Masonic affiliation, both from allusions in his letters and especially from the serious quality of the music he wrote for Masonic ceremonies in 1785 and for a Masonic cantata in 1791 (K. 623), his last completed work. In *Die Zauberflöte* Mozart wove the threads of many eighteenth-century musical ideas into new designs: the vocal opulence of Italian opera seria; the folk humor of the German Singspiel; the solo aria; the *buffo* ensemble, which is given new musical meaning; a new kind of accompanied recitative applicable to German words; solemn choral scenes; and even (in the duet of the two armed men in Act II) a revival of the Baroque chorale-prelude technique, with contrapuntal accompaniment.

Church Music

Given that Mozart's father worked as a musician for the archbishop of Salzburg and Wolfgang himself held similar appointments—first as concertmaster and later as organist—it was natural for Mozart to compose music for the church from an early age. However, with notable exceptions, his Masses, motets, and other settings of sacred texts are not counted among his major works. The Masses, like those of Haydn, were for the most part written in the typical symphonic-operatic idiom of the time, intermingled with fugues at certain customary places, and scored for chorus and soloists in free alternation, with orchestral accompaniment. The Requiem, K. 626, was Mozart's last work. It was commissioned by a wealthy nobleman, Count Walsegg, in July 1791, but Mozart was busy with *La clemenza di Tito* and *Die Zauberflöte* and made little progress until the fall. Left unfinished at Mozart's death, it was completed by his pupil and collaborator Franz Xaver Süssmayr (1766–1803), who added some instrumental parts to Mozart's draft and set the Sanctus, Benedictus, and Agnus Dei, in part repeating music that Mozart had composed for an earlier section.

Masses

Requiem

POSTLUDE

This chapter about Haydn and Mozart does not presume to cover the music of the late eighteenth century, for these two composers shared the limelight with a host of others. Some of their names may be familiar from the pages of this book, such as the opera composers Gluck and Salieri. To these may be added Georg Benda (1722–1795), Pasquale Anfossi (1727–1797), Niccolò Piccinni (1728–1800), Antonio Sacchini (1730–1786), Giovanni Paisiello (1740–1816), and Domenico Cimarosa (1749–1801). Among the instrumental composers, Ignaz Holzbauer (1711–1783), Luigi Boccherini (1743–1805), Carl Dittersdorf (1739–1799), and Leopold Anton Kozeluch (1747–1818) deserve mention. Some of these composers were also active in opera or Singspiel. Each of them contributed uniquely to the period and merits further attention. But Haydn and Mozart together ranged over all the genres practiced in the late eighteenth century, and their music represents the best that the period produced.

15

LUDWIG VAN BEETHOVEN
(1770–1827)

In 1792 George Washington was president of the United States; Louis XVI and Marie Antoinette were imprisoned by the leaders of the new French Republic; Viennese life, not yet under Napoleonic rule, presented an atmosphere of frivolous gaiety, at least on the surface; Haydn was at the height of his fame, and Mozart had been dead since the previous December. Early in November of 1792, the ambitious young composer and pianist Ludwig van Beethoven, then just under twenty-two years of age, traveled from the city of Bonn on the Rhine to Vienna, a five-hundred-mile journey that took a week by stagecoach. He ran short of money and for a while kept a detailed account of his finances. One of the entries in his notebook records an expenditure of twenty-five groschen [pennies] for "coffee for Haidn and me."

Haydn had stopped off at Bonn on his way to London in December 1790. He must have heard some of Beethoven's compositions because he encouraged the young man to come to Vienna for further study. Beethoven's lessons with Haydn began in late 1792 and continued until Haydn left in 1794 on his second visit to London. Beethoven then studied counterpoint for a year with Johann Georg Albrechtsberger (1736–1809), the author of a famous treatise on composition and one of the leading teachers of his day. He also took informal lessons in vocal composition from Antonio Salieri, who had been living in Vienna since 1766. His earliest music teacher had been his father, a singer in the chapel at Bonn, who pushed the boy's progress in the hope of making a second Mozart of him. When he was seventeen, Beethoven actually played for Mozart, who prophesied a bright future for him. Also, before going to Vienna, he had studied with the court organist in Bonn, Christian Gottlob Neefe (1748–1798), who was known for his Singspiel and songs.

Although some additional, mostly early, works are not included in the traditional count of Beethoven's compositions, they number 9 symphonies, 11 overtures, incidental music to plays, a violin concerto, 5 piano concertos, 16 string quartets, 9 piano trios, 10 violin sonatas, 5 cello sonatas, 32 large piano sonatas, many sets of piano variations, an oratorio, an opera, and two Masses, as well as arias, songs, and numerous lesser compositions. There is an obvious disparity when we compare these figures with the output of Haydn and Mozart: 9 symphonies, for example, to Haydn's 100-plus or Mozart's 60-plus. A partial explanation, of course, is that Beethoven's symphonies are longer and grander; but another reason is that Beethoven had nothing like the facility of Haydn and Mozart: he apparently wrote music with great deliberation, and sometimes only after periods of intense struggle. We can see this in his sketchbooks, which document the progress of a musical idea through various stages until it reaches the final form (see commentary, NAWM 106). The sketches for the Quartet Op. 131, for example, are three times as long as the finished work.

Another glimpse into Beethoven's working habits reveals the extent to which he was guided by what the Romantics called "inspiration." A young composer he befriended recalled Beethoven saying:

You will ask me whence I take my ideas? That I cannot say with any degree of certainty: they come to me uninvited, directly or indirectly. I could almost grasp them in my hands, out in Nature's open, in the woods, during my promenades, in the silence of the night, at the earliest dawn. They are roused by moods which in the poet's case are transmuted into words, and in mine into tones, that sound, roar and storm until at last they take shape for me as notes.[1]

Scholars have customarily divided Beethoven's works into three periods on the basis of style and chronology. During the **First Period**, to about 1802, Beethoven was assimilating the musical language of his time and finding his own voice as a composer. He wrote the six String Quartets Op. 18, the first ten piano sonatas (through Op. 14), the first three piano concertos, and the first two symphonies. The **Second Period**, in which his rugged individualism asserted itself, runs to about 1816 and includes the Symphonies Nos. 3 to 8, the incidental music to Goethe's drama *Egmont*, the *Coriolan* overture, the opera *Fidelio*, the last two piano concertos, the Violin Concerto, the Quartets Opp. 59 (the *Rasumovsky* Quartets), 74, and 95, and the Piano Sonatas through Op. 90. The **Third Period**, in which Beethoven's music generally became more reflective and introspective, includes the last five piano sonatas, the *Diabelli* Variations, the *Missa solemnis*, the Ninth Symphony, and the last great quartets.

First Period

Patrons

Beethoven established himself in Vienna with the help of contacts he made through his Bonn employer, the elector of Cologne, Maximilian Franz, whose brother was Habsburg Emperor Joseph II (reigned 1765–90). Several members of the Austrian, Bohemian, and Hungarian aristocracy encouraged and supported him. For a while, Beethoven had rooms in one of the houses of Prince Karl von Lichnowsky, with whom he traveled to Prague for concerts in 1796 and who sponsored concerts in his palace in Vienna. Prince Lobkowitz kept a private orchestra that played in Vienna and at his Bohemian country estates and bought rights to first performances of some of Beethoven's works. He, Prince Kinsky, and Archduke Rudolph—youngest brother of the reigning emperor Francis II and Beethoven's piano and composition student—joined in setting up an annuity for the composer so that he would stay in Austria when he got an attractive offer from Jerome Bonaparte, king of Westphalia. Many of Beethoven's works of this and later periods are dedicated to these patrons, as well as to the German-Bohemian Count Ferdinand

1. *Thayer's Life of Beethoven*, rev. and ed. Elliot Forbes (Princeton, Princeton University Press, 1967), pp. 851–52.

C H R O N O L O G Y		
1770	*Beethoven born in Bonn (December 16) Gluck, *Orphée et Euridice* in Paris (1774) American Declaration of Independence (1776)	Napoleon's forces occupy Vienna (1805– 09) *Beethoven's *Fidelio* performed unsuccess- fully (1805)
1780	Mozart, *Don Giovanni* in Prague (1787) French Revolution (until 1794) (1789)	*Premiere of Beethoven's Fifth and Sixth Symphonies; Goethe, *Faust*, Part I (1808) Death of Haydn (1809)
1790	Death of Mozart; Haydn, first *London* symphonies (1791) *Beethoven moves to Vienna (1792) Louis XVI and Marie Antoinette beheaded (1793)	**1810** Wellington defeats Napoleon at Waterloo; Jane Austen, *Pride and Prejudice* (1813) *Beethoven's *Fidelio* performed successfully; Congress of Vienna (1814) Invention of the metronome (1815)
1800	Haydn, *The Seasons* (1801) *Beethoven, Heiligenstadt Testament (1802) *Beethoven, *Eroica* Symphony (1803)	**1820** *Premiere of Beethoven's Ninth Symphony (1824) *Death of Beethoven (1827)

von Waldstein, and to Baron van Swieten. Beethoven sold a number of important works to a Leipzig publisher, played as a pianist in concerts that he or others organized, and gave piano lessons. In this way he managed to make a living as an independent musician and composer.

Beethoven dedicated his first three piano sonatas to Haydn; indeed, the themes and their treatment reveal his debt to the older composer. But his sonatas all have four movements instead of the usual three. Moreover, in the second and third sonatas Beethoven replaced the Minuet with the more dynamic Scherzo, a practice which he consistently used from then on. His choice of the uncommon key of F minor for the first sonata may have been suggested by a C. P. E. Bach sonata in that same key, but Beethoven's extensive use of the minor mode and the bold modulations in the first three sonatas are highly individual traits.

Piano sonatas

The Sonata Op. 7 in E♭ (1797) is especially characteristic, with its eloquent pauses in the Largo *con gran espressione* and the mysterious perpetual arpeggiations that appear in the *minore* trio of the third movement. Opus 10, No. 1 (published in 1798) and the *Sonate pathétique*, Op. 13 (published in 1799), both in C minor, have outer movements of a stormy, passionate nature (which Beethoven's predecessors associated with that key), and a calm, profound slow movement in A♭. In the *Pathétique*, the Grave introduction reappears twice in the first movement, and the theme of the rondo finale clearly resembles the second theme (in E♭ minor) of the first movement (see Rondo, NAWM 104). These features foreshadow the "cyclical" inter-movement connections in Beethoven's later works. Some of the harmonic characteristics in these early works, as well as Beethoven's frequent use of octaves and the thick

▲ The Lobkowitz Palace in Vienna, where under the sponsorship of Joseph Franz Maximilian Lobkowitz, Beethoven's *Eroica* Symphony was first performed at a private concert in 1804. Beethoven dedicated this symphony, as well as the Fifth and Sixth, to the nobleman. Engraving by Vincenz Reim. (*Vienna, Historisches Museum der Stadt Wien*)

full texture in the piano writing, may have been inspired by the piano sonatas of Muzio Clementi (1752–1832; see NAWM 105). Other possible influences include the piano sonatas of the Bohemian-born Jan Ladislav Dussek (1760–1812).

Chamber music

If Beethoven's piano writing owes stylistic features to both Clementi and Dussek, his art of developing motives and animating the texture contrapuntally follows Haydn's example. The six quartets of Opus 18 (composed 1798–1800) demonstrate this indebtedness but also show signs of competition with the master, who was still very active in this genre, and who dedicated his quartets to some of the same aristocratic patrons as Beethoven. In Opus 18, however, Beethoven's individuality shines through in the character of his themes, the frequent unexpected turns of phrase, the unconventional modulations, and some subtleties of formal structure.

Among the other chamber works from Beethoven's first period are the three Piano Trios of Op. 1; three Violin Sonatas, Op. 12; two Cello Sonatas, Op. 5; and the Septet in E♭ for strings and winds, Op. 20, which was played for the first time in 1800 and soon became so popular that Beethoven grew to dislike it.

First Symphony

Beethoven's Symphony No. 1 was premiered at a concert on April 2, 1800, on the same program with his Septet and a piano concerto, a Mozart symphony, an aria and a duet from Haydn's *Creation*, and improvisations by Beethoven at the piano. The four movements of the First Symphony are so regular in form that they could serve as textbook models. Beethoven's originality is evident in certain details: in the unusual prominence given to the woodwinds, in the character of the third movement—a scherzo, though labeled Minuet—and especially in the long and important codas of the other movements. The frequent marking *cresc.* $<$ *p* is but one example of the careful attention to dynamic shading that is essential to Beethoven's early style.

The long Adagio that introduces the first movement of the Second Symphony in D major (composed in 1802) announces a work conceived on a scale unknown in symphonic music at that time. The first movement contains a long coda that includes extensive new development of the principal material. The rest of the symphony has correspondingly large dimensions, with a profusion of thematic material held together in perfect formal balance. The Larghetto is especially remarkable for its multiplicity of themes and for its rich singing melody. The Scherzo and finale are, like the first movement, full of energy and fire. The finale is written in an enlarged sonata form with suggestions of a rondo in extra recurrences of the first theme, one at the end of the exposition and one at the coda.

Second Symphony

Carl Ludwig Junker Describes Beethoven's Playing and Improvising at the Piano, November 23, 1791:

66 The greatness of this amiable, soft-spoken man as a virtuoso may, in my opinion, be safely judged from his nearly inexhaustible wealth of ideas, the highly characteristic expressiveness of his playing, and the skill he displays in performance. I do not know that he lacks anything for the making of a great artist. I have often heard Vogler play by the hour on the pianoforte—of his organ playing I cannot speak, not having heard him on that instrument—and never ceased to wonder at his astonishing ability. But besides skill, Bethofen has greater clarity and profundity of ideas and of expression—in short, he speaks to the heart. He is as good at an adagio as at an allegro. Even the members of this remarkable orchestra [of the elector of Mainz] are, without exception, his admirers and are all ears when he plays. Yet he is exceedingly modest and free from all pretension. . . . His way of handling his instrument is so different from the usual that he gives the impression of having attained his present supremacy through a path that he discovered himself. 99

From Bossler's *Musikalische Korrespondenz*, adapted from Krehbiel's translation in *Thayer's Life of Beethoven*, rev. and ed. Elliot Forbes (Princeton: Princeton University Press, 1967), p. 105. Junker (1748–1797) was a writer on music and art and a composer.

Second Period

Within a dozen years after coming to Vienna, Beethoven was acknowledged throughout Europe as the foremost pianist and composer for piano of his time and as a symphonist on a par with Haydn and Mozart. His innovations were recognized, although they were sometimes dismissed as eccentricities. He was befriended by the highest noble families of Vienna and had devoted and generous patrons. Unlike other composers, Beethoven did not cringe or grovel before his patrons. He drove hard bargains with his publishers and sometimes offered the same composition to several at once. Although he wrote on commission, he dodged deadlines. He could afford, as he said, to "think and think," to revise and polish a work until it suited him.

Eroica Symphony

The Third Symphony, which Beethoven eventually named "Sinfonia Eroica" (Heroic Symphony) was immediately recognized as an important work, but its unprecedented length and complexity made it difficult at first for audiences to grasp. It marked, in fact, a radical departure in Beethoven's symphonic writing. The *Eroica* is not purely absolute or abstract music: it has a subject—the celebration of a hero—and expresses in music the ideal of heroic greatness. Even in Beethoven's time commentators complained that a new theme is presented in the development of the first movement and that certain passages are insistently dissonant (see full discussion in NAWM 106). The symphony begins, after two introductory chords, with an extremely simple theme on the notes of the E♭-major triad, but an unexpected C♯ gives rise to endless departures and developments. The other movements, aside from the Scherzo, are also unusually expansive. Moreover, the entire symphony has a rather dramatic flair.

Dramatization of themes in the Eroica

In the first movement particularly, the principal theme is treated almost like a character in a play, portrayed as striving, being opposed and subdued, but triumphing in the end. The most striking event is the recurrence of the syncopations first heard near the beginning, which culminate in the crashing, offbeat, dissonant chords of the development section. One of the most suggestive reappearances of the main theme is in the horn, just before the full orchestra sounds the complete dominant seventh to mark the arrival of the recapitulation. Early listeners accused the horn player of entering too soon; Carl Czerny, Beethoven's pupil, proposed this entrance be eliminated, and the French composer and Beethoven admirer Hector Berlioz even thought it was a copyist's mistake; but the sketches show that Beethoven contemplated this clever ploy from the very first draft.

Beethoven, Napoleon, and the Eroica

There is evidence that Beethoven intended to dedicate this symphony to Napoleon, his admired hero who promised to lead humanity into the new age of liberty, equality, and fraternity. According to the conductor Ferdinand

Ries, however, when Beethoven heard that Napoleon had proclaimed himself emperor (in May 1804), he angrily tore up the title page containing the dedication, disappointed that his idol proved to be an ambitious ruler on the way to becoming a tyrant. The story is an exaggeration; the title page of Beethoven's own score, which survives, originally read "Sinfonia grande intitolata Bonaparte" (Grand Symphony entitled Bonaparte), later corrected to read "Geschrieben auf Bonaparte" (composed on Bonaparte). On August 26, 1804, months after this alleged incident, Beethoven wrote to his publisher Breitkopf & Härtel: "The title of the symphony is really *Bonaparte*. . . ."[2] When the symphony was first published in Vienna two years later, it bore the title "Sinfonia Eroica . . . composta per festeggiare il sovvenire di un grand Uomo" (Heroic Symphony . . . composed to celebrate the memory of a great man). Whatever his feelings toward Napoleon, Beethoven conducted the symphony in Vienna in 1809 at a concert that Bonaparte was to have attended, and in 1810 he considered dedicating his Mass in C (Op. 86) to the emperor.

It is the second movement—the Funeral March—more than anything else in the symphony that links the work with France, the republican experiment there, and Napoleon. The customary slow movement is replaced by a march in C minor, full of tragic grandeur and pathos, and a contrasting "trio" in C major, brimming with fanfares and celebratory lyricism, after which the march returns, broken up with sighs at the end. At the opening of the Funeral March, the thirty-second notes of the strings imitate the sound of muffled drums used in the Revolutionary processions that accompanied heroes to their final resting place (Example 15.1).

Funeral March in the Eroica

EXAMPLE 15.1   Beethoven, Symphony No. 3, Funeral March

2. Emily Anderson, *Letters of Beethoven* (London, 1961), Letter no. 96.

EXAMPLE 15.1

Fidelio

Beethoven began work on his opera *Fidelio* almost immediately after finishing the Third Symphony, and the two works share the Revolutionary atmosphere. Not only was the rescue plot popular at the turn of the century, but also the libretto itself was borrowed from a French Revolutionary-era opera *Léonore ou L'amour conjugal* (Leonore, or Conjugal Love) in which Leonore, disguised as a man, rescues her husband from prison. Beethoven's music transforms this conventional material, making the chief character Leonore an idealized figure of sublime courage and self-denial. The whole last part of the opera glorifies Leonore's heroism and the great humanitarian ideals of the Revolution. Composing this opera gave Beethoven even more trouble than he had with his other works. The first performances of the original three-act version, *Leonore*, took place in November 1805, just after the French armies had marched into Vienna. Rearranged and shortened to two acts, the opera was brought out again the following March but immediately withdrawn. Finally, after still more extensive revisions, in 1814 a third version proved successful. In the course of all these changes, Beethoven wrote no fewer than four different overtures for the opera.

Rasumovsky Quartets

The three quartets of Opus 59 are dedicated to the musical amateur Count Rasumovsky, the Russian ambassador to Vienna, who played second violin in a quartet that was said to be the finest in Europe. As a compliment to the count, Beethoven introduced a Russian melody as the principal theme for the finale of the first quartet and another such tune in the third movement of the second quartet. These two quartets, composed in the summer and autumn of 1806, have such a new style that musicians were slow to accept them. When

Opus 59, No. 1

Count Rasumovsky's players first read through the Quartet No. 1 in F, they were convinced that Beethoven was playing a joke on them. The first movement is particularly charged with idiosyncrasies: single, double, and triple pedal points, frequent changes of texture—the melody accompanied sometimes by double stops or harmonically tense homorhythmic episodes—horn imitations, unmelodious passages exploiting the instruments' extreme ranges, fugues cropping up out of nowhere, and startling unison passages. These techniques are represented also in the other movements, but not in such great profusion. Clementi recalled saying to Beethoven, "Surely you do not consider these works to be music?" to which the composer replied with unusual self-restraint, "Oh, they are not for you, but for a later age."

The Fourth, Fifth, and Sixth Symphonies were all composed between 1806 and 1808, a time of exceptional productivity. Beethoven worked on the Fourth and Fifth Symphonies at the same time; the first two movements of the Fifth, in fact, were already done before the Fourth was completed. The two works are very different, as though Beethoven wished to express simultaneously two opposite poles of feeling. Joviality and humor mark the Fourth Symphony, while the Fifth has always been considered the musical projection of Beethoven's resolution "I will grapple with Fate; it shall not overcome me." The struggle for victory is symbolized in this symphony by the passing from C minor to C major and by the triumphant finale. The first movement is dom-

Middle symphonies

Fifth Symphony

Beethoven's Deafness

The impression Beethoven gave of being moody and unsociable had much to do with his increasing deafness. He began to lose his hearing around 1796, and by 1820 he was almost completely deaf. In the autumn of 1802 Beethoven wrote a letter, now known as the Heiligenstadt Testament, intended to be read by his brothers after his death. In it he describes in moving terms how he suffered when he realized that his malady was incurable:

> I must live almost alone like one who has been banished, I can mix with society only as much as true necessity demands. If I approach near to people a hot terror seizes upon me and I fear being exposed to the danger that my condition might be noticed. Thus it has been during the last six months which I have spent in the country. . . . what a humiliation for me when someone standing next to me heard a flute in the distance and *I heard nothing*, or someone heard a *shepherd singing* and again I heard nothing. Such incidents drove me almost to despair, a little more of that and I would have ended my life—it was only *my art* that held me back. Ah, it seemed to me impossible to leave the world until I had brought forth all that I felt was within me. . . . Oh Providence—grant me at last but one day of *pure joy*—it is so long since real joy echoed in my heart. . . .*

Thayer's Life of Beethoven, pp. 304–6.

inated by the four-note motive impressively announced in the opening measures, and the same motive recurs in one guise or another in the other three movements as well. The transition from minor to major takes place in an inspired passage that begins with the timpani softly recalling the rhythm of the four-note motive and leading without a break from the scherzo into the finale. Here the entrance of the full orchestra with trombones on the C-major chord has an electrifying effect. The finale of the Fifth Symphony adds a piccolo and a contrabassoon as well as trombones to the normal complement of strings, woodwinds, brass, and timpani.

Pastoral Symphony

The Sixth (*Pastoral*) Symphony was composed immediately after the Fifth, and the two were premiered on the same program in December 1808. Each of the *Pastoral*'s five movements bears a descriptive title suggesting a scene from life in the country. Beethoven adapted his descriptive program to the normal sequence of movements, inserting an extra movement (*Storm*) that serves to introduce the finale (*Thankful feelings after the storm*). In the coda of the Andante movement (*Scene by the brook*), flute, oboe, and clarinet join harmoniously in imitating bird calls—the nightingale, the quail, and, of course, the cuckoo (Example 15.2). All this programmatic apparatus is subordinate to the expansive, leisurely form of the symphony as a whole; the composer himself warned against taking the descriptions literally: he called them "expression of feelings rather than depiction."

EXAMPLE 15.2   Beethoven, Symphony No. 6: Scene by the Brook

Seventh Symphony

The Seventh and Eighth Symphonies were both completed in 1812. The Seventh, like the Second and Fourth, opens with a long slow introduction with remote modulations, leading into an Allegro dominated throughout by the rhythmic figure ♪. ♬ ♩. The second movement, in the parallel minor key of A, received so much applause at the first performance that it had to be repeated. The third movement, in the rather distant key of F major, is a

Hector Berlioz on Beethoven's Sixth Symphony, 4. Thunderstorm, Tempest:

66 *Storm, lightning.* I despair of trying to give an idea of this prodigious piece. You have to hear it to conceive the degree of truth and sublimity that musical painting can reach at the hands of a man like Beethoven. Listen, listen to these gusts of wind charged with rain, these deaf growlings of the basses, the high whistling of the piccolos that announce a terrible tempest about to unleash. The storm approaches, it spreads; an immense chromatic stroke starting in the higher instruments rummages down to the last depths of the orchestra, hitches on to the basses and drags them with it and climbs up again, shuddering like a whirlwind that overturns everything in its path. Then the trombones burst forth, as the thunder of the tympani redoubles in violence. This is no longer rain and wind; it is an appalling cataclysm, the great flood, the end of the world.

. . . . .

Veil your faces, poor great ancient poets, poor immortals. Your conventional language, so pure, so harmonious, cannot compete with the art of sounds. You are glorious in defeat, but vanquished. You did not know what we call today melody, harmony, the association of different timbres, instrumental colors, the modulations, the learned conflicts of inimical sounds that first combat each other, then embrace, our surprises of the ear, our strange accents that make the most unexplored depths of the soul reverberate. 99

Translated from Hector Berlioz, *A travers chants* (Paris, 1898), pp. 42–43.

scherzo, although it is not labeled as such. It is unusual because the trio (in D major) recurs a second time as in the Fourth Symphony, thus expanding the movement to a five-part form (ABABA). The finale, a large sonata-allegro with coda, has a particularly festal quality. By contrast with the huge scale of the Seventh Symphony, the Eighth reverts to more standard dimensions, aside from the long coda of the first movement and the still longer one of the finale. This is the most mercurial of all the nine symphonies, but its forms are extremely condensed. The second movement is a brisk Allegretto, while the third, by way of compensation, is a deliberately archaic Minuet instead of Beethoven's usual Scherzo.

Eighth Symphony

Beethoven's orchestral overtures are related in style to the symphonies, usually taking the form of a symphonic first movement. The *Leonore* Overtures aside, his most important works in this genre are *Coriolan* (1807), inspired by a tragic drama that was performed occasionally in Vienna, and *Egmont*, composed together with songs and incidental music for an 1810 performance of Goethe's play.

Overtures

Piano sonatas

Beethoven composed ten piano sonatas in the five years between 1800 and 1805. Among them are Op. 26 in A♭, with the funeral march, and Op. 27, Nos. 1 and 2, each designated as "quasi una fantasia"; the second is popularly known as the *Moonlight* Sonata. In Op. 31, No. 2 in D minor, the whole opening section of the first movement, with its rushing passages and sharp punctuation, has the character of a *recitativo obbligato*, anticipating that of the Ninth Symphony. The introductory *largo* arpeggio returns at the start of the development section and again at the beginning of the recapitulation, each time in expanded form and with new linkages to the surrounding music; its last appearance leads into an expressive recitative (see Example 15.3). The finale of this sonata is an exciting *moto perpetuo* in rondo form.

EXAMPLE 15.3   Beethoven, Piano Sonata Op. 31, No. 2

a. Opening

b. Beginning of development

c. Recitative before recapitulation

Waldstein *and* Appassionata *Sonatas*

Outstanding among the sonatas of this period are Op. 53 in C major (1804), called the *Waldstein* Sonata after the patron to whom it is dedicated, and Op. 57 in F minor (1805), usually called the *Appassionata* (Impassioned [Sonata]). Both have three movements—fast-slow-fast—and both exhibit the patterns of sonata form, rondo, or variations. But each of the formal schemes has been stretched in all directions to support the natural development and culmination of exceptionally intense themes. In the first movement of the

Waldstein, Beethoven managed to make the key of C major sound dark and brooding through the obstinate thundering of thick low chords, to which a figure high in the right hand answers like a flash of lightning (Example 15.4a). Then the storm clears, and a bright, chordally accompanied melody in E major glistens where a theme in the dominant is expected (Example 15.4b). The "normal" arrival of the dominant in the second part of the exposition is delayed until near the double bar, just in time to bring back the opening. In the recapitulation, the second theme is first heard in A major, and its restatement in C major is reserved for the coda.

EXAMPLE 15.4   Beethoven, Piano Sonata in C major, Op. 53, Allegro con brio

a.

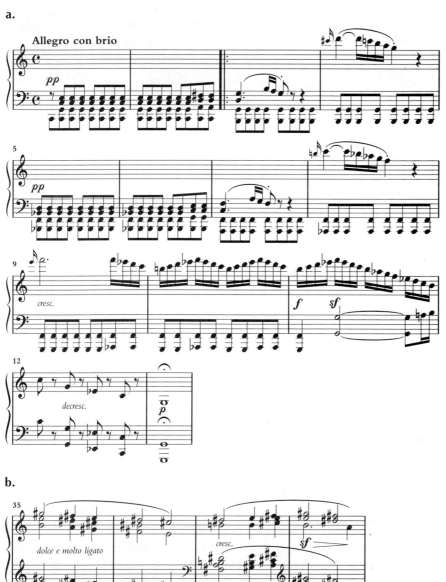

b.

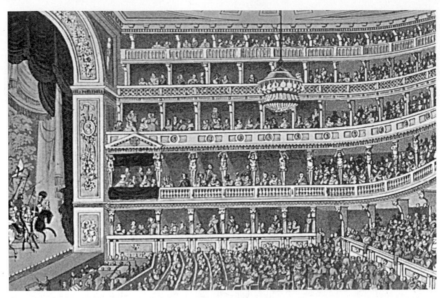

▲ The Theater an der Wien. Beethoven's famous four-hour concert of December 22, 1808, took place in this bitterly cold hall. The program included the first public performances of the Fifth and Sixth Symphonies, the first Vienna performance of the Fourth Piano Concerto, with the composer as soloist, and following some other pieces, the Choral Fantasy, Op. 80. Anonymous engraving, 1825. (*Vienna, Historisches Museum der Stadt Wien*)

After the *Waldstein* and the *Appassionata*, there were no more sonatas for five years. Then came the Sonata in F♯, Op. 78, which Beethoven once declared to be his favorite, and the somewhat programmatic Sonata Op. 81a. The latter was inspired by the departure from and return to Vienna of Archduke Rudolph, one of his patrons and pupils; its three movements are entitled *Lebewohl* (Farewell), *Abwesenheit* (Absence), and *Wiedersehn* (Return).

Piano concertos

As a pianist Beethoven naturally composed concertos to play at his own concerts. His first three piano concertos date from his early years in Vienna (No. 1 in C, No. 2 in B♭, No. 3 in C minor). His two largest works in this genre are the Concerto No. 4 in G major, Op. 58, composed in 1805–6, and the Fifth in E♭, known as the *Emperor* Concerto, which was composed in 1809 and first performed in Vienna three years later. The soloist, Carl Czerny (1791–1857), had studied piano with Beethoven and subsequently enjoyed a successful teaching career in Vienna, composing many studies and other works for the piano.

Beethoven retained Mozart's division of the concerto into three movements and the general outline of the Classic form, while greatly expanding the music's expressive range and dimensions. Some of Beethoven's most enchanting melodies appear in his piano concertos and his violin concerto, and they are all the more haunting because of unexpected harmonic turns. Virtuosity is demanded in the solo parts, which are continuously interwoven with the orchestra and assert their presence forcefully. For example, in Piano

Concertos Nos. 4 and 5, the soloist enters with a cadenza even before the orchestra's exposition begins, a technique Beethoven also applied in his Violin Concerto, Op. 61 in D major (1806).

Third Period

The years up to 1815 were, on the whole, peaceful and prosperous for Beethoven. His music was played regularly in Vienna, and he was celebrated both at home and abroad. Thanks to the generosity of patrons and the steady demand from publishers for new works, his financial affairs were in good order; but his deafness became a more and more serious trial. As it caused him to lose contact with others, he retreated into himself, becoming morose, irascible, and morbidly suspicious even toward his friends. Family problems, ill health, and unfounded apprehensions of poverty also plagued him, and it was only by a supreme effort of will that Beethoven continued composing. He wrote his last five piano sonatas between 1816 and 1821. He completed the *Missa solemnis* in 1822, the *Diabelli* Variations in 1823, and the Ninth Symphony in 1824, each after long years of labor. The final quartets, Beethoven's musical testament, followed in 1825 and 1826. At his death in 1827 he had plans for a tenth symphony and many other new works.

Characteristics of Beethoven's late style

By 1816, Beethoven had resigned himself to living in a soundless world of tones that reverberated only in his mind. More and more his compositions came to have a meditative character; the urgent sense of communication was replaced by a feeling of assured tranquillity, passionate outpouring by calm affirmation. The language became more concentrated, more abstract. Extremes meet: the sublime and the grotesque in the Mass and Ninth Symphony, the profound and the naïve in the last quartets. Classic forms remained, like the features of a landscape after a geological upheaval—recognizable here and there under distorted contours, lying at strange angles beneath the new surface.

In his late compositions, Beethoven deliberately worked out themes and motives until he had extracted every bit of meaning available from them. This is especially true in his variation techniques.

Variations

In Beethoven's late works, variations appear within the slow movements of the Piano Sonata Op. 106, the String Quartet Op. 132, and in the finale of the Ninth Symphony (after the introduction), to mention a few examples. Although he composed only one independent set for piano during this period—the *Thirty-three Variations on a Waltz by Diabelli*, Op. 120, completed in 1823—it surpasses anything in this genre since Bach's *Goldberg Variations*. Rather than altering the theme in a fairly straightforward manner, Beethoven transformed the very character of the theme, thus setting these variations apart from earlier ones. Diabelli's commonplace little waltz expands surpris-

Window

THE IMMORTAL BELOVED

My angel, my all, my very self—Only a few words today and at that with pencil (with yours)—Not till tomorrow will my lodgings be definitely determined upon—what a useless waste of time—Why this deep sorrow when necessity speaks—can our love endure except through sacrifices, through not demanding everything from one another; can you change the fact that you are not wholly mine, I not wholly thine—. . . .

In the summer of 1812, Beethoven wrote this impassioned letter to a woman whom he addressed as the Immortal Beloved, and whose identity posed a baffling riddle for generations of Beethoven biographers. Whether the letter was ever delivered was also a matter of speculation; dated July 6, but with no year, it was found among the composer's effects after his death. Although Beethoven had several close friendships with women, he never married; in fact, even his most serious romantic attachments were short-lived. Who, then, was his secret, undying love?

In a biography published 150 years after the composer's death, Maynard Solomon convincingly unravels the mystery of Beethoven's Immortal Beloved by re-creating a powerful web of circumstantial evidence from contemporaneous documents. He proposes that the woman was Antonie Brentano, a beautiful Viennese matron with four children whom Beethoven met in 1810, when she was thirty. (See her miniature portrait, painted on ivory, also found among Beethoven's possessions when he died.) Her husband was Franz Brentano, a merchant from Frankfurt who had obtained her father's permission to marry her when she was only eighteen years old. The couple resided far from Vienna in his native city, where Antonie missed her family and suffered periods of depression and mysterious physical ailments. During her father's illness and death in 1809, they moved back to Vienna and lived in her family's mansion. She persuaded her husband to open a branch of his business there and remained in Vienna for three years while she settled her father's affairs and disposed of his estate.

ingly into a world of variegated moods—solemn, brilliant, capricious, mysterious—ordered with due regard for contrast, grouping, and climax. Each variation is built on motives derived from some part of the theme, but altered in rhythm, tempo, dynamics, or context so as to produce a new design. The *Diabelli* Variations became the model for Schumann's *Symphonic Études*,

During this period (1810–12) Beethoven was a regular visitor to the Brentano household, where he attended the quartet concerts that were performed there and often played the piano himself. He dedicated several compositions to Antonie and, during her periods of gloomy withdrawal when she would admit no one else to her company, consoled her with his piano improvisations. At some point their attachment transformed itself into love, despite the looming prospect of Antonie's fated return to Frankfurt with her husband. It is probably no accident, then, that the letter to the Immortal Beloved—which eventually raises the issue of their living together—was written shortly after the final auction of her father's possessions.

If Antonie was willing to leave her husband and remain in Vienna rather than return to Frankfurt, Beethoven was unprepared for such a commitment. Ultimately, he renounced the possibility of a union so heavily weighted with conflicting ethical and emotional implications. But his anguish and ambivalence are apparent in this letter, written while en route to Karlsbad, where he was expecting to have a reunion with Antonie during the Brentanos' vacation that summer. Whatever happened during their meeting,* the two separated in the fall; the Brentanos went back to Frankfurt and Beethoven remained in Vienna. Although they kept in touch, they probably never saw each other again.

➤ Unsigned miniature on ivory of Antonie Brentano (ca. 1812).

---

*The planned climactic meeting in Karlsbad was at the center of the 1994 film *Immortal Beloved*, in which the event was aborted by fate. The film, however, so distorted the facts as we know them that the encounter, had it taken place, would have reunited Beethoven with his sister-in-law (widow of his deceased brother), whom the script outrageously hypothesized as Beethoven's true Immortal Beloved. Despite such liberties, the film's portrayal of Beethoven (played by Gary Oldman) and his music is very moving.

For further information, see Maynard Solomon, *Beethoven* (New York: Schirmer Books, 1977), especially Chapter 15 (pp. 158–89).

Brahms's *Variations on a Theme of Handel,* and many other nineteenth-century works in this genre.

Another feature of Beethoven's late style is a continuity achieved by intentionally blurring the divisions between phrases as well as divisions between sections in sonata forms and other movement types. A cadence falls on a weak

Continuity

beat, and its closing effect may be further lessened because the uppermost voice sounds the third or fifth scale degree rather than the tonic. The introduction may be in the same tempo as the Allegro and flow directly into it, as in the first movement of the Ninth Symphony. The wide-spaced harmonic arches and the leisurely march of melodies communicate a feeling of vastness in such movements as the Adagio of the Quartet Op. 127 or the *Benedictus* of the *Missa solemnis.*

Improvisatory passages

The improvisatory character of some passages may give us an idea of Beethoven's actual improvisations at the piano that so impressed his hearers (see vignette, page 355). This compositional style was forecast in the slow introduction to the Rondo of the *Waldstein* Sonata, Op. 53. At times a phrase is lingered over musingly, as in the slow movement of the Piano Sonata Op. 101; or a passage is measured freely, as in the Largo introduction to the finale of the Sonata Op. 106. Sometimes these reflective passages culminate in moments of instrumental recitative, as in the Adagio of the Sonata Op. 110 and in various transitions, as the one preceding the finale of the Ninth Symphony.

Fugal texture

Beethoven's late style takes on a universal quality through the prominent use of fugal texture. His sympathy for this technique came in part from his lifelong reverence for the music of J. S. Bach but was also perhaps a byproduct of his more meditative late style. There are numerous canonic imitations and learned contrapuntal devices in all the late works, but particularly in the fugatos that are incorporated in development sections—as in the finale of the Piano Sonata Op. 101. Many movements are predominantly fugal in conception—such as the finales of the Sonatas Opp. 106 and 110, the first movement of the Quartet in C♯ minor, Op. 131, the gigantic *Grosse Fuge* for String Quartet, Op. 133, and the two double fugues in the finale of the Ninth Symphony.

New sonorities

Beethoven commanded new sonorities in his last works, apparent, for example, in the widely spaced intervals at the end of the Piano Sonata Op. 110, or the extraordinary dark coloring of the orchestra and chorus at the first appearance of the words "Ihr stürzt nieder" (Throw yourselves down before Him) in the finale of the Ninth Symphony. Some of these experiments have been deemed unsuccessful because they almost require a miracle to make them "sound" in performance; the ideas seem too big for human capabilities to express. For this reason, early critics believed that Beethoven went too far in subordinating euphony and performability to the demands of his musical conceptions, perhaps because of his deafness. But whether we approve or condemn these passages, we have no reason to believe that even a Beethoven with perfect hearing would have altered a single note, either to spare tender ears or to make life easier for performers.

As with texture and sonority, so too with form in the instrumental works of Beethoven's third period: two of the last quartets and two of the final sonatas retain the external scheme of four movements, but the rest dispense with even this bow to tradition. The Sonata Op. 111 has only two movements, an Allegro in compact sonata form and an Adagio molto—a long set of variations on an arietta that is so eloquent and so complete that nothing further seems to be required. The Quartet Op. 131 has seven movements (the first two are in NAWM 107):

Quartet Op. 131

(1) A fugue in C♯ minor, Adagio ma non troppo e molto espressivo, ¢.

(2) Allegretto molto vivace, D major ⁶₈. This movement is in a compact sonata form, based on only one theme, a folklike tune first presented against a triple drone (Example 15.5).

(3) Eleven measures, Allegro moderato, in the spirit of a *recitativo obbligato*, functioning as an introduction to the following movement and modulating from B minor to E major, the dominant of the next movement.

(4) Andante, A major, ²₄. A theme made up of two double periods, with six variations and a coda that encloses an incomplete seventh variation.

(5) Presto, E major, ¢. Essentially a scherzo, though in duple rather than triple time, with a trio that returns twice in rondo fashion after the return of the scherzo, as in the Fourth and Seventh Symphonies.

(6) Adagio, G♯ minor, ³₄. Twenty-eight measures in the form ABB with coda, introducing the next movement.

(7) Allegro, C♯ minor, ¢, in sonata form.

EXAMPLE 15.5   Beethoven, String Quartet Op. 131: Allegro molto vivace

All this can only be forcibly reconciled with the Classic sonata scheme by calling (1) and (2) an introduction and first movement, (3) and (4) an introduction and slow movement, (5) a scherzo, and (6) and (7) an introduction and finale.

The most imposing works of the last period are the Mass in D, known as the *Missa solemnis*, and the Ninth Symphony. Beethoven regarded this Mass as his greatest work. It is a deeply personal yet universal confession of faith. The score incorporates far more musical and liturgical symbols in much more

Missa solemnis

detail than an uninformed listener can grasp. Written to celebrate the elevation of Archduke Rudolph to archbishop of Olmütz, it is, like Bach's B-minor Mass, too long and elaborate for ordinary liturgical use.

Debt to Handel

The choral treatment owes something to Handel, whose music Beethoven revered along with Bach's. Beethoven adapted the fugal subject of his *Dona nobis pacem* (a section of the Agnus Dei) from Handel's setting of "And He shall reign forever and ever" in the Hallelujah Chorus, and the lofty style of the whole is in the spirit of Handel. Handel's oratorios, however, were conceived as a series of independent numbers, without interconnecting themes or motives and without any definite plan of musical unity in the work as a whole. By contrast, Beethoven's Mass is a planned musical unit—a symphony in five movements, one on each of the five principal divisions of the Ordinary of the Mass: Kyrie in D, Gloria in D, Credo in B♭, Sanctus in D, and Agnus Dei in D. In this respect it resembles the late Masses of Haydn, and like them it freely combines and alternates choruses and solo ensembles in each movement. Beethoven's attention to musical form occasionally led him to take liberties with the liturgical text, such as the rondo-like recurrences of the word "Credo" with its musical motive in the third movement.

Ninth Symphony

The Ninth Symphony was first performed on May 7, 1824, on a program with one of Beethoven's overtures and three movements of his Mass. The large and distinguished audience applauded vociferously after the symphony. Beethoven did not turn around to acknowledge the applause because he could not hear it; one of the solo singers plucked him by the sleeve and directed

◀ Beethoven at age forty-eight. Chalk drawing by August von Klöber (1818). (*By permission of the Beethoven-Haus Bonn. Collection H. C. Bodmer*).

◄ Beethoven's signature, from a letter written in French to Thomas Broadwood, ca. 1817.

his attention to the clapping hands and waving hats and handkerchiefs, where-upon he finally realized the audience's reaction and bowed. The receipts at the concert were large, but so little remained after expenses that Beethoven accused his friends who had managed the affair of cheating him. A repetition two weeks later before a half-full house resulted in a deficit. Thus was the Ninth Symphony launched into the world.

The work's most striking innovation remains its use of chorus and solo voices in the finale. Beethoven had thought as early as 1792 of setting Schiller's *Ode to Joy*, but more than thirty years went by before he decided to incorporate a choral finale on this text in his Ninth Symphony. Consistent with his ethical ideals and religious faith, he selected stanzas that emphasize universal fellowship through joy, and its basis in the love of an eternal heavenly Father. Beethoven was troubled by the apparent incongruity of introducing voices at the climax of a long instrumental symphony. His solution to this aesthetic difficulty determined the unusual form of the last movement:

Form of Ninth Symphony finale

- A brief, tumultuous introduction, inspired by the operatic genre of *recitativo obbligato.*
- A review and rejection (by instrumental recitatives) of the themes of the preceding movements; proposal of the "joy" theme and its joyful acceptance.
- Orchestral exposition of the theme in four stanzas, *crescendo*, with coda.
- Return of the tumultuous opening measures.
- Bass recitative: "O Freunde, nicht diese Töne! sodern lasst uns angenehmere anstimmen und freudenvollere" (O friends, not these tones, but let us rather sing more pleasant and joyful ones).
- Choral-orchestral exposition of the joy theme, "Freude, schöner Götterfunken" (Beautiful divine spark of joy), in four stanzas, varied (including a "Turkish March"), and a long orchestral interlude (double fugue) followed by a repetition of the first stanza.
- New theme, for orchestra and chorus: "Seid umschlungen, Millionen!" (Join together, O millions!).
- Double fugue on the two themes.
- A brilliant Prestissimo choral coda, bringing back the Turkish percussion, in which the joy theme is repeated in strains of matchless sublimity.

POSTLUDE

Beethoven appeared on the scene when new and powerful forces, like the American and French Revolutions, were creating enormous social and political upheavals in the world that Haydn and Mozart had known. While building on musical conventions, genres, and styles of the Classic period, Beethoven effectively transformed this legacy into a body of works that would become models for composers of the Romantic period.

Only a few of Beethoven's contemporaries understood his late works, which in any event were so personal that they could hardly be imitated. His influence on later composers resulted mostly from the works of the middle period, especially the *Rasumovsky* Quartets, the Fifth, Sixth, and Seventh Symphonies, and the piano sonatas. Even in these works it was not the Classic element in Beethoven's style but the revolutionary element—the free, impulsive, mysterious, demonic spirit, the underlying conception of music as a mode of self-expression—that fascinated the Romantic generation. As E. T. A. Hoffmann wrote, "Beethoven's music sets in motion the lever of fear, of awe, of horror, of suffering, and awakens just that infinite longing which is the essence of romanticism. He is accordingly a completely romantic composer. . . ."[3] Hoffmann realized the importance of structure and control in Beethoven's music and in the works of Haydn and Mozart, whom he also called "romantic." (Perhaps he used the word as a general term of commendation.) Romantic or not, Beethoven was one of the great disruptive forces in the history of music. After him, nothing could ever be the same; he opened the gateway to a new world.

---

3. From an essay on "Beethoven's Instrumental Music," 1813; in *Source Readings in Music History: The Romantic Era* (New York: Norton, 1997), p. 153.

16

ROMANTICISM AND NINETEENTH-CENTURY ORCHESTRAL MUSIC

PRELUDE

"Classic" and "Romantic" are rough and imprecise labels; yet, like their counterparts "Renaissance" and "Baroque," we use them to help define chronological boundaries and to give us a starting point for discussing the music of these periods. The opposition of Classic to Romantic has caused confusion in the study of music history because the two are not entirely contradictory: the historical continuity between them is greater than any contrast. Thus, "Romantic" traits are found in some eighteenth-century music, and many of the "Classic" characteristics persist throughout the nineteenth century. We read that E. T. A. Hoffmann considered the instrumental music of Haydn, Mozart, and especially Beethoven "romantic" because he found it fantastic, idealistic, and marvelous. These were qualities he associated with the *romance*, a medieval tale or poem of adventure, written in one of the languages descended from Latin ("Roman"; hence, *romance* languages).

A principal tenet of **Romanticism** was that instrumental music could communicate pure emotion without using words. So the orchestra, with its infinite variety of colors and textures, became the medium *par excellence* of Romantic music. For this reason, our first chapter on Romanticism in music concentrates on the **Orchestral Music** of six great symphonic composers of the nineteenth century, treating them in the order of their births: Schubert, Berlioz, Mendelssohn, Liszt, Brahms, and Dvořák. We omit, among others, Robert Schumann, whose more original, nonsymphonic works will be discussed in the next chapter; Anton Bruckner, whose nine symphonies have a monumental character inspired by Beethoven's Ninth; and the Russian Piotr Il'yich Tchaikovsky, whose six symphonies and ever-popular ballet music reveal his mastery of orchestration and his cosmopolitan style. To be sure, all these composers had to come to terms with the towering figure of Beethoven in writing their own symphonies; but, as we will see in the Postlude, they accepted or rejected the Beethoven Legacy in different ways, according to their individual personalities and talents.

Romanticism

The great bulk of the music written between about 1770 and about 1900 lies on a continuum, employing a shared harmonic vocabulary and common conventions of harmonic progression, rhythm, and form. Some of the differences we perceive in comparing music of the Classic and Romantic periods are in degree only. Expression of feeling became more intense and personal as the 1800s progressed. The conventions of form and tonal relations exceeded limits that had once seemed reasonable. The imagination wandered into unexplored realms that sought to recapture a cherished past or to reach a visionary future. A spirit of longing, of yearning after an impossible fulfillment, haunted Romantic art (see Plate XI, facing page 418).

Music as a Romantic art

If remoteness and boundlessness are Romantic, then music is the most Romantic of the arts. Its sonoric landscape does not reflect the concrete world, and this independence makes music highly suited for suggesting the flood of impressions, thoughts, and feelings that became the special domain of Romantic art. The philosopher Arthur Schopenhauer (1788–1860) believed that music was the very image and incarnation of innermost reality, the immediate expression of universal feelings and impulses in tangible, definite form. Other nineteenth-century writers called instrumental music the ideal Romantic art because, being free from the burden of words, it could perfectly communicate pure emotion (see vignette, page 375).

Music and literature

Although instrumental music was held in the highest regard, poetry and literature occupied a central place in the thoughts and careers of many composers. The art song, or lied, was the genre in which Schubert, Schumann, Brahms, and others created a new and intimate union between music and poetry. Even the purely instrumental music of most Romantic composers was dominated by the lyrical spirit of the lied. Many leading composers, such as Berlioz, Schumann, and Liszt, were extraordinarily interested in literary expression and wrote distinguished essays on music; Wagner was a poet, essayist, and self-styled philosopher as well as a composer of music dramas. Similarly, leading Romantic novelists and poets wrote about music with deep love and insight or dabbled in music more directly: the novelist E. T. A. Hoffmann, for example, was a successful composer of operas.

Both the strong literary orientation of nineteenth-century composers and the ideal of instrumental music as the supremely Romantic mode of expression converged in the concept of *program music*. As Liszt and others used the term, program music referred to instrumental music accompanied by a printed concert program that laid out a poetic, descriptive, or narrative subject. Whether the "program" was detailed or merely suggestive, the music usually transcended its subject and could be understood and appreciated independently of the program. The Romantics also reconciled music with words by placing great importance on the instrumental accompaniment of vocal music, whether in the pianistic inventiveness of Schubert's lieder (see Chapter 17) or in the orchestral outpourings that enfold the voices of Wagner's music dramas (see Chapter 18).

Program music

Orchestral Music

Schubert (1797–1828)

Franz Schubert came from a humble family. His father, a pious, strict, but kind and honorable man, was a schoolmaster in Vienna. The boy's formal training in music theory was not systematic, but his environment, both at

---

Franz Liszt on Music as Direct Expression:

66 Music embodies *feeling* without forcing it to contend and combine with *thought*, as it is forced in most arts and especially in the art of words. If music has one advantage over the other media through which a person can represent the impressions of the soul, it owes this to its supreme capacity to make each inner impulse audible without the assistance of reason. Reason, after all, is restricted in the diversity of its means and is capable only of confirming or describing our affections, not of communicating them directly in their full intensity. To accomplish this even approximately, reason must search for images and comparisons. Music, on the other hand, presents at once the intensity and the expression of *feeling*. It is the embodied and intelligible essence of feeling, capable of being apprehended by our senses. It permeates them like a dart, like a ray, like a mist, like a spirit, and fills our soul. 99

From *Berlioz and His "Harold" Symphony* (1855), by Franz Liszt and Princess Caroline von Wittgenstein, adapted from the translation in *Source Readings in Music History: The Romantic Era* (New York: Norton, 1965), p. 109.

home and in school, was filled with music making. He was educated to follow his father's profession, but the son's heart lay elsewhere. After teaching school for three years (1814–17), Schubert devoted himself entirely to writing music. Constantly struggling against illness and poverty, he composed ceaselessly. "I work every morning," he said; "when I have finished one piece I begin another." In the year 1815 alone he wrote 144 songs. Schubert died at the age of thirty-one, and his tombstone was inscribed, "Music has here buried a rich treasure but still fairer hopes."

Given the short span of Schubert's composing career, his enormous output of works is doubly impressive: 9 symphonies, 22 piano sonatas, a multitude of short piano pieces for two and four hands, about 35 chamber compositions, some 200 choral works including 6 Masses, 17 operas and Singspiele, and more than 600 lieder—in all, nearly 1,000 separate works.

Unfinished Symphony

Schubert's *Unfinished* (in only two movements) has been called the first truly Romantic symphony. We are struck immediately by its haunting, colorful instrumental combinations. In the first movement, a quietly stirring figure in the strings that precedes, then combines with, a lyrical melody played *pianissimo* by the oboes and clarinets, is later joined by other woodwinds that help build to a *fortissimo* climax. Schubert produced noteworthy effects in the cello melody of the G-major second theme—with its syncopated accompaniment for violas and clarinets over the pizzicato of the double basses—and in the clarinet solo and the dialogue of clarinet and oboe that appear in the middle section of the slow movement.

C H R O N O L O G Y

1810	Goethe, *Faust,* Part I (1808)	**1850**	Bach-Gesellschaft founded
			*Liszt, *Les Préludes* and *Faust* Symphony
	Wellington defeats Napoleon at Waterloo;		(1854); Henry David Thoreau, *Walden*
	Jane Austen, *Pride and Prejudice* (1813)		Charles Darwin, *On the Origin of Species*
	Congress of Vienna (1814)		(1859)
	Invention of the metronome (1815)	**1860**	Leo Tolstoy, *War and Peace*
1820			Abraham Lincoln assassinated (1865)
	Premiere of Beethoven's Ninth Symphony	**1870**	
	(1824)		Claude Monet (1840–1926), *Impression:*
	*Mendelssohn, *Midsummer Night's Dream*		*Soleil levant* (1874) (see Plate XII, facing
	Overture (1826)		page 419)
	Death of Beethoven (1827)		*Brahms, First Symphony completed; Mark
	*Death of Schubert (1828)		Twain (1835–1910), *Tom Sawyer* (1876)
1830	*First performance of Berlioz, *Symphonie*	**1880**	
	fantastique		Metropolitan Opera House opened in New
	Victoria crowned queen of England (1837)		York (1883)
1840			Paris World's Fair (1889)
	New York Philharmonic Society founded	**1890**	
	(1842)		*Dvořák, Symphony No. 9, *From the New*
	Karl Marx and Friedrich Engels, *Communist*		*World* (1893)
	Manifesto (1848)		*Death of Brahms (1897)

In his "Great" Symphony in C major (No. 9, composed in 1828 and first performed in 1839), Schubert expanded his material almost to the breaking point; the "heavenly length" that Schumann admired (see vignette below) would be less heavenly if it were not for the beauty of Schubert's melodies and orchestral effects. Some of these effects remain unforgettable: two horns calling softly, as if from a distance, at the start of the slow introduction; the antiphony between strings carrying the first theme and winds playing quick repeating chords; the *pianissimo* trombones at the end of the exposition; the repeated g' of the horns in the slow movement as the strings vacillate among

> ### Great C-major Symphony

Schumann on Schubert's Symphony in C Major:*

❝ I must say at once that anyone who is not yet acquainted with this symphony knows very little about Schubert. When we consider all that he has given to art, this praise may strike many as exaggerated, partly, no doubt, because composers have so often been advised, to their chagrin, that it is better for them—after Beethoven—'to abstain from the symphonic form.' . . .

On hearing Schubert's symphony and its bright, flowery, romantic life, the city [of Vienna] crystallizes before me, and I realize how such works could be born in these very surroundings. . . . Everyone must acknowledge that the outer world—sparkling today, gloomy tomorrow—often deeply stirs the feeling of the poet or the musician; and all must recognize, while listening to this symphony, that it reveals to us something more than mere beautiful song, mere joy and sorrow, such as music has ever expressed in a hundred ways, leading us into regions that, to our best recollection, we had never before explored. To understand this, one must hear this symphony. Here we find . . . a suffusing romanticism that other works by Franz Schubert have already made known to us.

And then the heavenly length of the symphony, like that of a thick novel in four volumes. . . . How this refreshes, this feeling of abundance, so contrary to our experience with others when we always dread to be disillusioned at the end and are often saddened through disappointment. ❞

*Schumann discovered the unplayed manuscript of Schubert's Symphony in C major when he visited Schubert's brother Ferdinand in 1839. Through his intercession it was performed the same year at the Gewandhaus Concerts in Leipzig under the direction of Mendelssohn.

From *Neue Zeitschrift für Musik* 12 (1840):82–83, after the translation by Paul Rosenfeld in Robert Schumann, *On Music and Musicians*, ed. Konrad Wolff (New York: Norton, 1946), pp. 108–11.

the dominants of C, F, and D, and finally resolve (by way of the Neapolitan chord) in the dominant of A just before the return of the principal theme (measures 148–59; Example 16.1).

EXAMPLE 16.1   Franz Schubert, Symphony in C major: Andante con moto

Berlioz (1803–1869)

We have already encountered Hector Berlioz in his enthusiastic commentary on Beethoven's Sixth (*Pastoral*) Symphony (see vignette, page 361). Because his imagination tended to run in parallel literary and musical channels, Berlioz subtitled his first and most famous work, *Symphonie fantastique*, "Episode in the Life of an Artist" and provided it with an autobiographical program (see NAWM 108). Composed in 1830, only three years after Beethoven's death, the work is a musical drama without words. As Berlioz wrote, "The program should be regarded in the same way as the spoken words of an opera, serving to introduce the musical numbers by describing the situation that evokes the particular mood and expressive character of each." The literary influences in the program are too numerous to detail, although Goethe's *Faust* is conspicuous among them, and the supposed situations are depicted in the passionate prose of a young and sensitive artist.

Symphonie fantastique

Idée fixe

Berlioz brings back the opening theme of the first Allegro—the *idée fixe* or the obsessive image of the hero's beloved, according to the program—in all the other movements (Example 16.2). The first movement, *Reveries et*

EXAMPLE 16.2   Hector Berlioz, *Symphonie fantastique*: Allegro agitato e appassionato assai

passions, consists of a slow introduction followed by an Allegro in modified sonata form; the second is a waltz, replacing the Classic scherzo; the third is a pastorale, an Adagio in a large, two-part form (NAWM 108); the fourth movement is a macabre and descriptive orchestral *tour de force* (also in NAWM 108); and the finale, an introduction and Allegro, uses a transformation of the *idée fixe* and two other themes—one of them the chant sequence *Dies irae*—first singly, then in combination.

The *Symphonie fantastique* is original not only in bending the symphony to serve narrative and autobiographical purposes but also in presenting a dazzling musical vocabulary. It is partly a matter of details—melodies, harmonies, rhythms, phrase structures—and partly Berlioz's astounding ability to express the many shifting moods, the essential emotional content of his drama, in music that has great communicative power. His vivid aural imagination and his inventive orchestral sonorities shine through in nearly every measure. Berlioz achieved unity in the symphony as a whole—the kind of unity Beethoven forged in his Third and Fifth Symphonies—by introducing a recurring theme and by developing the dramatic idea through all of the five movements.

Berlioz's second symphony, *Harold en Italie* (1834; title suggested by Lord Byron's *Childe Harold*), is a set of four scenes imbued with the composer's recollections of an Italian sojourn. Each movement is connected by a recurrent theme, played by solo viola. The instrument is featured throughout,

Harold en Italie

Window

THE SYMPHONY ORCHESTRA

In the 1780s Haydn's orchestra at Eszterháza consisted of fewer than 25 instruments: a core of strings (10 violins, 2 violas, 2 cellos, and 2 basses) plus 2 oboes, 2 bassoons, 2 horns, and keyboard. The court orchestra in Mozart's Vienna was marginally bigger: it used a few more strings and 2 flutes in addition to the other winds. But only forty years later, Beethoven's Ninth Symphony was premiered in Vienna by a force of 61 players plus a large chorus. In addition to the strings (without keyboard, which was no longer necessary as a foundation for the orchestra), it called for a pair each of flutes, oboes, clarinets, bassoons, horns, trumpets, and trombones. By the 1830s, orchestras in Paris too had grown enormously and typically employed between 70 and 80 players, including some 50 strings (usually 24, 8, 10, 8). Berlioz scored his *Symphonie fantastique* for piccolo, 2 flutes, 2 oboes, English horn, 2 clarinets, bass clarinet, 4 bassoons, 4 horns, 2 cornets, 2 trumpets, 3 trombones, and 2 ophicleides (large, keyed brass instruments, eventually re-

though less prominently than in solo concertos; for this reason the great violinist Nicolò Paganini (1782–1840), who commissioned the work from Berlioz, refused to play it. In each movement the viola melody combines contrapuntally with the other themes, and the solo instrument continually blends with different orchestral groups in a ravishing display of sonorities. The finale explicitly sums up the themes of the preceding movements.

Roméo et Juliette

Five years after *Harold en Italie*, Berlioz produced his "dramatic symphony" in seven movements, *Roméo et Juliette*, for orchestra, soloists, and chorus. In adding choral parts to the orchestra, he was following Beethoven's example; but in this work the voices enter in the prologue and are used in three of the symphonic movements as well. Although the Classic order of movements can still be traced, the series of independent scenes approaches an unstaged opera or what the composer later called a "dramatic legend"— a genre he perfected in *La Damnation de Faust* (1864). Nonetheless, *Roméo et Juliette* is essentially a symphonic work.

Berlioz's influence

Berlioz's first three symphonies, especially the *Symphonie fantastique*, made him the initial leader of the Romantic movement's radical wing. All subsequent composers of program music—including Strauss and Debussy— would be indebted to him. Berlioz's orchestration initiated a new era: he enriched orchestral music with new resources of harmony, color, expression, placed by tubas) as well as a variety of percussion instruments (including bells) and 2 harps. In addition to the increase in numbers, changes in the construction of instruments greatly increased the power of the strings and the efficiency of the winds. At the same time, the expansion in the orchestra's size created a need for a permanent, baton-wielding conductor.

As orchestras became fuller and richer in texture and timbre, audiences at first condemned their "noisiness"; listeners complained that Beethoven's symphonies, for example, had too many notes. But when nineteenth-century ears became accustomed to the new complexity and volume of orchestral sound, Mozart's scores were considered too empty! The Romantic taste for monumentality and expressivity demanded still more volume, more brilliance, more color, and more variety. By the end of the nineteenth century the Vienna Philharmonic regularly had more than one hundred players, and many composers were still aiming to keep them all occupied.

The question arises: did the developing orchestra, like some gigantic machine, drive the composers to write bigger scores, or was it the composers themselves who pioneered the increasingly massive sonority of the symphony orchestra?

and form; and his use of a recurrent theme in different movements (as in the *Symphonie fantastique* and *Harold en Italie*) was an important impulse toward the development of the cyclical symphonic forms of the later nineteenth century. By example and precept he was the founder of modern orchestration and conducting.

Mendelssohn (1809–1847)

Felix Mendelssohn's two most important symphonies carry geographical subtitles—the *Italian* (No. 4, 1833) and the *Scottish* (No. 3, 1842). They preserve impressions he gained, both of sounds and landscapes, on trips to Italy and the British Isles. The *Italian* Symphony celebrates the south, sunny and vibrant. The slow movement suggests a procession of chanting pilgrims trudging along the road. In the finale, we can imagine people in the city squares dancing the spirited *saltarello*. The *Scottish* Symphony evokes the north, gray and somber, with the skirling of bagpipes and the sound of old heroic ballads. In both symphonies Mendelssohn skillfully fitted his melodious ideas into the regular Classic forms.

Unlike Berlioz's essentially vocal unfolding of the *idée fixe* in the *Fantastic* Symphony (Example 16.2), the equally expansive melody that opens the

Italian *Symphony*

Italian Symphony (Example 16.3) is thoroughly instrumental. Yet its sighing lurches and sequences and its repeated postponement of closure are inspired, like Berlioz's melody, by Italian opera. The second theme is similarly constructed. Assigned first to a clarinet-bassoon choir, then oboes and flutes, it is finally taken up by the strings. Mendelssohn practically forgoes these ideas in the development section, which is dominated by a sprightly Italian-flavored tune that returns at the end of the recapitulation, cleverly combined with the main theme. The trio of the (unlabeled) scherzo, in which a quartet of bassoons and horns hold forth, recalls similar ensembles in the trios of Beethoven's Third and Ninth Symphonies.

EXAMPLE 16.3   Felix Mendelssohn, Symphony No. 4 (*Italian*), Op. 90: Allegro vivace

Scottish Symphony

The four movements of the *Scottish* Symphony are played without pause. One portion of the slow introduction serves as a bridge to the second movement and to another, fragmentary motive. The Scottish flavor that pervades the entire work results not only from the trochaic rhythm of the "Scotch snap" in the second movement, but also from the pentatonic scales that underlie the themes. In Example 16.4 some of the principal melodic ideas are transposed to A minor/C major for easy comparison. These may be reduced to the two most common types of pentatonic scales found in folk music of the Hebrides Islands. The ornamental tones heard in Scottish bagpipe performances are represented in Mendelssohn's score by grace notes. His use of folk idioms reveals Mendelssohn's nostalgia for faraway places and illustrates the Romantic composer's interest in native music and local color. It also shows how strongly high-profile tunes determine the character of symphonic music in the Romantic period and, at the same time, how easily ethnic flavor can be diluted by lush harmonies and textures.

Overtures

Mendelssohn's peculiar genius for depicting musical landscapes is evident in his overtures *Die Hebriden* (The Hebrides), also called *Fingals Höhle* (Fingal's Cave, 1832), and *Meeresstille und glückliche Fahrt* (Calm Sea and Prosperous Voyage, 1828–32). Among his incidental music for plays, the overture for Victor Hugo's *Ruy Blas* (1839) is surpassed only by the incomparable

EXAMPLE 16.4   Felix Mendelssohn, Symphony No. 3 (*Scottish*): Op. 56

Midsummer Night's Dream Overture. Written in 1826 when the composer was only seventeen, that work set the standard for all subsequent concert overtures of the period. It remains a brilliant example of self-renewing perpetual motion by a large orchestra, tamed to tiptoe like a chamber ensemble. Although the overture is programmatic (in the same sense as Beethoven's *Pastoral* Symphony) and is certainly Romantic in its treatment of the orchestra and the quality of its imagination, Mendelssohn avoids extremes of feeling and never allows the extra-musical inspiration to disturb the musical balance. The program thinly veils the structure, lending charm to the view but not obscuring the outlines. Seventeen years later Mendelssohn wrote additional incidental music for a production of this Shakespeare play, including the picturesque Scherzo (NAWM 109).

Liszt (1811–1886)

The foremost composer of program music after Berlioz was Franz Liszt, who wrote twelve symphonic poems between 1848 and 1858 and a thirteenth in 1881–82. Liszt's term *symphonic poem* is significant: he did not call these works symphonies, presumably because they were relatively short and were not divided into separate movements in a conventional order. Instead, each presents a continuous form with sections contrasting in character and tempo;

Symphonic poem

a few themes are developed, repeated, varied, or transformed. These works are "poems" by analogy to word-poems. Not a drama, narrative, or prose exposition, the symphonic poem is an imaginative structure free of the conventions of traditional genres. The content and form may be suggested by a picture, statue, play, poem, scene, personality, or something else, but the subject is converted into music without specific reference to the details of the original. The title and, usually, a program, which may or may not have been written by the composer, identify the subject. So, for example, Liszt's *Hunnenschlacht* (The Battle of the Huns) is related to a mural painting, *Mazeppa* to a poem, *Hamlet* to Shakespeare's hero, *Prometheus* to the myth and also to a poem by Herder, and so on. The score of *Die Ideale* is liberally interspersed with quotations from Schiller's poem of that title, although Liszt changed the order of Schiller's passages to make them conform to his own musical plan.

The best of Liszt's symphonic poems, *Orpheus* and *Hamlet*, are concise musical portraits that originated as introductions to theatrical performances. The first, for Gluck's opera, was inspired by an Etruscan vase in the Louvre depicting Orpheus singing to the lyre; the second, an overture for Shakespeare's play, is a penetrating psychological study. Liszt's programs, like those of Berlioz, do not relate stories told in music but run parallel with them. The music represents an evocation of the ideas and states of feeling expressed in the different medium of the original subject.

Several of the symphonic poems grew out of concert overtures. Others are one-movement symphonies that contain lingering vestiges of sonata form and of the contrasts in mood and tempo found in the standard four-movement sequence. Liszt devised a method of unifying a composition by transforming a single motive to reflect the diverse moods needed to portray a programmatic subject. We call this method *thematic transformation*. In *Les Préludes* (1854; based on a poem of the same title by Alfonse-Marie de Lamartine [1790–1869]), he applied this method with notable artistic success. A three-note motive that has both a rhythmic and a melodic shape (Example 16.5a) is modified and expanded to take on different characters: amorphous, like a prelude (Example 16.5b); resolute (c); lyrical (d); stormy (e and f); excited (g); and martial (h). A more distant metamorphosis (i) serves as a contrasting theme and is itself subjected to transformations. Liszt used a similar method in his Piano Concerto in E♭, composed at about the same time (see page 401).

Thematic transformation

Les Préludes

EXAMPLE 16.5   Franz Liszt, *Les Préludes*

a. **Andante**   b. **Poco ritenuto**

The works that Liszt called symphonies are also programmatic. He dedicated his masterpiece, the *Faust* Symphony (1854), to Berlioz. It consists of three movements, labeled *Faust*, *Gretchen*, and *Mephistopheles*, with a finale (added later) for tenor soloist and men's chorus, setting the *chorus mysticus* that closes Goethe's drama. The first three movements correspond to the Classic plan: introduction and Allegro (in sonata form), Andante (three-part form), and Scherzo (three-part form, followed by a long additional development and coda). The first theme of the *Faust* movement uses one of Liszt's favorite chords—the augmented triad, here transposed sequentially downward through four chromatic steps so as to comprise all twelve notes of the chromatic scale (Example 16.6). Themes are interchanged among the movements and transformed in accordance with the program. The *Mephistopheles*

Faust *Symphony*

EXAMPLE 16.6   Franz Liszt, *Faust* Symphony: First Theme

movement, for example, is made up largely of sinister caricatures of the *Faust* themes (Berlioz similarly caricatured the *idée fixe* in the *Symphonie fantastique*), and the *Gretchen* melody is used as the principal theme of the finale. Liszt in this symphony most successfully combined a grandiose and momentous program with music of great inspiration, substance, and passion, in a form whose huge dimensions are justified by the scope and power of the generating ideas. The *Dante* Symphony (1856) is a shorter work in two movements—*Inferno* and *Purgatorio*—with a quiet concluding section for women's voices on the text of the *Magnificat*.

Liszt's influence   Liszt's influence was far reaching. Composers such as Bedřich Smetana (*Má vlast*), César Franck (*Psyché*), Camille Saint-Saëns (*Le Rouet d'Omphale*, *Danse macabre*), and Piotr Il'yich Tchaikovsky (*Francesca da Rimini*) appropriated the genre of the symphonic poem. Liszt's bold chords and chromatic harmonies helped form Wagner's style after 1854; and Liszt's manipulation of small sets of intervals and pitches enjoyed unexpected resonance in the twentieth century.

Brahms (1833–1897)

Johannes Brahms, by nature conscientious and severely self-critical, approached the composition of a symphony with great care and deliberation. His First Symphony, in C minor, Op. 68, was finished after some twenty years of work, in 1876, when Brahms was already in his forties. The second, in D major, Op. 73, appeared in 1877, and the last two (F major, Op. 90, and E minor, Op. 98) were composed in 1883 and 1885 respectively. Other late works for orchestra were his *Academic Festival Overture*, Op. 80 (1880) and the *Tragic Overture*, Op. 81 (1881). Brahms also left two piano concertos and the Violin Concerto, Op. 77 in D (1878), which ranks with Beethoven's concerto in the literature of this instrument; and the Double Concerto for violin and cello, Op. 102 in A minor (1887).

First Symphony   The First Symphony has the conventional sequence of movements—fast, slow, a light movement, and fast—the first and last having slow introductions. The third movement, like the corresponding movement in the Second and Third Symphonies, retains the lyrical rhythmic grace of an intermezzo rather than the intensity of the Beethoven scherzo. The key scheme of the symphony—C minor; E major; A♭ major and B major; and C minor and major—is characteristic of the late- and post-Beethoven eras in its use of the major-third relation and the shifts between minor and major. As in Beethoven's Fifth, the initial C minor gives way to a triumphant major at the end of the last movement. The opening theme of the first Allegro (Example 16.7) balances antecedent and consequent phrases in the top line, while the chromatically rising motive of the introduction is developed in the bass. Although this procedure is very much in the Classic tradition, the wide pitch-range reaching for ever new heights epitomizes Romantic melody.

EXAMPLE 16.7   Johannes Brahms, Symphony No. 1, Op. 68: Allegro

The opening measures of the Third Symphony illustrate the wide melodic span particularly well. We also find the characteristic cross-relation between the minor and major forms of the tonic triad (see Example 16.8). The conflict between the two modes recurs in the last movement, which begins in F minor and settles in F major only in the coda. At the statement of the second theme, another typical Brahmsian clash occurs, between two diverse simultaneous meters: the accompaniment in four and the melody in six (Example 16.9).

Third Symphony

EXAMPLE 16.8   Johannes Brahms, Third Symphony, Op. 70: Allegro con brio, Outline of First Theme

EXAMPLE 16.9   Johannes Brahms, Third Symphony, Op. 70, IV: Allegro

Brahms began the Fourth Symphony by setting out a chain of thirds, in which all the notes of the harmonic minor scale are used serially before any is repeated (see Example 16.10). The thematic statement in the first violin continues with a similar series, this time rising from the keynote *E* to *C*,

Fourth Symphony

completing an eight-measure phrase. Another series of thirds accompanies the melodious second subject, and at the start of the recapitulation Brahms unfolds the initial series of thirds in augmentation.

EXAMPLE 16.10   Johannes Brahms, Fourth Symphony, Op. 98: Allegro non troppo

The finale of this work is a 32-variation passacaglia/chaconne, a form that reflects Brahms's fascination with Baroque music. It is at once a set of variations on a melody and on a harmonic pattern. The variations are laid out in a broad three-part form, the middle section consisting of four quiet variations in $\frac{3}{2}$ meter (in effect, at half of the surrounding $\frac{3}{4}$). The diversity among the variations of figuration and mood is balanced by a feeling of continuous, controlled movement throughout.

Dvořák (1841–1904)

Of the nine symphonies by the Czech composer Antonín Dvořák, No. 7 in D minor (1885) is considered his best. The work is rich in thematic ideas; its prevailingly tragic mood is relieved only by the G-major trio of the Scherzo. The Symphonies No. 6 in D major (1880) and No. 8 in G major (1889) are more relaxed in spirit, with fresh folklike melodies and rhythms and many fine touches of orchestration. No. 9 (*From the New World*), which Dvořák wrote in 1893 during his first sojourn in the United States, is the most familiar. For this symphony, the composer consciously used themes suggested by Native American melodies and, especially, by Negro spirituals that he heard sung in New York by Harry T. Burleigh. Among Dvořák's other orchestral music is a fine cello concerto that remains a standard in the repertoire.

POSTLUDE

Any composer living in Vienna during the first three decades of the nineteenth century walked in Beethoven's shadow. Such was the case with Schubert, for example, who did not attempt a large-scale symphony until his *Unfinished* (No. 8) in B minor, abandoned in 1822 and not performed until 1865. After a bow to Beethoven's Third in the introductory theme, Schubert launched into a songful melody quite unlike the typical first themes of his day. As Schubert's lyrical outpourings were not suited to Beethovenian development, he compromised with the Classic tradition by treating the more economical introductory theme, rather than the tuneful first theme, in the development section as well as in the coda. In this way,

▲ Liszt at the piano: painting (1840) by Joseph Danhauser in the Nationalgalerie, Berlin.
From left to right: Alexandre Dumas, Hector Berlioz, George Sand, Paganini, Rossini, Liszt,
and the countess Marie d'Agoult. Note Beethoven's bust on the piano. (*Corbis-Bettmann*)

Schubert could meet his listeners' expectations without compromising his
lyrical style.

Beethoven's *Pastoral* Symphony gave Berlioz the license to shape a
Classic form around a set of feelings or passions. In the *Pastoral*, Beethoven paints a tableau of emotions created by a day in the country: contemplative delight in nature, apprehension as a storm approaches, terror at the
storm's fury, and joy and gratitude for the fresh, washed calm that follows.
In the *Symphonie fantastique*, Berlioz arouses the passions by his thoughts
and fantasies about a woman whose love he hopes to win. The slow
movements of both works evoke an idyllic pastoral atmosphere, with dialogues among piping shepherds or cowherds. On a musical level, the
Eroica's monumentality and spacious conception released Berlioz from the
earlier confines of the Classic symphony. Beethoven had subjected the
main theme in both the Third and Fifth Symphonies to a series of exciting
adventures; that gave Berlioz a precedent to invent the *idée fixe*, a melody
that he used in several movements to represent the heroine. But instead of
a four-note motive that invites development, this melody has the long line
of an operatic aria that can be extended and ornamented but that resists
fragmentation. For his dramatic symphony *Roméo et Juliette* (1839),
Berlioz used Beethoven's Ninth Symphony as a model for a work that
combined an orchestra, soloists, and chorus in an unstaged concert drama.

By contrast, Felix Mendelssohn was able to resist Beethoven's influence, thanks to his rigorous training in the Classic forms and his study of Bach and Handel. As a pupil of Carl Friedrich Zelter (1758–1832) he wrote thirteen symphonies for strings alone that gave him a mastery of form, counterpoint, and fugue and helped determine his personal style.

Brahms's reluctance to put a major symphonic work before the public is notorious. As we have seen, he worked on his First Symphony on and off for more than twenty years, beginning in 1855. Concerning the specter of Beethoven, Brahms exclaimed in 1870: "I shall never compose a symphony! You have no idea how someone like me feels when he hears such a giant marching behind him all the time."[1] However, far from wanting to write "Beethoven's Tenth"—as the conductor Hans von Bülow dubbed Brahms's First—the composer deliberately set out to cut a fresh path. In this work, the slow introductions to the first and final movements gradually present the principal thematic material, even before their respective Allegros begin. This was a new idea, and linking all the movements through references to the opening slow introduction also gave Brahms's First a strong organic coherence.

Although Richard Wagner (1813–1883) was not a symphonist but an opera composer, he too came under Beethoven's spell, believing that Beethoven's Ninth Symphony pointed the way to the music of the future. Wagner imagined that the Ninth's choral finale was an admission of music's need for poetry. And even though Beethoven had not renounced the symphony in favor of music drama, Wagner credited Beethoven with opening the way to the "totally unified artwork" (*Gesamtkunstwerk*)—the universal music drama:

> The last symphony of Beethoven is the deliverance of music from its own nature to become a universal art. It is the human gospel of the art of the future. Beyond it no advance is possible; only the perfect artwork of the future can follow: the universal drama, the key to which Beethoven has wrought for us.[2]

The fuller story of Wagner's music dramas will be told in Chapter 18.

1. Max Kalbeck, *Johannes Brahms* (Berlin: Deutsche Brahms-Gesellschaft, 1921), 1:165.

2. Richard Wagner, *Gesammelte Schriften*, ed. Julius Rapp (Leipzig: Hesse & Becker, n.d. [1914?]), 9:103–4.

17

Solo, Chamber, and Vocal Music in the Nineteenth Century

Romantic composers seemed intent on testing the limits of musical expression, which meant pushing to extremes such elements as dynamic shadings, harmonic logic, formal boundaries, even the physical capabilities of performers. One pair of opposites they explored with equal enthusiasm was the monumental and the miniature: at the same time that orchestras became larger and more colorful (see window, pages 380–81), nineteenth-century composers cultivated many different and more intimate genres for solo piano, solo voice, and chamber ensemble. In addition to writing hundreds of monumental works for orchestra, they also produced thousands of smaller pieces—piano sonatas, chamber works, and lieder—among which are the characteristic miniatures that portray a mood or communicate a sentiment in a matter of minutes.

The piano, much enlarged and strengthened since Mozart's day, became the perfect instrument for conveying repertory from either end of the spectrum: concertos of grandiose proportions or brief statements of fleeting impressions. It was capable of producing a full, firm tone at any dynamic level, of responding in every way to demands for both expressiveness and virtuosity. Composers developed new ways of writing for the instrument, such as splitting the accompaniment between two hands, reinforcing the melody by simulating the orchestral technique of doubling, and calling for extended legato effects with the help of the pedal. For all these reasons, many Romantic composers of orchestral music—Schubert, Mendelssohn,

Robert Schumann, Liszt, Brahms—also devoted their energy to writing **Solo Music for Piano**, while others—like Chopin—made it the sole focus of their creative activity.

The medium of **Chamber Music** was not as congenial to many Romantic composers. It lacked the intimate personal communication of the solo piano or the solo voice on the one hand, and the glowing colors and powerful sound of the orchestra on the other. It is therefore not surprising that the arch-Romantics Berlioz, Liszt, and Wagner contributed nothing to the repertory of chamber music, nor that the best nineteenth-century chamber works came from those composers who felt closest to the Classic tradition—Schubert, Brahms, and, to a lesser degree, Mendelssohn and Schumann.

Vocal Music is the third genre to be discussed in this chapter, in particular, the German art song or **The Lied**, which became a favorite outlet for intense personal feelings. In Schubert's works, for example, it was the perfect antidote to the "heavenly length" of his symphonies. At once the most suitable medium for both the literary and the lyrical tendencies of Romanticism, the lied enjoyed a brilliant period of efflorescence in the nineteenth century—one that has never been matched.

Solo Music for Piano

Much Romantic piano music was written in dance forms, such as waltzes, mazurkas, and polonaises; the last two are Polish dances that became popular in Parisian high society. Also characteristic were short lyrical pieces that appeared under many different names—ballades, nocturnes, impromptus, scherzos, etc.—and were nearly always intended to evoke a specific mood or scene. Although the principal longer works were concertos, variations, fantasias, and sonatas, many of these also contained mood pieces among their movements.

Schubert

In addition to marches, waltzes, and other dances, Franz Schubert wrote fourteen short pieces that became for piano literature what his lieder were to the vocal repertory. Each of his six *Moments musicaux* (D. 789)[1] and eight Impromptus (D. 899, 935) creates a distinctive mood, and the works became models for every subsequent Romantic composer of intimate piano pieces. Schubert's most important larger works for the piano are his eleven completed

---

1. Schubert's works are best identified by the number assigned to them in *Schubert: Thematic Catalogue of All His Works in Chronological Order* by Otto Erich Deutsch and Donald R. Wakeling (London and New York, 1951); corrections and additions by O. E. Deutsch in *Music and Letters*, 34 (1953):25–32; German trans., rev., enlarged by Walter Dürr, Arnold Feil, Christa Landon, and others as *Franz Schubert: Thematisches Verzeichnis seiner Werke in chronologischer Folge von Otto Erich Deutsch*, Neue Ausgabe Sämtlicher Werke, 8/4 (Kassel: Bärenreiter, 1978).

sonatas and a Fantasia in C major (1822) on a theme adapted from his song *Der Wanderer*. The *Wanderer Fantasie* (D. 760), unlike most of his other compositions for piano, makes considerable demands on the player's technique. Its four movements, which are linked together, center around the Adagio and Variations; the theme is the song itself. The remaining movements use motives from the song as well.

Sonatas

The music of Haydn and Mozart more than Beethoven's influenced Schubert's sonatas. By using "substitute" dominants, for example, and introducing three keys in his expositions instead of two, Schubert departs in subtle ways from the standard Classic patterns. The thrust of his writing is more lyric than dramatic, as his expansive melodies do not lend themselves to motivic development. In composing his last three piano sonatas (all 1828) Schubert was obviously aware of Beethoven's works, as witness the stormy first movement of the Sonata in C minor (D. 958) and the finale of the Sonata in B♭ (D. 960), which begins like the finale of Beethoven's Quartet Op. 130. But these are superficial similarities; Schubert is nowhere more independent, more the incomparable lyric master, than in these sonatas. The last of these, in B♭, undoubtedly his greatest work for the piano, opens with a long singing melody, doubled at the lower octave (Example 17.1). The slow movement is in C♯ minor (the enharmonic lowered mediant key), with a middle section in A major. The delicately varied ostinato rhythm of this movement is typical of Schubert, as are the expressive suspensions and the unexpected shifts between major and minor in the coda.

EXAMPLE 17.1   Franz Schubert, Sonata in B♭: Molto moderato

Mendelssohn

Felix Mendelssohn was himself a virtuoso pianist. His piano music requires a fluent technique, but in general the style is elegant, sensitive, even restrained, as befits Mendelssohn's more classical temperament in general. His larger compositions for piano comprise two concertos, three sonatas, preludes and

◄ Grand piano by Anton Walter and Son, Vienna, ca. 1810. (*Yale University, Collection of Musical Instruments*)

fugues, variations, and fantasias. The preludes and fugues reveal Mendelssohn's interest in the music of J. S. Bach. (The performance he conducted in Berlin [1829] of the *St. Matthew Passion* helped spark a revival of Bach's music, which led eventually to the publication of his complete works in forty-seven monumental volumes.)

A certain elfin lightness and clarity in scherzo-like movements, a quality unique to Mendelssohn's orchestral music as well, is evident in the familiar *Andante and Rondo Capriccioso*, Op. 14, and in the brilliant *Capriccio* in F♯ minor, Op. 5 (1825). Mendelssohn's most popular piano works were the forty-eight short pieces issued at intervals in six books under the collective title *Lieder ohne Worte* (Songs without Words; most of the names attached to the separate pieces were supplied by publishers). The title itself is typical of the Romantic period. Here, along with a few tunes that now seem faded and sentimental, are many distinguished examples of the Romantic miniature: the *Gondola Song* in A minor (Op. 62, No. 5), the delightful little Presto in C major known as the *Spinning Song* (Op. 67, No. 4), the *Duetto* in A♭ (Op. 38, No. 6), or the tenderly melancholic B-minor melody of Op. 67, No. 5.

Lieder ohne Worte

Robert Schumann (1810–1856)

After university studies in law, Robert Schumann devoted himself with enthusiasm to becoming a concert pianist. An injury to his right hand cut short this career. He then turned his energies wholly to composition and to the Leipzig *Neue Zeitschrift für Musik* (New Journal of Music), which he edited from 1834 to 1844. His essays and reviews became an important force in the Romantic movement; he was one of the first to recognize the genius of Chopin and Brahms as well as Schubert's instrumental music. All of Schumann's published compositions (Opp. 1–23) up to 1840 were for piano, and, except for his one concerto (1845), they include most of his important works for that instrument.

Schumann was a master of the miniature, and the bulk of his piano compositions are short character pieces, often grouped into loosely organized cycles that are colorfully named: *Papillons* (Butterflies), *Carnaval*, *Phantasiestücke* (Fantasy Pieces; see NAWM 110), *Kinderscenen* (Scenes from Childhood), *Kreisleriana*, *Novelletten*, *Nachtstücke* (Night Pieces), *Faschingsschwank aus Wien* (Carnival Fun from Vienna), and *Album für die Jugend* (Album for the Young). The titles he gave to the collections and to separate pieces suggest that Schumann wanted listeners to associate them with extra-musical poetic fancies. This attitude was typical of the period, and its significance is not diminished at all by Schumann's admission that he usually wrote the music before he thought of the title. More than any other composer, he instilled in his music the depths, contradictions, and tensions of the Romantic spirit; it is by turns ardent and dreamy, vehement and visionary, whimsical and learned. Both in his literary writings and in a piano work entitled *Davidsbundlertänze*, the different facets of Schumann's own nature are personified in the figures of Florestan, Eusebius, and Raro, members of an imaginary league called the *Davidsbund*—a league that took its name from the biblical David and campaigned against musical Philistines. Florestan was the impulsive revolutionary, Eusebius the youthful dreamer, and Raro the wise, mature master, but they all gave voice to Schumann the composer.

Schumann gave each of the *Phantasiestücke* (Fantasy Pieces) a whimsical title; what binds them together is their flights of fantasy. *Grillen* (Whims, NAWM 110a) typifies Schumann's approach to composition at the time. It is built entirely of four-measure phrases that join to form five distinct musical periods or modules, which recur in the rondo-like pattern ABCBA–DE–ABCBA. Although the periods are subtly linked through rhythmic, melodic, and harmonic motives, they are essentially independent blocks of music. The periods are repeated intact and can be joined front to back or back to front; that is, A can proceed to B, B to A, C to B, and so forth. Like many of Schumann's short pieces, *Grillen* has a triple-time dance flavor in which the middle section (DE) functions as a trio.

Character pieces

Phantasiestücke

Chopin (1810–1849)

Among the piano music in dance forms, the works of Fryderyk Chopin stand out for their sheer beauty and sensuality. Chopin wrote almost exclusively for the piano. Although he lived in Paris from 1831, he never stopped loving his native Poland or grieving over its political misfortune. His mazurkas, suffused with the rhythms, harmonies, forms, and melodic traits of Polish popular music, are among the earliest and best examples of Romantic music inspired by national idioms. He incorporated the "Lydian" raised fourth,

Mazurkas

Polonaises

characteristic of Polish folk music, in his earliest works. To some extent Chopin's polonaises may also be regarded as a manifestation of his Polish nationalism. Since entering Western European music during Bach's time, the polonaise had, inevitably, acquired a conventional character. But the chivalric and heroic spirit of his native land glows anew in some of Chopin's polonaises—particularly those in A♭ (Op. 53) and F♯ minor (Op. 44).

Performing style

Most of Chopin's pieces are introspective and, within clearly defined formal outlines, suggest the quality of improvisation. An infrequent public performer, Chopin was not theatrically overwhelming as a pianist, and other virtuosos have emphasized the heroic side of his music more than he himself could or would have. All his works, however, demand of the player not only a flawless technique and touch but also an imaginative use of the pedals and a discreet application of *tempo rubato*, which Chopin described as a slight pushing or holding back of the right-hand part while the left-hand accompaniment continues in strict time.

Nocturnes

The nocturnes, impromptus, and preludes are Chopin's most soulful works. He got both the name and the general idea of the nocturnes—descriptive pieces that evoke the quiet and/or fretful dreaminess of night—from the Irish pianist and composer John Field (1782–1837), whose nocturnes parallel Chopin's in a number of ways. Although Field anticipated some of Chopin's mannerisms, he could not match the rich harmonic imagination that so powerfully supports Chopin's lyrical lines, as in the E♭ Nocturne (compare NAWM 111 and 112).

Preludes

Chopin composed his preludes at a time when he was deeply immersed in the music of Bach. Like the preludes in *The Well-Tempered Keyboard*, these brief, sharply defined, mood pictures utilize all the major and minor keys, though the circle of fifths determined their succession—C major, A minor, G major, E minor, and so on—whereas Bach's were arranged in rising chromatic steps—C major, C minor, C♯ major, C♯ minor, etc. Chopin's rich chromatic harmonies and modulations, which influenced later composers, are evident in many of the preludes, most notably Nos. 2, 4, 8, and the middle sections of Nos. 14 and 24.

Ballades and Scherzos

Chopin projected his ideas onto a larger canvas in the ballades and scherzos. He is the first composer known to have used the title *ballade* for an instrumental piece. His works in this genre—especially Op. 23 in G minor and Op. 52 in F minor—capture the mood swings of the narrative ballads by contemporary poets (see page 406), filled with romantic adventures and supernatural incidents. The principal scherzos are his Op. 20 in B minor and Op. 39 in C♯ minor. These show no trace of this genre's original connotation of playfulness; they are wholly serious, vigorous, and passionate works, organized—as are the ballades—in forms that grow organically from the musical ideas. On an equally grand scale but even more varied in content is the great *Fantasia* in F minor (Op. 49), a worthy companion to the fantasias of Schubert and Schumann. The *Polonaise-Fantaisie*, Op. 61, Chopin's last large work for the piano, and the Cello Sonata, Op. 65, point in directions he would probably have explored had he lived longer than his thirty-nine years.

Chopin's études—twelve in each of Opp. 10 and 25, and three without opus number—are important landmarks in defining the piano idiom. Because études are intended primarily to develop technique, each one as a rule is devoted to a specific technical skill pursued through repetition of a single figure. Among the difficulties exercised in Op. 25 are parallel diatonic and chromatic thirds in the right hand (No. 6), parallel sixths in the right hand (No. 8), and chromatic octaves in both hands (No. 10). In No. 11, a brilliant yet highly evocative étude, the right hand spins out a perpetual filigree of sixteenth notes against a vigorous march theme in the left hand (Example 17.2). Through much of the piece the right hand's passage work alternates between chromatic appoggiaturas or passing notes and chord tones. Chopin's études are not only intensely concentrated technical studies, but also transcendent poetic statements, successfully combining virtuosity with significant artistic content. In this respect, Liszt and Brahms followed Chopin's lead.

Études

EXAMPLE 17.2 Fryderyk Chopin, Étude, Op. 25, No. 11

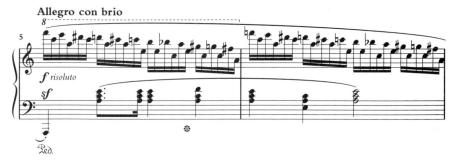

Liszt (1811–1886)

One of the foremost musical personalities of his day, Franz Liszt was born in Hungary, son of an official in the service of Prince Nicholas Esterházy. He studied piano with Carl Czerny in Vienna and at the age of eleven began a dazzling career as a concert virtuoso that lasted, with a few interruptions, until 1848. During most of this time he made his home in Paris. From 1848 to 1861 he was court music director at Weimar, where he encouraged new music by conducting performances of many important works, among them the premiere of Wagner's opera _Lohengrin_ in 1850. Several well-publicized love affairs with women of elevated social status, and honors showered upon him all over Europe, added glamour to his fame as pianist, conductor, and composer. From 1861 until about 1870 Liszt resided chiefly in Rome, where he took minor orders in the Catholic Church. The remainder of his life was divided among Rome, Weimar, and Budapest.

Window

A BALLAD OF LOVE

The novelist George Sand (Aurore Dudevant, 1804–1876) adopted her male pseudonym after she left her husband and moved to Paris, where she eventually met Fryderyk Chopin. She was forward and free-thinking; he was fastidious and frail. She was a devoted mother who smoked cigars and wore men's clothing; he suffered from tuberculosis and required solitude and mothering, though he enjoyed the company of aristocratic friends. Despite their differences in age and experience—she was six years older than he and immensely more worldly—they developed a romantic relationship that coincided with his most productive years as a composer.

A prolific correspondent and diarist, Sand described Chopin's creative process in her memoirs as a combination of effortless improvisation and painstaking revisions:

His musical composition was spontaneous and miraculous. [Ideas] would come to him unexpectedly and without effort. They simply burst forth out of his piano, sublime and complete. . . . But then began the most heartbreaking labor I have ever seen, consisting of a succession of struggles, uncertainties, and impatience to recapture certain details of the theme he had heard. What he had conceived as a whole he analyzed too much in trying to write down, and his dismay at not being able to capture it exactly again threw him into a kind of despair. He would shut himself up in his room for whole days at a time, weeping, pacing back and forth, smashing his pens, repeating or changing one measure a hundred times, . . . He sometimes spent six weeks on one page, only to finish by writing it exactly as he had sketched it at the first draft.*

As Chopin's manuscripts show no sign of such extraordinary efforts, Sand may have exaggerated—indeed, "romanticized"—his creative process under the assumption that genius was always accompanied by only the most titanic labors.

The couple's liaison lasted nine years, during which time they lived partly in Parisian society and partly at Nohant, the quiet country estate that Sand had inherited. Their holiday-escape to Majorca during the winter of 1838–

---

*Histoire de ma vie (Paris, 1854, 7/1928), Vol. 4, p. 470; adapted from the translation by William G. Atwood, *The Lioness and the Little One* (New York: Columbia University Press, 1980), pp. 136–37.

39 turned into a terrible ordeal. Though Chopin managed to complete his Twenty-four Preludes (Op. 28) there, his health was permanently damaged by the bad weather and primitive living conditions. Nevertheless, they spent several more peaceful and productive years together after returning to France. Then, overwhelmed by intrigues involving a rivalry between Sand's two grown children, the lovers' affection for one another gradually dwindled and by 1847 they were separated. Alone and physically ailing, Chopin lost all interest in composing and died two years later at the age of thirty-nine.

A charming film—*Impromptu* (1991), in which Hugh Grant portrays the ethereal composer and Judy Davis his tempestuous seducer—dramatizes the beginning of their love affair and makes very effective use of Chopin's glorious music.

◄Fryderyk Chopin, age thirty-six (probably copied from the Ary Scheffer portrait, 1846). (*Music Division, The New York Public Library at Lincoln Center, Astor, Lenox, and Tilden Foundations*)

►George Sand (Amantine-Aurore-Lucile Dupin, baroness Dudevant), age thirty-three (by Julien, ca. 1837). (*Music Division, The New York Public Library at Lincoln Center, Astor, Lenox, and Tilden Foundations*)

➤ Hector Berlioz and Carl Czerny (standing), with Liszt at the piano and violinist Heinrich Wilhelm Ernst at his right. The creator of this 1846 lithograph, Joseph Kriehuber (1800–1876), observes from the left.

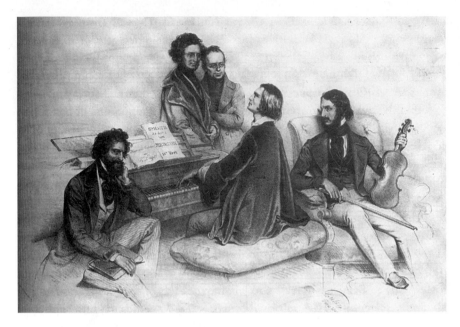

Style

Liszt's cosmopolitan career was matched by his eclectic style, the result of many factors and influences. His Hungarian roots show not only in his compositions based on or inspired by national melodies, but also in his fiery, dynamic, and impulsive temperament. Superimposed on these influences were his early Viennese training and a strong strain of French literary Romanticism, with its ideal of program music as represented by the works of Berlioz; many of Liszt's pieces have explicit programmatic titles, as we have seen in the orchestral works. He built his piano style on that of several impressive Viennese and Parisian virtuosos, adding his own vocabulary of stunning effects to theirs. He adopted as well the lyricism of Chopin's melodic line, his *rubato* rhythmic license, and his harmonic innovations, again amplifying and enhancing them.

Paganini's influence

In Paris Liszt came under the spell of the great Italian violinist Nicolò Paganini (1782–1840), one of the most hypnotic artists of the nineteenth century (see illustration, page 389). Stimulated by Paganini's fabulous technical virtuosity, Liszt resolved to accomplish similar miracles with the piano. He pushed the technique of the instrument to its furthest limits both in his own playing and in his compositions. He directly imitated the master in his six *Études d'exécution transcendante d'après Paganini* (Transcendental Technical Studies based on Paganini, 1851), transcribing four of Paganini's solo violin Caprices, Op. 1, and his *La Campanella* from the Violin Concerto No. 2 in B minor.

Transcriptions

Much of Liszt's piano music consists of arrangements: transcriptions of Schubert's songs, Berlioz's and Beethoven's symphonies, Bach's organ fugues, excerpts from Wagner's music dramas, and fantasies on operatic airs. These pieces were useful in their day for bringing important works to a wide audience unacquainted with the originals. Also, by transferring orchestral idioms to the piano, Liszt demonstrated new possibilities for that instrument. Liszt also wrote piano music that makes free use of national tunes. Chief among these are nineteen *Hungarian Rhapsodies*, based on traditional Hungarian melodies and ornamentation styles.

National elements

Liszt's compositions for piano and orchestra include two concertos, E♭ major and A major, the *Fantasia on Hungarian Folk Melodies* (1853), and *Totentanz* (Dance of Death, 1849), a paraphrase on the plainsong *Dies irae*. The four movements of the Piano Concerto in E♭ are linked together by the same process of thematic transformation that we observed in his orchestral work, *Les Préludes* (see pages 384–85).

Concertos

In Liszt's Sonata in B minor (1853)—one of the outstanding piano compositions of the nineteenth century—four themes are worked out in one unbroken movement that is subdivided into three sections, analogous to the three movements of a Classic sonata. The themes are transformed and combined in a free rhapsodic order, but one that is perfectly suited to the thematic material. In this work Liszt successfully adapted the cyclic strategy of the symphonic poem.

Sonata in B minor

In some of his late works, Liszt experimented with harmonies that surprisingly anticipate late-nineteenth- and twentieth-century developments. He was one of the first composers to make extensive use of augmented triads (see Example 16.6, page 385), which are prominent in the B-minor Sonata and in the late piano piece *Nuages gris* (1881; Gray Clouds, NAWM 113), along with other unconventional harmonies.

Late works

Chamber Music

Of necessity this will be an incomplete survey of nineteenth-century chamber music, concentrating on a few works by two of the most Classic among the Romantic composers: Schubert and Brahms.

Schubert

Schubert wrote his first quartets, modeled after Mozart and Haydn, primarily for the pleasure of his circle of friends. The most popular work from his earlier period is the *Trout* Quintet for piano, violin, viola, cello, and bass (1819), so called because of the Andantino variations, inserted between the scherzo and the finale, on his own song *Die Forelle* (The Trout). The quintet's slow movement is a masterpiece of serene, simple beauty. Schubert's mature period in chamber music begins in 1820 with an Allegro in C minor, D. 703, commonly called the *Quartettsatz*, intended as the first movement of a string quartet that he never completed. Three important works followed—the Quartets in A minor, D. 804 (1824), in D minor, D. 810 (1824–26, nicknamed "Death and the Maiden"), and in G major, D. 887 (1826).

Last three quartets

The A-minor Quartet begins with a long singing melody that calls out for words, while the lower strings provide harmony and rhythmic ostinatos for thirty-one measures. Then, out of the first few notes of the melody, Schubert builds exciting transitional episodes, the second theme section, and most of the development section with a variety of textures, returning from time to time to the opening texture. The two inner movements have quotations of melodies from Schubert's own works—in one case a song, showing how readily Schubert incorporated his lieder melodies into an instrumental context. The finale is a cheerful Allegro in Hungarian style, contrasting sharply with the dark mood of the preceding three movements.

The Quartet in D minor is grimly serious. The main ideas are distributed among the instruments, and its central movement is a set of variations on Schubert's gripping song *Der Tod und das Mädchen* (D. 531, Death and the Maiden). The G-major Quartet, on a larger scale than the other two, offers a remarkable instance of Schubert's alternating major and minor forms of the triad (Example 17.3), reversed and differently colored at the recapitulation.

EXAMPLE 17.3   Franz Schubert, Quartet in G major, D. 887: First Movement

Schubert's masterpiece of chamber music is the String Quintet in C major, D. 956, written during the last year of his life. The added instrument is a second cello, providing a low tessitura that was particularly appealing to the Romantic sensibility. Schubert obtained some of the most exquisite effects from this combination. The ideas and the way they are set forth and developed in the first movement are truly symphonic in conception. The beautiful E♭-major melody of the secondary thematic section is heard in the cello before it reaches the first violin. Its recapitulation in A♭, a third down from the tonic (just as E♭ is a third up), completed a characteristic tonal scheme in the nineteenth century. The quintet has the profound lyricism, the unobtrusive contrapuntal mastery, the long melodic lines (for example, the first fifteen measures of the Adagio), and the wealth of harmonic invention that characterize the late piano sonatas. The finale, like that of the Quartet in A minor, is in a lighter style, relaxing the tension built up by the first three movements.

String Quintet in C major

EXAMPLE 17.4   Franz Schubert, Quintet in C major, D. 956: Allegretto

Not only are the themes playful but so are the modulations; witness the rapid shift from E♭ minor to B major to C major by way of enharmonic and chordal common tones (Example 17.4).

Brahms

The giant among nineteenth-century composers of chamber music, Brahms is the true successor of Beethoven in this medium—as he was in orchestral music. Not only is the quantity of his production impressive—twenty-four works in all—but the quality as well, including at least a half-dozen master-pieces. The variety of combinations is interesting: string quartets, quintets (including one with clarinet), and sextets, piano trios and quartets—for various ensembles involving violin, viola, cello, or Waldhorn (a natural horn, without valves) with piano—and some sonatas for either violin, cello, or clarinet with piano.

Piano Quintet   Opus 34 (1864) in F minor, so stunningly successful as a piano quintet, is the third metamorphosis of this work. Brahms originally composed it as a string quintet with two cellos. He later arranged it effectively for two pianos, and then Clara Schumann, herself a successful composer of chamber music with piano, advised him to combine the string and piano sonorities for the final version. The first movement is a powerful, closely knit Allegro in sonata

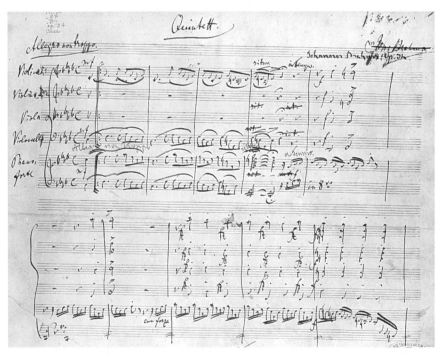

▲ The opening of the Brahms Piano Quintet, Op. 34, in the composer's hand. (*The Gertrude Clarke Whittal Foundation Collection, Music Division, Library of Congress. Reproduced by permission of the Library of Congress*)

form. Brahms's treatment of the opening idea (Example 17.5a) during the exposition aptly illustrates "developing variation," a technique associated with Brahms. In diminution, the theme becomes a piano figure against string chords (b), a lyrical melody in the first violin (c); then, with note values doubled and the figure transformed, it is subjected to close imitation in the two violins (d). The key relationships are remote: the second theme group, in C♯ minor, is recapitulated in F♯ minor; the slow movement, in A♭, has a middle section in E major.

EXAMPLE 17.5   Johannes Brahms, Piano Quintet in F minor, Op. 34: Allegro non troppo

The spirit and even the themes of the quintet's third-movement Scherzo (NAWM 114) recall Beethoven's Fifth Symphony, which is also in C minor. The opening of Beethoven's movement definitively spells out the key; by contrast, Brahms's A♭-major melody over an insistent *C* pedal clouds the tonal feeling. The ambiguity is not cleared up until the broadly arched, soaring theme has unfolded in the first violin and reached the dominant of C minor. Both composers' trios are in C major, but Beethoven invented truly contrasting material and textures, whereas Brahms developed the same ideas as in the Scherzo. The robust rhythms and the fleeting hints of a hurdy-gurdy in its persistent pedal points give the entire Brahms movement an earthy quality that is true to the Beethovenian tradition. The rousing Finale is preceded by a broad *poco sostenuto.*

Later works

Brahms's string quartets date from the 1870s; remembering his reluctance to bring out a symphony, we note with interest that his final String Quartet, Op. 67 in B♭, dates from 1876, the year of his first symphony. Outstanding among Brahms's later works are the two Piano Trios, Op. 87 in C major (1882) and Op. 101 in C minor (1886); the String Quintet in G major, Op. 111 (1890); and the moving Clarinet Quintet in B minor, Op. 115 (1891), one of the glories of the literature for this instrument.

Sonatas

The sonatas with piano form a special category of Brahms's chamber music. There are three for violin, two for cello, and two for clarinet. All except the first Cello Sonata, Op. 38 (1862–65), are late works. The first two Violin Sonatas, in G major, Op. 78 (1878–79), and in A major, Op. 100 (1886), contain some of Brahms's most lyric and melodious writing; the third, in D minor, Op. 108 (1887), is on a more symphonic scale. The two Clarinet Sonatas of Op. 120, written in 1894, are among the most mature achievements of the composer.

Vocal Music: The Lied

Romantic traits were already apparent in the German lied by the end of the eighteenth century, principally through the influence of a new type of song, the *ballad*. Most ballads were fairly long poems, alternating narrative and dialogue in a tale filled with romantic adventures and supernatural incidents. Romantic ballads demanded a musical treatment quite different from the short, idyllic, strophic lied of the eighteenth century. Their greater length necessitated a greater variety of themes and textures, which in turn required some means of unifying the whole. Moreover, the music needed to capture and enhance the contrasting moods and movements of the story. The ballad, then, expanded on the lied both in its form and in the range and force of its emotional content. The role of the piano rose from accompaniment to equal partner with the voice in supporting, illustrating, and intensifying the meaning of the poetry. By the early nineteenth century the lied had become a vehicle that demanded the utmost powers of a composer.

Although many of the nineteenth-century composers we have encountered so far wrote songs, here we will concentrate on two undisputed masters of German lieder—Schubert and Robert Schumann—and introduce a new composer, Clara Wieck Schumann.

Schubert

Schubert's songs reveal his supreme gift for creating beautiful melodies, a talent that few composers have possessed so fully. Many of his melodies have the simple, artless quality of folksong (for example, *Heidenröslein, Der*

▲ Schubert at the piano accompanying a singer in the home of Joseph von Spaun. Sepia drawing by Moritz von Schwind, 1868. (*Vienna, Schubert Museum of the City of Vienna*)

Lindenbaum [NAWM 116], *Wohin?*, *Die Forelle*). Others are suffused with an indescribable Romantic sweetness and melancholy (*Am Meer, Der Wanderer, Du bist die Ruh'*). Still others sound declamatory, intense, and dramatic (*Aufenthalt, Der Atlas, Die junge Nonne, An Schwager Kronos*). Every mood or nuance of feeling finds spontaneous and perfect expression in Schubert's wonderful melodic stream, which flows as purely and as copiously in the songs as it does in the instrumental works.

Along with a genius for melody Schubert possessed an uncanny feeling for harmonic color. His complex modulations, sometimes embodying long passages in which the tonality is kept in suspense, powerfully underline the dramatic qualities of a song text. Striking examples of harmonic boldness may be found in *Gruppe aus dem Tartarus* and *Das Heimweh*, a song that also illustrates the Schubertian device of hovering between the major and minor forms of the triad. Masterly use of chromatic coloring within a prevailing diatonic sound is another Schubert characteristic (*Am Meer, Lob der Thränen*). His modulations characteristically move from the tonic toward flat keys, and the mediant or submediant is a favorite relationship. Other modulations may take off from a chord in the mode opposite to the normal one—for example, the sudden introduction of a chord with a minor third where the major third is expected. These are but a few of the hundreds of procedures and instances that demonstrate the inexhaustible harmonic richness of Schubert's music.

Harmonic style

Many of Schubert's lieder are in strophic form, in which the music is repeated for each stanza either literally (as, for example, in *Litanei*) or with slight variation (*Du bist die Ruh'*). Others, particularly those on longer texts, may alternate between declamatory and arioso style but are always unified by recurring themes and are built on a carefully planned tonal scheme (*Fahrt*

Form

zum Hades, Der Wanderer). The form, however complex, always suits both the poetical and musical requirements of the text.

Accompaniments

Equally rich and ingenious are the piano accompaniments. Very often a piano figuration is suggested by some pictorial image in the text (as in *Wohin?* or *Auf dem Wasser zu singen*). Schubert designed such pictorial features not only to illustrate but also to enhance the mood of the song. So the accompaniment of *Gretchen am Spinnrade* (Gretchen at the Spinning Wheel, NAWM 115)—one of the earliest (1814) and most famous of the lieder—suggests not only the whir of the spinning wheel by a constant sixteenth-note figure in the right hand and the perpetual motion of the treadle by the left hand, but also the agitation of Gretchen's thoughts as she sings of her beloved in Goethe's epic poem *Faust*. Similarly, in *Der Erlkönig* (The Erlking), one of Schubert's relatively few ballads—also on a Goethe text—the pounding octave triplets in the accompaniment depict at once the galloping of the horse and the frantic anxiety of the father as he rides "through night and wind" with his frightened child clasped in his arms. The delirious boy imagines that he sees the legendary Erlking, enticing him to a land where he will be comforted by the swaying, dancing, and singing of the Erlking's daughters. Schubert has characterized in an unforgettable manner the three actors in the drama: the concerned father, the bewitching Erlking, and the increasingly terrified child.

Gretchen am Spinnrade

Der Erlkönig

Der Doppelgänger

An entirely different style of accompaniment appears in *Der Doppelgänger* (The Ghostly Double): long, somber chords, with a recurrent sinister melodic motif in low triple octaves, below a declamatory voice part that rises to a powerful climax before sinking in a despairing phrase. With awesome effectiveness, Schubert depicts the ghostly horror of the scene—in which the poet meets his double staring in the moonlight at the abandoned house where his sweetheart had once lived—using heavy, obsessive, dark chords revolving fatally about the tonic of B minor except for one brief, lurid flash of D♯ minor near the end.

Texts

Schubert drew on the works of many poets for his texts: from Goethe alone he took fifty-nine poems, setting some of them more than once. Some of Schubert's finest lieder are found in his two song-cycles on poems by Wilhelm Müller, *Die schöne Müllerin* (The Beautiful Miller, 1823) and *Winterreise* (1827). The *Schwanengesang* (Swan Song, 1828), not intended as a cycle but published as such posthumously, includes six songs on poems by Heinrich Heine. Schubert sometimes chose texts of lesser literary quality, but his music could glorify even commonplace poetry.

Winterreise

Winterreise (Winter's Journey) consists of twenty-four poems by Müller that express the nostalgia of a lover revisiting in winter the haunts of a failed summer romance. In *Der Lindenbaum* (The Linden Tree, NAWM 116), the poet dwells on the memory of the tree under which he used to lie dreaming of his love. Now, as he passes it, the chilly wind rustles the branches, which seem to be urging him back there once again. The music is in a modified strophic form, each strophe of music setting two stanzas of the poem.

Robert Schumann

Despite his Romantic lyrical qualities and harmonic color, Schubert nearly always maintained a certain Classic serenity and poise. By contrast, Robert Schumann—his first important successor among the many lied composers—rode the full restless tide of Romanticism. His melodic lines are warm and expressive, sounding less spontaneous than Schubert's, and the accompaniments are of unusual interest.

Some of Schumann's finest lieder are his love songs. In 1840, the year of his long-delayed marriage to his beloved Clara Wieck, he produced over one hundred lieder, including two cycles: *Dichterliebe* and *Frauenliebe und -leben* (Women's Love and Life). *Dichterliebe* (A Poet's Love) consists of sixteen songs on poems selected from the more than sixty in Heinrich Heine's *Lyrisches Intermezzo* (1823 and later editions). Neither Heine's collection nor Schumann's cycle has an encompassing narrative, but the theme of unrequited love runs through the poems. In the first song of the cycle, *Im wunderschönen Monat Mai* (In the Marvelous Month of May, NAWM 117a) the poet confesses a springtime love that is possibly not returned. The tonal ambiguity and tension between voice and piano reflects the ironic spirit of Heine's poem as well as the pessimistic outlook of the cycle as a whole. The appoggiaturas and suspensions that begin almost every other measure underline the bittersweet anxiety expressed in the text. The lover's defiant attitude in *Ich grolle nicht* (I Bear No Grudge, NAWM 117b) demands a more declamatory, less tuneful, approach. The strong, octave-reinforced bass line and the emphatic chords in the right hand concentrate the expression in the piano part. The harmonic momentum and coloring depend greatly on secondary dominants and on altering to minor chords that would normally be major in the key and vice versa. The four-measure piano prelude and postlude are characteristic of the songs from this cycle.

Dichterliebe

Clara Schumann (1819–1896)

Clara Wieck Schumann had a remarkable career as a pianist, composer, sponsor of other composers' music, wife of Robert Schumann, mother of eight, and close friend of Brahms. From an early age, she was trained to become a concert pianist by her father, Friedrich Wieck. Recognized as a child prodigy from her first public appearance in Leipzig at the age of nine, she toured throughout Europe and earned the praise of Goethe, Mendelssohn, Chopin, Paganini, and Schumann. Although she curtailed her concertizing after marrying Schumann and while raising a large family, she continued to perform, compose, and teach throughout her long life. Her works include an early piano concerto (1835–36), a piano trio (1846), many pieces for piano, and several collections of lieder. Among the latter, those of Op. 23 (1853) are particularly original. No. 3, *Geheimes Flüstern hier und dort* (Secret Whispers Here and There, NAWM 118), is one of six songs that Clara Schumann

▲ Clara Schumann and Joseph Joachim, who were close friends and gave concerts together. Print after a chalk drawing by Adolph von Menzel (1854). (*Zwickau, Robert-Schumann-Haus*)

composed on poems from the cycle *Jucunde* by Hermann Rollett. The uniform mood of the three stanzas, dominated by an image of the forest whispering to the poet, permits a strictly strophic setting. A continuous sixteenth-note broken-chord motion in $\frac{3}{8}$ sets up a backdrop of rustling leaves and branches for expressing the poet's reliance on the forest as a refuge and a communicator of life's secrets. The closing lines of the poem refer to unfulfilled passion that can only be revealed in song.

POSTLUDE

A chronology has not been included in this chapter; instead, it might be useful at this point to review, decade by decade, some of the events, activities, and compositions that have been presented here and in the previous chapter in order to gain an overview of the period.

The 1820s saw the first performance of Beethoven's Ninth Symphony, Mendelssohn's *Midsummer Night's Dream* Overture, and the composition of Schubert's mature piano sonatas and chamber works, as well as of his song cycles *Die schöne Müllerin* and *Winterreise*. By 1830, the year of the first performance of the *Symphonie fantastique*, Beethoven and Schubert were dead; Berlioz and Chopin were rising stars; Liszt, Paganini, and Clara Wieck (still a child) were stunning concert audiences with their prodigious talents; and Brahms had not yet been born. During the 1830s,

Mendelssohn wrote his *Italian* Symphony and *Hebrides* Overture, and
Schumann composed all of his important piano music. In 1840, the year
of Schumann's *Dichterliebe*, he and Clara Wieck were married.

By 1850, when the Bach Society was founded, Mendelssohn (who had
been an important figure in the revival of Bach's music) and Chopin were
already deceased; Liszt's concert career was over and he had embarked on
the composition of his earliest symphonic poems, a genre that would occupy him during the next decade. The 1850s also saw the appearance of
Liszt's Piano Sonata in B minor, his orchestral *Les Préludes*, and his *Faust*
Symphony; the death of Robert Schumann; and the publication of
Brahms's first chamber pieces and some of Clara Wieck Schumann's piano
music and lieder. In the next decades Clara and Brahms became close
friends and Brahms produced the bulk of his chamber music, perfecting
his technique of "developing variations." In the 1870s and 1880s Brahms
composed his four symphonies and several important concertos. He died
in 1897, having survived Clara Schumann by one year and Liszt by
eleven. Four years earlier, in 1893, Dvořák had made his first trip to the
New World.

A final chronological note: While the nineteenth century may seem to
present a host of contradictory tendencies, personalities, and developments, students may perhaps appreciate the fact that the three musical
giants who towered over the century in many ways—Bach (in spirit),
Beethoven, and Brahms—entered and left the historical stage in absolutely
alphabetical order!

18

Opera, Music Drama, and Church Music in the Nineteenth Century

In the aftermath of the French Revolution and because of the success of Gluck and his followers, Paris became the operatic capital of Europe during the first half of the nineteenth century. Following Napoleon's defeat at Waterloo the Bourbon monarchy was restored in 1815. Many of those who had fled the city returned, and musical life became reestablished; a new theater for French opera was built in 1821. The government continued to subsidize opera and concerts, and the royal family contributed informally to opera and benefit concerts. But with the increasingly large and powerful middle class thronging the opera theaters in search of excitement and entertainment, a new kind of opera came into being, designed to appeal to the relatively uncultured audiences. **French Grand Opera**, as this genre came to be called, was as much spectacle as music, consistent with the fashion that had prevailed in France since the time of Lully, but newly infused with Romantic elements, such as rescue plots and huge choral scenes.

Italian Opera in the nineteenth century grew out of an established tradition, healthily grounded in the life of the nation. Italy succumbed less than northern countries did to the seductions of the Romantic movement, and composers there were less tempted to try new and radical experiments. Romantic elements permeated Italian opera only gradually, and never to the same degree as in Germany and France. Moreover, as opera was the only important Italian musical outlet during this period, the genius of the nation was largely concentrated on this one genre. While that tended to encourage a conservative attitude, composers such as Rossini, Donizetti, Bellini, and especially **Giuseppe Verdi** created a distinctly Italian genre of Romantic opera.

As a composite art form, opera integrated music and literature. This interaction, so typical of nineteenth-century Romanticism, developed most fully in the German-speaking lands. Without the long-established tradition that Italian opera enjoyed, German opera was more open to experimentation. At the root of **German Romantic Opera** was the Singspiel, exemplified at its best by Mozart's *Die Zauberflöte* (The Magic Flute). In the early nineteenth century, the Singspiel soaked up Romantic elements from French opera, while keeping and even intensifying its specific national features. Both trends culminated in **Richard Wagner**, one of the crucial figures in nineteenth-century music, **and the Music Drama**, the new fusion of music, poetry, and theater he forged to rival traditional opera.

As expected, **Church Music** in the nineteenth century was more or less influenced by Romantic tendencies, depending on the aesthetic attitude of the composer and the intended function of the work. Although some symphonic composers wrote relatively modest settings of sacred texts, others outdid Beethoven's monumental *Missa solemnis* in setting liturgical texts on such a colossal scale that these works can only be appropriately performed in a concert hall.

French Grand (and Not-So-Grand) Opera

The leaders of French *grand opera* were the librettist Eugène Scribe (1791–1861) and the composer Giacomo Meyerbeer (1791–1864). Two of their operas established the genre: *Robert le Diable* (Robert the Devil, 1831) and *Les Huguenots* (The Huguenots [a group of French Protestants], 1836). Meyerbeer's penchant for integrating crowd scenes, public ceremonies, and confrontations on stage is most evident in Act II of *Les Huguenots*. Although his musical ideas are sometimes commonplace, he often managed the solo, choral, and orchestral forces with broad strokes of extraordinary dramatic effectiveness. Such grand-opera proceedings were admired and emulated by Verdi and others.

Meyerbeer

Among the most productive composers of grand opera around 1830 were François Auber (*La Muette de Portici*, The Mute Girl of Portici, also known as *Masaniello*, 1828), Gioachino Rossini (*Guillaume Tell*, 1829), and Jacques Fromental Halévy (1799–1862), whose masterpiece was *La Juive* (The Jewess, 1835). These works incorporate in the music a grandeur of structure and style that conveys more than just the plot. The French ideal of grand opera stayed

Other grand operas

Les Huguenots, Closing Scenes of Act II

*A*gainst the historical backdrop of the religious wars in France during the sixteenth century, Queen Marguerite de Valois tries to reconcile the Protestants and Catholics through a peace-making marriage between the Catholic maiden Valentine and the Protestant Raoul. A timpani solo introduces the oath of peace, sung in unison, unaccompanied and *pianissimo*, by the leaders of the two factions. The chorus, *fortissimo* with orchestra, interjects, "Nous jurons" (we swear) three times. In an extended a cappella ensemble in four parts the leaders hail the benefits of harmony among peoples. Only the militant Protestant Marcel defies the others as he vows to make war on Rome and her soldiers. As the orchestra rejoins the singers on a diminished-seventh chord, Marguerite's voice floats above all the others, crowning the scene with coloratura. Later, when Raoul rejects Valentine as a prospective wife, and the truce between the opposing factions breaks down, Marcel in the midst of the fury triumphantly bellows a phrase of the Lutheran chorale *Ein' feste Burg ist unser Gott* (A mighty fortress is our God).

alive to some extent throughout the nineteenth century, influencing the work of Bellini, Verdi, and Wagner. The grand-opera tradition also survives in such twentieth-century works as Darius Milhaud's *Christophe Colomb*, Samuel Barber's *Antony and Cleopatra*, and John Corigliano's *The Ghosts of Versailles*.

Opéra comique

Side by side with grand opera, the opéra comique pursued its course in France during the Romantic period. As in the eighteenth century, the technical difference between the two was that opéra comique used spoken dialogue instead of recitative. Apart from this, the differences were primarily those of size and subject matter. The opéra comique was less grand than grand opera, required fewer singers and players, and was written in a much simpler musical idiom. Its plots, as a rule, presented straightforward comedy or semiserious drama instead of the historical pageantry of grand opera. Examples of opéra comique include works by François Auber, who in *Fra Diavolo* (Brother Devil, 1830) and other comic operas mingled humorous and Romantic elements in tuneful music of considerable originality.

Opéra bouffe

Another strain of French light opera appeared around midcentury, during the reign of Napoleon's nephew Louis, who proclaimed himself Emperor Napoleon III in 1851. While censorship controlled the serious theaters, the *opéra bouffe* could freely satirize the society of the Second Empire. This new genre (not to be confused with the eighteenth-century Italian opera buffa) emphasized the smart, witty, and satirical elements of comic opera. Its founder was Jacques Offenbach (1819–1880), who managed to introduce a can-can for the gods in his opéra bouffe, *Orphée aux enfers* (Orpheus in the Underworld, 1858). Offenbach's work influenced developments in comic opera elsewhere, including the operettas of W. S. Gilbert (librettos) and Arthur Sullivan (music) in England (*The Mikado*, 1885), and of Johann Strauss the Younger (1825–1899; *Die Fledermaus* [The Bat], 1874) and many others in Vienna.

Still another type of French opera during this period might best be termed *lyric opera*, which lies somewhere between light opéra comique and grand opera. Like the opéra comique, its main appeal is through melody; its subject matter is romantic drama or fantasy, and its general scale is larger than that of the opéra comique, although still not so huge as that of the typical grand opera. By far the most famous example of this genre remains Gounod's *Faust*, which was first staged in 1859 as an opéra comique (that is, with spoken dialogue) and later arranged by the composer in its now familiar form with recitatives. Gounod wisely restricted himself to Part I of Goethe's drama, which deals chiefly with Faust and Gretchen's tragic love affair. The result is a work of just proportions in an elegant lyric style, with attractive melodies that are moderately expressive.

A landmark in the history of French opera was the *Carmen* of Georges Bizet (1838–1875), first performed at Paris in 1875. Like the original version of *Faust*, *Carmen* was classified as an opéra comique simply for technical reasons—it contained spoken dialogue (later set in recitative by another composer)—and without regard for the stark realism of its drama. Bizet's rejection of a sentimental or mythological plot signaled a narrow but important anti-Romantic move toward realism in late-nineteenth-century opera. In its Spanish setting and Spanish rhythms and tunes, however, *Carmen* typifies exoticism, a vein running through the whole Romantic period and evident in some other French operas and ballets of the period. The music of *Carmen* has an extraordinary rhythmic and melodic vitality. It is spare in texture and beautifully orchestrated, obtaining stunning dramatic effects with the most economical means.

The dramatic works of Hector Berlioz do not belong to any of the categories discussed above, which is one reason that his contribution to French Romantic opera has only recently been recognized. His most important dramatic work, *La Damnation de Faust* (1846), was not even intended for stage performance. Like the *Symphonie fantastique* and *Roméo et Juliette* (see Chapter 16), it is a symphonic drama whose connecting plot is considered familiar to all, thereby permitting the composer to choose only those scenes most suitable for musical treatment and assuring the maximum variety with the greatest possible compactness. Unlike the two earlier works, however, *La Damnation de Faust* has no lingering resemblance to the formal structure of the Classic symphony. Its unity is a function of Berlioz's own musical style, depending hardly at all on recurring themes or motives.

The crown of Berlioz's dramatic works is his five-act opera *Les Troyens*,

Lyric opera

Gounod's Faust

Bizet's Carmen

Berlioz

La Damnation de Faust

Les Troyens

composed in 1856–58. Its first part, *La Prise de Troie* (The Capture of Troy), was not staged until 1890; the second part, *Les Troyens à Carthage* (The Trojans at Carthage), had a few performances in Paris in 1863. The text, by Berlioz himself, is based on the second and fourth books of Vergil's *Aeneid*, with only the essential action presented in a series of mighty scene-complexes. Berlioz condensed the narrative and used various appropriate occasions to introduce ballets, processions, and other musical numbers. Although its outward form and its use of a historical (or legendary) subject give *Les Troyens* the appearance of a grand opera of the 1830s, nothing could be further from the glitter of a work like Meyerbeer's *Huguenots*. The drama preserves the antique, epic quality of Vergil's poem, and the music speaks in the same accents. Not a note is there for mere effect; the style is severe, almost ascetic by comparison with Berlioz's earlier works. At the same time every passion, every scene and incident, is brought to life intensely and on a heroic scale. *Les Troyens* represents the Romantic consummation of the French opera tradition descended from Lully, Rameau, and Gluck.

Italian Opera

Rossini

The principal Italian composer of the early nineteenth century, Gioachino Rossini (1792–1868) had a pronounced gift for melody and a flair for stage effect, which brought him quick success. Between the ages of eighteen and thirty he produced thirty-two operas and other assorted works for voices and/ or instruments. Among his best serious operas were *Tancredi* (Venice, 1813), *Otello* (Naples, 1816), and *La donna del lago* (Naples, 1819; adapted from Sir Walter Scott's novel, *Lady of the Lake*).

Rossini excelled at writing comic opera, and many of them sound as fresh today as they did when he first wrote them—especially *La scala di seta* (The Silken Ladder; Venice, 1812), *L'Italiana in Algeri* (The Italian Woman in Algiers; Venice, 1813), *La Cenerentola* (Cinderella; Rome, 1817), and *La gazza ladra* (The Thieving Magpie; Milan, 1817). His masterpiece, *Il barbiere di Siviglia* (The Barber of Seville; Rome, 1816), ranks with Mozart's *Figaro* and Verdi's *Falstaff* among the supreme examples of Italian comic opera.

Rossini's style

Rossini's style combines an inexhaustible flow of melody with animated rhythms, clear phraseology, and well-shaped though sometimes unconventional structure of the musical period. His spare texture and orchestration respect the quality of the individual instruments, and his harmonic schemes are not complex but often original. He shares with other early-nineteenth-century composers a fondness for bringing the mediant keys into close juxtaposition with the tonic. A combination of beautiful melody, wit, and comic description appears in the justly famous *Una voce poco fa* (A voice a short while ago, NAWM 120) from *Il barbiere di Siviglia*. This multi-sectional aria illustrates how Rossini achieved the illusion of action by changing tempo and style. He usually juxtaposed two separate lyrical sections–an opening *canta-bile*, often called a *cavatina*, and a faster, more brilliant conclusion, called a *cabaletta*. Although Rossini was no revolutionary, he did encourage certain reforms, such as replacing the piano or harpsichord in *recitativo secco* with an orchestral accompaniment, and attempting to curb his singers' excessive embellishments by writing out the coloratura passages and cadenzas.

Quickly paced ensemble scenes constitute the dramatic core of comic opera, and Rossini managed these with sparkle and gusto. In these scenes and elsewhere he frequently used a simple but effective device, the crescendo: building up excitement by repeating a phrase, often having it sung louder and higher each time. The crescendo, a prominent feature of many of Rossini's popular overtures as well, virtually became his trademark.

In 1824 Rossini settled in Paris, where he became the darling of an elite circle of intellectuals (see illustration, page 389). There he brought out new versions of two earlier works, adapting them to French taste by giving more importance to the chorus and the orchestra. He also wrote the grand opera *Guillaume Tell* (1829) before retiring and resting on his operatic laurels for the remaining forty years of his life, during which time he wrote only sacred music, songs, and albums of piano pieces.

One of the most prolific Italian composers of the second quarter of the century was Gaetano Donizetti (1797–1848), who turned out some seventy operas, as well as hundreds of works in other genres. His most enduring operas were *Lucrezia Borgia* (1833) and *Lucia di Lammermoor* (1835); the

Donizetti

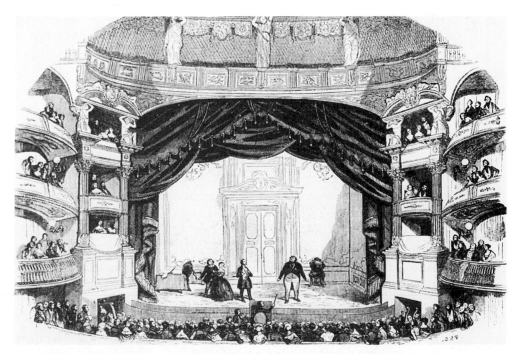

▲ A scene from the second act of Gaetano Donizetti's *Don Pasquale* as performed at the Théâtre italien in Paris in 1843. Engraving from the Leipzig *Illustrirte Zeitung.*

opéra comique, *La Fille du regiment* (The Daughter of the Regiment; Paris, 1840); and the *buffo* operas *L'elisir d'amore* (The Elixir of Love; 1832) and *Don Pasquale* (1843). Donizetti had some of Rossini's instinct for the theater and his talent for melody, and in *Don Pasquale* he created a work that is in a class with *Il barbiere*. On the whole, though, his music—composed very rapidly and with a view to immediate success—is often formulaic in harmony, rhythm, and orchestration. Yet, Donizetti was the immediate historical forerunner of Verdi; both were attuned to the taste and judgment of the Italian public, and their work is deeply rooted in the life of the people.

Bellini

If Donizetti was the commoner, Vincenzo Bellini (1801–1835) may be called the aristocrat of his period. Of his ten operas, all serious, the most important are *La Sonnambula* (The Sleepwalker, 1831), *Norma* (1831), and *I Puritani* (The Puritans, 1835). His style represents the utmost in refinement; the harmony is sensitive, and the intensely expressive melodies have a breadth, a flexibility of form, and a tinge of sadness that we associate with the nocturnes of Chopin. *Casta diva*, the cavatina from *Norma* (NAWM 121), exemplifies these qualities.

Giuseppe Verdi (1813–1901)

The career of Giuseppe Verdi by itself practically constitutes the history of Italian music for the fifty years following Donizetti. Except for the Requiem and a few other pieces, all of Verdi's published works were written for the stage. The year 1839 saw the first production of his twenty-six operas, 1893 the last. At no point did Verdi break with the past or experiment radically with new theories. He worked steadily to refine his goals and techniques, and in the end he carried Italian opera to its greatest heights.

Such a straight path, so different from the course of musical affairs farther north, was possible because of Italy's long, unbroken operatic tradition. Italians loved opera. The only Romantic issue that much affected their music was nationalism, and here Verdi was uncompromising: he believed wholeheartedly that each nation should cultivate its own, native music. He maintained a resolute independence in his personal musical style and deplored the influence of foreign (especially German) ideas in the work of his younger compatriots. Many of his early operas contain choruses that were politically inflammatory, thinly disguised appeals to his compatriots struggling for national unity and against foreign domination during the stirring years of the *Risorgimento* (national rebirth). Verdi's name became a patriotic symbol and a rallying cry: "Viva Verdi" to Italian patriots stood for "**Viva V**ittorio **E**manuele **R**e **d'I**talia!"—"Long live Victor Emanuel, king of Italy!"

Verdi's treatment of opera as human drama (in contrast to the Germans' emphasis on romanticized nature and mythological symbolism) revealed a

XI. J. M. W. Turner (1775–1851) painted *Music Party, East Cowes Castle* about 1835. Known mainly for his misty seascapes, here the artist depicts the congenial atmosphere of a country house on the Isle of Wight. The women enjoy a quiet moment of music making, to which the red color and the flash of light in the center lend warmth, while the black dress of the pianist hints at a serious performance.   (*CLORE COLLECTION, TATE GALLERY, LONDON / ART RESOURCE, NY*)

XII. Claude Monet (1840–1926) entered *Impression: Soleil levant* (Sunrise) along with eight other works in an exhibition he helped to organize for the Société Anonyme des Artistes Peintres, Sculpteurs, Graveurs, Etc. (Association of artist-painters, sculptors, engravers, etc.) in 1874. A critic headlined his mocking review "Exhibition of the Impressionists," and thus the term was launched. Instead of mixing his colors on a palette, Monet juxtaposed them on the canvas to capture a fleeting moment of the early light of day. Apart from the rowboats in the foreground, the tall ships, smokestacks, and cranes blend into the misty blue-gray background against a reddish sky. (*PARIS, MUSÉE MARMOTTAN / ART RESOURCE, NY*)

deeply ingrained national trait. He conveyed this human drama directly and primarily by means of the singing voice (in contrast to the orchestral and choral luxuriance of French grand opera). His independence was not, of course, absolute. Apart from the influence of Beethoven, whom he revered above all composers, and the obvious indebtedness to his predecessors Donizetti, Bellini, and Rossini, Verdi learned much from the harmony and orchestration of Meyerbeer. But before adopting any stylistic influence, Verdi first fully assimilated it and made it part of his own language.

Verdi's creative life falls roughly into three periods, the first culminating in 1853 with *Il trovatore* (The Troubadour) and *La traviata* (The Fallen Woman). Around this time many of his operas told intimate stories of personal tragedy, such as *Luisa Miller* (1849), and were influenced by French culture. *Rigoletto* (1851) and *Traviata* (1853) were adapted by Verdi's librettist, Francesco Piave, from plays by Victor Hugo (*Le Roi s'amuse*, The King Enjoys Himself) and Alexandre Dumas the Younger (*La Dame aux camélias*, The Lady of the Camelias), respectively. (See illustration, page 389, in which Dumas and George Sand appear with Liszt and others in their Parisian circle.)

Early operas

Certain structural features appeared in Verdi's early operas and were retained throughout his career, even in his later works. Typically, each opera has four main divisions: either four acts, or three acts with a prologue. The second and third divisions have important ensemble finales, while a big duet usually figures in the third division. The fourth often opens with a *preghiera* (prayer scene) or similar meditation for a soloist (preferably the heroine), often accompanied by the chorus. Choruses are more notable in the early operas.

Dramatic structure

Many of the features found in the early period are summed up in *Il trovatore*, one of Verdi's most popular works. The diverse resources that he now commanded are plainly in evidence in the first scene of Part IV (see NAWM 122). These include solo utterances, both declamatory and lyrical, sometimes broken by sobs; colorful orchestration, which paints the gloomy scene, depicts a funeral march, and imitates the sounds of a death knell and of the troubadour's lute (the latter accomplished with harps); and an off-stage, a cappella chorus chanting a Latin prayer. One is reminded of Meyerbeer's handling of similar forces. The progression from near-speech to high levels of lyricism displays the versatility of Verdi's talent and his dramatic instinct in avoiding the separate "numbers" or set pieces, formal transitions, and ritornellos that were still used by Bellini and Rossini.

Il trovatore

Ventures into grand opera—*Les Vêpres siciliennes* (The Sicilian Vespers, 1855) and *Don Carlos* (1867), both premiered in Paris—characterize Verdi's second period, ending with *Aida* (1871). Operas appeared less frequently now, as Verdi was indulging in a certain amount of cautious experimentation. Solo, ensemble, and chorus are more freely combined in the dramatic scheme, harmonies become more daring, and the orchestra is treated with greater care and originality. Comic roles are introduced in *Un ballo in maschera* (A

Second-period operas

Masked Ball, 1859) and *La forza del destino* (The Power of Destiny, 1862; revised 1869). At crucial points in both these operas, Verdi brought back distinctive themes or motives introduced earlier in the score. Such "reminiscence motives," already common among other composers and used previously in *Rigoletto*, help unify the work both dramatically and musically. All the advances of the second period are gathered up in *Aida*, which unites the heroic quality of grand opera with solid dramatic structure, vivid character delineation, pathos, and a wealth of melodic, harmonic, and orchestral color.

Reminiscence motives

Late works

Verdi's late works number only two—*Otello* (1887) and *Falstaff* (1893)—but they are in a class by themselves. Sixteen years had elapsed since the premiere of *Aida* in Cairo, Egypt, the year after the opening of the Suez Canal. A number of important works had appeared during this interval, among them Verdi's own Requiem, Bizet's *Carmen*, all four of Brahms's symphonies, Wagner's *Ring* cycle and *Parsifal*. Wagner's music was performed in Italy, and Meyerbeer's operas were frequently heard there as well. The publisher Giulio Ricordi, eager to see Verdi give Italian opera a boost, proposed *Otello* in a projected new libretto by Boito, who had scored a success in Bologna with his own opera *Mefistofele*. The final libretto, based on Shakespeare's tragedy and incomparably the best that Verdi ever set, presents a powerful human drama that the music penetrates, sustains, and intensifies at every turn.

Otello

Verdi began *Otello* in 1884, four years after he received the first draft of Boito's libretto; it was produced at Milan in 1887. This new work, so long in

◄ Otello approaching Desdemona's bed in Verdi's *Otello*, Act IV. Special *Otello* issue of *L'illustrazione italiana*, February 1887. (*Milan, Ricordi, Archivio Storico*)

The act opens with a brief prelude, scored only for winds. The absence of strings lends an eerie quality that keeps us suspended in operatic time, between past and future. When the curtain rises, Desdemona and her confidante, Emilia, talk about Otello's strange behavior; Desdemona apprehensively gets ready for bed. Passages marked "recitativo," with sparse chords in the orchestra, alternate with melodious outpourings that pick up motives previewed in the prelude. Desdemona sings a sad song she learned from her mother's maid about a woman, abandoned by her lover, who asks that her funeral garland be cut from a willow tree. The melody of the first line of this "Willow Song," *Piangea cantando* (She wept singing), was already heard in the prelude. Between the strophes, she issues instructions to Emilia and even interrupts her song with comments. After Desdemona bids Emilia good night, an instrumental epilogue dwells on a motive from the prelude played against an ominous chromatic descending tremolo marked *ppppp*. In the second scene (a *preghiera*), which flows imperceptibly out of the first, Desdemona says her nightly *Ave Maria* (Hail Mary) kneeling before an image of the Virgin. She sings at first on a reciting tone, then breaks into a lyrical aria. The third scene again follows without pause: Desdemona sleeps as an instrumental prelude accompanies Otello's stealthy entrance. The prelude announces motives that will be developed by the orchestra during the couple's strained dialogue and during the actions, carefully marked in the score, that lead to her slaying. The most prominent of these motives is a staccato turn-figure in the violas punctuated by a muffled bass drum (Example 18.1a) and a reminiscence of the love duet of Act I (Example 18.1b). The reminiscence motive, originally sung to the words "un bacio" (a kiss), here accompanies the enactment of Otello's final couplet in Shakespeare's play:

> I kissed thee ere I killed thee. No way but this,
> Killing myself, to die upon a kiss.

EXAMPLE 18.1 Giuseppe Verdi, *Otello*, Act IV, Scene 3: Motives

gestation, was clearly Verdi's response to the changed musical situation, for, despite his deliberate isolation, he was sensitive to new currents. On the surface it differs from the earlier operas chiefly in the continuous development of unifying motives in the orchestra and in the unbroken flow of the music within each act; it is not cut up into separate pieces. Closer inspection reveals that the traditional scheme of declamatory and lyrical solos, duets, ensembles, and choruses is still present. But these units are arranged in larger scene-complexes in which the lyrical high points are imbedded in long stretches of recitative-like blank verse, set in a *parlante* or declamatory style and interspersed with more melodious passages that serve as transitions to the next musical pinnacle. Each act, therefore, has a musical continuity that reinforces the inexorable sweep of its dramatic content; only when the curtain comes down at the end of the act may we exhale and applaud. Act IV, set in Desdemona's bedroom and ending in her murder by Otello, is a wonderful example of this musical continuity.

Falstaff

If *Otello* was the consummation of Italian tragic opera, *Falstaff* (1893) holds a parallel place in comic opera. As *Otello* transformed dramatic lyrical melody, so *Falstaff* transformed that characteristic element of opera buffa, the ensemble. Carried along over a nimble, fine-spun, endlessly varied orchestral background, the comedy speeds to its climaxes in the great finales of the second and third acts. At times Verdi seems to be satirizing the entire Romantic century, himself included. The last scene culminates in a fugue on the words "Tutto nel mondo è burla. / L'uom è nato burlone"—"All the world's a joke. We are all born fools."

German Romantic Opera

German Romantic opera was initiated by *Der Freischütz* (The Marksman) by Carl Maria von Weber (1786–1826), first performed at Berlin in 1821. This opera typifies the genre, which usually involves humble folk caught up in supernatural incidents against a background of wilderness and mystery. The plots are often similar to fairy tales. Musical styles and forms resemble those of other countries, although the use of simple folklike melodies introduces a distinctly German national element. German opera also displays increasingly chromatic harmony, the use of orchestral color for dramatic expression, and an emphasis on the inner voices of the texture (in contrast to the Italian stress on melody).

Der Freischütz

In *Der Freischütz*, rustic choruses, marches, dances, and airs mingle in the score with full-bodied arias in the Italian style. The finale of Act II, the "Wolf's Glen" scene (see full discussion in NAWM 123) illustrates how Weber ingeniously exploited the orchestra to depict the scene's eerie natural setting. It also incorporates elements of the *melodrama*, a genre of musical theater that combined spoken dialogue with background music. *Der Freischütz*'s immense

▲ Setting by Carl Wilhelm Holdermann for the Wolf's Glen scene in Weber's *Der Freischütz* (Weimar production of 1822). As Caspar casts the bullets, Max looks around with growing alarm, while "night birds crowd around the fire" and the "cracking of whips and the sound of galloping horses is heard." (*Weimar, Staatliche Kunstsammlungen, Schlossmuseum*)

popular success, based both on its appeal to national sentiment and on the beauty of its music, was not matched either by Weber's later works or by those of his immediate followers, including Heinrich Marschner (1795–1861) and Albert Lortzing (1801–1851).

Richard Wagner (1813–1883) and the Music Drama

For Richard Wagner, the outstanding composer of German opera, the function of music was to serve the ends of dramatic expression, and all his important compositions are for theater. His first triumph came with *Rienzi*, a five-act grand opera performed at Dresden in 1842. The following year Dresden saw a production of *Der fliegende Holländer* (The Flying Dutchman), a Romantic opera in the tradition of Weber and Marschner. The success of these two works led to Wagner's appointment as director of the Dresden Opera.

Der fliegende Holländer

The lines of development that Wagner followed in his later works were established in *Der fliegende Holländer*. The libretto—written, like those of all his operas, by the composer himself—is based on a legend. The action takes place against a stormy sea, and the hero is redeemed through the unselfish love of the heroine, Senta. Wagner's music is most vivid in its depiction of the storm and of the contrasting ideas of curse and salvation, which are clearly set forth in Senta's ballad, the central number of the opera. The themes of the ballad appear in the overture and recur elsewhere throughout the opera.

Lohengrin

After *Der fliegende Holländer* came *Tannhäuser* (Dresden, 1845) and *Lohengrin*, first performed under Liszt's direction at Weimar in 1850. *Lohengrin* is the last important German Romantic opera; it also embodies several changes prophetic of subsequent music dramas. The story comes from medieval legend and folklore, but Wagner's treatment is generalized and symbolic. Lohengrin may represent divine love descending in human form, and Elsa the weakness of humanity unable to receive with faith the offered blessing. Such a symbolic interpretation is suggested by the Prelude, which depicts the descent of the Holy Grail and its return to Heaven.

The orchestration of *Lohengrin* is at once fuller and more subdued than his earlier works; the music flows more continuously, with fewer traces of separate numbers. The well-written choruses are combined with solo singing and orchestral background into long, unified musical scenes. Wagner's new style of declamatory, arioso melody appears more often. The technique of recurring themes is further developed and refined, particularly with respect to the motifs associated with Lohengrin and the Grail and the motif of the forbidden question, heard first in Act I, Scene 3, at Lohengrin's words "Nie sollst du mich befragen" (You must never ask me [my name and origins]; Example 18.2). Like Weber, Wagner used tonality to help organize both the drama and the music: Lohengrin's key is A major, Elsa's A♭ or E♭, and that of the evil personages F♯ minor. The style on the whole is diatonic, with modulations usually toward the mediant keys.

EXAMPLE 18.2   Richard Wagner, *Lohengrin*: Act I, Scene 3

Essays and librettos

Political unrest in Germany during 1848–49 persuaded Wagner to emigrate to Switzerland, which became his home for the next ten years. Here he found the leisure to formulate his theories about opera and to publish them in a series of essays, the most important of which is *Oper und Drama* (Opera and Drama, 1851, revised 1868). At the same time, he was writing the poems of a cycle of four dramas with the collective title *Der Ring des Nibelungen*

Wagner Sums Up His Early Career in a Letter to a Friend:

❝ Despite a serious scholarly education, I kept in close touch with the theater in my younger years. These coincided with the last years of Carl Maria von Weber, who periodically performed his operas in the same city of Dresden. I owed my first musical experiences to this master, whose airs filled me with enthusiastic admiration and whose personality greatly fascinated me. His death in a distant land [London, June 5, 1826] filled my child's heart with dread. I became aware of Beethoven just as I learned of his death [March 26, 1827], not long after Weber's. I then came to know his music also, drawn to it first by the puzzling reports concerning his death. Stirred by these deep impressions, a pronounced inclination for music kept growing in me. But it was only after broader studies introduced me to classical antiquity and awoke my urge to write poetry that I began to study music systematically. . . .

Rossini once asked his teacher whether an opera composer needed to learn counterpoint. The teacher, thinking of modern Italian opera, replied that he did not, and the pupil gladly desisted. After my teacher [Christian Theodor Weinlig, cantor of the Thomaskirche in Leipzig] had taught me the most difficult contrapuntal methods, he said to me, "You may never have to write a fugue, but being able to write one will give you technical self-reliance and will make everything else seem easy." Thus trained, I embarked on a career as a music-director in a theater [at Würzburg in 1833] and began to set to music opera librettos I had written [e.g., *Die Feen*]. ❞

Richard Wagner, *Zukunftsmusik* (Music of the Future), a letter to a friend, François Villot, as a preface to a prose translation into French of four of Wagner's librettos, Paris, September 15, 1860. Trans. from Wagner, *Gesammelte Schriften*, ed. Julius Rapp (Leipzig: Hesse & Becker, 1914), 1:183. For a translation of the entire essay, see *Richard Wagner's Prose Works*, trans. William Ashton Ellis (London: William Reeves, 1907), 3:295–345.

(The Ring of the Nibelungs). The music of the first two—*Das Rheingold* (The Rhine Gold) and *Die Walküre* (The Valkyrie)—and part of the third, *Siegfried*, was finished by 1857; the entire cycle was completed with *Götterdämmerung* (The Twilight of the Gods) in 1874, and the first complete performance took place two years later in a theater built in Bayreuth according to Wagner's specifications.

During a break from composing *Siegfried*, Wagner wrote *Tristan und Isolde* (1857–59), and during another, *Die Meistersinger von Nürnberg* (The Mastersingers of Nuremberg, 1862–67). His last work was *Parsifal* (1882).

Wagner believed in the absolute oneness of drama and music—that the

> **Der Ring des Nibelungen**

The Ring of the Nibelungs: A Brief Overview

*T*he four dramas, woven out of stories from Norse legends, are linked by a common set of characters and musical motives. The "Ring" of the title refers to a ring that the gnome Alberich fashioned out of gold he stole from the Rhine, where it was guarded by the Rhine maidens. Wotan, the ruler of the gods, with the help of the trickster Loge, manages to retrieve the ring from Alberich and captures, in addition, a hoard of gold, which he uses to pay for the construction of his new castle. But Alberich has put a curse on the ring that will make its wearer subject to misery and murder. In the course of the four dramas the curse is fulfilled and the Rhine maidens get back the ring.

Gesamtkunstwerk

two are organically connected expressions of a single dramatic idea (unlike conventional opera, in which song predominates and the libretto serves mainly as a framework for the music). Poetry, scenic design, staging, action, and music all work together to form what he called a *Gesamtkunstwerk* (total or composite artwork). He considered the action of the drama to have an inner and an outer aspect. The orchestra conveys the inner aspect, while the sung words articulate the outer aspect—the events and situations that further the action. The orchestral web is, then, the chief factor in the music, and the vocal lines—not arias with accompaniment—are only part of the complete musical texture.

In Wagner's music dramas, the music is seamless throughout each act, not formally divided into recitatives, arias, and other set pieces, thus accelerating a growing tendency toward continuity in nineteenth-century opera. Yet, broad scene divisions remain, and we can distinguish between recitative-like passages with orchestral punctuation and others of arioso melody with continuous orchestral scoring. Moreover, the drama is occasionally interrupted—or adorned—with scenes that are decidedly operatic and not strictly necessary to the plot.

The Leitmotif

Wagner achieved coherence within the continuity of the action and music by means of the *Leitmotif,* a musical theme or motive associated with a particular person, thing, emotion, or idea in the drama. The association is established by sounding the leitmotif (usually in the orchestra) at the first appearance on stage or mention of the subject, and by its repetition at subsequent appearances or citations. Often the significance of a leitmotif can be recognized from the words to which it is first sung. But the leitmotif is more than a musical label, for it accumulates significance as it recurs in new contexts; it may recall an object in situations where the object itself is not present; it may be varied, developed, or transformed as the plot develops; similar motifs may suggest a connection between the objects to which they refer; motifs may be contrapuntally combined; and, finally, by their repetition, motifs may help unify a scene or an opera as recurrent themes unify a symphony.

Wagner's idea of music drama and his use of leitmotifs is illustrated in *Tristan und Isolde*, for example. The story comes from a medieval romance by Gottfried von Strassburg, a less typical source for Wagner than the Norse mythology used in the *Ring*, but more in the mainstream of Romantic art. Example 18.3 shows the leitmotifs of *Tristan* in the order of their appearance in the last section of Act I, Scene 5, from the entrance of the sailors (NAWM 124). The text sung at the leitmotif's most characteristic appearance is given along with the motif.

EXAMPLE 18.3   Richard Wagner, *Tristan und Isolde*: Leitmotifs

▲ The Bayreuth Festival Theater, designed by Otto Brückwald, incorporated Wagner's ideals for the production of music drama. There he was able to produce the *Ring* in its entirety for the first time in August 1876. *Parsifal* (1882) was written for this theater, which continues to be the stage for the Bayreuth Festival today.

Wagner's use of the leitmotif differs from the use of reminiscence motives by composers such as Weber, Verdi, and others. Wagner's motifs themselves are for the most part short, concentrated, and intended to characterize their object at various levels of meaning. The first motif of Example 18.3d, for example, is identified with the longing that Tristan and Isolde feel for each other, now intensified by the love potion. At the same time the harmonic progression from the dominant seventh of A minor to the chord on the sixth degree—the deceptive-cadence pattern first heard in the prelude—symbolizes the very essence of the drama, a love doomed to remain unfulfilled. Another and more important difference, of course, is that Wagner's leitmotifs are the basic musical substance of the score. He uses them not once in a while but constantly, in close alliance with every step of the action.

Endless melody   Wagner's leitmotifs also serve as material for forming his "endless melodies," which are not the foursquare phrases set off by caesuras and cadences of earlier composers. The leitmotifs, their development, their restatements and variants, and the connective tissue linking them form the stuff of "musical prose" with which Wagner wanted to replace the "poetic" rhythms of symmetrical phrases. The impression we have of "endless melody" results from the ongoing continuity of line, unbroken by the stops and restarts of Classic musical syntax. Act I, Scene 5 of *Tristan,* in which Tristan and Isolde fall in love under adverse circumstances, demonstrates the effective intertwining of action, scenery, and musical forces. (See NAWM 124 for a detailed discussion of the scene, illustrating how the motives and harmonic progressions acquire meaning and symbolize the dramatic situation.)

Few works in the history of Western music have so deeply impacted succeeding generations of composers as *Tristan und Isolde.* Especially in its harmony we see the culmination of a personal style that was influenced in the 1850s by the chromatic idiom of Liszt's symphonic poems. The complex chromatic alterations of chords in *Tristan,* together with the constant shifting of key, the telescoping of resolutions, and the blurring of progressions by means of suspensions and other nonharmonic tones, produces a novel, ambiguous kind of tonality that can be explained only partially in terms of the harmonic system of the previous two centuries. This departure from the Classic conception of tonality in such a conspicuous and musically successful work can today be viewed historically as the first step toward the breakdown of tonality and the establishment of new systems of harmony that marked the development of music after 1890 (see Chapter 21).

Wagner's influence

If Wagner's work affected all subsequent opera, his peculiar use of mythology and symbolism could not be successfully imitated. But his ideal of opera as a drama of significant content, with words, stage setting, visible action, and music all working closely together to further the central dramatic purpose—the idea of the *Gesamtkunstwerk*—profoundly influenced later composers. Almost equally influential was his technical method of writing continuous music ("endless melody"), which minimized divisions within an act and charged the symphonic orchestra with maintaining continuity with the help of leitmotifs. As a master of orchestral color Wagner had few equals, and here also his example was imitated by composers of the late nineteenth and early twentieth century.

Church Music

The tension between Romantic musical energy, at times so flamboyant, and sacred themes was a problem for composers of church music in the nineteenth century. A case in point is Berlioz, whose magnificent religious works—the *Grande Messe des morts* (Requiem, 1837) and the *Te Deum* (1855)—were intended for special occasions. Their nature is wholly original: they are dramatic symphonies for orchestra and voices using poetically inspiring texts that happen to be liturgical. The tradition to which they belong is not ecclesiastical but secular and patriotic; their historical forebears are the great musical festivals of the French Revolution. Both works are huge, not only in

Berlioz

C H R O N O L O G Y

1800		1860	
	Goethe, *Faust,* Part I (1808)		Abraham Lincoln assassinated (1865)
1810		1870	Opening of the Suez Canal
	*Rossini, *Il barbiere di Siviglia* (1816)		*Verdi, *Aida* in Cairo, Egypt (1871)
1820			*Bizet, *Carmen* (1875)
	*Weber, *Der Freischütz* (1821)		*First performance of Wagner, *Der Ring des
1830	First performance of Berlioz, *Symphonie		Nibelungen,* Bayreuth; Brahms, First
	fantastique*		Symphony (1876)
	*Meyerbeer, *Les Huguenots* (1836)	1880	
1840			*Death of Wagner; Metropolitan Opera
	*Wagner, *Der fliegende Holländer* (1843)		House opened in New York (1883)
	Marx and Engels, *Communist Manifesto*		Gilbert and Sullivan, *The Mikado* (1885)
	(1848)		*Verdi, *Otello* (1887)
1850		1890	
	*Verdi, *Il trovatore* and *La traviata* (1853)		Death of Brahms (1897)
	*Berlioz, *Te Deum* (1855)	1900	
	*Offenbach, *Orphée aux enfers*; Berlioz, *Les		*Death of Verdi (1901)
	Troyens* (1858)		
	*Wagner, *Tristan und Isolde*; Darwin, *On the		
	Origin of Species* (1859)		

length and in the number of performers they require, but in grandeur of conception and brilliance of execution. For example, the Requiem calls for a massive choir and an orchestra of 140 players, including 4 brass choirs, 4 tam-tams, 10 pairs of cymbals, and 16 kettledrums to accompany the chorus at "Tuba mirum" in the *Dies irae.* Moreover, Berlioz obtains many superb musical effects in his control of these forces, again showing his genius for orchestration.

Liszt

The big sacred scores of Liszt, like those of Berlioz, were also created for special occasions: the Festival Mass (1855) for the consecration of a cathedral in Hungary, and the Mass for the coronation of the king of Hungary in 1867. Their scale and style correspond to Liszt's own ideal of Romantic sacred music, which he outlined in 1834, but which he never quite welded into a consistent style in his church music:

> For want of a better term we may call the new music "humanitarian." It must be devotional, strong, and drastic, uniting on a colossal scale the theatre and the church, at once dramatic and sacred, splendid and simple, ceremonial and serious, fiery and free, stormy and calm, translucent and emotional.[1]

Cecilian movement

Toward the middle of the century an agitation for musical reform arose within the Roman Catholic Church. The Cecilian movement, named after St. Cecilia, the patron saint of music, was stimulated in part by a Romantic

1. Reprinted in Liszt, *Gesammelte Schriften* (Leipzig, 1881), 2:55–57.

interest in music of the past. This helped bring about a revival of the sixteenth-century a cappella style and the restoration of Gregorian chant to what was thought to be its pristine form.

Anton Bruckner (1824–1896) succeeded as no one before him in uniting the spiritual and technical resources of the nineteenth-century symphony with a reverent and liturgical approach to the sacred texts. His Masses and symphonies have in common many qualities and even some musical themes. A solitary, simple, profoundly religious person, who was thoroughly schooled in counterpoint, Bruckner served as organist of the Cathedral at Linz and from 1867 as court organist in Vienna. Bruckner composed his D-minor Mass in 1864 and a larger one in F minor in 1867; like all his works, they were subjected to numerous revisions. The influence of the Cecilian movement is apparent in some of Bruckner's motets—for example, the strictly modal Gradual *Os justi* (1879) for unaccompanied chorus, or the *Virga Jesse* (NAWM 119), written in a modernized diatonic style.

Bruckner

Two Italian opera composers, Gioachino Rossini (1792–1868) and Giuseppe Verdi (1813–1901), made important contributions to church music in the nineteenth century. It is fashionable nowadays to stigmatize Rossini's *Stabat Mater* (1832, 1841) as gaudy, and indeed its operatic style was expressly forbidden in 1903 by the famous encyclical of Pope Pius X, *Motu proprio*. But these standards would also have excluded the Masses of Haydn, Mozart, Beethoven, Schubert, and Bruckner from church use, in addition to those of Berlioz, Liszt, and Verdi. Rossini's *Stabat Mater* remains a serious and well-crafted composition that contains some excellent choral writing, especially in the opening and closing numbers. The style of the questionable operatic arias was not intended by the composer nor perceived by his public to be flippant or inappropriate. His *Petite Messe solennelle* is another fine example of nineteenth-century church music.

Rossini

Verdi composed his Requiem (1874) in memory of Alessandro Manzoni (1785–1873), author of *I promessi sposi*, the most famous Italian novel of the nineteenth century. The Requiem is an immense work, deeply moving, vividly dramatic, and thoroughly Catholic in spirit.

Verdi

The main strength of the nineteenth-century oratorio lay in its use of the chorus, and there its descent from Handel is obvious. Mendelssohn, Brahms, and Bruckner wrote compellingly for chorus. Brahms's *Ein deutsches Requiem* (A German Requiem, 1868), for soprano and baritone soloists, chorus, and orchestra, has for its text not the liturgical words of the Latin Requiem Mass but Old Testament passages of meditation and solace in German, admirably chosen by the composer himself. Brahms's music, like that of Schütz and Bach, is inspired by a deep concern with mortality and hope for Heaven. In the German Requiem, these solemn thoughts are expressed with intense feeling and clothed with the opulent colors of nineteenth-century harmony, regulated always by spacious formal architecture and guided by Brahms's unerring judgment for choral and orchestral effect.

The Romantic oratorio

POSTLUDE

Although worlds apart in their compositional styles, the two giants of nineteenth-century opera, Verdi and Wagner, together transformed opera once more into drama. Having absorbed the innovations of grand opera, each went on to cultivate his own national style and to become the proverbial "last word" in opera and music drama.

Every Verdi opera, from *Nabucco* to *Falstaff*, combines primitive, earthy, elemental emotional force with directness, clarity, and—beneath all its refinement of detail—fundamental simplicity. Verdi's relation to the Romantic movement was complex: on the one hand, his music epitomized the expression of human emotion; on the other, it betrayed his completely unsentimental attitude toward nature. Unlike the northern Romantics, he depicted natural settings and phenomena—the storm music in *Rigoletto* and *Otello*, for example, or the exotic atmosphere in *Aida*—in a concise, almost formalized way, like the landscapes in Renaissance Italian paintings. All his interest lay in humanity, and consequently in the expressiveness of the human voice. Nature was there to be used, not worshiped. This was a logical attitude for Verdi, who was an avid and successful farmer.

Wagner's significance is threefold: he brought German Romantic opera to its consummation; he created a new genre, the music drama, in which all elements contributed meaningfully to the composite work of art (*Gesamtkunstwerk*); and, because he so thoroughly exploited chromaticism for expressive purposes, he hastened the dissolution of tonality through the harmonic idiom of his late works. Composers after Wagner found there was no turning back. His music remains overwhelmingly powerful and arouses in its listeners that all-embracing state of ecstasy, at once sensuous and mystical, toward which all Romantic art had been striving.

Finally, church music from this period was characterized by the monumentality of large choral and orchestral forces and the colorful dramatic treatments typical of opera on the one hand; and by the retrospective and more sober goals of the Cecilian movement on the other.

19

EUROPEAN MUSIC FROM THE 1870S TO WORLD WAR I

PRELUDE

Europe was relatively peaceful and stable in the late 1800s, but increasing social unrest and international tension marked the first two decades of the twentieth century, culminating in the First World War (1914–18). The same period saw radical experiments in the musical realm, which also aroused uneasiness and tension in concert audiences. Composers challenged the conventions of tonality that had ruled in the eighteenth and nineteenth centuries, effectively bringing the Classic-Romantic period to a close.

Wagner held an enormous fascination for European musicians in the last quarter of the nineteenth century. Many composers came under his spell, even as most of them consciously struggled to find their own styles while making use of his advances in music. Composers in **The German Tradition** continued to cultivate the solo song with piano accompaniment, the symphony and symphonic poem, and opera. Meanwhile, the rise of **Nationalism** prompted some composers to search for an independent, native voice, especially in Russia and the countries of Eastern Europe, where the dominance of German music was felt as a threat to homegrown musical creativity. **New Currents in France**, too, were at least in part sparked by nationalism, although they took many different paths, the most radical of which was cleared by Debussy. Finally, new trends also emerged in **Italian Opera** in the late nineteenth century, involving more realistic librettos and greater naturalism.

The German Tradition

Hugo Wolf

Songs

Hugo Wolf (1860–1903) continued the German tradition of the solo song with piano accompaniment, bringing to it certain Wagnerian elements. He produced most of his 250 lieder in short periods of intense creative activity between 1887 and 1897, after which the composer suffered a mental breakdown. They were published in six principal collections, each devoted to a single poet or group of poets.

In choosing his poems Wolf displayed fine literary discernment and an even greater regard for the text than earlier German songwriters. He concentrated on one poet at a time, and he placed the poet's name above his own in the titles of his collections, indicating a new ideal of equality between words and music derived from Wagner's music dramas. Like Wagner, Wolf had no use for the folksong type of melody, and little use for the strophic structures that were so characteristic of other German composers. Unlike Wagner, his accompaniments never overwhelm the voice. In short, Wolf adapted Wagner's methods with discrimination; he achieved a balanced fusion of voice and instrument without sacrificing either to the other.

A good illustration of such balance is his setting of *Kennst du das Land?* (Do You Know the Land?, NAWM 125). The singer's line, which is not organized into periodic melodic phrases, always preserves a truly vocal and speechlike character. As in Wagner's work, continuity is sustained by the instrumental part rather than the voice. The chromatic voice-leading, appoggiaturas, anticipations, and the wandering tonality are clearly inspired by the idiom of *Tristan*.

Wolf obtains equally beautiful effects in a sensitive diatonic style, for example in some of the songs from his *Spanisches Liederbuch* (1891). His treatment of pictorial images is always restrained but at the same time highly poetic and original. Only close study reveals the remarkable variety of fine psychological and musical details found in Wolf's songs.

Gustav Mahler

Career

Gustav Mahler (1860–1911), another admirer of Wagner, forged a successful career writing symphonies and orchestral lieder. An eminent interpreter as well, Mahler conducted at numerous opera houses, among them Prague, Leipzig, Budapest, and Hamburg. He served as director of the Vienna Opera from 1897 to 1907 and led the New York Philharmonic Society from 1909 to 1911, composing mainly in the summers between busy seasons of conducting.

Works

Of Mahler's five song-cycles for solo voices with orchestra, the best known is *Das Lied von der Erde* (The Song of the Earth, composed in 1908). He com-

▲ Caricature of Gustav Mahler as conductor by Hans Schliessmann in the *Fliegende Blätter* of March 1901. The German captions read (top) "A hypermodern conductor" and (bottom) "Kapellmeister Kappelmann conducts his Diabolical Symphony." Between 1907 and 1911 Mahler conducted at the Metropolitan Opera and led the New York Philharmonic Society. (*Collections of the Gesellschaft der Musikfreunde in Wein*)

pleted nine symphonies and left a tenth unfinished (it has since been completed by others). He repeatedly revised his first six symphonies and would probably have reworked the later ones had he lived longer.

Mahler's symphonies are long, formally complex, and programmatic. They require an enormous group of performers. The Second Symphony, first performed in 1895, calls for a huge string section, seventeen woodwinds, twenty-five brasses, six kettledrums and other percussion instruments, four or more harps, and an organ, in addition to soprano and alto soloists and a large chorus. The Eighth, composed in 1906–7 and popularly known as "the Symphony of a Thousand," demands an even larger array of players and

Instrumentation of symphonies

singers. But the size of the orchestra tells only part of the story. Mahler showed great imagination and daring in combining instruments, comparable in this respect only to Berlioz. (See Chapter 16, pages 379ff., and window, pages 380–81.) His continuing activity as a conductor allowed him to perfect details of scoring in the light of practical experience. Instances of his skill in orchestral effects, ranging from the most delicate to the most overwhelmingly gigantic, abound in all the symphonies. Mahler's instrumentation is an intrinsic part of the composer's musical language, as are his extremely detailed indications of phrasing, tempo, and dynamics, and his occasional use of unusual instruments (such as mandolins in *Das Lied von der Erde* and the Seventh and Eighth Symphonies, and sleigh bells in the Fourth).

Programmatic content of symphonies

Programmatic content, although usually not explicit, is almost always present in Mahler's symphonies. Quotations from and references to some of his own songs, the presence of obviously pictorial details, and the overall plan of each work combine to suggest that the composer had extra-musical ideas in mind like those ascribed to Beethoven's Third and Fifth Symphonies. Thus, Mahler's Fifth moves steadily from the funereal gloom of the opening march to the triumph of the Scherzo and the joy of the finale. The Sixth, by contrast, is his "tragic" symphony, culminating in a colossal finale in which heroic struggle, undermined by a persistent A-minor tonality, seems to end in defeat and death. In the Seventh two slow movements of "night music" frame a scherzo that is a ghost of a waltz. The polyphonic textures of the Eighth Symphony pay tribute to J. S. Bach (one of Mahler's musical guides). It ends in a grand chorale, the *Chorus mysticus*, based on the closing scene of Part II of Goethe's *Faust*. The Ninth, Mahler's last completed symphony (1909–10), conjures up a mood of resignation mixed with bitter satire, a strange and sad farewell to life, symbolized by deliberate reference to the *Lebewohl* (farewell) theme of Beethoven's Piano Sonata Op. 81a.

Use of voices

Following the examples of Beethoven, Berlioz, and Liszt, Mahler used voices as well as instruments in four of his symphonies. The Second and Eighth Symphonies make the most extensive use of sung text. The Second, known as the *Resurrection* Symphony, culminates (like Beethoven's Ninth) in a monumental setting for soloists and chorus of a Resurrection ode by the nineteenth-century German poet Friedrich Gottlieb Klopstock.

Tonal organization of symphonies

The Fourth Symphony begins in one key (G major) and ends in another (E major), a trait that is consistent with Mahler's feeling for the special significance of various tonalities. This disposition also contributed to a weakening sense of traditional tonal harmony. Other symphonies shaped this way are the Fifth (C♯ minor to D major), Seventh (B minor to E to C major), and Ninth (D major to D♭ major).

Songs with orchestral accompaniment

With the *Kindertotenlieder* (Songs of Dead Children) of 1901–4, a song cycle for solo voice and orchestra on poems by Friedrich Rückert, Mahler began the change in style that characterized his last two symphonies and *Das Lied von der Erde*. The typically full, crowded textures of the earlier works are replaced by a more austere idiom. For example, the first song of the cycle,

Mahler's Fourth Symphony

Mahler once remarked that to write a symphony was to "construct a world." Indeed, among his most popular symphonies, Mahler's Fourth suggests its own variegated "world." It is shorter than some of his others, most lightly orchestrated, almost conventional in form, and altogether more accessible. Its first movement observes many of the Classic constraints. The exposition, in G major, has clearly articulated theme sections: a squarely phrased principal theme (Example 19.1a), a lyrical second theme on the dominant (Example 19.1b), and a playful closing theme, also on the dominant (Example 19.1c). Unexpected, though, is the repeat of the opening before the development section and its failure to appear with the return of the tonic in the recapitulation.

EXAMPLE 19.1 Gustav Mahler, Symphony No. 4: First Movement, a) first theme; b) second theme; c) closing theme

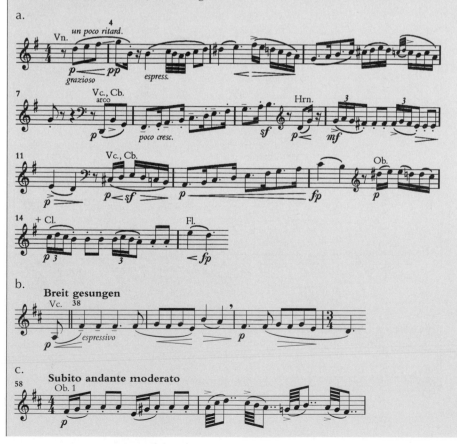

Mahler's precise use of instruments is well displayed in his orchestration of this opening material. After a three-measure introduction by an ensemble of flutes, clarinets, and sleigh bells, phrases of the long, winding melody are assigned successively to the first violins, cellos paired with double basses, French horns, and oboes paired with clarinets (Example 19.1a). When motives are later reassigned to different instruments, they sometimes sound ironic or distorted. For example, in an intricately contrapuntal passage in the development section (Example 19.2), fragments of bass motives are given to the trumpet and upper woodwinds, and the three marked repeated notes of the lyrical second theme first heard in the cellos (Example 19.1b) become ghostly apparitions in the soft woodwinds, harp harmonics, and *pianissimo* cymbal claps (19.2, measures 202, 204). Though the original ideas are dismembered and recombined as in a Classic development, the listener experiences something more like a fevered dream in which remembered images pop up from the subconscious in strange and distorted guises. The recapitulation then has the effect of restoring sanity, lucidity, and logic.

EXAMPLE 19.2   Gustav Mahler, Symphony No. 4: First Movement

The second movement, in $\frac{3}{8}$, is a musical representation of the Dance of Death, a favorite subject in old German paintings. A solo violin—the strings retuned a whole tone higher than normal—suggests the medieval fiddle of a certain grisly folklore demon. After this grim scherzo, the slow movement is down-to-earth in its mournful and at times impassioned lyricism. Two sections are each restated with variations, followed by a coda in which an unexpected outburst momentarily shatters the calm. The second of the melodic themes illustrates Mahler's technique of intensification, not through Wagnerian sequences, but, like Brahms, through seeking ever higher levels of pitch with wider strides, returning each time to the original starting point (Example 19.3).

EXAMPLE 19.3   Gustav Mahler, Symphony No. 4: Third Movement, Leidenschaftlich—Appassionato

The last movement, composed years before the others, is a song on a text from the early-nineteenth-century folk collection *Des Knaben Wunderhorn* (The Boy's Magic Horn) that presents a child's vision of Heaven. Here the jingling open fifths and running figures of the first-movement introduction, where they sounded out of place, find their true habitat and disclose their inspiration in the lines "Wir tanzen und springen, Wir hüpfen und singen" (We dance and leap, we skip and sing). This music serves as an interlude between the strophes of the song.

Nun will die Sonn' so hell aufgeh'n (Now the Sun Will Rise Again, NAWM 126), achieves a chamber-music transparency through its spare use of instruments, which allows the delicate counterpoint to shine through. The post-Wagnerian chromatic harmony, here stripped to its bare essentials, acquires unaccustomed freshness and clarity.

Das Lied von der Erde (The Song of the Earth) is based on a cycle of six poems translated from the Chinese. The texts alternate between frenzied grasping at the dreamlike whirl of life and resigned sadness about having to part from all its joys and beauties. Just as Mahler called on the human voice in his symphonies to complete his musical thought with words, here he called on the orchestra to sustain and supplement the tenor and contralto solos, both in accompaniment and in extensive connecting interludes. The exotic

Das Lied von der Erde

atmosphere of the words is lightly suggested by details of instrumental color and the use of the pentatonic scale. *Das Lied von der Erde* epitomizes hallmarks of Mahler's genius. Nowhere else did he so perfectly define and balance the two sides of his personality—ecstatic pleasure and morbid foreboding—a dualism that also characterizes the autumnal mood of the late nineteenth century.

Richard Strauss

The most famous German composer around 1900 was Richard Strauss (1864–1949). Like Mahler, Strauss was a celebrated conductor. Trained under Hans von Bülow, he held positions in the opera houses of Munich, Weimar, Berlin, and Vienna, and in the course of numerous tours conducted most of the great orchestras of the world. He received many official honors both at home and abroad and was universally recognized as the dominant figure in German musical life during the first part of the century. Whereas Mahler became the last in the long line of German symphonists that extended from Haydn to Bruckner, Strauss followed more in the footsteps of Berlioz and Liszt in cultivating the symphonic poem.

Types of symphonic programs

A symphonic poem may present one of two kinds of program. The philosophical program lies in the realm of general ideas and emotions; Liszt's *Les Préludes* and most of his other symphonic poems have such programs. In the other type, which we may call descriptive, the composer represents in music specific nonmusical events; Berlioz wrote many programs of this kind. The two types cannot be strictly differentiated, since philosophical programs often include descriptive elements, and descriptive programs usually convey a more general message as well.

Music lends itself quite well to the philosophical type of program, which probably lies behind many compositions that are not acknowledged as program music: Beethoven's Fifth Symphony, for example, and the purely instrumental symphonies of Mahler, among others. By contrast, the descriptive type of program is more difficult to reconcile with the essentially abstract nature of music. The danger of producing a work of little artistic merit is greatest when the event being described is quite definite and specific or when natural sounds are concerned. The skillful composer must absorb the imitated events and sounds into a musical whole using the procedures of absolute music. Successful examples are the bird sounds in Beethoven's *Pastoral* Symphony, the distant thunder in Berlioz's *Symphonie fantastique,* and the depiction of Resurrection day in Mahler's Second Symphony.

Symphonic poems

Strauss wrote symphonic poems with both philosophical and descriptive programs. His best works of the first type are *Tod und Verklärung* (Death and Transfiguration, 1889) and *Also sprach Zarathustra* (So Spoke Zoroaster, 1896). *Till Eulenspiegels lustige Streiche* (Till Eulenspiegel's Merry Pranks, 1895) and *Don Quixote* (1897) are highly descriptive early works. *Don Juan*

(1889) is Strauss's first completely mature work; vividly descriptive, it is music of tremendous verve, with brilliant orchestration. *Ein Heldenleben* (A Hero's Life, 1889) is openly autobiographical, a mocking and defiant challenge to Strauss's critics, whom he caricatures in cacophonous passages while glorifying his own deeds and triumphs with citations from his early works.

Zarathustra, a symphonic poem of the philosophical type, is a musical commentary on the celebrated prose-poem by the philosopher-poet Friedrich Nietzsche. In choosing a subject from this author, whose ideas on the *Übermensch* (superman) were agitating all of Europe at the end of the century, Strauss revealed a good nose for publicity. Nietzsche's original four-part poem proclaimed that the Christian ethic of exalting the humble and poor should be replaced by the ideal of an aristocratic and moral superman who is above good and evil. Strauss had the prologue to Nietzsche's poem printed before the score. He also placed titles from the book at the head of musical sections: "Of the Inhabitants of the Unseen World," "Of the Great Longing," "Of Joys and Passions," "Dirge," "Of Knowledge," "The Convalescent," "The Dance Song." Without a close reading of the poem itself, a listener could hardly make sense of this. Nietzsche's ideas, therefore, served chiefly to stimulate Strauss's musical imagination.

Zoroaster's (Zarathustra's) opening address to the sun in the prologue—"Great star, how happy would you be if you did not have those whom you light up?"—must have inspired Strauss's splendid opening passage, which became a commonplace after it was quoted in the soundtrack of the film *2001*. A deep *C* in the organ pedal and contrabassoon, accompanied by soft tremolos in the basses, is followed by a trumpet fanfare and a tutti C-minor chord that turns to major when the passage is immediately repeated. Another obvious programmatic device is the fugue theme, which uses all twelve notes of the chromatic scale (see Example 19.4) to symbolize the all-embracing dark realm of *Wissenschaft* (science, learning, knowledge). The symbolism is reinforced by the low-lying thick sound of the fugal exposition given to the basses and cellos, each divided in four parts.

Also sprach Zarathustra

EXAMPLE 19.4   Richard Strauss, *Also sprach Zarathustra*: Fugue Subject

In *Till Eulenspiegel*, which is among the descriptive types of symphonic poems and the popular favorite, Strauss developed a comic program in music of unfading freshness and melodic attractiveness. The realistic details of Till's adventures (specified by a few marginal notes that the composer added to the printed score) are so thoroughly blended into the musical flow that the work

Till Eulenspiegel

could easily be heard simply as a character sketch of a particularly appealing rascal, or even more simply as a piece of musical humor, reminiscent of Haydn. A further suggestion of Haydn lies in Strauss's indication that *Till* is "in rondo form." It is not a rondo in the Classic sense, but rondo-like because the two *Till* themes keep recurring in an endless variety of guises, enlivened by shrewd touches of instrumentation. In no other work does Strauss seem so unrestrained, so spontaneous, as in this merry musical tale.

Don Quixote

If *Till* is a children's tale that Strauss turned into a sophisticated but sentimental mock-heroic epic, *Don Quixote* is very much an adult comedy, an instrumental dramatization of Cervantes's picaresque novel. As the rondo was appropriate to Till, who remains the same fool after each successful prank, so the variation fits the adventures of the knight Don Quixote and his squire Sancho Panza (see excerpt in NAWM 127), whose personalities are shaped by their frustrating experiences. We are no longer in a world of merry pranks but in one of split personalities and double meanings. The wry humor and cleverness in *Don Quixote* lie not so much in the apt depiction of real things as in the play with musical ideas. Much of this work has a chamber-music sound because it was conceived in contrapuntal lines, and its themes attach to particular solo instruments. "Variations" here does not mean preserving a melody or harmonic progression and its form through a number of statements. Rather, the themes of the two main characters are transformed so that the beginnings of the themes sprout new melodic continuations.

Operas

Strauss came to feel, like Beethoven, Berlioz, Liszt, Wagner, and Mahler, that he needed words to supplement the language of music, so he transferred his powers of depiction and characterization almost exclusively to opera. In that genre, he dealt with subjects, actions, and emotions stranger than any attempted in opera before. These stimulated him to create harmonically complex and dissonant musical idioms that greatly influenced two later developments: the growth of musical expressionism (see pages 502–3) and the dissolution of tonality in German music.

Salome

Strauss leaped into fame as an opera composer in 1905 with *Salome*, a setting of Oscar Wilde's one-act play in German translation. In this decadent version of the biblical story, Salome entices Herod, with her famous dance of the seven veils, to deliver the head of John the Baptist so that she can kiss his cold lips. With orchestral splendor, novel rhythms, and keenly descriptive harmonies, Strauss captured the macabre tone and atmosphere of the drama with such expressive force as to lift it to a plane where artistry outweighs perversion.

Der Rosenkavalier

Der Rosenkavalier (The Rose-Bearing Cavalier, 1911), on an excellent libretto in three acts by Hofmannsthal, takes us into a sunnier world of elegant, stylized eroticism and tender feeling in the aristocratic, powdered-wig milieu of eighteenth-century Vienna. *Der Rosenkavalier* is Strauss's operatic masterpiece. The sultry harmonies of *Salome* and the cacophonies of *Elektra* are softened. The mock-Romantic, sensuous melodic curves, the novel harmonic

Strauss's *Elektra*

With *Elektra* (1908), Strauss began his long and fruitful collaboration with the Viennese playwright Hugo von Hofmannsthal (1874–1929) that would result in seven different operas. For Hofmannsthal's version of Sophocles' play, which dwells throughout its long single act on the emotions of insane hatred and revenge, Strauss conceived music with shrill dissonance and apparent harmonic anarchy that outdid anything previously experienced in an opera house. The anarchy is only apparent, however. In spite of *Tristan*, audiences in 1909 still expected chords sounding like dominants to resolve to a tonic, which Strauss's seldom do. The prevailing chromatic harmony is offset by some dissonant polytonal passages and tonal sections that are purely diatonic. The sound of the harmony emanates from a single germinal chord (Example 19.5a), thereby anticipating a technique used by later twentieth-century composers. The score is further unified by leitmotifs and by the association of certain keys with particular characters or situations: B♭ with Agamemnon, E♭ with Chrysothemis, and a C–E complex with Elektra's triumph. Strauss frequently set up chord relationships at the interval of a tritone as in the Elektra motive (Example 19.5b). Dissonances most often occur in the meeting of contrapuntal lines but are sometimes chosen deliberately for their shock value.

EXAMPLE 19.5   Richard Strauss, *Elektra*: Harmony

a. The germinal chord of *Elektra*

b. Elektra motive

▲ Setting for Act III of Richard Strauss's *Der Rosenkavalier*, designed by Alfred Roller for the original 1911 Vienna production. The legend below reads, "Private room in a small inn." (*By permission of Boosey & Hawkes, Inc.*)

twists, the magical orchestral colors, and a lively sense of comedy are couched in a deceptively simple diatonic style derived from South German dances and folksongs. The human voice is once again prominent. Woven into the orchestral background and alternating with much cleverly wrought *parlando* dialogue are melodious arias, duets, and trios. These ensembles do not really fall into separate numbers as in the Classic opera but still depart significantly from the Wagnerian (and earlier Straussian) singing that was purely declamatory or, at most, arioso and that was dominated by the orchestra. The whole score, with its mingling of sentiment and comedy, overflows with the light-hearted rhythms and melodies of Viennese waltzes.

Nationalism

Nationalism in nineteenth-century music was marked by an emphasis on literary and linguistic traditions, an interest in folklore, a large dose of patriotism, and a craving for independence and identity. A sense of pride in a language and its literature formed part of the national consciousness that led, respectively, to German and Italian unification. Up to a point, Wagner and Verdi chose subject matter that reflected their patriotic feelings, but neither one was narrowly national in this respect. It was the character of Verdi's operas that made him a symbol for national unity (see Chapter 18, page 418). Neither composer cultivated a style that was ethnically German or Italian. Brahms arranged German folksongs and wrote folklike melodies. Haydn, Schubert, Schumann, Strauss, and Mahler all made conscious use of folk idioms, if not always those of their native countries. The Polish elements in Chopin and the Hungarian-Gypsy traits in Liszt and Brahms were for the most part exotic accessories to cosmopolitan styles. Nationalism was not really an issue in the music of any of these composers.

The search for an independent, native voice—one important aspect of nationalism—was keenest in England, France, the United States, Russia, and the countries of Eastern Europe whose composers wished to be recognized as equals of those in the Austro-German orbit. By employing native folksongs and dances or imitating their musical character, composers could develop a style that had ethnic identity. Although individual composers in these countries differed in their interest in a nationalist agenda, it is convenient to deal with both nationalists and non-nationalists in this section.

Russia

Until the nineteenth century, secular art music in Russia was largely in the hands of imported Italian, French, or German composers. The first composer recognized by both Europeans and Russians as an authentic native voice and an equal of his Western contemporaries was Mikhail Glinka (1804–1857). He established his reputation in 1836 with the patriotic opera *Zhizn za tsarya* (A Life for the Czar). Some of the recitative and melodic writing has a Russian character, attributable to modal scales, quotation of folksongs, and folklike idiom. Glinka's second opera, *Ruslan and Lyudmila* (1842), contains many imaginative uses of the whole-tone scale, chromaticism, dissonance, and variation technique applied to folksongs.

Glinka

Meanwhile, Tchaikovsky (1840–1893), trained in Germany and writing in a cosmopolitan style, was not particularly interested in furthering the nationalist cause, although he chose Russian subject matter. He wrote a great deal of music for the stage, including background music, ballet music, and operas, such as *Eugene Onegin* (1879), notable for its penetrating portrayal of passions and for the way numerous themes grow from a germ-motive first announced in the orchestral prelude. In another opera, *The Queen of Spades* (1890), Tchaikovsky matched the ghoulish atmosphere of Pushkin's story and re-created the spirit of the eighteenth-century Russia of Catherine the Great by borrowing musical ideas from that period.

Tchaikovsky

In the second half of the nineteenth century five leading Russian composers banded together in a group known as "the Mighty Handful," that is, the mighty five: Alexander Borodin (1833–1887), Modest Musorgsky (1839–1881), Mily Balakirev (1837–1910), César Cui (1835–1918), and Nikolay Rimsky-Korsakov (1844–1908). All of them except Balakirev had unconventional training in music, but it would be wrong to call them amateurs. They admired Western music but felt alienated from the St. Petersburg Conservatory, founded in 1862 by Anton Rubinstein (1829–1894), a Germanic dogmatist. They were disillusioned with the academic musical establishment

The Mighty Handful

César Cui on the Russian Mighty Handful:

❝ We formed a close-knit circle of young composers. And since there was nowhere to study (the Conservatory didn't exist) our *self-education* began. It consisted of playing through everything that had been written by all the greatest composers, and all works were subjected to criticism and analysis in all their technical and creative aspects. We were young and our judgments were harsh. We were very disrespectful in our attitude toward Mozart and Mendelssohn; to the latter we opposed Schumann, who was then ignored by everyone. We were very enthusiastic about Liszt and Berlioz. We worshipped Chopin and Glinka. We carried on heated debates (in the course of which we would down as many as four or five glasses of tea with jam), we discussed musical form, program music, vocal music and especially operatic form. ❞

Trans. from Cui, *Izbrannye stat'i* by Richard Taruskin in "Some Thoughts on the History and Historiography of Russian Music," *Journal of Musicology* 3 (1984):335.

and found little worthwhile in the exercises and prizes that it fostered. Seeking a fresh approach, they called on the materials nearest at hand, namely folksong, modal and exotic scales, and folk polyphony.

Musorgsky

The greatest of the Mighty Handful, Modest Musorgsky earned a living as a clerk in the civil service and received most of his musical training from Balakirev. His principal works are a symphonic fantasy *Night on Bald Mountain* (1867); the set of piano pieces *Pictures at an Exhibition* (1874, later orchestrated by Ravel); the song cycles *The Nursery* (1872), *Sunless* (1874), and *Songs and Dances of Death* (1875); and the operas *Boris Godunov* (first performed in 1874) and *Khovanshchina*, which was completed by Rimsky-Korsakov in 1886.

Musorgsky's individuality shines through every aspect of his music. He followed the accents of Russian speech as closely as possible, and therefore his vocal music generally lacks lyrical melodic lines and symmetrical phrasing. Although Musorgsky quoted actual folk tunes only occasionally (as in the Coronation scene of *Boris*), Russian folksong was rooted in his musical nature even more deeply than in Borodin's.

Musorgsky's songs are among the finest of the nineteenth century. His use of nonfunctional harmonic progressions in *O konchen prazdnyi* (The Noisy Days are Over, NAWM 128), from the cycle *Sunless*, intrigued Debussy, who borrowed an accompaniment pattern for his *Nuages* (NAWM 131; see Example 19.9, page 454).

Musorgsky's harmony was highly original and indeed revolutionary. Unfettered by traditional procedures and unpracticed in manipulating standard formulas, he labored at the piano to work out his innovative progressions; these, along with his rhythms, may have been culled from his memories of polyphonic folk singing. His harmonic vocabulary remains limited, but his apparently simple progressions convey precisely the effect he wanted, and resist conventional analysis (see Example 19.6).

EXAMPLE 19.6   Modest Musorgsky, *Boris Godunov*: End of Act II

Lord! You do not wish the death of a sinner. Forgive the soul of guilty Czar Boris!

The realism that was so prominent in nineteenth-century Russian literature found an echo in Musorgsky's opera *Boris Godunov*—not only in the way he imitated the spoken word, but in the lifelike musical depiction of gestures and, in the choral scenes, the sound and stir of the crowds. The psychological insight displayed in the songs on a miniature scale is also applied with equal mastery in depicting the Czar's character. Like other Russian com-

Boris Godunov

posers, Musorgsky built his effects by the repetition and accumulation of single impressions, not by thematic development to a climax. Rather than continuously developed action, *Boris* is a series of episodes welded together by an epic thread and the central figure of the Czar.

Rimsky-Korsakov

Nikolay Rimsky-Korsakov forms a link between the first generation of Russian composers—Glinka and the Mighty Handful—and those of the early twentieth century. In the 1880s he led some Russian musicians away from the insular Balakirev circle toward a style that was based on broader, more eclectic methods and resources, but was still strongly impregnated with national idioms. He proved his abiding interest in national music not only by arranging and editing folksongs but by incorporating them and their characteristic turns and harmonies into his own compositions. Particularly in his late works, he experimented with whole-tone and octatonic scales (comprised in the first case entirely of whole steps and, in the second, of alternating half and whole steps) and with parallel chord progressions such as those used in improvised polyphony.

Abandoning an early career in the navy, Rimsky-Korsakov served from 1871 as professor of composition at the St. Petersburg Conservatory and was also active in Russia as a conductor. To supplement his rather sketchy musical training under Balakirev, he studied counterpoint on his own. His compositions include symphonies, chamber music, choruses, and songs, but his principal works are symphonic poems and operas. His music, in contrast to the intense dramatic realism of Musorgsky's, is distinguished by lively fantasy and bright orchestral colors. The *Capriccio espagnol* (1887), the symphonic suite *Sheherazade* (1888), and the *Russian Easter Overture* (1888) are outstanding examples of his genius for orchestration; he systematized his teachings on this subject in a treatise published in 1913. In the two most important of his fifteen operas—*Sadko* (1897) and *The Golden Cockerel* (first performed in 1909)—he alternated a diatonic, often modal style with a lightly chromatic, fanciful style suggestive of their fairy-tale worlds.

Rimsky-Korsakov's leading pupils were Alexander Glazunov (1865–1936), the last of the Russian nationalists and a minor master of the symphony, and Igor Stravinsky (see pages 481ff.), whose early works are descendants of Rimsky-Korsakov's style and orchestral technique.

Rakhmaninov

Sergei Rakhmaninov (1873–1943), like Tchaikovsky, cultivated a late Romantic, sweepingly passionate, melodious idiom. He was not interested in the national movement, and, indeed, left Russia in 1917, never to return. Apart from numerous songs and piano pieces his most notable works remain the Second Piano Concerto (1901), the Third Piano Concerto (1909), the Second Symphony (1906–7), the symphonic poem *The Isle of the Dead* (1907), and *Rhapsody on a Theme of Paganini* for piano and orchestra (1934).

Skryabin

Alexander Skryabin (1872–1915), influenced by the chromaticism of Liszt and Wagner, and to some extent also by the mood-evoking methods of impressionism (see page 456), gradually evolved a complex harmonic vocabulary all his own. A concert pianist, he began by writing nocturnes, preludes, études, and mazurkas in the manner of Chopin. The growth of this language can be followed step by step in his ten piano sonatas, of which the last five, composed 1912–13, dispense with key signatures and drift toward atonality. He replaced the common tonal hierarchy with a complex chord chosen to serve as the root of a work's melodic and harmonic material. These chords contain one or more tritones, and some, like the "mystic" chord of his symphonic poem *Prometheus*, have whole-tone properties (see Example 19.7). The last chord in Example 19.7, the basis of his piano work *Vers la flamme* (1914; NAWM 129), is heard in several transpositions and finally, with an added third, in the introductory section. Traditional formal articulations dissolve in a stream of strange, colorful, and sometimes magnificent sound effects.

EXAMPLE 19.7   Alexander Skryabin, Chord Forms

Two of Skryabin's most original compositions are orchestral works, the *Poem of Ecstasy* (1908) and *Prometheus* (1910). During the playing of the latter, the composer wished the concert hall to be flooded with changing light. Skryabin aspired to a synthesis of all the arts with the aim of inducing states of mystic rapture. He had no important disciples, though his radical antitonal tendencies doubtless encouraged others to take this path.

Nationalism in Other Countries

Among the lands of central Europe, Bohemia had for centuries been politically attached to Austria and so, unlike Russia, had always been in the mainstream of European music. The two principal Bohemian or Czech composers of the nineteenth century were Bedřich Smetana (1824–1884) and Antonín Dvořák (see Chapter 16, page 388). Although they leaned toward nationalistic subjects in their program music and operas (for example, Smetana's *Bartered Bride*, 1866), their musical language was basically European. By contrast, the Czech composer Leoš Janáček (1854–1928) consciously renounced the styles of western Europe in his works after 1890. He anticipated Bartók in deliberately collecting folk music, and his own mature style grew out of the rhythms and inflections of Moravian peasant speech and song. His operas include *Jenůfa* (1903) and *The Cunning Little Vixen* (1924).

Bohemia

Nationalism in Norway is represented by Edvard Hagerup Grieg (1843–

Norway

1907), whose best works are his short piano pieces, songs, and incidental orchestral music to plays. A national character emerges most clearly in the songs on Norwegian texts, the choruses for men's voices Op. 30, the four Psalms for mixed chorus Op. 74, many of his *Lyric Pieces* for piano (ten collections), the four sets of piano arrangements of folksongs, and especially the *Slåtter* (Norwegian peasant dances that Grieg arranged for the piano from transcripts of country fiddle playing). His piano style, with its delicate grace notes and mordents, owes something to Chopin, but the all-pervading influence in his music is that of Norwegian folksongs and dances, reflected in his modal turns of melody and harmony, frequent drone basses (suggested by old Norwegian stringed instruments), and the fascinating combination of $\frac{3}{4}$ and $\frac{6}{8}$ rhythm in the *Slåtter*. These national characteristics blend with Grieg's sensitive feeling for harmony in a personal, poetic music that has not lost its freshness.

Finland

The great Finnish composer Jean Sibelius (1865–1957) was devoted to the literature of his country, particularly the *Kalevala*, the Finnish national epic, which he mined for use in his vocal works and symphonic poems. It is easy to imagine that much of his music—"somber," "bleak," and "elemental" are favorite adjectives—was inspired by his profound love of nature, and particularly aspects typical of northern countries. Surprisingly, he does not quote or imitate folksongs in his works. Unlike Grieg, who was essentially a miniaturist, Sibelius is best revealed in his symphonies, symphonic poems (for example, *The Swan of Tuonela* and *Finlandia* from the 1890s), and the Violin Concerto (1903).

England

Nationalism came comparatively late to English music. Edward Elgar (1857–1934) was the first English composer in more than two hundred years to enjoy wide international recognition. His music is not touched by folksong in the least, nor do its technical characteristics derive from the national musical tradition. Yet it "sounds English," perhaps because Elgar's typical melodic line resembles the intonation patterns of British speech. The oratorio *The Dream of Gerontius* (1900) remains his most important choral work. Elgar also composed a number of excellent orchestral scores, including the *Enigma Variations* (1899). His musical idiom is late Romantic: from Brahms and Wagner he derived his harmonic style, from Wagner the system of leitmotifs in his oratorios and perhaps also his persistent sequential repetitions. The English musical renaissance signaled by Elgar took a nationalist turn in the twentieth century, when Ralph Vaughan Williams (1872–1958) and Gustav Holst (1874–1934) became the leaders of a new English school, which will be introduced in the following chapter.

Spain

Felipe Pedrell (1841–1922) sparked a comparable nationalist revival in Spain with his editions of sixteenth-century Spanish composers and his operas, chief of which was *Los Pirineos* (The Pyrenees, composed 1891). Further nationalist impetus came from the works of Isaac Albéniz (1860–1909), whose piano suite *Iberia* (1909) used Spanish dance rhythms in a colorful virtuoso

C H R O N O L O G Y	
1870	**1890**
*Founding of the National Society for French Music (1871)	*Fauré, *La Bonne Chanson* (1892)
*Claude Monet (1840–1926), *Impression: Soleil levant* (1874) (see Plate XII, facing page 419)	*Debussy, *Prélude à l'après-midi d'un faune* (1894)
*Musorgsky, *Boris Godunov* (1874)	*Strauss, *Also sprach Zarathustra* (1896)
First performance of Wagner, *Der Ring des Nibelungen*, Bayreuth; Brahms, First Symphony (1876)	Death of Brahms (1897)
	*Sibelius, *Finlandia* (1899)
	1900
Thomas Edison invents the phonograph (1877)	Death of Verdi (1901)
	*Puccini, *Madama Butterfly* (1904)
	*Mahler, *Das Lied von der Erde* (1908)
1880	**1910**
	*Strauss, *Der Rosenkavalier* (1911)
Death of Wagner (1883)	First World War (1914–18)
Dvořák, Seventh Symphony (1885)	Death of Debussy (1918)
Verdi, *Otello* (1887)	
Paris World's Fair (1889)	

style. The principal Spanish composer of the early twentieth century, Manuel de Falla (1876–1946), collected and arranged national folksongs, and his earlier works—the opera *La vida breve* (Life Is Short, composed 1905), for example, and the ballet *El amor brujo* (Love, the Sorcerer, 1915)—are imbued with the melodic and rhythmic qualities of Spanish popular music. *Nights in the Gardens of Spain*, three "symphonic impressions" for piano and orchestra (1916), testify both to national sources and the influence of Debussy, who was himself inspired by Spanish local color, among other exotic musics (see below).

New Currents in France

France, too, showed concern for the recovery of its national musical heritage and the encouragement of its native composers. The National Society for French Music was founded at the end of the Franco-Prussian War in 1871. Its purpose was to give performances of works by French composers, and the society can be credited with a marked rise, both in quantity and quality, of symphonic and chamber music. It also sought to revive the great French music of the past through editions and performances of Rameau, Gluck, and the sixteenth-century composers. The Schola Cantorum, founded in Paris in 1894, introduced broad historical studies in music, in contrast to the narrow technical training (emphasizing opera) that had prevailed at the century-old Conservatory. These and similar activities allowed France to regain a leading position in music during the first half of the twentieth century.

Three interdependent lines of development occurred in French music from 1871 to the early 1900s: (1) the eclectic, cosmopolitan tradition, transmitted through César Franck and carried on by his pupils; (2) the specifically French tradition, transmitted through Camille Saint-Saëns and continued by his pupils, especially Gabriel Fauré; and (3) a later tradition, rooted in the second, led by Debussy in directions that could hardly have been predicted.

Cosmopolitan tradition, Franck

César Franck (1822–1890) worked mainly in the conventional instrumental genres—symphony, symphonic poem, sonata, variations, chamber music—and oratorio. He shaped and developed his themes in traditional ways, but he enriched his essentially homophonic texture by contrapuntal means. Underlying all his work was his warm religious idealism and his belief in the serious social mission of the artist. Because he worked out his ideas logically and deliberately avoided extremes of expression, his music may be termed anti-Romantic. Franck introduced some mildly chromatic innovations in harmony and systematically applied the cyclical method.

French tradition

The French tradition, the second of the three "schools" outlined above, is essentially cool and Classic, regarding music as sonorous form rather than spontaneous expression. Order and restraint are fundamental. Instead of emotional displays and musical depiction it relies on subtle patterns of tones, rhythms, and colors. The music sounds more lyric or dancelike than narrative or dramatic. It is economical, simple, and reserved rather than profuse, complex, and grandiloquent. It delivers no message about the fate of the cosmos or the state of the composer's soul. French composers as far apart in time and temperament as Couperin and Gounod wrote this kind of music. Perhaps because Berlioz did not compose such music, he was not a success in France.

Gabriel Fauré (1845–1924) was a founder of the National Society for French Music and the first president of the Independent Musical Society, which branched off from the parent association in 1909. After studying composition with Saint-Saëns from 1861 to 1865, Fauré held various posts as an organist. He became professor of composition at the Paris Conservatoire in 1896 and its director from 1905 to 1920, when he resigned because of a hearing loss.

Fauré

Fauré's refined, highly civilized music embodies the aristocratic qualities of the French tradition. Primarily a composer of lyric pieces, solo piano and chamber music, he wrote a few works in larger forms, including the *Requiem* (1887), incidental music to Maeterlinck's play *Pelléas et Mélisande* (1898), and the operas *Promethée* (1900) and *Pénélope* (1913). His music is not remarkable for color—he was not particularly skilled at orchestration. Simple lyrical melody, which avoids any display of virtuosity, remained the basis of his style.

Fauré's songs

Fauré's nearly one hundred songs, set largely to texts by his countrymen, reveal his musical personality most fully. In his maturity, from about 1885, Fauré added innovations in harmony to his flowing, supple melodies. *Avant que tu ne t'en ailles* (Before you depart, NAWM 130) from the cycle *La Bonne Chanson* illustrates some of his melodic and harmonic idiosyncrasies, which include ambiguous tonality and a kind of melodic neutrality; these combine to give his music a certain equilibrium and repose that is the opposite of the emotional unrest in Wagner's music. In Example 19.8 the chords consist mainly of dominant sevenths and ninths, as in Wagner, but the tension melts as one chord fades into another and the unresolved seventh or ninth becomes a wayward member of another chord.

EXAMPLE 19.8   Gabriel Fauré, *Avant que tu ne t'en ailles*

What joy in the fields of ripe wheat.

Fauré's music has often been described as Hellenic, its clarity, balance, and serenity recalling the Classic spirit of ancient Greek art. Such qualities appear not only in his more intimate works, but also in his opera *Pénélope* (where they are particularly appropriate to the subject, the wife of Odysseus) and in the *Requiem.* After 1910 Fauré's style became even more concentrated, his textures more austere (as in the song cycle *L'Horizon chimérique* and the Tenth Barcarolle), and his lines more contrapuntal (Second Quintet, Thirteenth Nocturne). Through his pupil Ravel and through the famous teacher Nadia Boulanger (1887–1979), who was also his student, Fauré influenced countless later composers.

Claude Debussy (1862–1918), the leader of the third stream of French music discussed in this chapter, became one of the most potent influences on the entire course of twentieth-century music. One aspect of his style— often overemphasized at the expense of other important traits—is summed up in the term *impressionism* (see window, page 456), but various early influences contributed to the formation of Debussy's style as well. The immediate background included Franck, Saint-Saëns, and the witty and original

Debussy

Emmanuel Chabrier (1841–1894), but contemporary French painters and poets had at least as much impact on his thinking. Debussy's admiration for Wagner was coupled with revulsion against his bombastic rhetoric and his attempts to expound philosophy in music. Debussy found potential new directions, for example, in Russian music, especially Musorgsky's *Boris* and his songs. Grieg also influenced Debussy, and after 1900 Ravel did as well, especially his piano music. The lure of Spain, inspired in part by Chabrier's *España* and Ravel's *Habanera,* is evident in the *Soirée dans Grenade* (No. 2 of *Estampes*) and the *Iberia* movement of the orchestral *Images* (1912). From the French tradition Debussy inherited his refined sensibilities, his aristocratic taste, and his anti-Romantic conception of music's function. In his last works he turned with renewed conviction to the heritage of Couperin and Rameau.

Debussy's Nocturnes

Debussy's most celebrated orchestral work, *Prélude à l'après-midi d'un faune* (Prelude to the Afternoon of a Faun, 1894), is based on a poem of Mallarmé. He followed it with *Nocturnes* (1899) and the symphonic sketches *La Mer* (1905). The first movement (*Nuages*) of the orchestral *Nocturnes* illustrates Debussy's new idiom—impressionism—and reveals certain sources of his style as well. *Nuages* (Clouds, NAWM 131) begins with a chordal pattern borrowed from Musorgsky's song *O konchen prazdnyi* (The Noisy Days Are Over, NAWM 128), but Musorgsky's alternating sixths and thirds are replaced by the starker sounding fifths and thirds (see Example 19.9a). As in Musorgsky we feel an impression of movement but no harmonic direction, a perfect analogy for slowly moving clouds. To articulate disparate segments of the piece, Debussy used descending parallel seventh and ninth chords (Example 19.9b). Like Musorgsky and Fauré, Debussy did not use chords to shape a phrase by tension and release; instead he conceived each chord as an in-

EXAMPLE 19.9   Chord Progressions in *Nuages* (Debussy) and *The Noisy Days Are Over* (Musorgsky)

a.

b.

dependent unit in a phrase whose structure was determined more by melodic shape or color value than by the movement of the harmony. Debussy usually maintained a tonal focus—a kind of key center—but he systematically neutralized the common tonal relationships between chords, which gives much of his music a serene, floating quality. The middle section of *Nuages* had a more exotic source—the Javanese *gamelan*, an orchestra made up mainly of gongs and percussion, that Debussy heard at the 1889 World's Fair in Paris. Simulating the *gamelan* texture, Debussy gave the flute and harp a simple pentatonic tune, while the other instruments were assigned a static background.

Debussy's orchestration

Debussy's orchestration admirably suits his musical ideas. His works require a large orchestra, but it is seldom used to make a loud sound. Strings are frequently divided and muted, and harps add a distinctive touch. Among the woodwinds, the flute (especially in the low register), oboe, and English horn are featured in solos. Horns and trumpets, also often muted, are heard in short *pianissimo* phrases. Percussion instruments of many types—kettledrums, large and small drums, large and small cymbals, tam-tams, celesta, glockenspiel, xylophone—provide still another source of color. Debussy's orchestral technique is well illustrated in the *Nocturnes*: the clarity of the full ensemble in *Fêtes*; and the magic of rich, subdued instrumentation in *Nuages* (NAWM 131) and *Sirènes*, supplemented in *Sirènes* by a wordless chorus of women's voices.

Debussy's piano music

Pianistic counterparts of all these devices are found in Debussy's piano music, which—along with Ravel's—constitutes the most important early-twentieth-century literature for that instrument. The chord structure is often veiled by figuration and by the blending effect of the damper pedal. No mere listing of technical features can suggest the sparkling play of color, the ravishing pianistic effects, the subtle poetic fancy these pieces display. Debussy's principal impressionistic piano works occur in collections published between 1903 and 1913: *Estampes*, two books of *Images*, and two books of *Préludes*.

Impressionism, of course, is only one aspect of Debussy's style; a Hellenistic or Classic detachment, as in Fauré, also distinguishes many of his compositions. Examples may be heard in the piano music: the early *Suite Bergamasque* (1893), the suite *Pour le piano* (1901), and the delightful *Children's Corner* (1908). The String Quartet (1893) fuses Debussy's harmonic and coloristic traits with Classic forms and cyclic treatment of themes. In his only completed opera, *Pelléas et Mélisande* (1902), Debussy set a symbolist play by Maurice Maeterlinck (1862–1949). The veiled allusions and repressed sexuality of the text are perfectly matched by the strange, often modal harmonies, subdued colors, and constricted expressivity of the music. The voices, in fluent recitative, are supported but never dominated by a continuous orchestral background, while the instrumental interludes connecting the scenes carry on the mysterious inner drama.

Pelléas et Mélisande

The changes that Debussy introduced in harmonic and orchestral usage

IMPRESSIONISM

T he word *impressionism* was initially applied to a French school of painting that flourished during the last quarter of the nineteenth century. Its chief representative was Claude Monet (1840–1926), whose work entitled *Impression: Soleil levant* (Impression: Sunrise) first appeared in an 1874 group exhibition in Paris (see Plate XII, facing page 419). A disapproving critic, perturbed by the apparent lack of form and rigor in Monet's technique, reacted by coining the term "impressionists," which by extension included Camille Pissarro (1830–1903) and Edouard Manet (1832–1883), and eventually Auguste Renoir (1841–1919) and Edgar Degas (1834–1917) as well. Generally, their style was characterized by an attempt to capture fleeting moments painted directly from nature. Consequently, they popularized outdoor painting and specialized in representing sunlight and water, two of the most

Debussy's influence

made him one of the great seminal forces in the history of music. To name the composers who at one time or another came under his influence would be to name nearly every distinguished composer of the early and middle twentieth century. Such a list, in addition to Ravel and all others of French nationality, would include Skryabin, Strauss, Falla, Puccini, Janáček, Stravinsky, Bartók, Berg, Webern, Hindemith, and Orff, all of whom also developed their own personal languages. Composers for whom impressionism had a more conspicuous or lasting effect were the Alsatian-born American Charles Martin Loeffler (1861–1935), the Swiss-American Ernest Bloch (1880–1959), the American Charles Griffes (1884–1920), the Pole Karol Szymanowski (1882–1937), the Englishman Arnold Bax (1883–1935), and the Italian Ottorino Respighi (1879–1936).

Satie

Erik Satie (1866–1925) spearheaded a movement that was anti-impressionist, though not altogether anti-Debussy. Some of Satie's early piano pieces (for example, the three *Gymnopédies* of 1888) anticipated the unresolved chords and quasi-modal harmonies of impressionism in an ostentatiously plain texture. By 1891 he was writing chords in parallel motion built on perfect fourths. Surrealistic titles headed his piano caricatures written between 1900 and 1915: *Trois morceaux en forme de poire* (Three Pieces in the Form of a Pear), *Embryons desséchés* (Dehydrated Embryos), and the like. The scores contain running commentary and tongue-in-cheek directions to the player:

formless yet luminous phenomena in nature. Similarly, their musical counter-parts, Debussy and his followers, aimed to evoke moods and sensuous impressions mainly through harmony and tone color rather than through melodic linearity and form. Some of Debussy's titles, many of which evoke glimmering images, are revealing in themselves: *La Mer* (The Sea), *La Cathédrale engloutie* (The Sunken Cathedral), *Nuages* (Clouds), *Sirènes* (Water Nymphs), *La Fille aux cheveux de lin* (The Girl with the Flaxen Hair), etc.

Unlike earlier program music, impressionism did not seek to express deeply felt emotion or tell a story but to elicit a mood, a passing sentiment, an atmosphere. It used enigmatic titles, reminiscences of natural sounds, dance rhythms, characteristic bits of melody, limpid harmonies, shimmering orchestral colors, and the like to suggest the subject. Musical impressionism relies on allusion and understatement in contrast to the forthright, energetic, and sometimes overstated outpourings of the Romantics. Because it depends on subtlety and nuance for effect, and requires listeners to suspend their sense of direction and their expectations of narrative, impressionism is for many an acquired taste. For others, it is the ultimate in sensuous "mood music."

pp en un pauvre souffle (pianissimo, short of breath), *avec beaucoup de mal* (with much difficulty). Some of these satirized the impressionistic titles and directions of Debussy. But the comic spirit lives also in the music itself—spare, dry, capricious, brief, repetitive, parodistic, and witty in the highest degree. Satie's biting, antisentimental spirit, economical textures, and severe harmony and melody influenced the music of his compatriots Milhaud, Honegger, and Poulenc, among others.

Maurice Ravel (1875–1937) hints at his move away from Debussy by the historical references in the titles of his first two piano compositions—*Menuet antique* (1895), *Pavane pour une infante défunte* (Pavane for a Deceased Princess, 1899)—and in his last, *Le Tombeau de Couperin* (Memorial for Couperin, 1917). Although Ravel adopted some impressionist techniques, he was more attracted to clean melodic contours, distinct rhythms, and firm structures; his harmonies, while complex and sophisticated, are functional.

Ravel

In the Menuet from *Le Tombeau de Couperin* (NAWM 132), originally written for piano, Ravel achieved a classic simplicity of musical form, using conventional cadences to demarcate the short phrases and sections of the binary dance form. The orchestration is finely detailed: strings constantly change from *arco* (bow) to pizzicato or from a unison to a divided texture, not to mention special effects such as harmonics and muted passages. Mutes also mask the color of the horns and trumpets. Rather than the soft edges of

Le Tombeau de Couperin

▲ The opening page of Debussy's autograph manuscript for *Prélude à l'après-midi d'un faune*, with a dedication by the composer to Gaby Dupont dated 1899. This short score shows the intended instrumentation. The tempo is given as Assez lent, but the edition based on Debussy's conducting score of 1908–13 reads Très modéré. (*Robert Lehman Collection*)

impressionism, we hear well-defined phrases, contrapuntal lines, and a transparency that recalls Mozart more than Couperin.

Ravel's partiality for Classic forms is clearest in works such as the *Sonatine* (1905) for piano as well as in the various chamber pieces, which include a quartet (1903), a piano trio (1914), a sonata for violin and cello (1922), and one for violin and piano (1927). His most markedly impressionistic works for piano are the *Jeux d'eau* (1901), the five pieces titled *Miroirs* (1905), and the three titled *Gaspard de la nuit* (1908). Other impressionist works are the orchestral suite *Rapsodie espagnole* (1907) and the ballet *Daphnis et Chloé* (1909–11).

Like Debussy, Ravel was a brilliant colorist who orchestrated several of his own piano pieces (see NAWM 132). He also absorbed ideas from elsewhere, adapting them to his own use with as much assurance as he adapted impressionism. He used folk melodies from various countries in his *Chansons madécasses* (Songs of Madagascar, 1926), Viennese waltz rhythms in the "choreographic poem" *La Valse* (1920), jazz elements in the *Concerto for the Left Hand* (1930), and Spanish idioms in the rousing *Bolero* (1928), which became a musical best-seller.

Italian Opera

One of the most characteristic musical "isms" of the late nineteenth century was *verism* (*verismo*) in Italian opera. Literally "truthism," it is sometimes translated as "realism" or "naturalism." The librettos present everyday people in familiar situations acting violently under the impulse of primitive emotions. Veristic opera is the innocent grandparent of the television and movie thriller. Among the best examples of this genre are two works usually paired in performance, *Cavalleria rusticana* (Rustic Chivalry, 1890) by Pietro Mascagni (1863–1945) and *I Pagliacci* (The Clowns, 1892) by Ruggiero Leoncavallo (1858–1919). Though short-lived, verism had some parallels or repercussions in France and Germany, and its progeny still live in the repertory around the world.

Verismo

Only some of the operas of Giacomo Puccini (1858–1924) fall into this category. In such works as *Tosca* (1900) and *Il tabarro* (1918), Puccini achieved a musical style appropriate to the realistic libretto. Musical ideas grow out of the action, as if recitative suddenly sprouted melody. From a large harmonic palette—parallel chords, augmented triads, added sixths, whole-tone scales, chromatic alterations, all within a base of functional and even Wagnerian harmony—he applied the most suitable devices in a fluid succession that is sometimes seamless and sometimes abrupt. Puccini had a flair for representing swift action as well as for the lyrical pause. He paid great

Puccini

◄ Theatrical poster (1899) by Adolfo Hohenstein for Giacomo Puccini's *Tosca*, premiered in Rome in 1900. Illustrated is the highly dramatic scene at the end of Act II in which Tosca, having killed the malefactor Scarpia, places lighted candles beside his head and a crucifix on his chest. (*Milan, Museo Teatrale alla Scala*)

attention to mood, both psychological and external—the Japanese local color in *Madama Butterfly* (1904), for example, the Chinese flavor in *Turandot* (1926), and the aura of the Parisian Latin Quarter in *La Bohème* (1896). Most of all, Puccini was a successful eclectic who combined a late-Romantic taste for intense emotion with realism and exoticism.

POSTLUDE

In this chapter we have studied some of the most important composers and trends preceding the outbreak of the First World War. Foremost among the Germans were Mahler and Strauss. Mahler had inherited the whole Romantic tradition of Berlioz, Liszt, Wagner, and, of course, its Viennese branch consisting of Beethoven, Schubert, Brahms, and Bruckner. A restless experimenter with wide-ranging interests, he expanded the symphony, the symphony-oratorio, and the orchestral lied; at the same time he beat a path to a new age by influencing the Viennese composers of the next generation—Schoenberg, Berg, and Webern. Whereas Mahler essentially adhered to the traditional symphony and its musical architecture, even while admitting many programmatic and operatic elements, Strauss attached himself to the more radical Romantic genre of the symphonic poem and eventually even dared to write operas in the wake of Wagner's domination of that genre.

The rise of nationalism stimulated new bursts of native musical creativity in many countries, Russia and France being among the most significant for later developments in Western music. In Russia Musorgsky emerged as the most original and influential of the group of five composers known as the Mighty Handful. In France a revival nurtured by several factors and traditions, not the least of which was a renewed interest in its own great musical past, produced a number of fine composers. France's musical revival also deposited on the doorstep of the twentieth century a genius of the first rank—Debussy—who blazed a new trail that enabled composers of all nationalities to escape from the long shadows of influence cast by Wagner and the Romantics.

20

The European Mainstream in the Twentieth Century

Europe between the two world wars (1918–39) enjoyed a peace made uneasy by increasing international tension. The Austro-Hungarian Empire was split into independent states—Austria, Czechoslovakia, Hungary, Yugoslavia, and Romania—where democracy mostly gave way to authoritarian rule. In Russia the Bolsheviks—radical Marxist revolutionaries—had seized power by 1917 and set up a dictatorship. Fearing a similar "proletarian" revolution, Benito Mussolini and the Fascists took over the Italian government in 1922. In Germany, Adolf Hitler and the National Socialists (Nazis) took advantage of the weakened Weimar Republic (1918–33) to turn the chancellorship, which Hitler had won in a legitimate election, into a dictatorship. The Nazis, in a fierce arousal of latent anti-Semitism, passed laws to deprive people of Jewish origin of their citizenship and all other rights, driving many intellectuals, writers, artists, composers, and scholars into exile. The Spanish Civil War (1936–39) and its aftermath, the totalitarian rule of Francisco Franco, practically closed that country off from the rest of the world until the mid-1970s.

These movements and events tended to isolate even neighboring areas from each other: Germany from Austria, Hungary from Austria and its Slavic neighbors, and these from Russia. England and France distanced themselves from Italy and the German-speaking countries, and the Western Hemisphere from Europe. As we will see, the course of music history followed suit, inevitably branching into divergent paths.

Although bold musical innovations marked the period 1914–30, the seeds for many of the changes were sown earlier. Musorgsky and Debussy had cultivated a harmony of static blocks that eliminated the tension and relaxation of dominant and tonic, dissonance and resolution. Others had questioned the validity of themes and development and explored different ways to focus compositions, such as unifying chords or pitch collections, or contrasting tone colors. Non-Western musics and the traditional (folk) music of Eastern Europe offered composers resources free of such familiar constraints as fixed meters and conventional tonal relationships. "Exotic" scales, such as the pentatonic and whole tone, lacked the leading tones that demanded particular melodic and chordal successions. The traditional music of Eastern Europe and Russia offered modal melodies and polyphonic practices that did not fit Western conventions. Complex meters, alternating duple and triple, introduced novel rhythmic irregularities. Composers also imitated the open form of performance-oriented music that had no clear beginning or end, such as Indonesian and other traditional musics.

Technological factors also played a significant role in musical changes throughout the interwar period. Recordings, radio, and eventually television spawned an unparalleled growth in the size of the audience listening to music, and these new technologies tended to bring contemporary music closer to ordinary people. Leading composers were invited to provide background music for films, theater, and dance. Once wider audiences were within reach, Germany cultivated *Gebrauchsmusik*—workaday music—for use by school groups or other amateurs. Similar movements arose elsewhere, such as "proletarian" music in the Soviet republics. Hungary, under the musical leadership of composer Zoltán Kodály, sought to make music serve the people, and set up an educational program based on folksong, a method that later spread to other countries, especially the United States. Technology also facilitated the collection and preservation of folk idioms from the more remote corners of the world, thereby immeasurably increasing the available vocabulary of musical sounds. Then, too, technological advances spurred the neo-Classic movement (see below) by bringing about widespread dissemination of the standard repertory from Vivaldi to Prokofiev, as well as other "serious" music from the more remote past to the very present.

After the war, government censorship in Russia and Germany attempted to "protect" the public from the new, more sophisticated art music. In Poland, the Nazi occupation drove all artistic activity underground between 1939 and 1945, when a musical renaissance began, only to be bent in ideological directions during the Stalinist period from 1949 to 1956. Elsewhere, the gulf between what the concert-going public would tolerate and the output of avant-garde composers continued to widen, especially after 1950.

It is not practical to deal with this complex century of European music chronologically. Partly because of the wars and political movements, different regions and individual nations pursued widely divergent trends and styles. However, certain practices—such as art music borrowing folk materials—crossed geographical boundaries. In this discussion national movements that exploited their own **Ethnic Contexts**, particularly in central and Eastern Europe, are considered first. Then we look at similar trends in countries within **The Soviet Orbit**, and in **England** and **Germany**. Next we take up **Neo-Classicism in France**, essentially an anti-Romantic trend. Finally we turn to **Stravinsky**, whose influence pervaded Europe and America into the 1950s. The innovations of Arnold Schoenberg, who embarked on his radical course early in the twentieth century, were not much evident until after World War II. Consequently, his music will be discussed in the next chapter.

Ethnic Contexts

The distinctive character of ethnic music in central and eastern Europe became an important resource for composers in the first half of the twentieth century. Recording technology and speedier communication made the differences among traditional cultures evident to a wider public. Recording also led to more complete documentation of ethnic music than had been possible previously. Researchers in the field no longer collected folk music by clumsily transcribing it into conventional notation but instead recorded it on disks and tapes; then they analyzed the collected specimens using techniques developed in the new discipline of ethnomusicology. Rather than trying to absorb folk idioms into more or less conventional styles by smoothing out their "irregularities" and making them fit the rules of art music, composers came to respect their uniqueness and drew inspiration from these idioms to create new styles, while at the same time expanding their own tonal and rhythmic vocabularies.

Central Europe saw some of the earliest efforts toward a scientific study of folk music. Janáček's pioneering work in the Czecho-Slovak region (see page 449) was soon followed by that of two Hungarian scholar-composers, Béla Bartók (1881–1945) and Zoltán Kodály (1882–1967).

Bartók

Béla Bartók made important contributions as a music ethnologist, performer, and composer. He published nearly two thousand traditional tunes, chiefly from Hungary, Romania, and Yugoslavia—only a small part of what he had collected in expeditions ranging over central Europe, Turkey, and North Africa. He wrote books and articles on this music and arranged and created original works based on traditional tunes. He cultivated a style that fused, more intimately than ever before, folk elements with highly developed

◄ Béla Bartók in 1907, recording Slovakian folksongs on an acoustic cylinder machine in the Hungarian village of Zobordarázs. (*Collection of Ferenc Bónis*)

techniques of art music. He was also a virtuoso pianist who taught piano at the Budapest Academy of Music from 1907 to 1934. His *Mikrokosmos* (1926–37)—153 piano pieces in six books of graded difficulty—remains a work of great pedagogical value that also summarizes Bartók's own style and presents in microcosm the development of European music in the first third of the twentieth century. Finally, he was one of the composers active between 1910 and 1945 whose music has endured.

Bartók first manifested a personal style about 1908, shortly after he became interested in traditional songs. Compositions from this period include the First Quartet (1908), the one-act opera *Duke Bluebeard's Castle* (1911), and the *Allegro barbaro* for piano. Like many other twentieth-century composers, Bartók often treated the piano more as an instrument of percussion than as a provider of tuneful melodies and full-textured harmonies (which the Romantics had done). By 1917, the year he wrote the Second Quartet, he had thoroughly absorbed the influences from late Romanticism and impressionism into a combination of characteristic rhythmic vigor, exuberant imagination, and elemental folk qualities. His compositions of the next ten years show him pushing toward the limits of dissonance and tonal ambiguity, reaching the furthest point with his two Violin Sonatas of 1922 and 1923.

Bartók's early works

The later works of Bartók are the most widely known. The Second Violin Concerto (1938) and the Concerto for Orchestra (1943) represent masterpieces in large form. Other works of the late period are the Fifth and Sixth Quartets (1934, 1939), the *Mikrokosmos,* the *Music for Strings, Percussion, and Celesta* (1936), the Sonata for Two Pianos and Percussion (1937), the Divertimento for string orchestra (1939), and the Third Piano Concerto (his last completed composition, 1945).

Bartók's late works

Bartók's style

Bartók combined contrapuntal textures, thematic development, and sensitivity to the purely sonorous value of chords in a way that is true to the Western musical heritage. With these he blended melodic lines derived from or inspired by eastern European traditional music. Powerful motoric rhythms are characteristically inflected by irregular meters and offbeat accents. His intense drive toward expression is always balanced by a strong formal design. His textures may be prevailingly homophonic or made up of fiercely independent contrapuntal lines, including free use of imitative, fugal, and canonic techniques (as in No. 145 of the *Mikrokosmos* or the first movement of *Music for Strings, Percussion, and Celesta*). Frequently, one or more of the interweaving lines is enriched by parallel voices moving in chord streams.

Bartók's harmony

Bartók's harmony is in part an incidental result of contrapuntal movement. It develops from the character of the melodies, which may be based on pentatonic, whole-tone, modal, or irregular scales (including those found in traditional music) as well as the regular diatonic and chromatic scales. All kinds of chords appear, from triads to combinations built on fourths and other more complex constructions. Bartók often gave pungency to a chord by adding dissonant major or minor seconds (see Example 20.1a). Sometimes seconds are piled up in tone clusters, as in the Piano Sonata, the First Piano Concerto (Example 20.1b), and the slow movement of the Second Concerto.

EXAMPLE 20.1　Examples of Bartók's Chords with Seconds and Tone Clusters

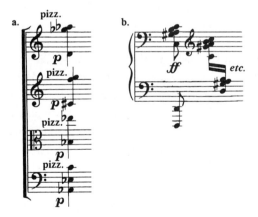

Bartók's tonal organization

Most of Bartók's music is tonal in the sense that a fundamental key center recurs, though it may be obscured for considerable stretches by either modal or chromatic means, or both. Occasionally, and especially in the works of the 1920s, Bartók wrote simultaneously on two or more harmonic planes—a procedure that resulted in so-called *polytonality*—but he did not aim systematically at negating tonality. Moreover, though he sometimes composed a theme that included up to twelve different tones in a row (as in the first movement of the Second Violin Concerto), or otherwise used all the notes of the chromatic scale in a single phrase (as in the opening of the Third and Fourth Quartets), he never systematically used Schoenberg's serial technique

XIII. The *Temptation of Saint Anthony,* one of the scenes from the Isenheim altarpiece by Matthias Grünewald (d. 1528). Paul Hindemith's opera *Mathis der Maler* (Matthias the Painter, 1934–35), first performed in Zurich just before World War II) is based on incidents from Grünewald's life. In Scene 6 of the opera (NAWM 136), the despairing painter is tormented by visions resembling the remarkably expressionistic demons in this panel from the sixteenth-century altarpiece.   (*COLMAR, MUSÉE D'UNTERLINDEN. ERICH LESSING / ART RESOURCE, NY*)

XIV. Ernst Ludwig Kirchner (1880–1938), *Street Scene,* 1914, revised 1925. Feathered hats were the sign of the streetwalker in Berlin. The bright red and yellow of the woman in the foreground and the pastel green of the one in the back contrast sharply with the black suits and hats of the men. All walk in isolation, avoiding human contact, an expressionist commentary on the social breakdown in urban communities. (*NIMATALLAH/ART RESOURCE, NY*)

(see Chapter 21). In some of Bartók's late works tonality is defined by relatively familiar procedures—particularly in the Third Piano Concerto, the Concerto for Orchestra, and the Second Violin Concerto. More commonly, however, the tonal field is less definite and the relations within it harder to grasp. The quartets, for example, are built around keynotes as points of departure and return, but the intervening relationships generally cannot be explained in explicitly tonal terms.

Bartók's *Music for Strings, Percussion, and Celesta*

*M*usic for Strings, Percussion, and Celesta (1936) illustrates several aspects of Bartók's approach to composition. The main tonality of the first and last movements is A, with an important secondary center at the augmented fourth D♯ (rather than the conventional dominant E). The second movement is in C, with a similar tritonic subcenter on F♯. The third movement (Adagio; see NAWM 133) is indeterminate, fluctuating in the region C–F♯ (the two keys equidistant on either side from the main tonality of the work). Some of the principal themes of the four movements and all of the final cadences clearly bring out this tritone relationship (Example 20.2), which is common in works by Bartók and many other twentieth-century composers.

EXAMPLE 20.2 Béla Bartók, *Music for Strings, Percussion, and Celesta*

IV. Theme

(bass: A Major I⁶₄)

Several other aspects of this work, including its use of "mirror form" and traditional ethnic styles, are discussed in NAWM 133. Example 20.3a shows a typical Serbo-Croatian folksong, whose idiom is imitated in the first measures of the Adagio molto, presented in 20.3b. Later in the movement instruments play in textures that imitate the sound of Bulgarian dance orchestras. Another ethnic influence may be heard in Bartók's adoption of the Bulgarian dance rhythm 2 + 3 + 3 in portions of this movement.

EXAMPLE 20.3 Relationships between Folk and Art Styles in Bartók, *Music for Strings, Percussion, and Celesta*

The music of Zoltán Kodály, more narrowly national, is less thorough-going than Bartók's in integrating folk and art styles. His most famous compositions, the *Psalmus hungaricus* for tenor soloist, chorus, and orchestra (1923) and the Singspiel *Háry János* (1926), are rich in allusions to plainchant, Renaissance and Baroque polyphony, and ethnic Hungarian music. Kodály's most pervasive influence has been in music education. His method of teaching children through a movable-*do* solfège system has been adopted in many primary schools in Europe and North America.

Kodály

The Soviet Orbit

National influences of various sorts were prominent in much music from the Soviet republics. But, despite official encouragement of nationalism, several leading composers—Sergey Prokofiev (1891–1953) and Dmitri Shostakovich (1906–1985) among them—cultivated international styles. So, although Prokofiev's *Scythian Suite* for orchestra (1916), his cantata *Alexander Nevsky* (originally a film score, 1938), and his opera *War and Peace* (1941), as well as Shostakovich's opera *Lady Macbeth* (1934) draw on Russian material, neither composer was a nationalist in the narrow meaning of the word.

Prokofiev lived outside Russia from 1918 to 1934. During these years abroad, he toured in Europe and America as a pianist and fulfilled a variety of commissions as a composer, among them an opera for Chicago, *The Love for Three Oranges* (1921), and ballets for the choreographer and impresario Sergei Diaghilev in Paris. His style did not change radically once he settled permanently in Russia, but he took to heart the charge of "formalism" that was directed at him, as well as at Shostakovich and others, by the Soviet critics and party leaders in 1948. By "formalism" critics meant music that did not celebrate the revolutionary ideology and its heroes nor reflect the working-class experience through an accessible "socialist realism." Prokofiev in his own defense said that he sincerely strove for a language that was clear and appealing (see vignette, page 470).

Prokofiev

Among Prokofiev's works, the *Classical* Symphony (1918) reveals some of his inventive mixing of earlier materials and formal plans in fresh contexts—melodies that are essentially tonal with wide skips and long sweeping lines, and triadic harmony full of strange inversions, unusual spacings, and jarring juxtapositions. The Third Piano Concerto (1921) is among the best of his early works; the symphonic suite *Lieutenant Kijé* (arranged from music for a film, 1934), the "symphonic fairy tale" *Peter and the Wolf* for narrator and orchestra (1936), and the ballet *Romeo and Juliet* (1935–36) have become widely popular.

Prokofiev's Symphonies No. 5 (1944) and No. 7 (1951–52) bear witness to his successful search for clear melody—they are triumphs of lyricism, without being saccharine or banal. He was fond of building excitement by repe-

Prokofiev on the Importance of Melody:

66 I have never questioned the importance of melody. I love melody, and I regard it as the most important element in music. I have worked on the improvement of its quality in my compositions for many years. To find a melody instantly understandable even to the uninitiated listener, and at the same time an original one, is the most difficult task for a composer. He is beset by a great multitude of dangers: he may fall into the trivial or the banal, or into the rehashing of something already written by him. In this respect, composition of complex melodies is much easier. It may also happen that a composer, fussing over his melody for a long time, and revising it, unwittingly makes it over-refined and complicated, and departs from simplicity. I fell into this trap, too, in the process of my work. 99

Prokofiev, Letter to Tikhon Khrennikov, Secretary of the Union of Composers, 1948, trans. William W. Austin, *Music in the 20th Century* (New York: Norton, 1966), pp. 459–60.

tition—a device that also allows his listeners to appreciate the richness of his novel subordinate ideas as they are played against the recurring main themes. He never ceased to pursue structural clarity and refinement, despite his admission that he had been infected by "formalism" in the West.

Shostakovich

Dmitri Shostakovich (1906–1985) broke upon the international musical scene at the age of nineteen with his First Symphony (1926), and although every one of his subsequent symphonies (he wrote fifteen altogether) was enthusiastically received, only the Fifth (1937) and Tenth (1953) have won a prominent place in the repertoire. He received his education and spent his entire career within the Soviet system, where he was treated generously, though he was not immune to official criticism. His opera *Lady Macbeth of Mtsensk*, which enjoyed some success in St. Petersburg (1934, then called Leningrad), New York, Cleveland, London, Prague, Zurich, and elsewhere, was withdrawn after being condemned in the Moscow newspaper *Pravda* in 1936. In Act IV, Scene 9 (NAWM 135), Katerina ("Lady Macbeth") and Sergey, who have murdered her husband, are marched off to Siberia with other prisoners; the passage displays the realistic and often satirical musical portrayal of violence and sex that offended the Soviet leaders.

Post-Soviet music

Although the Union of Soviet Socialist Republics did not break up until 1991, the state began to relax its control over culture well before that—in the 1970s and 1980s. Scores and recordings from western Europe and America were difficult to get, but a number of young composers managed to become familiar with pieces by avant-garde composers from outside the Soviet orbit.

The policy of *glasnost*, or openness, intensified the interest in foreign developments and permitted both Russian and Western audiences to become acquainted with composers who had been working quietly for decades without much official recognition. Although these creative efforts were not "post-

Shostakovich's Fifth Symphony

*S*ome considered the Fifth Symphony, because of its optimistic outlook, easy communicativeness, and boisterous finale, a concession to the "socialist realism" required by the Communist Party. But by any standards it is a masterpiece of symphonic composition, holding to the traditional architecture of the genre yet displaying both sweep and grandeur. It opens majestically with a two-measure canon in the strings on a theme with a French-overture rhythm, but the bold leaps and chromaticism take it out of the courtly atmosphere (Example 20.4). As the dotted rhythms continue in the lower strings, a soaring melody resembling those of Prokofiev takes the foreground in the violins. The second theme is subtly related to the opening by the expansion of both intervals and durations. A formal closing theme, when taken up by the piano (an instrument not heard until then), marks the beginning of a classic development section. This includes a march episode, which is very characteristic of Shostakovich. The remaining movements are a Scherzo (not so marked), a Largo for reduced orchestra, and an Allegro non troppo that fully utilizes the big orchestra. This symphony illustrates how Shostakovich welded the national heritage (coming largely through Tchaikovsky) to the main European tradition, the influence of Mahler being particularly evident.

EXAMPLE 20.4   Dmitri Shostakovich, Fifth Symphony: Moderato, measures 1–4

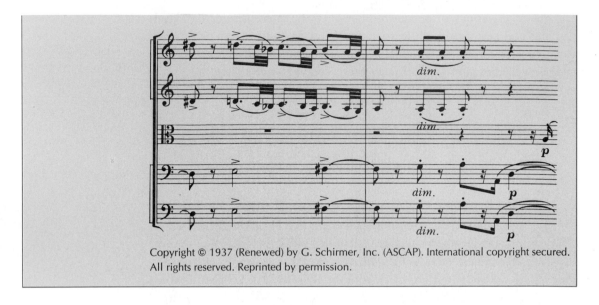

Soviet" in the chronological sense, they were so in spirit. Among the most notable are Alfred Schnittke and Sofia Gubaidulina.

Schnittke

Alfred Schnittke (b. 1934) spent almost all of his career in the Soviet Union, where he was known to the public chiefly for his film music, before taking up residence in Hamburg. His approach, by his own admission, is polystylistic—he incorporates music from the Baroque to the present, including his own earlier creations, as well as popular music. The Concerto Grosso No. 1 (1976–77) for two violins, harpsichord, prepared piano, and string orchestra recalls several Baroque genres: prelude, toccata, recitative, and cadenza. The harmonic idiom, however, is entirely modern. The fifth movement, Rondo, surrealistically juxtaposes gypsy-tango episodes against distortions of a main subject inspired by Corelli.

Gubaidulina

Sofia Gubaidulina (b. 1931), who was not well known in her own country and was not permitted to travel to the West before 1986, attained international stature shortly thereafter. Born and trained in the Tatar Republic, she moved to Moscow in 1954, when she began eight years of study at the national conservatory. Almost all her works have a spiritual dimension, and even the titles of her instrumental pieces reveal a Christian inspiration (*Introitus, In croce, Offertorium, Jubilatio, De profundis*).

The spiritual element is deeply rooted in Gubaidulina's sonata for violin and cello, *Rejoice!*, written in 1981 but not performed until 1988 in Finland. Its five movements are inspired by eighteenth-century devotional texts. The sonata, according to the composer, expresses the transcendence from ordinary reality to a state of joy, and relies particularly on the passage from a fundamental note to its harmonics to embody this transition. The fifth movement (NAWM 134), inscribed with the text, "Listen to the still small voice within," is a study in chromatics, tremolos, and harmonics, particularly glissandos

C H R O N O L O G Y	
1900 Debussy, *Nocturnes* (1899) Sigmund Freud (1856–1939), *The Interpretation of Dreams* The Wright brothers, Wilbur (1867–1912) and Orville (1871–1948), first successful airplane flight (1903) Puccini, *Madama Butterfly* (1904) Strauss, *Salome* (1905) *Bartók, First String Quartet; Mahler, *Das Lied von der Erde* (1908) *Vaughan Williams, *Fantasia on a Theme of Thomas Tallis* (1909) **1910** *Stravinsky, *Le Sacre du printemps*; Marcel Proust (1871–1922), *Remembrance of Things Past* (1913) World War I (1914–18) Albert Einstein (1879–1955), general theory of relativity (1916) *Prokofiev, *Classical* Symphony (1918) **1920** T. S. Eliot (1888–1965), *The Waste Land* (1922)	*Milhaud, *La Création du monde* (1924) International Musicological Society founded at Basel; Charles Lindbergh, solo flight across the Atlantic (1927) *Weill, premiere of *The Threepenny Opera* (1928) New York stock market crash; worldwide depression (1929) **1930** Franklin D. Roosevelt (1882–1945), president of the United States; Adolf Hitler (1889–1945), chancellor of Germany (1933) *Hindemith, *Mathis der Maler* (See Plate XIII, facing page 466); American Musicological Society founded in New York (1934) *Shostakovich, Fifth Symphony; Pablo Picasso (1881–1973), *Guernica* (1937) **1940** World War II (1939–45) **1950** *Stravinsky, *The Rake's Progress* (1951) **1960** *Britten, *War Requiem* (1961)

from low fundamental notes in the cello to their higher harmonics. Typically, Gubaidulina did not rely on any underlying system or model for this composition, but on a series of intuitive choices from her rich personal store of resources.

England

The foremost English composer in the first half of the twentieth century was Ralph Vaughan Williams (1872–1958), whose works include nine symphonies and other orchestral pieces, songs, operas, and a great many choral pieces. Amid all the variety of dimensions and forms, Vaughan Williams's music drew inspiration from both national sources—English literature and traditional song, hymnody, and earlier English composers such as Purcell and Tallis—and the European traditions of Bach and Handel, Debussy and Ravel. From 1904 to 1906 Vaughan Williams served as musical editor of the new *English Hymnal*. Concerning this experience he wrote long afterward in his *Musical Autobiography*: "Two years of close association with some of the best (as well as some of the worst) tunes in the world was a better musical edu-

Vaughan Williams

cation than any amount of sonatas and fugues." He modestly neglected to add that he himself composed a half-dozen new tunes, one of which was the well-known hymn *For All the Saints* (Example 20.5a).

EXAMPLE 20.5   Examples of Themes by Ralph Vaughan Williams

a. Hymn tune, *Sine nomine*

b. *Pastoral* Symphony, Fourth Movement

c. *Pastoral* Symphony, Third Movement

d. *Pastoral* Symphony, First Movement

Reprinted by permission of G. Schirmer, Inc. on behalf of J. Curwen & Sons, Ltd.

Among Vaughan Williams's important early works is the *Fantasia on a Theme of Thomas Tallis* (1909) for double string orchestra and string quartet. Here the antiphonal sonorities and the rich texture of unadorned triads in parallel motion are heard within a modal framework that also characterized many of his later compositions. The *London* Symphony (1914, revised 1920) is a loving evocation of the sounds and atmosphere of the city, a program symphony in the same sense as Mendelssohn's *Italian.* In Vaughan Williams's *Pastoral* Symphony (1922) a wordless melisma in unbarred free rhythm for solo soprano appears at the beginning and in shortened form at the close of the last movement (Example 20.5b). It exemplifies a type of melody with gapped scales—here of pentatonic character—that often occurs in his music. Equally characteristic and folklike is the trumpet tune in the trio of the third movement (Example 20.5c). His contrapuntal treatment of parallel chords is especially effective (Example 20.5d).

Britten

Benjamin Britten (1913–1976), the most prolific and well-known English composer of the mid–twentieth century, is distinguished especially for his choral compositions, songs, and operas. Among the choral works are *A Boy Was Born* (1935), *A Ceremony of Carols* (1942), and *Spring* Symphony (1947). His most celebrated operas are *Peter Grimes* (1945) and *The Turn of the Screw* (1954). Britten's hallmarks are simplicity dressed up in orchestral finery, and adherence to tonal and diatonic means colored with modal and chromatic elements.

One of Britten's most acclaimed works, the *War Requiem* (1961), received worldwide attention following its first performance at Coventry Cathedral, which had just been newly erected beside the bombed-out shell of the old cathedral. An impressive, large work for soloists, chorus, boys' choir, and orchestra, it is a setting of the Latin text of the Requiem Mass alternating with verses by Wilfred Owen, a young English soldier who was killed in France in 1918. The music incorporates many modern features in a very individual way.

Germany

Germany, the country that harbored the most aggressive nationalism in the years between the two wars, had been at the center of music developments for so long that it hardly needed to assert itself as a musical culture. Yet the Nazis did try to enforce a kind of national purity. This policy led, in the end, to the dissolution of its creative forces, as some of its most talented musicians, whether Jewish or not, took refuge abroad.

Hindemith

Paul Hindemith (1895–1963) was important not only as a composer but also as a teacher and theorist. His book, *The Craft of Musical Composition*, presents both a general system of composition and an analytical method. His work as a teacher—at the Berlin School of Music (1927–37), the Yale University School of Music (1940–53), and the University of Zurich (after 1953)—influenced generations of musicians and composers.

Hindemith thought of himself first as a practicing musician. An experienced solo, orchestral, and ensemble player of the violin and viola, he learned to play many other instruments as well. As a composer he represented a mid-twentieth-century link in the German cosmopolitan line of Beethoven, Schumann, and Brahms; additional influences in his work came from Bach, Handel, Schütz, and the German sixteenth-century lied composers. But, disturbed by the widening gulf between composers and an increasingly passive public in the late 1920s and early 1930s, Hindemith undertook to compose *Gebrauchsmusik*—music for use, as distinguished from music for its own sake. For example, much of Hindemith's music was composed for teaching purposes. The title *Klaviermusik: Übung in drei Stücken* (Piano Music: Three Practice Pieces, 1925) is reminiscent of Bach's *Clavier Übung*, and *The Well-Tempered Keyboard* served as a model for Hindemith's *Ludus tonalis* (Tonal Play, 1942) for piano. Subtitled "Studies in Counterpoint, Tonal Organization, and Piano Playing," *Ludus* consists of twelve fugues, one in each key, with modulating interludes; the whole set is framed by a Prelude (C–F♯) and Postlude (F♯–C).

**Mathis
der Maler**

Hindemith's works from the 1930s display a quality of almost Romantic warmth, along with less dissonant linear counterpoint than he used in his earlier works and more systematic tonal organization. Compositions from this decade include the opera *Mathis der Maler* (Matthias the Painter, 1934–35, first performed in Zurich, 1938) and the symphony *Mathis der Maler* (1934), probably the best known of all Hindemith's works, composed while he was working on the libretto of the opera. Hindemith's libretto of *Mathis der Maler* is based on the life of Matthias Grünewald, the painter of the famous Isenheim altarpiece (see Plate XIII, facing page 466). Composed in Germany while Hindemith was under attack from the Nazi government, the opera examines the role of the artist in times of stress. In the libretto (Scene 6; see NWM 136), Mathis leaves his studio to join the rebellion against the nobles (Peasants' War of 1525). In despair over the defeat of the peasants, Mathis is tormented by visions resembling the strange figures in the altarpiece. The restless, tortured chromatic line of the melody is a fine example of German expressionism (Example 20.6; for discussion of expressionism, see page 495, and window, pages 502–3).

EXAMPLE 20.6 Paul Hindemith, *Mathis der Maler*: Scene 6

Hindemith's compositions after 1940 include the Fifth and Sixth Quartets (1943, 1945), the *Symphonic Metamorphoses* on themes of Weber (1943), a "requiem" on words of Walt Whitman (*When lilacs last in the dooryard bloom'd*), and other choral works. The opera *Die Harmonie der Welt* (The Harmony of the World) was begun in the 1930s but set aside when the composer came to the United States because there seemed no chance of having it performed. In 1952 he composed a three-movement orchestral symphony on the subject and then continued work on the opera, which was finally presented at Munich in 1957.

Kurt Weill (1900–1950) had two careers, one as an opera composer in Berlin and another as a Broadway composer in New York. In Berlin he embraced a kind of *Gebrauchsmusik* in the sense that he did not aim to produce masterpieces but rather to promote social programs and ideologies, entertaining common people rather than elite intellectuals. He collaborated with a number of playwrights, most notably Bertolt Brecht, who supplied the text for the two operas that made Weill's reputation: *Aufstieg und Fall der Stadt Mahagonny* (Rise and Fall of the City of Mahagonny, 1927–29, revised 1929–31) and *Die Dreigroschenoper* (The Threepenny Opera, 1928).

Weill

The most famous product of the Brecht-Weill collaboration remains *Die Dreigroschenoper* (The Threepenny Opera), based on the text of Gay's *Beggar's Opera* (see page 297 and NAWM 90), although only one air was borrowed from Pepusch's score. At the premiere in Berlin in 1928, the orchestra consisted of eight musicians who played twenty-one instruments. The cast starred

Die Dreigroschenoper

Weill's *Mahagonny*

Weill's opera *Mahagonny* was first performed in 1930 at Leipzig rather than Berlin, where it would have been found too shocking. Its form was that of a number opera: lyrical scenes for individual characters, with some choruses and ensembles. The pit orchestra included two saxophones, piano, banjo, and bass guitar as well as winds and timpani, while three saxophones, zither, a bandoneon (accordion), strings, and brass played in the stage orchestra. The intent is satirical and the means include sophisticated takeoffs on American popular songs. The plot revolves around several fugitives from justice who build Mahagonny, a place dedicated to pleasure, free of legal or moral taboos, but they soon discover their city is a hell rather than a paradise on earth. Many of the theater people in Weill's circle sat on the political left and were bent on exposing the failures of capitalism, which the decadent city of Mahagonny exemplified.

▲ Lotte Lenya in a scene from Kurt Weill's *The Threepenny Opera*, New York production, mid-1950s. (*Photo by Neil Fujita, 1956. Yale University Music Library. Used by permission*)

an unknown actress, Lotte Lenya, whom Weill had married in 1926 and who was to become his favorite interpreter and after his death a champion of his work. The music parodied rather than imitated American hit songs, which were then the rage in Europe. Weill intended the surrealistic juxtaposition of the eighteenth-century ballad texts, European dance music, and American jazz to be provocative as well as appealing; he also wanted to explore "new expressive possibilities for simple human actions and relationships."[1]

The original production ran for over two years, and within five years of the premiere *Dreigroschenoper* enjoyed more than ten thousand performances in nineteen languages. It was banned from the stage as decadent by the Nazis in 1933, when Weill left for Paris; soon after that he emigrated to the United States and devoted himself mostly to musical comedies and operettas. The most successful were *Knickerbocker Holiday* (1938), *Lady in the Dark* (1940), *One Touch of Venus* (1943), *Street Scene* (1946), the college opera *Down in the Valley*, and the musical tragedy *Lost in the Stars* (about apartheid in South Africa, 1948). He wrote occasional "art music," such as his *Four Songs of Walt Whitman* (1942).

1. Kurt Weill, "Korrespondenz über *Dreigroschenoper*," *Anbruch* 11 (January 1929):24, trans. in Stephen Hinton, "*Neue Sachlichkeit*, Surrealism, *Gebrauchsmusik*" in *A New Orpheus, Essays on Kurt Weill*, ed. Kim H. Kowalke (New Haven: Yale University Press, 1986), p. 74.

Neo-Classicism in France

The term *neo-Classicism* is something of a misnomer. Composers who took part in this movement did not necessarily go back only to Classic genres, styles, and forms; they also imitated earlier models from the Baroque and Renaissance periods. Prokofiev's *Classical* Symphony (1918) was truly neo-Classic, a parody of a Haydn symphony and, as with most parodies, the intention was partly humorous, partly nostalgic. But Stravinsky's "neo-Classic" *Dumbarton Oaks* Concerto (1938; see page 489) was actually neo-Baroque because it took as its model the Vivaldi-Bach concerto grosso. A great many other mid-twentieth-century works hark back to earlier procedures in less obvious ways. Beethoven often lurks behind Hindemith's instrumental works, for example. Many composers tried to absorb the more experimental elements from previous decades while maintaining their continuity with tradition. They held to some recognizably familiar features of the past—such as tonal centers (defined or alluded to, often in quite new ways), melodic shape, and goal-oriented movement of musical ideas—while incorporating fresh and unfamiliar elements. Arthur Honegger, Darius Milhaud, Francis Poulenc, and Igor Stravinsky illustrate these trends in France.

Honegger

Arthur Honegger (1892–1955) excelled in music of dynamic action and graphic gesture, expressed in short-breathed melodies, strong ostinato rhythms, bold colors, and dissonant harmonies. Born in France of Swiss parentage, he resided in Paris after 1913. Honegger's "symphonic movement" *Pacific 231,* in which he aimed not to imitate the sound but to translate into music the visual and physical impression of a speeding locomotive, was hailed in 1923 as a sensational piece of modernistic program music. His principal orchestral works are five symphonies (1931–51).

Honegger became an instant celebrity with the concert performance in 1923 of his oratorio *King David,* which had appeared two years earlier in an original stage version. This work signals the rise of an important new genre, a compound of oratorio and opera. *King David* may be popular because the choruses, written for amateurs, are easy to sing, the rhythmic and formal patterns, conventional; the few harmonic audacities are mingled with familiar consonant diatonic writing; and the action is illustrated pictorially by vivid music that captures some of the aura of the Bach Passions.

Milhaud

Darius Milhaud (1892–1974), a native of Aix-en-Provence in southern France, created a gracious memorial to his native region in the *Suite provençale* for orchestra (1937), which incorporates melodies from works by the early-eighteenth-century composer André Campra. Milhaud produced an immense quantity of music, composing with a facility rare in the twentieth century. His works include piano pieces, chamber music (his eighteen string quartets are especially notable), suites, sonatas, symphonies, film music, ballets, songs, cantatas, and operas. A great contrast exists between the frivolity, mockery, and satire of the ballets—*Le Boeuf sur le toit* (The Ox on the Roof,

1919) and *Le Train bleu* (The Blue Train, 1924)—and the cosmic earnestness of the opera-oratorio *Christophe Colomb* (1928) or the religious devotion of the (Jewish) *Sacred Service* (1947). Milhaud did not subscribe to theories or systems; rather, he was receptive to many kinds of stimuli, which he spontaneously converted to musical expression: Brazilian folk melodies and rhythms, for example, in the orchestral dances (later arranged for piano) *Saudades do Brasil* (Souvenirs of Brazil, 1920–21). Saxophones, ragtime syncopations, and the blues found their way into the ballet *La Création du monde* (The Creation of the World, 1924). Milhaud's music is essentially lyrical, a blend of simplicity and ingenuity, clear and logical in form, and addressed to the listener as objective statement, not personal confession.

Milhaud's polytonality

Like many composers of his time, Milhaud frequently employed polytonality, as in Example 20.7a, where two lines of melody and planes of harmony, each in a distinct and different key, sound simultaneously. We see another example from the slow movement of the Twelfth Quartet (1945), as shown in Example 20.7b: in the first two measures the four instruments trace triads in four different keys (starting from the first violins: A–G–D–E♭).

EXAMPLE 20.7   Polytonality in Works of Darius Milhaud

a. *Saudades do Brasil*, I: No. 4, *Copacabaña*

b. String Quartet No. 12: Second Movement

Saudades: © 1922, renewed 1950 by Editions Max Eschig. Used by permission of the publisher. Sole representative U.S.A., Theodore Presser Company. Quartet: © 1948 by Editions Salabert. Reprinted by permission of G. Schirmer, Inc.

The compositions of Francis Poulenc (1899–1963), many in small forms, revel in an ingratiating harmonic idiom; they are infused with the grace and wit of the Parisian popular chansons, and wed satirical mimicry to fluent melody. His comic opera *Les Mamelles de Tiresias* (The Breasts of Tiresias, 1940) is a good example. His *Concert champêtre* (Pastoral Concerto) for harpsichord or piano and small orchestra (1928) evokes the spirit of Rameau and Domenico Scarlatti. Among his other compositions are a Mass in G for chorus a cappella (1937), several motets, other choral works, and numerous songs. His three-act opera *Dialogues des Carmelites* (Dialogues of the Carmelites, 1956), a serious, effective setting of an unusually fine libretto by Georges Bernanos, has entered the repertory of many opera houses.

Poulenc

Stravinsky

In the course of a long career, Igor Stravinsky (1882–1971) not only participated in, but also actually began, some of the most significant musical developments of the first half of the twentieth century. As a result, his influence on three generations of composers has been enormous. Born in Russia in 1882, he went to Paris in 1911, moved to Switzerland in 1914, to Paris again in 1920, to California in 1940, and lived in New York after 1969 until his death in 1971. Stravinsky's principal early compositions include three ballets commissioned by Sergei Diaghilev (1872–1929), the founder and director of the Russian Ballet, which reigned in Paris from 1909 to 1929 as a European institution that attracted many leading artists. For Diaghilev and Paris, Stravinsky wrote *The Fire Bird* (1910), *Petrushka* (1911), and *Le Sacre du printemps* (The Rite of Spring, subtitled "Scenes of Pagan Russia," 1913).

Career

The Fire Bird stems from the Russian nationalist tradition and has the exotic orientalism and sensuous orchestration of Stravinsky's teacher, Rimsky-Korsakov. *Petrushka*, rich in Russian traditional songs and polyphonic textures, brings a touch of *verismo* to its carnival scenes and characters, while the alert rhythms, bright orchestral colors, and lean counterpoint tested paths that Stravinsky would later explore further. *Le Sacre*, the most famous composition of the early twentieth century, provoked a notorious riot at its premiere in Paris (see vignette, page 484), though in the long run this and the other two ballets for Diaghilev were to enjoy more public favor as concert works than Stravinsky's later compositions.

Early works

Le Sacre struck listeners as the height of primitivism; one of Stravinsky's associates called it "a pastorale of the pre-historic world." Its novelty consisted not only in the rhythms but even more in the previously unheard orchestral effects and chordal combinations, and in the ruthless logic and elemental power with which all these were combined.

Sacre du printemps

Despite a large number of folksong quotations in *Le Sacre*, the audience

*P*etrushka contains many stylistic ingredients that remain identified with Stravinsky. The opening scene of the ballet, a fair in St. Petersburg during the climactic week of carnival, presents blocks of static harmony against which repetitive melodic and rhythmic patterns shift abruptly as the spotlight draws attention from the general scene to particular groups of dancers, each given its characteristic music: a band of tipsy revelers, an organ grinder with a dancer, a music-box player with another dancer, the puppet theater. Seemingly unconnected musical events succeed each other without transition, and only the frequent return of the opening music (Example 20.8) makes the scene a unit.

EXAMPLE 20.8   Igor Stravinsky, *Petrushka*: First scene

The Russian and popular carnival atmosphere is enhanced throughout the ballet by the quotation and elaboration of several folk tunes. Rather than working these quotations into artful arrangements, as previous Russian composers had done, Stravinsky restored them to their ethnic environment. For example, the Easter song from the Smolensk region that accompanies the drunken merrymakers, taken from Rimsky-Korsakov's 1877 collection of traditional songs, avoids the dominant-tonic harmony of Rimsky's version; Stravinsky rearranged the song to sound like folk heterophony, in which voices sing in parallel fifths and octaves (Example 20.9), often against drones. Similarly the Russian Dance and Song of St. John's Eve in the duet between the Moor and the Ballerina recall a Balkan improvising orchestra, the winds and strings playing rapid repetitive figurations, while the harps imitate the plucked and strumming sounds of a balalaika ensemble.

EXAMPLE 20.9   Igor Stravinsky, *Petrushka*: Second part, Easter Song

The notorious *Petrushka* broken chord (Example 20.10) near the opening of the second scene (Petrushka's room) can be explained as a juxtaposition of two tonalities, an interpretation Stravinsky himself once offered. More recently scholars have acknowledged the passage as one of many uses by Stravinsky of the octatonic scale that alternates whole tones and semitones—*C–C♯–D♯–E–F♯–G–A–A♯*—with the *D♯* and *A* omitted. *Petrushka* also hints at the rhythmic innovations that will be so striking in *Le Sacre*—for example, at the end of the third scene, where the meter changes from $\frac{4}{8}$ to $\frac{5}{8}$ to $\frac{6}{8}$ to $\frac{5}{8}$, etc., and silences take the place of expected downbeats.

EXAMPLE 20.10   Igor Stravinsky, *Petrushka*, Opening of Second scene

was put off by certain features in both the music and the scenario, which calls for the sacrifice of an adolescent girl chosen by her ancient tribe to marry the sun god; in order to save the earth, she must dance herself to death. The most unusual passage (Example 20.11) is in the second scene, the *Danse des adolescentes* (Dance of the Adolescent Girls, NAWM 137). The lower strings, divided, play the equivalent of an E-major triad, while the upper strings, also divided, sound a first-inversion seventh chord on E♭. The barring is regular

EXAMPLE 20.11   Igor Stravinsky, *Le Sacre du printemps: Dance of the Adolescent Girls, Augurs of Spring*

**Stravinsky Recalls the First Performance
of *Le Sacre du printemps*, May 29, 1913:**

❝ That the first performance of *Le Sacre du printemps* was attended
by a scandal must be known to everybody. Strange as it may seem,
however, I was unprepared for the explosion myself. The reactions of
the musicians who came to the orchestra rehearsals were without inti-
mation of it and the stage spectacle did not appear likely to precipitate
a riot. . . .

Mild protest against the music could be heard from the very beginning of the performance. Then, when the curtain opened on the group
of knock-kneed and long-braided Lolitas jumping up and down [*Danse
des adolescentes*], the storm broke. Cries of "*Ta gueule*" ["Shut up!"] came
from behind me. I heard Florent Schmitt shout "*Taisez-vous garces du
seizième*" ["Be quiet, you bitches of the sixteenth"]; the *garces* of the
sixteenth arrondissement [the most fashionable residential district of
Paris] were, of course, the most elegant ladies in Paris. The uproar
continued, however, and a few minutes later I left the hall in a rage. . . .
I arrived in a fury backstage, where I saw Diaghilev switching the house
lights off and on in a last effort to quiet the hall. For the rest of the
performance I stood in the wings behind Nijinsky holding the tails of
his jacket, while he stood on a chair shouting numbers to the dancers,
like a coxswain [to help the dancers keep track of the steps, as the
commotion in the audience drowned out the sound of the
orchestra]. ❞

Stravinsky in *Expositions and Developments* (New York: Doubleday, 1962), pp. 159–64.

but marked with an extraordinary pattern of syncopations and accents, these
being reinforced by eight horns doubling the notes of the strings. The accents
regroup the eighth notes as follows: $9 + 2 + 6 + 3 + 4 + 5 + 3$, destroying
any feeling of metrical regularity. Yet while the spectator-listener is utterly
disoriented metrically and rhythmically, the music is cleverly conceived for
ballet, since the passage makes an eight-measure period and the dancers can
continue to count four-measure phrases. The electrifying results were more
than a genteel Parisian audience in 1913 could tolerate!

1913–23

The forced economy of wartime was partly responsible for Stravinsky's
turn in the years 1913 to 1923 from the large orchestra toward small combinations of instruments to accompany stage works. For *L'Histoire du soldat*
(The Soldier's Tale, 1918) he called for solo instruments in pairs (violin and
bass, clarinet and bassoon, cornet and trombone) and a battery of percussion

played by one person. In *Les Noces* (The Wedding, 1917–23), he wrote for four pianos and percussion. *Pulcinella* (1919–20) requires a small orchestra with strings divided into concertino and ripieno groups. The Octet for Wind Instruments (1922–23) was also part of this trend. *Ragtime* (see illustration, page 489) and *Piano Rag Music* were early examples of the composer's fascination with jazz (followed up in the *Ebony Concerto* of 1945), an interest reflected also in the instrumentation and rhythms of *L'Histoire.*

In the works between the Octet and the opera *The Rake's Progress* (1951), Stravinsky adopted the neo-Classic approach, revealing his preference for balance, coolness, objectivity, and absolute (in contrast to program) music. At the same time, he turned away from Russian folk music and back to earlier Western art music as a source for imitation, quotation, or allusion. The work that symbolized the transformation of his style around 1920 was *Pulcinella*, a ballet for which Diaghilev asked Stravinsky to arrange some eighteenth-

Stravinsky's neo-Classicism

➤ "Painted maiden"; costume sketch by Nicholas Roerich for the original production of Stravinsky's ballet, *Le Sacre.* Compare Stravinsky's description of the adolescent girls as "knock-kneed and long-braided Lolitas" (see vignette, page 484, and window, page 486). (*A. A. Bakhrushin State Central Theatrical Museum, Moscow*)

Window

NIJINSKY'S LOST BALLET

A handsome Russian dancer and choreographer, Vaslav Nijinsky (1888–1950), in collaboration with Diaghilev and Stravinsky (see page 481), burst colorfully upon the sedate, pastel world of classical ballet in Paris during the second decade of the twentieth century. In 1912, the year before the notorious premiere of Stravinsky's *Le Sacre du printemps* (The Rite of Spring), audiences had been scandalizd by Nijinsky's first choreographed ballet, set to Debussy's symphonic poem *Prélude à l'après-midi d'un faune* (see page 454). In that work, Nijinsky himself danced the role of the faun, a mythological creature who is half man, half goat. The ballet was starkly original in its sensuous atmosphere and sexually suggestive movements, and in portraying the faun's visions of ethereal nymphs.

The next year, encouraged by Diaghilev and intent on pursing his own unique course, Nijinsky created the perfect counterpart on stage to Stravinsky's galvanizing score of *Le Sacre*. According to an account by one of the dancers, Nijinsky was bent on reproducing every note of the music in his choreography, thereby emphasizing the jarring impact of the orchestra's explosive rhythms and unpredictable harmonies. The effect was further enhanced by the set and costume designs of the Russian-born painter Nicholas Roerich, who transformed his ideas about the prehistory of his native land and its primitive cultures into bold colors and exotic shapes. The costumes were loose-fitting garments with headbands, hand painted with geometric patterns that were repeated in the steps and angular movements of the dancers. Nijinsky's choreography was similarly unorthodox and shocking, completely defying the audience's expectations and the graceful attitudes of classical ballet. As Stravinsky implied in his description of the first performance (see vignette and illustration, pages 484–85), not only did the dancers representing the "Lolitas" or tribal maidens wear pigtails, but they also moved awkwardly, in "knock-kneed" fashion, with their toes turned in. At one point,

century music to accompany a theatrical scenario using traditional or stock characters. Stravinsky threw himself into music by Pergolesi (and music erroneously attributed to him), eventually reworking a number of sonata movements and arias in a manner at once faithful to the older models and true to his own sensibilities. He later spoke of this experience as his "discovery of the past, the epiphany through which the whole of my late work became they appeared to stalk across the stage in exaggerated frontal poses, their silhouettes resembling a row of clumsy storks!

Not surprisingly, however, Nijinsky's original choreography, unlike Stravinsky's music, did not survive. Although forms of dance notation exist, they are relatively inaccurate compared to music notation and, in any case, were not employed in this instance; and the work itself predated the use of film or video camera by many years. But in the 1980s, the choreographer Robert Joffrey became interested in the possibility of reconstructing the ballet's scenic designs and choreography through a variety of different sources that were painstakingly rediscovered and assembled by a pair of dedicated scholars: the annotated rehearsal score that had belonged to one of Nijinsky's principal dancers; some hastily drawn figures sketched by a young artist who attended the chaotic premiere; a number of the original costumes, which had made their way to England (Diaghilev's Russian Ballet company brought the production to London briefly, where it curiously received almost no notice); Roerich's paintings and records of his stage designs, collected in a New York museum; verbal material in the form of interviews and memoirs; and the largely indignant reviews by those critics who witnessed firsthand what was probably the most revolutionary artistic event of the century. These efforts resulted in an amazing 1987 production by the Joffrey Ballet, which accurately recaptured (and preserved on videotape) the exuberant spirit, if not all the details, of Nijinsky's lost ballet. Although today's concert audiences react more calmly than the Parisian public did, they still experience this work as powerfully fascinating.

➤ Tableau with dancers; painting by Nicholas Roerich of one of his set designs for the original production of Stravinsky's *Sacre*. (*State Russian Museum, St. Petersburg*)

possible."[2] Other excursions into the past led to borrowings and allusions in numerous works: to Bach-style counterpoint in the Octet, to Bach's keyboard concertos in the Concerto for Piano and Winds (1924), to Tchaikovsky in the ballet *Le Baiser de la fée* (The Fairy's Kiss, 1928), to Weber in the Capriccio

2. Stravinsky and Craft, *Expositions and Developments*, pp. 128–29.

The Rake's Progress

The subject of *The Rake's Progress* (1951) was suggested by a series of engravings by eighteenth-century painter and satirist William Hogarth; the libretto is by W. H. Auden and Chester Kallman. In keeping with the eighteenth-century subject, Stravinsky adopted the convention of recitatives, arias, and ensembles. For example, in the card-game scene that will decide the fate of the hero, Tom Rakewell, the duet between Tom and Nick Shadow (the Devil in disguise) is introduced by a five-measure Baroque-style ritornello in which two flutes play in thirds throughout over clarinet arpeggios and a pseudo–basso continuo. The duet itself is accompanied mostly by harpsichord, but there are interludes resembling *recitativo obbligato* that involve either the wind or string choir of the orchestra (Example 20.12). Rakewell's vocal line, which is accompanied by broken chords in strict rhythm, is full of Mozart-like turns and appoggiaturas. The accompaniment has a bitonal flavor.

EXAMPLE 20.12   Igor Stravinsky, *The Rake's Progress:* Act III, Scene 2, Duet, *My heart is wild with fear*

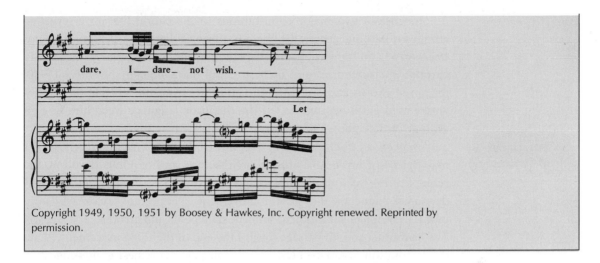

for piano and orchestra (1929), to Bach's Brandenburg concertos in the *Dumbarton Oaks* Concerto (1938), and to Machaut's Mass in his Mass (1948).

But Stravinsky's most significant debt was to the eighteenth-century Classic tradition. Genres, forms, and styles from that period served as prototypes for the Piano Sonata (1924), the Serenade in A (1925), the Symphony in C (1940), and the Symphony in Three Movements (1945). These works are basically diatonic and adhere to tonal centers and areas, if not to major and minor keys or dominant-tonic polarities. Moreover, the first movement of the Symphony in C clearly follows the traditional sonata form of the Classic period.

► Title page designed by Picasso for Stravinsky's piano arrangement of *Ragtime*, published by J. & W. Chester, London, 1919. (© *1997 Estate of Pablo Picasso / Artists Rights Society [ARS], New York*)

Stravinsky's two major contributions to the choral literature reveal an affinity for Baroque genres: the opera-oratorio *Oedipus rex* (Oedipus the King, 1927) on a Latin translation and adaptation of Sophocles' tragedy, for soloists, narrator, men's chorus, and orchestra; and the *Symphony of Psalms* (1930) for mixed chorus and orchestra on Latin texts from the Vulgate Bible. Stravinsky used Latin because he felt the ritualistic language freed him to concentrate on its "phonetic" qualities.

Symphony of Psalms

Symphony of Psalms is one of the great works of the twentieth century—a masterpiece of invention, musical architecture, and religious devotion. Baroque features include the ubiquitous ostinato constructions and the fully developed fugue of the second movement ("Expectans expectavi Dominum"), complete with tonic-dominant statements and answers, and strettos. The haunting ostinato passage toward the end of the third movement, "Laudate Dominum in sanctis Ejus," is harmonically the richest in its application of the ostinato device (Example 20.13). Here an ostinato bass of four half-notes overlaps the $\frac{3}{2}$ pattern of the choral setting, creating many different vertical combinations of the pitches in the E♭-major scale. This type of diatonic kaleidoscope has been dubbed "pandiatonicism."

EXAMPLE 20.13 Igor Stravinsky, *Symphony of Psalms:* "Laudate Dominum" (winds and strings omitted)

© Copyright 1931 by Edition Russe de Musique. Copyright renewed. Copyright and renewal assigned to Boosey & Hawkes, Inc. Revised edition © copyright 1948 by Boosey & Hawkes, Inc. Copyright renewed. Reprinted by permission.

In his compositions of the 1950s Stravinsky very gradually and judiciously adapted some techniques of the Schoenberg school, which will be explored in the next chapter. These works include the Septet (1953), the song *In memoriam Dylan Thomas* (1954), the *Canticum sacrum* (1955), the ballet *Agon* (1954–57), and *Threni* (1958), for voices and orchestra on texts from the Lamentations of Jeremiah. He further explored this technique in *Movements* (1959) and the *Orchestra Variations* (1964).

POSTLUDE

In sum, the European mainstream in the twentieth century incorporated many different trends. Bartók and Kodály (Hungary), Prokofiev and Shostakovich (USSR), Vaughan Williams and Britten (England), Hindemith and Weill (Germany), and others continued to cultivate musical styles that employed national folk idioms or otherwise reflected nationalist tendencies. Various movements, including neo-Classicism, which took hold quite naturally in France, combined innovations from the early part of the century with principles, forms, and techniques from the past, especially the Baroque and Classic eras. Some composers, most notably Milhaud and Stravinsky, participated to some extent in one or more of these movements. Still other composers, such as Arnold Schoenberg (1874–1951), explored altogether new paths, as we will now discover.

21

ATONALITY, SERIALISM, AND RECENT DEVELOPMENTS IN TWENTIETH-CENTURY EUROPE

PRELUDE

Because some of the trends presented in this chapter grew out of late German Romanticism, we must return to the end of the nineteenth century to trace the origins of certain compositional procedures not discussed so far, such as *atonality*, *twelve-tone*, and *serial* methods.

The word *atonal* describes music that is not based on the harmonic and melodic relationships revolving around a key center; it is the opposite of tonal, which characterizes most music of the eighteenth and nineteenth centuries, roughly from J. S. Bach to Richard Strauss. Much late-Romantic music, especially in Germany, tended toward atonality. Chromatic melody lines and chord progressions—in the music of Wagner, for example—resulted in passages with no perceived tonal center; but these passages, relatively short and exceptional, were still anchored in a tonal context. From the heavily chromatic, though still tonal, idiom of Wagner, Arnold Schoenberg (1874–1951) cleared a new path, through atonality, toward serial music.

Serial composition refers to Schoenberg's method of arranging all twelve tones of the chromatic scale in a series (twelve-tone row) that avoids establishing consonant or harmonic relationships. Twelve-tone music, however, is not necessarily atonal; it may observe a tonal center. The new compositional method was developed between the two world wars by **Schoenberg and His Followers**, Alban Berg (1885–1935) and Anton Webern (1883–1945). **After Webern**, some composers—notably Olivier

Messiaen (1908–1992)—methodically applied serialism to other aspects of composition, such as rhythm, dynamics, and form. But Messiaen, who was French, also cultivated a highly personal style that distinguished him from his Viennese contemporaries, and contributed to the eventual relaxation of strict serial composition.

Recent Developments in twentieth-century Europe include the discovery of new electronic resources and technologies, which have inevitably influenced compositional method; and an increased reliance on the role of the performer to help determine the elements of the composition. The first trend allows composers to have more control than ever before over their work: once a sound is executed electronically and recorded on tape, it remains unchanged; in this way, the mediating presence of a performer can be completely eliminated. By contrast, the second tendency allows more room for change and the element of chance, which some composers have purposefully cultivated by adopting the technique of *indeterminacy*. At its most extreme, indeterminacy allows the performer to make all-important decisions that affect the actual shape, and not merely the surface details, of a composition. In this case our basic notion about what constitutes a musical composition must be revised.

Schoenberg and His Followers

Born in Vienna of poor, Hungarian-Jewish parentage, Arnold Schoenberg (1874–1951) was largely a self-taught musician who learned composition by exchanging ideas and performing with friends. He embarked on a very personal aesthetic journey, with an unorthodox approach to his craft that eventually attracted a nucleus of composition students—most notably Alban Berg and Anton Webern. They remained artistically loyal to him and, through their own success, helped to spread his reputation. Escaping the growing Nazi threat in 1933, Schoenberg continued his career in the United States, where he accepted a professorship at the University of California in Los Angeles.

Schoenberg's career

Schoenberg's music may be divided into four approximate, overlapping compositional periods: tonal (until about 1908); transitional (1905–12) and atonal (1908–23); serial (1923–36); and stylistically diverse (after 1936). The second and third periods had particularly important consequences for twentieth-century music.

The music of the first period is tonal and, as we have noted, originated in late German Romanticism. Schoenberg's earliest important work, the string sextet *Verklärte Nacht* (Transfigured Night, 1899), is in a chromatic idiom growing out of *Tristan*, while the symphonic poem *Pelleas und Melisande* (1903) owes much to Gustav Mahler and Richard Strauss. With the huge symphonic cantata *Gurrelieder* (Songs of Gurre) for five soloists, narrator,

First period

four choruses, and large orchestra (1901, orchestration completed 1911), Schoenberg outdid Wagner in emotional fervor, and Mahler and Strauss in complex scoring.

Second period

We hear a new musical direction in Schoenberg's second-period works, which include the first two Quartets (D minor and F♯ minor, 1905 and 1908), the first *Kammersymphonie* (Chamber Symphony, 1906) for fifteen instruments, the *Five Orchestral Pieces*, Op. 16 (1909), two sets of short piano pieces (Op. 11, 1908 and Op. 19, 1911), a cycle of songs with piano accompaniment, *Das Buch der hängenden Gärten* (Book of the Hanging Gardens, 1908) for soloist and orchestra, *Erwartung* (Expectation, 1909), and a dramatic pantomime *Die glückliche Hand* (The Lucky Hand, 1911–13). In these works Schoenberg turned away from post-Romantic gigantism. He chose small instrumental combinations or, in large orchestra works, a soloistic treatment of instruments or swift alternation of colors (as in the *Five Orchestral Pieces* and *Erwartung*). Concurrently, rhythm and counterpoint became more complex, the melodic line fragmented, and the composition as a whole more concentrated and compact. For example, in the First Quartet, all the themes of its one-movement cyclical form, even the material of subsidiary voices, evolve from a few germinal motives through variation and combination.

Atonality

Schoenberg had explored the extreme possibilities of chromaticism within the limits of tonality in the *Gurrelieder* and *Pelleas*. After that, it was an easy step to cut loose altogether from a key center and treat all twelve notes of the octave as equal, instead of regarding some of them as chromatically altered tones of a diatonic scale. Without a keytone, harmonies ceased to have conventional functions—already foreshadowed in the free chord successions of Debussy—and any combination of tones could constitute a chord not requiring resolution, a situation Schoenberg called "the emancipation of the dissonance." Schoenberg proceeded gradually from tonality obscured by extreme chromaticism to atonality with free dissonance. The piano pieces of Opus 11, the last movement of the Second Quartet (apart from the final cadence in F♯), and the piano pieces of Opus 19 mark the transition to atonality.

Pierrot lunaire

Pierrot lunaire (Moonstruck Pierrot, 1912; see Nos. 8 and 13, NAWM 138), from Schoenberg's second period, is his best-known composition of the prewar era. It is a setting of twenty-one songs drawn from a larger poetic cycle published in 1884 by the Belgian symbolist poet Albert Giraud and later translated into German. Scored for a woman's voice with a chamber ensemble of five players and eight instruments, it calls for flute (doubling piccolo), clarinet (bass clarinet), violin (viola), cello, and piano. The poet imagines himself as the clown Pierrot; he expresses all aspects of himself through the symbol of a moonbeam, which is capable of taking many shapes and colors. Instead of the comic adventures of Pierrot the clown, however, the poet invents a gruesome fantasy. The voice throughout the cycle declaims the text

Sprechstimme

in a so-called *Sprechstimme* (speech-voice; also called *Sprechgesang*, or speech-

Arnold Schoenberg on Artistic Expression:

❝ Art is a cry of distress from those who live out within themselves the destiny of humanity, who are not content with it but measure themselves against it, who do not obtusely serve the engine to which the label 'unseen forces' is applied, but throw themselves into the moving gears to understand how it works. They are those who do not turn their eyes away to protect themselves from emotions but open them wide to oppose what must be attacked. They do, however, often close their eyes to perceive what the senses do not convey, to look inside of what seems to be happening on the surface. Inside them turns the movement of the world; only an echo of it leaks out—the work of art. ❞

From "Aphorismen" in *Die Musik*, Berlin, 9. Jahrgang, Vol. 36 (1909–10):159.

song), only approximating the written pitches but closely following the notated rhythm. To achieve this effect Schoenberg used the sign ♩̽. The result is a kind of eerie distortion of both speech and song, which effectively expresses the poet's innermost, often tortured feelings. Because of this emphasis on subjective expression, *Pierrot lunaire* is among Schoenberg's most stunning *expressionist* works (see window, pages 502–3).

The early atonal piano pieces of Opus 19 (1911) were quite brief; the composer did not have to face the problem of how to unify formally a composition without words until his attempt at creating larger works. By 1923, after six years during which he published no music, Schoenberg had formulated a new unifying "method of composing with twelve tones which are related only with one another." The essential points of the theory of this twelve-tone ("dodecaphonic") technique may be summarized as follows: the basis of each composition is a *row* or *series* consisting of the twelve tones or pitch classes of the octave arranged in an order the composer chooses; the tones of the series may be used both successively (as melody) and simultaneously (as harmony or counterpoint), in any octave and with any desired rhythm; the row may be used not only in its original or "prime" form but also in intervalically inverted form, in retrograde order (backward), or retrograde inverted form, and in transpositions of any of the four forms; and the composer must use all twelve pitches of the series before going on to use the series in any of its forms again.

The first works that reveal Schoenberg's deliberate use of tone rows were the five piano pieces in Opus 23 (1923), of which, however, only the last has a complete row of twelve tones. Over the next few years he perfected his technique with the Serenade, Op. 24; Suite for Piano, Op. 25; Wind Quintet, Op. 26; the Third Quartet (1926); and the *Variations for Orchestra* (1928).

Third period

Twelve-tone method

Pierrot lunaire

*S*ome of the songs in *Pierrot* rely on constructive devices such as canons to achieve unity, since they cannot depend on chord relationships within a tonality for this purpose. One example is No. 8, *Nacht* (Night, NAWM 138a), which Schoenberg called a passacaglia. But it is an unusual passacaglia because the unifying motive, a rising minor third followed by a descending major third, appears constantly in various note values throughout the parts of the texture. The relentless ostinato becomes a fitting artistic emblem of Pierrot's obsession with the giant bats that enclose him in a frightening trap, thereby shutting out the sun.

No. 13, *Enthauptung* (Beheading, NAWM 138b), displays a different technique. Instead of thematic development we hear what sounds like free improvisation, responsive only to the changing message of the text. Here Pierrot imagines himself beheaded by the moonbeam for his crimes. The opening measures sum up the poem's imagery (see the translation in NAWM 138) with a cascade of notes in both the bass clarinet and viola to depict the sweep of the scimitar. The passage that follows evokes the atmosphere of a moonlit night; Pierrot scurries to avoid the dreaded moonbeam, while augmented chords in the piano suggest his knees knocking together. Here, and in other works from this period, Schoenberg depended largely on the text to establish a measure of continuity.

Most of the works Schoenberg wrote after coming to America in 1933, particularly the Violin Concerto (1936) and the Fourth Quartet (1937), also employ tone rows. Schoenberg's fourth-period works are varied. "In olden [and tonal] style" is his Suite for String Orchestra (1934). In the *Ode to Napoleon* and the Piano Concerto (both 1942), he approached a synthesis of his own system with some elements of orthodox tonality; but these pieces are less characteristic than other late works, such as the String Trio (1946) and the *Fantasy for Violin and Piano* (1949), both of which employ serialism.

Fourth period

Moses und Aron

In 1930–32 Schoenberg composed the first two acts of a three-act opera, *Moses und Aron*, on his own libretto. Although the score remains uncompleted, the opera has entered the repertory. Against the Old Testament background, Schoenberg presents the tragic conflict between Moses, the philosopher-mystic, as mediator of the word of God, and Aron, the statesman-educator who acts as Moses' interpreter to the people. Moses is unable to communicate his vision, while Aron, who can communicate, does not rightly understand it. Symbolically, Moses speaks—in *Sprechstimme*—but does not sing; his speech turns to music at only one moment, when Moses warns Aron,

▲ Autograph short score of the opening measures of Schoenberg's *Moses und Aron.* "Hz"
stands for woodwinds, "Bl" for brass, "Str" for strings, and "Schlg" for percussion. (*Copyright
1957 by B. Schott's Söhne, Mainz. Copyright renewed. All rights reserved. Used in the territory of the world excluding the U.S., Canada and Cuba by permission of European American
Music Distributors Corp., agent for B. Schott's Söhne*)

"Purify your thought: set it free from earthly things, dedicate it to Truth" (Act I, Scene 2). Example 21.1 reveals Moses' solemn proclamation of these words in a style at once reminiscent of Wagner and yet using a strict twelve-tone row.

EXAMPLE 21.1   Arnold Schoenberg, *Moses und Aron*: Act I, Scene 2

Rei-ni-ge dein Denk-en,   lös es von Wert-los-em,   wei - he es   Wahr - em:

Schoenberg's *Variations for Orchestra*

Generally acknowledged to be among Schoenberg's finest works, the *Variations for Orchestra* (1926–28; see NAWM 139) illustrate the blending of traditional procedures with the twelve-tone technique. Following an introduction, in which the row is surrounded in a veil of mystery that creates an expectant mood, we hear a twenty-four-measure theme. Four forms of the twelve-note row (Example 21.2) determine the pitch successions of the melodic subject in the cello, while the same four forms in reverse order supply the harmonic accompaniment to this melody. The subject is clearly laid out in motives employing groups of three to six notes of the row, and these are given distinct rhythmic shape, so that their rhythms, when heard with different pitches in the course of the theme, contribute to the overall cohesion. Example 21.1 shows the first half of the theme, with numbers to indicate the pitch order in the four forms of the row given below the theme. The first three motives use up the row in its original state (P-0, the Principal [P] form at the original pitch, represented by 0, i.e., zero half-steps of transposition). The harmony for each of the motives is drawn from the same numbers of the row but in the Inversion (I) transposed up a major sixth to the ninth half-step (I-9). As the first group of motives had 5, 4, and 3 different pitches respectively, the second group has the reverse, 3, 4, and 5 pitches. The melody is now drawn from the Retrograde (R) of the Inversion at the ninth half-step (RI-9), which had previously furnished the accompaniment.

EXAMPLE 21.2 Arnold Schoenberg, *Variations for Orchestra*, Op. 31: Forms of the Twelve-Tone Row, First Half of Theme

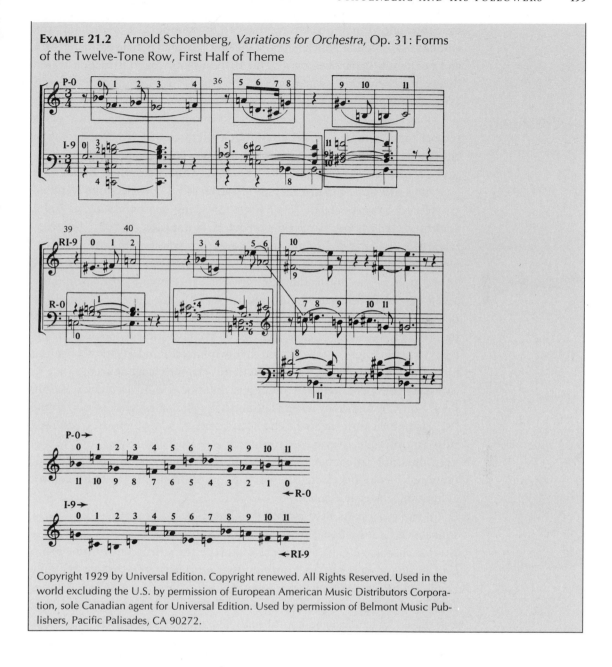

Moses und Aron is as much oratorio as opera. The choruses of the people of Israel play a large part. A group of six solo voices (in the orchestra pit, not on the stage) represents the Voice of God, in *Sprechstimme* like Moses. In the most picturesque part of the score—the complex of solos, choruses, and dances in the big scene depicting the worship of the Golden Calf (Act II)—rhythm, instrumental color, and sudden contrasts combine in a spectacle of oriental splendor and dramatic effect. The entire opera is based on a single tone row, one form of which is represented in Example 21.1. *Moses und Aron* embodies a profound philosophical conception in appropriate dramatic form and powerfully expressive music. The towering unity of construction makes this work its composer's masterpiece and earns it a place, alongside Berg's *Wozzeck,* among the great operas of its time.

Alban Berg

Alban Berg (1885–1935), Schoenberg's famous pupil, adopted most of his teacher's methods of construction. But he used them with freedom and often chose tone rows that allowed for tonal-sounding chords and chord progressions. Moreover, Berg invested the technique with a warmth of feeling that gives it greater appeal than it had in the hands of other twelve-tone composers. His chief works are the *Lyric Suite* for string quartet (1926); a Violin Concerto (1935); and two operas, *Wozzeck* (composed 1917–21, first performed 1925) and *Lulu* (composed 1928–35, the orchestration not quite completed at Berg's death).

Wozzeck

Wozzeck is the outstanding example of expressionist opera (for more about expressionism, see window, pages 502–3). The libretto, arranged by Berg from fragments of a drama by Georg Büchner (1813–1837), presents the soldier Wozzeck as a hapless victim of his environment, despised by his fellow men, betrayed in love, driven finally to murder and suicide. The music is continuous throughout each of the three acts, the changing scenes (five in each act) being connected by orchestral interludes as in Debussy's *Pelléas.* Berg's music is unified by several leitmotifs, by pitch-class sets (as in Example 21.3) identified with the main characters, and by adaptations of traditional closed forms: suite, rhapsody, song, march, passacaglia, and symphony. Moreover, the third act contains five so-called inventions: on a theme (six variations and fugue); on a note (the pitch *B*); on a rhythm; on a chord; and on a duration (the eighth note).

In the vocal parts Berg moved fluidly between ordinary speech, *Sprechstimme,* and conventional singing. There are passages of stylized realism—snoring chorus, gurgling water, a tavern orchestra with an out-of-tune piano caricaturing a waltz motive from Strauss's *Rosenkavalier*—that are skillfully employed for expressionistic purposes. The grim, ironic, symbolical action is supported throughout by a wealth of musical invention. The orchestration is ever varied, ingenious, and appropriate. The music's formal clarity and concentration intensify the impact of the graphic descriptions and dramatic confrontations.

Anton Webern

If Berg's music represents the warm, lyrical side of Schoenberg's compositional approach, the music of Anton Webern (1883–1945), Schoenberg's other celebrated pupil, personifies the cool, constructive side. Webern wrote no opera and never used *Sprechstimme.* Economy and extreme concentration reign. His mature compositions unfold by imitative counterpoint, often strictly canonic. He used inversion and rhythmic shifts, but avoided sequences and, for the most part, repetitions. The melodic outline of the generating "cells" usually involves intervals that exclude tonal implications, such as major sevenths and minor ninths. Textures are stripped to bare essentials.

Wozzeck, Act III, Scene 3

*A*ct III, Scene 3 (NAWM 140), a wild polka, presents the invention on a rhythm. Wozzeck sits in a tavern singing and drinking. He asks Margret, the barmaid, to dance with him. After they dance, she sits on his lap and sings a song, in the midst of which she notices blood on his hand. Wozzeck becomes agitated and obsessed with this blood, for just before entering the tavern he murdered his unfaithful mistress, Marie. At the beginning of the scene a barroom piano announces both the rhythmic theme and a set of six pitches (Example 21.3). The pitch-set, nearly a whole-tone scale, recurs frequently throughout the opera. The music of this scene is constructed like a medieval isorhythmic motet. The set of eight durations is continually reiterated, sometimes in diminution, sometimes in augmentation, pervading the entire texture, even the voices.

EXAMPLE 21.3 Alban Berg, *Wozzeck*: Act III, Scene 3

Rhythmic patterns are complex, often based on simultaneous duple and triple divisions of all or part of a measure. The dynamics, specified down to the finest gradations, seldom rise above the level of *forte*.

Most remarkable is Webern's instrumentation. A melodic line may be distributed among different instruments so that only one or two—seldom more than four or five—successive tones are heard in the same timbre. The result is a texture made up of sparks and flashes of color. Special effects— pizzicato, harmonics, tremolo, muting, and the like—are common in all of Webern's works. His striving for color and clarity often led him to choose unusual combinations, as in the Quartet Op. 22 for violin, clarinet, tenor saxophone, and piano, or the three songs Op. 18 for soprano, E♭ clarinet, and guitar.

Webern's instrumentation

Intense concentration resulted in short compositions. Not all are so brief as the *Six Bagatelles* for string quartet, Op. 9, or the Five Pieces for Orchestra, Op. 10 (both 1913), which average respectively about 36 and 49 seconds for each movement (No. 5 of Op. 10 runs only 19 seconds). But even "larger" works like the Symphony (1928) and the String Quartet (1938) require only eight or nine minutes' playing time.

Webern's brevity

Webern, like Schoenberg, passed through the stages of late-Romantic

Window

EXPRESSIONISM

During the second decade of the twentieth century a group of German painters espoused a movement called *expressionism*. Real objects or people were represented in grossly distorted ways in order to reflect the artists' feelings about their surroundings and themselves (see, for example, *Street Scene* [1914, revised 1925] by Ernst Ludwig Kirchner [1880–1938]; Plate XIV, facing page 467). Similarly, contemporary composers used distorted melodies, violently graphic musical images, discordant harmonies, fragmented rhythms, and exaggerated speech inflections to express their own (or their chosen poets' or librettists') often nightmarish visions of the world. Schoenberg and his pupil Alban Berg were two leading exponents of expressionism in music.

Where *impressionism* (another term first used in connection with painting) aimed to capture objects of the sensual, external world as perceived at a given moment (see window, Chapter 19), expressionism sought to represent *inner* experience, to explore the hidden world of the psyche. Expressionism developed from the subjectivity of Romanticism; it differed from Romanticism in the kind of introspective experience it aimed to portray and in the means chosen to portray it. Expressionism dealt with the emotional life of the modern person—isolated, helpless in the grip of poorly understood forces, prey to inner conflict, tension, anxiety, fear, and elemental, irrational drives. That is also how Schoenberg's fellow Viennese, Sigmund Freud, conceived the deepest level of memory and emotional activity in his *Interpretation of Dreams* (1900). Expressionism also revealed the tormented soul rebelling against established order and accepted forms. One of Schoenberg's own self portraits (for he was also a painter)—depicted with his back to the viewer—suggests the alienation of the artist from society and its conventions.

Webern's three periods

chromaticism, free atonality, and organization by tone rows, the last beginning with the three songs of Op. 17 (1925). With few exceptions his works, about equally divided between instrumental and vocal, are in chamber style. His chief instrumental compositions are the Symphony, Op. 21 (1928; see NAWM 141), the String Quartet, Op. 28, the Concerto for Nine Instruments, Op. 24 (1934), and the Piano Variations, Op. 27 (1936). For voices he wrote numerous collections of solo songs—some with piano, others with small ensembles—and a few choral pieces, notably *Das Augenlicht* (Light of the Eyes, 1935) and two cantatas (1939, 1943) for soloists, chorus, and orchestra. These

Because of such subject matter, expressionist art insisted upon desperate and revolutionary modes of utterance. Both characteristics are evident in Schoenberg's *Pierrot lunaire* (1912), a work of tremendous emotional force that is written in a dissonant, rhythmically and melodically fragmentary, non-thematic musical idiom, for which Schoenberg invented an entirely new type of vocal declamation, *Sprechstimme* (see pages 494–95). Schoenberg's *Erwartung* (1909) and *Die glückliche Hand* (1911–13), and Berg's opera *Wozzeck* (1917–21) are also expressionist compositions. In none of these works did the composer aspire to make music that was either pretty or naturalistic. Instead, he deployed the most forceful and direct means, no matter how disfigured—whether in music, subject matter, text, scenic design, or lighting—to communicate the particular, compelling, innermost thought or feeling that he ventured to express.

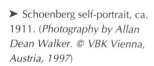 Schoenberg self-portrait, ca. 1911. (*Photography by Allan Dean Walker. © VBK Vienna, Austria, 1997*)

cantatas, and also the *Variations for Orchestra*, Op. 30 (1940), are written in a more relaxed and expressive style than Webern's previous works. They employ serial technique but include homophonic as well as contrapuntal texture. Webern's use of serial technique may be observed in the first movement of his Symphony, Op. 21 (see NAWM 141 for detailed discussion).

Webern's output was small. Although he received little acclaim during his lifetime, recognition of his work grew steadily in the years after World War II, and his music launched important new developments in Italy, Germany, France, and the United States.

Webern's influence

After Webern

By the 1950s many composers, including Stravinsky, had accepted Schoenberg's twelve-tone system in principle, modifying and adapting it to their own
purposes. It was Webern, however, more than anyone else, who anticipated
and stimulated a movement that came to be associated with a group of young
composers centered about the "holiday courses for new music" in the city of
Darmstadt. These courses began immediately after the end of the war, in 1946.
At a memorial concert of his works at Darmstadt in 1953, Webern was hailed
as the father of the new movement.

Darmstadt movement

Many of the ideas fostered at Darmstadt spread throughout the musical
world and stimulated experiments by composers in other countries, including, eventually, Eastern Europe. But every composer worked independently,
striking out in new directions, cultivating a personal language and style. There
was no allegiance to one consistent body of principles, no well-defined "common practice," as there had been in the eighteenth and nineteenth centuries.
Pierre Boulez (b. 1925) of Paris and Karlheinz Stockhausen (b. 1928) of Cologne, both pupils of Olivier Messiaen (see page 505), became the two principal composers of the Darmstadt group.

Total serialism

Even before 1950, composers applied the principle of Schoenberg's tone
rows to musical elements or parameters other than pitch. Thus arose "total
serialism": if the twelve tones of the chromatic scale could be serialized, so
also could duration, intensity, timbre, and texture. In the eighteenth and
nineteenth centuries, all these elements had been interdependent, combined
in certain accepted melodic, harmonic, rhythmic, dynamic, and instrumental
patterns. Now a series of pitches could be combined with a series of one or
more of the other factors, as Messiaen did in his *Mode de valeurs et d'intensités*
(the third of the *Quatre Études de rythme* for piano, 1949). By similar means,
a composer could achieve serial control over every detail of a composition.
Naturally, the relationships among the parameters had to be worked out in
a way that made sense musically, not merely mathematically.

Boulez

The rigidity of total serialism soon relaxed. In Boulez's *Le Marteau sans
maître* (The Hammer without a Master, 1954, revised 1957), for example, the
seemingly fragmented style and serial method fuse with a sensitive musical
realization of the text, verses from a cycle of surrealist poems by René Char.
The work has nine short movements interspersed with instrumental "commentaries." The ensemble—a different combination in each movement—
comprises alto flute, xylorimba, vibraphone, guitar, viola, and a variety of
soft percussion instruments. The ensemble produces a translucent scrim of
sound, all in the middle and high registers, with effects often suggestive
of Balinese music. The contralto vocal line, characterized by wide melodic
intervals, glissandos, and occasional *Sprechstimme*, is often the lowest voice

in the texture, and relates in a deliberate way to particular instruments in the ensemble.

Olivier Messiaen (1908–1992) was an influential, unique, and unclassifiable figure. Born in Avignon, Messiaen studied organ and composition in Paris and became professor of harmony at the Conservatoire there in 1942. His many distinguished pupils, besides Boulez and Stockhausen, included the Italian Luigi Nono (b. 1924), the Netherlander Ton de Leeuw (b. 1926), and many other important composers of their generation.

Messiaen

It is a tribute to the quality of Messiaen's teaching that each of his pupils went his own way, indicating that Messiaen was not the founder of a school of composition in the ordinary sense of the word. He was one of the first to experiment with total serialism. In *Quatre Études de rythme* (1949) each pitch of an unordered twelve-tone set is assigned a duration, dynamic value, and type of attack. Moreover the note values are so arranged that each is one thirty-second longer than the previous one.

Besides numerous works for piano and for his own instrument, the organ—such as the *Méditations sur la mystère de la Sainte Trinité* (Meditations on the Mystery of the Holy Trinity, 1969)—Messiaen's principal compositions include the *Quatuor pour la fin du temps* (Quartet for the End of Time) for violin, clarinet, cello, and piano (first movement in NAWM 142), written at a German military prison camp in 1941 for performance by the composer and three fellow-prisoners; *Trois petites liturgies pour la Présence Divine* (Three Short Liturgies of the Divine Presence) for unison chorus of women's voices and small orchestra (1944); a symphony *Turangalîla* in ten movements for large orchestra (1948); *Cinq rechants* (Five Refrains) for unaccompanied chorus of mixed voices (1949); and *Chronochromie* (literally, "Time-Color") for orchestra (1960).

The Quartet for the End of Time is a study of time: measured, finite time, and timelessness or eternity. Although the quartet lacks a text, it is actually a piece of sacred music, as are many of Messiaen's works. Religion is not so much on the surface as it is the motivation and goal of his creative efforts. Nature is also ever present in his compositions, often in the form of birdsong, as here in the opening dialogue between a blackbird (clarinet) and a nightingale (flute). The rhythm, which has a pulse but no regular meter, is also reminiscent of nature (see NAWM 142 for discussion of Messiaen's rhythmic devices).

Quatuor pour la fin du temps

Messiaen's music is highly personal. At the same time a certain mystical detachment calls our attention to its unusual technical features. He worked mainly within a rich homophonic texture or with sweeping gestures, sometimes in counterpoint against one another. He drew melodic and harmonic material from a variety of sources, among them the plainchant modes, conventional tonality, octatonic scales, and pitch-sets. He often used contrasts of timbre to serve a structural function. His complex vertical combinations sometimes incorporate the upper partials of a fundamental, as in the organ

Messiaen's style

C H R O N O L O G Y				

	*Schoenberg, *Verklärte Nacht*; Debussy, *Nocturnes* (1899)	**1930**	
1900	Sigmund Freud (1856–1939), *The Interpretation of Dreams*		*Schoenberg, *Moses und Aron* (1932)
	Puccini, *Madama Butterfly* (1904)		Hindemith, *Mathis der Maler*; Franklin D. Roosevelt (1882–1945), president of the United States; Adolf Hitler (1889–1945), chancellor of Germany; Schoenberg arrives in the U.S. (1933)
	Strauss, *Salome* (1905)		
	Bartók, First String Quartet; Mahler, *Das Lied von der Erde* (1908)		
1910			Shostakovich, Fifth Symphony; Pablo Picasso (1881–1973), *Guernica* (1937)
	*Schoenberg, *Pierrot lunaire* (1912)	**1940**	World War II (1939–45)
	Stravinsky, *Le Sacre du printemps* (1913)		*Messiaen, *Quartet for the End of Time* (1941)
	*Ernst Ludwig Kirchner (1880–1938), expressionist painting *Street Scene* (1914) (See Plate XIV, facing page 467)	**1950**	
	World War I (1914–18)		Stravinsky, *The Rake's Progress* (1951)
	Albert Einstein (1879–1955), general theory of relativity (1916)		*Death of Schoenberg (1951)
1920			*Boulez, *Le Marteau sans maître* (1954)
	Milhaud, *La Création du monde* (1924)		*Stockhausen, *Gesang der Jünglinge* (1956)
	*Berg, premiere of *Wozzeck* (1925)		*Varèse, *Poème électronique* at the Brussels World's Fair (1958)
	*Schoenberg, *Variations for Orchestra* (1928)	**1960**	*Penderecki, *Threnody for the Victims of Hiroshima* (1960)
	*Webern, Symphony, Op. 21; Weill, premiere of *The Threepenny Opera* (1928)		Britten, *War Requiem* (1961)
	New York stock market crash; worldwide depression (1929)		President John F. Kennedy assassinated (1963)
		1970	
			Death of Stravinsky (1971)

stops called mixtures. Rhythmic pedals akin to isorhythm, mirror-patterns of note values, and extra durations within the measure create an impression of a fluid, nonmetrical stream of ideas.[1]

Recent Developments

New timbres

Music after Webern incorporated an increasingly large number of unaccustomed sounds. Earlier, the most revolutionary "new sounds" were the piano "tone clusters," employed by the American Henry Cowell (1897–1965) in the 1920s, and the "prepared piano" of John Cage (1912–1993) in the 1940s (see Chapter 22). Now, other unfamiliar sounds were produced by new uses of conventional instruments, such as the flutter-tongue technique on wind instruments, as well as glissandos, harmonics, and *col legno* (playing with the wood part of the bow) on strings. Composers sometimes demanded spoken

1. These means are described in detail in Messiaen's *The Technique of My Musical Language* (Paris, 1944), trans. John Satterfield (Paris: Leduc, 1956).

and whispered sounds of vocalists and even instrumentalists. New instruments, such as the vibraphone and the *Ondes Martenot*, appeared in the orchestra. The percussion group enjoyed a major expansion, often including instruments drawn from Asian or African musics.

Edgard Varèse (1883–1965) wrote music in which timbre played a most important role. For Varèse, sounds as such were the essential structural components of music, more basic than melody, harmony, or rhythm. In his *Ionisation* (1931), composed for a huge battery of percussion instruments (including piano and bells) along with chains, anvils, and sirens, Varèse created a form defined by contrasting blocks and masses of sound. Some of his late works (*Déserts*, 1954; *Poème électronique*, 1958) utilized new sound resources that became available soon after the middle of the century (for more on Varèse, see Chapter 22).

No development after 1950 attracted more public attention or held greater potential for far-reaching changes in the world of music than the use of electronically produced or manipulated sounds. In the so-called *musique concrète* of the late 1940s, the raw material consisted of recorded musical tones or other natural sounds that were transformed in various ways by mechanical and electronic means and then assembled on tape for playback. The next step was to replace or supplement sounds of natural origin by sounds generated electronically in a studio. One of the most prominent early electronic compositions, Stockhausen's *Gesang der Jünglinge* (Song of the Youths, 1956), as well as many of his later works in this medium, used sounds from both sources. *Musique concrète* and electronic music encouraged listeners to accept sounds not produced by voices or musical instruments.

Musique concrète

Electronic resources

The new medium freed composers from all dependence on performers and empowered them to exercise complete, unmediated control over the sound of their compositions. Much of the new music already demanded minute shadings of pitch, intensity, and timbre that could be notated only approximately in a score, as well as extremely complex rhythms that could barely be realized by performers. Besides, the specially qualified personnel and lengthy rehearsal time required to perform this music was scarce. But in the electronic studio, every detail could be accurately calculated and recorded. Moreover, a whole new realm of possible sounds was now available—including sounds not producible by any "natural" means. Composers in Europe, America, and Japan industriously exploited all these advantages. Further possibilities (and problems) arose when tape recordings were combined with live performers.

Diminished role of performers

Electronic music was at first produced by combining, modifying, and controlling the output of oscillators, then recording these sounds on tape. The composer had to splice the tapes and mix their output, sometimes in combination with recorded sounds of physical objects in motion or of musicians, speakers, singers, etc. Electronic sound synthesizers were developed

New technology

Synthesizers

to make the process much easier. Composers could call on pitches from a music keyboard, and with switches and knobs control harmonics, waveform, resonance, and location of sound sources. By the 1980s, electronic keyboards combined with computers made synthesized music accessible to composers outside the large electronic studios that had been set up in the 1950s and 1960s. Through computers, composers could define and control all the parameters of pitch, timbre, dynamics, and rhythm, and the characteristics thus digitally encoded could be translated directly into music through a MIDI (Musical Instrument Digital Interface) technology developed for this purpose.

Experimentation with live performers improvising against synthesized or computer-generated music is now commonplace. Equipment and software programs permit the computer to respond to music played either on a synthesizer or on an instrument according to formulas decided by the composer. Imitative polyphony, nonimitative polyphony, music on one or more rhythmic or melodic ostinatos, heterophony, and a variety of other textures can be generated by the composer at a synthesizer keyboard in "real time," that is, as actually played and listened to, rather than laboriously prepared in advance and tape-recorded.

Influence of electronic music

Electronic and synthesized music has not superseded live music and is not likely to do so. A good many composers have not worked at all, or to any important extent, with electronic media. Nonetheless, electronic sounds stimulated the invention of new sound effects obtainable from voices and conventional instruments, a development that is especially noticeable in the music of Krzysztof Penderecki and the Hungarian composer György Ligeti.

Spatial effects

In both electronic and live music, many composers worked with the idea of dispersing the various sound sources throughout a concert hall in order to manipulate space as an additional dimension of music. This effect, of course, was not altogether a new discovery. Antiphonal singing of plainchant, the *cori spezzati* and the choral-instrumental canzone and sinfonie of the sixteenth-century Venetians, and the Requiem of Berlioz had exemplified the same fascination with spatial relationships. A more recent example was Bartók's *Music for Strings, Percussion, and Celesta* of 1936 (NAWM 133), which required a particular placement of players and instruments.

In the second half of the twentieth century, composers began to use space with more calculation and inventiveness than ever before. They might place two or more groups of instruments on different parts of the stage, or locate loudspeakers or performers at the sides or back of the hall, above or below the level of the audience, or even in the midst of the audience. Varèse's *Poème électronique* at the Brussels Exposition in 1958 was projected by 425 loudspeakers ranged all about the interior space of Le Corbusier's pavilion (see illustration, page 509), while moving colored lights and projected images accompanied the music. Direction and location in space suddenly became a factor in the overall form of a work.

▲ Philips Pavilion, Brussels World's Fair, 1958. Edgard Varèse collaborated with the architect Le Corbusier to fill this building with the sound of *Poème électronique*, composed at the Philips laboratories in Eindhoven. (*Photograph Courtesy The Museum of Modern Art, New York*)

From the end of the seventeenth century, Western music utilized a set of twelve equidistant semitones systematically dividing the space of an octave. Proposals at one time or another for including more tones in the octave came to no practical end. In practice, however, shifting pitches have always been used, such as glissandos in singing and on stringed instruments. Sounds outside the twelve semitones of the tempered scale were common in minute adjustments by string players, but more recently composers sometimes required quarter-tones or other microtones, as in Berg's *Chamber Concerto* (1925). Fuzzy pitch characterized the *Sprechstimme* of Schoenberg and Berg. Now, however, distinct pitches and intervals can be supplemented by a *continuum*, an unbroken range of sound from the lowest to the highest audible frequencies, without distinguishing separate tones of fixed pitch. The sirens in Varèse's *Ionisation* and similar electronic sounds in his later works provide striking examples of a composer's use of the pitch continuum. Other examples are the glissandos of the *Ondes Martenot*, used in Messiaen's *Turangalîla* symphony, and the frequent glissando effects on traditional instruments in the music of Penderecki and others. Related to this is the use of complex or unpitched nonmusical sounds, from whatever source, as elements in composition.

The pitch continuum

The *Threnody for the Victims of Hiroshima* (1960) for fifty-two string instruments by Krzysztof Penderecki (b. 1933) expands the conventional resources of the orchestra in numerous ways. Players may choose pitches relative to the instrument's range, such as "the highest note," rather than specific notes. When particular pitches are called for, they may progress by quarter-tones or their multiples. String players may bow between the bridge and the tailpiece or arpeggiate on four strings behind the bridge (that is, where the pitch is not controlled by the left hand), or bow on the bridge or tailpiece itself, or strike the sound board. Different groups of instruments are assigned narrow pitchbands that may gradually become narrower or wider or move by glissando to a different level. The score gives few definite pulses or note values, the intervals of time measured by units of clock time. The beginning and ending sections give the players the greatest latitude, while the middle section is the most precisely notated and has the most intense variety of sound. Despite the individual freedom, the composer carefully controlled the outcome. The entire pitched and unpitched world, animate and inanimate, wailing and weeping at once, often in polychoral and antiphonal calls and responses, seems to mourn in this dirge.

The music of György Ligeti (b. 1923) achieved world renown through Stanley Kubrick's science-fiction film *2001*, which used excerpts from three of his works, *Atmosphères* (1961), the Requiem (1963–65), and *Lux aeterna* (1966). Listeners were impressed that this music was in constant motion, yet static both harmonically and melodically. *Atmosphères* begins with fifty-six muted strings, together with a selection of woodwinds and horns playing simultaneously all the notes of the chromatic scale through a range of five octaves. Instruments imperceptibly drop out until only the violas and cellos remain. An orchestral tutti follows with a similar panchromatic layout, but out of it emerge two clusters: one, in the strings, made up of the diatonic "natural" notes of the chromatic scale, contrasts with the other, a pentatonic cluster of the "flat" notes in the woodwinds and horns. Similar textures, peppered with vibratos, sudden changes of dynamics, and string harmonics, and saturated with churning, dense canonic imitations, continue throughout the piece.

When we compare a work such as Penderecki's *Threnody* with Ligeti's *Atmosphères*, we are struck by the similarity of effect achieved through different strategies of control: Penderecki often left the choice of pitches or durations to the individual players, while Ligeti carefully notated both, forming a mosaic of precisely chiseled parts.

Throughout the history of Western music, composer and performer have constantly interacted, employing those factors (such as pitch and relative duration) that the composer could specify by notation and those left to the performer, either by convention or because adequate notational signs were lacking. In the twentieth century some composers tried to exercise near-total control over performance by a plethora of detailed indications for dynamics, manner of attack, tempo—through frequent metronome marks—pauses, and rhythms. But total control became possible, or nearly possible, only in all-electronic works, where the performer was eliminated. In fact, the range of gradations and fluctuations between control (exercised by the composer) and freedom (exercised by the performer) widened in the twentieth century.

The indeterminate features in twentieth-century music do not originate—as they did in the sixteenth century—from deliberately giving performers a conventional choice, such as to play or sing the notated music, or by leaving certain things to performers by purposely or inevitably using imprecise notation, as in the nineteenth century. Rather, the degree of control, or *determinacy*, and freedom, or *indeterminacy*,[2] may be programmed for each composition. This may take the form of indeterminate sections, somewhat like the Baroque or Classic cadenza, within a composition otherwise fixed by the score. Or the composer may specify more or less exactly a series of distinct musical events, leaving their succession partly or wholly unspecified. In such an "open" form, the performer (soloist, member of a group, or conductor) may either determine the order of the events by choice or be led by means of certain devices into an apparently chance or random order. The performer may also, both within an event and in choosing the order of events, be guided by reactions to what others in the group, or even members of the audience, are doing. In short, the possibilities of indeterminacy, of modes of interaction between freedom and authority—the extent to which chance can be controlled—are limitless.

Indeterminacy

The European composer who worked most consistently in this domain is Karlheinz Stockhausen (b. 1928). (He was indebted to the American John Cage for stimulating his interest in this medium; see Chapter 22.) A look at two of his compositions may help clarify some of the procedures. The score of *Klavierstück XI* (Piano Piece No. 11; 1956) consists of nineteen short segments of notation displayed on a large sheet (about 37 by 21 inches). These segments can be put together in various ways as the player's eyes happen to light on one after another. Certain directions are given for choosing and linking the segments played: not all need be played, and any may be repeated. When in the course of a performance the pianist plays any one segment a third time, the piece ends.

Stockhausen

The setup in Stockhausen's *Opus 1970* is a little more complicated. This piece is performed by four players—piano, electric viola, electronium, and tam-tam—and four loudspeakers.

> Each of the four players has a magnetophone [tape recorder] on which, for the whole of the recording period [or performance], a tape, prepared differently for

---

2. Indeterminacy (John Cage's term) is used here, in preference to the more restricted term "aleatory" (from the Latin *aleae* = dice), to cover everything from improvisation within a fixed framework to situations where the composer gives only the minimum of directions to the performer or exercises only the minimum of choice in composition.

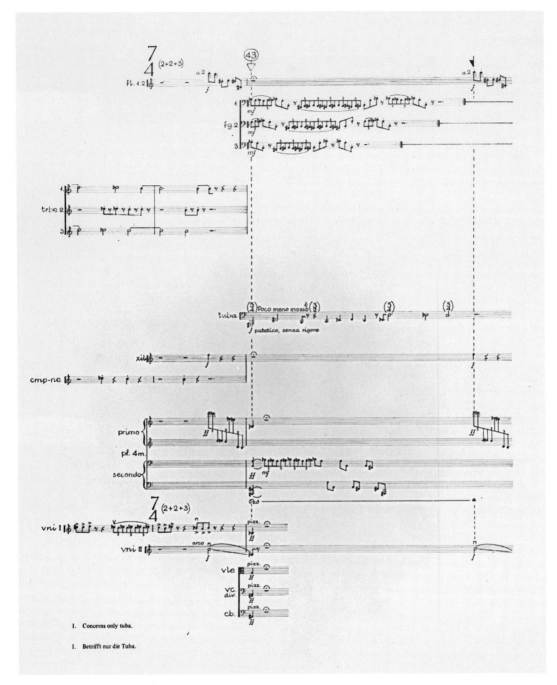

▲ Witold Lutosławski, Symphony No. 3 (1983), p. 46. The composer employed a full arrowhead to indicate the signal that the conductor gives the entire orchestra to initiate a section that is played together. The half-arrowhead marks a signal to selected *ad libitum* players. The music written in regular measures, such as that for the three trumpets, is governed by the conventional correspondence of parts; the music written without bars is played freely with respect to durations but accurately with respect to pitches. (*Copyright 1984 by J. W. Chester/ Edition Wilhelm Hansen, London, Ltd. Copyright held by Polskie Wydawnictwo Muzyczne, Cracow, Poland. All Rights Reserved. Used by permission*)

each of the players, continuously reproduces fragments of music by Beethoven. The player opens and shuts the loudspeaker control [i.e., regulates the volume] whenever he wishes.[3]

A new element here is the incorporation of fragments (transformed but immediately recognizable) from Beethoven. The intention is, in Stockhausen's words, "not to interpret, but to hear familiar, old, preformed musical material with new ears, to penetrate and transform it with a musical consciousness of today." This aim represents a new way of relating music of the present to that of the past. "Quotation" music is also exemplified in the works of George Rochberg (b. 1918) and Lukas Foss (b. 1922) in America (see Chapter 22), Peter Maxwell Davies (b. 1934) in England, and Hans Werner Henze (b. 1926) in Germany.

The Polish composer Witold Lutosławski (1913–1994) made selective use of indeterminacy. A graduate in composition and piano of the Warsaw Conservatory, he was deeply influenced by Bartók in his own early folkloristic works. Later Lutosławski briefly adopted a personal version of the twelve-tone serial method. With *Venetian Games* (1961), he began to give some leeway to performers, while insisting very much on his own authorship of the entire composition. In his String Quartet (1964), for example, the players begin a section together, but each plays a pitch-determined part in the notated rhythm independently, without a coordinated tempo or meter, introducing hesitations, ritards, and accelerations as individual expressive interpretations, until the next checkpoint is reached. Then, at a signal from one of the players, they begin again together. Performances of such a short section may differ hardly at all.

Lutosławski

In Symphony No. 3 (1983) Lutosławski uses a similar procedure, except that the conductor signals the beginning of each section. Some sections are *ad libitum*, permitting the individual orchestral player to dwell upon a figure or develop a motive in the manner of a soloist playing a cadenza (see facsimile, page 512). At times eight stands of violins, guided by the prescribed pitches but only approximate durations, go their own way like tendrils of a vine, each scaling its own adventurous peak. These passages achieve a freedom and eloquence hardly possible through precise notation.

One by-product of indeterminacy is the variety of new kinds of notation. Scores range all the way from fragments of conventional staff notes, through purely graphic suggestions of melodic curves, dynamic ranges, rhythms, and the like, to even more impressionistic and meager directives. One main consequence of indeterminacy is that no two performances of a piece are identical. The difference, whether small or great, between one performance and another is not merely a matter of interpretation but a substantive difference in musical content and order of presentation. A recording of such a work captures only one particular performance. Consequently, we must alter our

New notation

New concept of composition

3. Wilfried Daenicke: from the record jacket DGG 139–461 SLPM.

traditional definition of "a composition." In effect, this type of composition does not exist as such, but only as a performance, or as the sum of its possible performances.

POSTLUDE

The first half of the twentieth century witnessed a progressive breakup of the tonal harmonic system that had prevailed for the preceding two hundred years. Schoenberg, at first intuitively and later methodically with his twelve-tone rows, introduced a radically new conception of musical structure and, with his "emancipation of the dissonance," in effect abolished the traditional distinction between consonance and dissonance. As the century progressed Schoenberg's serial method was applied to all elements of musical design before being combined with other, freer methods of composition. Traditional ideas about musical sound and even about the art of composition itself have also been altered in this century—by the introduction of new timbres and instruments, by the expansion of the pitch continuum and experimentation with spatial effects, by the application of various electronic media and technologies, and by the concept of indeterminacy in the creation of musical compositions. As a result, new and different modes of interaction have modified the customary roles of composer and performer.

22

The American
Twentieth Century

PRELUDE

The United States led the production of new music in the second half of
the twentieth century. The number of serious composers—Americans by
birth or choice—the volume, strength, and originality of their creative output, and the important fresh directions nurtured here, made America the
center for new musical developments.

Twentieth-century American music was in large measure an extension
of European music, and many of Europe's leading composers for political,
professional, or personal reasons spent a significant portion of their creative years in the United States. The most prominent were Bartók, Hindemith, Stravinsky, Schoenberg, Varèse, Weill, and Milhaud; others, such as
Penderecki and Boulez, paid shorter visits. Some of these European composers had a host of American pupils, though it would be wrong to say
that they founded "schools" of composition. One of the forums where
American and European composers interacted was the Berkshire (now
Tanglewood) Music Center in western Massachusetts. Each summer since
1940, the Center has awarded scholarships to promising young composers
and brought to the Berkshires eminent figures from inside and outside the
country to teach. Starting in the 1920s a steady stream of Americans went
to Europe to study composition, many with Nadia Boulanger in Paris, who
continued her classes there and in Fontainebleau until her death in 1979
at the age of ninety-two. Among those who studied with her were Aaron
Copland, Virgil Thomson, Roy Harris, Walter Piston, Ross Lee Finney,

▲ Virgil Thomson, Walter Piston, Herbert Elwell, and Aaron Copland at the home of Nadia Boulanger (inset), June 1926, before a concert of works by young American composers. Elwell, less famous than the other three, was head of composition and theory at the Cleveland Institute of Music and music critic of the *Cleveland Plain Dealer* (1932–64). (*Photo by Thérèse Bonney. Virgil Thomson Papers, Yale University Music Library. Boulanger portrait courtesy of Louise Talma. Used by permission*)

Elliott Carter, and Philip Glass. These exchanges contributed to the Europeanization of American music.

In other ways American twentieth-century music remained true to the traditions of its colonial and indigenous past and to the multicultural ethnic mix that was only partly European. **Traditional Music** occupied a prominent place in American history: Protestant psalmody and hymnody; British folk and popular songs; African and African-American spiritual songs, rhythms, and textures. Another strain that made America's music recognizably different from that of other continents was its **Vernacular Styles**: ragtime, blues, jazz, swing, wind-band music, country music, cowboy songs, rock, musical comedy songs, and sentimental ballads. All of these traditions lie behind, or alongside of, the **Foundations for an American Art Music**—art music being music aimed at a relatively small, concert-going public and requiring some effort to understand. Composers

Since 1945 have continued to draw on an increasing array of options from the past or have rejected these in favor of new experiments, some of which have been more long-lived than others, as we will see.

Traditional Music

The earliest music making in the American colonies that is documented in writing remains the singing of psalms. In fact, the very first book printed in North America was the Bay Psalm Book (*The Whole Booke of Psalmes Faithfully Translated into English Metre*), published in Boston in 1640. Congregations were taught and encouraged to read notes and not to depend simply on rote learning. Later, singing schools established during the eighteenth century trained a core of amateurs to sing psalm settings and anthems in parts. The availability of such singers became an invitation for composers to write new music.

Music in the colonies

William Billings (1746–1800), the most prominent of these composers, left a significant body of music and writings. His *New-England Psalm-Singer* (1770) contains 108 psalm and hymn settings and 15 anthems and canons for chorus. He issued several more collections, including *The Continental Harmony*, in 1794. Most of Billings's settings were "plain tunes," that is, homophonic four-part harmonizations of his newly invented melodies, such as the famous "Chester," a patriotic song for which he also wrote the text.

W. Billings

◄ The frontispiece to William Billings's *New-England Psalm-Singer* (1770). Surrounding the a cappella singers at the table is a canon for six voices with a ground bass to be sung "by three or four deep voices." Engraving by Paul Revere.

▲ *Washington-Street*, arranged by William Billings in *The Continental Harmony* (Boston: Isaiah Thomas and Ebenezer T. Andrews, 1794). After a mainly note-against-note opening, a single voice begins a series of entrances in free imitation, or "fuging style." (*Yale University Music Library. Used by permission*)

But his later collections showed a preference for "fuging tunes," which contain sections of free imitation. Billings declared his independence from the normal rules of counterpoint, claiming that he had devised a set of rules better suited to his aims and method. Indeed his settings, as exemplified in the fuging tune *Washington-Street* (see facsimile above), exhibit numerous parallel fifths and octaves (for example, measures 1–2, 3, 3–4, 5, 6, 7, and 10), as well as chords without thirds (measures 5, 8, and 11). Other hymns are spiced with unconventional dissonances. The rugged character of the music matches Billings's colorful and eccentric personality.

Immigration and its influences

Moravians

Outside New England, diverse immigrant groups brought with them or later imported elements of their religious and secular music. Most notable were the Moravians, German-speaking Protestants from Moravia and Bohemia, the regions of Austria-Hungary that eventually became the Czech and Slovak republics. They settled in Bethlehem (Pennsylvania), Salem (North Carolina), and surrounding areas. Embellishing their church services with concerted arias and motets, the Moravians also collected substantial libraries of imported music, which fostered chamber-music making.

Immigration from Germany intensified after the 1848 revolution and crop failures there caused many musicians and music teachers to leave. Eventually, Germans (and Americans who had studied in Germany) dominated the teaching of composition and music theory in American conservatories and universities. Hermann Kotzschmar, a refugee from Germany in 1848 who settled in Portland, Maine, taught organ and composition to Harvard's first professor of music, the composer and organist John Knowles Paine (1839–1906).

Lowell Mason (1792–1872) was one of the most influential of the German-educated musicians. Born of a musical family in Medfield, Massachusetts, he was a partner in a dry-goods firm in Savannah, Georgia, when he began studying music with Frederick Abel, who had just come from Germany. Mason became president of the Boston Handel and Haydn Society in 1827 and led the founding in 1833 of the Boston Academy of Music, dedicated to the musical instruction of children. He deplored the crude music of the Yankee tunesmiths, leaning rather toward a correct and modest European style, in which he set some 1,200 original hymn tunes as well as arrangements of others. Even today, many Protestant hymnals contain more than a dozen of his melodies and arrangements. As superintendent of music for the public schools of Boston, he introduced music into the regular curriculum, prompting other cities to follow suit.

L. Mason

While Mason was reforming New England hymnody, the Yankee tunes were kept alive in the south, transcribed in collections such as *Kentucky Harmony* (1816), *The Southern Harmony* (1835), and *The Sacred Harp* (1844). The last included some spiritual songs and others used in Southern revival meetings. So-called Negro spirituals, although they had a pre–Civil War history, were not published until after the war, when *Slave Songs of the United States* (1867) appeared. The Fisk Jubilee Singers of the all-black Fisk Univer-

▲ The original Fisk Jubilee Singers, photographed in London, 1873, during their European tour. Founded at Fisk University in Nashville, Tennessee, the group consisted of black student musicians who performed spirituals and other songs in four-part harmony. Their example inspired other "jubilee" groups to form. (*Photographs and Prints Division. Schomburg Center for Research in Black Culture, The New York Public Library, Astor, Lenox, and Tilden Foundations*)

sity in Nashville, Tennessee, popularized these songs in the 1870s through their polished and enthusiastic performances in concert tours on both sides of the Atlantic.

Brass and wind bands

The instrumental counterparts of the singing schools were the town, village, and school bands. The earliest of these became attached to military units, but in the nineteenth century local bands cropped up everywhere, and no parade was complete without one or more. The wind band became one of the fixtures of American life; every high school, not to mention college, had one. By the 1960s there were fifty thousand wind bands in schools throughout the country.

Sousa

The repertory of early-nineteenth-century bands consisted of marches, quicksteps (fast marches), dances including the two-step (in march time), waltzes, polkas, arrangements of songs, such as those of Stephen Foster (1826–1864), and display pieces often scored for special soloists. The most famous of the bandmaster-composers was John Philip Sousa (1854–1932), who in 1880 became leader of the U.S. Marine Band. In 1892 he organized his own band, which toured throughout the world. A highly skilled composer of marches himself, he wrote more than a hundred, including the famous *Stars and Stripes Forever* (1897). Edwin Franko Goldman (1878–1956), a pupil of Dvořák, also composed many marches and pioneered the training of bandmasters. He and his son, Richard Franko Goldman (1910–1980), acquainted the American public with this repertory and promoted the idea of the summer town-band concert through the nationally broadcast Goldman Band summer series from New York's Central Park.

Brass bands and dance orchestras were the main training grounds for African-American musicians. Black bands occupied an important place in both black and white social life in New Orleans, Baltimore, Memphis, Newark, Richmond, Philadelphia, New York, Detroit, Chicago, and other cities early in the twentieth century and even before. These bands performed from notation and did relatively little improvisation, although they played with a swinging and syncopated style that distinguished them from white bands. Among the leaders who attracted national and international attention was James Reese Europe (1881–1919). Europe's band created a sensation in Paris, and the French Garde Républicaine tried in vain to imitate its sound.

Vernacular Styles

Ragtime

Among the dances played by both the brass and concert bands were pieces in ragtime, sometimes in march-and-trio form. Ragtime apparently originated in the cakewalk, a couples dance marked by strutting and acrobatic movements that was popular in minstrel-show finales. Musically, ragtime's most prominent feature was syncopation against a regular bass rhythm. This syncopation, often involving silence on a downbeat, derived from the "clapping" or "patting" *Juba* of American blacks, a survival of African drumming and hand-clapping. The emphasis on offbeats reflects the complex cross-rhythms common in African music. Piano and band pieces identified as cake-walks, "rags," or "ragtime" were first published in the 1890s. The success of *Maple Leaf Rag* (Example 22.1) by Scott Joplin (1868–1917), son of an ex-slave musician, added momentum to the ragtime craze. Soon the syncopated rhythms found their way into music for ballroom dancing, reflected in new steps such as the turkey trot and chicken glide, evolving eventually into the most enduring of them, the foxtrot.

EXAMPLE 22.1   Scott Joplin, *Maple Leaf Rag*

Blues

The origin of the blues is obscure. Well before 1900 black singers in the rural south—especially in Georgia, Mississippi, and Tennessee—were heard singing laments in a style that later became known as blues. The subject might be the loss of a lover or a job, or simply general desperation. The text usually consisted of two-line stanzas, with the first line repeated and the last rhyming with the first. The use of "blue" notes, a slight lowering of the third, seventh, and sometimes the fifth degrees of the major scale, may have been an attempt to approximate within the equal-tempered system a West African pentatonic scale. The chordal accompaniment, by a guitar, piano, or band, however, is an adaptation of European triadic harmony.

Jazz

Black musicians in their own circles had been improvising *choruses*, that is, variations on blues, ragtime, and other tunes, for years. It was only after this style was performed outside the culture in which it grew up that jazz became recognized as a distinct phenomenon. When white orchestras—such

Form of the Blues

*E*arly blues used a variety of period lengths and successions of chords. Eventually the preferred form distributed the tonic, subdominant, and dominant chords over a period of twelve measures, as shown in Example 22.2. The accompanist or an instrumental soloist, such as a cornet player, usually improvised "breaks" at the ends of lines, and this has been likened to the choral responses of African music. Bessie Smith's rendering of *St. Louis Blues* by W. C. Handy with Louis Armstrong on cornet, recorded in 1925, exemplifies this style of music and performance.

EXAMPLE 22.2 W. C. Handy, *St. Louis Blues*

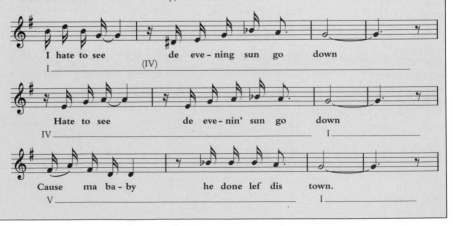

as Tom Brown's "Dixieland Jass Band, Direct from New Orleans," which played in Chicago in 1915—began imitating this practice, it was evident that a new kind of music had emerged, different from ragtime and blues particularly in the way it was performed. Instead of playing the music "straight," observing the rhythms and textures of the model, players improvised arrangements that distinguished one musician from another and one performance from another.

The essence of jazz is improvisation on an existing tune or scheme—it is very much a player's art. Group improvisation, practiced particularly in New Orleans, resulted in a counterpoint of improvised melodic lines alternating with improvised solo episodes in which the rest of the ensemble supplied a rhythmic and harmonic background. A typical New Orleans ensemble, such as Joseph ("King") Oliver's Creole Jazz Band of the 1920s, consisted of cornet(s), clarinet, trombone, piano, banjo, and drums. In later combos trumpets substituted for the cornets, and saxophones replaced or doubled the clarinet.

Improvisation

The fashion for larger bands that began in the 1920s was propelled in part by the availability of larger performance spaces for jazz: supper clubs, ballrooms, auditoriums, and theaters. White musicians, such as Paul Whiteman and Benny Goodman, as well as blacks, such as Fletcher Henderson, Louis Armstrong, Duke Ellington, and William "Count" Basie, organized *big bands*, which typically comprised sections of trumpets, trombones, reeds, including saxophones and clarinets, sometimes a violin, and a "rhythm section" of bass, piano, guitar, and drums. Although solos were still improvised, the basic plan of a piece was written down as an orchestration or *chart* by an arranger, who was sometimes the leader but more often a member of the band or a skilled orchestrator. For example, Henderson arranged for Goodman both before and after his own band broke up. In addition to instrumental pieces, which were jazz-oriented, more and more of the big-band repertory was taken over by popular songs in which the band both accompanied a singer and elaborated on the song through clever, harmonically adventurous arrangements that featured one or another of the band's sections. The arrangers and leaders, modeling their style on the black bands, developed a swinging manner—an uneven rendering of a series of equal note values—that led to their music being called *swing*. It was intended for dancing as well as casual listening, but some ambitious compositions commanded an attentive audience, such as Ellington's *Mood Indigo* (1930) or his *Concerto for Cootie* (1940).

Big bands

Arrangers

While the big-band arrangements and the thoroughly scored jazz compositions downplayed improvisation, the most essential element of jazz, the *bebop* or *bop* style of the 1940s and 1950s and the freer idioms of jazz that followed it inspired a kind of music that was planned in advance but realized in largely improvised performance. Bebop and post-bop styles often were not based on standard songs but on newly created music. Bebop admitted techniques that were outside the common vocabulary of popular music, some of which were borrowed from classical music—non-chordal dissonance, chro-

Bebop

▲ King Oliver's Creole Jazz Band, 1923. Left to right: Honoré Dutrey, trombone; Baby Dodds, drums; King Oliver, cornet; Louis Armstrong, slide trumpet; Lil Hardin (later Armstrong), piano; Bill Johnson, banjo; Johnny Dodds, clarinet. (*William Ransom Hogan Jazz Archives, Tulane University*)

maticism, complicated and conflicting rhythms that were not danceable, irregular phrase structures, modality, atonality, and unaccustomed instrumental effects. Performances in which one of the players was essentially the composer are preserved on recordings that have become classics, that are listened to over and over again, analyzed, and reviewed in critical essays. Some of the composer-performers were trumpeters John Birks ("Dizzy") Gillespie (1917–1993) and Miles Davis (1926–1991); saxophonists Charlie ("Bird") Parker (1920–1955), John Coltrane (1926–1967), and Ornette Coleman (b. 1930); and pianists Thelonious Monk (1917–1982), Bill Evans (1929–1980), and Cecil Taylor (b. 1933). They and many others created music that deserves to be heard as serious art.

Modern Jazz

While jazz got its start in cities, rural areas nurtured other kinds of music. One type was the hillbilly-country music of the southeast, which was at first based on traditional narrative and lyrical Anglo-American ballads and fiddle tunes. Partly through commercial sponsorship of the recording and broadcast industry, hillbilly combined with the western cowboy themes and manners popularized by the Texan Gene Autry, to produce *country-and-western*, often called *country* music. Typically the singer strummed the accompaniment on the guitar. Bands were later formed to support the singers, but, unlike the big bands that inspired them, these groups were dominated by violins and guitars (eventually electric and pedal-steel guitars) rather than trumpets and saxophones. The bands also adapted some of the practices of jazz, notably its

Country music

driving and syncopated rhythms and virtuoso improvisations. A different approach was taken by Roy Acuff, whose weekly radio show from Nashville in the 1940s, *Grand Ole Opry*, promoted conservative religious sentiments. From this background emerged two country-and-western stars of the 1960s, Hank Williams and Johnny Cash.

The urban-black counterpart to this music was called *rhythm-and-blues*, a music-trade term that embraces a variety of genres common in the post–World War II years. The most characteristic of these is performed by small groups consisting of a vocalist or vocal quartet, a piano, organ, or electric guitar, string or electric bass, and drums. It is distinguished from traditional blues by an insistent rhythm, with emphasis on the second and fourth beats—the backbeats—whining treble guitar, mannered articulation of the lyrics, and repetitive amplified bass line. *Hound Dog* (1952) by Willie Mae ("Big Mama") Thornton (1926–1984) received wide recognition through the version recorded by Elvis Presley (1935–1977) in 1956.

Rhythm-and-blues

The two guitar-dominated genres just described merged during the 1950s into the popular interracial movement originally called *rock-and-roll* and later shortened to *rock*. This music was launched in the 1955 film *Blackboard Jungle* with the hit song *Rock around the Clock* by Bill Haley (1925–1981). It had the unrelenting beat of rhythm-and-blues and the milder guitar background of country-and-western. Elvis Presley enjoyed phenomenal success in the late 1950s and early 1960s with a southern, insinuating version of this amalgamation. The texts, most often concerned with sex, were delivered in an explosive, raucous, sometimes wailing, shrieking, or shouting voice, though there were also gentle ballads, often about teenage love, sung in a deliberately subdued mode. The instrumentation of rock-and-roll consisted of amplified or electric guitars for both rhythm and melody, with saxophones inserting jazz-like responses. Additional harmony, rhythmic effects, and ostinatos were supplied by an organ or synthesizer. An eclectic version of the idiom developed by the British quartet The Beatles achieved unprecedented success starting in 1964, when they first toured the United States. The group included two creative songwriters, John Lennon (1940–1980) and Paul McCartney (b. 1942), who continued on their own after The Beatles broke up in 1970.

Rock-and-roll

The Broadway musical or *musical comedy* reflected the fashions popular at any given time and supplied new "standard" songs for adaptation by other vernacular styles. The genre differed in important ways from other plays with songs, such as the ballad opera, opéra comique, Singspiel, or operetta. The production and the plot were built around the songs, vocal ensembles, and dances, all of which determined the success or failure of the enterprise. Although George M. Cohan (1878–1942) wrote the music for his own lyrics and plays, and Cole Porter (1891–1964) wrote his own witty lyrics, most shows were the products of short-term collaborations or long-standing teams. For example, Richard Rodgers (1902–1979) collaborated with the lyricist

Musical comedy

Lorenz Hart (1895–1943) and later with Oscar Hammerstein II (1895–1960); Frederick Loewe (1904–1988) wrote music for the books and lyrics of Alan Jay Lerner (1918–1986). In 1944 a young assistant conductor who became an overnight celebrity after brilliantly directing the New York Philharmonic Symphony during Bruno Walter's illness saw his Broadway musical *On the Town* open the same year for a run of 463 performances. This was Leonard Bernstein (1910–1990), who was to enjoy one of his greatest popular successes and creative achievements with *West Side Story* (1957), with lyrics by Stephen Sondheim (b. 1930).

Although these successful shows consisted of many components, including stage sets, choreography, costumes, and lighting designs, in most cases the music and lyrics are all that have survived (apart from cinematic versions of a few shows like *Oklahoma*, *My Fair Lady*, and *West Side Story*). It is easy to forget that *Smoke Gets in Your Eyes* and *All the Things You Are*—two "standards" for jazz improvisation—are songs from theater pieces by Jerome Kern (1885–1945), and are among the thousand or so such creations that he left. Similarly, an even larger number by Irving Berlin (1888–1989), including *A Pretty Girl Is like a Melody*, from *Ziegfeld Follies of 1919*, are from Broadway shows. George Gershwin (1898–1937), who began as a songwriter rather than a theater person, by 1924 had three hits on lyrics by his brother Ira in the show *Lady, Be Good*: the title song, *Fascinating Rhythm*, and *The Man I Love*. Gershwin's *Porgy and Bess* (1935), which he called a "folk opera," has been produced both as a musical and as an opera, erasing the boundary between so-called popular or vernacular traditions on the one hand, and classical or cultivated traditions on the other. In the same way, his *Rhapsody in Blue* (1924) bridged the gulf between popular music and the concert hall by combining the languages of jazz and Lisztian Romanticism.

Foundations for an American Art Music

Ives

Charles Ives (1874–1954) became the first distinctively American art-music composer to gain eminence. He studied with his father, a bandmaster and church musician, and at Yale with Horatio Parker (1863–1919). Although his musical training was solid, his aesthetic aims did not coincide with those of the musical establishment; so, while he continued to compose, he went to work in a relative's insurance business and later started his own firm. Public recognition of Ives's musical achievements came only in the 1930s, many years *Ives's works* after he had created a body of highly original works. Mostly unperformed and unpublished, his pieces anticipated some of the radical developments of twentieth-century music: free dissonance, polytonality, polyrhythm, and experimental form. Almost all were written between 1890 and 1922, and they include some two hundred songs, five violin sonatas and other chamber music, two piano sonatas, five symphonies, and other orchestral music. His most famous work was the second piano sonata, *Concord, Mass., 1840–60* (1911–15), which he described as "impressionistic pictures" of the so-called transcendentalist writers Ralph Waldo Emerson and Henry David Thoreau, who were associated with the time and place of Ives's title.

Conventional and unconventional elements either mingle or stand side by side in Ives's works: fragments of folksongs, dance tunes, gospel hymns, as well as motives from Beethoven and Bach emerge from a complex, rhapsodic, uniquely ordered flow of sound. Sometimes Ives first quotes fragments of a tune, then gradually pieces together a full statement. Two or more familiar tunes are often strung together or sounded simultaneously in a humorous, surprising, or shocking way. Ives also quotes tunes in the ordinary way, to support a text he is using or to illustrate an extramusical program. His song *They Are There!* (NAWM 143), composed for unison chorus and orchestra in 1917—the year the United States sent troops to fight alongside the Allies in World War I—illustrates several of these techniques.

Ives's style

Ives's work has been of incalculable importance to younger generations of American musicians. He questioned the value of traditional forms and thematic unity, setting meter and tonality adrift. He indulged in apparently irrational tone clusters, allowing several independent layers of sound to coexist without a harmonic relationship. He admitted melodies from the sacred and secular, popular and artistic realms as equally valid material for his compositions. He gave performers a chance in certain compositions to choose between several options. In all these departures from convention, Ives set an example for later composers, challenging them to shun conformity and experiment with these tactics (see vignette, page 528).

Ives's influence

Carl Ruggles (1876–1971; see Plate XV, facing page 538), both a friend of Ives and a kindred spirit, was fiercely independent of all influences, including those of the American past. Although conscious of both Schoenberg's and Berg's methods, he struck out on an atonal path all his own. His best-known composition, *Sun-Treader* (1926–31) for a large orchestra, is dominated by the tritone and semitone, the latter most often used in octave-displacements, which makes the music strident, always reaching for new goals.

Ruggles

That Henry Cowell (1897–1965) was a Californian is significant, because it shows that the musical frontier had reached the West Coast. He balanced the northeastern composers' European orientation with one that looked inward to the American midwest and outward to Asia. In the 1920s Cowell embarked on a search to obtain new effects from the grand piano. In *The Aeolian Harp* (1923) the strings of the piano are strummed by the player while holding down three- and four-note chords on the keyboard. Soft harp-like broken chords emerge, not so elusive or mysterious but still resembling

Cowell

Cowell's special piano effects

Charles Ives on Americanism in Music:

❝ If a man finds that the cadences of an Apache war-dance come nearest to his soul—provided he has taken pains to know enough other cadences, for eclecticism is part of his duty; sorting potatoes means a better crop next year—let him assimilate whatever he finds highest of the Indian ideal so that he can use it with the cadences, fervently, transcendentally, inevitably, furiously, in his symphonies, in his operas, in his whistlings on the way to work, so that he can paint his house with them, make them a part of his prayer-book—this is all possible and necessary, if he is confident that they have a part in his spiritual consciousness. With this assurance, his music will have everything it should of sincerity, nobility, strength, and beauty, no matter how it sounds; and if, with this, he is true to none but the highest of American ideals (that is, the ideals only that coincide with his spiritual consciousness), his music will be true to itself and incidentally American, and it will be so even after it is proved that all our Indians came from Asia. ❞

From "Epilogue," in Charles Ives, *Essays Before a Sonata and Other Writings*, ed. Howard Boatwright (New York: Norton, 1961), pp. 79–80.

those of the wind-driven Aeolian harp, which was popular in Asia and the United States. In *The Banshee* (1925), an assistant holds the damper pedal down while the pianist plays glissandos with both hands, sometimes in opposite directions, at other times sustaining a note or several at once by rubbing the lower strings along their length. The sustained notes in this piece form a whole-tone scale that adds to its "exotic" flavor.

Cowell's tone clusters

Cowell is remembered most for his tone clusters, which he used in *The Tides of Manaunaun* (1912; Manaunaun was the legendary Irish sea-god), written when he was fifteen, *Advertisements* (1914), and *Piano Piece* (1924). The tone clusters are obtained by striking the keys with the fist or forearm, thereby creating harmonies based on the interval of the second. He later applied tone clusters to orchestral music, as in *Some More Music* (1917) and the Piano Concerto (1929).

In his later compositions, Cowell made use of Irish folk music, rural hymns and fuging tunes, non-Western music, and even non-Western instruments such as the Indian tabla and the Japanese koto. Cowell promoted music by his contemporaries as well as his own through the periodical *New Music*, in which he published scores by Ruggles and Ives, among others.

Crawford Seeger

Cowell also published the works of Ruth Crawford (1901–1953). She joined the circle around Ruggles through Charles Seeger, the composer and pioneering musicologist with whom she studied composition and whom she married in 1931. She was most productive as a composer in Chicago between 1924 and 1929 and in New York between 1930 and 1933. One of her most successful works from the Chicago period was the Violin Sonata (1926; see the second movement, Bouyant, in NAWM 144). In her New York period she experimented with serial techniques, including their application to parameters other than pitch. Later she collaborated with writer Carl Sandburg and folklorists John and Alan Lomax, editing American folksongs from field recordings; she also published many folk transcriptions and arrangements in which she was faithful to the songs' native contexts.

The French-born Edgard Varèse (1883–1965) moved to New York in 1915 after a short career as a composer and conductor in Paris and Prague. Apart from brief sojourns in Europe, he remained in New York for the rest of his life. Varèse celebrated his adopted country in his first major work, *Amériques* (1918–21). Its fragmentary melodies and loose structure betray links to Debussy, whom he knew and who approved of his independent spirit. Even more, *Amériques* points in the direction of Varèse's future work: his concerns with the manipulation of sound masses more than with themes and their development. Next came a series of compositions that laid down a new agenda: *Offrandes* (1921), *Hyperprism* (1923), *Octandre* (1923), *Intégrales* (1925), *Ionisation* (for percussion only, 1931), and *Ecuatorial* (1934). In these works, Varèse aimed to liberate composition from conventional melody, harmony, meter, regular pulse, recurrent beat, and traditional orchestration. Instead, he deployed individual and massed instrumental ensembles as the raw material of organized sounds. In his compositions from the 1920s, nonpitched percussion sounds and pitches, played mostly by winds, collide, balance, intersect, attract, repel, speed up, slow down, combine, split up, crystallize, diffuse, and expand and contract in range, volume, and timbre. A great variety of percussion instruments, some drawn from non-Western cultures, others—such as the siren—from city life, are given key roles in these works, acting independently as equals to the winds and strings.

Aaron Copland (1900–1990) integrated national American idioms into his music with technical polish. He was the first of many American composers to study with Nadia Boulanger in Paris (see illustration, page 516). Jazz idioms and dissonance figure prominently in some of his earlier works, such as the *Music for the Theater* (1925) and the Piano Concerto (1927). These were followed by compositions of a more reserved and harmonically complex style, including the Piano Variations of 1930. In a desire to appeal to a larger audience, Copland turned toward simplicity, diatonic harmonies, and the use of traditional song—Mexican folksongs in the brilliant orchestral suite *El Salón Mexico* (1936), cowboy songs in the ballets *Billy the Kid* (1938) and *Rodeo* (1942). The school opera *The Second Hurricane* (1937) and scores for

Varèse

Varèse's style

Copland

Copland's early works

Two measures from *Intégrales* demonstrate how pitch, duration, register, dynamics, and instrumental color interact (Example 22.3). The B♭ has been sounding in the clarinet from the very first measure of the piece when the pitch classes on either side, *A* and *B*, collide with it in the piccolos. A moment later these sustained tones are simultaneously joined by more semitone intervals in the muted trombones—*C* against the *B*, *E* against *E♭*—while the ninth *B♭–B* in the woodwinds is confronted and counterpoised by the ninth *C–C♯* in the trombones. Meanwhile, rolls on the tenor drum, strokes on the rim (R) and membrane (M) of the muffled snare drum, and thumb-beats on the tambourine offer their own characteristic versions of the passage of time. Later, a fanfare rudely intrudes, Ives-like, into the athematic surroundings. In this almost constantly explosive, expletive, and exclamatory medium few relaxing moments exist; it is the music of urban noise and clashes, reflecting the midtown New York scene that Varèse heard and saw from his apartment.

EXAMPLE 22.3   Edgard Varèse, *Intégrales*: Andantino

a number of films (including *Our Town*, 1940) represent the *Gebrauchsmusik* of this period—that is, music composed specifically "for use."

Copland reached the apex of his trend toward simpler music in *Appalachian Spring* (1944), first written as a ballet with an ensemble of thirteen instruments but better known in the arrangement as an orchestral suite (see excerpt in NAWM 145). The work incorporates variations on the Shaker hymn *'Tis the Gift to Be Simple*. The song (NAWM 145a) is subtly transfigured and its essence is absorbed in music that sincerely and simply expresses the pastoral spirit in authentically American terms. The wide spacing of chords and the empty octaves and fifths suggest country fiddling.

Copland's later works encompassed numerous styles. On the one hand, a new large-scale synthesis appeared with the Third Symphony (1946), which has no overt program, though some of its tunes are suggestive of folksongs. On the other, the finely wrought chamber-music idiom of the Piano Sonata (1941) evolved from the style of the Piano Variations. In the songs on *Twelve Poems of Emily Dickinson* (1950), and more markedly in the Piano Quartet (1950), the Piano Fantasy (1957), and the orchestral *Inscape* (1967), Copland adopted some features of twelve-tone technique. After 1970 he was more active as a conductor and lecturer than as a composer. Despite the various influences reflected in the range of styles he employed, Copland retained an unmistakable artistic identity. His music preserves a sense of tonality, though not always by traditional means. His rhythms are lively and flexible, and he was adept at obtaining new sounds from simple chords by exploiting instrumental color and spacing. Through encouragement, counsel, and by example, he influenced many younger American composers, among them Leonard Bernstein, Lukas Foss, and David Del Tredici.

Copland's later works

Copland's style and influence

A more self-conscious nationalist, Roy Harris (1898–1979) wrote music that suggests at its best (as in the Third Symphony, 1939) something of the rugged simplicity of Walt Whitman's poetry. Some of his works embody actual folk themes, for example in the choral *Folk Song Symphony*, his fourth of fourteen symphonies (1940). His sweeping modal melodies and transparent counterpoint impart a sense of the expansiveness associated with the American West. His orchestral music sounds American also because of its wind-band scoring. A student of early music, Harris was fond of fugue and ostinato procedures.

Harris

Virgil Thomson (1896–1989), a witty and caustic critic as well as a composer, returned to the simplicity of the colonial past and its hymnody in his *Variations and Fugue on Sunday School Tunes* (1926) and the *Symphony on a Hymn Tune* (1928). He spent many years in Paris, and although he studied with Nadia Boulanger, his model became Satie, whom he met in 1922 and whose playfulness, directness, and striving for simplicity he imitated. He found a kindred soul in another American expatriate, Gertrude Stein, whose opera libretto, *Four Saints in Three Acts*, he set in 1928. Its music is a sophisticated tongue-in-cheek mix of Protestant hymns, patriotic tunes, tangos,

V. Thomson

waltzes, and marches. *The Mother of Us All* (1947), also a collaboration with Stein, is based on the life of the suffragette Susan B. Anthony. The repetitive, stripped-down, triadic accompaniments anticipate the minimalists of the 1970s and 1980s, while the vocal parts reveal an uncanny facility for turning speech into music (see Example 22.4, and vignette, page 533).

EXAMPLE 22.4   Virgil Thomson, *The Mother of Us All*: Act I, Scene 2, *Susan B. Anthony is my name*

Virgil Thomson on Setting Words to Music:

❝ My hope in putting Gertrude Stein to music had been to break, crack open, and solve for all time anything still waiting to be solved, which was almost everything, about English musical declamation. My theory was that if a text is set correctly for the sound of it, the meaning will take care of itself. And the Stein texts, for prosodizing in this way, were manna. With meanings already abstracted, or absent, or so multiplied that choice among them was impossible, there was no temptation toward tonal illustration, say, of birdie babbling by brook or heavy heavy hangs my heart. You could make a setting for sound and syntax only, then add, if needed, an accompaniment equally functional. I had no sooner put to music after this recipe one short Stein text than I knew I had opened a door. ❞

From "Langlois, Butts, and Stein" in *Virgil Thomson* by Virgil Thomson (New York: Knopf, 1966), p. 90.

Likewise incorporating specifically American idioms is the *Afro-American Symphony* (1931) of William Grant Still (1895–1978). The opening movement, in sonata form, has a first theme in twelve-bar blues structure. The third movement (NAWM 146) is a colorful, syncopated, cleverly orchestrated, dancelike scherzo. The lowered third and seventh "blue notes" are prominent

Still

➤ Virgil Thomson looking over Gertrude Stein's shoulder at the score of their *Four Saints in Three Acts*. (*Virgil Thomson Papers, Yale University Music Library. Used by permission*)

C H R O N O L O G Y

1940	World War II (1939–45)
	*Copland, *Appalachian Spring* (1944)
	Britten, *Peter Grimes* (1945)
	*Menotti (b. 1911), *The Medium* (1946)
	Arthur Miller (b. 1916), *Death of a Salesman* (1949)
1950	Korean War (until 1953)
	*Cage, *Music of Changes* (1951)
	*Death of Charles Ives (b. 1874) (1954)
	Boulez, *Le Marteau sans maître* (1955)
	Rock around the Clock from *Blackboard Jungle* (1955)
	Stockhausen, *Gesang der Jünglinge* (1956)
	*Bernstein, *West Side Story* (1957)
	Orbit of first Sputnik (1957)
	*Schuller, *Seven Studies on Themes of Paul Klee* (1959)
1960	Penderecki, *Threnody for the Victims of Hiroshima*
	*Brown, *Available Forms I* (1961)
	Vatican Council II (1962)
	U.S. president John F. Kennedy assassinated (1963)
	Martin Luther King Jr. awarded Nobel peace prize (1964)
	*Babbitt, *Philomel* (1964)
	*Rochberg, *Nach Bach* (1966)

	*The Beatles, *Sergeant Pepper's Lonely Hearts Club Band* (1967)
	USSR invades Czechoslovakia (1968)
	Astronauts walk on the moon (1969)
	Woodstock Rock festival (1969)
1970	*Crumb, *Ancient Voices of Children*
	U.S. president Richard Nixon resigns (1974)
	End of U.S. involvement in Vietnam (1975)
	*Glass, *Einstein on the Beach* (1976)
	Films, *Star Wars* and *Close Encounters of the Third Kind* (1977)
	Premiere of completed *Lulu* by Berg (1979)
1980	Publication of *The New Grove Dictionary of Music and Musicians*, edited by Stanley Sadie
	*Death of John Lennon (b. 1940) (1980)
	Sandra Day O'Connor, first woman Supreme Court justice (1981)
	Compact disc becomes favored format (1985)
	*Adams, *Nixon in China* (1987)
1990	Union of East and West Germany
	*Death of Miles Davis (b. 1926) (1991)
	Dissolution of the Union of Soviet Socialist Republics (1991)
	Corigliano, *The Ghosts of Versailles*, a centenary commission by the New York Metropolitan Opera (1991)

melodically and harmonically, particularly in the transformations of the opening motive, which evolves into a sixteen-bar tune accompanied by offbeat banjo chords that punctuate the orchestral texture.

Price

Florence Price (1888–1953) adapted the antebellum *Juba* folk dance as well as melodic and harmonic elements reflecting her black musical heritage—particularly the pentatonic scale of many spirituals—in several of her large works, outstanding among which are the Piano Concerto in One Movement (1934) and the First Symphony (1931).

National vs. cosmopolitan elements

In the music of most American composers of this period the genuinely national element is not easily isolated or defined, because it is blended with cosmopolitan style features of European music. One obvious sign, of course, is the choice of American subjects for operas, cantatas, or symphonic poems, as in the *American Festival Overture* (1939) of William Schuman (1910–1992), and in his *William Billings Overture* (1943), which borrowed some tunes from Billings. But most often nationalism is injected more subtly. It may show itself in a certain forthrightness and optimism or in the flowing, unconstrained color and melody of the *Serenade for Orchestra* (1954) and *Umbrian Scene* (1964) by Ulysses Kay (1917–1995). But some eminent American composers wrote habitually in a language that cannot be considered national in any narrow sense of the word. Howard Hanson (1896–1981) was an avowed neo-Romantic with a style influenced by Sibelius. Walter Piston (1894–1976) composed chamber music and symphonies in a sturdy and sophisticated, craftily wrought, and lucid neo-Classic idiom, of which his Third Symphony (1948) is a beautiful example.

Since 1945

Abstract Idioms

Roger Sessions (1896–1985) employed the serial method freely in his Sonata for Unaccompanied Violin (1953) and later works. However, it hardly affected his consistent method of continuous motivic development. His music, stoutly individual, intense, and complex, is dissonant and chromatic. His nine symphonies, rarely performed, are among the best of the post–World War II years. The Second Symphony (1946) is a particularly powerful, almost stridently expressionistic work. The first movement begins as though in sonata form, with distinct first- and second-theme sections and development, but there is no formal recapitulation—indeed, the avoidance of literal repetition is characteristic of the work. A vigorous and distinctive theme announced in

Sessions

Roger Sessions on the Limitations of the Serial Method:

❝ Once the initial choice has been made, the series will determine the composer's vocabulary; but once the vocabulary has been so determined, the larger questions of tonal organization remain. My own strong feeling is that, while these questions must certainly be answered in terms not alien to the nature of the series, it is not serialism as such that can ever be made to account for them. I do not mean at all that I am opposed in principle to the idea of basing the structure entirely on the series itself, as Webern and others have tried to do. What I am saying is that even in structures so based, the acoustical effect seems to me to derive in the last analysis not from the manipulation of the series as such, but from the relationships between notes, as the composer has by these means set them up. . . . The series governs the composer's choice of materials, only the composer's ear and his conception determine the manner or the effect of their usage. ❞

Quoted in Andrew Imbrie, "Roger Sessions, In Honor of His Sixty-fifth Birthday," in *Perspectives on American Composers*, ed. Benjamin Boretz and Edward T. Cone (New York: Norton, 1971), p. 64.

a trumpet solo (brasses are prominent throughout the movement), continually mutates into new forms. The densely contrapuntal scoring keeps the large orchestra almost constantly busy.

Carter

The compositions of Elliott Carter (b. 1908) demonstrate an equally personal style, with notable innovations in the treatment of rhythm and form. Beginning with his Cello Sonata (1948), Carter experimented with what he called *metric modulation* in which a transition is made in a performer's part from one tempo and meter to another through an intermediary stage that shares aspects of the previous and subsequent rhythmic organization. Carter further developed this device in the First String Quartet (1950–51). While one player continues in the previous tempo, another speeds up, which imparts to each a distinctly individual profile. This counterpoint of sharply differentiated lines was inspired in part by Ives's collages quoting familiar hymns and popular music and by the cross accents heard in English madrigals. The continuous pulse and rhythmic variety invest each part with remarkable fluency and consistency as well as independence.

In the Quartet No. 2 (1959; Introduction and Allegro fantastico, NAWM 147), each instrumental part takes on a personality that interacts with others in the ensemble as if in a dramatic work, where different characters play off against one another. The tempo modulations are still present but less frequent. A trend toward expressionistic writing is evident here and even more in the Variations for Orchestra (1955), a piece rich in motivic contrasts and interplay of what Carter called "musical behaviors," referring to the character both of particular instruments and of episodes in a larger work. The Piano Concerto (1964–65), written in Berlin in the shadow of the newly built Wall dividing the city, continued the dynamic confrontation. This tragic work pits the piano with a supporting concertino of seven instruments against the full orchestra in an irreconcilable bout in which each of the two groups is assigned different pitch-trichords and metronomic speeds.

The post-Webern vogue

Although Schoenberg had a small following after settling in California, the twelve-tone method acquired its most ardent devotees not through any personal contact with its European practitioners but through fascination with the works of Schoenberg's pupil Anton Webern. Without a strong university network, Webern's advancement as the model for the 1950s would surely not have gained such strength and diffusion among young North American composers. These artists embraced Webern's lean, transparent, objective, formally clear, concentrated approach in which harmony and melody annihilated each other—partly as a rebellion against the Americanists, partly as a new phase of the neo-Classic movement (see Chapter 20, pages 479ff.). The abstract, symmetrical structures and the systematic handling of small motivic units held particular appeal for those composers who wanted to insulate their art music from other influences, particularly their own involvement in jazz, musical comedy, arranging, or film.

Babbitt

Milton Babbitt (b. 1916) was one such American composer. He studied

The University as Patron

A peculiarity of contemporary composition in North America is its close association with universities. In Europe composers have been partly supported by the state through radio networks, composers' unions (in socialist countries), research centers, festivals, annual subsidies, and grants. But in the United States and Canada steady employment in universities and colleges has given them time to compose, a ready audience, and, often, access to nearby or campus performing organizations. Of the composers just considered, only Copland and Carter had no steady university association. In the 1990s commissions by symphony orchestras, opera companies, individual performers (aided by the National Endowment for the Arts), and foundations have freed some composers from teaching institutions.

Contrary to popular wisdom, university composers have generated notable avant-garde experiments, not staid "academic" music. The universities did, however, tend to isolate composers from the public and make them independent of its support (see vignette, page 539). Walter Piston was associated with Harvard. The presence of Paul Hindemith at Yale between 1940 and 1953 turned its School of Music into a nest of his disciples. Among them, Mel Powell (b. 1923), once a jazz pianist with Benny Goodman, became the first dean of the California Institute of the Arts, and Norman Dello

▲ Paul Hindemith teaching a composition class at the Yale University School of Music, 1953. In the foreground Sam di Bonaventura (b. 1920), at right Yehudi Wyner (b. 1929). Wyner directed the music program at the State University of New York in Purchase and has taught at Yale, Brandeis, and Tufts Universities. Di Bonaventura was professor of music at George Mason University in Virginia. (*The Paul Hindemith Collection, Yale University Music Library. Used by permission*)

Joio (b. 1913) was influential nationally as the head of the Contemporary Music Project, which placed young composers in high schools to write for school ensembles.

The University of California at Berkeley, which had links to Harvard, came under Stravinsky's influence, though Roger Sessions injected a different point of view when he taught there between 1944 and 1952. Nearby Mills College in Oakland was a sinecure for Darius Milhaud between 1940 and 1970; among his pupils were Dave Brubeck (b. 1920), Pauline Oliveros (b. 1932), and Steve Reich (b. 1936).

The University of California at Los Angeles became the hub of Schoenberg's influence from 1936, when he was appointed professor, until his death in 1951. Princeton was also dominated by the teachings of the Schoenberg school, particularly through the influence of Roger Sessions, who was appointed professor in 1953, and his student Milton Babbitt (b. 1916), who became the principal theorist of the twelve-tone method. Through a grant from the Rockefeller Foundation, Columbia and Princeton Universities established a pioneering center for electronic music in 1959 to which many composers from the U.S. and abroad were invited. From this studio issued the electronic works of Otto Luening (1900–1996), Mario Davidovsky (b. 1934) of Argentina, and Jacob Druckman (1928–1996), and it was there that Varèse put the finishing touches on his *Déserts*, composed years before in Paris.

The Universities of Illinois and Michigan were also important centers, where the annual festivals of contemporary music served as forums for both avant-garde and traditional approaches. At the University of Michigan at Ann Arbor, Ross Lee Finney (1906–1997), who had studied with Boulanger and Alban Berg, was a mentor to talents as different as George Crumb (b. 1929) and Roger Reynolds (b. 1934). At the University of California at San Diego, Reynolds became the first director of the Center for Music Experiment, a magnet for multimedia and electronic innovation. Stanford University took the lead in computer-assisted composition under the guidance of John Chowning (b. 1934), whose success inspired Boulez to inaugurate a similar program in Paris.

with Sessions and received all his education in the United States (mathematics and music, both of which he taught at Princeton). Babbitt furthered serial composition through his analysis of twelve-tone rows as mathematical sets. He described the principles of this method in numerous articles and through his teaching. In his Three Compositions for Piano (1947), Babbitt subjected both pitch and duration to serial control for the first time, anticipating similar experiments by Messiaen, Boulez, and Stockhausen.

Babbitt went beyond the practices of Schoenberg and his circle to realize new potentials of the twelve-tone system. At the same time he became an

XV. *The Sun-Treader,* a portrait of Carl Ruggles by Thomas Hart Benton (1889–1938). *Sun-Treader* was the title of an important one-movement orchestral work that Ruggles wrote be
tween 1926 and 1931.   (*T. H. BENTON AND R. P. BENTON TESTAMENTARY TRUSTS / LICENSED BY
VAGA, NEW YORK, NY*)

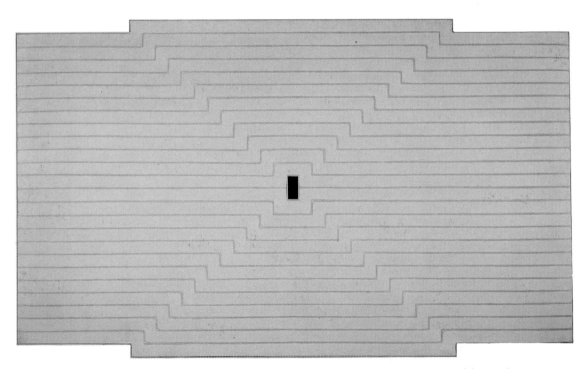

XVI. Frank Stella (b. 1936), *Six Mile Bottom* (1960). This painting is representative of the trend known as minimalism, which limits the subject of a work to the repetition of a simple geometric pattern of shapes or colors. (*© 1997 FRANK STELLA/ARTISTS RIGHTS SOCIETY (ARS), NY*)

outspoken proponent of the composer's right to be indifferent to the public's likes and dislikes. He expressed this attitude in a 1958 essay entitled by a magazine editor "Who Cares if You Listen?" (see vignette below).

New Sounds and Textures

The exploration of new sounds begun by Cowell and Varèse was taken up by several composers. Conlon Nancarrow (1912–1997) in Texarkana, Arkansas, eventually settled in Mexico but kept in touch with developments in American jazz and the music of Africa and India. These interests merged in his experiments with complex rhythms that could not be adequately expressed in notation. The player piano of his day used perforated paper rolls to activate the keys. By punching out the holes himself, Nancarrow was able to control precisely the keys of a player piano, producing time- and pitch-intervals between notes that were beyond the capability of human hands either because of their speed or their rhythmic quirkiness. He wrote more than thirty studies for the Ampico player piano, which could respond to the roll's instructions with

Nancarrow

Milton Babbitt on Composers and Their Audience:

❝ Why refuse to recognize the possibility that contemporary music has reached a stage long since attained by other forms of activity? The time has passed when the normally well-educated man without special preparation can understand the most advanced work in, for example, mathematics, philosophy, and physics. Advanced music, to the extent that it reflects the knowledge and originality of the informed composer, scarcely can be expected to appear more intelligible than these arts and sciences to the person whose musical education usually has been even less extensive than his background in other fields.

I dare suggest that the composer would do himself and his music immediate and eventual service by total, resolute, and voluntary withdrawal from his public world to one of private performance and electronic media, with its very real possibility of complete elimination of the public and social aspects of musical composition. By so doing, the separation between the domains would be defined beyond any possibility of confusion of categories, and the composer would be free to pursue a private life of professional achievement, as opposed to a public life of unprofessional compromise and exhibitionism. ❞

From Milton Babbitt, "Who Cares if You Listen?," *High Fidelity*, 8/2 (February 1958), pp. 39–40, reprinted in Elliott Schwartz and Barney Childs, *Contemporary Composers on Contemporary Music* (New York: Holt, Rhinehart & Winston, 1967), pp. 243–50.

respect to dynamics as well as pitch and duration. Some of these pieces are obviously influenced by jazz, others employ canons and ostinato figures. Before electronic and computer means could accomplish similar feats, Nancarrow offered the ear exciting new experiences.

Partch

Harry Partch (1901–1974) undertook a ruggedly individualistic, single-minded search for new sonic media. He gave up equal temperament and Western harmonic and contrapuntal practices in the 1920s to seek a wholly new system inspired partly by various traditional and non-Western musics—ancient Greek, Chinese, Native American, Jewish, Christian, African, and rural American. He designed and built new instruments that could play his octave-scale of forty-three notes based on just intonation. Among his instruments were cast-off cloud-chamber bowls used in particle physics, a large kithara-like string instrument, and marimbas. In his multimedia works of the 1950s, these instruments accompany speaking and chanting voices as well as dancing by singer-actor-dancers. *Oedipus–A Music-Dance Drama* (1951) and *Revelation in the Courthouse Park* (1962), based on Euripides' *The Bacchae*, aspired to the elusive ideal of the Greek tragedy.

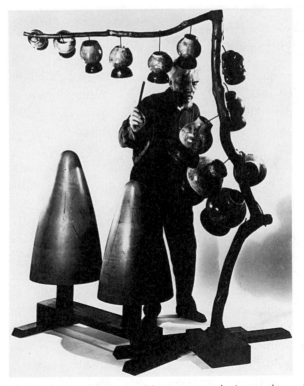

▲ Harry Partch playing the gourd tree, one of the instruments he invented to realize his music, mostly monophonic, based on the just (untempered) scale. Beside him are two cone gongs. Among his other novel instruments were cloud-chamber bowls, originally used to trace particles in nuclear-physics experiments, and a variety of marimbas and modified guitars.

Johnston

Ben Johnston (b. 1926), who worked with Partch and performed on his instruments, continued Partch's pursuit of just intonation and microtones, that is, intervals smaller than the semitone. But unlike the just-intonation idealists of the Renaissance, who wanted all the consonances to sound pure (as in the simple ratios of string lengths, such as 3 : 2 for the fifth), Johnston targeted the odd-numbered intervals: thirds, fifths, sevenths, etc. His *Sonata for Microtonal Piano* (1965) permits the hearer to savor in melody, arpeggios, and chords the justly tuned thirds, fifths, and their compounds, while seconds, fourths, sixths, octaves, tenths, twelfths, and fourteenths sound out-of-tune. The slow movement, which has a Middle Eastern flavor because of the melodic microtones against the purely consonant double drones, is particularly moving and fresh. In his Quartets Nos. 1 and 2 (1959, 1964), Johnston combined this approach with serial procedures.

Crumb

George Crumb (b. 1929) has been most imaginative in coaxing new sounds out of ordinary instruments and objects. In *Ancient Voices of Children* (1970), a cycle of four songs and two instrumental interludes based on texts by Federico García Lorca, unusual sound sources include a toy piano, a musical saw, and a number of instruments rarely heard in concerts, namely harmonica, mandolin, Tibetan prayer stones, Japanese temple bells, and electric piano. Special effects are also obtained from conventional instruments; for example, players must bend the pitch of the piano by applying a chisel to the strings, or thread paper in between the harp strings, or tune the mandolin a quarter-tone flat. *Black Angels* (1970; NAWM 148) derives special sound effects from everyday concert instruments. In this work a string quartet is electronically amplified to produce a surrealistic effect of dreamlike juxtapositions. The composer also explored unusual means of bowing, such as striking the strings near the pegs with the bow, holding the bow in the manner of viol players, and bowing between the left-hand fingers and the pegs; he also used glissandos, *sul ponticello*, and percussive pizzicato.

Electronic music

The absence of a performer in purely electronic music has hindered its acceptance, since the public responds more warmly to performers than to composers. When composers no longer depend on performers to realize their music, they also lose promoters and communicators. Even so, a significant body of purely electronic music is being created, particularly now that a personal computer or work station combined with a synthesizer can achieve what once required a big studio. Still, in the field of classical music, synthesizers are used more to compose music in notation for performers to realize than in direct communication with listeners.

Nevertheless, the combination of prerecorded tape and live performers is a familiar phenomenon in concerts and continues to evolve technologically. One of the most moving early examples was Milton Babbitt's *Philomel* (1964; first section in NAWM 149), for soprano soloist with a tape that incorporates a kind of distorted echo of her own voice together with electronic sounds.

Babbitt's *Philomel* (1964)

*T*he poem of Babbitt's partly electronic composition *Philomel*, written expressly for this setting by John Hollander, is based on a story by Ovid (*Metamorphoses* 6:412–674). Procne, wife of Tereus, king of Thrace, is eager to see her sister Philomela after many years and sends Tereus to fetch her. On the return trip Tereus rapes Philomela in a Thracian wood and cuts out her tongue to prevent disclosure, but his guilt is exposed nevertheless. Angry, he pursues the two sisters, but before he can catch them, all three are transformed: Tereus into a hoopoe bird, Procne into a swallow, and Philomela—whose voice is restored in her metamorphosis—into a nightingale. The vocal sections are answered by the tape voice, and both are accompanied by synthesized sounds; the score gives evidence that every detail was worked out in serial terms (see detailed discussion in NAWM 149).

Druckman

Similarly, Jacob Druckman, working in the Columbia-Princeton Electronic Music Studio, produced a series of dramatic dialogues between live performers and recorded electronic music: *Animus I* (1966) for trombone, *Animus II* (1968) for female voice and percussion, and *Animus III* (1969) for clarinet. (After the 1970s Druckman's major compositions were for conventional ensembles, such as the string quartet and symphony orchestra.)

Influence of jazz

Many composers, both European and American, introduced aspects of jazz into their concert music. Debussy, Ravel, Stravinsky, Hindemith, and Milhaud at one time or another imitated the rhythms of jazz, its typical harmonies, or its improvisational manners of playing the trumpet, saxophone, or percussion. But they did not write whole pieces or even parts of works that insiders would recognize as jazz and that also fit into the concert repertory. However, George Gershwin's *Rhapsody in Blue* (1924) accomplished this feat unselfconsciously. Similarly, Duke Ellington's more ambitious compositions, such as *Black, Brown and Beige* (1933–43), used symphonic means as a natural extension of his jazz ideas.

Schuller and "third stream" music

In the 1950s there was a deliberate quest by certain composers who were conversant with both kinds of music to merge the two. One of the most successful of these, Gunther Schuller (b. 1925), called this combination "third stream." In his *Seven Studies on Themes of Paul Klee* (1959), the third, *Kleiner Blauteufel* (Little Blue Devil, NAWM 150a), is unmistakably in jazz style, though the blues pattern is reduced from twelve bars to nine and there are unexpected asymmetries of rhythm. It is a genre picture in the same way that another of the studies, *Arabische Stadt* (Arab Village, NAWM 150b), places the hearer in a North African market, enraptured by the slightly off-tune nasal woodwinds playing in unison with bowed and plucked strings. In Schuller's *Transformation* (1957), a twelve-tone context becomes transformed into a full-blown modern jazz piece.

Composers not associated with the third-stream movement or with popular music have also used jazz as a model. One of the most unusual examples is Milton Babbitt's *All Set* (1957), written for a seven-piece jazz ensemble and dedicated to Schuller. Its title is a pun on the jazz term "set" (a performing session on stage) and on the concept of Babbitt's all-combinatorial pitch-class set—a hexachord that can be combined with any one of its possible transformations (retrograde, inversion, retrograde-inversion) or with one of its transpositions to produce a twelve-tone row (see page 495). Although highly disjunct and totally controlled through set-manipulations, the music has the improvisatory character of jazz, with saxophone, trumpet, and trombone riffs, a rhythmic background of cymbals, hi-hat, vibraphone, and drum-set, and even drum solos.

Babbitt, **All Set**

Joining the third stream from the direction of jazz is the pianist Anthony Davis (b. 1951), leader of a free jazz ensemble, Episteme. This improvising group became the orchestral nucleus for his opera *X: The Life and Times of Malcolm X* (1984), which enjoyed a successful New York premiere at the City Opera in 1986. The opera does not so much merge jazz and classical styles as juxtapose them. The solo roles are declaimed syllabically against a lightly orchestrated background that develops motives in an idiom that is sometimes expressionistic, and at other times agitated and Stravinskyesque. The many choruses elaborate on text-driven rhythmic figures, stylizing the obsessive chanting of street demonstrators. Improvised jazz breaks out only occasionally, as in a Harlem scene at the end of Act I. The music of *X* is a cosmopolitan product of a university-trained composer whose roots are in modern jazz.

Random techniques of all kinds, which John Cage summed up in the term *indeterminacy* (discussed in Chapter 21; see pages 500ff.), raised questions about the nature and purposes of music. When a composer abandons control over all elements of a composition, the listener simply hears sounds as sounds, enjoying (or not) each as it comes along, not trying to connect one sound with preceding or following ones, not expecting the music to communicate feelings or meanings of any kind. The sounds may not even be limited to intentional ones—any mistake or accidental noise from anywhere that occurs in the course of a performance is perfectly acceptable. Value judgments become irrelevant and musical time becomes simply duration, something that can be measured by a clock.

John Cage and indeterminacy

However strange such an aesthetic may seem and however much its practice encourages sheer dilettantism, it has a tenable basis in the philosophies of East Asia. The enigmatic John Cage, the chief proponent of these principles of indeterminacy, has stood in the forefront of new musical developments in both America and Europe since the late 1930s. Indeed, his influence in Europe was greater than that of any other American composer.

Cage's 4′33″

Cage's most extreme surrender to chance was *4′33″* (Four Minutes and Thirty-three Seconds, 1952), in which the performer or performers sit silently for a period of time while noises in the concert hall or from outside constitute the music. The piece implies that musical silence is not true silence, that there are always environmental sounds worth contemplating, and that nature is the greatest creator of music. In other works, Cage also abdicated the composer's

Cage's interest in Chinese thought

decision making to various chance devices, such as the Chinese *I Ching* (Book of Changes), which was allowed to determine the pitches in *Music of Changes* (1951). Beginning from about 1956, he moved more and more toward complete openness in every aspect of composition and performance, by offering performers options, as in his *Variations IV* (1963): "for any number of players, any sounds or combinations of sounds produced by any means, with or without other activities." The "other activities" might well include dance and theater. All this coincided with Cage's growing interest in Zen Buddhism; more important, it was symptomatic of the increasing tendency for Western artists—and for Western civilization generally—to become more open to the ideas and beliefs of other great world cultures.

E. Brown

Among Cage's protégés were Morton Feldman (1926–1987) and Earle Brown (b. 1926). Brown's approach was partly inspired by the mobiles of Alexander Calder, in which the material was always the same but a spectator's perception of it constantly changed. His *Available Forms I* (1961) for eighteen players and *Available Forms II* (1962) for large orchestra divided into two groups realize a musical parallel by giving the musicians completely scored fragments—with some leeway in the choice of pitches—that are played in the order and tempos (including accelerations and decelerations) determined by the conductor(s). This procedure permits a spontaneity and multiplicity of perceptions that could not be achieved through normal notation.

Influence of Asia

The musics of Asia, frequently heard in North America since 1960, stimulated composers to cultivate a simpler style in which subtleties of melody, intonation, and rhythm could be brought to the fore. The controlled improvisation on Indian ragas, with their alternating patterns of rhythmic units, microtonal intervals, drones, and rhapsodic figurations, was one source of inspiration. The cool, entrancing, repetitive, contemplative music of the Javanese and Balinese gamelans presented a model of complex structures that depend on reiteration of simple rhythmic and melodic patterns. Synthesizers provided an easy means to improvise over prerecorded rhythms and melodic motives. Rock music, which itself absorbed elements of jazz, blues, folk, electronic music, and Asian idioms, was the common experience of most composers born after the 1930s. They were enticed by rock's directness, hypnotic rhythms, consonant harmonies, repeated phrases, and ostinatos.

Whether pursuing simplicity or reacting to the complexity of serial music,

a number of composers took up what is now known as *minimalism*. The term
was apt, because their vocabulary, whether rhythmic, melodic, harmonic, or
instrumental, was intentionally limited. The term as well as the direction may
owe something to the New York group of visual artists who designed cyclic
and repetitive structures consisting of simple elements such as lines and dots
(see, for example, Frank Stella's *Six Mile Bottom*, Plate XVI, facing page 539).
The lengths, however, of many of the musical compositions or improvisations
and the durations of particular gestures—in contrast to the compression and
constant change of most serial music—was anything but minimal.

La Monte Young (b. 1935) and Terry Riley (b. 1935), two pioneers in this
movement, combined improvisation with electronic media. Riley experimented at an electronic studio in the 1960s with tape loops containing many
repetitions of short phrases against a continuous regular pulse and piling these
up on one another. Steve Reich (b. 1936) developed a quasi-canonic procedure in which musicians play the same material slightly out of phase with
each other. He was led to this methodology by superimposing tapes of the
same speaking voice in such a way that one tape got out of step with the other
by moving slightly faster. He applied the idea to two pianos in *Piano Phase*
(1967), and in *Violin Phase* (1967) he juxtaposed a live violinist with a second
one on tape. The piece evolved into a published version (1979) for four violinists or for a single violinist with three synchronous recording tracks
(NAWM 151).

Philip Glass (b. 1937), who had published twenty works by the time he
completed degrees at the University of Chicago and The Juilliard School and
finished his studies with Nadia Boulanger, withdrew all of them after working
with the Indian sitarist Ravi Shankar in Paris. Glass's works since the mid-
1960s were deeply influenced by the rhythmic organization of Indian music;
they emphasized melodiousness, consonance, and the simple harmonic progressions and abundant amplification of rock music. His one-act, four-and-
a-half-hour opera *Einstein on the Beach*, a collaboration with Robert Wilson
(scenario and staging), received its premiere at the Metropolitan Opera House
in 1976. Two other operas followed: *Satyagraha* (1980), about Gandhi's non-
violent struggle, and *Akhnaten* (1984), about an Egyptian pharaoh martyred
for his monotheistic worship of the sun god. Otherwise he wrote mainly for
his own ensemble.

Einstein is non-narrative and has no sung text other than solfège syllables.
The orchestra consists of electronic keyboard instruments, woodwinds, and
a solo violin (in deference to the real Einstein's enthusiasm for the instrument). Glass has won the admiration of a large and diversified audience that
includes concert-goers, frequenters of art galleries (where the music is sometimes played), rock enthusiasts, and the record-buying public. His *The Voyage*
(1992), commissioned by the Metropolitan Opera to commemorate the five
hundredth anniversary of Columbus's trip to the New World, uses a full
orchestra. Its recitatives and arias and its multi-layered rhythms and ostinatos

Minimalism

Reich

Glass

*I*n the version for a single violinist and three-track tape, the performer first records the music reproduced in Example 22.5a over and over again for one to five minutes. Then, after rewinding the tape, the violinist superimposes repetitions of the same pattern of notes, but now four eighth-notes ahead of the first track (see Example 22.5b). The performer then rewinds the tape again and records the pattern four eighth-notes ahead of track 2. The best three to seven repetitions are made into a tape loop, resulting in the ostinato shown in Example 22.5c and d, which serves as a background for further improvisation.

EXAMPLE 22.5   Steve Reich, *Violin Phase*

a. measure 1

b. at measure 7

c. at measure 18

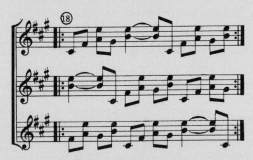

d. at measure 18

came closer to meeting the expectations of opera-goers than his previous stage works.

Leading up to his successful minimalist opera, *Nixon in China* (1987), John Adams (b. 1947) wrote the light, provocative *Grand Pianola Music* (1982), which bent the Beethoven piano-style to sound like a pianola and in which Adams recalled from his youth the gospel music and band marches he played in New Hampshire. *Fearful Symmetries* (first performed 1988) was written for an ensemble—also used in the opera—dominated by saxophones, brass, and winds, with strings, synthesizer, and relentless percussion in the background. As in the opera, short, repetitious, and pulsating ideas constantly evolve and modulate, particularly by semitone. Adams avoided monotony by continually shuffling instrumental colors and pitting conflicting rhythmic patterns, beats, and syncopations against one another. His later music returned to more traditional harmonic and contrapuntal means.

J. Adams

The Mainstream

To speak only of the newest, most prominent, or most novel trends would not do justice to the large proportion of "mainstream" composers. This term does not mean that they share a set of beliefs about music or aesthetics; rather, they compose in a great diversity of styles within a generally conservative and somewhat retrospective posture. Tonality or at least the maintenance of a tonal center often, though not necessarily, characterizes their music. Because they wish to communicate with a large public, these composers offer listeners more accessible features—a thread that can be followed through identifiable themes, musical designs that are perceptible rather than hidden, programmatic subjects or titles—and strike a balance between lyricism and liveliness, expression and logic, caution and risk. The successful middle-of-the-roaders have also discovered the secret of inspiring performers to champion their music: creating works that musicians are eager to play more than once.

Among this group are three composers noted particularly for their vocal music: Samuel Barber (1910–1981), Ned Rorem (b. 1923), and Gian-Carlo Menotti (b. 1911). Barber's *Dover Beach* (1931) for baritone and string quartet is marked by the intense lyrical flow that characterizes his later music, such as the cycle *Hermit Songs* (1952–53), his opera *Antony and Cleopatra* (which opened the new Metropolitan Opera House in 1966), and his ever popular *Adagio for Strings* (1936). Rorem's songs, which number in the hundreds, have become favorites in vocal recitals because of their sensitive setting of English poetry. Menotti's operas descended from the Italian tradition of Puccini and Mascagni familiar to opera-goers. But in his own librettos he put aside the old Romantic and veristic plots in favor of dramatic situations that modern audiences could identify with: *The Medium* (1946), *The Telephone* (1947), *The Consul* (1950), and *The Saint of Bleecker Street* (1954) all enjoyed popular success.

Barber

Rorem

Menotti

Among the younger generation, two women may be singled out for hew-

▲ Philip Johnson, the architect of Tycon Towers (1983–88) in Vienna, Virginia, blends in his design elements from the past, such as columns and arches, with patterns of glass and concrete. This approach, sometimes called "post-modern," rejects the stark glass walls and undecorated facades of many mid-twentieth-century buildings. (*Photograph by Richard Payne, FAIA*)

Tower

ing to their own middle paths and avoiding the extremes. Joan Tower (b. 1938) is regarded by some as eclectic because of the variety of approaches she chooses. But she can more correctly be called "inclusive," for she plucks expressive resources out of a rich bouquet gathered as a performer in her contemporary-music ensemble, the Da Capo Chamber Players. *Amazon* (for orchestra, 1977–82) traverses several seemingly incompatible idioms as we hear impressions of the great river of South America, where the composer grew up, but these diverse sources present a unified whole thanks to the force of her personality and purpose. Ellen Taaffe Zwilich (b. 1939) sometimes

Zwilich

found her idiom in the innate character and capability of an instrument, as she did in her *Concerto Grosso 1985* for trumpet and five players and in the Sonata in Three Movements for Violin and Piano (1973–74). Alternatively, her approach may be born of the occasion, as in *Symbolon*, written for the New York Philharmonic's tour of the Soviet Union in 1988. *Symbolon* in Greek meant a "sign" or "token," and more specifically in the plural, the halves of a bone or coin that two persons broke between them as a symbol of friendship. The composer handed her hosts their half of the token in the form of subtle stylistic allusions in the piece to Shostakovich. Her Symphony No. 1 (1982) earned her the first Pulitzer Prize in Music awarded to a woman.

Post-modern styles

A number of architects, such as Robert Venturi, Philip Johnson, and Cesar

Pelli, turned away from the faceless glass facades of the mid–twentieth century by incorporating elements of earlier styles into essentially modern designs, a mixture that became known as "post-modern." This term may fit better than "collage" to describe a similar technique in recent music.

Rochberg

George Rochberg (b. 1918), who had earlier depended on serial methods, constructed a quilt from the music of Mozart, Beethoven, Mahler, Webern, Varèse, Stockhausen, and previously composed works of his own in *Music for a Magic Theater* (1965). In the Fantasy for harpsichord or piano *Nach Buch* (According to Bach, 1966; NAWM 152), he adopted the style of a Baroque

Rochberg and Bach Compared

*L*ike Bach, Rochberg begins with an arpeggio followed by a typical double-dotted effect and a descending appoggiatura (Example 22.6). But where Bach's arpeggio contains only the notes of the E-minor triad, Rochberg's contains all twelve notes of the chromatic scale. Similarly, the arpeggio that resolves the appoggiatura includes all of the notes of Bach's chord but in addition B♭, E♭, and B. The most characteristic trichord of the piece contains both a fourth (or fifth) and a tritone, for example descending A–E–B♭ and B–F♯–C.

EXAMPLE 22.6

a. Johann Sebastian Bach, Partita No. 6, BWV 830: Toccata

b. George Rochberg, *Nach Bach*

toccata and quoted short passages from J. S. Bach's Partita No. 6 for keyboard, BWV 830.

Del Tredici

One of the most remarkable re-creations of an earlier musical world is David Del Tredici's *In Memory of a Summer Day* (*Child Alice*, Part One, 1980). In a soaring, passionate transformation of the work's principal melody (Example 22.7), Del Tredici (b. 1937) translated Wagner's *Liebestod* into modern—but not too modern—terms without borrowing any of Wagner's motives, only his manner of developing them, his harmony, and his brilliant orchestration. The resemblance of the theme to the "kiss" motive in Verdi's *Otello* may be accidental. The aim of the backward look seems in this case to be communication rather than parody or irony (see vignette below). Del Tredici, a student of Earl Kim and Roger Sessions at Princeton, established his contemporary credentials by composing atonal music before beginning his extended series of works (1968–86) on Lewis Carroll's *Alice's Adventures in Wonderland* and *Through the Looking Glass*. *Final Alice* (1975) is brilliantly

David Del Tredici on Composing *Final Alice*:

❝ About halfway through the piece, I thought, 'Oh my God, if I just leave it like this, my colleagues will think I'm crazy.' But then I thought, 'What else can I do? If nothing else occurs to me I can't go against my instincts.' But I was *terrified* my colleagues would think I was an idiot. . . . People think now that I wanted to be tonal and have a big audience. But that was just not true. I *didn't* want to be tonal. My world was my colleagues—my composing friends. . . . The success of *Final Alice* was very defining as to who my real friends were. I think many composers regard success as a kind of threat. It's really better, they think, if *nobody* has any success, to be all in one boat.

Composers now are beginning to realize that if a piece excites an audience, *that doesn't mean it's terrible*. For my generation, it is considered vulgar to have an audience really, *really* like a piece on a first hearing. But why are we writing music except to move people and to be expressive? To have what has moved us move somebody else?

Right now, audiences just reject contemporary music. But if they start to like *one* thing, then they begin to have perspective. That will make a difference, it always has in the past. The sleeping giant is the audience. ❞

From an interview with John Rockwell, in *New York Times*, Sunday, October 26, 1980, Section D, pp. 23, 28.

scored for soprano, orchestra, and a "folk group" of two soprano saxophones, mandolin, banjo, and accordion. Here the manner owes more to Richard Strauss than to Wagner, but in the midst of this determinedly Romantic tonal writing we also hear folklike episodes and others that are atonal, all fused into a compound of irresistible charm.

EXAMPLE 22.7   David Del Tredici, *In Memory of a Summer Day*: Allegretto

POSTLUDE

Of the four basic characteristics in Western music that began taking shape in the eleventh century—composition, notation, principles of order, and polyphony—some have been altered and others restored by twentieth-century developments. *Composition*, in the sense that a work of music exists apart from any particular performance, has in some quarters given way to controlled improvisation, which was the practice in antiquity and the early Middle Ages. As to *notation*, the score in many cases is now less than ever a definitive set of directions. The performer, instead of being only a mediator between composer and audience, is sharing in the creation of a work with the composer, as was true until the eighteenth century. *Principles of order* have been challenged by indeterminacy, allowing an outside force to impose the succession of musical events, as liturgy and ritual did in earlier times and still do in many situations. *Polyphony* and to a lesser extent *harmony*, though transformed, remain. What the twentieth century has witnessed has been a realignment of values and means, rather than a revolution.

The radical changes that have come and gone affected only a small number of listeners. The audience for "serious" music has never been more than a small fraction of the population. That audience is still relatively small, and within it the audience for the new and experimental is even smaller. Composers who write in a difficult, unfamiliar idiom cannot expect a large popular following.

Most composers have always cared about their audience, and in the last quarter of the twentieth century more and more composers addressed their works to the public rather than to other composers, connoisseurs, and analysts. A concern with the gap between composer and listener has led to simplification and even minimalization of content. Hybrid styles have sprung from marriages between art music and popular, ethnic, non-Western, and traditional musics. Composers are once again letting the organization of music be heard instead of concealing it. Finally, they have built bridges between the familiar music of the past and that of the present.

GLOSSARY

Within a definition, terms that are themselves defined in this glossary are printed in SMALL CAPITALS. Terms that are special to a narrow topic are explained in the text and are not included here, nor are terms that are defined in general dictionaries. Page numbers following the definitions refer to selected discussions in the text that concern the defined term.

Language abbreviations: Fr. = French; Ger. = German; Gr. = Greek; It. = Italian; Lat. = Latin; Port. = Portuguese; Sp. = Spanish. *Also:* sing. = singular; pl. = plural.

Accidental   Sign that calls for altering the pitch of a note: raising it one half step by a sharp, ♯, lowering it by a flat, ♭, or canceling a previous such sign by a "natural," ♮ (pp. 33–34, 77, 131, 174).

Ad libitum (Lat. "at pleasure")   Details of execution left to the discretion of the performer (pp. 242, 512, 513).

Affection   Fixed state of mind, such as rage, fear, or wonder, not unlike a persistent emotion (pp. 172–73, 188, 207, 248).

Agrément (Fr. "charm")   ORNAMENT in French music, usually indicated by a sign (pp. 199, 236, 237).

Air   (1) Tune. (2) Tuneful song in a French stage work, usually in a dance METER (pp. 214, 259–60). (3) English or French art song with lute or viol accompaniment (pp. 138–39, 149).

Alberti bass   Broken-CHORD accompaniment named after Domenico Alberti, a composer who used it frequently (p. 293).

Allemande, alman   Dance in moderate duple METER, often the first dance of a SUITE (pp. 144, 199, 200, 233, 234).

Anthem   MOTET-like composition on an English text (p. 159).

Antiphonal   Pertaining to a method of performance in which one group answers another (pp. 24, 27, 193–94).

Aria (It. "air")   (1) Tune or formula for singing poetry (pp. 177, 178, 206). (2) Strophic song (pp. 178, 181). (3) Songful monologue or duet in an OPERA or other vocal work (pp. 184, 209).

Arioso (It. "airy")   (1) Short for *recitativo arioso,* "tuneful RECITATIVE" (p. 211). (2) Free lyric passage not formally organized as an aria (pp. 218–19).

Arpeggio (from It. *arpa* "harp")   Broken-CHORD FIGURE (p. 549).

Atonal (atonality)   Pertaining to music that avoids a TONAL center but is not built on SERIAL principles (pp. 492, 494–95).

Aulos   Single or double-reed wind instrument of the ancient Greeks (p. 5).

Ballad opera   Eighteenth-century English comic play with songs in which new texts are set to familiar tunes (p. 297).

Ballade   (1) One of the French FORMES FIXES of the fourteenth and fifteenth centuries, each stanza having an overall aabC form (pp. 70, 71, 95). (2) Instrumental piece inspired by the genre of narrative poetry (p. 396). (3) Composed setting of a narrative poem (pp. 406, 408; also called ballad).

Ballet   Entertainment in which both professionals and guests danced; later, a stage work danced by professionals (pp. 143, 183–84, 213, 481–84, 485–87).

Bar form   Song form in which the first melodic component is sung twice with different texts (AA); the remainder (B) is sung once (p. 41).

Baroque (from Port. *barroco* "misshapen," as in a bulbous pearl)   (1) Bizarre, extravagant (p. 170). (2) Period of music history from ca. 1580 to ca. 1730.

Basse danse   Family of dances, some duple, some triple, or a mixture of the two, whose music was often IMPROVISED over a TENOR CANTUS FIRMUS (p. 144).

Basso continuo   A base line serving as a foundation for IMPROVISED CHORDS that filled in the HARMONY in music of the BAROQUE period (p. 174; also, its system of NOTATION). See also FIGURED BASS.

Bel canto (It. "beautiful singing")   Smooth, fluent, vocal line that shows off the singer's voice (pp. 186, 207).

Blue notes   Lowered third, seventh, and sometimes fifth degrees of the MAJOR SCALE, used especially in African-American music (p. 522).

Blues   (1) Standard 12–bar chord progression: I-I-I-I-IV-IV-I-I-V-V (or IV)-I-I (p. 522). (2) African-American vocal genre (p. 522).

Bridge   See **Transition**.

Cadence   Melodic or harmonic succession that closes a musical phrase, section, or composition (pp. 74, 92, 142). A cadence may be evaded by preparing the close but then moving on (pp. 122–23).

Cadenza (It. "cadence")   IMPROVISED passage usually placed just before the end of a piece or section (pp. 344, 417, 513).

Camerata   Circle of intellectuals and amateurs of the arts that met in Florence at the home of Giovanni Bardi in the 1570s and 1580s (pp. 177, 179).

Canon (Gr. *kanōn* "rule")   (1) Rule for performing music, particularly for deriving more than one voice from a single line of notated music, as when several voices sing the same MELODY, entering at certain intervals of time or singing at different speeds simultaneously (pp. 109–11). (2) Composition in which the voices enter successively at determined pitch and time intervals, all performing the same melody (p. 267).

Cantata (It. "sung")   (1) Chamber composition for solo voice containing RECITATIVES and ARIAS (pp. 190–92, 218–20). (2) Church cantata; see **Sacred concerto**.

Cantus firmus (Lat. "plain chant"; pl. *cantus firmi*)   PLAINCHANT or other MELODY used as a basis for a POLYPHONIC composition (pp. 56, 64–65, 94–97, 121–22).

Canzona   In the sixteenth century an instrumental chanson; later, a piece for ensemble in several sections or tempos (pp. 146–47, 202–3).

Chaconne (Fr.; Sp. *chacona*; It. *ciaccona*)   (1) Dance song in triple time, originating in Latin America. (2) A type of variation form having a repeating base line and harmonic pattern. (3) Stately French dance made popular by Lully's stage music (pp. 187, 236).

Chanson (Fr. "song")   Secular French song, either of popular origin or composed anew, usually arranged POLYPHONICALLY (pp. 71, 93, 135–36).

Chant   See **Plainchant**.

Choirbook   Large-format manuscript or printed book of music NOTATION easily read by the choir standing around it (pp. 60, 107, 109).

Chorale   STROPHIC hymn comprised of a simple, metrical tune and rhyming verses in German, used in the Lutheran Church (pp. 152–53, 222–23).

Chorale prelude   Organ arrangement of a CHORALE played before the congregation sings it (pp. 232–33).

Chord   Three or more simultaneous pitches heard as a single entity (p. 258).

Chromatic (chromaticism)   (1) One of the GENERA of Greek music (p. 8). (2) Pertaining to a MELODY or SCALE that uses successive half steps (pp. 131–32, 175–76, 429).

Classic, classical   (1) Art music as opposed to VERNACULAR or entertainment music. (2) Period or style from ca. 1730 to ca. 1820 (pp. 287, 373).

Clausula (Lat. "end, concluding sentence or verse")   (1) CADENCE. (2) Phrase of PLAINCHANT. (3) Measured ORGANUM set to MELISMATIC fragment of PLAINCHANT (p. 52–53).

Clavecin   French term for harpsichord (p. 199).

Coda (It. "tail")   A supplementary ending to a composition (pp. 308, 355).

Collegium musicum   Ensemble or orchestra made up mostly of amateurs such as university students (p. 243).

Commedia dell'arte   Professional, IMPROVISED Italian comedy of the sixteenth and seventeenth centuries using standard characters (p. 295).

Concertato (adj. from It. *concertare* "to agree upon or act together")   (1) Concerted, that is, joining instruments and voices (p. 188). (2) Performing as a soloist, contrasting with a group, as in *violino concertato* (p. 246).

Concertino (It. "little concerto")   Ensemble of few solo instruments, as opposed to CONCERTO GROSSO, large ensemble with numerous players to a part (pp. 246, 253).

Concerto (It.; Fr. *concert*; Eng. *consort*)   (1) Ensemble of instruments or voices. (2) Composition for instruments or voices. (3) Composition in which one or more solo performers join an orchestral ensemble (pp. 189, 193, 195, 202, 246–47, 252–53). See also **Sacred concerto**.

Concerto for few voices   See **Sacred concerto**.

Concerto grosso (It. "large concerto")   (1) TUTTI or RIPIENO—the full orchestra in a CONCERTO. (2) Composition for a full orchestra or for such an orchestra alternating with a small group of soloists, the CONCERTINO (pp. 246, 279).

Concitato (It. "excited")   Style in which a single note or CHORD is rapidly repeated, mixed with fanfares, to suggest belligerence and battle (p. 189).

Conductus (pl. *conductus*)   (1) Medieval MONOPHONIC song, usually sacred, on rhythmical Latin verse (p. 36). (2) Measured POLYPHONIC setting of an original MELODY (pp. 54–56).

Consonance (consonant)   INTERVAL or CHORD that has a stable, agreeable sound. In the Middle Ages only octaves, fifths, and fourths were considered consonant; later, thirds and sixths were included (pp. 45–46, 86, 97, 103).

Consort   See **Concerto.**

Continuo   See **Basso continuo.**

Contrafactum (pl. *contrafacta*)   Composition in which a new text is substituted for the original one—for example, a sacred text for a secular one (pp. 150, 152).

Counterpoint (contrapuntal)   Artful combination of two or more simultaneous melodic lines (pp. 103, 162–65).

Cross-relation, false relation   (1) The juxtaposition of a pitch in one voice followed by a CHROMATIC ALTERATION of that pitch (or its replicate) in another voice. (2) The succession of two pitches in different voices forming a TRITONE (pp. 210–387).

Courante, corrente   Fast-moving dance in a moderately fast triple METER (p. 234).

Da capo aria   Two-section ARIA form. The first section is repeated after the second section's close, which carries the instruction *da capo* (It. "from the head") (pp. 211–12, 299).

Development   Process or section in which a subject is taken apart, combined with other ideas, and reworked (p. 320).

Diatonic   (1) One of the GENERA of Greek music (p. 8). (2) Pertaining to a MELODY or SCALE that mixes whole tones and semitones without consecutive half steps.

Diminution   (1) Uniform reduction of note values in a MELODY or phrase. (2) Type of embellishment involving replacing a long note with a run or other FIGURE composed of short notes (p. 241; also called "division").

Discant (Lat. "singing apart")   (1) TREBLE part, also called "discantus." (2) IMPROVISED or written POLYPHONY in which voices move at same speed, particularly when all are measured (pp. 47, 50, 52).

Dissonance (dissonant)   (1) INTERVAL or CHORD that is disagreeable or that requires RESOLUTION. Seconds, TRITONES, and sevenths, and chords containing them are considered dissonant (pp. 97, 103). (2) A note not belonging in a chord, a nonharmonic tone (p. 175).

Divertissement (Fr. "entertainment, diversion")   Entertaining episodes of BALLET, tuneful AIRS, and spectacle within serious French OPERAS (pp. 214, 259).

Division   See **Diminution.**

Dominant   Fifth degree of a MAJOR or MINOR scale.

Drone   Note or notes, usually in the bass, sustained throughout an entire piece or section (pp. 47, 329).

Double (Fr. "double")   Immediate embellished repetition of a piece, such as movement of a SUITE (pp. 235, 267).

Duplum (Lat. *duplus* "double")   Voice part in early POLYPHONY set against a TENOR (p. 54).

Dynamics   Variation of loudness and intensity (pp. 147, 311).

Empfindsamkeit (Ger. "sentimentality, sensitivity"; adj. *empfindsam*)   Quality of restrained passion and melancholy in eighteenth-century music (pp. 208, 308–10).

Enharmonic   (1) One of the GENERA of Greek music (p. 8). (2) Pertaining to a MELODY or SCALE that uses steps smaller than a semitone (p. 131). (3) Pertaining to a change in the NOTATION and function of a single pitch, as from E♭ to D♯.

Episode   Free, connecting passage, especially in a FUGUE, that does not state the principal subject (p. 230).

Étude   Exercise to develop instrumental technique, or composition devoted to a particular technical skill (p. 397).

Exposition Section of a FUGUE, SONATA, or CONCERTO in which the main subject or subjects are announced (pp. 230, 308, 313, 317–19).

Expressionism Exaggerated and extreme subjectivity in artistic expression (pp. 476, 495, 502–3).

Falsobordone (It. "false bass") Method of IMPROVISING four-part HARMONY against a PSALM TONE in the TREBLE, resulting in a succession of mostly ROOT-position CHORDS (p. 114).

Fancy Fantasy for a solo instrument or ensemble (p. 146).

Fantasia (It. "fantasy") Instrumental composition lacking a strict form, often IM-PROVISATORY. (2) Instrumental piece developing an abstract subject, often invented by the composer (pp. 144–45, 202). See also FANCY.

Fauxbourdon (Fr. "false bass") Scheme for IMPROVISING a third part between a PLAINCHANT in the TREBLE and a lower voice. The outer voices form parallel sixths, while the middle voice is a fourth below the PLAINCHANT, though they start and end phrases with an octave mediated by a fifth (pp. 86, 88).

Figure, figuration Melodic pattern, usually ORNAMENTAL, made of commonplace material such as SCALES, ARPEGGIOS, and turns, not distinctive enough to be considered a MOTIVE or THEME (p. 241).

Figured bass THOROUGHBASS with numbers to indicate the intervals above it that form the required CHORDS (p. 174).

Final Step of a mode that is the normal closing note of a PLAINCHANT or TENOR part (pp. 32, 33).

Finale Last movement of a work or the closing scene of an act in an OPERA (pp. 321, 325).

Folk music See **Traditional music**.

Formes fixes (Fr. "fixed forms") Schemes of poetic and musical repetition used in the late Middle Ages, such as VIRELAI, RONDEAU, and BALLADE (pp. 69, 71).

French overture See **Ouverture**.

Fret Raised strip of material, such as leather, which guides and aids the stopping of strings on a fingerboard (p. 142).

Fuging tune Arrangement of hymn using free IMITATION (pp. 518, 528).

Fugue, fuga (fugal) (Lat. and It. "flight") Composition or section of a composition in which a subject is answered or repeated successively by several parts (pp. 116, 202, 230).

Galant (Fr. "elegant") (1) Smart, chic, sophisticated. (2) Light, HOMOPHONIC early eighteenth-century style of music that treats CONTRAPUNTAL rules freely (p. 288).

Galliard Lively dance in triple meter that usually followed a PAVANE (pp. 143–44, 199).

Gebrauchsmusik (Ger. "utilitarian music") Music for amateurs, children, and workers to play and sing (p. 476).

Genera (Lat. "classes"; sing. *genus*) In ancient Greek music, three classes of MELODY or ways of tuning the TETRACHORD: DIATONIC, CHROMATIC, and ENHARMONIC (pp. 8, 131).

Gesamtkunstwerk (Ger. "composite or integrated artwork") Theatrical work envisioned by Richard Wagner that unites poetry, scenery, staging, action, and music, all working toward a dramatic goal (pp. 426, 429).

Gigue (Eng. *jig*) Quick dance usually in triple METER (p. 235).

Grand concerto See **Sacred concerto**.

Grand motet (Fr. "large motet") Seventeenth- and eighteenth-century French SACRED CONCERTO for soloists, double choruses, and orchestra (p. 222).

Ground bass   Pattern of bass notes repeated as a foundation for HARMONY (pp. 187, 216–17). See also OSTINATO, CHACONNE, and PASSACAGLIA.

Gruppo   Early Italian word for TRILL (p. 178).

Harmonic   (1) High thin tone produced by lightly touching the string, such as of a violin, at ½, ⅓, ¼, etc., of its length. (2) Overtone, or partial, of a vibrating string or air column. (3) **Harmonic** system, or **harmonics**, among the ancient Greeks, was the study of matters concerning pitch (p. 8).

Harmony   Aspect of music that pertains to simultaneous combinations of sounds, particularly CONSONANT ones.

Hemiola (from Gr. *hemiolios* "one and a half")   Three beats against two in an equivalent amount of time, whether between voices or successive MEASURES, as in one measure of $\frac{3}{2}$ against, or alternative with, two measures of $\frac{3}{4}$ (pp. 76, 181, 234).

Heterophony   Same MELODY performed simultaneously in more than one way, for example, simply and ORNAMENTED (p. 4).

Hexachord   Set of six pitches.

Hocket (Lat. *hoquetus;* Fr. *hoquet* "hiccup")   Device of splitting a melodic line between two voices, or a composition based on this device (pp. 66, 69, 73, 76).

Homophony (homophonic)   Music in which the HARMONY is chordal and not made up of distinctive lines (pp. 89, 114).

Homorhythmic   Having the same RHYTHM, as when several voices sing the same syllables with the same durations (p. 114).

Humanism   Movement in the RENAISSANCE to revive ancient Greek and Roman culture (pp. 99, 101, 103).

Imitation   Device of repeating a MOTIVE or MELODY announced in one part in a second or more parts, often at a different pitch level and not always exactly (p. 116).

Imitation Mass   Mass in which movements are based on a single POLYPHONIC model, such as a MOTET or MADRIGAL, all of whose voices may be borrowed or reworked (p. 118; also called "parody Mass").

Impressionism   Style that evokes moods and sensuous impressions through HARMONY and tone color (pp. 456–57).

Improvisation (improvised)   Spontaneous invention of music, embellishment, or accompaniment while performing (pp. 4, 39, 144–46, 200–1, 240, 511–13, 522–24).

Indeterminacy   Freedom from a composer's NOTATIONAL prescription (pp. 511–13, 543–44).

Intermedio   Pastoral, allegorical, or mythological interlude of vocal and instrumental music performed before and between the acts of a spoken comedy or tragedy (pp. 176, 178).

Intermezzo   A brief comic operatic work performed between the acts of a serious OPERA (pp. 295–96).

Interval   Distance in pitch between two notes.

Inversion   (1) Shifting the position of the notes in a CHORD so that a different one is the lowest. (2) Reversing the upward or downward direction of melodic INTERVALS while maintaining their size. (3) In COUNTERPOINT, placing a part above a given part that had been below it.

Isorhythm (Gr. "same rhythm")   Repetition in a voice part (usually the TENOR) of an extended pattern of durations throughout a section or an entire composition (pp. 64–65, 67–68).

Just intonation   Method of tuning that affords both perfect and imperfect CONSONANCES in their purest form as demonstrated by the simple ratios of their frequencies, such as $3:2$ for the perfect fifth and $5:4$ for the major third (pp. 540–41).

Key See **Tonality**.

Key signature Sharp(s) or flat(s) placed on line(s) or space(s) at the beginning of each staff.

Kithara Large lyre-shaped instrument of ancient Greece, having between five and eleven strings (p. 5).

Lauda (Lat. *laudare* "to praise") Italian devotional song (pp. 70, 124–25).

Leitmotif (Ger. "leading motive") Musical THEME or MOTIVE associated with a person, thing, emotion, or idea in a drama (pp. 426–28).

Libretto (It. "booklet") Literary text for a musical stage work (pp. 185, 216, 345, 424).

Lied (Ger. "song"; pl. *lieder*) German song, such as a POLYPHONIC part-song or an accompanied art song (pp. 139–40, 406–10, 439–40).

Ligature NEUME-like shape used to indicate a short rhythmic pattern in the NOTATION of the twelfth to the sixteenth centuries (pp. 50, 60).

Madrigal (It. *madrigale* "song in the mother tongue") (1) Fourteenth-century Italian VERSE form and its musical setting having two or three stanzas followed by a RITORNELLO (p. 72). (2) Sixteenth-century Italian poem having any number of lines, each of seven or eleven syllables (pp. 125–26). (3) POLYPHONIC or CONCERTATO setting of such a poem or of a canzona, sonnet, etc. (pp. 128–35). (4) English part-song imitating the Italian models (pp. 136–38).

Major scale DIATONIC succession of notes with a major third as the third step.

March Piece in duple METER to accompany military stepping.

Masque English entertainment in which guests and professionals joined in a dance performance, sometimes including RECITATIVES, songs, and choruses (p. 216).

Measure Metrical unit set off by barlines.

Meistersinger (Ger. "master singer") German singer and composer of songs practiced by fourteenth- to sixteenth-century burgher-musicians' guilds (pp. 42, 139).

Melisma (melismatic) Flowing passage of many notes sung to a single syllable, particularly of PLAINCHANT (pp. 24, 28, 30–31).

Melodrama Theatrical genre that combined spoken dialogue with background music (p. 422).

Melody (1) Succession of tones perceived as a coherent line. (2) Tune. (3) Principal part accompanied by other parts or CHORDS.

Meter Pattern of beats in a MEASURE, such as $\frac{3}{4}$.

MIDI (Musical Instrument Digital Interface) Type of synthesizer that translates the characteristics of pitch, timbra, dynamics, and rhythm (these having been digitally encoded through a computer) directly into music (p. 508).

Minimalism Type of music deliberately limiting musical material and vocabulary, often marked by continual repetition of a short MELODY, FIGURE, or CHORD with only slight variation (pp. 545–47).

Minnesinger (Ger. "singer of love") Composer or singer of medieval German song, particularly about love (p. 41).

Minor scale DIATONIC succession of notes with a minor third as the third step and optional lowered sixth and seventh steps.

Minuet Dance in triple METER usually followed by a second minuet, called "Trio," after which the first minuet returns (p. 320).

Mode (1) MELODY type characterized by a certain FINAL or ending pitch, a particular arrangement of tones and semitones, and an approximate range (pp. 7, 32–34). (2) Rhythmic pattern of two or three short and longer durations—for example, Mode 1, long-short (p. 79).

Modulation   Change from one TONALITY to another in the course of a composition.

Monochord   Instrument used to locate INTERVALS through dividing and measuring lengths of its single string (p. 11).

Monody   Accompanied solo song (pp. 177–78, 189–90).

Monophony (monophonic)   Unaccompanied MELODY (pp. 4, 44, 177).

Motet (from Fr. *mot* "word")   POLYPHONIC vocal composition, most often on a sacred text (pp. 56–60, 64–66, 93, 221–22).

Motetus   DUPLUM or TRIPLUM voice part in early POLYPHONY to which words are set.

Motive   Short melodic or rhythmic idea.

Motto   (1) Musical idea that recurs (p. 94). (2) Introduction of the main idea in the voice, prior to the completion of the instrumental RITORNELLO, in what is called a "motto ARIA" (p. 210).

Musica ficta (Lat. "feigned music")   (1) Practice of raising or lowering by a semitone the pitch of a written note in a POLYPHONIC TEXTURE, particularly at a CADENCE, for the sake of smoother HARMONY or stronger part movement (p. 77).

Musique concrète (Fr. "concrete music")   Natural sounds stored, combined, modified, and arranged (p. 507).

Neo-Classicism   Movement in the twentieth century to revive forms, genres, and styles of the eighteenth century (pp. 479, 485).

Neume   Sign placed above a syllable to indicate the pitch height of one or more PLAINCHANT notes (p. 23).

Notation   Writing down of music, usually on a staff of lines, using signs that define the pitch, duration, and other qualities of sound (pp. 22–23, 48, 80–81, 138–39, 513).

Office   Monastic ritual celebrated at certain hours of the day and night (pp. 20–21).

Opera (operatic) (It. "work")   Dramatic stage composition, ordinarily in two or more acts.

Opera buffa (It. "comic opera")   Italian full-length comic OPERA sung throughout (pp. 294–98).

Opéra comique (Fr. "comic opera")   French full-length comic OPERA with spoken dialogue instead of RECITATIVE (pp. 297, 414, 415, 418).

Opera seria (It. "serious opera")   Serious Italian OPERA of the eighteenth century, purged of comic scenes and characters (pp. 298–302).

Opus (Lat. "work"; pl. *opera*)   A composition or set of compositions.

Oratorio   Composition for solo singers, chorus, and instruments, usually dramatic and on a biblical or religious subject (pp. 194–95, 282–84).

Orchestration   (1) Art of assigning musical material to individual instruments. (2) The product of this process (pp. 324–25, 455).

Ordinary (Lat. *ordinarium missae* "the ordinary of the Mass")   Texts and PLAINCHANTS of a Mass that remain the same throughout the church calendar, such as the Kyrie and Gloria (pp. 22, 93–94).

Ordre (Fr. "order")   French collection of pieces that are mostly in dance rhythms, such as a SUITE (pp. 235–36).

Organum   IMPROVISED or written voice part sung against a PLAINCHANT, or the work resulting from this procedure (pp. 45–54).

Ornament, ornamentation, ornamented   Decorative element, such as a TRILL or turn, written or IMPROVISED, that adds expression, charm, or variety to a melodic line (pp. 189, 236–37, 241–42).

Ostinato   Short melodic FIGURE persistently repeated, most often in the bass (pp. 147, 187–88).

Ottava rima (It. "eighth-line rhyme")   Stanza of eight eleven-syllable lines having the rhyme scheme a b a b a b c c (p. 187).

Ouverture (Fr. "opening")   (1) French OVERTURE in two-part form, the first slow and majestic with dotted rhythms, the second quick, fluent, and FUGAL, after which the first section is often recalled (p. 215). (2) A SUITE having such an introduction (pp. 245–46).

Overture   Introduction to a stage work, ORATORIO, or instrumental SUITE; later also a brief orchestral work in one movement (pp. 243–44, 382–83).

Parody Mass   See **Imitation Mass**.

Partbook   Volume containing the music for a single vocal or instrumental part of a POLYPHONIC ensemble (pp. 106–7).

Partita   Single VARIATION of a THEME or a set of such variations (pp. 205–6, 233, 267–68).

Passacaglia (It.; Sp. *passecalle*; Fr. *passecaille*)   Pattern of pitches, usually in triple meter and minor mode, serving as a foundation for HARMONY and suitable for supporting instrumental or vocal variations (pp. 187–88, 236).

Passion   Setting of a New Testament account of the crucifixion of Jesus (pp. 225, 273–74).

Pastoral   Poetic genre to which the early OPERA LIBRETTOS, such as *Euridice* of 1600, belonged (pp. 179, 181).

Pavane (Eng.; Fr. *pavana*; It. *paduana*)   Slow, stately dance in duple METER, often followed by a GALLIARD (pp. 139, 143–44).

Periodicity   Quality of being organized in discrete phrases and periods (pp. 292–93).

Petit motet (Fr. "little motet")   French version of the SACRED CONCERTO for few voices (p. 222).

Phrygian cadence   CADENCE in which the lowest voice descends by a semitone and the highest ascends by a whole tone (pp. 77, 240).

Pitch-class   One of twelve pitches of the CHROMATIC SCALE without reference to register, such as C when it refers to any C (p. 495).

Plainchant, plainsong (Lat. *cantus planus*)   Monophonic sacred chant or song of the Christian church, performed in free rhythm.

Polychoral   TEXTURE in which two or more choruses alternate and join together (pp. 147, 193–94).

Polyphony (polyphonic)   Musical TEXTURE consisting of two or more lines of MELODY (p. 44). See also COUNTERPOINT.

Polytonality   Combination of two or more lines of melody that are in different TONALITIES (pp. 466, 480).

Prelude   Introductory piece in an OPERA, SUITE, or independent instrumental composition (pp. 144, 396).

Prima pratica   See **Seconda pratica**.

Program music   Music that is descriptive, narrative, or that develops a nonmusical subject (pp. 375, 378–81, 383–84, 440).

Prologue   Dramatic scene or speech before the beginning of a spoken or musical stage work (p. 181).

Proper (Lat., *proprium de tempore* "proper of the time")   Texts and PLAINCHANTS of the Mass that are assigned to particular days in the church calendar (pp. 22, 28, 30, 46).

Psalm tone   Formula for chanting psalms on a reciting tone, which varies with the MODE (pp. 26–27).

Quodlibet (Lat. "whatever you please")   Composition juxtaposing several borrowed melodies (p. 267).

Recapitulation   Section of a movement in which the subjects announced in the EXPOSITION are reviewed in the tonic key (pp. 308, 313, 320).

Récitatif mesuré (Fr. "measured recitative")   Songful RECITATIVE in French seventeenth- and eighteenth-century OPERA that maintained a uniform METER (p. 214).

Récitatif simple (Fr. "simple recitative")   Speechlike RECITATIVE in French seventeenth- and eighteenth-century OPERA that frequently shifted between duple and triple METERS (p. 214).

Recitative (from It. *stile recitativo* "recitative style")   A manner of singing approaching speech (pp. 179–80). See also RECITATIVO SEMPLICE and RECITATIVO OBBLIGATO.

Recitativo obbligato   Orchestrally accompanied RECITATIVE, later called *recitativo accompagnato* or *recitativo stromentato* (pp. 211, 282, 369, 488).

Recitativo semplice   RECITATIVE accompanied only by BASSO CONTINUO, later called *recitativo secco* (It. "dry recitative") (pp. 211, 282, 417).

Refrain   In a song, a recurring line (or lines) of text, usually set to a recurring MELODY (pp. 38, 71, 136, 209).

Renaissance (Fr. "rebirth")   (1) Period in art and cultural history, ca. 1350–1600. (2) Period of music history, ca. 1450–1600, dominated by the rebirth of secular musical activity and the ideals of antiquity (pp. 99–105).

Requiem   Mass for the dead (pp. 31, 349, 429–30, 431).

Resolution (resolve)   Relief of DISSONANCE through CONSONANCE, as in a SUSPENSION or in a dissonant seventh followed by a consonant sixth.

Responsorial   Pertaining to chanting in which a chorus answers a soloist.

Rhythm   Pattern of short and long durations.

Ricercare   At first an IMPROVISED PRELUDE, later, a sedate FUGAL piece on one or more subjects (pp. 146, 201–2).

Ripieno (It. "full")   (1) TUTTI as opposed to solo, usually in a CONCERTO (pp. 174, 246).

Ritornello (It. "refrain")   (1) Closing pair of lines in a fourteenth-century Italian MADRIGAL, usually contrasting in music and meter with the madrigal's stanzas (p. 75). (2) Instrumental interlude between sung strophes (pp. 181, 189). (3) Instrumental introduction or interlude in an ARIA, CONCERTO movement, or similar piece (pp. 212, 247, 272).

Rococo (from Fr. *rocaille* "rockwork")   Delicate architectural arabesques and similar features in music, as in the highly ORNAMENTED clavecin music composed around 1700 (pp. 287–88).

Romanesca   Formula for singing OTTAVE RIME (pp. 147, 187, 206).

Romantic   (1) Quality of free, imaginative storytelling characteristic of the nineteenth-century French *roman* (romance). (2) Period in music covering all but the first and last decades of the nineteenth century (pp. 372–75).

Root   Lowest note of a CHORD built up by successive thirds.

Rondeau (Fr.; pl. *rondeaux*)   One of the FORMES FIXES usually in the form ABaAabAB (capital letters indicating a REFRAIN) (pp. 70, 71, 76–77, 78–79).

Rondo Form used mostly in classic- and romantic-period instrumental FINALES in which an opening A section returns following each of several contrasting sections; for exampe, A B A C A B A (pp. 325, 344, 442).

Rubato (It. *tempo rubato* "stolen time") Advancing or delaying a beat, or slowing down and speeding up, usually for expressive effect, before restoring the regular beat or TEMPO (pp. 179, 396, 400).

Sacred concerto Composition on a sacred text for one or more soloists and instrumental accompaniment, with chorus (*grand concerto*) or without (*concerto for few voices*) (pp. 188, 193–94). See also GRAND MOTET and PETIT MOTET.

Sarabande Slow dance in triple METER often emphasizing second beat (p. 235).

Scale Series of pitches in ascending or descending order.

Scherzo (It. "joke") Jesting type of movement that evolved from the MINUET (pp. 325, 327, 392, 396).

Seconda pratica (It. "second practice") Monteverdi's term for a type of COUNTERPOINT that permits license to express the feelings of a text, also called STILE MODERNO; Monteverdi called the stricter counterpoint *prima pratica* (pp. 133, 135, 172). See also STILE ANTICO.

Sequence (1) Immediate repetition of a pattern of MELODY or HARMONY on successive levels of pitch (p. 239). (2) Type of Latin verse and plain chant composition originating in the ninth century (p. 30–31).

Serial (1) Pertaining to method of composition, either with rows or with series of twelve tones or PITCH-CLASSES (pp. 492–93, 495–507). (2) Also applied to other parameters, such as duration, DYNAMICS, TIMBRE, TEXTURE (pp. 504–5).

Sinfonia (It. "symphony") Italian ensemble piece, OVERTURE, orchestral PRELUDE, or SYMPHONY (pp. 228, 307, 311, 316).

Singspiel (Ger. "sing-play") Spoken play interspersed with songs, choruses, instrumental music (pp. 217–18, 297–98, 348–49).

Solmization Pedagogic scheme for learning to sing melodies at sight by assigning the syllables *ut, re, mi, fa, sol, la* to a SCALE of six notes in which *mi-fa* is the only semitone (p. 34).

Sonata (from It. *sonare* "to play") (1) Literally, a piece to be played on one or more instruments. (2) After ca. 1650, a work in several movements for church use (*sonata da chiesa*) or a SUITE of dances for secular use (*sonata da camera*) (pp. 203–205, 237–40). (3) After ca. 1750, an ambitious work in several movements for one or two solo instruments (pp. 305–7, 309–10, 317–19).

Sonata form Form used mostly in classic- and romantic-period first movements, usually consisting of an EXPOSITION, DEVELOPMENT, and RECAPITULATION of a limited number of themes (pp. 317–19).

Sprechstimme (Ger. "speech-voice") Approximate speechlike intonation of written pitches according to the notated rhythm (pp. 494–95).

Stile antico (It., "severe style" or "old style") CONTRAPUNTALLY correct, serious, POLYPHONIC style of sacred music codified by Zarlino and practiced by Palestrina and his followers (pp. 168, 192, 208, 220).

Stile moderno (It. "modern style") Early-seventeenth-century manner of composition with BASSO CONTINUO that applied COUNTERPOINT rules freely (pp. 192, 195). See also SECONDA PRATICA.

Stop Mechanism on an organ or harpsichord to turn on or off the sounding of certain sets of pipes or strings.

Stopping Pressing a string down to the fingerboard or FRET to shorten the length of the vibrating portion.

Stretto IMITATION of a subject at a close time-interval, even before the complete subject has been stated, as in a FUGUE (p. 231).

Strophic Pertaining to poetry in which stanzas (strophes) are in equivalent form, permitting them to be sung with a single MELODY; such a poem set to music in this way.

Style brisé (Fr. "broken style") Technique in lute and keyboard composition or performance of splitting a CHORD into a succession of individual notes (pp. 199, 200).

Suite Set of pieces, usually dances (pp. 233–36, 245–46).

Suspension DISSONANCE caused by a voice that moves from a CONSONANT to a dissonant relationship with a sustained note, which then descends a step to RESOLVE the dissonance (pp. 167, 175).

Syllabic Pertaining to a style of compositon or performance in which one note is sung to each syllable of text (p. 248).

Symphonia (Latinized Gr. "sounding together") (1) Ensemble piece for chorus and instruments (pp. 197–98). (2) SINFONIA.

Symphonic poem One-movement orchestral work based on a program or non-musical subject (pp. 383–84, 440).

Symphony Work for orchestra in several movements.

Syncopation Displacing the normal recurrence of a strong beat either by elongating or accentuating a normally weak beat (p. 520).

Synthesizer Electronic instrument that generates musical sounds (pp. 508, 541, 544).

Tablature NOTATION showing graphically the location of the FRETS on a lute, viol, or similar instrument that must be STOPPED to produce the music (pp. 138, 142, 143, 147, 200).

Temperament Instrumental tuning that reduces or increases the INTERVAL size of some CONSONANCES to make others more pleasing. *Equal temperament* has equal tones and semitones which makes it possible to play in any key (pp. 231, 266). See also JUST INTONATION.

Tempo (It. "time") Slowness or quickness of performance.

Tenor (Lat. *tenere* "to hold") (1) Voice part that holds the principal melody, or CANTUS FIRMUS, sometimes in long-held notes (pp. 47, 56, 64–65, 94–97). (2) Voice whose compass is approximately from c' to g''. (3) Reciting tone in a MODE or PLAINCHANT (pp. 26, 33).

Tetrachord (1) In Greek and medieval theory, series of four notes spanning a fourth (pp. 8, 131). (2) In modern theory, set of four pitches (pp. 188, 217, 339).

Texture Interweaving, spacing, and contrasting of vocal and instrumental parts or groups of them—for example, HOMOPHONIC, POLYPHONIC, POLYCHORAL textures (pp. 96–97, 174, 205, 238, 500, 503).

Theme Musical subject of a composition or section, or of a set of VARIATIONS (pp. 148, 337).

Thoroughbass See **Basso continuo**.

Timbre Characteristic color or sound of an instrument or voice.

Time signature Sign or numerical proportion, such as $\frac{3}{4}$, placed at the beginning or in the course of a composition to indicate the METER or MEASURE (pp. 80–81).

Toccata Introductory instrumental piece in IMPROVISATORY style; later, such a piece containing FUGAL sections or serving as a prelude to an independent fugue (pp. 145–46, 200–201, 228–30, 263–64).

Tombeau (Fr. "tomb") Musical tribute to a dead composer or musician (pp. 200, 457, 459).

Tonality (tonal) (1) From ca. 1600, means by which music is organized around a central pitch to which the other pitches of a major or minor scale are related (pp. 176, 240). (2) The central pitch of a composition.

Tone cluster (1) Collection of notes obtained by striking piano keys with the hand or forearm (p. 506). (2) In instrumental music, a piling up of dissonant tones, usually major and minor seconds, within a chord (p. 466).

Tonic The first and central note of a MAJOR or MINOR SCALE.

Tonos (Gr.; pl. *tonoi*) In Greek music, a SCALE at a certain pitch level, similar to a modern TONALITY. Tonoi were given ethnic names, such as Dorian, Phrygian, and Lydian; some writers recognized seven, others thirteen or fifteen (p. 34).

Traditional music Music indigenous to an ethnic or national group; folk music, consisting mainly of anonymous songs, dances, and patriotic music (pp. 38, 45, 86, 464, 481–82, 528).

Tragédie lyrique (Fr. "lyrical tragedy") French seventeenth- and eighteenth-century music drama, often modeled on contemporaneous spoken tragedies (pp. 213, 258).

Transcription Arrangement of a piece for an instrumental medium different from the original, such as a reduction of an orchestral score for piano (pp. 400–1).

Transition Section, usually occurring in SONATA FORM, having no subject of its own serving as a bridge between thematic statements (pp. 308, 317–18).

Treble (1) Pertaining to highest part. (2) Highest voice or part.

Trecento (from It. *mille trecento* "1300") Period of the fourteenth century in Italian art and music history (pp. 63–64, 70, 72–77).

Triad CHORD consisting of three CONSONANT notes.

Trill Rapid alternation between a tone and its neighbor.

Trillo Vocal ORNAMENT consisting of a rapid repetition of the same pitch (p. 179).

Triplum (Lat. *triplus* "triple") Third part in early POLYPHONIC texture, the others being the TENOR and DUPLUM.

Tritone INTERVAL spanning three whole tones, such as *F* to *B*.

Trope (noun and verb) (1) Passage of text added to the original words of a PLAIN-CHANT, particularly to furnish words for singing a MELISMA. (2) Interpolation of both new text and new MELODY in an existing composition (pp. 30, 31).

Troubadour Poet-composer of MONOPHONIC song in Provencal (*langue d'oc*) in twelfth- and thirteenth-century southern France (pp. 36–41).

Trouvère Poet-composer of MONOPHONIC song in Old French (*langue d'oïl*) in twelfth- and thirteenth-century northern France (pp. 36–41).

Tutti (It. "all") (1) Instruction to an ensemble that all should play. (2) In a CON-CERTO, denotes the orchestra, as opposed to the soloist(s) (p. 246).

Twelve-tone row Ordered series of twelve different PITCH-CLASSES (pp. 492, 495).

Variation Reworking of an existing tune, song, AIR, ARIA, or THEME, often in a series of movements called "variations" (pp. 147–48, 205–7, 232, 233, 267, 365–67).

Verismo (It. "realism") Type of OPERA in which ordinary people are portrayed in passionate and violent situations (pp. 450, 481).

Vernacular music Popular, entertainment, and show music not intended for the concert hall (pp. 520–526).

Verse (1) Line of poetry. (2) Strophe or stanza of a hymn. (3) Sentence of a Psalm, which consists of two parallel statements or versicles.

Vibrato Slight fluctuation of pitch in performing a single note.

Virelai French FORME FIXE in which each stanza has the form AbbaA (capital letters indicating the REFRAIN) (p. 71).

Virtuoso (It. "virtuous") Musician who excels in technical ability.

INDEX

A **boldface** page number indicates the primary discussion of the entry. *Italics* refer to illustrations or music examples.

a cappella singing, 414, 419, 431, *517*
A chantar, Beatriz de Dia, 40
Abel, Fredrick, 519
Abendmusiken, 222
Académie Royale de Musique (Paris), 213
academies, 126, 171, 177, 190, 220, 244–45, 250
Accademia degli Unisoni, 190
accidentals, 131. *See also musica ficta*
  in church modes, 33–34
  figured bass, 174
  and *musica ficta,* 77
Acuff, Roy, 525
Ad organum faciendum, 46
Adam de la Halle, 38, *38*
Adams, John, 547
Aeolian Harp, The, Cowell, 527–28
Aeschylus, 5
affections, **172–73,** 188, 207, 241, 248, 271, 293, 299
affetti, 204
African-American music, 388, 516, **519–24,** 533–34
Afro-American Symphony, Still, 533–34
Agnus Dei, **22,** 29, 67
agréments, **199,** *236,* 237, 246, 260
Ahimè, dov'è 'l bel viso, Arcadelt, 128
Aida, Verdi, 419, 420, 432
air, English, **138–39,** 149
air, French, 214, 259–60, 336
air, Italian, 177, 178, 179
Akhnaten, Glass, 545
Albéniz, Isaac, 451
Alberti, Domenico, 293, 306
Alberti bass, 293
Albinoni, Tomaso, 247
Albrechtsberger, Johann Georg, 350
Alceste, Gluck, 303–304
Alcina, Handel, 281, 300
Alcuin of York, 29
aleatory music, 511n. *See also* indeterminacy
Alexander Nevsky, Prokofiev, 469
All Set, Babbitt, 543

alla breve, 119, 164
Alleluia, **22, 28–29,** 30, 46, 48
Alleluia Justus ut palma, 46
Alleluia Pascha nostrum, 48, 56–57
Alleluia Pascha nostrum, Léonin, 48, 50–53
allemande (alman), 144, 199, 200, 233, **234,** 235, 267
Allgemeine musikalische Zeitung, 275
Alma Redemptoris Mater, Dufay, 93
Almira, Handel, 276
Also sprach Zarathustra, Strauss, 440, **441**
amateur music and musicians, 126, 138, 236, 328, 479, 517
Amati, Niccolò, 228
Amazon, Tower, 548
Ambrose, Saint, 9, 13
Ambrosian chant, 13–14
Amériques, Varèse, 529
amor brujo, El, Falla, 451
Amours mi font souffrir–En mai, quant rose est florie–Flos filius, 57, 58, 60
Ancient Voices of Children, Crumb, 541
Andante and Rondo Capriccioso, Mendelssohn, 394
Andromeda, Manelli, 184
Anfossi, Pasquale, 349
Anglebert, Jean Henri d', 200
Anglican church music. *See under* church music, Reformation
Animus series, Druckman, 542
Anonymous IV, 53
anthems, **159,** 283, 517
antica musica ridotta alla moderna prattica, L', Vicentino, 131
antiphonal music, 193, 194, 508. *See also* polychoral music
antiphonal psalmody, 24, **27**
Antiphonale, 23, 27
antiphons, **20,** 21, 24–25, 26, **27–28,** 30, 44, 90, 124, 157, 158. *See also* Marian antiphons
  fauxbourdon settings of, 88, 89
  three-part, 89

Apotheosis of Lully, The, Couperin, 243
Appalachian Spring, Copland, 531
Appassionata Sonata, Beethoven, 362
appoggiaturas, 241, 254, 260, 309, 337, 397, 409, 434
Aquinas, Saint Thomas, 14
Aquitanian polyphony, 46–47
Arabs, poetry of, 37
Arcadelt, Jacques, 127, **128,** 149
arcicembalo, 131
arciorgano, 131
Arco, Livia d', 126
Aria di Ruggiero, Frescobaldi, 206
Ariadne musica, Fischer, 231
arias. *See also* air, Italian
  in cantatas, 271, 272
  in church music, 194
  da capo, **211–12,** 218, 224, 225–26, 282, 296, 299–300, *301,* 302, 303
  forms of, 209, 210
  influence on Baroque instrumental music, 198
  opera buffa, 296
  opera seria, 298–300, *301,* 302, 303
  in oratorios, 283
  in Passions, 274
  recitative *vs.,* 173, 184, 186
  sacred, 218, 224
  seventeenth-century, 185–86, *189,* 207, 209, 218, 225
ariettes, 297
arioso, 185, **211,** 224
Ariosto, Ludovico, 126, *183,* 184, 185, 281
Aristides Quintilianus, 6, 101
Aristotle, 5, 6, 7–8, 101, 103
Aristoxenus, 8, 12, 103
Armida, Haydn, 332
Armide, Gluck, 304
Armide, Lully, 214, 215, 304
Armstrong, Louis, 522, 523, *526*
arrangements
  of big band music, 523
  of French ballet music, 199

ars antiqua, 61, 63
Ars cantus mensurabilis, Franco of
    Cologne, 60
ars combinatoria, 342
ars nova, 61, 63, **64–71,** 82
Ars nova, Philippe de Vitry, 63
ars subtilior, 78–79
Art de toucher le clavecin, L', Couperin,
    237
*Art of Fugue, The. See Kunst der Fuge,
    Die*
Artusi, Giovanni Maria, 133, 134–35
astrology and music, 15
astronomy and music, 6, 7, 11, **14–15**
atonality, **492,** 494–95. *See also* serial
    music
Attaingnant, Pierre, 106, **135,** 136, 143,
    144
Auber, François, 413, 414
Auden, W. H., 488
audiences, and twentieth-century music,
    537, 539, 545, 550, 551–52
Aufstieg und Fall der Stadt Mahagonny,
    Weill, 477
augmentation, 231
Augustine, Saint, 9, 10, 14, 17
aulos, *4,* 5
Austrian music. *See* German music
Autry, Gene, 524
Available Forms I, Brown, 544
Available Forms II, Brown, 544
Avant que tu ne t'en ailles, Fauré,
    452–53
Ave Maria. . . virgo serena, Josquin, 116,
    117
Ave virgo virginum, 55–56
Avignon, 62, 76

Babbitt, Milton, 536, 538–39, 542, 543
Bach, Anna Magdalena, 265
Bach, Carl Philipp Emanuel, 307, *309,*
    309–10, 312
    sonatas of, 288, 353
Bach, Johann Christian, **312–13,** 336,
    343–44
Bach, Johann Christoph, 261
Bach, Johann Sebastian, 150, 168–69,
    188, 222, 249–50, **260–76,** *261,*
    286, 308, 312, 431
    cantatas of, 224, **270–73**
    chorale preludes of, 157
    influence on other composers, 338,
        368, 394, 396, 436, 473, 475, 476,
        487, 489
    instrumental (non-keyboard) music
        of, 267–68
    Italian influence on, 239
    keyboard music of, 201, 231, **265–67,**
        476, 550
    Mass of, 274
    melody of, 291
    orchestral music of, 246, 268
    organ music of, 206, 262–65, 400
    Passions of, 152, *153,* **273–74,**
        275–76, 479
    quotations from, 527, 549–50
    reception of, 274–76, 394, 411
    Scheibe on, 275
Bach, Wilhelm Friedemann, 264,
    308–309

Bach Gesellschaft (Society), 276, 411
Baiser de la fée, Le, Stravinsky, 487
Balakirev, Mily, 445, 446, 448
ballad opera, 297
ballade style, 70, 91
ballades
    Burgundian, 95
    of Chopin, 396
    double, 70
    fifteenth-century, 93
    medieval, 69, **70, 71,** 73, 82, 91
ballads
    eighteenth-century, 406
    medieval, 37
    nineteenth-century, 392, 406, 408
ballata, 72, **73,** 74, **75,** 81, 82, 91
Ballet comique de la reine, 143
ballets
    eighteenth-century, 289
    in operas, 208, 213–15, 258, 282
    seventeenth-century, 183–84, 189,
        213–15
    sixteenth-century, 143
    of Tchaikovsky, 374
    twentieth-century, 451, 459, 469, 480,
        481–84, 485–87, 491, 529, 531
ballett, 136, 137
balletto, 125
balli, 189
ballo in maschera, Un, Verdi, 419–20
Banchetto musicale, Schein, 199
Banshee, The, Cowell, 528
Bar form, 41
Barber, Samuel, 414, **547**
barbiere di Siviglia, Il, Rossini, 416–17,
    418
barcarolles, 453
Bardi, Giovanni, 177, 179
Baroque, 170–286
    affections in, 172–73
    Brahms influenced by, 388
    cantatas in, 190–91, 208, 218–20,
        223–24, 226, 270–73
    church music in, 171, 192–98,
        218–25, 226, 228–32, 262–65,
        269–74
    concertos in, 227, 228, 246–47,
        252–55, 268, 278–79, 286, 313
    counterpoint in, 174, 208, 268
    dance suites in, 199–200, 227, 228,
        233–36, 242, 243, 245–46, 247,
        267
    historical background of, 170–71
    influence on twentieth-century
        composers, 472
    instrumental music in, 172, 173,
        198–207, 227–48, 252–55, 260,
        278–79
    musical style in, 172–76
    opera in, 176–86, 209–18, 250, 251,
        257–60, 276–78, 280–82
    oratorios in, 194–95, 220, 221, 276,
        279, 282–85
    Passions in, 225, 273–74
    patronage in, 170–71
    sonatas in, 305
    vocal chamber music in, 186–92
baroque, 170
Bartók, Béla, **464–68,** *465,* 491, 515
    Debussy's influence on, 456

folk music studies of, 449, 464
    influence on other composers, 508,
        513
Bartoli, Cosimo, 100, 105
Bartolozzi, Therese Jansen, 331
baryton, 318
Basie, William "Count," 523
Basil, Saint, 9
basse danse, 144
basse fundamentale, 258
basso continuo, **174,** 176, 207, *236,* 243,
    311
    in church music, 193, 226
    in recitatives, 179, 181, 211
    in trio sonatas, 204, *205,* 238
basso ostinato, **187,** 209, 216–17, 490
bassoon, 174
Bax, Arnold, 456
Bay Psalm Book, 517
Bayreuth Festival Theater, *428*
Beatles, The, 525
Beatriz, Comtessa de Dia, 40
bebop, 523–24
Bedford, John of Lancaster, duke of, 88
Beethoven, Ludwig van, 308, **350–72,**
    370, 373, 411, 460
    Bach's influence on, 368
    Berlioz's views on, 361
    chamber music of, 351, 352, 354 (*See
        also under* string quartets, below)
    choral music of, 351, 352, 369–70,
        413
    church music of, 351, 352, 365, 431
    concertos of, 351, 352, 364–65
    deafness of, 359, 365, 368
    Handel's influence on, 370
    Haydn's influence on, 350, 353, 354,
        370
    Immortal Beloved of, 366–67
    influence on Mahler, 436
    influence on other composers,
        366–67, 372, 374, 386, 388–89,
        393, 405, 419, 425, 475, 479
    opera of, 351, 352, **358**
    overtures of, 351, 352, 361
    patrons of, 352–53, 358, 364
    quotations from, 513, 527, 549
    sonatas of, 339, 351, 352, 353–54,
        362–64, 365, **368–69,** 372, 436
    string quartets of, 351, 352, **354,**
        358–59, 365, **368, 369,** 372, 393
    style periods of, 352, 365
    symphonies of, 289, 351, 352,
        354–57, 359–61, *364,* 365, 368,
        370–71, 372, 378, 379, 380, 381,
        383, 388–89, 400, 405, 410, 436,
        440
    teachers of, 350–51
    use of Alberti bass, 293
Beggar's Opera, The, Gay, 277, 297, 477
bel canto, 186, 207
Belle, bonne, sage, Cordier, 76–77,
    78–79
Bellini, Vincenzo, 413, 414, **418,** 419
bells, 81
Benda, Georg, 349
Benedicamus Domino, 47
Benedict, Sir Julius, 351
Beneventan chant, 13
Benevoli, Orazio, 193–94

Berg, Alban, 492, 493, **500**, 502–503, 509
  Debussy's influence on, 456
  influence on other composers, 538
  Mahler's influence on, 460
Berkshire Music Center (Tanglewood), 515
Berlin, 290, 312
Berlin, Irving, 526
Berlioz, Hector, 305, 356, 373, *389,* 392, *400,* 410, 452
  Beethoven's influence on, 389
  choral music of, **429–30,** 431, 508
  influence on other composers, 380–81, 436, 446, 460
  operas of, **415–16**
  symphonies of, **378–81,** 386, 400, 440
  writings on music of, 361, 374
Bernanos, Georges, 481
Bernart de Ventadorn, 39, 40–41
Bernini, Gian Lorenzo, 171, 196–97
Bernstein, Leonard, 526, 531
big bands, 523
Billings, William, 517–18, 534
Binchois, Gilles, 86, 90, **91,** *92,* 108
birdsong, 505
bitonality, 481, 483
Bizet, Georges, 415, 420
Black, Brown and Beige, Ellington, 542
Black Angels, Crumb, 541
black music. *See* African-American music; non-Western music
Bloch, Ernest, 456
Blow, John, 216, 217, 220
blues, 480, 516, **522,** 523, 533–34, 542
Boccaccio, Giovanni, 63, 72, 73
Boccherini, Luigi, 349
Boethius, Anicius Manlius Severinus, **10–12,** *11,* 15, 17, 19, 32, 34, 101
Bohème, La, Puccini, 460
Bohemian music, 388, 449
Boito, Arrigo, 420
Bolero, Ravel, 459
Bologna, 171, 220, 243, 246, 247
Bonaparte, Jerome, King of Westphalia, 352
Bonaparte, Napoleon, 356–57
Bonaventura, Sam di, *537*
Bonne Chanson, La, Fauré, 452–53
Bonno, Giuseppe, 289
Bononcini, Giovanni, 300
Book of Common Prayer, 159
bop, 523
Bordoni, Faustina, 300–301, *302*
Boris Godunov, Musorgsky, 446, **447–48,** 454
Borodin, Alexander, 445, 446
borrowing. *See also* quotation
  in Baroque music, 202, 268, 271, 284–85, 303
  in medieval music, 55, 56, 64, 94–95
  in Renaissance music, 111, 118, 119
Boston, 519
Boulanger, Nadia, 453, 515, *516,* 529, 531, *538,* 545
Boulez, Pierre, **504–505,** 515, 538
Bourgeois, Loys, 154
Brahms, Johannes, 373, 394, 409, 444–45
  Beethoven's influence on, 367, 386

chamber music of, 392, **404–406,** 411
choral music of, 431
clarinet music of, 406
concertos of, **386,** 411
influence on other composers, 439, 450, 460, 475
lieder of, 374
overtures of, 386
piano music of, 392, 397
sonatas of, 406
symphonies of, **386–88,** 411, 420
Brandenburg Concertos, Bach, 268, 271, 489
branle gay, 144
Brecht, Bertolt, 477
Brentano, Antonie, 366–67, *367*
Brentano, Franz, 366–67
breve, 80
Britten, Benjamin, 475, 491
Broschi, Carlo. *See* Farinelli
Broschi, Riccardo, 281
Brosses, Charles de, 251
Brown, Earle, 544
Brown, Tom, 523
Brubeck, Dave, 538
Bruckner, Anton, 373–74, **431,** 460
Brückwald, Otto, *428*
Brunelleschi, Filippo, 93
Buch der hängenden Gärten, Das, Schoenberg, 494
Büchner, Georg, 500
Bull, John, *148*
Bülow, Hans von, 440
Burgundian music, 83–85, 87, **91–98,** 100
  cadence formulas in, 92
  chansons, 93
  court chapel, 84–85, 87, 91
  genres and style, 91–92
  Masses, 93–97
  motets, 93
  rhythm in, 93, 95–96
  voice combinations in, 91, 93, 95, 98
Burleigh, Harry T., 388
Burney, Charles, 278, 300, *302,* 311
Busenello, Giovanni Francesco, 185
Busnois, Antoine, 110–11
Buti, Francesco, 184
Buxtehude, Dietrich, **222,** 247, 248, 262
  chorale variations of, 232
  passacaglias and ciaconas of, *187,* 206
  toccatas of, 201, **230,** 264
Byrd, William, **167–68**
  church music of, 159, 168
  keyboard music of, 140, 143, 147–48
Byzantium, 12, 13, 17

cabaletta, 417
caccia, **72–73,** 75, 82
Caccini, Francesca, 183–84
Caccini, Giulio, *173,* 177, **178–79,** 184, 189–90
Caccini, Margherita, 183
Caccini, Settimia, 183
cadences
  in Baroque music, 175
  Burgundian, 92, 95
  in chant, 26–27
  chromatically altered, 77
  deceptive, 428

double leading-tone, 77
  in eighteenth-century music, 292
  evaded, 116, **122,** *123, 132,* 201
  in fifteenth-century music, 103, 104, 119
  in French chanson, 136
  Landini, 74, 92
  in organum, 53
  perfect, 124
  Phrygian, 77, 240
  rhymed, 68–69
  in sixteenth-century music, 130
  tones, 67
cadenzas, 240, 268, **344,** 417, 511, 513
  of Beethoven, 365
  for eighteenth-century arias, 299
  of Mozart, 344
Cage, John, 506, 511n, **543–44**
cakewalk, 520–21
Caldara, Antonio, 220
Calder, Alexander, 544
Calvin, Jean, 150, 151, 153–54
Calzabigi, Raniero de, 289, 303
cambiata, 164
Camerata, Florentine, 177, 179
Campion, Thomas, 138
Campra, André, 479
Can vei la lauzeta mover, Bernart de Ventadorn, 39
Canonical Hours, **20–21,** 23, 27
canons, 72, **109–10,** 162
  of Bach, 267
  cancrizans (crab), 109
  mensuration, 110–11, 116
  retrograde, 109
  in twentieth-century music, 496, 500, 510, 517, 540, 545
canso, 39, 40
cantatas, **190,** 207
  of Bach, 270–73
  Baroque, 190–91, 208, 218–20, 223–24, 226, 270–73
  Lutheran, 208, 223–24, 226
  twentieth-century, 469, 493–94, 502–503
canticle, **20,** 21
cantilena texture, **70,** 82, 83, 91, 93
cantus firmus, **56,** 61, 89
  chorales as, 232
  in isorhythmic motets, 64–65, 67, 68
  in Masses, 94–97, 108, 111, 116, 121–22, 158, 162
cantus firmus variations, 206
canzon villanesca, 125canzone, **146–47,** 149, 202–203, 228, 238, 239, 508
canzonets, 136, 137, 181, 186, 189
canzonettas, 125
Capriccio, Stravinsky, 487, 489
Capriccio espagnol, Rimsky-Korsakov, 448
Caravaggio, Michelangelo Merisi da, 127
Carissimi, Giacomo, 190, **194–95,** 218, 220, 283
Carmen, Bizet, 415, 420
carols, 86
Carroll, Lewis, 550
Carter, Elliott, **515–16,** 536, 537
Cash, Johnny, 525
Castor et Pollux, Rameau, 257, 260
castrati, 280–81, 299, 301

catch, 220
Catherine the Great, Empress of Russia, 289
caudae, 55
Cavalieri, Emilio de', 194
Cavalli, Pier Francesco, 186
cavatina, 417
Cazzati, Maurizio, 220
Cecilian movement, 430–31, 432
Cento concerti ecclesiastici, Viadana, 194
Cervantes, Miguel de, 442
Cesti, Antonio, 186, 190, 218
Chabrier, Emmanuel, 454
chace, 72–73, 75
chaconne, 147, 187, 227, **236,** 247, 268, 388. *See also* passacaglia
Chamber Concerto, Berg, 509
chamber music. *See also* instrumental music; *specific genres and composers*
    Baroque, 171, 186–92, 208, 227, 228, 243
    eighteenth-century, 309–10, *312*
    of Romantic period, 391, 392, 401–406, 410–11
Chambonnières, Jacques Champion de, 200
Champion des dames, Le Franc, 88, 90, 91
chance music. *See* indeterminacy
Chandos anthems, Handel, 283
chanson de geste, 36
chansonniers, 37, *38*
chansons
    Burgundian, 91, **93,** 97, 110, 112
    fifteenth-century, 108, 119
    Franco-Flemish, 110–11, 112–13
    French sixteenth-century, 125, 135–36, 149
    influence on canzone, 202–203
    instrumental performances of, 140
    medieval, 68, 69, 71
    Odhecaton anthology, 106–107, 112
    Parisian, 135
chansons balladées, 68
Chansons madécasses, Ravel, 459
chant, **13–16, 18–35,** 40, 44, 46
    accidentals in, 23, 33–34
    antiphonal, 24, 27–28
    classification of, 24
    Council of Trent revisions of, 161
    dialects of, 13, 17
    direct, 24
    in fifteenth-century Burgundian music, 93, 94, 95
    forms of, 26, 29
    Gregorian, 16, 17, 29
    influence on twentieth-century music, 505
    liturgical books of, 23
    liturgy and, 19–23
    for Masses, 21–22, 28–29
    melismatic, 19–20, 24, 26, 28, 30–31, 52, 53
    melody in, 24, 26, 30
    modern editions of, 161
    neumatic, 24, 30
    notation of, 22–23, *24,* 26, 42
    for Office, 20–21, 26–28
    organ settings of, 207

performance practice of, 23, 25, 28
purpose of, 19
range of, 23
responsorial, 24, 28, 48, 50
revival of, 431
rhythm of, 26
syllabic, 19, 24, 26, 29
tenor in, 26, 33, 47
text setting in, 24, 26
transmission of, 14–15, 18, 19, 22–23, 29–30
Chant des oiseaux, Le, Janequin, 136
Char, René, 504
Charlemagne, Emperor, 29
Charles, VI, Holy Roman Emperor, 303
Charles I, duke of Bourbon, 106
Charles the Bold, duke of Burgundy, 83–84, 87
Charles V, King of France, 67, 112
Charpentier, Marc-Antoine, 220–21
charts, 523
Chaucer, Geoffrey, 63, 66
Cherubini, Luigi, 305
Chester, Billings, 517–18
choirbooks, 60, 107
Chopin, Fryderyk, 394, **398–99,** *399,* 409, 410–11
    influence on other composers, 446, 449, 450
    piano music of, 392, **395–97,** 418
    sonatas of, 397
choral music. *See specific composers and genres*
chorale cantatas, 271–72
chorale fantasias, **232,** 274
chorale motets, 153
chorale partitas, 227, **232,** 262
chorale preludes, 153, *157,* 227, **232–33,** 349
    of Bach, 262, 264–65
chorale variations, 207, **232,** 233
chorales, 150, **152,** 156, *157,* 169, 222–23, 226, 271–72, 274, 414
    contrafacta, 152
    organ, 207, 227, 228, 231–32, 247
    polyphonic settings of, 152–53, 195, 197
    tune sources for, 152
choruses, jazz, 522
Chowning, John, 538
Chrétien de Troyes, 41
Christ lag in Todes Banden, Bach, 271
Christ lag in Todes Banden, Luther, 152
Christian church, early. *See under* church music, early Christian
Christina, Queen of Sweden, 238, 244–45
chromaticism
    in Baroque music, 175–76, 239
    in bebop, 523–24
    of Brahms, 386
    of Chopin, 396
    in eighteenth-century music, 259, 288
    of Franck, 452
    in German opera, 422
    of Haydn, 328, 331
    of Liszt, 385
    of Schoenberg, 494
    in sixteenth-century music, 131–32, 134, 149

of Strauss, 441, 443
of Wagner, 429, 432, 492
of Wolf, 434
Chrysostom, Saint John, 9
church music, Baroque, 171, 192–98, 208, 218–25, 228–32, 250, 262–65, 269–74
    Lutheran, 222–25, 226, 228–32, 262–65, 269–74
    Roman Catholic, 193–95, 218–22, 226, 250
church music, Counter-Reformation, 151, 158–69
church music, early Christian, 3, 8–16, 27
    Byzantine, 13
    Church Fathers' philosophy of, 9, 10, 14, 16
    Eastern, 13
    instruments' exclusion from, 12
    Jewish liturgical influence on, 12
    non-Roman (Western) liturgies, 13
    Roman dominance of, 3, 13, 15–16, 18–19
church music, eighteenth-century, 332–33, 349, 517–18
church music, Lutheran
    eighteenth-century, 262–65, 269–74
    seventeenth-century, 195–98, 222–25, 226, 228–32
    sixteenth-century, 139, 150, 151–53
church music, nineteenth-century, 413, 429–31, 432, 518–19
church music, Reformation, 150–58, 168–69
    Anglican, 151, 157–58, 159, 168
    French (Calvinist), 151, 153–56
ciacona. See chaconne
Cimarosa, Domenico, 349
Cirillo, Bernardino, 100, 102, 128
Claeszoon, Pieter, 154–55
Clarinet Quintet in A, Mozart, 340
clarinet sonatas, 406
classic, 287
Classic style, eighteenth-century. *See* eighteenth-century music
Classical Symphony, Prokofiev, 469, 479
clausula, **52–53,** 56–57, 61
    substitute, 54, 56–57
clavecin. See harpsichord
clavicembalo, 142
clavichord, 82, 142, 228
clavichord music, 233–37, 247, 265–67, 309–10, 330
Clavier-Übung, Bach, **264,** 267, 274, 476
Clement of Alexandria, 9
Clementi, Muzio, 354, 359
Cleofide, Hasse, 300–302
Cleonides, 8, 101
Clock Symphony, Haydn, 324
coda, 308, 355
Coffee Cantata, Bach, 273
Cohan, George M., 525
col legno, 506 Coleman, Ornette, 524
Collects, 22
Collegia musica, 243
color, **65,** 67
Coltrane, John, 524
Combattimento di Tancredi e Clorinda, Monteverdi, 189

comic opera. *See opera buffa; opera comique*
commedia dell'arte, 295
Communion, 28
Compline, 21
Comus, Lawes, 216
Concert champêtre, Poulenc, 481
Concert spirituel, 290, 322
concertato madrigal, 188, 189
concertato medium, **188**, 207, 246, 274
concertino, 246
concerto delle donne, 126, 129, 131, 183
Concerto for the Left Hand, Ravel, 459
concerto grosso, 240, **246**, 268, 279, 479
Concerto Grosso 1985, Zwilich, 548
Concerto Grosso in G minor, Vivaldi, 253–54
Concerto Grosso no. 1, Schnittke, 472
concertos. *See also* piano concertos; violin concertos; violoncello concertos
of J. C. Bach, 312–13
Baroque, 188–89, 227, 228, 246–47, 252–55, 268, 278–79, 286, 288, 291, 343
eighteenth-century, 290, 312–13
for few voices, 194, 195
grand, 193–94
of Mozart, 337–38, 343–44
nineteenth-century, 410–11
sacred, 171, **188**, 193–94, 195, 207, 222, 226
concerts, public, 184, 185, 216, 222, 250, 251, 290, *410*, 412
concerts, sacred, 216
Concerts de la Loge Olympique, 322
Concerts français, 290
Concord, Mass., 1840–60, Ives, 527
Conditor alme siderum, Dufay, 93
conductus
monophonic, **36**, 53, 61, 64
polyphonic, 44, 53, **54–56**, 67, 86, 89
Confessions, St. Augustine, 9, 10, 17
consonance and dissonance. *See also* chromaticism; harmony
of Bach, 265
in Baroque music, 172, 173, 175
in bebop, 523–24
of Billings, 518
in early polyphony, 45–46
in fifteenth-century music, 83, 86, 97, 98, 103
in fourteenth-century music, 67
in Greek music, 8
of Haydn, 333
of Monteverdi, 181
of Palestrina, 164
of Peri, 179
of Rameau, 259, 260
in sixteenth-century music, 97, 131, 133–34, 135, 146, 149
of Strauss, 443
tuning and, 231
in twentieth-century music, 494, 514, 541
consorts, of instruments, 141, 202
Contemporary Music Project, 538
Continental Harmony, The, Billings, 517, *518*
continuo instruments, 174, 227, 238

contrafacta, 150, **152**
Copland, Aaron, 515, *516*, **529, 531**, 537
influence on other composers, 531
Coprario, John, 202
Cordier, Baude, 76–77, 78–79
Corelli, Arcangelo, 175, 243, **244–45**, 248, 472
concertos of, 246, 247
influence of, 254, 263, 264, 276, 279, 286
sonatas of, **238–40**, 242, 244–45, 253
cori spezzati, 193, 508
Corigliano, John, 414
Cornaro family, 196–97
Corneille, Pierre, 213
cornett, 81, *105*, 141, 147
corrente, 234, 267
Così fan tutte, Mozart, 340, 344–45, **348**
Council of Trent, 30, 31, **158–60**, 165
Counter-Reformation, music of the, 151, 158–69
counterpoint
Baroque, 174, 192, 208, 268, 286
of Beethoven, 368
of Billings, 518
in fifteenth-century music, 103, 108
of Haydn, 323, 326
imitative, 110, 112, 114, 115, 119, 151, 202, 203, 215, 230
jazz, 523
of Mozart, 342–43
Palestrina style, 151, 162–65, 192, 316
in twentieth-century music, 476, 498, 500–501, 503, 505–506, 508, 536
country music, 516, **524–25**
Couperin, François, 247, 248, 452, 454
keyboard music of, 200, **234, 235–36**, 288
trio sonatas of, 242–43
vocal music of, 222
Couperin, Louis, 200
couplets, 328
courante, 144, 199, 200, 233, **234**, 235, 267
court chapels, 84–85, 87, 91, 104, 113
cowboy songs, 516, 529
Cowell, Henry, 506, 527–28, 539
Craft of Musical Composition, The, Hindemith, 475
Creation, The. See Schöpfung, Die
Création du Monde, La, Milhaud, 480
Credo, **22**, 29, 67
Creole Jazz Band, 523
cross relations, 210, 387
Cruda Amarilli, Monteverdi, 134–35
Crumb, George, 538, **541**
Crusades, 42, 43
Cui, César, 445, 446
cymbals, 81
Czech music. *See* Bohemian music
Czerny, Carl, *266*, 356, 364, 397, *400*

da capo aria, **211–12**. *See also* arias; ariettes
Da Ponte, Lorenzo, 345, 346
dall'Abaco, Evaristo Felice, 247
Damnation de Faust, La, Berlioz, 380, 415
dance, social, 143

dance music. *See also* ballets; suites, Baroque
American popular, 520–21, 523
Baroque, 173, 199–200, 228
early ballate as, 73
medieval, 37–38, 42, 82
nineteenth-century, 392, 395–96
Renaissance, 143–44, 149
dance pairs, 143, 231
Danket dem Herrn, denn er ist sehr freundlich, Buxtehude, 232
Dante Alighieri, 15, 63
Dante Symphony, Liszt, 386
Darmstadt movement, 504
Datemi pace, o duri miei pensieri, Rore, 129–30
Davidovsky, Mario, 538
Davidsbundlertänze, Schumann, 395
Davies, Peter Maxwell, 513
Davis, Anthony, 543
Davis, Miles, 524
De harmonia musicorum instrumentorum opus, Gaffurio, 102
De institutione musica, Boethius, 10–12
de Leeuw, Ton, 505
De profundis clamavi ad te, Josquin, 115
Debussy, Claude, 433, **453–56**, *458*, 461, 463, 486, 494, 500, 529, 542
Berlioz's influence on, 380
influence on other composers, 451, 455–56, 473
Musorgsky's influence on, 446, 454
Degas, Edgar, 456
Deidamia, Handel, 282
Del Monte, Cardinal, 127
Del Tredici, David, 531, 550–51
Dello Joio, Norman, 537–38
des Prez, Josquin. *See* Josquin des Prez
Descartes, René, 245
Déserts, Varèse, 507, 538
development, 308, 313, **320**, 321
Devin du village, Le, Rousseau, 297
Diabelli Variations, Beethoven, 352, **365–67**
Diaghilev, Sergei, 469, 481, 484, 485, **486–87**
Dialogo della musica antica et della moderna, Galilei, 177
Dialogues des Carmelites, Poulenc, 481
Dichterliebe, Schumann, 409, 411
Dido and Aeneas, Purcell, *188*, 216–17
Dies irae, 31, 379, 401, 430
diminution, 241
discant, *47*, 50, 52, 53, 54, 91–92
English, 86, 88
Discorso sopra la musica de' suoi tempi, Giustiniani, 129
dissonance. *See* consonance and dissonance
Dittersdorf, Carl, 349
divertimentos, 337
divertissements, 214, 259
Divine Comedy, Dante, 63
division, 241
Dodekachordon, Glareanus, 103
Don Giovanni, Mozart, 344, **346–48**
Don Juan, Strauss, 440–41
Don Quixote, Strauss, 440, **442**
Donizetti, Gaetano, 413, **417–18**, 419
Doppelgänger, Der, Schubert, 408

double, 235, 267
Dover Beach, Barber, 547
Dowland, John, **138–39,** 140, 148
Doxology, 27, 28
dramma giocoso, 346
Dreigroschenoper, Die, Weill, 477–78
Druckman, Jacob, 538, 542
Drumroll Symphony, Haydn, 325
drums, 81, *144*
Dufay, Guillaume, 86, 90, **91,** *92,* **93,** *94,* **95–97,** 108
Dumas, Alexandre, the Younger, *389,* 419
Dumbarton Oaks Concerto, Stravinsky, 479, 489
D'ung aultre amer, Ockeghem, 110–11
Dunstable, John, 86, 88–90
Durazzo, Giacomo, 289, 303
Durch Adams Fall ist ganz verderbt, Bach, 265
Dussek, Jan Ladislav, 354
Dvořák, Antonín, 373, **388,** 411, 449, 520
dynamics, **147,** 179, 391, 417, 501
  in eighteenth-century music, 309, 310, **311,** 321, 324, 330, 355

Easter, 30, 31, 48, 152
Ecstasy of Saint Teresa, The, Bernini, 196–97
education, music
  ancient Greece, 5, 7
  Baroque, 172, 250, 251, 264–65, 266, 269
  medieval, 15–16, 19, 29–30, 34, 36, 43
  nineteenth-century, 519
  seventeenth-century, 517
  sixth-century, 11
  twentieth-century, 463, 469, 515–16
Edward VI, King of England, 158
Egmont, overture and incidental music to, Beethoven, 352, 361
eighteenth-century music, 249–349. *See also* Haydn, Franz Joseph; Mozart, Wolfgang Amadeus
  Baroque music compared with, 291
  chamber music, 309–10
  church music, 332–33, 349
  concertos in, 312–13
  emotions in, 293–94, 310–11
  internationalism in, 288–91
  operas, 289, 294–305, 314
  orchestra in, 311
  Romantic traits in, 373
  sonatas, 305–307, 309–10, 330–31
  string quartets, 325–30, 339
  style characteristics of, 291–94
  symphonies, 307–308, 311–12, 316–25, 340–43
Ein deutsches Requiem, Brahms, 431
Ein' feste Burg ist unser Gott, Luther, 152, 414
Ein Heldenleben, Strauss, 441
Eine kleine Nachtmusik, Mozart, 337
Einstein, Alfred, 335
Einstein on the Beach, Glass, 545
Eleanor of Aquitaine, 39, 40–41
electronic music, 493, **507–508,** 511, 513, 514, 538, **541–42,** 545, 546

Elektra, Strauss, 442, 443
Elgar, Edward, 450
Elizabeth I, Queen of England, 158, 159
Ellington, Edward Kennedy "Duke," 2, 523, 542
Embryons desséchés, Satie, 456
Emerson, Ralph Waldo, 527
Emperor Concerto, Beethoven, 364
empfindsamer Stil, 287, **288,** 308–310, 331
English Hymnal, 473–74
English music
  Baroque, 202, 208, 216–17, 220, 276–85
  eighteenth-century, *291,* 297, 313
  fifteenth-century, 83, 86, 88–91
  medieval, 13, 29, 46, 86
  nineteenth-century, 415, 450
  opera, 208, 216–17, 276–77, 280–82, 297
  operas, 475
  operettas, 415
  Renaissance, 125, 136–39, 144, 146, 147–48, 149, 157–58, 167–68
  twentieth-century, 450, 464, 473–75, 491
English Suites, Bach, 267
Enlightenment, 288–90. *See also* eighteenth-century music
Enrico detto il Leone, Steffani, 210
ensemble finales, 345, 419
ensemble music. *See also* chamber music; *specific composers and genres*
  Baroque, 202, 203–204, 228, 237–48
  sixteenth-century, 106–107, 126, 129, 146–47
Entführung aus dem Serail, Die, Mozart, 258, 338, 344, **348**
Epitaph of Seikilos, 4, *6,* 7
equal temperament, 231, 266
Ercole I, duke of Ferrara, 118
Erlkönig, Schubert, 408
Eroica Symphony, Beethoven, *354,* **356–57,** 389
Este family, 105, 126, 132
Esterházy, Anton, 319
Esterházy, Nicholas, *317,* 318–19, 397
Esterházy, Nicholas II, 319, 332
Esterházy, Paul Anton, 316, 318
ethos, **7,** 9, 103
études, 397, 400
Euclid, 12, 101
Eugene IV, Pope, 91, 93
Eugene Onegin, Tchaikovsky, 445
Euridice, Caccini, 177, 179, 181
Euridice, Peri, 177, 179–80, 181
Euripides, 5, 176, 540
Europe, James Reese, 520
Evans, Bill, 524
exoticism, 415, 432, 439–40, 445, 451, 454, 459, 460, 463, 481, 528. *See also* non-Western musics
exposition, 230, 308, 313, **317–19**
expressionism, 442, 476, 495, 500, **502–503,** 526

fa-las, 136
faburden, 88

Falla, Manuel de, **451,** 456
falsobordone, 114
Falstaff, Verdi, 416, 420, **422**
fancy, 146
Fantasia on a Theme of Thomas Tallis, Vaughan Williams, 474
fantasias and fantasies
  of Bach, 262, 263–64
  Baroque, 202, 227
  of Chopin, 396–97
  of Liszt, 401
  of Mendelssohn, 394
  of Mozart, 339
  of Schubert, 393
  of Schumann, 395
  sixteenth-century, 144–45, 146, 149
  twentieth-century, 474, 531, 549
Fantasy for Violin and Piano, Schoenberg, 496
Farewell Symphony, Haydn, 322
Farinelli, 277, 280–81, *281*
Fauré, Gabriel, **452–53,** 454, 455
  influence on other composers, 453
Faust, Goethe, 385, 408, 436
Faust Symphony, Liszt, 385, 411
fauxbourdon, **86, 88,** 89, 92, 93, 98, 115, 130
Fearful Symmetries, Adams, 547
Feldman, Morton, 544
Fenice fù, Jacopo de Bologna, 72, 75
Ferrabosco, Alfonso, the Younger, 202
Ferrante I, King of Naples, 103
Ferrara, 126, 129, 131, 183
Ferrari, Benedetto, 184
fiddle, tenor, *85*
Fidelio, Beethoven, 352, 358
Field, John, 396
figuration, 241
figured bass, *173,* 174, *236,* 240. *See also* basso continuo
Final Alice, Del Tredici, 550–51
finale, 321, 325
finalis (final), 32, 33
Fingals Höhle, Mendelssohn, 382
Finney, Ross Lee, 515, 538
Finnish music, 450
Fiori musicali, Frescobaldi, 201
Fire Bird, The, Stravinsky, 481
first-movement form, 317–29
Fischer, J. K. F., 231
Fisk Jubilee Singers, 519–20
Fitzwilliam Virginal Book, 147
Five Pieces for Orchestra, Webern, 501
fliegende Holländer, Der, Wagner, 423–24
Florence, 72, 93, *94,* 126, 171, 183
  Camerata, 177, 179
Florilegium, Muffat, 246
Flow, my tears, Dowland, 139, 140, 143, 148
flute, transverse, 81, 141, *144*
flute music, 238, 267–68
folk music. *See also* non-Western musics
  influence on Haydn, 324
  influence on nineteenth-century music, 382, 388, 395–96, 400, 444–48, 449
  influence on twentieth-century music, 449–51, 463, 464–69, 481, 482, 527, 528, 529, 531

Italian, 250
  medieval, 38, 45, 86
Folk Song Symphony, Harris, 531
For All the Saints, Vaughan Williams,
  474
Forkel, Johann Nikolaus, 275, 292, 294
form. *See also* sonata form
  of Bach's cantatas, 271–72
  of Bach's fugues, 264
  of ballades, 71, 93
  of ballate, 75
  Bar, 41
  of Baroque concerto, 246–47, 264
  of Baroque sonata, 239–40
  in Beethoven's late works, 367–69,
    371
  binary, 236, 240, 306, 308
  of blues, 522
  of caccia, 71
  of chants, 26, 29
  concerto, 313
  cyclical, 381, 401, 452, 494
  of da capo aria, 211–12, 299–300
  in eighteenth-century music, 292
  of eighteenth-century symphonies,
    316–21
  of French chanson, 135
  of fugues, 230–31
  in Haydn's string quartets, 328
  mirror, 468
  multi-movement, 67, 93–94
  open, 511
  ottave rime, 187
  of pavane, 139
  in Romantic music, 391
  of rondeaux, 71, 93, 110
  of rondo, 325
  of sequences, 30
  sonata, 308
  strophic, 39, 41, 42, 186, 187, 209,
    407, 408
  of toccatas, 229–30
  of troubadour and trouvère songs,
    37–38, 39–40
  in twentieth-century music, 463
  of virelais, 71
"formalism," 469, 470
formes fixes, **69, 71,** 82, 110, 112
fortepiano, 309, 330
Foss, Lukas, 513, 531
Foster, Stephen, 520
4′33″, Cage, 544
Four Saints in Three Acts, Thomson,
  531–32
foxtrot, 521
Fra Diavolo, Auber, 414
Francis I, Holy Roman Emperor, 289
Francis I, King of France, 135
Francis II, Holy Roman Emperor, 352
Franck, César, 386, **452,** 453
Franco-Flemish music, 100, **105–18,**
  120, **121–24,** 136, 139, 151, 152,
  165–67
  cadences in, 122, *123*
  canons, 109–10
  chansons, 112–13, 136
Franco of Cologne, 60
Franconian motet, 56
Franconian notation, 80
Frankish Empire, 29–30

Franz Joseph I, Holy Roman Emperor,
  329
Frederick the Great, King of Prussia,
  268, 289, 301, *309,* 312
Freemasonry, 289, 338, 348
Freischütz, Der, Weber, 422–23
French music. *See also* Burgundian
  music; Franco-Flemish music
  ars nova, 62–63, 64–71
  Baroque, 199–200, 208, 212–15,
    220–22, 228, 233–37, 242–44,
    255–60
  eighteenth-century, 297, 305
  late fourteenth-century, 63–64, 75–77
  medieval, 36–41, 44, 46–60
  nineteenth- early twentieth-century,
    433, 451–60
  nineteenth-century, 378–81, 389,
    412–16
  opera, 208, 212–15, 257–60, 286, 297,
    305, 412–16, 452, 453, 455, 481
  opéra bouffe, 414–15
  opéra comique, 414, 415
  orchestral music, 378–81, 389
  sixteenth-century, 135–36, 143, 149,
    153–56
  twentieth-century, 464, 479–81, 491,
    504–507
French overture, **215,** 216, 245, 259,
  260, 341
  in chamber music, 239, 243, 331
  in church music, 271
French Suites, Bach, 267
Frescobaldi, Girolamo, 175, **201,** 206,
  242
Freud, Sigmund, 502
Friedrich August II, King of Poland, 274
Froberger, Johann Jakob, 175–76, 200,
  201, 234
From the New World, Dvořaaak, 388
frottola, **124–25,** 126, 128, 135
fuga, 202
fugal imitation, **116,** 119
fuging tunes, 518, 528
fugues
  of Bach, 264, 265–67, 268, 338, 400
  Baroque, 227, 228, 230–31, 235, 239,
    247
  of Beethoven, 368
  of Handel, 476
  of Haydn, 326
  of Mendelssohn, 394
  of Stravinsky, 490
  toccata and, 173, 201
Fux, Johann Joseph, 316, 334

Gabrieli, Giovanni, 147, 193, 195, 243
  motets of, 172
Gabrielli, Caterina, 289
Gaffurio, Franchino, 101–103
gagliarda. See galliard
galant style, 249, 273, 287, **288,** 293, 326
Galilei, Vincenzo, 177, 231
galliard *(gagliarda),* 143–44, 199
Gallican chant, 13
gamelan, 455, 544
Garcia Lorca, Federico, 541
Gassmann, Florian, 289
Gaultier, Denis, 199–200
Gaultier, Ennemond, 199

Gay, John, 277, 477
Gebrauchsmusik, 463, **476,** 477, 531
Geheimes Flüstern hier und dort, C. W.
  Schumann, 409–10
Geistliche Chormusik, Schütz, 197
Geistliche Konzerte, Schein, 195
genera, 8
genere rappresentativo, 189
George I, King of England, 276
German music
  Baroque, 200, 207, 208, 217–18, 220,
    222–25, 228, 233, 234, 243,
    244–46, 247, 260–76
  of Beethoven, 350–72
  chamber music, 401–406
  eighteenth-century, 297–98, 308–12,
    315–49
  late nineteenth- to early twentieth-
    century, 433, 434–44, 460
  lieder, 374, 406–10
  medieval, 29, 41–42
  nineteenth-century, 375–78, 381–83,
    386–88, 390, 391–95, 401–11,
    413, 444–45
  opera, 208, 217–18, 297–98, 332, 338,
    348–49, 358, 413, 422–20, 432,
    442–44, 461, 476, 477–78, 496,
    498–501
  orchestral music, 375–78, 381–83,
    386–88, 390
  piano music, 392–95
  Renaissance, 125, 139–40, 151–53
  twentieth-century, 463, 464, 475–78,
    491, 493–504
  in the United States, 518
"German" sixth chord, 328
Gershwin, George, 526, 542
Gershwin, Ira, 526
Gesamtkunstwerk, 426, 429, 432
Gesang der Jünglinge, Stockhausen, 507
Gesualdo, Carlo, **132–33,** 149, 175
Gewandhaus concerts, 290
Giasone, Cavalli, 186
Gibbons, Orlando, *148,* 159
gigue, 199, 200, 233, **235,** 240, 267
Gilbert, William S., 415
Gillespie, John Birks "Dizzy," 524
Giotto, 63
Giraud, Albert, 494
Giulio Cesare, Handel, 277, 282
Giustiniani, Vincenzo, 129
Glareanus, Heinrich, 103
Glass, Philip, 516, 545, 547
Glazunov, Alexander, 448
Glinka, Mikhail, **445,** 446, 448
Gloria, **22,** 29, 30, 46, 67
Gloria patri, 28
Gluck, Christoph Willibald, 287, 289,
  338, 345, 349, 451
  influence on Mozart, 336
  operas of, 297, **303–305,** 384, 412,
    416
glückliche Hand, Die, Schoenberg, 494,
  503
Goethe, Johann Wolfgang von, 289, 409
  dramas of, 361, 378, 385, 408, 415,
    436
Goldberg Variations, Bach, 267, 274
Golden Cockerel, The, Rimsky-Korsakov,
  448

Goldman, Edwin Franko, 520
Goldman, Richard Franko, 520
Goliard songs, 35
Gonzaga family, 105, 126, 133
Goodman, Benny, 523, 537
Gorzanis, Giacomo, 231
Gott erhalte Franz den Kaiser, Haydn, 329
Goudimel, Claude, 155–56
Gounod, Charles, 415, 452
Goûts-réünis, Le, Couperin, 242, 243
Gradual, **22, 28,** 46, 48, 431
Graduale, 23
Gradus ad Parnassum, Fux, 316, 334
grand concerto, 193–94
Grand Ole Opry, 525
Grand Pianola Music, Adams, 547
Grande Messe des morts, Berlioz, 429–30, 508
Grandi, Alessandro, 194, 198
grands motets, 222
Graun, Johann Gottlieb, 312
Greek music, ancient, 2–3, **4–8,** 99, 100
    astronomy and, 6, 14–15
    drama and, 5
    education and, 5, 7
    ethos doctrine in, 7, 9
    instruments in, 5
    intervals in, 6, 8
    and Italian theater music, 176–77, 179, 180, 195
    modes in, 7, 34, 102, 103
    mythology and, 4, 7
    poetry and, 4, 6–7
    politics and, 8
    powers of, 4, 7, 8, 16
    rhythm in, 7
    scales in, 8
    surviving examples of, 4, 6, 7
    theory, 3, 4, 6–8, 10, 12, 14, 16, 19, 43, 101
    virtuosity and, 5, 7, 8
Gregorian chant and liturgy, 3, 8, **15–16,** 17, 29, 42, 43, 431. *See also* chant
Gregory I, Pope, 15, *22*
Gregory II, Pope, 16
Gregory XIII, Pope, 161
Gretchen am Spinnrade, Schubert, 408
Grétry, André Ernest Modeste, 297
Grieg, Edvard Hagerup, **449–50,** 454
Griffes, Charles, 456
Grillen, Schumann, 395
Griselda, A. Scarlatti, 211–12
ground bass. *See* basso ostinato
Grünewald, Matthias, 476
gruppi, 178
Guarini, Anna, 126
Guarini, Giovanni Battista, 126
Guarneri, Giuseppe Bartolomeo, 228
Gubaidulina, Sofia, 472–73
Guerre, La, Janequin, 136
Guerre des bouffons. See Querelle des bouffons
Guido of Arezzo, **34–35,** 90
Guidonian hand, 34, *35*
guitar music, 524–25
Gurrelieder, Schoenberg, 493–94
Gutenberg, Johann, 107
Gymnopédies, Satie, 456

Haffner, Sigmund, 340
Haffner Symphony, Mozart, 340
Halévy, Jacques Fromental, 413
Haley, Bill, 525
Hamburg, 218, 276
Hamlet, Liszt, 384
Hammerstein, Oscar, II, 526
Handel, George Frideric, 220, 239, 250, **276–85,** *277,* 286, 288, 297
    borrowings of, 284–85
    Burney on, 278
    choral style in, 283–84
    influence on other composers, 333, 370, 431, 473, 475
    instrumental music of, 278–79
    Italian influences of, 210, 240, 242
    operas of, 276–78, 280–82, 300, *302*
    oratorios of, 276, 282–85, 370
Handel and Haydn Society, 519
Handy, W. C., 522
Hanson, Howard, 535
Harmonic Elements, Aristoxenus, 8
Harmonice musices odhecaton A. See Odhecaton
harmonics, 8
Harmonics, Ptolemy, 12
Harmonie der Welt, Hindemith, 477
harmony
    in Baroque music, 172, 174–76
    in Baroque variations, 206
    of Billings, 518
    blues, 522, 533–34
    in early English music, 86
    in eighteenth-century music, 288, 292–93, 310
    of Fauré, 452–53
    in fifteenth-century music, 97, 112, 114, 119
    in German opera, 422
    in Romantic music, 391
    in sixteenth-century music, 125, 128, 130, 131, 135–36, 158
    in toccatas, 229
    tonal, 176
    in twentieth-century music, 463
Harold en Italie, Berlioz, 379–80, 381
harp, 81, *85, 92*
harpsichord, 82, 142
    as continuo instrument, 174
    two-manual, 227, 228, *233*
harpsichord music
    of Bach, 265–67
    Baroque, 172, 199, 200, **233–37,** 247, 248, 268
    of Haydn, 330
    of Rameau, 260
    of Scarlatti, 306–307
Harris, Roy, 515, 531
Hart, Lorenz, 525–26
Háry János, Kodály, 469
Hasse, Johann Adolph, 275, 289, **300–302**
Hassler, Hans Leo, 139, 152, *153*
Haydn, Franz Joseph, 287, 308, **315–34,** 349, 372, 373, 444, 479
    Bach's influence on, 275
    baryton music of, 318
    Beethoven compared with, 351
    Beethoven influenced by, 350, 353, 354, 370

and Freemasonry, 289
Handel's influence on, 333
humor of, 327–28, 330, 332
influence on other composers, 393, 401, 442, 443
Masses of, 332–33, 431
Mozart compared with, 315, 337, 340, 341, 349
Mozart influenced by, 336, 338, 339
operas of, 331–32
oratorios of, 319, 331, 333–34, 354
orchestra of, 311, 318, 322, 324–25, 380
patrons of, 316, 318–19
sonatas of, 330–31
string quartets of, 319, **325–30,** 339
symphonies of, **316–25,** 340
trios of, 319
use of Alberti bass, 293
Haydn quartets, Mozart, 339
Hebrew scriptures, 4
Hebrides Overture, Mendelssohn, 382, 411
Heiligenstadt Testament, Beethoven, 359
Heimweh, Das, Schubert, 407
Heine, Heinrich, 408–409
hemiola, **76,** 181, 234
Henderson, Fletcher, 523
Henrici, Christian Friedrich, 273
Henry II, King of England, 40–41
Henry VIII, King of England, 150, 151, 158, 159
Henze, Hans Werner, 513
Herder, Johann Gottfried von, 384
heterophony, 4. *See also* texture
Hildegard of Bingen, 32
Hiller, Johann Adam, 290, 298
Hindemith, Paul, **475–77,** 479, 491, 515, *537,* 542
    Debussy's influence on, 456
Hippolyte et Aricie, Rameau, 257, 260
Histoire du soldat, L', Stravinsky, 484–85
historia, 225
history, importance of, 1–2
Hofer, Andreas, 193
hocket, **66,** 69, 73, 76
Hoffmann, E. T. A., 372, 373, 374
Hofmannsthal, Hugo von, 442, 443
Hogarth, William, 488
Hollander, John, 542
Holst, Gustav, 450
Holy Communion, 21
Holzbauer, Ignaz, 349
Homme armé, L', 162. *See also Missa L'homme armé* entries
homophony. *See also* texture
    eighteenth-century, 517
    fifteenth-century, 86, 89, 92, 98, 114–15, 119
    sixteenth-century, 125, 128, 136
Honegger, Arthur, 457, **479**
Horizon chimérique, L', Fauré, 453
Hugo, Victor, 382, 419
Huguenots, Les, Meyerbeer, 413, **414,** 416
humanism, 63, 99, **101,** 103, 114, 122, 149
Hungarian music, 463, 491
Hungarian Rhapsodies, Liszt, 401
Hunnenschlacht, Liszt, 384

hymns
  American, 516, 517–18, 519, 531
  Byzantine, 13
  of Dufay, 93
  early Christian, 12
  early Greek, 7
  fauxbourdon settings of, 88
  of Haydn, 329
  medieval, 44, 54, 56
  in Roman liturgy, 20, 26
  sixteenth-century, 158
  three-part, 89

Iberia, Albéniz, 450–51
Iberia, Debussy, 454
Ich grolle nicht, Schumann, 409
Ideale, Die, Liszt, 384
idée fixe, **378–79**, 381, 386, 389
Idomeneo, Mozart, 336
Im wunderschöne Monat Mai,
  Schumann, 409
Images, Debussy, 454, 455
imitation
  descriptive, 136, 209 (*See also*
    program music)
  in fifteenth-century music, 92, 98,
    108–109
  sixteenth-century, 116, 128
  in sixteenth-century Masses, 122
imitation, theory of, 7
imitation Mass, **118**. *See also* Masses
imitative counterpoint. *See under*
  counterpoint
impressionism, 448, 453, 454, 455,
  456–57, 459, 502
impromptus, 392, 396
improvisation, 511n
  of ancient Greek music, 4, 16
  in Baroque music, 174, 200–201, 204,
    228–30, 240, 241–42, 277–78
  of Beethoven, 354, 355, 367, 368
  blues, 522
  of Chopin, 398
  on chorale tunes, 153
  in eighteenth-century music, 301–302
  fourteenth-century, 70
  jazz, 522–24
  medieval, 18, 44, 46, 51, 61, 140
  of Mozart, 336
  Renaissance, 143, 144–46, 178, 179
  of troubadour and trouvère songs, 39
  in twentieth-century music, 508, 511–
    13, 544, 545, 546, 551
In ecclesiis, Gabrieli, 193
In Memory of a Summer Day, Del
  Tredici, 550, *551*
incidental music
  of Beethoven, 352, 361
  of Fauré, 452
  of Mendelssohn, 382–83
  of Purcell, 216
incipit, 56
incoronazione di Poppea, L', Monteverdi,
  184–86, 209
Indes galantes, Les, Rameau, 257,
  258–59, 260
indeterminacy, 493, **511**, **513**, 514, 527,
  543–44, 551
India, Sigismondo d', 190
Ingegneri, Marc'Antonio, 133

initium, 26Innocent XI, Pope, 244
Innsbruck, ich muss dich lassen, Isaac, 152
instrumental music. *See also* keyboard
    music; *specific composers,
    instruments, and genres*
  ancient Greek, 5
  Baroque, 171, 172, 173, 175–76,
    198–207, 227–48, 252–55, 260,
    278–79
  Burgundian court, 85, 87
  categories of, 121, 143–48u, 198,
    227–28
  eighteenth-century, 290, 305–13, 314
  fifteenth-century, 93
  fourteenth-century, 64, 70, 81
  in motets, 56
  Romantic period, 373–89, 391–406
  sixteenth-century, 121, 126, 138,
    140–48, 149
instrumentation and orchestration
  of Bach, 268, 272
  Baroque, 242
  of Beethoven, 360
  of Berg, 500
  of Berlioz, 379, 380–81, 430
  of big bands, 523
  of Brahms, 436
  of Crumb, 541
  of Debussy, 455
  in eighteenth-century music, 311
  of Fauré, 452
  of Haydn, 322–23, 324–25, 332
  idiomatic writing and, 172
  of jazz combos, 523
  of Lully, 215
  of Mahler, 435–40
  of Mendelssohn, 382
  of Mozart, 340, 345–46, 347, 381
  of Rameau, 260
  of Ravel, 457, 459
  of rhythm and blues groups, 525
  of Rimsky-Korsakov, 448
  of rock-and-roll, 525
  of Rossini, 416
  of Schoenberg, 494
  of Schubert, 376, 377–78
  of Schütz, 198
  in sixteenth-century music, 147
  of Strauss, 441–42
  of Stravinsky, 481
  in twentieth-century music, 506–507,
    509, 514
  of Varèse, 529
  of Verdi, 419, 422
  of Vivaldi, 253
  of Wagner, 424, 429
  of Weber, 422
  of Webern, 500
  of Weill, 477
instruments. *See also specific instruments*
  ancient Jewish, 12
  Baroque, 172
  consorts of, 141, 202
  continuo, 174, 227, 238
  and early Christian church, 12
  early Greek, 5
  fourteenth- and fifteenth-century,
    81–82
  "high" and "low," 81
  Renaissance, 141–42

Intégrales, Varèse, 529, **530**
intermedi (intermezzi), 176, 178
intermezzo, 295–96
international style, 83–85, 91, 98, 100,
    118, 120, 288–89, 290–91
Introit, **22**, **28**, 30, 31
Inventions, Bach, 265
"*Io parto*" *e non più dissi*, Gesualdo,
    132
Ionisation, Varèse, 507, 509, 529
Iphigénie en Aulide, Gluck, 304, 305
Iphigénie en Tauride, Gluck, 304
Ippolito ed Aricia, Traetta, 303
Ireland, 29
Isaac, Heinrich, 111–12, 152
Islam, 29, 42
isorhythmic motets, **64–65**, 66, 67, *68*,
    81, 82, 88, 89–90, 93, 95
Israel in Egypt, Handel, 283, 284
Istituzioni harmoniche, Le, Zarlino, 103,
    130, 131, 164
Italian music. *See also* Italian opera
  Baroque, 171, 172–95, 201–206,
    209–12, 218–19, 228, 237–41,
    243, 246–47, 262–63
  eighteenth-century, 306–307, 336
  Renaissance, 104–105, 158–65
  sixteenth-century, 120–21, 124–35,
    145–47, 149
  trecento, 63–64, 70, 72–77
Italian opera
  Baroque, 176–86, 208, 209–12, 250,
    251, 276–78, 280–82
  eighteenth-century, 294–97, 298–303,
    332, 344–48
  nineteenth-century, 412–13, 416–22,
    433, 459
  opera buffa, 290, 294–98, 313–14
  opera seria, 290, 295, 298–302
  twentieth-century, 459–60
  verismo, 433, 459–60
Italian Symphony, Mendelssohn,
    381–82, 411, 474
Ite, missa est, **22**, 67
Ives, Charles, **526–27**, 528
  influence on other composers, 527,
    536

Jacopo de Bologna, 72, 75
Jacques de Liège, 63, 66
Jacquet de la Guerre, Elisabeth-Claude,
    200, 234–35
Jahreszeiten, Die, Haydn, 319, 333, 354
Janáček, Leoš, **449**, 456, 464
Janequin, Clément, 136
jazz, 459, 485, 516, **522–24**, 529, 540,
    542–43
Jenkins, John, 202
Jephte, Carissimi, 194–95
Jephtha, Handel, 283, *285*
Jerome, Saint, 9
Jeu de Robin et de Marion, Adam de la
    Halle, 38
Jewish liturgy, 27
Jewish music, early, 12
Joan of Arc, 88
Joffrey, Robert, 487
Johannes de Garlandia, 53
John, King of Bohemia, 65–66
John, King of England, 40

Johnson, Philip, 548, *548*
Johnson, Dr. Samuel, *291,* 297
Johnston, Ben, 541
Jommelli, Nicolò, 303, 304
jongleurs, 36
Joplin, Scott, 521
Joseph II, Holy Roman Emperor, 289, 352
Josquin des Prez, 100, 105, **111–18,** *116,* 121, 151, 168
    chansons of, 112–13
    Masses of, 107, 116, 118
    motets of, 103, 114–16, *117*
    text setting of, 112–15
Juba, 521, 534
jubilus, 28, 30
Juive, La, Halévy, 413
Julius III, Pope, 160, *161*
Junker, Carl Ludwig, 355
Jupiter Symphony, Mozart, 340–41, 342

Kalevala, 450
Kallman, Chester, 488
Kay, Ulysses, 534
Keiser, Reinhard, 218, 220
Kennst du das Land?, Wolf, 434
Kentucky Harmony, 519
Kern, Jerome, 526
kettledrum, 81, *144*
keyboard music. *See also* clavichord
    music; harpsichord music; organ
    music
    of Bach, 265–67
    Baroque, 200–207, 233–37
    sixteenth-century, 145–46, 147–48
Kim, Earl, 550
Kindertotenlieder, Mahler, 436, 439
King David, Honegger, 479
Kinsky, Prince, 352
Kirchenlied, 150. *See also* chorales
Kirchner, Ernst Ludwig, 502
kithara, 5
Klaviermusik: Übung in drei Stücken, Hindemith, 476
Klavierstück XI, Stockhausen, 511
Klinger, Friedrich Maximilian, 321
Klopstock, Friedrich Gottlieb, 436
Koch, Heinrich Christoph, 343
Köchel, Ludwig von, 335
Kodály, Zoltán, 463, 464, **469,** 491
kortholt, 141
Kotzschmar, Hermann, 518
Kozeluch, Leopold Anton, 349
Krieger, Johann Philipp, 224
krummhorn, 141
Kubrick, Stanley, 510
Kuhnau, Johann, 224
Kunst der Fuge, Die, Bach, **268,** 274, 275, 338
Kyrie, **22,** 26, 29, 30, 46, 67

La Pouplinière, Alexandre-Jean-Joseph
    Le Riche de, 255–59
Lady, Be Good, Gershwin, 526
Lady Macbeth of Mtensk, Shostakovich, 469, 470
Lagrime mie, B. Strozzi, 191, *192*
lais, 68
Lalande, Michel-Richard de, 222
Lamartine, Alfonse-Marie de, 384

Lamentation, Froberger, 200, 234
Lamentations, falsobordone technique
    in, 115
Lamentations, Tallis, 158
Landini, Francesco, **73–74,** 81, 82
langue d'oc, 36
langue d'oïl, 37 *Lascia, deh lascia,* A.
    Scarlatti, 218, *219*
Lasso, Orlando di, 130, 139–40, 149, 153, **165–67,** 168
laude, 70, 124–25
Lauds, 21, 222
Lawes, Henry, 216
Le Corbusier, 508, *509*
Le Franc, Martin, 88, 90, 91
Le Jeune, Claude, 156
Leçons de ténèbres, Couperin, 222
Legrenzi, Giovanni, 238, 251, 263
Leipzig, 260–61, 262, 269–74, 290
Leitmotifs, **426–28,** 443, 450, 500
Lennon, John, 525
Lenya, Lotte, 478
Leoncavallo, Ruggero, 450
Léonin, 44, 47, **48,** 50
Leonore overtures, Beethoven, 358, 361
Leopold II, King of Bohemia, 344
Lerner, Alan Jay, 526
Liber de arte contrapuncti, Tinctoris, 103
Liber usualis, 23, *24–25*
liberal arts, 10, 14
liberazione di Ruggiero dall'isola d'Alcina,
    La, F. Caccini, 183
Libro de musica de vihuela de mano
    intitulado El Maestro, Milán, 145
Lichnowsky, Karl von, 352
Lied von der Erde, Das, Mahler, 434, 436, **439–40**
lieder
    of Mahler, 434, 436, 439–40, 460
    nineteenth-century, 19, 374, 375, 376, 392, **406–10,** 410–11
    Renaissance, 139–40, 149
    of Wolf, 434
Lieder ohne Worte, Mendelssohn, 394
ligatures, 50, 60
Ligeti, György, 508, **510**
Lindenbaum, Der, Schubert, 406–407, 408
Liszt, Franz, 373, **383–86,** *389,* **397,** *400,* 410–11, 445
    choral music of, 430, 431
    influence on other composers, 386, 446, 448, 460
    piano music of, 392, **400–401**
    symphonic poems of, 384, 429, 440
    symphonies of, 385–86
    writings on music of, 374, 375
Little Notebooks, Bach, 264–65
liturgical books, 23. *See also specific types*
liturgical drama, **31–32,** 36, 176
liturgies, **20**
    Lutheran, 150–51
    Roman, 19–23, 43
Lobkowitz, Joseph Franz Maximilian, 352, *354*
Locke, Matthew, 202
Loeffler, Charles Martin, 456
Loewe, Frederick, 526
Lohengrin, Wagner, 397, **424**
Lomax, Alan, 529

Lomax, John, 529
London, 276–78, 290, *291,* 297, 313, 319, 323–25, 333. *See also*
    English music
London symphonies, Haydn, 321, 322, **323–25,** 340
London Symphony, Vaughan Williams, 474
long, 80
Lortzing, Albert, 423
Louis VII, King of France, 40
Louis XII, King of France, 113
Louis XIV, King of France, 170, 208, 212–13, 221–22, 255
love songs
    Burgundian, 93
    fourteenth-century, 63, 68, 82
    Minnesinger, 41
    of Schumann, 409
    troubadour and trouvère, 38–40, 43
Ludus tonalis, Hindemith, 476
Luening, Otto, 538
Luisa Miller, Verdi, 419
Lully, Jean-Baptiste
    influence of, 243, 244–45, 257, 259
    operas of, **213–15,** 226, 236, 304, 305, 416
lute, 81, *105,* 126, 127, 135, **142,** 145, 146
    as continuo instrument, 174
lute music, 172, 199–200, 207, 231
lute songs, **138–39,** 145, 149
Luther, Martin, 100, 150, 151–52, 154
Lutheran church music. *See* church
    music, Lutheran
Lutosławski, Witold, *512,* **513–14**
Luzzaschi, Luzzasco, 131–32
lyre, 5

Ma fin est mon commencement et mon
    commencement ma fin, Machaut, 70
Machaut, Guillaume de, 2, **65–70,** *69,* 82, 93
Madrigali guerrieri et amorosi,
    Monteverdi, 189
madrigals
    concertato, 188–89
    English, 136–38, 536
    instrumental performances of, 140
    of Monteverdi, 189
    of Schütz, 195
    seventeenth-century, 174, 188–90, 207
    sixteenth-century Italian, 120, **125–26, 128–35,** 140, 149, 172, 178
    trecento, **72,** 75, 82, 125
    Venetian, 193
Maeterlinck, Maurice, 452, 455
Magic Flute, The. See Zauberflöte, Die
Magnificat, **21,** 157, 158
    Burgundian, 91
    falsobordone technique in, 114
    fauxbourdon settings of, 88
Magnus liber organi, 48, **50–53,** 56
Mahler, Gustav, **434–40,** *435,* 444, 460–61
    Bach's influence on, 436

influence on other composers, 471, 493–94
quotations from, 549
Maldere, Pierre van, 289
Mallarmé, Stéphane, 454
Mamelles de Tiresias, Les, Poulenc, 481
Manelli, Francesco, 184
Manet, Edouard, 456
Mannheim school, 255, 311, 314
Mantua, 126, 129
Manzoni, Alessandro, 431
Maple Leaf Rag, Joplin, 521
Marcello, Benedetto, 299
marches, 520
Marenzio, Luca, **130–31,** 172
Marian antiphons, 21, *24–25,* 28, 157
Marie Antoinette, Queen of France, 303, 322
Marini, Biagio, 204
Marino, Giambattista, 184
Marot, Clément, 154
Marriage of Figaro, The. See nozze di Figaro, Le
Marschner, Heinrich, 423
Marteau sans maître, Le, Boulez, 504
Martianus Capella, 10
Martini, Giovanni Battista, 313, 336
Mary, Queen of England, 158, 159
Mascagni, Pietro, 450, 547
Mason, Lowell, 519
masque, 216
mass media, 1, 463, 464
Masses, 19, 20, **21–23, 28–29,** 42. *See also entries under Messe and Missa; Requiem; specific composers*
of Bach, 274
Baroque, 208, 220
of Beethoven, 351, 352, 365, 368, 369–70
of Bruckner, 431
Burgundian, 83, 91, **93–97**
cantus firmus (*See below under* tenor)
chants for, 28–29, 48
English, 83, 88, 89, 94, 157, 158, 168
fifteenth-century, 119
Franco-Flemish, 120, 121
German, 151–52
of Haydn, 332–33, 370
imitation (parody), 118
of Josquin, 116, 118
of Liszt, 430
liturgy of, 21–22
Lutheran, 264, 270
of Machaut, 67–68
motto, 94
of Mozart, 349
naming of, 108–109
of Ockeghem, 107–109
Ordinary of, **22,** 23, 29, 30, 46, 67, 88, 93–94
of Palestrina, 161–65
polychoral, 193
polyphonic settings of, 46
Proper of, **22,** 23, 28, 30, 46
Requiem, 31
symbolism of, 12, 20
tenor (cantus firmus), **94–97,** 108, 111, 116, 118, 121–22, 158, 162
mathematics and music, 6, 7, 12, 14, 32

Mathis der Maler, Hindemith, 476
Matins, 21, 222
Maugars, André, 221
Maximilian Franz, Elector of Cologne, 352
mazurkas, 392, 395–96
McCartney, Paul, 525
mediatio, 26
Medici family, 104, 105, 112, 126, 179
medieval drama, 19, 32, 38. *See also* liturgical drama
Meeresstille und glückliche Fahrt, Mendelssohn, 382
Mei, Girolamo, 176–77
Mein G'muth ist mir verwirret, Hassler, 152, *153*
Meistersingers, **42,** 139
melismas
in ballatas, 74
in Burgundian music, 92, 93
in chant, 24, 28, 30–31
in fifteenth-century music, 89
in organum, 46–47, 54
in Renaissance English music, 158
in rondeaux, 70
in troubadour and trouvère songs, 39
melodrama, 422
melody
in ancient Greek music, 4, 7, 16
chant, 14–15, 24, 26, 28, 30
in early polyphony, 46, 54
in eighteenth-century music, 288, 291–92, 299, 300, 310
galant style, 288
in Minnelieder, 41
in motets, 57
Renaissance, 158
of troubadour and trouvère songs, 39–40
for variation sets, 148
melos, 6
Mendelssohn, Felix, 275–76, 373, **381–83,** 409, 410–11
Bach's influence on, 394
chamber music of, **392**
choral music of, 431
incidental music of, 382–83
influence on other composers, 446
overtures of, 382–83
piano music of, 391, **393–94**
symphonies of, 381–83, 474
Menotti, Gian Carlo, 547
mensuration, 80
Menuet antique, Ravel, 456
Mercure de France, 322
Merulo, Claudio, 145–146, 201
Messe de Notre Dame, Machaut, 67, 93
Messiaen, Olivier, 492–93, **505–506,** 509, 538
influence on other composers, 504, 505
Messiah, Handel, 277, 283, 333, 338, 370
Metastasio, Pietro, 289, **298,** 299, 300
metric modulation, 536
Meyerbeer, Giacomo, 413, **414,** 419, 420
Michelet, Jules, 99
microtonal music, 509, 540–41
Middle Ages, 18–98. *See also specific composers and topics*
ars nova in, 64–71

ars subtilior in, 78–79
astronomy and music in, 14–15
Burgundian music in, 91–98
chant in, 18–35, 40
education in, 29–30, 34, 36
English music in, 86–90
instruments in, 81–82
music theory in, 19, 32–35, 43, 44, 45, 63, 77
notation in, 80
polyphony in, 43–61
secular song in, 18, 19, 35–42
trecento music in, 70, 72–77
MIDI (Musical Instrument Digital Interface), 508
Midsummer Night's Dream, A, incidental music for, Mendelssohn, 383, 410
"Mighty Handful," The, 445–48, 461
Milan, 12, 13–14
Milán, Luis, 144–45
Milhaud, Darius, 414, 457, **479–80,** 491, 515, 538, 542
Military Symphony, Haydn, 324
Mille regretz, Josquin, 112–13
Milton, John, 15, 216, 333
minim, 80, 81
minimalism, 532, 545–47, 552
Minnesinger, 41
minstrels *(ménestrels),* **36,** 85minuet, 255, **320,** 325, 327, 329–30
Missa ad fugam, Palestrina, 162
Missa Ave regina caelorum, Dufay, 95
Missa Caput, Ockeghem, *108*
Missa De plus en plus, Ockeghem, 108
Missa Hercules dux Ferrariae, Josquin, 116, 118
Missa L'homme armé super voces musicales, Josquin, 116
Missa Malheur me bat, Josquin, 118
Missa mi-mi, Ockeghem, 108–109
Missa Papae Marcelli, Palestrina, 160, 162–65
Missa prolationum, Ockeghem, 109, *110,* 111
Missa Repleatur os meum, Palestrina, 162
Missa Se la face ay pale, Dufay, 95–97, 108
Missa solemnis, Beethoven, 352, 365, 368, **369–70,** 413
Mode de valeurs et d'intensités, Messiaen, 504
modes, Byzantine, 13
modes, church, 19, 26, **32–34,** 42, 44, 103, 165
accidentals in, 33–34
authentic and plagal, 32–33
final in, 32, 33
in Minnelieder, 41
ranges of, 33
in sixteenth-century music, 124
tenor in, 33
in troubadour and trouvère songs, 39
modes, Greek, **7,** 34, 102, 103
modes, rhythmic, 44, 48, **49–50,** 54, 57, 58, 60, 61
Moments musicaux, Schubert, 392
monasteries, 14–15
Monet, Claude, 456

Monk, Thelonious, 524
Monn, Georg Matthias, 311
monody (genre), **177–78,** 189–90, 207
monophony (texture), **4,** 16, 44, 177.
    See also texture
    fourteenth-century, 64, 70, 72
    sixteenth-century, 152, 154–55
Monsigny, Pierre-Alexandre, 297
Monte, Philippe de, 130
Monteverdi, Claudio, 192, 193, 207
    influence on Schütz, 198
    madrigals of, **133–35,** 149, 172, 189
    operas of, **181–83, 184–86,** 209
    Vespers of, 194
Morales, Cristóbal de, 113
morals and music, 7–8, 9, 10, 11, 15, 16,
    151, 153–55, 158–60
Moravians, 518
mordents, 241
Morley, Thomas, **136,** 137
Morzin, Count, 316
Moses und Aron, Schoenberg, 496–500
motets. *See also* motets, thirteenth-
    century
    ars nova, 63, 64–66, 81–82
    Baroque, 174, 208, 220, 221–22, 226
    Burgundian, 83, 91, *92,* 93
    chorale, 152
    of Dunstable, 89–90
    English, 157, 158
    fifteenth-century, 90, 119
    Franco-Flemish, 120, 121
    grand and petit, 222
    isorhythmic, **64–65,** 66, 67, *68,* 81, 82,
        88, 89–90, 93, 501
    of Josquin, 114–16
    Latin, 166–67, 168
    Lutheran, 195
    of Machaut, 66
    nineteenth-century, 431
    polychoral, 193
    of Poulenc, 481
    of Schütz, 197–98
    tenors of, 64–65, 66, 67, *68,* 89–90
    Venetian polychoral, 193
motets, thirteenth-century, 44, 53, 54,
    56–60, 60, 61
Mother of Us All, The, Thomson, 532
motto beginning
    in arias, 210
    in Masses, 94
Mozarabic chant, 13
Mozart, Constanze, 346
Mozart, Leopold, 334, *335,* 336,
    346–47
Mozart, Marianne ("Nannerl"), 334,
    335, 346
Mozart, Wolfgang Amadeus, 287, 308,
    315, 316, **334–49,** *335,* 372, 373
    J. C. Bach's influence on, 313, 336
    J. S. Bach's influence on, 275, 338
    Beethoven compared with, 351
    cadenzas of, 344
    church music of, 349, 431
    concertos of, 313, **343–44**
    and Freemasonry, 289
    Handel's influence on, 338
    Haydn compared with, 315, 337, 340,
        341, 349
    Haydn's influence on, 336, 338, 339

influence on other composers, 393,
    401, 446, 459
Italian influence on, 336
Masses of, 349
on opera librettos, 345
operas of, 258, 289, 298, 336, **344–49,**
    413, 416
quotations from, 549
relationship with father, 346–47
serenades of, 337
sonatas of, 306, 336–37
string quartets of, 327, 339
string quintets of, 340
symphonies of, **340–43,** 354, 381
teachers of, 336
use of Alberti bass, 293
Muffat, Georg, 246
Müller, Wilhelm, 408
music drama. *See under* Wagner,
    Richard
Music for a Magic Theater, Rochberg,
    549
Music for Strings, Percussion, and Celesta,
    Bartók, 465, 466, **467–68,** 508
Music for the Theater, Copland, 530
Music of Changes, Cage, 544
"music of the spheres," 14–15
music theory. *See* theory, music
Musica enchiriadis, 45
musica ficta, **77,** 90, 163
musica humana, 11, 15
musica instrumentalis, 11
musica mundana, 11, 15. *See also* "music
    of the spheres"
Musica transalpina anthology, 136
musical comedies, 478, 516, **525–26**
Musical Offering, A, Bach. *See*
    Musikalisches Opfer
musical rhyme, 69
Musikalische Exequien, Schütz, 197
Musikalisches Opfer, Bach, 268, 274
musique concrète, 507
Musorgsky, Modest, 445, **446–48,** 461,
    463
    influence on other composers, 446,
        454

Nach Bach, Rochberg, 549–50
Nancarrow, Conlon, 539–40
Naples, 171
    opera in, 208, 211–12, 295
Napoleon III, Emperor, 414
Narváez, Luys de, 113
National Endowment for the Arts, 537
National Society for French Music, 451,
    452
nationalism, 297
    in nineteenth-century music, 401,
        418, 433, **444–51,** 461
    in twentieth-century music, 462,
        464–69, 473–75, 481, 491, 529,
        531–34
Nations, Les, Couperin, 242
Neapolitan sixth chord, 239, 378
Neefe, Christian Gottlob, 351
neo-Baroque, 479, 481, 487, 488–89,
    490, 491
neo-Classicism, 463, 464, **479–81,**
    485–89, 491, 535, 536
neo-Romanticism, 487, 535

Nero, Emperor, 3
Neue Zeitschrift für Musik, 394
Neumeister, Erdmann, 223–24, 271
neumes, **23.** *See also* notation
New Music (periodical), 528
New Orleans, 523
New World Symphony, Dvořák, 388
New York, 520
Nicomachus, 10, *11*
Nietzsche, Friedrich, 441
Nights in the Gardens of Spain, Falla,
    451
Nijinsky, Vaslav, 484, **486–87**
nocturnes, 392, 396, 418, 453
Nocturnes, Debussy, 454–55
Non avrà ma' pietà, Landini, 74, 75
non-Western musics, 527, 528, 529, 539,
    540, 541, 544, 552
    African, 521, 522, 539
    Indian, 528, 539, 544, 545
    Indonesian (Balinese, Javanese), 455,
        463, 504, 544
Nono, Luigi, 505
Norma, Bellini, 418
North Africa, 29
Norwegian music, 449–50
notation
    "black" and "white," 81
    of chant, 22–23, *24,* 26, 42
    of chant rhythm, 23
    choirbook, 60
    "colored," 81
    of early polyphony, 44, 46, 51
    fifteenth-century, 111
    fourteenth-century, 63, 64, 75, 76,
        78–79, **80–81,** 82
    Franconian, 60, 80
    of Goliard songs, 35
    lute songs, 138–39
    medieval, 18, 48
    neumatic, 23, 50
    of organum purum, 48
    polyphonic conductus, 55
    of rhythmic modes, 48, 49–50
    score, 55, 60, 174
    seventeenth-century, 173
    staff, 23, 35
    tablature, *138,* 142, *200,* 207
    thoroughbass, 174, 176
    of troubadour and trouvère songs, 39
    of twentieth-century music, 495,
        510–11, *512,* 513, 551
Notker Balbulus, 31
Notre Dame organum, 44, 47, **48–54**
Nouvelles suites de pièces de clavecin,
    Rameau, 260
nozze di Figaro, Le, Mozart, 344,
    345–46, 418
Nuages, Debussy, 446, 454–55, 457
Nuages gris, Liszt, 401
Nun komm, der Heiden Heiland, Bach,
    271
nuove musiche, Le, Caccini, 178–79,
    189–90
Nuper rosarum flores, Dufay, 93, *94*

O Care, thou wilt despatch me, Weelkes,
    136–37
O crux, splendidior cunctis astris,
    Willaert, 122–24

O Haupt voll Blut und Wunden, 152
O konchen prazdnyi, Musorgsky, 454
O magnum mysterium, Victoria, 165, 166
O Mensch, bewein' dein' Sünde gross, J. S. Bach, 157
O quam tu pulchra es, Grandi, 194
Obrecht, Jacob, 111–12, 113
Ockeghem, Johannes, **105–11,** *109,* 114
octatonic scale, 448, 483, 505
Octet for Wind Instruments, Stravinsky, 485, 487
Ode for St. Cecilia's Day, Purcell, 220
Ode to Napoleon, Schoenberg, 496
Odhecaton, 106–107, 112
Oedipus—A Music-Dance Drama, Partch, 540
Oedipus rex, Stravinsky, 490
Offenbach, Jacques, 415
Offertory, 28
Office, **20–21,** 23, 42, 45, 48, 194
  chants for, 26–28
Ohimè dov'è il mio ben, Monteverdi, 187
Oklahoma, Rodgers, 526
"Old Hundredth," 156, *157*
Old Roman chant, 13
Oliver, Joseph "King," 523, *526*
Oliveros, Pauline, 538
Ondes Martenot, 507, 509
Opella nova, Schein, 195
Oper und Drama, Wagner, 424
opera-ballet, 258
opéra bouffe, 414–15
opera buffa, 290, **294–98,** 313–14, 332, 418
  of Mozart, 345, 348
opéra comique, 297, 414, 415, 418
Opera of the Nobility (London), 277, 280
opera seria, 290, 295, **298–302,** 416
  of Mozart, 336, 344
operas. *See also specific composers and operas*
  American, 526, 529, 531–33, 543, 545, 547
  ballad, 297
  Baroque, 171, 176–86, 207, 208, 209–18, 225, 250, 251, 257–60, 276–78, 280–82
  Bohemian, 449
  choruses in, 260, 303, 304, 419, 497, 543
  eighteenth-century, 289, 290, 294–305, 314, 332, 336, 344–49
  English, 208, 216–17, 276–77, 280–82, 297, 475
  forerunners of, 176–77
  French, 208, 212–15, 257–60, 286, 297, 305, 412–16, 452, 453, 455, 481
  German, 208, 217–18, 297–98, 332, 338, 348–49, 358, 413, 422–29, 432, 442–44, 461, 476, 477–78, 496, 498–501
  grand, 412, 413–14, 416, 419–20, 432
  Hungarian, 465
  Italian (*See* Italian opera)
  lyric, 415
  nineteenth-century, 412–20, 432

overtures for, 243–44, 248, 259, 303, 307, 358 (*See also* French overture; sinfonia)
  reform of, 290, 302–305, 314
  rescue, 358
  Russian, 445, 447–48, 469, 470
  sacred, 194
  Spanish, 450, 451
  of Stravinsky, 485, 488–89
  subjects for, 184, 185, 213–14, 418–19, 422, 424
  twentieth-century, 414, 461, 465, 469, 470, 475, 476, 477–78, 481, 496, 498–501, 526, 529, 531–33, 543, 545, 547
operettas, 415
Opus 1970, Stockhausen, 511, 513
oral transmission, 18, 28, 35
oratorio Passion, 225
oratorios
  Baroque, 171, 190, 194–95, 207, 220, 221
  of Beethoven, 351
  chorus in, 283
  of Elgar, 450
  of Handel, 276, 277, 282–85, 370
  of Haydn, 333–34, 354
  nineteenth-century, 431
  of Stravinsky, 490
orchestra. *See also* instrumentation and orchestration
  of Berlioz, 380–81
  of Corelli, 245
  eighteenth-century, 311
  of Haydn, 318, 380
  of Lully, 244
  Mannheim, 311
  nineteenth-century, 380–81
  in operas, 303
  of Vivaldi, 253
orchestral music, Baroque, 227, 243–47, 252–55, 278–79. *See also specific composers and genres*
Ordo virtutum, Hildegard, 32
ordres, 234, **235–36,** 242
Orfeo, Monteverdi, 181–83, 185
Orfeo, Rossi, 184
Orfeo ed Euridice, Gluck, 303–304
Orff, Carl, 456
organ, 142
  Baroque, 227, 228, *232*
  with chorales, 153
  as continuo instrument, 174
  enharmonic, 131
  pedals for, 82, 142
  portative, 74, 81, 82, *92,* 142
  positive, 82, *85,* 142, *223*
organ chorales, 227, 228, 231–37, 247. *See also* chorale preludes
organ music
  Baroque, 172, 193, 201–202, 207, 228–33, 247, 248, 262–65
  of Messiaen, 505–506
  sixteenth-century, 140, 145–46
organetto, 74, 82
organum, 44, **45–54,** 56, 61
  early, 45–48
  florid, 46–47, 53, 54, 61
  manuscript sources of, 46, 47, *51*
  Notre Dame, 47, 48–54

  oblique motion in, 45
  parallel, 45, 61, 88
  organum duplum, **47,** *51*
  organum purum, **47,** 48, 51, 53
  organum quadruplum, 53, 54
  organum triplum, 53, 54
Orgelbüchlein, Bach, 264–65
Origen, 9
ornamentation
  Baroque, 199, 204, 206, *236,* 237, 240, 241–42, 246, 248, 254, 260
  of chant, 25
  in eighteenth-century music, 299, 301–302, 309–10
  of Monteverdi, 189
  in nineteenth-century music, 417
  in sixteenth-century music, 134, 178, 179
  of troubadour and trouvère songs, 39
Orontea, Cesti, 186
Orphée aux enfers, Offenbach, 415
Orpheus, Liszt, 384
ostinatos, 147, 187–88, 540. *See also* basso ostinato
Otello, Verdi, **420–22,** 432, 550
ottave rime, 187, 206
ouverture. See French overture
Ouvertures, Bach, 268
overtures, 448, 534. *See also* French overture; sinfonia; *sinfonia*
  of Beethoven, 351, 352, 358, 361
  of Brahms, 386
  of Handel, 278
  of Mendelssohn, 382–83
  opera, 243–44, 248, 259, 303, 307, 358
Ovid, 542
Owen, Wilfred, 475

Pachelbel, Johann, 222
Pacific 231, Honegger, 479
paduana. See pavane
Paganini, Nicolò, 380, *389,* 400, 409, 410
Paine, John Knowles, 518
Paisiello, Giovanni, 349
Palestrina, Giovanni Pierluigi da, 151, **160–65,** *161*
  style and influence of, 161–62, 168, 192, 316
Pallavicino, Carlo, 210
pandiatonicism, 490
papal chapel, 15, 113, 128, 160
Paris, 256–57, 290, 314, 322, 412, 417, 451, 481, 484, 486
Paris symphonies, Haydn, 321, *322*
Parker, Charlie "Bird," 524
Parker, Horatio, 526
Parnassus, or the Apotheosis of Corelli, Couperin, 242, 243
partbooks, 106–107
Partch, Harry, *540,* 540–41
Parthenia anthology, 148
partitas, **205–206,** 233, 267–68
passacaglia, 147, 187, 188, 206, 227, **236,** 247, 388, 496. *See also* chaconne
Passacaille ou Chaconne, Couperin, 236
passamezzo, 143, 231
  antico and *moderno,* 147
Passions, **225**

Passions (*continued*)
    of Bach, 152, *153*, **273–74,** 275–76, 479
Pastoral Symphony, Beethoven, 360, 361, 378, 383, 389
Pastoral Symphony, Vaughan Williams, 474–75
pastorals, 179, 181
pastourelle (pastorela), 38
patronage
    Baroque, 170–71, 179, 183, 184, 185, 196–97, 212–13, 244, 250, 255, 261–62, 276
    of Beethoven, 352–53, 358, 364
    eighteenth-century, 290, 303, 315, 316, 318–19
    fifteenth-century, 83–86, 95
    fourteenth-century, 70, 72, 76
    Renaissance, 104, 118, 121, 126, 129, 132, 133, 160
Pavana Lachrymae, Byrd, 139, 140, 143, 148
pavane, **139,** 143–44, 147, 199
Peasant Cantata, Bach, 273
pedagogy. *See* education, music
pedal point, 231
Pedrell, Felipe, 450
Pelléas et Mélisande, Debussy, 455, 500
Pelleas und Melisande, Schoenberg, 493, 494
Pelli, Cesar, 548–49
Penderecki, Krzysztof, 508, 509, **510,** 515
Pénélope, Fauré, 452, 453
pentatonic scale, 382, *383,* 440, 455, 463, 466, 475, 522, 534
Pepusch, John Christopher, 477
percussion, 507, 529, 540, 541
perfectio, 50
Perfidissimo volto, Caccini, 173, 179
performance practice
    of Baroque music, 172, 174, 179, *236,* 237, 240, 241–42, 246, 254
    of cadenzas, 344
    of chant, 23, 25, 28
    of chorales, 153
    of eighteenth-century music, 299, 301–302, 309
    of fourteenth-century music, 64, 77, 81
    of Italian madrigal, 126, 127
    of liturgical drama, 31
    of nineteenth-century music, 396, 417
    of seventeenth-century opera, 209
    of sixteenth-century music, 134, 135, 140, 178–79
    of troubadour and trouvère songs, 39
    of twentieth-century music, 506–507, 508, 510–11, 514, 527–28, 541
Pergolesi, Giovanni Battista, 486
    intermezzi of, **295–96,** 299, 300, 305
Peri, Jacopo, 177, *178,* **179–80,** 181, 184
periodicity, musical, 292–93
Pérotin, 44, 47, 48, **53–54,** 55, 56
petit motet, 222
Petrarch, Francesco, 120, 125, 126
Petrucci, Ottaviano, 104, 106–107, 112, 125, 143
Petrushka, Stravinsky, 481, **482–83**
Peverara, Laura, 126

Phantasiestücke, Schumann, 395
Philidor, Anne Danican, 290
Philidor, Français André Danican, 297
Philip the Good, duke of Burgundy, 83–84, 91
Philippe de Vitry, 63, 64
Philomel, 541, **542**
piano, 391, *394,* 506, 527–28
piano concertos
    of Beethoven, 351, 352, 364–65
    of Mozart, 313, 338, 343–44
    of Romantic period, 386, 393, 401, 409, 448
    twentieth-century, 465, 466, 467, 469, 487, 496, 528, 530, 534, 536
Piano Phase, Reich, 545
piano quintets, 401, 404–405
Piano Rag Music, Stravinsky, 485
piano sonatas
    of Beethoven, 339, 351, 352, **353–54,** 362–64, 365, **368–69,** 372
    of Haydnm, 330–31
    of Mozart, 336–37
    of Romantic period, 393, 401, 406, 410, 411
    twentieth-century, 449, 466, 489, 527, 531
piano trios
    of Beethoven, 351, 354
    of Ravel, 459
    of Romantic period, 406, 409
Piano Variations, Copland, 529, 531
Piave, Francesco, 419
Piccinni, Niccolò, 305, 349
Pièces de clavecin, Jacquet de la Guerre, 234–35
piedi, 75
Pierrot lunaire, Schoenberg, 494–95, **496,** 503
Pietà (Venice), 250, 251, 253
Pietism, 222–23
Pissarro, Camille, 456
Piston, Walter, 515, *516,* 535, 537
pitch continuum, 509–10
Pius X, Pope, 431
plainchant, 18. *See also* chant
Plato, 6, 7–8, *11,* 14, 101, 103
Play of Daniel, 31–32
Play of Herod, 31–32
player piano, 539–40
Pleyel, Ignaz, 323, 324
Poème électronique, Varèse, 507, 508, *509*
poetry. *See also* text setting
    ballads, 406
    Bar form, 41
    cantata texts, 223–24, 271, 273
    chanson de geste, 36
    formes fixes, 69
    and French opera, 213, 214
    and Greek music, 4, 5, 6–7
    meters in, 55
    Minnesinger, 41–42
    Mozart's views on, 345
    ottave rime, 187, 206
    Petrarchan movement, 125, 126, 129
    recitation of, 178
    Roman de Fauvel, 64
    and Romantic music, 374–75
    set by Schubert, 408
    troubadour and trouvère, 37–39

Polish music, 463
Politics, Aristotle, 7
polkas, 520
polonaise, 392
Polonaise-Fantasie, Chopin, 396–97
polonaises, 396
polychoral music, 147, 193–94
polyphony, **44,** 86, 172. *See also* texture; *specific genres*
    fourteenth-century, 67, 70
    manuscript sources of, 72
    medieval, 30, 43–61
    secular music, 63
polytonality, 466, 480
Porgy and Bess, Gershwin, 526
Porpora, Nicola, 277, 280, 300, 316
Porporino. *See* Uberti, Antonio
Porter, Cole, 525
post-modernism, 548–51
Poste, La, Gaultier, 199
Poulenc, Francis, 457, 479, **481**
Powell, Mel, 537
Practica musice, Gaffurio, 102
praeludium. *See* preludes; toccatas
Praeludium in E, Buxtehude, 230
Prato, Giovanni Gherardi de, 72, 73, 74
preambulum, 144
preghiera, 419, 421
Prélude à l'après-midi d'un faune, Debussy, 454, *458,* 486
preludes, **144,** 146, 149, 173. *See also* chorale preludes
    of Bach, 263–64, 265–66, 267
    Baroque, 227, 228, 230
    of Chopin, 396, 399
    of Debussy, 455
    of Mendelssohn, 393–94
Préludes, Les, Liszt, 384, 401, 411, 440
preludio, 239
"prepared piano," 506
Presley, Elvis, 525
Price, Florence, 534
prima pratica, 172
Primavera Concerto, Vivaldi, 253
printing and publishing
    early Renaissance, 104, 106–107, 112, 119
    sixteenth-century, 125, 126, 143, 144, 152
program music, **375,** 378–81, 383–84, 385–86, 389, 395, 400, 424, **440,** 449. *See also* affections; rhetoric; text setting
    Baroque, 260, 265
    of Beethoven, 360, 361
    of Haydn, 333–34
    impressionist, 457
    of Mahler, 436
    of Strauss, 440–42
    twentieth-century, 474, 479, 547
Prokofiev, Sergey, **469–70,** 479, 491
prolation, 80–81
Prometheus, Skryabin, 449
Provençal language, 37, 38–39
Prussian quartets, Haydn, 328
psalm tones, **26–27,** 194
Psalmen Davids, Schütz, 196–97
psalms
    American adaptations of, 516, 517
    antiphonal performances of, 193

in early Christian services, 12
falsobordone technique in, 114–15
fauxbourdon settings of, 88
of Grieg, 450
in Jewish services, 12, 20, 27
Reformation settings, 151, 154–56
responsorial, 13
in Roman liturgy, 20, 26–28, 42
of Schütz, 196–97
seventeenth-century, 193
Psalmus hungaricus, Kodály, 469
Psalters, 151, 154–56
psaltery, 81
Ptolemy, Claudius, 12, 14, 101
publishing. *See* printing and publishing
Puccini, Giacomo, 456, **459–60,** 547
Puchberg, Michael, 338
Pugnani, Gaetano, 289
Pulcinella, Stravinsky, 485–86
Purcell, Henry
    influence on other composers, 473
    operas of, 216–17, 226
    sonatas of, 239, 240
    viol music of, 202
    vocal works of, 220
Pushkin, Alexander, 445
Pythagoras, 6, 7, *11,* 12, 14

quadrivium, **10,** 14
Quam pulchra es, Dunstable, 89–90
Quantz, Johann Joachim, 288–89, 290
quarter tones, 509, 510
quartets, 501, 505. *See also* piano
    quartets; string quartets
Quartettsatz, Schubert, 401
Quatre Études de rythme, Messiaen, 505
Quatuor pour la fin du temps, Messiaen,
    505
Queen of Spades, The, Tchaikovsky, 445
Quem quaeritis in praesepe, 31
Quem quaeritis in sepulchro, 31
querelle des bouffons, 295, 305
quickstep, 520
Quinault, Jean-Philippe, 213–14, 304
quodlibet, 267
quotation, 486–87, 489, 513, 527, 536,
    549–50. *See also* borrowing

Racine, Jean, 213
ragtime, 480, 485, 516, **520–21,** 522, 523
Ragtime, Stravinsky, 485, *489*
Rake's Progress, The, Stravinsky, 485,
    488–89
Rakhmaninov, Sergei, 448
Rameau, Jean-Philippe, 249, **255–60,**
    257, 286, 451, 454, 481
    instrumental music of, 260
    operas of, 257–60, 303, 305, 416
    theoretical works of, 256, 258, 288
rap, 19
rappresentazione di Anima et di Corpo,
    La, Cavalieri, 194
Raspona, La, Legrenzi, 238
Rasumovsky quartets, Beethoven, 352,
    358–59
rauschpfeife, 141
Ravel, Maurice, 454, **457, 459,** 542
    Debussy's influence on, 456
    Fauré's influence on, 453
    influence on other composers, 473

realization, figured bass, 174
recapitulation, 308, 313, **320**
récitatif mesuré, 214
récitatif simple, 214recitative style. *See*
    stile recitativo
recitatives. *See also stile recitativo; specific*
    types
    aria *vs.,* 184, 186
    in cantatas, 218, 271, 272
    in church music, 194
    English, 216
    French, 214
    German, 217–18
    of Handel, 282
    of Haydn, 332
    influence on Baroque instrumental
        music, 198
    of Monteverdi, 181
    Neapolitan, 211
    in *opera buffa,* 296
    in *opera seria,* 298, 302–303
    in oratorios, 283
    in Passions, 274
    of Rameau, 259
    rhythm in, 173
    seventeenth-century, 207, 225
recitativo accompagnato, 211, 272
recitativo arioso, 211
recitativo obbligato, **211,** 282, 296, 362,
    369, 371, 488
recitativo secco, **211,** 272, 282, 417
recitativo semplice, 211
reciting tone, 26, 33
recorder, 81, *105,* 141
Reformation, 150. *See also* church
    music, Reformation
refrain. *See also* ritornello
    in balletts, 136
    in *formes fixes,* 69, 71, 82
    in seventeenth-century arias, 209
    in troubadour and trouvère songs, 38,
        42, 63
Regina caeli laetere, Dunstable, *89*
Reich, Steve, 538, 545, 546
Rejoice!, Gubaidulina, 472–73
religion and music. *See also* church
    music *headings*
    eighteenth-century, 288
    fourteenth-century, 66–67
    Middle Ages, 62–63
    twentieth-century, 544
reminiscence motives, 420, 421, 428
Renaissance, 99–169
    English music in, 125, 136–39, 144,
        146, 147–48, 149, 157–58,
        167–68
    Franco-Flemish music in, 111–18,
        120, 121–24, 136, 139
    French music in, 135–36, 143, 149,
        153–56
    German music in, 125, 139–40,
        151–53
    historical background of, 99
    instrumental music in, 140–48, 149
    Italian music in, 104–105, 120–21,
        124–35, 145–47, 149, 158–65
    meaning of, 99
    musical culture of, 99–100, 101–105
    patronage in, 104, 118, 121, 126, 129,
        132, 133

printing in, 104, 106–107, 125, 126,
    143, 144
Spanish music in, 144–45, 147, 165
texture in, 157–58
theory in, 101–103
tuning in, 103
Renoir, Auguste, 456
Renzi, Anna, 209, *209*
Republic, Plato, 7, 14
Requiem, 31
Requiem, Berlioz, 429–30, 508
Requiem, Fauré, 452, 453
Requiem, Mozart, 349
Requiem, Verdi, 418, 420, 431
"rescue" operas, 358
Respighi, Ottorino, 456
responsorial psalmody, 13
responsories (respond), **20,** 24, 28, 46,
    48, 90
Resurrection Symphony, Mahler, 435,
    436
Resvellies vous et faites chiere lye, Dufay,
    93
Revelation in the Courthouse Park,
    Partch, 540
Reynolds, Roger, 538
Rhapsody in Blue, Gershwin, 526, 542
Rhaw, Georg, 152
rhetoric, musical, 191
Rhétorique des dieux, La, Gaultier, 200
rhythm, modes of, 44, 48, **49–50,** 54, 57,
    58, 60, 61
rhythm-and-blues, 525
rhythm and meter
    in Baroque dance suites, 233–35
    in Baroque music, 173
    in bebop, 524
    Bulgarian, 468
    in Burgundian music, 92, 95–96
    in canzone, 146
    of chaconne, 187, 236
    in chant, 23, 26
    in conductus, 36, 55, 56
    in dance music, 143–44, 144, 199
    duple, 69, 112, 119
    in early polyphony, 46
    in eighteenth-century music, 288,
        310
    in fifteenth-century music, 112, 114
    in fourteenth-century French music,
        63, 78–79, 80–81, 82
    in French overtures, 215, 239
    in French recitative, 214
    in Greek music, 7
    hemiola, 76, 181, 234
    hocket, 66, 69, 73, 76
    isorhythm, 64–65, 66, 67, *68,* 82, 89,
        95, 501, 505
    in jazz, 523
    in minimalist music, 545
    in Minnelieder, 41
    in motets, 57, 58, 60
    in organum, 48, 49–50, 54
    in Parisian chanson, 135
    in passacaglia, 187
    in rhythm and blues, 525
    in seventeenth-century arias, 209
    syncopation, 68, 69, 76, 520–21, 525
    in toccatas, 229
    trochaic, 382

rhythm and meter (*continued*)
  of troubadour and trouvère songs, 39
  in twentieth-century music, 463, 507
  in variations, 148
Ricercar dopo il Credo, Frescobaldi, 201
ricercare (ricercar), 144, 146, 149,
    201–202, 230, 266–67
Richard I, King of England, 40–41
Ricordi, Giulio, 420
Rienzi, Wagner, 423
Ries, Ferdinand, 356–57
Rigoletto, Verdi, 419, 420, 432
Riley, Terry, 545
Rimsky-Korsakov, Nikolay, 445, **448**
  influence on Stravinsky, 481, 482
Rinaldo, Handel, 277, 281, 282
Ring des Nibelungen, Der, Wagner, 420,
    424–26
Rinuccini, Ottavio, 177, 179, 181
ripieno, 174, 246
ripresa, 75
ritornellos, **189,** 207
  in cantatas, 272
  in church music, 220
  in concertos, **247,** 253, 254, 313, 343
  in da capo arias, 212, 300
  in early opera, 181
  in opera, 419, 488
Rochberg, George, 513, 549–50
rock-and-roll, 516, **525,** 544
rococo, 287–88
Rodgers, Richard, 525–26
Roerich, Nicholas, *485,* 486–87
Roger, Estienne, 241
Rollett, Hermann, 410
Roman de Fauvel, 64, *65*
Roman Empire, 2–3, 8–9, 10
romance, 373
romanesca bass and variations, 147, 187,
    206
Romantic period, 373–461
  chamber music in, 401–406, 452, 455
  choral music in, 429–31, 432
  lieder in, 19, 406–10, 434, 436,
    439–40
  operas in, 412–29, 432, 447–48, 450,
    459
  orchestral music in, 373–89, 434–42,
    445, 446, 448, 449–50
  piano music in, 392–401
Romanticism, 372, 373, 374–75, 432. *See
    also specific composers, genres,
    and topics*
Rome, 171, 244–45, 247
  church music in, 13, 15–16, 160
  opera in, 184
  St. Peter's Basilica in, 193–94
Roméo et Juliette, Berlioz, 380, 389, 415
rondeaux, 69, **70, 71,** 76–77, 78–79, 82,
    110
  Burgundian, *92,* 93
rondo, 325, 344, 442
Rore, Cipriano de, 122, 125, **129–30,**
    149, 168, 172
Rorem, Ned, 547
Rose, liz, Machaut, 69, 70, 71
Rosenkavalier, Der, Strauss, 442, 444
Rossi, Luigi, 184, 190, 218
Rossini, Gioachino, *389,* 413, **416–17,**
    418, 419, 425, **431**

Rousseau, Jean-Jacques, 297, 305
Rowlandson, Thomas, *291*
Royal Academy of Music (London),
    276, 277
Rubinstein, Anton, 445
Rückert, Friedrich, 436
Rudolph, Archduke, 352, 364, 370
Ruggiero variations, 147, 206
Ruggles, Carl, **527,** 528, 529
Rule of St. Benedict, 20
Ruslan and Lyudmila, Glinka, 445
Russian Easter Overture, Rimsky-
    Korsakov, 448
Russian music
  nineteenth-century, 433, 445–48, 461
  opera, 445, 447–48, 469, 470
  twentieth-century, 448–49, 463, 464,
    469–73, 491

Sacchini, Antonio, 349
Sachs, Hans, 42
sackbut, 81, 141, 147
Sacrae symphoniae, G. Gabrieli, 147
Sacre du printemps, Le, Stravinsky, 481,
    483–84, *485,* 486–87
sacred concertos, 171, **188,** 193–94, 195,
    207, 222, 226
Sacred Harp, The, 519
Sadko, Rimsky-Korsakov, 448
St. Gall, monastery of, 30, 31
St. John Passion, Bach, 273–74
St. Louis Blues, Handy, 522
St. Matthew Passion, Bach, 152, *153,*
    273–74, 275–76, 394
Saint-Saëns, Camille, 386, 452, 453
Salieri, Antonio, 289, 349, 350
Salome, Strauss, 442
Salomon, Johann Peter, 319, 321, 323
saltarello, 143, 231
Salve Regina, 21, *24–25,* 28
Salzburg, 334, 335
Sammartini, Giovanni Battista, 303, 308,
    336
Sanctus, **22,** 29, 67
Sand, George, *389,* 398–99, *399*
Sandburg, Carl, 529
Sannazaro, Jacopo, 126
sarabande, 199, 200, 233, **235,** 267
Sarum Use, 13
Satie, Erik, **456–57,** 531
Saudades do Brasil, Milhaud, 480
Scarlatti, Alessandro, 226, 244, 276, 282,
    306
  cantatas of, 218
  operas of, 211–12
Scarlatti, Domenico, 260, 481
  sonatas of, 306–307
Scheibe, Johann Adolph, 275
Scheidemann, Heinrich, 202
Scheidt, Samuel, 202, **207,** 232
Schein, Johann Hermann, 195, 199
scherzos, 325, 327, 392, 396
Schiller, Johann von, 289, 371, 384
Schleicht, spielende Wellen, Bach, 273
Schmitt, Florent, 484
Schnitger, Arp, 228
Schnittke, Alfred, 472
Schobert, Johann, 336
Schoenberg, Arnold, 464, 466, 492,
    493–500, 502–503, 509, 514, 515

influence on other composers, 491,
    536, 538
  Mahler's influence on, 460
Schola Cantorum, 451
schöne Müllerin, Die, Schubert, 408,
    410
Schopenhauer, Arthur, 374
Schöpfung, Die, Haydn, 319, **333–34**
Schubert, Franz, 373, **375–78,** 394, *407,*
    410, 444, 460
  Beethoven's influence on, 388–89
  chamber music of, 376, 392, **401–404**
  choral music of, 376
  church music of, 431
  lieder of, 374, 375, 376, 392, 400,
    406–407
  piano music of, 376, 391, **392–93**
  Schumann on, 377
  sonatas of, 339
  symphonies of, 376–78, 388–89
Schuller, Gunther, 542–43
Schuman, William, 534
Schumann, Clara Wieck, 404, **409–10,**
    410, 411
Schumann, Robert, 373, 444
  Beethoven's influence on, 366
  chamber music of, 392
  influence on other composers, 446,
    475
  lieder of, 374, **409**
  piano music of, 391, **394–95**
  writings on music of, 374, 377, 394
Schütz, Heinrich, 193, 194, **195–97,** 222,
    225, 431
  influence on other composers, 475
Schwanengesang, Schubert, 408
Scipione, Handel, 282
Scotland, 29
Scott, Sir Walter, 416
Scottish Symphony, Mendelssohn, 381,
    382
Scribe, Eugène, 413
scuole, 250
Se la face ay pale, Dufay, 95–97
Second Vatican Council, 16
seconda pratica, 133, 135, 172
secular songs. *See also* chansons
  in conductus style, 56
  fifteenth-century, 88–89, 91
  of Middle Ages, 18, 19, 30, 31, **35–42**
  seventeenth-century, 189–90
  sixteenth-century, 121
Sederunt principes, Pérotin, 53, 54
Seeger, Charles, 529
Seeger, Ruth Crawford, 528–29
Sei concerti per il cembalo o piano e forte,
    J. C. Bach, 313
Seikilos song, 4, *6,* 7
semibreve, 80, 81
semiminim, 80
Senfl, Ludwig, 139
Septet, Stravinsky, 491
septets, 354
Sequence, 46
sequences, harmonic, 239
sequences, liturgical, **30–31,** 36, 42, 44,
    46, 54, 56, 68, 152. *See also Dies
    irae; Stabat Mater*
Serenade for Orchestra, Kay, 534
serenades, 337

serial music, **492–93, 495–507,** 513, 514
    American, 529, 535–39, 541, 542, 543
    of Stravinsky, 491, 504
    total serialism, 504–505, 538
Sermisy, Claudin de, 135–36
Serse, Handel, 282, 300
serva padrona, La, Pergolesi, 295, 305
Service, Anglican, 159
Sessions, Roger, 535–36, 538, 550
Seven Studies on Themes of Paul Klee,
    Schuller, 542–43
Sforza family, 105, 113
Shakespeare, William, 15, 384, 420, 422
Shankar, Ravi, 545
shawm, 81, 141
Sheherazade, Rimsky-Korsakov, 448
Shostakovich, Dmitri, 469, **470, 471–72,**
    491, 548
Sibelius, Jean, **450,** 535
Silbermann, Gottfried, 228
sinfonias, 228, 237, **307,** 311, 316, 508
    of Vivaldi, 252, 255
Sinfonie, Bach, 265
Sing joyfully unto God, Byrd, 159
singing schools, 517
Singspiel, **217–18,** 297–98, 338, 344,
    348–49, 413
Sirènes, Debussy, 455, 457
Six Bagatelles, Webern, 501
Skryabin, Alexander, **448–49,** 456
Slåtter, Grieg, 450
Slave Songs of the United States, 519
Smetana, Bedřich, 386, 449
Smith, Bessie, 522
Smoke Gets in Your Eyes, Kern, 526
"socialist realism," 469, 471
Soler, Antonio, 307
Solesmes, Benedictine Abbey of, 16
solmization, 19, **34,** 90
sonata da camera, 228, 237–38, 239–40
sonata da chiesa, 146–47, 205, 228,
    237–38, 239, 242, 243, 279, 317
Sonata for Microtonal Piano, Johnston,
    541
sonata form, **308, 317–19,** 325, 326
*Sonata per il violino per sonar con due
    corde,* Marini, 204
Sonata pian' e forte, G. Gabrieli, 147
sonata-rondo, 325, 344
sonatas. *See also* piano sonatas; trio
    sonatas; violin sonatas;
    violoncello sonatas
    of Bach, 267–68
    Baroque, 203–205, 227, 228, 237–40,
        242–43, 247
    canzona distinguished from, 203–204
    eighteenth-century, 290, **305–307,**
        309–10
    ensemble, 237–38, 243
    sixteenth-century, 147, 149
    solo, *238,* 240
    of Vivaldi, 253
Sonate pathétique, Beethoven, 339, 353
Sonaten für Kenner und Liebhaber, C. P.
    E. Bach, 309–10
Sonatine, Ravel, 459
Sondheim, Stephen, 526
Song of Roland, 36
*Songs without Words. See Lieder ohne
    Worte*

sonority. *See* texture
Sophocles, 5, 176, 443, 490
Sousa, John Philip, 520
Southern Harmony, The, 519
Spain, Arabic poetry in, 37
Spanisches Liederbuch, Wolf, 434
Spanish music, 450–51, 454
    Baroque, 187
    Renaissance, 144–45, 147, 165
spatial dimensions in music, 508, 514.
    See also antiphonal music
Speculum musicae, Jacques de Liège, 63,
    66
spinet, 142
spirituals, 519–20
Spontini, Gasparo, 305
Sprechstimme (Sprechgesang), **494–95,**
    496, 500, 503, 504, 509
Squarcialupi Codex, 72
Stabat Mater, Haydn, 331
Stabat Mater, Rossini, 431
Stadtpfeifer, 243
Stamitz, Johann, 311
Steffani, Agostino, 210
Stein, Gertrude, 531, 532, *533*
Stella, Frank, 545
stile antico, 168, 192, 208, 220, 274
stile concertato. See concertato medium
stile concitato, 189
stile moderno, 192, 195
stile recitativo, 177–78, **179,** 180, 184–85,
    221. *See also* recitative
Still, William Grant, 534–35
Stockhausen, Karlheinz, 504, 505, 507,
    511, 513, 538
    quotations from, 549
Stradella, Alessandro, 218, 220
Stradivari, Antonio, 228
Strassburg, Gottfried von, 427
Strauss, Johann, the Younger, 415
Strauss, Richard, **440–44,** 460–61
    Berlioz's influence on, 380
    Debussy's influence on, 456
    influence on other composers, 442,
        493–94, 551
Stravinsky, Igor, 2, 464, 479, **481–91,**
    515, 542
    Debussy's influence on, 456
    influence on other composers, 538
    Rimsky-Korsakov's influence on, 448,
        481, 482
    serial music of, 491, 504
Street Scene, Kirchner, 502
stretto, 231
Striggio, Alessandro, 181
string quartets
    of Beethoven, 351, 352, 354, 358–59,
        365, 368, 369, 372, 393
    of Brahms, 406
    of Debussy, 455
    of Haydn, 319, **325–30,** 339
    of Mozart, 327, 339
    of Ravel, 459
    of Schubert, 401–403, 404
    twentieth-century, 465, 466, 467, 476,
        480, 494, 495, 496, 500, 501, 502,
        513, 536, 541
string quintets, 403–404
    of Mozart, 340
String Trio, Schoenberg, 496

strophic variation, 186, 189
Strozzi, Barbara, 190–91, *191, 192*
Strozzi, Bernardo, 190, *191*
Strozzi, Giulio, 190, 191, *209*
Sturm und Drang, 310–11, 321
style brisé, 199, 200
style galant. See galant style
Suite for String Orchestra, Schoenberg,
    496
Suite provençale, Milhaud, 479
suites, Baroque, 143–44, 199–200, 214,
    227, 228, **233–36,** 242, 243, 247
    of Bach, 267, 268
    of Handel, 278
    orchestral, **245–46,** 268
sul ponticello, 541
Sullivan, Arthur, 415
Sun-Treader, Ruggles, 527
Sunless, Musorgsky, 446
Surprise Symphony, Haydn, 324
Susato, Tilman, 136
suspension, 167, 175
Süssmayr, Franz Xaver, 349
Sweelinck, Jan Pieterszoon, 156, 202,
    207, 232
Swieten, Gottfried van, 333, 338, 353
swing, 516, **523**
Switzerland, 29, 30
Symbolon, Zwilich, 548
Symphoniae sacrae, Schütz, 197–98
symphonic poems, **383–84,** 386, **440**
    of Liszt, 383–84, 401, 411, 429
    of Rakhmaninov, 448
    of Rimsky-Korsakov, 448
    of Sibelius, 450
    of Strauss, 440–42, 461
Symphonie fantastique, Berlioz, **378–79,**
    380, 381, 386, 389, 410, 415, 440
symphonies. *See also* specific composers
    of Beethoven, 351, 352, 354–57,
        359–61, *364,* 365, 368, 370–71,
        372, 378, 379, 380, 381, 383,
        388–89
    eighteenth-century, 290, 307–308,
        311–12, 316–25, 340–43, 381
    of Mahler, 435–39, 440
    nineteenth-century, 376–82, 385–89,
        410–11, 431, 450, 460
    twentieth-century, 448, 450, 469–70,
        471–72, 473, 474–75, 479,
        489–90, 501, 502–503, 505, 509,
        512, 513, 527, 531, 533–34,
        535–36, 548
Symphony in C, Stravinsky, 489
Symphony of Psalms, Stravinsky, 490
synthesizers, 508, 541, 544
Syria, 12, 27, 29
Szymanowski, Karol, 456

tabarro, Il, Puccini, 459
tablatures, *138,* 142, 143
    keyboard, 207
    lute, 147, *200*
Tabulatura nova, Scheidt, 207
talea, **65,** 66, 67
Tallis, Thomas, **158,** 159, 168, 473
Tant que vivray, Sermisy, 135–36
Tasso, Torquato, 126, 184, 185, 189,
    250, 281
Tate, Nahum, 216

Taverner, John, 158
Taylor, Cecil, 524
Tchaikovsky, Piotr Il'yich, 374, 386, **445**, 471, 487
Te Deum, Berlioz, 429
teatro alla moda, Il, Marcello, 299
Teatro San Cassiano (Venice), 184, 185
Tecum principium, 27
Telemann, Georg Philipp, 269
temperament. *See* tuning and temperament
tempo rubato, 179, 396, 400
tenors
    in chant, 26, 33, 47
    instrumental, 81
    in Masses, 91, 94–97, 121–22
    motet, 56, 58, 64–65, 66, 67, *68,* 81, 89–90
    in organum, 54
    in polyphonic conductus, 55
Teresa of Avila, Saint, 196–97
terminatio, 26
tetrachords, **8,** 16, 131, 188, 217, 339
text setting
    in ancient Greek music, 177
    in Baroque music, 172–73, 176
    in chant, 24, 26
    in English madrigals, 137
    in fifteenth-century music, 103–104
    in *formes fixes,* 69, 71
    of French chanson, 135–36
    in frottole and laude, 125, 126
    in madrigals, 125–26
    in motets, 56–57, 60
    in polyphonic conductus, 55–56
    in seventeenth-century Italian opera, 211
    in sixteenth-century music, 122, 131, 149
    trecento music, 72–73, 74
    in Venetian opera, 186
texture. *See also* heterophony; homophony; monophony; polyphony
    in Baroque dance suites, 234–35
    in Baroque music, 174
    basso continuo, 207, 226
    cantilena, 70, 82, 83, 91, 93
    in concertos, 246
    in da capo arias, 300
    in eighteenth-century music, 310, 312
    in fifteenth-century music, 108, 112, 114, 118–19
    five-part, 215
    four-part, 95
    of Franco-Flemish chansons, 136
    of French chanson, 135
    galant style, 288
    in German opera, 422
    layered, 96–97, 98
    in madrigals, 126
    in motets, 58, 67
    in nineteenth-century lieder, 406
    in polyphonic conductus, 55–56
    in Renaissance music, 157–58, 174
    in seventeenth-century opera, 211
    in sixteenth-century music, 121, 124
    style brisé, 199, 200
    in synthesized music, 508

of trio sonatas, 205, 238, 239, 247–48
of Venetian music, 193
thematic transformation, 384, 401
theme and variations. *See also* chorale variations; *romanesca*
    Baroque, 199, **205–207,** 227, 232, 233, 236, 267
    of Beethoven, 351, 365–67
    of Brahms, 367, 388
    of Elgar, 450
    of Haydn, 322, 329
    of Mendelssohn, 394
    of Mozart, 336
    Renaissance, 140, 143, 147–48, 149
    strophic, 186, 189
    twentieth-century, 498, 503, 530, 531, 536
Theorica musice, Gaffurio, 102
theory, music
    ancient Greece, 3, 4, **6–8,** 10, 12, 14, 16, 101, 179
    Baroque, 175, 176, 258
    eighteenth-century, 288, 316, 334
    fourteenth-century, 63, 64, 77
    medieval, 19, 32–35, 43, 44, 45
    of Rameau, 258
    Renaissance, 101–103, 130, 131
    twentieth-century, 475, 538
They Are There!, Ives, 527
third-stream music, 542–43
Thomson, James, 333
Thomson, Virgil, 515, *516,* **531–33,** *533*
Thoreau, Henry David, 527
Thornton, Willie Mae "Big Mama," 525
thoroughbass. *See* basso continuo
Three Compositions for Piano, Babbitt, 538
Threni, Stravinsky, 491
Threnody for the Victims of Hiroshima, Penderecki, 510
Tides of Manaunaun, The, Cowell, 528
Till Eulenspiegels lustige Streiche, Strauss, 440, 441–42
timbre, 506–507, 514
    organ, 228
time signatures, 80–81
Tinctoris, Johannes, 103
'Tis the Gift to Be Simple, 531
toccatas, **145–46,** 149, 173, 175–76, 227, **228–30,** 247, 550
    of Bach, 262, 263–64
    of Frescobaldi and Froberger, 200–201, 242
tombeau, 200
Tombeau de Couperin, Le, Ravel, 457, 459
Tomkins, Thomas, 159
tonality, major-minor, 176, 239, 240, 246, 306, 308, 466, 492
tone clusters, 466, 506, 527, 528
toni, 32
tonoi, 34
Tonus peregrinus, 26
Torelli, Giuseppe, 246–47, 253
Tosca, Puccini, 459, *460*
Totentanz, Liszt, 401
Tower, Joan, 548
Trabaci, Giovanni Maria, 203
Tract, **28,** 46
traditional music. *See* folk music

Traetta, Tommaso, 303, 336
tragédie lyrique, **213,** 226, 258, 304, 336
Traité de l'harmonie, Rameau, 256
transcriptions, piano, 400–401
Transformation, Schuller, 543
Trauersinfonie, Haydn, 321
trecento music, 63–64, **70, 72–77**
trilli, 179
trills, 241
trio sonatas, **205,** 238, **239, 239–43,** 247–48
tripla, 199
Tristan und Isolde, Wagner, 425, **427–29,** 434, 443, 493
Tristis est anima mea, Lasso, 166–67
tritone, 33, 45, 77
Triumphes of Oriana anthology, 137
trivium, 10
trobairitz, 19, **36–41**
Trois morceaux en forme de poire, Satie, 456
tropes, **30,** 31, 42, 44, 46, 47, 57, 61
troubadours, 19, **36–41,** 42, 43
Trout Quintet, Schubert, 401
trouvères, 19, **36–41,** 42, 43, 63, 68, 71, 82
trovatore, Il, Verdi, 419
trovatori, 70
Troyens, Les, Berlioz, 415–16
trumpet, 141, *144*
trumpet, slide, 81
Tu solus, qui facis mirabilia, Josquin, 114–15
tuning and temperament
    Baroque, 231, 266
    equal, 231, 266
    just intonation, 540–41
    Renaissance, 103
    in twentieth-century music, 509, 514, 540–41
Tuotilo, 30
Turandot, Puccini, 460
turba, 225
Turmsonaten, 243
tutti, 246
twelve-tone music, 492, 495. *See also* serial music
twentieth-century music, 462–517, 522–52. *See also* neo-Classicism; serial music; *specific composers and genres*
    historical background of, 462–63
    musical trends in, 463–64
    technology in, 463, 464, 493, 507–508, 514

Uberti, Antonio, 301
Umbrian Scene, Kay, 534
Un bacio di mano, Mozart, *341*
Unfinished Symphony, Schubert, 376, 388–89
United States, 463, 469, 515–52
    colonial music of, 517–18, 531
    Dvořák influenced by music of, 388
    eighteenth- and nineteenth-century music in, 516, 518–20
    twentieth-century music in, 478, 515–17, 522–52
    universities' support of composers in, 536–39

vernacular music in, 516, 531–34, 542–43, 547
Ut queant laxis, 34

Valse, La, Ravel, 459
vanitas paintings, 154–55
Varèse, Edgard, **507,** 508, *509,* 515, **529, 530,** 538, 539, 549
variation canzona, 203
variations. *See* theme and variations
Variations for Orchestra, Carter, 536
Variations for Orchestra, Schoenberg, 495, 498–99
Variations for Orchestra, Webern, 503
Variations IV, Cage, 544
vaudevilles, 297
Vaughan Williams, Ralph, 450, **473–74,** 491
Venetian Games, Lutosławski, 513
Venetian school, 171, 192–93, 508
Venice, 171, 243, 250–52
  opera in, 184–86, 208, 209–10, 295
  St. Mark's Church in, 122, 129, 133, 147, 171, 192–93, 250
Venturi, Robert, 548
Verdi, Giuseppe, 418, 428, 444
  Beethoven's influence on, 418
  choral music of, 418, 420, **431**
  operas of, 413, 414, 416, **418–23,** 432, 444, 550
Vergil, 216, 416
verismo, 450, 481
Verklärte Nacht, Schoenberg, 493
Vers la flamme, Skryabin, 449
verse anthem, 159
Vespers, 21
Vespers, Monteverdi, 194
Viadana, Lodovico, 194
vibraphone, 507
vibrato, 142
Vicentino, Nicola, 131, 149
Victimae paschali laudes, 30, 152
Victoria, Tomás Luis de, **165,** *166,* 168
vida, 40
vida breve, La, Falla, 451
vielle, 81
Vienna, 220, 289, 290, 298, 311, 314, 316, 319, *333,* 338, 350, 352, *364,* 377, 388
vihuela, 145
vihuela de mano, 142
villanella, 125
Vingt-cinquième ordre, Couperin, 236
viol, *105,* 138, 141, 142, 202
viol music, 236
viola, 379–80
viola da gamba, 174, 199, 238, 268
violin, 147, 154, *155,* 186, 228
violin concertos
  Baroque, 246–47
  of Beethoven, 364, 365
  of Mozart, 337–38
  nineteenth-century, 386, 400
  twentieth-century, 450, 465, 466, 467, 496, 500
  of Vivaldi, 254
Violin Phase, Reich, 545, 546

violin sonatas
  of Bach, 267–68
  Baroque, 204–205, 207, 238–40, 248
  of Beethoven, 351, 354
  of Mozart, 337
  nineteenth-century, 406
  twentieth-century, 459, 465, 527, 529, 535, 548
violoncello, 174
violoncello concertos, 388
violoncello music, 267
violoncello sonatas, 351, 354, 397, 406, 536
virelais, 68, 69, 70, **71,** 73, 82
Virga Jesse, Bruckner, 431
virginal, 142
virginalists, 147–48
virtuosity
  Baroque, 172, 201, 218, 229–30, 232, 240, 248, 260
  of Beethoven, 355
  in eighteenth-century musicm, 299, 301–302, 344
  fourteenth-century, 67
  and Greek music, 5, 7, 8
  in nineteenth-century music, 364–65, 391, 393, 396, 397, 400
  Renaissance, 126, 129, 142, 148
Visigothic chant, 13
Vitali, Giovanni Battista, 238
Vitali, Tommaso Antonio, 238
Vitry, Philippe de. *See* Philippe de Vitry
Vivaldi, Antonio, 239, 249, **250–55,** *252,* 286
  concertos of, 247, **252–55,** 279, 288, 291
  influence on Bach, 262–63
  influence on other composers, 479
  operas of, 251–52
vocal ranges
  fifteenth-century, 91, 108
  medieval, 55
voice combinations
  in fifteenth-century music, 91, 95, 98, 108
  in fourteenth-century music, 70
  in sixteenth-century madrigals, 126
volta, 75
vox organalis, 45–46
vox principalis, 45–46
Voyage, The, Glass, 545, 547

Wachet auf, Bach, 272–73
Wagenseil, Christoph, 311
Wagner, Richard, 392, 444, 460
  influence on other composers, 429, 433, 434, 448, 450, 454, 492, 493–94, 497, 550
  Liszt's influence on, 386
  operas and music dramas of, 375, 397, 400, 413, 414, 420, **423–29,** 432, 434, 443
  writings on music of, 374, 424–25
Waldstein, Count Ferdinand von, 352–53
Waldstein Sonata, Beethoven, 362–63, 368

walking bass, 210
Walsegg, Count, 349
Walter, Johann, 152
waltz, 392, 444, 459, 520
Wanderer, Der, Schubert, 407, 408
Wanderer Fantasie, Schubert, 393
War of the Buffonists. *See querelle des bouffons*
War Requiem, Britten, 475
Washington-Street, Billings, 518
Watteau, Jean, 286
Webb, Daniel, 293
Weber, Carl Maria von, **422–23,** 425, 428, 487
Webern, Anton, 492, 493, **500–503**
  Debussy's influence on, 456
  influence on other composers, 503–504, 536
  Mahler's influence on, 460
  quotations from, 549
Weelkes, Thomas, **136–37,** 159
Weill, Kurt, **477–78,** 491, 515
Weinlig, Christian Theodor, 425
Well-Tempered Keyboard, The. See wohltemperirte Clavier, Das
Wert, Giaches de, 130
West Side Story, Bernstein, 526
Western Wynde Mass, Taverner, 158
Whiteman, Paul, 523
Whitman, Walt, 477, 531
whole-tone scale, 445, 448, 449, 463, 466, 528
Wieck, Friedrich, 409
Wilbye, John, 136
Wilde, Oscar, 442
Willaert, Adrian, 120, **122–24,** 129, 133, 149, 164, 168, 193
  madrigals of, 125, 128
William Billings Overture, Schuman, 534
William IX, Duke of Aquitaine, 40
Williams, Hank, 525
Wilson, Robert, 545
Winchester Troper, 46
wind bands, 516, **520**
Winterreise, Schubert, 408–409, 410
Wohin?, Schubert, 407, 408
wohltemperirte Clavier, Das, Bach, 231, **265–66,** 274, 275, 396, 476
Wolf, Hugo, 434
women's vocal ensembles, 126, 129, 183
Wozzeck, Berg, **500–501,** 503

X: The Life and Times of Malcolm X, Davis, 543

Yonge, Nicholas, 136
Young, La Monte, 545

Zachow, Friedrich Wilhelm, 224, 276
Zarlino, Gioseffo, 103, 122, 124, 130, 131, 164, 172
Zauberflöte, Die, Mozart, 289, 345, **348–49,** 413
Zelter, Carl Friedrich, 275
Zwilich, Ellen Taaffe, 548